T0366291

UNIVERSITY
of the
CUMBERLANDS:

125 ALUMNI CAREERS

James H. Taylor

authorHOUSE®

AuthorHouse™ LLC
1663 Liberty Drive
Bloomington, IN 47403
www.authorhouse.com
Phone: 1-800-839-8640

© 2014 James H. Taylor. All rights reserved.

No part of this book may be reproduced, stored in a retrieval system, or transmitted
by any means without the written permission of the author.

Disclaimer: Biographical information for this book was gathered from Cumberland College's 100 year history,
A Bright Shining City Set on a Hill, and past Cumberland College and University of the Cumberlands alumni
publications. Every attempt was made to contact each person to update the biographical information. Information
on the persons who were not reached is printed as it appeared in the alumni publication from which it was drawn.

Names and careers listed in the 125 Alumni Career Categories are taken from the University's
Alumni Directories and Alumni records.

Published by AuthorHouse   05/13/2014

ISBN: 978-1-4918-7251-2 (sc)
ISBN: 978-1-4918-7252-9 (e)

Library of Congress Control Number: 2014905129

Any people depicted in stock imagery provided by Thinkstock are models,
and such images are being used for illustrative purposes only.
Certain stock imagery © Thinkstock.

This book is printed on acid-free paper.

Because of the dynamic nature of the Internet, any web addresses or links contained in this book may have changed
since publication and may no longer be valid. The views expressed in this work are solely those of the author and do
not necessarily reflect the views of the publisher, and the publisher hereby disclaims any responsibility for them.

Contents

iv

About the Author

James Harold Taylor arrived on the Cumberland College campus as a traditional student of age 18. Growing up in Waterford Township, Michigan near Detroit, he worked full-time during his senior year of high school at Pontiac Motor Division loading trucks for teamsters and boxcars for United Auto Workers while maintaining honor roll status.

The old-fashioned values of hard-work and honesty have driven Taylor while in college and in employment. Remaining at Cumberland after graduation he taught speech, argumentation, and debate. His duties have included serving as Assistant to the President, Director of Alumni Activities, Director of Admissions, and Director of Development. For a short time, he served as Vice President for Development at Scarritt College in Nashville, Tennessee, before returning to Cumberland as Vice President for Development and eventually as President.

Taylor holds two doctorate degrees: one in higher education and administration from Nova University in Ft. Lauderdale, FL and a second in general studies from George Peabody College of Vanderbilt University in Nashville, TN.

 Under his leadership, the endowment has increased from $6,775,349 in 1980 to over $70 million. Every building on campus has been renovated and updated during Taylor's tenure.

The land holdings on campus have increased from twenty acres and fifteen buildings in 1980 to one hundred acres and forty-two buildings during the Taylor administration. The main campus footprint consists of 1.2 million square feet of usable space. The off campus properties have grown from 8,000 acres to 13,000 in land, admittedly roughly contoured land with not much of a way to develop it at this time. University acquisitions include multiple rental properties comprising thirty-seven apartment units and fourteen houses. In addition, the University leases and operates an 11,000 square foot facility for the Northern Kentucky Campus, the Richard Knock School of Lifelong Learning.

University enrollment figures (FTE) for the 1979-80 school year totaled 1,924. Today the FTE stands around 4,000 with the most dramatic increase in school history coming in 2009 with the rapid addition of new undergraduate and graduate programs. Today headcount enrollment has reached an all-time high of nearly five thousand combined undergraduate and graduate students.

Dr. Taylor dedicates over 180 days per year on the road visiting donors and attending meetings and conferences representing the University and often represents SACS in program reviews of some 30+ colleges and universities to date.

Although there have been many defining moments during the Taylor administration, the most significant came when Taylor and his wife, Dinah, lost their son, Jim, at the age of 18 in a single car accident in 1991. Time and again, the Taylors have reached out to others who have lost loved ones at the peak of adolescence through bereavement groups, extending compassion where needed and providing inspiration at life's lowest point. As a testament to their work, three domed murals painted by Cumberland alumnus, Jerry Wayne Taylor, Class of '72, stand in memoriam on campus.

During Taylor's tenure the graduate programs have expanded from one to seven. New undergraduate academic programs have also expanded, athletic facilities built or updated, classroom buildings built or updated, parking lots constructed, infrastructure replaced or increased, internet technology added, endowment funds increased, retirement packages enhanced, faculty, staff, and retiree recognition programs added, and many other programs too numerous to list added or enhanced. Taylor's imagination and perception have certainly paid off for the University in his 34 years as president.

UNIVERSITY of the CUMBERLANDS:

125 ALUMNI CAREERS

Reflections

Since becoming President on August 1, 1980, I've thoroughly enjoyed what I believe to have been and continues to be a remarkable journey made possible in large measure by my understanding wife, Dinah, and a capable staff, wonderful faculty and the joy our students and alumni bring to our service. My wife has always been by my side and she has done it all with class.

Our vice presidents and department heads, our maintenance and kitchen staff, our work study students and support staff have been almost always a delight to work with over these productive decades. Any shortcomings otherwise should in all probability lie at my feet. I know I stand on the shoulders of those who have gone before. One compelling reason to construct this reflection of alumni accomplishments is to answer the age old question, "Can anything good come out of Nazareth?"

Indeed, enlightened, productive, tax-paying citizens have come from these beautiful mountains and have gone on to distinguished roles in Kentucky, throughout the nation and around the world.

This has been an exciting journey in faith with a substantive number of heads, hearts and hands making it all possible. For almost forty some years I've spent almost 180 nights each year on the road, seeing as many people as possible in different locations throughout the United States, those with whom we could arrange appointments. My wife often accompanies me on my travel throughout the nation as we seek support, visit alumni, conduct work for the accrediting agency, work with foundations, corporations and others seeking good-will in our friend raising efforts.

So many of our alumni have made such significant and substantial contributions to our beautiful mountain area, to our great nation and to the world, so much so that we fondly say the sun never sets on the work of our alumni. Arguably other countless numbers of alumni could have been justifiably selected for this publication, yet those selected are the ones who most commonly come to my mind including the 125 categories representing one category for each of the first 125 years of the University's history. If your name should have been included and was inadvertently omitted then you know who you are. Clearly every alumnus has made a contribution but limited time and space precludes our ability to recognize each alumnus for his or her contribution, although I've tried to list our alumni by profession at the end of this book and hope we have not overlooked you or your contribution.

This publication has required the assistance of a number of folks as we compiled the names and gathered the information and located the pictures.

Of course, we found that a number of the original 100 alumni honorees have now passed away. The information from the book compiled in 1988 when we celebrated our 100th year of service is included without revision on those folks.

Others in the original 100 named alumni were included with updated biographical information as provided by the alumnus or family member.

Feature stories published in *Cumberland Today* for the last 25 years were reviewed and biographical information collected on those alumni. Again that information was mailed to the alumnus for review and update if possible. Information that we were unable to confirm is included as obtained from the *Cumberland Today* story or other printed information.

Other information was gleaned from alumni records, scripts from various alumni programs, newspaper stories and from information published on the internet.

While we have listed information on a number of alumni, we are aware that there are so many others who should have been included. I apologize now for not including you if you are an alumnus who was not included and I assure you that the oversight was not intentional.

The compilation of this information took a number of hands. I would like to thank our Alumni Director, **Dave Bergman**, and his assistant, **Stephanie Taylor**, for their many hours of research and compilation of information. I also thank **Sherry Roaden** and **Alice Bowling**, my administrative assistants, for their typing and assistance in locating pictures. Further, **Alyssa Burke**, assistant in Multimedia, spent countless hours searching for and scanning pictures. And finally, I must provide overwhelming appreciation to **Sue Wake**, our Vice President for Advancement, who worked endlessly and tirelessly over the past twelve months in producing this publication. She has performed yeoman's service in this area as well as in so many other areas. My hat is off to her for this laudable accomplishment among others.

While we have written about quotable notables, I've often felt one of the greatest contributions a mother could make would be as a stay at home mom while the children were growing up; though, granted, that is almost impossible in this two bread winner economy.

As I think about almost 50 years of association with Cumberland, I remember wanting to pinch myself on more than one occasion to make sure what I was seeing on national television was what I was seeing, or to ensure what I was experiencing personally was real and not a dream. Was what I was seeing, what I was seeing? Was it an illusion or a real live human experience? You should read this publication and judge for yourself.

On and on this remarkable saga goes, but perhaps it would be best to begin with the first four graduates before we get to the stellar accomplishments of other graduates this institution has produced. On and on it will go with stories about Generals, an Admiral, the governors, a Congressman, college and university presidents, medical doctors, scientists, engineers, researchers, outstanding graduates going on the Harvard, MIT, Princeton and so forth. The roster of our alumni reads like a Who's Who.

No doubt the story we are telling about the contribution of a relatively small university in Appalachia is a remarkable story by any measure and clearly vindicates the faith of our founding fathers who envisioned young people from humble homes coming forth its shining portals their faces radiant with the light of learning.

I marvel and rejoice at the accomplishment of our alumni. So many tell me their acceptance to Cumberland was an answer to prayer, a chance of a lifetime, an opening to the American Dream. What admission to and completion of a college education accomplishes is incalculable with greater earnings, better health care, more civic and church and community participation, earning $1.2 million on average more over a lifetime than a person with only a high school degree.

We must ask ourselves, "Where would any of us be today if not for Cumberland?" Indeed, the best way to cushion life is still a college education.

An investment in your alma mater is like investing in stock – as the value increases the worth of your degree increases.

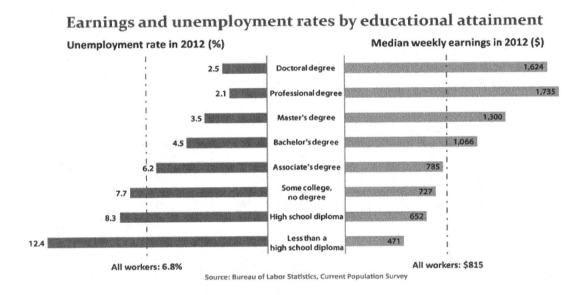

Earnings and unemployment rates by educational attainment

Unemployment rate in 2012 (%)		Median weekly earnings in 2012 ($)
2.5	Doctoral degree	1,624
2.1	Professional degree	1,735
3.5	Master's degree	1,300
4.5	Bachelor's degree	1,066
6.2	Associate's degree	785
7.7	Some college, no degree	727
8.3	High school diploma	652
12.4	Less than a high school diploma	471
All workers: 6.8%		All workers: $815

Source: Bureau of Labor Statistics, Current Population Survey

Our History

While many colleges and universities could die tomorrow and it would not make a significant difference in educational opportunities for the people of Appalachia, that is not so for Cumberland -- an institution which stands in stark contrast to the discordant sameness of most institutions since 1888. This is what makes UC-Cumberland College different from, other than, better than or what UC does differently from others and does uniquely alone. UC's traits and characteristics taken separately may not provide distinction, but when combined, they make UC-Cumberland College unique among higher education institutions.

The distinct early history of the College can be seen in the *Stained Glass Windows* commissioned in 1992 for the Gatliff Chapel. The windows on the main floor depict the history of the college and the windows on the balcony, the life of Christ. In the foyer are pictures of angels playing mountain dulcimers reflecting mountain culture. The window in the tower was dedicated to the memory of James H. Taylor, II.

STATESVILLE STAINED GLASS, INC.
STATESVILLE, NORTH CAROLINA
Artist, Les Whicker

History of Cumberland College
The three windows depict our campus and its extension into the Appalachian area. The Cumberland College seal is replicated in the center window and is depicted as radiating to the people throughout the surrounding community of farmlands, mountains, highways, and river.

Bottom Windows

Ancil Gatliff and James Perry Mahan, 1888
At the December 1887 meeting of the Mt. Zion Association and at the urging of General Green Clay Smith, Dr. Ancil Gatliff pledged the first $1,000 toward the building of a new school, Williamsburg Institute. The offer of this gift prompted others at the meeting to give $4,500 toward the cost of beginning the school. Mrs. Gatliff cried because she had no idea where the money would come from to pay the $1,000 pledge. However, a few months later, Dr. Gatliff and his neighbor, James Mahan, were watching a big piece of coal from a new

mine burn on the grate. Gatliff said to Mahan, "If that turns out alright (sic), we can build that college, can't we? The coal mine was a good one, and Dr. Gatliff was able to pay this pledge plus many more.

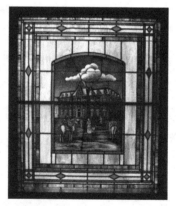

Roburn Hall/E.S. Moss Hall, 1889
Men worked all night long to ensure the Williamsburg Institute was ready for occupancy. **R. C. Medaris**, who was there on the opening day, recalled: "On Saturday before the school was to open the next Monday, we worked till midnight, and then we arose at midnight, Sunday night, and went to the school building and began getting everything ready for the opening. About seven o'clock the good ladies brought us our breakfast and we ate heartily of it. When the 200 happy boys and girls were coming in at the front door, we were sweeping the rubbish out at the back. We were dirty and tired but we stayed on the grounds until about noon."

On that opening day, January 7, 1889, the vision, faith, hard work, sacrifice, and struggle to found the college became a reality as the students arrived on foot, on horseback, and by wagon.

William James Johnson, 1892

William James Johnson was the Institute's first president, but soon became so involved in raising money for the Institute that he gave up the presidency to raise $15,000 for the endowment to match the gift of John D. Rockefeller and to raise funds with which to build a boarding hall (Johnson Hall). One can imagine Johnson on horseback, wading streams, crossing turbulent rivers, climbing mountains in the rain, snow, and sleet, raising money, and begging for the Institute. Johnson reported: "My heart swells with gratitude when I think of those little boys and girls all over the state who gave me their last copper or made pledges and are now doing little jobs to pay them."

Johnson was successful in his work and raised the funds to pay the Institute's debt, complete and enlarge Roburn Hall, build a boarding hall, and establish an endowment of almost $50,000.

Gray Brick Building, 1906

The Gray Brick Building, originally known as the Reuben D. Hill Building, was constructed in 1906 at a cost of $20,000 and was a part of Highland College's Williamsburg Academy. In 1907, Williamsburg Institute purchased Highland College's three buildings (the Gray Brick Recitation Building, Dixie Hall and the Manual Training Building) from the Congregational Church for $40,000.

For many years the Gray Brick Building served not only as the recitation building, but also as the administrative building at the college.

Early Classroom, 1914

The early classrooms were functional and well-equipped to meet the needs of the students including those studying in the areas of domestic science (cooking, sewing), commerce, art, and manual

training (bench work, mechanical drawing, cabinet making, house building, blacksmithing).

The Viaduct, 1920

The Viaduct, constructed in 1920, joined the two hills on which the Cumberland College campus was constructed. The hill to the left of the Viaduct was the site of what was formerly known as Highland

College and the hill to the right, Williamsburg Institute. From the time the Institute purchased Highland College until the Viaduct was constructed, access to one side of the campus from the other side was gained by crossing the ravine.

The old water tower, donated to the college by Dr. Gatliff, can be seen in the background.

Mountain Outreach

Today Cumberland College extends far beyond the two hills on which the campus is built to the surrounding community of hills and hollows. One program of service is entitled Mountain Outreach.

Through this program students and other volunteers build and repair homes for the poor, the indigent and the elderly. In addition, through this program families are also supplied with wells for safe, clean drinking water. The Mountain Outreach

program was recognized by President George Bush as his 220th Point of Light.

Science Laboratory

The science laboratories at Cumberland College

today are unequalled on any comparable size college campus thanks to the generosity of friends of the college who provided funds for the modern equipment as well as an endowment for the upkeep and replacement of the equipment.

Student Work Program

The student work program at Cumberland College is

as old as the college itself. The first President William James Johnson wrote, "We have some students who are living on forty cents a week and are dependent on working nights and mornings to make it, and, if they fail, they have either to beg, starve, or leave. Most of them leave."

The tradition of student work continues today with the students doing a multitude of jobs to help pay their own way. No task is too menial or too backbreaking for a student who truly wants an education.

President George W. Bush in his letter to the college in April, 1990, noted: "One's greatest dreams can be realized through self-discipline, imagination, perseverance, and hard work. These principles have inspired the students and staff of Cumberland College during its first century, and I am sure that they will continue to do so in the future."

Student Service

When President Jimmy Carter visited Cumberland College in April, 1990, he reminded the college family that Cumberland College "never forgets the moral and ethical and service basis of an education. . . . We can be successful in life as measured by achievement: wealth, fame, recognition on the one hand; but combine that with the more important things in life: humility and love. . . . It's only when we have the courage to look at ourselves and say:

what can we do that exceeds what we are presently doing; what can we do to expand our hearts, to expand our lives, to reach out to others that we can have that joy and that peace that transcends what we previously imagined. So service to others may seem to be a sacrifice, but usually it turns out to be life's greatest blessing."

The Beginning

The vision to establish the university must be credited to four individuals, General Green Clay Smith, Reverend R. C. Medaris, Dr. Edwin Smith Moss and Dr. Ancil Gatliff.

Green Clay Smith's roots were in Madison County, Kentucky, home of his grandfather. Smith's father  was a Richmond attorney. Smith served as a Civil War General, Governor of Montana and a presidential candidate in 1876 but he left all that to become a Baptist minister. It was in this capacity that he provided the inspiration for and helped to found the Williamsburg Institute. In fact, prior to the Mount Zion Association meeting in December 1887 Smith, John Wesley Siler, Gatliff and Medaris met to discuss the possibility of founding the Institute. To help Medaris, who was charged with raising the funds for the Institute, Smith urged Gatliff to pledge $1,000.[1] Smith's obituary read:

> *His zeal and wisdom and sympathy enabled the struggling men who are trustees of Williamsburg Institute to bring this noble institution into being. We honor him because he was a General and Governor and Moderator of the General Association of Kentucky, the successful pastor, evangelist, and lecturer; and then we love him because he was our friend and brother and helped. No military honors, no towering shaft of marble we could build for him would ever equal the monument already erected in the Williamsburg Institute.[2]*

 In 1887 the Committee on Education of the General Association of Kentucky retained **R.C. Medaris** as the financial agent for the Institute. While R. C. Medaris pastored the First Baptist Church of Williamsburg; he also provided the leadership to get the Institute underway. A pastor from age 17,

Medaris is described as "full of the Spirit of God and (of) zeal for his cause. . ."[3]

 **Edwin Smith Moss**, a surgeon who studied medicine under Dr. Ancil Gatliff and formally trained at the University of Louisville, was a leader in the Williamsburg Community. He served as one of the first Trustees of the Institute as appointed by the Mount Zion Association of Baptists. Moss, Smith and Medaris helped to secure the land on which to build the Institute and Moss was elected temporary chairman of the Board. He served on the Board for 15 years.[4]

Ancil Gatliff helped to found the Institute and served  as the president of the Board from 1889 until his death in 1918. At the December 1887 meeting of the Mount Zion Association Gatliff pledged $1,000 toward the building of the Institute which served as the impetus for the raising of $4,500 before the meeting closed. Neither Gatliff nor his wife knew where they would get the money for the pledge.[5] A short time later, Gatliff and a neighbor, **Jim Mahan**, began a successful mining operation that provided the funds with which to pay the pledge.[6] The Institute's first building known as the Recitation Building (Roburn Hall later named Moss-Roburn Hall) opened its doors on January 7, 1889.

The Railroad

As the Appalachian ballad exclaims, "The train doesn't stop here anymore." From the middle 1950's through the early 1980's the second largest migration of people took place as they left the mountains to work in factories in Cincinnati, Dayton and Detroit. This migration was only surpassed by the Oakies fleeing the Dust Bowl from which *The Grapes of Wrath* was developed. But back to the railroad and King Coal.

The Institute's solicitors traveled by horseback and by train to gather funds "to give an opportunity for a first-class education at rates that are compatible with the means of the mountain people."[7] In 1898 the L&N Railroad issued a pass to the Institute's solicitor, **H.H. Hibbs**, to travel by railroad to solicit funds for the school, and in 1907 Hibbs convinced the railroad to build a road to Gatliff's new mines so that coal could be mined, sold and shipped out with a portion of the proceeds going to support the Institute.[8]

These acts of kindness by the L&N Railroad (extending the railroad to Dr. Gatliff's mine and providing the pass for Mr. Hibbs) were two of a series of favors the Company performed for the College. The railroad company also provided transportation for students, visitors, and faculty alike to and from Williamsburg as well as giving land and gifts to the College. (Interstate 75 performs a similar function today as the railroad did one hundred years ago by providing access to and from the campus.)

The College's relationship with the railroad company exists even today. On 9 August 1986, **Richard D. Sanborn**, President and Chief Executive Officer of CSX Railway, was awarded an honorary doctorate from Cumberland College in appreciation for all the railroad company had done for the College since its inception. Two other CSX employees have been recognized by Cumberlands with honorary degrees. **Alvin R. Carpenter** served as President and Chief Executive Officer at CSX Transportation, Inc. from 1992 to July 1999; then as Vice Chairman of CSX Corporation from 1999 to 2001. **Clarence W. Gooden** has been the Chief Commercial Officer and Executive Vice President for Sales and Marketing at CSX Corporation since 2004. He also served as Chief Operating Officer of CSX Corporation and Chief Executive Officer and President of CSX Intermodal.

It is undeniable that the development of the coal mines in Whitley County and the moving of the coal by railroad were instrumental in the building of this university, a relationship that has continued over the years. In fact, the Chair of our Board of Trustees, **Jim Oaks**, is the retired Vice President of CSX transportation.

James C. Oaks received a Bachelor of Science degree from University of Alabama, Gadsden, and an Honorary Doctor of Laws Degree from Cumberland College.

He serves as President of James C. Oaks, LLC and is a member and chair of the University of the Cumberlands Board of Trustees. In addition, he serves on the Board of Directors of Lynch Consulting Group, Inc. and R. J. Corman Railroad Group, LLC. Oaks also holds membership with CSX Corp. Capitol Connections, Pittsburg Traffic Club and the American Railway Engineering and Maintenance Association.

Dr. Oaks has previously served as a Deacon at First Baptist Church, Corbin, Kentucky; President of Southern Kentucky Economic Development Corporation, on the Boards of Directors of Kentucky Baptist Hospitals, Inc., First National Bank and Trust, Union Planters Bank, and National Mining Association. Oaks has been a member of the Transportation Committee of the Kentucky Coal Council, was appointed by the Governor of Kentucky as Executive Director of the United States Department of Defense Special Task Force for Coal, has served as a Commissioner for the Commonwealth of Kentucky Department of Corrections and as a member of the Forward in The Fifth Committee.

He retired from CSX Corporation in 1999 after serving various positions for more than 45 years. At the time of retirement he was serving as Vice President for Coal Development.

Dr. Oaks and his wife, Hazel, make their home in Jacksonville, Florida. They have two children; Aleatha Oaks and James C. Oaks, Jr., and one grandchild, Haley.

Richard D. Sanborn, a native of Sanbornville, NH, graduated from the University of New Hampshire in 1957 and received a law degree from Harvard in 1960. He had a career in the railroad industry that spanned 27 years. In January 1989, he became chairman and chief executive officer of Conrail. Previously, he was President of Distribution Services, Inc. for the CSX Corporation. Sanborn had also worked at the Atlantic Coast Line Railroad, Seaboard Coast Line and the Louisville & Nashville Railroad. On August 9, 1986, Sanborn was awarded an honorary doctorate from Cumberland in appreciation for all the railroad company had done for the College since its inception. Cumberland is deeply indebted to Sanborn and the CSX Railway for their support of the College and its programs. Sanborn passed away suddenly on February 12, 1989 at the age of 52.

Jim Terry, and alumnus of Cumberlands, was long-time legal counsel for the old L&N Railroad (now CSX).

Coal

"You load 16 tons and what do you get? Another day older and deeper in debt. Saint Peter don't you call me cause I can't go, I owe my soul to the company store." Our founders were not Robber Barons. They actually invested in creating the college and developing health care. Amazingly it was mountain scrip redeemable only at the company store which kept people in the mining camps and was legal until the late 1950s.

The College has been intimately related to the coal business from the beginning and for a time offered an associate's degree in Mining Technology. It was **Jay Gould** looking down from his New York office who decided to put the railroad through Williamsburg, thus changing the lives of mountain youth.[9]

In the Taylor years, an analogy was used in many of the fund raising letters, comparing our students to diamonds since diamonds are formed when a piece of coal is subjected to pressure for a period of time. Taylor's letter notes:

It's much like we do here at Cumberland College, turning unlikely-looking youngsters – diamonds in the rough – into trained, educated men and women who go back home, most of them, to provide leadership and service in their native Appalachian mountains.

Coal and coal mining play a large part in the Institute's founding but also in the history of the  institution now known as University of the Cumberlands. In 1933 the college was deeded the Whitley County land and the coal rights originally purchased by American industrialist, **Henry Clay Frick,** from Faraday Coal and Coke Company. Frick's heirs deeded the land and all mineral rights to Harvard, Princeton and Massachusetts Institute of Technology after Frick's passing. The Ivy League schools later relinquished the land and its coal rights retaining the oil and gas rights.[10] The coal mined from this land has produced millions of dollars in coal royalty for the institution during coal's heyday.

The Board of Trustees gave much of the credit for securing this coal land from Harvard, Princeton, and Massachusetts Institute of Technology to Mr. **A. T. Siler**, attorney and trustee, and since that time numerous attempts have been made to secure the gas and oil rights on the property from Harvard, Princeton, and Massachusetts Institute of Technology to no avail. Mr. A. T. Siler served as Trustee of the

 Institute from 1901 until his death in 1953. His motto, "Be Somebody," was the creed by which he lived. In addition to being an attorney and trustee, he served as county school superintendent, railroad commissioner, congressional district chairman, bank president, and president of Kentucky Baptists.[11]

James B. Cheely. Born in Williamsburg, Kentucky to Doris and Beulan E. Cheely. Received an AA Degree from Cumberland College in 1932 and an AB degree from Duke University in 1934. Was Manager of the Southern Collieries, Inc. coal mine and later president of Regal Mining Company in Lake City, Tennessee in 1957. Cheely became director of low-rent housing and urban renewal in Clinton, Tennessee until his retirement in 1975. He is married to Imogene Thompson. He has three children, 6 grandchildren, and 2 great grandchildren. Cheely served the First Baptist Church of Clinton as a Sunday School Superintendent, teacher, a deacon and as treasurer. James' father was **B. E. Cheely**, once a member of the Board of Trustees of Cumberland

College, a great supporter and a true friend of the college. James and the entire Cheely family have left a mark on Cumberland College and on the area in which Cumberland College is located. Cheely's grandfather was **T. B. Mahan,** who served as president of the trustees of Cumberland College.

Mr. **Thomas Jefferson Roberts** (1890 -1959), a trustee of Cumberland College from 1936 until his

death in 1959, served as treasurer of the College (1942-1959) and as secretary and treasurer of the Board of Trustees (1939-1959). Roberts had served as secretary and treasurer of many coal companies, and since most of the trustees were coal men, they had great confidence in him.

Mr. Roberts was a soft-spoken, tactful man; he did not take credit for the things he did. He was a sound businessman and an advisor to people who had money and authority, yet he was also their friend. His son **Gorman Roberts**, a Harvard graduate in business, was a partner at J. J. B. Hilliard and Lyons. Like his father, he was respected by the high and mighty as well as by the common man. A very polite and capable man, **Gorman Roberts** has also served as a trustees and advisor to the College.

Historically, T. J. Roberts is given the credit as the man who accumulated the "nest egg" for the

construction of the Gatliff Building. He held a vision for transferring the College from junior to senior college status. He managed the college's land very well. Respected for his financial genius, his vision still impacts the College today. At the time of his death in 1959, T. J. Roberts was president of the Bank of Williamsburg.

Roberts loved young people, and he felt that Cumberland College was providing a quality Christian education for youngsters who wanted to attend. He was devoted to the College. In May 1960, the trustees decided to name the College's cafeteria as a memorial to Mr. Roberts who had given such faithful and effective service. The building had, in fact, been made possible largely by his efforts and financial genius.

T. J. ROBERTS DINING HALL
The T. J. Roberts Dining Hall is a modern building housing a dining area capable of seating 800, a reception room, and a well-equipped kitchen. With cafeteria style service, around 1,500 people may dine over a two-hour period.

The Roberts Dining Hall, erected in 1958, is named for Mr. T. J. Roberts, who rendered faithful and efficient service to the College. Much thought was given to naming the building for Dr. Creech, the former president, but Mr. Roberts was most deserving, and it was most fitting to have the structure named for him. After all, he had created the "nest egg" for the Gatliff Building and for this building and had successfully guided the College for nearly two decades in its financial affairs.

The Opening

Students arrived on horseback, on foot and by wagon that first day. The Founding Fathers "envisioned young people from humble homes coming forth its shining portals their faces radiant with the light of learning." The first building, now known as Moss - Roburn Hall, was constructed under unusual circumstances. The trustees and other friends worked right up to the time that the students arrived on that first day, January 7, 1889, to get the building ready for the students.[12]

Also present that morning was **John Wesley Siler**, one of the first Trustees, sponsoring, encouraging, and pushing forward. Siler said, "Go forward young men, this school will never die. We will pass on, but the college itself will live."[13]

The first four graduates, **A. J. Meadors, A. S. Petrey, L. B. Parker, and E. L. Stephens**, were all successful in their chosen fields. These men were and are typical of the graduates produced by this University.

A. S. Petrey (bottom row, left) was an Instructor of A Grammar at Williamsburg Institute from 1893-1897. He did missionary work in Hazard and Perry County, organizing twelve churches in the area including the First Missionary Baptist Church of Hazard in 1898. His interest in education work led him to found and become president of the Hazard Baptist Institute in 1902.

E. L. Stephens (bottom row, middle) taught as an Instructor of A Grammar, Rhetoric and History, and Algebra at the Williamsburg Institute 1894-1901. He studied for and passed the bar exam and became a prominent attorney in Williamsburg, Kentucky.

A. J. Meadors (bottom row, right) entered the field of education and taught in the elementary grades of the Williamsburg Institute for one year, 1895-96, Instructor of A Grammar. He moved on to become a principal of a high school in Arkansas and later President of Conway Female College, Conway, AR. According to the University of Central Arkansas historical archives, Meadors Hall was erected in 1937 to honor Andrew Jackson Meadors, UCA's first academic dean. This position is known today as "Provost." Meadors joined the faculty of UCA in 1909 and became dean in 1921. He served in this capacity until 1942. Before retiring, he served briefly as Interim President.

L. B. Parker (standing) became a minister and was at one time supply pastor of the Williamsburg Baptist Church. Reverend Parker served as pastor at several churches in the Midwest including Illinois, Kansas, Kentucky, Missouri, Nebraska, Oklahoma and Texas. The early graduates of Williamsburg Institute are much like the graduates of today. There is a steady flow of students in Williamsburg who dedicate themselves to academic excellence, civic service and spiritual growth. It is this well roundedness in Cumberland graduates that enables selfless growth in service to others.

Early Financial Supporters

No one would have imagined that a little school nestled in the foothills of the Appalachian Mountains in Kentucky would attract the attention that it has over the years, but this special purpose institution has been shown favor by God and by man. Two of its earliest financial supporters were from outside the area **John D. Rockefeller** and **Andrew Carnegie**.

John D. Rockefeller gave through the American Baptist Education Society and later through the

General Education Board. In 1891 Rockefeller gave $4,500 to the Institute's endowment. Mr. **Wallace Buttrick**, Rockefeller's personal representative, when asked why the support was given, responded that the gift "was justified by the fact that this is a mountain school, in the mountains, of the mountains, and by the mountains."[14] Between 1891 and 1906 Rockefeller's gifts paid directly to the Institute totaled $23,508.42 to the Institute, no small sum. In later years gifts totaling $113,500 were made by the John D. Rockefeller Foundation for Higher Education to the General Education Board and distributed to the Institute and to the College (after the name was changed from Williamsburg Institute to Cumberland College).[15]

Andrew Carnegie, who during his lifetime gave over $60 million to public libraries, also pledged $18,000 during the College's early years. Rockefeller's and Carnegie's interest in lumber, coal and the railway business are probably what attracted them to the Institute.[16]

Help from within the community continued as well. **Ezra Stephens** of Hartford, Connecticut, a member of the Institute's Board of Trustees, had pledged $40,000 to construct the Stephens Building.[17] On the

basis of this pledge the Trustees bought the property

of Highland College for $40,000. Stephens paid $10,000 on his pledge but then failed in business during the 1907 panic. This left a $30,000 debt. By 1912 the debt with accrued interest amounted to $41,000, but the Institute's history praises Stephens for his pledge rather than condemning his inability to pay. Through this misfortune the local trustees learned to attempt great things for God and to expect great things from God. Without Stephens, the Institute may never have acquired the Highland College property or the endowment.[18]

No avenue of aid from the outside seemed open. The Trustees and friends arose to the emergency and the

entire indebtedness was raised without leaving Williamsburg. The funds received from Rockefeller and Carnegie and $50,000 from the estate of **John Wesley Siler**, the Institute's treasurer since its beginning, the endowment rose to $275,000 by 1912.[19] Dr. Gatliff gave $16,000 and Mrs. J. P. Mahan $10,000.

Famous People

Several famous names are associated with our institution.

Harlan Sanders began his Kentucky Fried Chicken business in Corbin, Kentucky, 15 miles north of the campus. While Sanders did not attend Cumberland, his nephew did. In 1997 when Mrs. Sanders passed away, she included our college in her Will for around $100,000.

Duncan Hines married alumna **Clara Wright**, '23,

the daughter of **Arkley Wright** who served Cumberland's first academic dean. **Clara Wright** was born in 1904 to Arkley and Annie Wright. Her father, Arkley Wright was a teacher in the northeastern Kentucky town of Carrollton. Her mother died in 1905, and her father remarried and in time Clara had five step-brothers. Arkley Wright came to Cumberland in 1911 to teach Latin and history. He left Cumberlands in 1914 but returned in 1920 to serve as Academic Dean.

Arkley Wright left his position as Academic Dean in 1924 but remained as a faculty member teaching history. He later taught at LMU and served as superintendent in Hopkinsville and in Williamsburg.

Upon graduation from

high school in about 1919, Clara enrolled at Cumberland and was graduated in 1923. She taught in the Carroll and Harlan County school systems. In 1929 she moved to Bowling Green and found steady employment as a recorder in the admissions office of Western Kentucky State Teachers College. She remained a member of the administration until 1932, when she left the college to become a secretary for Clarence Nahm to whom she was married until his death in 1944.

In 1946, Clara married the famous Duncan Hines, and they travelled the country visiting restaurants. Based on their experience, some establishments would get the coveted "Recommended by Duncan Hines" sign to hang outside the restaurant. This brought attention to these establishments and more business. Clara also assisted her husband in getting various high-quality foods and eventually baked goods to houses across the country and nationwide. Duncan Hines made Clara the chairman of the Duncan Hines Foundation and the *de facto* editor of *Adventures in Good Cooking.*[20]

While the estate was left to Cornell's Duncan Hines School we are, nonetheless, fortunate to be associated with the name.

During his lifetime **Bing Crosby** funded a Youth Fund Loan. One of our alumni, **Bill Thompson** was

chosen to receive that loan in 1976 and was rewarded with a trip to Pebble Beach, California, to attend the Pebble Beach Open and meet personally with Mr. Crosby. Bill's wife, Susan accompanied him.

Reverend William (Bill) Frank Thompson graduated from Cumberland College in 1977 with a degree in biology. He was the recipient of the 1976 Bing Crosby Youth Fund Loan which is sponsored by the 3M Corporation. As the loan recipient, Bill and his wife Susan were welcomed to the Bing Crosby Open at Pebble Beach, California by Mr. Crosby. Reverend Thompson attended seminary at Southern Seminary in Louisville, Kentucky and has worked and ministered to students all of his adult life.

Reverend and Mrs. Thompson served 15 years as church planting missionaries in Taiwan. They began serving at Euclid Avenue Baptist Church in Bristol, VA in 2003. Bill is the Minister of Youth and Education while Susan is the Director of Preschool and Children Ministries. They have three children and five grandchildren.

Scientists

You've often heard the old saying, "He's no rocket scientist." Well, here we produce graduates who are rocket scientists – among other brilliant minds. They remind me of a young man from Appalachia who wrote *October Sky*, which was later made into a movie. That young man was a coal miner's son. The young man, Homer Hickman, went from a mining camp in a small West Virginia town to aeronautics engineer at NASA.

Being born in a mining camp or up a mountain hollow should not stop a youngster who has brains and is willing to work. Parents then, as now, prefer their children go to college rather than to the coal mines.

Who knows what Einstein may reside just over the mountain, waiting to be brought out to a life of service or when a cure for cancer could come from a youngster living up a mountain hollow.

The number of students studying the sciences at Cumberlands is far greater than you will find at most universities. A full 31% of our students major or minor in biology, chemistry, physics, or mathematics preparing for careers in the sciences or in one of the medical professions. What a contrast with the household named large universities having only 5% to 7% in these areas.

We understand the value of the sciences. Indeed, America's prosperity to a large extent depends upon the STEM programs. Like the space shuttle leaving Cape Canaveral, the thrust required is several times the power required for the remaining portion of the trip. It's like the first four years toward the college degree which propels our students forward for the rest of their lives as they reach for the stars and are propelled through constellations because someone cared enough to provide scholarship assistance.

To accommodate the large number of students studying in the STEM areas, the science building that was constructed in the 1960's was renovated in 2005, 2006 and 2007 and a new addition was added to the building in 2008. This addition was built as a replica of Monticello, Thomas Jefferson's home, and houses the biology department. The renovated areas house the chemistry, physics, mathematics and physician assistant departments.

Terry E. Forcht, although not an alumnus of Cumberlands, is one of Kentucky's leading entrepreneurs. He is the founder, Chairman and CEO of Forcht Group of Kentucky, a management services company employing more than 2,100 people in Kentucky, Indiana and Illinois. Dr. Marion C. Forcht is controlling co-owner of Forcht Group of Kentucky. Included among the companies under the Forcht Group of Kentucky are Forcht Bank, which operates 30 banking centers in Whitley, Laurel, Knox, McCreary, Pulaski and six other Kentucky counties; Kentucky National Insurance Company; Kentucky Home Life Insurance Company; nine nursing homes throughout East and Southeast Kentucky; two weekly newspapers, the Corbin News-Journal and the Hamburg Journal; 20 radio stations; and My Favorite Things, a gift and furniture store in Lexington.

The Terry and Marion Forcht Medical Wing accommodates our Physician Assistant program.

Dr. Terry Forcht is a native of Louisville and holds two degrees from the University of Louisville: a

Bachelor of Science degree and a Juris Doctorate degree from the University's School of Law. He also earned a Master of Business Administration degree from the University of Miami, Florida. In 1964 Dr. Terry Forcht came to the Williamsburg area to serve as a chairman of the Commerce Department at Cumberland College. Three years later he began a law practice in Corbin, Kentucky. Although no longer practicing law, Dr. Terry Forcht remains a member of the Whitley County and Kentucky Bar Associations. He is a Past President of the Whitley County Republican Party and former candidate for a seat in the Kentucky House of Representatives. He is also a member of the Kentucky Broadcasters Association and the University of Louisville Alumni Association, and currently serves on the Board of Directors of the Kentucky Chamber of Commerce and the Kentucky Economic Development Board.

Although not a Cumberlands alumnus, we like to consider **Marion C. Forcht** as one of our own. A graduate of Atherton High School, and a Louisville native, Dr. Forcht serves as controlling owner and president of Key Insurance Agency, a position she has held since 1983. Key Insurance maintains offices in Corbin, Lexington and Williamsburg. Further, she serves on the boards of Kentucky National Insurance Company, the Sanders-Brown Center on Aging Foundation at University of Kentucky, and the Kentucky Hemophilia Association. In January, 2005, former Governor Ernie Fletcher appointed Dr. Marion Forcht to the Historic Properties Advisory Committee, which provides continuing supervision of the Governor's Mansion, the State Capital, Berry Hill Mansion, and the old Governor's Mansion. She is a trustee of Grace on the Hill United Methodist Church in Corbin and has been a member of the Republican Women's Club since 1965. For her public and professional accomplishments, Dr. Marion Forcht was named one of the outstanding Young Women of America in 1973.

In April of 2005, Dr. Terry Forcht was awarded an Honorary Doctor of Laws Degree from University of the Cumberlands, and Dr. Marion Forcht received an Honorary Doctor of Laws Degree from University of the Cumberlands on April 21, 2008. She currently is a member of the University of the Cumberlands Board of Trustees.

The Forchts have been married for 53 years. They are the parents of four children, Ted, Brenda, Laurie and Deborah, and grandparents to 11 grandchildren.

Terry and Marion believe in giving back to their church and community. In addition to being active members of Grace on the Hill United Methodist Church in Corbin, their major gifts have included: $3 million to their alma mater, the University of Louisville, to establish the Forcht Center for Entrepreneurship in the School of Business; $1 million to University of the Cumberlands to fund the Forcht Medical Studies Wing of the science building; $300,000 to the State of Kentucky to finance the completion of the Capitol Rotunda murals in Frankfort, and $100,000 to University of the Cumberlands to help fund the new entrance of campus currently under construction.

One Cumberland physics professor, Dr. **Larry Newquist**, spent a summer at NASA Langley Research Center in Hampton, Virginia, conducting research of "the effects of particle shape on backscatter using a non-spherical particle scattering computer code. This lidar system could eventually be used to monitor emissions from the High Speed Civil Transport (HSCT) aircraft which would fly in the stratosphere."[21]

Dr. Lawrence Newquist earned the first of three degrees in Physics in 1981, with a B.A. from Knox College in Galesburg, Illinois. In 1983 and 1990, respectively, he completed an M.S. and a Ph.D. in Physics, both at the University of Missouri. Since coming to Cumberland in 1991, Dr. Newquist has been active in developing presentations with a particular emphasis on exciting elementary and high school students with the possibilities of physics. Newquist is a passionate recruiter of outstanding mathematics and physics students for the University and also takes his astronomy show on the road to various school-age groups. Within the community, he works tirelessly for the Boy Scouts, Girl Scouts and Rogers' Explorers programs.

He demonstrates his dedication to advanced student research in all disciplines by serving as Chair of the Committee for Presidential Scholars Research. In 1997, Dr. Newquist presented a talk entitled "Organization and Analysis of Lidar Data Obtained from the Contrails of a Boeing 737" at the NASA Langley Research Center in Hampton, VA.

Cumberland alumnae **Lawanna Miracle Scoville**, '72, a native of Loyall, KY, was twelve years old when she made her first visit to Cumberland College for the Southeastern Kentucky Regional Science Fair. The grand prize was the college scholarship that Cumberland provided to the Grand Champion. During the next three years, she attended three International Science Fair competitions. She also traveled to Detroit, San Francisco, and Fort Worth winning fourth place one year. *Seventeen* magazine picked her as one of the seventeen girls to model for their outstanding teenager's edition in 1969. Scoville was also Miss Southeastern Kentucky and Mountain Laurel Princess and through her efforts collected enough scholarship money to provide a free education at Cumberland. She graduated *Summa Cum Laude* in three years with a bachelor's degree in biology/chemistry. Scoville also went on to earn a master's in education and Rank I in Teaching.

Scoville received the 1989 Presidential Award for Science Teaching and was invited to the White House to accept her award. That same year World Book Encyclopedia chose her as the World Book Science Teacher of the Year and she traveled to Seattle, Washington, to receive this award. In 1990 with the recommendation of Dr. Jim Taylor, she was invited to apply for the Selby Chair for Academic Enrichment. The Selby Foundation did a national search for a teacher to live in Sarasota, Florida, to work with and inspire the children and teachers in the area of science. Scoville was offered the position and moved to Sarasota for a year. She completed her career at North Laurel High School in London, KY. Scoville and her husband, **John Scoville**, a 1970 alum of Cumberland, reside in East Bernstadt, KY and are both retired educators.

Hailing from the Jellico Community, **Charles Barton** attended Jellico High School, and during his junior year made the startling discovery that he had already acquired full credit to receive his high school diploma. Unable to attain his diploma with three years of high school, he dropped out without graduating. His older sister, Myrtle Nicholson (Mrs. G.O. Nicholson), a secretary working at Cumberland, encouraged him to attend Cumberland, and he did for a year, 1929-1930. Barton went on to pursue a

bachelor's degree in 1933 and a master's degree in 1934 from the University of Tennessee. Afterwards, Barton received his Ph.D. in analytical chemistry from the University of Virginia in 1939.

He later found his calling at the Oak Ridge National Laboratory (ORNL) where he specialized as a reactor chemist until his retirement in 1977. Barton was a renowned inventor and patent holder; his contributions in developing the liquid fluoride thorium reactor (LFTR) led to a 'step' in developing nuclear reactors for submarines and aircraft carriers.

His first major invention was the construction of a photo spectrometer as part of his Ph.D. project. Building the spectrometer from scratch, Barton perfected every minute detail in his project, even going as far as learning to grind glass to form the lenses needed for his machine.

After his passing on January 31, 2009, Charles Barton left behind a legacy long to be remembered.

University of the Cumberlands received a bequest from the late Barton to support alumni recommended scholarships. Barton's sons, Charles Barton, Jr., of Dallas, TX, and David Barton, of Greenville, TX, traveled to Williamsburg to present their father's gift in the amount of $51,632 to the University. They expressed their appreciation for their father and for the University where their father had first attended college.

Robert Pittman graduated from Cumberland in 1961with a B.S. in biology. He was assigned to man the Space Flight Center, Houston, Texas in October, 1965, as a member of the flight support team. He served during the flights of Gemini 6 through 12 and for the Apollo 11, which was the first lunar landing. In 1969, Pittman was reassigned to the A.F. Eastern Test Range for the NASA Unmanned Program, Atlas Centaur. He was then reassigned as Program Manager of the Apollo Program for the remainder of the program which included Apollo 15, 16 and 17. At the conclusion of the Apollo Program, Pittman continued as Program Manager for Sky Lab Program. This program entailed the launching of the orbiting space laboratories, the crews that manned them and the recovery of the shuttle vehicle which boosted the crews into orbit.

Billy D. Janeway '66 served as a member of the civilian corps at the Manned Spacecraft Center in Houston as an aerospace technologist. From Four Mile, KY, one of Janeway's assignments in Texas was to assist the flight of Apollo 14 astronauts as they manned the nation's sixth flight to the moon. Janeway is married to the former **Helen Clendaniel**, '66.

Shaft of Steel from The World Trade Center

How did a shaft of steel from Ground Zero end up planted adjacent to Independence Hall on our campus? **Andy Croley**, our County Coroner, worked at the World Trade Center after 9-11. In honor of Andy's work, he was given the shaft of steel from the World Trade Center, and two NYC first responders, NYC Police Office Lt. **John Bushing** and NYC Fireman **John Fila** of Firehouse 54, who Andy worked with at Ground Zero came to campus for the dedication of the shaft of steel in memory of all those who lost their lives on 9-11.

As the campus has been expanded over the last 33 years, every attempt has been made to unify the appearance by blending the architecture of the buildings. Hutton School of Business was constructed in 2004 and named to honor Edward Hutton. The building was constructed as a replica of Independence Hall. Inside the building is a miniature replica of the Liberty Bell donated to the University by friend and Trustee, Jo Cochran. Outside in Patriot Park is the shaft of steel, an additional Liberty Bell, the American Flag and two statues: George Washington and Thomas Jefferson.

Although not an alumnus of Cumberlands, **Andy Croley** was named an Honorary Alumnus at Homecoming 2013. Croley is a graduate of

Williamsburg High School in 1991, and he grew up on the edge of campus. He attended Carson Newman in Jefferson City, TN where he played football. After an injury in 1992, Andy left Carson-Newman and completed his degree in Mortuary Science at Mid-America College. Additionally, Andy has earned a degree in Aeronautical Science from Emory Riddle University and holds a master's degree in forensic science. In 2010 and 2011, Andy served as an associate professor at the University of the Cumberlands in the Criminal Justice Department.

Andy is the third generation to operate the Croley Funeral Home in Williamsburg. In addition to the Funeral Home, Andy is an elected public official. He holds the office of Whitley County Coroner. As Coroner, Andy sponsors various educational programs for the youth. He volunteers in all of the local schools educating students about drug prevention. Recently, Andy has started a new program called "Win 1 Way." This will support the existing "Win Drug Free Program." Along with

Andy's professional life, he has a strong commitment to his civic and community endeavors. Andy serves on the University of the Cumberlands Board of Visitors, UNITE board, First Priority, Airport Board, Child Fatality Board and is the founder and current Chairman of the Border Bowl.

Andy and his wife, **Tracy Davis Croley**, '98, spend their time with their busy children, Alicyn (11) and Jerrod (8) doing all the things necessary to give them what they need. Andy and his family are members of the Corbin Presbyterian Church.

Colan Harrell graduated from Cumberland in 1981

with his bachelor's degree. Over the years, Harrell has served the community in numerous capacities and is currently the Sheriff of Whitley County. He was a member of the Kentucky State Police from 1969 to 2009 and worked as Police Detective for 35 years.

Harrell has also served as a member of Cumberland's Alumni Board of Directors. During the 7th annual Forcht Group of Kentucky Center for Excellence in Leadership event on, April 3, 2012, Harrell received a Principled Leadership Award for his commitment and motivation in providing outstanding service in response to crisis situations and his dedication to making the world a safer place to live.

Steve Newell, of Barbourville, KY, earned his Bachelor of Science in Allied Health and Psychology from Cumberland in 2003. He worked as the Student

Services Coordinator for the Southern Area Health Education Center before pursuing a career in the area of law enforcement. In 1996, Newell joined the Kentucky State Police (KSP) working in several capacities within the agency, including Executive Security, where he provided executive protection for the Governor of the Commonwealth of Kentucky.

After leaving the KSP, Newell was appointed by former Governor Paul Patton to the position of Special Assistant to the Governor and held several positions within the Governor's Executive Cabinet. For the past nine years, Newell has been employed as an Investigator/Agent with the Kentucky Alcoholic Beverage Control (ABC).

Newell, who resides in Lexington, KY, currently serves as a Board Member of the Kentucky Peace Officers Association, a member of the Kentucky Narcotics Officer Association, and is active in several other civic and professional organizations.

Jason S. Ellis was born the son of the late Denny Ellis and Pam Deerwester. Ellis grew up in Batavia, Ohio with two sisters - playing on various all-star teams and summer leagues.

Ellis entered Cumberland College in 1998 and his collegiate baseball career began in 1999 and by spring 2002, Ellis had rewritten many school records at Cumberlands, staking claim to one of the most impressive baseball resumes on the diamond for Cumberlands.

Ellis remains Cumberlands all-time career batting average leader, all-time career leader in hits, all-time career leader in doubles, all-time career leader in homeruns and all-time runs batted-in. He also played in 186 games which is also a career record. Ellis also holds the following team records for a season: he is third in batting average for a season, first in hits, first in doubles, third in home runs, and first in games played. Adding to this remarkable list of statistics is the fact that he was a leader on and off the field, leading by example. Coach Brad Shelton said of Ellis, "Offensive statistics aside, Jason changed the game defensively by shutting down the opposition's running game as catcher."

Upon leaving Cumberlands Ellis was signed by the Cincinnati Reds Minor League professional baseball team, and he played with the Reds in Sarasota, Florida and in Billings, Montana from 2002 -2005. In 2005, Ellis began a career in law enforcement gaining employment with the Bardstown City Police

Department. He was the only K-9 Officer with the Canine Unit from 2008-2013. On the job, Ellis received the Governor's Award for Impaired Driving Enforcement for 2007 and 2008. He also received the Officer of the Year Award in 2008.

Officer Ellis was closing out a late work shift and on the way home Memorial Day Weekend 2013 when he stopped to help what appeared to be a stranded motorist in the roadway. The life of an unsuspecting Ellis doing a good deed was taken senselessly by unknown sources and later found in his cruiser. Ellis leaves behind his wife of seven years, **Amy Phillips Ellis**, a 2005 Cumberland alumna, and their two sons, Hunter and Parker.

Perseverance

A statue of our 16th U.S. President Abraham Lincoln stands in the courtyard between The Gatliff Building and the Bennett Building (formerly the Gray Brick Building). At the base of the statue is recorded a lesson on **Perseverance** that not only describes Lincoln but also serves as a lesson for the students who attend our institution.

He failed in business in '31.
He was defeated for State Legislator in '32.
He tried another business in '33. It failed.
His fiancée died in '35.
He had a nervous breakdown in '36.
In '43 he ran for Congress and was defeated.
He tried again in '48 and was defeated again.
He tried running for the Senate in '55. He lost.
The next year he ran for Vice President and lost.
In '59 he ran for the Senate again and was defeated.
In 1860, the man who signed his name A. Lincoln was
Elected the 16th President of the United States.

The difference between history's boldest accomplishments and
its most staggering failures is often, simply, the diligent will to persevere.[22]

Three of the longtime teachers and administrators of the Institute were **Denison graduates**: Professor **E.E. Wood** - President, **P. R Jones** – Chemistry teacher, and **Gorman Jones** – professor of French and history.[23] Two other Denison graduates, **F. D. Perkins** and **Laurence C. Irwin** taught in the early years.[24]

At one time four of the faculty were **Phi Beta Kappa**: E. E. Wood, Gorman Jones, J. T. Fitzgerald and A. R. Evans.

The list of faculty of the University employed on January 1, 2013, can be found in Appendix G.

National Television

I recall Mike Wallace's interview of two fellow classmates, **Don Mantooth** and **Ernie Harris**, on the popular show **"Sixty Minutes."** Ernie had reported a mountain superintendent of schools who had hired some 200 of his relatives in this expose' while Don Mantooth had pointed out the work being done in an Israeli mission. Both caused me to beam with pride. Much later, in fact in 2012, another alumnus, **Adam Sulfridge**, working as a journalist uncovered corruption in the Whitley County Sheriff's office which also aired as a "Sixty Minutes" story. Also in 2012, alumnus **Mike Wilson** '94 was featured on NBC's Rock center with Brian Williams in an unforgettable story of adoption. The Wilson's inspiration continues through myLifespeaks, an outreach ministry they fund.

The campus was abuzz in 2001 when one of our lady basketball players, **Erin Kelley**, was proposed to on national television. **The Sally Jessie Raphael Show** was live from New York City and the proposal was aired on the **Times Square electronic board**. This was such an unusual proposal and I'll never forget it. The title of the Dec. 27 "Sally Jesse Raphael" show was "Will You Marry Me in 2002?" But 2003 alumna and former Cumberland women's basketball player **Erin (Kelly) Robinson** sat backstage at the New York City studio thinking she was there for a completely different reason. Not long before her trip to the Big Apple, her now-husband, Mike Robinson, told her that he had won a poetry contest and was invited to the "Sally" show. Being a committed girlfriend, and not passing up the chance to go to New York, she accompanied him on the trip. Now she was waiting for Sally to call her out on stage. As Sally called Kelly onstage her heart was pounding, "like I was going out for the last game of the season." Sally revealed that Robinson actually brought her to the show to make a surprise proposal. On a big screen in the middle of Times Square read the words, "I LOVE YOU, WILL YOU MARRY ME, ERIN?" He then got down on one knee and quoted the poem he had written, a proposal. Kelly was completely shocked. Her reaction was that of astonishment. Excitedly she declared, "I cannot wait to marry this man!"[25]

For over a week in 2011, lady basketball player, **Stephanie Quattrociocchi**, was featured on **ESPN** and about every other television network for her 86 foot three pointer basket. This was such a spectacular event that it dominated the sports world for over a week. Indeed we had a ceremony during which time we officially marked the spot on our basketball floor which will be seen by others for decades to come. Then, too, in the fall of 2011, one of our football players, **Drew Yeargin**, delivered a Big-Time clean hit in a game with UVA-Wise made a hit that was seen and heard around the world on **You Tube** with over 150,000 views.

I never dreamed while I was watching the news on TV about the 26,000 Sudanese boys who walked to Ethiopia seeking refuge, referred to as the Lost Boys of Sudan, that one of those boys would one day be a student on our campus running track and cross country.

Then, too, even today you can turn on the TV and see former Cumberlands biology professor, Dr. **Robert Hancock**, on the Discovery Channel leading students on research trips to study mosquitos. On campus he was known as the Mosquito Man.

Reverend **Robert Donald Mantooth** started his adult life with the ambition of being an architect and that was what he initially studied as an undergraduate at Auburn University. Later, he felt called to full-time ministry and came to study theology at Cumberland. During the summer of 1966, Mantooth served as a Baptist Student Union summer missionary in Israel. He graduated from Cumberland in 1967 and went on to receive two advanced degrees from Southern Baptist Seminary in Louisville, a Bachelor of Divinity and a Doctor of Ministries. For nine years, he and his wife, Suzanne served as missionaries to Israel and served as co-directors of the Baptist Village Camp and Conference Center near Tel Aviv. He also served as mission administrator and business manager of the Baptist Mission office in Jerusalem.

Upon their return to the United States, Mantooth served as pastor of First Baptist Church in Morehead, KY for thirty years before retiring in 2013. Continuing his love of architecture, he led the remodeling of the sanctuary and fellowship hall at First Baptist; designed more than forty local homes and designed or remodeled commercial facilities for local businesses. He took a leadership role in the First Baptist Church's establishment of Clearfield Baptist Church and designed nineteen churches across Kentucky and Tennessee. Mantooth was president of the local chapter of Habitat for Humanity for five years and was intimately involved in the building of ten of the forty plus houses built. He has sponsored and taken volunteer groups on summer mission trips to Prague to work on the International Baptist Seminary.

Mike Wilson is a 1994 alumnus of Cumberland. Wilson and his wife, Missy, began "myLIFEspeaks" in 2006 as a way for them to share a story of hope and helping others overcome adversity in their own lives by using the story of their son, Lane, who has severe special needs. In January 2012, they launched the myLIFEspeaks Campus in Neply, Haiti providing a home to children who have been orphaned or abandoned--both typically developing children and special needs children. Mike has been traveling to Haiti regularly since 2003 and leading short-term mission trips to Haiti since 2005. Mike and Missy

have three biological sons and have adopted two daughters from the country of Haiti and have another daughter who currently lives and works in Haiti with the myLIFEspeaks organization as the Child Intake Coordinator. They were featured on **NBC's Rock Center** with Brian Williams on January 12, 2012 in an unforgettable story of adoption. Wilson has been travelling full-time and speaking to groups of all sizes since 2008. He is passionate about helping others "Park Their Hearts" around the globe and watching people learn to live for something BIGGER than themselves. Wilson was inducted into Cumberlands Alumni Hall of Honor in 2012 for his service.

That lifetime moment, the dream of seeing herself on ESPN, came true on January 22, 2011 for **Stephanie Quattrociocchi** '11, Cumberlands senior guard and native of Windsor, Canada. All it took was for the 5-foot-7 senior to heave in an 86-foot buzzer beater to end the first half of Cumberlands game. The real story though is Stephanie herself and her character, drive, determination, perseverance, and will to succeed in everything she does.

The "Shot Seen 'Round the Nation", which was the **ESPN SportsCenter** No. 1 Play of the Day on January 22 and then the No. 1 Play of that Weekend as well. On ESPN.com's "Best of the Best" poll, Stephanie dominated for seven consecutive polls. Her reign ended on February 7, 2011 when a play from the Super Bowl nudged her out. The support for Quattro and the shot warranted ESPN to schedule a live chat with her on SportsCenter. Not only did ESPN notice Quattrociocchi's feat, but the video went gone viral and now has over 200,000 views on YouTube.

Quattrociocchi played on Cumberlands' women's basketball team from 2006 through 2011 before being graduated with a major in English and minor in communication arts. Following graduation,

Quattrociocchi has assisted Multimedia and Sports Information with various assignments including writing news releases, keeping stats and co-announcer of women's basketball games on the radio.

University of the Cumberlands Football player, **Drew Yeargin** was featured on **ESPN's Numbers Never Lie** after his big-time hit on a UVA-Wise Wide Receiver. The Patriots (Cumberlands) defeated the Cavaliers (UVA-Wise) by a score of 42-13 on September 10th, 2011.

Cumberlands faculty member, **Barry Vann,** has been interviewed on numerous radio and television shows including Fox News Channel's "Spirited Debate" with Lauren Green, "The Mancow Experience," "Science Fantastic" with Michio Kaku and "Ecotopia," with Stephen and Susan Tchudi. His sixth book, Puritan Islam: The Geoexpansion of the Muslim World, is housed in the Marine Corps Research Library, The Federal Bureau of Investigation Academic Library, and the Defense Intelligence Agency.

Grant Doepel, '11, spent the summer of 2009 as an intern at **Fox News Channel's** headquarters in

Washington, D.C. He worked for *America's News Headquarters* and primarily wrote scripts for the news anchors, Brian Wilson and Shannon Bream, and booked political guests for the program. Although he received no monetary compensation, Grant received a priceless experiential education that went far beyond the classroom. One of the first things people asked Grant was, "How did you get to do this?" In the spring of 2009, while checking out the news on Fox News Channel's website, Grant noticed a link labeled "Interns-FNCU." On impulse, he clicked on it and learned that FNCU (Fox News Channel University) was recruiting for summer internships. The Webpage stated, "Fox News is looking for motivated, ambitious students who are seeking to expand their knowledge, improve their skills and kick start their career. Push the envelope of career possibilities and gain an edge in this competitive industry. The strong-willed need only apply." Grant immediately sent out his resume. Two weeks later, Krista Gambacorta, from Fox, called to set up a phone interview. He was thrilled just to be

interviewed and asked where he would like to work. His immediate response was "Washington, D.C." A few days later, in an e-mail message, he was offered an internship.

During his time at Cumberland, Doepel pursued a double major in communication arts and journalism and a double minor in music and political science, served as the editor of the campus newspaper, *The Patriot*; the anchor of the *Patriot Report*, an online news program; host of a political talk show on the campus radio station, WCCR, entitled, *Your World Today*; co-anchor of the *Patriot Report* on WCCR, a member of the production staff of *Cumberland Idol*, UC's own version of the hit reality show and was an accomplished pianist for several campus events.

For four months, **Aleer Akol Duot** and roughly 26,000 southern Sudanese boys, which are now

referred to as the **"Lost Boys of Sudan,"** hiked to the safety of Ethiopia. Over half were captured or died along the way, mainly due to hunger, disease, dehydration, attacks from wild animals, or enemy gunfire. Those individuals that were successful in their journey to the Ethiopian refugee camp narrowly escaped the violent civil war that erupted in Sudan in 1988. Aleer traveled with his sixteen-year-old brother to Ethiopia in 1988. The long and torturous journey seemed to be impossible. Blisters began to form on the young boys' feet, but most were too weak or too exhausted to carry the injured. "Many boys were left to die because they could not walk any further," comments Aleer.

"We stayed at the camp in Ethiopia for almost four years, until another war broke out." adds Aleer. The boys were forced to go back to their war-torn country of Sudan. More boys lost their lives on the treacherous journey, especially at the crossing of the Gila River. "There were not enough boats for everyone," remembers Aleer. "Some drowned; some were shot, while others were eaten by crocodiles." Aleer finally arrived in southern Sudan, but only remained there a very brief period before he was forced out by the North's gunfire.

The boys decided to walk to Kenya, another three month trip, where there was another refugee camp for the southern Sudanese people. Aleer remained at this camp for eight years. An International Rescue Committee began to select boys through a random lottery and place them with families in the United States. Out of 9,000 boys, 3,000 would be able to resettle in America. In the year 2000, Aleer received news that he was chosen at the age of 16. Just before leaving Kenya, Aleer's mother and sister showed up at the refugee camp. He did not know who they were because he had not seen them since he was four. Aleer was placed with a family in Phoenix, Arizona. He was enrolled in high school and began running Cross Country and Track his sophomore year. He went on to run at a junior college in Phoenix, where they won Nationals both years. Aleer was then recruited to run for the University of the Cumberlands. He graduated from Cumberland with a bachelor's degree in public health in 2011.

Meet our Generals, Admirals and other Heroes

Today our students are educated in the principles of leadership through the Hutton Leadership Program named for Dr. **Edward L. Hutton,** a business man and entrepreneur who took an interest in our university and its students. Dr. Hutton believed that every student needs to know and understand how to lead and how to serve.

Army Major General **Kenneth S. Dowd** assumed duties as the Director of Logistics Operations for the Defense Logistics Agency in August, 2012. Prior to assuming his current position, he served as Commander, 1st Theater Sustainment Command at Camp Arifjan, Kuwait, U.S. Army Central Command, Operation Iraqi Freedom, Kuwait, and Operation Enduring Freedom, Afghanistan.

A native of Abington, Pennsylvania, Major General Dowd was graduated from Cumberland in1979 with a bachelor's degree in history. He also received his commission through the ROTC program. He also holds a master's degree in logistics management from the Florida Institute of Technology and is a graduate of the United States Army War College. His other military schools include the Quartermaster basic and advanced courses; Logistics Executive Development Course, the U. S. Army Command and General Staff College, Fort Leavenworth, Kansas, and the Armed Forces Staff College, Norfolk, Virginia.

Major General Dowd served in numerous assignments, starting in 1979 as Battalion Motor Officer, 702nd Maintenance Battalion, 2nd Infantry Division, 8th United States Army, South Korea. Later positions include Battalion Motor Officer; Commander, Headquarters and Headquarters Company, 4th Supply and Transportation Battalion; S-2/3, 3rd Support Battalion, 4th Infantry Division (Mechanized), Fort Carson, Colorado; Deputy Chief of Staff for Logistics, G-4, U.S. Army, Washington, D.C.; Logistics Staff Officer, and later Supply and Service Management Officer, U.S. Army Logistics Management Center, Fort Lee; Operations Chief, Supply and Services, Director of Logistics and Deputy Director, Engineering and Logistics, Sharpe

Army Depot, Lathrop, California; Support Operations Officer; Executive Officer, 3rd Forward Support Battalion; and Chief, Division, Materiel Management Center, Division Support Command, 3rd Infantry Division (Mechanized), U.S. Army Europe and 7th Army, Germany.

Major General Dowd assumed command of the 299th Forward Support in June 1996, deploying to Bosnia in support of Operation Decisive Edge. In June 2001 Major General Dowd commanded the Division Support Command, 1st Armored Division, U.S. Army Europe and 7th Army, deploying in support of Operation Iraqi Freedom, Iraq. His next assignment was as Acting Deputy Chief of Staff, and later as Assistant Deputy Chief of Staff, G-4, United States Army Europe and Seventh Army, Germany. In August 2004, Major General Dowd returned to Washington, DC, to become the Executive Officer to the Deputy Chief of Staff, G-4, U.S. Army.

His joint assignments include Logistics Plans Officer, J-4, United States Atlantic Command, Norfolk, Virginia; Director, Logistics, Engineering and Security Assistance, J4, U.S. Pacific Command, Camp H.M. Smith, Hawaii. In 2007 he served as Director for Logistics, J-4, United States Central Command, MacDill Air Force Base, Florida.

Major General Dowd's awards included the Distinguished Service Medal, the Defense Superior Service Medal, the Legion of Merit with One Oak Leaf Cluster; Bronze Star Medal; Defense Meritorious Service Medal, the Meritorious Service Medal with five Oak Leaf Clusters; Army Commendation Medal with five Oak Leaf Clusters; the Army Achievement Medal with two Oak Leaf Clusters, and the Army Staff Identification Badge.

Dowd is married to the former Jennie Elmore, and they have one son, Cody, and a daughter, Correy.

Captain **Dwight Lyman Moody**, a native of Packard, attended Cumberland College before entering the United States Naval Academy in 1931. After being graduated from the Academy, Moody served various

naval assignments from Assistant Navigator to Commanding Officer. During his career Moody earned several commendations including the American Defense Service Medal with Star and the World War II Victory Medal.

After having survived the rigors of war, Moody's death occurred several years later as a result of an extreme reaction to the sting of a bumblebee.

Colonel **Ronald B. Stewart** was graduated from Cumberland College in 1953 and from the University of Kentucky School of law in 1959.

In 1954 Stewart enlisted in the Army where his interest in law was heightened. He served various posts as counsel. In 1969 Colonel Stewart began his military judicial service which lasted until 1985. He holds the record of the longest period of continuous judicial service in U. S. Army history serving not only here in the States but also in Vietnam, Europe, the Middle East, and Panama.

Stewart was born in Williamsburg, Kentucky; son of Edna Moore Stewart and Walter Stewart. He did his post graduate legal training at The Judge Advocate General's School at University of Virginia and The National Judicial College in Nevada.

Stewart retired from the U.S. Army as Colonel in 1985, following a longer period of continuous judicial service that any other Military Judge in U.S. Army history. He retired from the Kentucky Judiciary in 1999. He is a member of various legal and professional associations and has received the Legion of Merit, Bronze Start and numerous military awards and decorations. He was named "The Outstanding Judge in the United States on a Court of Special Jurisdiction" by the American Bar

Association as the National Conference of Special Court Judges in 1984.

Stewart is married to **Carolyn Asher Stewart,** 1953, and they have two sons and one grandson.

Major General **Charles G. Calloway** was reared in Whitley County and attended Cumberland College

from the eighth grade through one year of college. In 1925 Calloway received an appointment to the US Military Academy and was graduated in 1929. Calloway married Marian Dalrymple in 1930. She was a graduate of Cumberland College. General Calloway served with McArthur in Australia, New Guinea and the Philippian Islands and with the Army General Staff in Washington, D.C. during World War II. In 1954 Calloway was promoted to the rank of Brigadier General and given command of the New Research and Development Command. In 1957 he received the rank of Major General. In 1960 Calloway was moved to the Army General Staff, Washington, D.C. where he remained until his retirement in 1961.

Brigadier General **Roy W. Easley** was born in Frankfort and was graduated from Williamsburg Institute. He joined the Army's First Officers'

Training Camp in 1917 and by June 1918 was commissioned a First Lieutenant. In 1921 he made the rank of Captain and organized and commanded Company "D" of the Kentucky National Guard. In 1931 he was promoted to Major and then to Lieutenant Colonel, Kentucky National Guard; and in 1936 to Colonel, Kentucky National Guard. During World War II, Easley was assistant division commander of the 38th "Cyclone" division in the Philippines. He received the bronze star and other honors.[26]

Major General **Floyd L. Parks** was born in Louisville but moved to Lily as a child and then to Williamsburg. He attended Williamsburg Institute and Cumberland College before being graduated from Clemson College in South Carolina. He enlisted in the army in 1918 and was graduated from Yale University in 1924 with a degree in mechanical engineering while continuing his army career.

Parks served as an instructor at Camp Meade for one year before being sent to Hawaii. In 1941 as a Lieutenant Colonel he became Secretary, General Staff of the General Headquarters. He then served as Chief of Staff of Army Headquarters, Ground Forces in Washington, D.C.; Assistant Division Commander 9th Infantry Division; Chief of Staff, Headquarters, First Allied Airborne Army in Europe. As Commander of the First Airborne Army Parks participated in the crossing of the Rhone at Wesel in March 1945 in what is said to have been the largest airborne force lifted in one day during the war. **Parks was also responsible for leading the U.S. troops into Berlin on July 1, 1945** and he made the arrangements for the U.S. personnel at the Potsdam Conference and was commended by President Truman for his preparations. General Parks was Chief Commander of the Allied Kommandantantura, the military governing body of Berlin, and he was responsible for the inauguration of policies and procedures to improve the relationships among the occupation forces.[27]

"Admiral **Charles A. Blakely** was once a barefoot boy from Briar Creek but later he became the highest ranking Naval Officer whoever emerged from the state of Kentucky, so far as I have learned from any available source."[28]

Blakely was a Williamsburg Academy graduate in the class of 1897. During the Spanish American War he volunteered in the Infantry before attending the United States Naval Academy. He served in World War I and received the Distinguished Service Medal from the United States

and The Distinguished Service Order from Great Britain after commanding the U.S.S. Denver, the U.S.S. Michigan and the U.S.S. O'Brien.

In 1936 he completed aviation training and became the first man to have experience in submarines, surface vessels and aerial flight. He served as commanding officer of the Naval Air Station at Pensacola, of the Scouting Force Aircraft Squadrons, of the 11th Naval District and of the Naval Operating Base in San Diego. He retired in 1942 as a Vice Admiral.[29]

General **Benjamin R. Baker** was the nephew of Bessie M. Rose, graduate and longtime professor at Cumberland. Son of graduates Barney W. and Mary

Rose Baker and brother of graduate, Colonel John Baker. Baker was born at Hazard, KY and was graduated from Cumberland College, US Navy V-12 program, Berea College, M.D., University of Louisville, MS., (Surgery), Temple University. He retired from the United States Air Force as a Major General. Baker was the recipient of Distinguished Service Medal and Bronze Star. He served the US Department of Defense as Deputy Assistant Secretary for Health Programs & Resources.

While not an alumnus, Major General **Donald C.**

Storm has a strong connection with Cumberlands over the years. He was appointed as the Adjutant General of the Commonwealth of Kentucky by Governor Ernie Fletcher on Dec. 9 2003 and served in that position until Dec. 11 2007. Storm began his military career in 1970 as an enlisted soldier, serving with Military Assistance Commander Vietnam. After leaving active duty in 1972, he enlisted in the Kentucky Army National Guard and has been employed full time by the Guard since 1974. Since he was commissioned as an

Infantry officer in 1981, the General has commanded and served in staff officer positions at the company, battalion, brigade, and state headquarters level. His senior-level leadership assignments include: Director of Army Personnel; State Surface Maintenance Manager, Director of Plans, Operations and Training; and State Counter-Drug Coordinator. Gen. Storm served as the Kentucky Army Guard's Chief of Staff from October 2001 to December 2003. Storm has received numerous awards and decorations.

Major General James R. "Ron" Mason was assigned as the Commander, 35th Infantry Division (Mechanized), Fort Leavenworth, Kansas, in November 2003 and was promoted to Major General on December 6, 2003. Major General Mason assumed command of the Division after commanding Task Force Eagle and Multinational Brigade (North), Stabilization Force 13, for the NATO peacekeeping mission in Bosnia-Herzegovina.

Major General Mason received his commission through OCS in 1974. He is a graduate of the Infantry Basic and Armor Advanced Courses, the Command and General Staff College and other military schools including the Army War College. His assignments have included command of units at Platoon, Company, Battalion and Brigade levels. His staff assignments have included Intelligence Officer, Logistics Officer, Operations and Training Officer, Adjutant, Chief of Plans, Operations and Support and Deputy Director of Personnel Kentucky Army National Guard.

Mason has received numerous meritorious awards and decorations throughout his career, as well as several foreign awards and decorations.

Major General Mason retired December 2006 and resides in Middlesboro Kentucky with his wife, Helen.

Meet our Governors

Like a flower that sprouts and grows, you never know what our graduates will become until they've gone out into the world to do such marvelous things. Two of our graduates became Governors of Kentucky, one a democrat and one a republican.

Bert T. Combs, the Democratic Governor of Kentucky from 1959-1963, attended Cumberland College from 1929-1931. He had an active career  serving as Commonwealth Attorney, 31st Judicial District Kentucky, 1950-1951; Judge, Court of Appeals, Kentucky, 1951-1955; Governor, Commonwealth of Kentucky, 1959-1963; and Judge, United States Court of Appeals, 6th District, 1967-1970. He practiced law with the firm Wyatt, Tarrant, and Combs, Louisville, Kentucky, until his unfortunate death from hypothermia on December 3, 1991, as a result of being swept away in a flash flood.

Combs is commonly credited with the construction of I-75 through Kentucky, the founding of the community and technical college system, bringing educational television to our state and perhaps his most important achievement, the Kentucky Education Reform Act (KERA). KERA came about as a result of Combs' representation of 66 poor school districts challenging the state's method of financing public education. The state's Supreme Court ruled the state's system unconstitutional, and the General Assembly revamped the education system in three areas: finance, governance and curriculum. KERA's objective is to provide equal educational opportunities for all Kentucky children no matter the wealth of the district in which they reside.

Combs was graduated from Cumberland College in 1930. Here are some of his thoughts as expressed in an interview in 1980, when he was recognized as an outstanding alumnus at Homecoming.

"I learned about Cumberland College fifty years ago. I was seventeen at the time. I lived in Manchester in Clay County. I had finished high school at Manchester. I had absolutely no prospects for a job or going to college. There were seven in my family, seven children. My father managed to feed and house us and that was about it. So my mother and a friend of hers, who taught business school, shorthand and typing and so on, got me to take shorthand and typing from this lady. And so then they decided they would send me to college. They didn't know where, but Mrs. Benge knew about Cumberland, and said, 'You need to go to Cumberland College, it's a good school, and it won't cost very much, and that's where you need to go.' But I said, 'It will cost something, and I don't have anything.' She said, 'I am gonna get you a job. I can get you a job in Williamsburg with a coal mine.' She knew somebody in one of the coal companies. And so a little later she said, 'You have a job waiting for you.' My mother and her friend pushed me on a bus and said, 'You are going to Cumberland College.'

So I got on the bus in Manchester with a blue serge suit and a long bill cap (the kids wore long bill caps in those days). I came to Williamsburg and came up and enrolled. This was the second semester 1929, and this was January. The next day I went to the office of this coal company. I have forgotten the name of it, but they didn't know anything about Bert Combs, of course, or they didn't know anything about a job for anybody like me. So here I was. I was enrolled and had been assigned in classes. I hadn't attended any classes, but I had absolutely no money.

Dr. J. L. Creech was president at the time and somebody said to me, 'There is a little money in a fund for emergency purposes and why don't you see Dr. Creech.' Creech said, 'Well, I don't know. I want you to write something for me.' He gave me two pieces of paper and told me to write two or three sentences on each piece of paper. He said, 'Come back in three days.'

I went back in three days, and he loaned me $100. So I stayed in Cumberland. This is, of course, a personal story; but the point is at that time and through the years there have been hundreds and even thousands of young people in this part of Kentucky in the Appalachian region that couldn't have gone to

College except that Cumberland was here and Cumberland cooperated to make it possible for those kids to stay in college. I remember Dr. Creech said in one of the specimens he wanted me to write, 'Cumberland College educates the youth of the mountains.' That's exactly the truth, and I'm certain except for Cumberland I would have never gone to college.

I think Cumberland has done an outstanding job in making it possible for the youth of this region to obtain a college education. Of course, when I was here it was a two-year college, but with what I got at Cumberland that enabled me to go to another institution and also taught me that education was important; that without knowledge you cannot compete. It's just that simple, and I think a practical example is that from the early 30's until the middle 60's, it may be the early 70's, the youth of this region, and that means the leaders, the potential leaders, were leaving this part of Kentucky. For the last ten years, since 1970, they have been coming back, and the trend is very definitely now in a return to this region of the country, and I think the educational institutions are largely responsible for that. Without educational facilities these people would not come back to eastern Kentucky. They would leave, and they would stay.

When I was here we had a dedicated and fortunately educated group of faculty members that I think would measure up to any faculty anywhere. They were men and women of dedication, and more importantly, of vision, and they had the ability to transmit that dedication and a desire in their students to continue their education. And those faculty members had this philosophy in mind: Some people look at things as they are and say so what, and others dream of what might be and say, why not. And those ladies and gentlemen dreamed of what might be and were not ashamed of it, and they said, why not. They were idealists. Ideas, of course, are like stars. You don't reach them with your hands, but they knew that although they couldn't reach the stars, like a sailor in the ocean if they set their course on those stars and dedicated themselves with their vision and their energy, they would reach the proper destination.

When I was here I fired the furnace in Felix Hall. Dr. Creech was a bachelor and he lived in that Hall, first door on the right when you went in. We didn't need any thermometer; he was the thermometer. He was a good thermometer, and if I let that heat vary five degrees, up or down, I immediately heard about it from Dr. Creech.

To me Cumberland College is unique in that if a young person has average ability to learn, a desire to learn, and is willing to work, he or she can go to Cumberland College, at least I found it that way, and I'm certain it is still that way.

In addition to making it possible for hundreds, perhaps thousands of young people to go to college, students received at Cumberland a solid foundation in art, sciences, history, and literature, and the kind of training that is so important, if not absolutely necessary, for a person who is going to be competitive in whatever area, industry, or profession he takes up. The teachers here taught the importance of patriotism and religion, but they didn't do it to the extent that it causes reaction. Students, I think, were encouraged to practice high morals and high ethics.

I see a very great future for Cumberland College. It is now the biggest private institution of higher learning in Kentucky. It, of course, has been a four-year institution for several years now. It is still dedicated to the principles on which it was founded, but it has kept up with changes in the world. It has increased greatly, of course, in its enrollment. They have a very imaginative, a very capable, a very progressive president, President Taylor. They have an excellent supporting staff, and I have kept up with it enough to know that they still have a faculty of dedication and vision, many of whom, in particular, have the ability to instill in young people the feeling that the pursuit of knowledge is important in itself, is an end in itself for that matter.

And so I see with that combination and with the dedication and the desire to continue to educate many young people of Appalachia on the same basis that the College has followed since its founding, I believe Cumberland College will perform a great role in the future, not only for students of Appalachia, but across Kentucky and across this country.

Cumberland has a dedicated, imaginative, capable President, a fine supporting staff, and perhaps more importantly, a faculty dedicated to instilling in young people a desire to learn and to become good citizens. But we still have a lot of work to do. I know Cumberland College, although successful, has problems and will always have problems because that's part of life, but the problems today ought to be the progress of tomorrow, and from tomorrow's progress each of us ought to be in a position to say, 'I had a part, even though perhaps a small part, in building a bigger and better Cumberland College'[30]

Edwin Porch Morrow was reared in a family of politicians. His father, Thomas C., was defeated in

the Kentucky governor's race in 1883. Morrow's uncle, William O. Bradley, was Kentucky's first Republican governor. Morrow was elected governor in 1919 and still holds the distinction of being the only governor elected from Pulaski County.

Morrow was born a twin in 1877. He attended Cumberland prior to serving in the Spanish American War in 1898. After contracting typhoid fever, Morrow was discharged from the army in 1899. In 1902 Morrow was graduated from the University of Cincinnati with a degree in law.

Morrow earned a reputation as a successful criminal defense lawyer in Lexington after successfully defending a black man accused of murder.

In 1910 Morrow was appointed by President Taft to serve as US Attorney for the Eastern District of Kentucky. Following an unsuccessful run for the U.S. Senate in 1912, Morrow also lost the governor's race in 1915. In 1919, however, he was successful and became the 40th governor of Kentucky. Morrow is known as Kentucky's "law and order" governor. He signed the bill ratifying the U.S. Constitution's 19th Amendment in Kentucky, created the state's first Department of Labor, enforced the law against carrying concealed weapons, and called for the creation of colleges at Morehead and Murray.

After leaving the office of governor, Morrow continued his public service with numerous civil rights organizations, on the US Railroad Labor Board and later the US Board of Mediation. He sought the U.S. senate seat again in 1934 but was defeated.

Morrow married Katherine Hale Waddle on June 18, 1903 in Somerset. The couple had two children, Edwina Haskell and Charles Robert. Morrow passed away suddenly in 1935 from a heart attack.[31]

Eugene Siler reminds us that Morrow was from Somerset as was Senator John Sherman Cooper. Cooper had once talked with Morrow about a political career and Morrow gave Cooper this advice, "Be gentle with the people – always be gentle with the people."[32]

Meet a few of our Judges, Justices and a Congressman

Mr. A.T. Siler always had a cigar in his pocket, wore a rose in his lapel, and carried a cane. It is told that one day a gentleman asked Siler why he had a cigar in his pocket since he never smoked, why he had a rose in his lapel since he never smelled it, and why he carried a cane since he never used it for walking? Siler responded that he did these things because they made him feel like somebody.

Eugene E. Siler, Sr., the son of A. T. Siler, was graduated from Cumberland College in 1920 and from the University of Kentucky in 1922. He studied law at Columbia University and practiced law in Williamsburg. He was a judge of the Court of

Appeals of Kentucky, 1945-1949, and a United States Congressman, representing the Fifth District in Kentucky, 1955-1965. Siler also ran for governor in 1951, but was defeated. He was elected as Moderator of the General Association of Baptists in Kentucky in 1952 and served two years. Siler served as a member of Cumberland College's Board of Trustees from 1946 to 1965 and as a Deacon and Sunday School teacher at Williamsburg's First Baptist Church. According to Congressman Carroll Hubbard, addressing the graduating class of Cumberland College in May, 1984, it was Eugene Siler, Sr. who led this nation's Congress to place the words, "One Nation Under God," in our pledge to the flag of the United States. Congressman Siler can also be credited as the first Congressman to speak out against the Vietnam conflict, calling it a "great mistake," and, as a Congressman, he voted against the sending of troops to Vietnam in 1964. Mr. Siler passed away in December, 1987. Siler was well known for his strong Baptist beliefs, openly opposing the use of alcohol, profanity and cigarettes, and in his law practice never took cases involving alcohol and divorce.[33]

To honor Congressman Siler, the University constructed and dedicated Eugene E. Siler Hall in 1985 to house 100 male students.

Eugene Siler, Jr., although not an alumnus, is the grandson of Mr. A. T. Siler and the son of Congressman Eugene E. Siler and a native of Williamsburg. He attended Vanderbilt University and was graduated *cum laude* in 1958 with a B.A. He attended law school at the University of Virginia, receiving an LL.B. degree in 1963. He also has two LL.M. degrees from Georgetown University and the University of Virginia.

Judge Siler served as an officer on active duty in the U.S. Navy from 1958-60. He later retired as a Commander in the U.S. Naval Reserve.

He began his private law practice in Williamsburg in 1964 with his father. He was elected Whitley County Attorney and served in that position from 1965 until 1970 when he was appointed United States Attorney for the Eastern District of Kentucky by President Nixon.

In 1975, Judge Siler was appointed by President Ford to the United States District Court for the Eastern and Western Districts of Kentucky. He was later appointed to the United States Court of Appeals for the Sixth Circuit in 1991 by President Bush.

He was given the 1992 Outstanding Judge of the Year Award by the Kentucky Bar Association. In 1992, he was sent by the U.S. State Department to Lithuania, to assist the judiciary and bar association in that country in making the transition from a Communist to a democratic system.

Although not an alumnus, Judge Siler has served as a Trustee and Chairman of the Board of the University of the Cumberlands. He is currently a Board member for Baptist Healthcare.

Judge Siler is married to the former **Chris Minnich**, a graduate of Cumberland College. They have two sons, Gene Siler, III and Adam T. Siler.

Judge Siler still lives in Williamsburg and has offices in London and Cincinnati. He is a member of the

First Baptist Church in Williamsburg, where he serves as a deacon, trustee and Sunday School teacher.

Judge **Jerry D. Winchester** is a native of McCreary County, Kentucky and a coal miner's son.

With encouragement from his father and a scholarship to Cumberland, Winchester enrolled in

the fall of 1959. During the school year, he cleaned the Gray Brick Building (now known as the Bennett Building). In the summer, he worked any job he could get, painting houses half a day, lifeguarding at the city pool and driving a gas truck. Money earned

was used to pay for tuition.

Looking back on his time at Cumberland, Winchester said he was challenged by teachers who did not want him to simply get through college, but to succeed above and beyond the standards. He also spoke of teachers who wanted to expand student experiences and outlooks.

After graduating from Cumberland in 1963, Winchester was recruited for training at the Wright Patterson Air Force Base in Dayton, Ohio. He began his career as a math teacher at McCreary County High School and in 1967 he earned his law degree and gained employment with the FBI. Winchester served as a special agent for five years. He began practicing law in Corbin, Kentucky in 1971 and then served as the Commonwealth Attorney for twelve years. Governor Martha Lane Collins appointed Winchester as Circuit Court Judge which he held until retiring in 2007. Since then, he has served as Senior Judge and is the longest sitting judge in Whitley County.

Judge Winchester and his wife, Nell, reside in Corbin. They celebrated their 50th wedding anniversary on June 29, 2013.

Robert Boone Bird, a 1924 graduate, served the Kentucky Supreme Court, Court of Appeals 1957-1965. From 1960-1962 he served as Chief Justice.

Judge **Pleas Jones** Wife: Marie Jones. Two sons: Pleas David Jones, Gorman Jones. The Honorable

Pleas Jones was graduated from Cumberland College in 1934. He then attended the University of Kentucky Law School. He was a veteran of World War II. Judge Jones served this area and its people in

a host of positions: school teacher, circuit court clerk, county judge, commonwealth attorney, and circuit judge. In 1973, Judge Jones was appointed to the State Court of Appeals, then Kentucky's highest court, and in 1976,

when the court system was reorganized, he was appointed Supreme Court Justice from the Third Appellate District, a post he held until 1979. Judge Jones was an active member of Williamsburg's Main Street Baptist Church, where he served as Sunday School teacher, church treasurer, and chairman of the Building and Finance Committee. He also served as Commander of Williamsburg's American Legion post, president of Williamsburg's Lions Club, president of the Kentucky Society of the Sons of the American Revolution, and member of the Rotary Club, Masons, and Shriners.

Judge **Ronald Blaine Stewart** (See Meet our Generals, Admirals and Other Heroes)

Buzz Carloftis, class of 1973. Carloftis was graduated with a major in political science and a minor in German. He earned the Master of Arts in Political Science degree from Eastern Kentucky University. Carloftis has served as judge-executive for Rockcastle County since October, 1993, having been appointed by Governor Jones to fill a term of his predecessor. Judge Carloftis is now the longest serving county judge in Rockcastle County's 204-year history, and has the third longest continuous tenure in Kentucky. Recently Rockcastle County was recognized by the state's Economic Development Cabinet as having created the largest number of new jobs in Kentucky based upon per capita population. He steered 40% of Rockcastle's tax revenues toward economic development, had the County purchase and renovate a manufacturing building and built another building for job growth. In addition, a number of parks have been created under his leadership, along with four new fire departments.

Meet a few of our Doctors

With 30% of our students enrolled in STEM programs (science, technology, engineering and mathematics) our graduates find easy access to medical school, pharmacy school, veterinary medicine school, engineering school and other professional schools.

At one time all Wayne County doctors were our alumni: **Dr. Mack Roberts, Dr. John Simmons, Dr. Lyle Matthews, and Dr. William Kelsey**.

Jimmy Kamso-Pratt, can be considered a diamond in the rough. Pratt came to Cumberlands from a mud hut in Sierra Leone and went on to become both a Ph.D. and M.D. Pratt was named doctor of the year several years ago in Tennessee. He is now serving his Sierra Leone with free medical clinics.

Jimmy Kamso-Pratt is a native of Freetown, Sierra Leone, West Africa. While attending a Christian high school in Sierra Leone, Pratt met a man who worked for the Peace Corps who suggested Pratt  attend Cumberlands. Pratt was the first in his family to finish high school and go to college. Though Pratt knew he wanted to serve in some capacity, it wasn't until he attended Cumberland that becoming a doctor became a possibility. Dr. Kamso-Pratt received his Bachelor of Science degree in biology from Cumberland, graduating with high honors; his Ph.D. from Louisiana State University, and he did postdoctoral work at Meharry Medical Center in Nashville. He received his medical degree from the University of Tennessee, Memphis in 1993 and completed his postgraduate residency training at the University of Tennessee Medical Center, Department of Family Medicine, in Knoxville. Dr. Pratt is Board Certified in Family Medicine. Pratt has been practicing medicine at East Jackson Family Medical Center in Jackson, TN for over a decade and a half. He divides his time between the clinic in Tennessee and his mission work in Sierra Leone, Hands to Hearts, which provides free medicine and healthcare services to those in need and educates the country's less privileged children. The situation in Sierra Leone was recorded in the movie, **Blood Diamond.**

Mack Roberts, Born in Wayne County. Married to Alma Dolen, three daughters, and four grandchildren. Cumberland Junior College, University of Louisville. Janitor on the third floor of Felix Hall. Taught in a

one room rural school in Wayne County. County Health Officer of Wayne County. Interned one year at St. Joseph's Hospital in Lexington. Private practice in Monticello. Valedictorian in. high school, Member of the Wayne County Medical Society, the Kentucky Medical Association, the American Medical Association, the 50 Year Club of American Medicine, Elk Spring Baptist Church, and President of the Monticello Banking Company. Class Agent.

Paul Ray Smith, a native of Pineville, KY, graduated from Cumberland in 1949. After graduation, Smith taught third grade for one year. He then went to the University of Kentucky to finish his  bachelor's degree. He gained his medical license in 1957 from the University of Louisville Medical School. Soon after, Smith enlisted in the United States Air Force, serving as a flight surgeon from 1958-1960. When he returned, he set up his practice in London, KY. He served as team physician for the London High School football team and the Laurel High School (now South Laurel High School) football team. Dr. Smith retired in 1998 after 41 years of service.

Dr. Smith is the current CME Medical Director at Southern Kentucky AHEC and works in a free clinic, once a month, for uninsured persons.

He has served as an elder at London's First Christian Church and as chairman of the church board. Dr. Smith and his wife, Ann (Hollin) Smith, a 1956 alumna, reside in London, Kentucky.

Amir Tabatabai first learned of Cumberland while a student at Oneida Baptist Institute. At Cumberland  he had a double major in biology and chemistry. In 1989 he did undergraduate research from Columbia University. While at Cumberland he participated in the Student Government Association, American Chemical Society, Clowns for Christ, International Student Club, Baptist Student Union, and Medical Careers Club. Amir was also a lab assistant for the Biology Department.

Amir attended the University of Louisville Medical School and graduated cum laude in 1994. He did his residency in internal medicine in St. Louis in 1997. He also did fellowship training in hematology and oncology at Washington University in 2000. Dr. Tabatabai has been an Oncologist at York Hospital in York, PA since 2000.

Dr. Amir Tabatabai lives in York, Pennsylvania and has two sons.

Doris Spegal of DeMossville, Kentucky earned her  associate's degree from Cumberland in 1937. She then transferred to the University of Louisville and took one more year of college and four years of medical school and graduated in 1942 with an M.D.

Spegal started in the private practice of pediatrics in Dallas, Texas, in 1945. She was appointed Professor of Pediatrics at the local medical school, a post she held for twenty years. She taught senior students in the clinic, usually one day per week for a month, two times each year. Spegal was accepted as a training union director for a department of teenagers for several years and often planned her vacations to attend the teenage summer camps as the camp doctor. She developed a set of lectures on parenting and did these for many school PTA's. In 1989, Spegal was inducted into Cumberland's Alumni Hall of Honor.

Charles E. Freeman. Born and grew up in Williamsburg, Kentucky. Williamsburg High School, Cumberland College (2 year), Illinois College of Optometry (O.D. degree), Pennsylvania College of Optometry, graduate work, Continuing education annually. Practiced optometry in  Williamsburg starting in 1950. Member: American Optometric Association; Kentucky Optometric Association; Eastern Kentucky Optometric Society; Veterans of Foreign Wars; First Baptist Church. Past member: Deacon Board of First Baptist Church; City Council of City of Williamsburg. Cumberland College: Past member of the Board of Trustees; Past chairman, Board of Trustees.

James Croley, III earned a Bachelor of Science  degree from Cumberland in 1972, where he majored in biology, minored in chemistry, and was graduated with honors. Dr. Croley is one of the most respected ophthalmologists in the United States. He attended medical school at the University of Miami in Florida. After an internship at Baptist Medical Centers in Birmingham, Alabama, he served his residency at the University of Alabama Eye Foundation Hospital, where he was named Chief Resident and House Staff Representative. Now residing in Cape Coral, Florida, he is an ophthalmologist at his own practice, Cataract and Refractive Institute of Florida.

"… one thing I know, that, whereas I was blind, now I see." Dr. James Croley, III, has received numerous awards and honors for his work and is an active participant in causes related to sight. He also was a pioneer in telemedicine, developing software to enable access to medical care in rural communities in the United States.

Desiring to provide exceptional care to his patients, Dr. Croley developed an electronic medical records computer program for doctors to use in their offices and a patient eye care education web site called TotalEye.org. He decided from the very beginning that a portion of the income raised from this website would be donated to his alma mater. When asked what spurred this decision, Dr. Croley stated, "I believe in the mission that Cumberland has in helping students from the area get an outstanding education." Although he is miles and miles away, Dr. Croley continues to give back.

He is past president of the Florida Society of Ophthalmology and has served on its board for over 15 years. Dr. Croley was a member of the Council for the American Academy of Ophthalmology for 6 years and served on the Ophthapac Committee for 5 years. The Lions Club of American honored Dr. Croley with the Melvin Jones Award for his work in providing free eye care for the needy. Dr. Croley served on the board of directors at the Kentucky Mountain Laurel Festival, and he has been awarded the distinction of Kentucky Colonel. He currently serves on the University's Board of Visitors.

Darrel Estle Rains - "And God said, Let there be light: and there was light. And God saw the light: that it was good…" Darrel Estle Rains first saw the light of day on September 28, 1939, in diminutive Emlyn in southeastern Kentucky, and whether he knew it or not, light was to become the dominant theme of his life. First it was the loving light in the eyes of proud parents, Robert and Lula Rains. Later, that light was supplemented by the pleased glow on the faces of teachers, such as P.R. Jones as they one by one recognized his inherent intelligence, strength of character, and unusual determination to learn. And then along the way came the light of self-discovery: Darrel saw clearly by the time of his graduation from Williamsburg High School in 1957 that his life's path was to be, had to be, in medicine. "A wise man will hear, and will increase learning:

and a man of understanding shall attain unto wise counsels…" Darrell began his pre-med training at Cumberland College in the fall of 1957, entering with many of his high school classmates: Siler, Byrd, Early, Chambers, Grant, Jones, King, Broyles, Yancy, West… He lived at home, studied hard, earned A's, and became increasingly committed to a career in medicine. He also lived in the light, further developing a religious faith and an aggressive self-discipline that stirred the respect of even the most macho of his friends. In 1959, the Lamp of Higher Education was passed to the University of Kentucky after Darrel graduated from Cumberland; there he roomed with his old friend, Jimmy King. By now his enthusiasm for medicine and achievement had been fanned to white-hot intensity. He worked at the UK Medical School doing genetics research while also carrying a full class load. He consistently urged his close friends (many of them former classmates at Cumberland) to study hard and to develop demanding personal goals. And he took his own advice, graduating with honors in 1961. All three medical schools where he made application for admission

accepted Darrel; he chose to remain at the University of Kentucky. In medical school, Darrel continued to strain for the stars. Characteristically, he didn't want to become just another doctor- he wanted to provide Kentuckians with the quality of medical care that they would expect to receive at only the best metropolitan medical centers. In 1965, after four years of intensive study, Darrel achieved the first part of his bright dream; he received his M.D. degree. The second part was equally tough. To make sure he had all the skills necessary to give his patients complete medical care. Darrel did residencies in not one but three fields: General Practice (John Gaston Hospital in Memphis), Psychiatry (Rollmans Psychiatric Hospital in Cincinnati), and his major field, Ophthalmology (Eye Foundation Hospital in Birmingham). It took five more years, but finally Darrell knew he was fully prepared to being his medical practice. "… one thing I know, that, whereas I was blind, now I see." The first few years of Darrel's practice were spent in hospital emergency rooms. Then in 1974, he renewed his friendship with Dr. James Parrott, a Corbin native and classmate from UK, and his wife, Phyllis, by opening an ophthalmology practice in Hopkinsville, Kentucky, where Dr. Parrott was working as a Radiologist. Darrel was joined there by his brother, Ken, who provided complementary services as an Optician. Darrel's reputation for excellence quickly spread, and physicians from all over Kentucky, Missouri, Tennessee, Alabama, Ohio, and Indiana sent patients to Hopkinsville for eye surgery. They gave Darrel the "tough" cases, and in return he gave his patients unexcelled professional care along with healthy measures of love and compassion. In many instances, the blind were literally made to see. Darrel had achieved his dream- he was providing his patients with the best medical care in the world. Over a relatively short span of remarkably productive years, this "Man of Light" had many great achievements. Among them were: Dr. Rains was one of the first doctors in the world to do outpatient surgery for cataracts, using as a scalpel the exquisitely pure light from a laser; Dr. Rains built his own laser system and used it for patient care at a time when this technology was considered to be strictly a research tool. He was ten years ahead of his profession; Dr. Rains had his own research effort, the development of laser surgery techniques for diabetic patients; Dr. Rains published his work in internationally acknowledged medical journals, some with co-authors at major medical schools. "And if I go and prepare a place for you, I will come again, and receive you unto myself; that where I am, there ye may be also." But even as Dr. Darrel Rains was bringing hope and healing and joy to others, dark storm clouds of ill health were gathering in his own life. In December of 1977, Darrel was forced to have a double heart valve replacement at a hospital in Birmingham. Shortly thereafter, in January of 1979, a heart transplant operation was performed on him at Stanford University. And finally, on October 20, 1982, one of the world's leading Ophthalmologists died. Then, surely, his triumphant and shining spirit encountered another great Healer, One who once said, "... I am the Light of the world..." Darrel's wife, Sheila, and sons, Derrick, Brian, and Gavin, are grateful to Cumberland College for helping Darrel develop his extraordinary vision, creativity, and determination." James Gover ('59)

Another alumnus who has worked tirelessly to assist those who have poor sight is **Jerry Wayne Barker.** Barker was graduated from Cumberland College in 1996 with a major in biology and a minor in chemistry. One year after leaving Cumberland, he became a laboratory processing assistant and team leader at Baptist Hospital in Knoxville, Tennessee. This led to him serving a yearlong position as Technical Director of the East Tennessee Lions Eye Bank. For six years (1998-2004) Barker gained

valuable business and technical knowledge as Director of Clinical Services of North Carolina Eye Bank in Winston Salem, North Carolina.

His big move occurred in June 2004, when Barker founded Ocular Systems in Winston Salem, North Carolina, which is an independent firm specializing

in the processing and delivery of corneal tissue for transplantation. He defined, developed and launched an ophthalmic medical device product to support domestic and international ophthalmic surgeons. While engaged in all aspects of the

company both domestic and international, Barker networks with business contacts and is the driving force behind company sales while managing the executive team responsible for the strategic vision for the organization.

Barker has held Certified Eye Bank Technician (CEBT) credentials through the Eye Bank Association of America since 1998, and he is on the North Carolina Biotechnology Center Advisory Board. In 2011, Barker was inducted into Cumberlands Alumni Hall of Honor as the Young Alumnus Award Recipient.

Although not an alumnus of Cumberlands, one of our professors, **Travis Freeman,** caught the attention of

movie producers. His unconditional love for football and his faith in Christ gave him motivation after developing meningitis and becoming **totally blind**.

Freeman was challenged at the

tender age of twelve when he lost his sight. The Corbin native was the typical middle school boy whose life was consumed by football and friends. But he contacted a deadly disease that kills nearly 70% of people affected and usually leaves the remaining 30% in a vegetated state. He, however, was lucky and pulled through. His case is the second case in the world where only the eyes were affected. Even though he was only twelve years old, he still tried to maintain a positive outlook on life. What he wanted more than anything was to play football. And play he did with the help of the quarterback and the encouragement of the team.

He continued to play football throughout the rest of his middle school career and through high school. With the help and motivation given to him by his Coach, he played the position of center on the Corbin High School football team. His teammates would help him and tell him where to go during the plays of the game. They were always trying to help protect him which is true team work.

Years after high school, he received a phone call from the mother of a friend and former teammate. She wanted to create her first screen play about his life. He agreed to it and the film "23 Blast" was made. The movie's title was adopted from an old high school football play they used which they called, "23 Blast."

Although many view Dr. Travis Freeman as a hero, he remains humbled throughout everything. He says that he is just a regular guy living his life. About a year after Freeman finished his Ph.D. in Expository Preaching at The Southern Baptist Theological Seminary, he came to UC during the spring of 2013 to be an adjunct instructor of religion.

He is enjoying his teaching experience at the University of the Cumberlands and hopes to make it his permanent home.

Harold L. Moses is the son of Mrs. Catherine H. Smith (Franklin, Tennessee) and Mr. Ernest Moses (deceased), formerly of Gatliff and Pleasant View, Kentucky. Married to Linda Hardeman. Four

children – Jeanne, Jill, William, and Timothy. Attended Gatliff Elementary School, Pleasant View High School and Cumberland College ('54-'56) and received a B.A. degree in Chemistry from Berea College. Attended Vanderbilt University Medical School, Nashville, Tennessee, receiving an M.D. degree. After residency training in pathology at Vanderbilt University Hospital, he served in the U.S. Public Health Service as Surgeon

(Lieutenant Commander) at the National Institutes of Health in Bethesda, Maryland. He entered academic medicine and has held faculty positions at Vanderbilt University School of Medicine as Assistant and Associate Professor and Mayo Medical School as Associate and Full Professor. He was also Consultant in Pathology at the Mayo Clinic during this time and was Chairman of the Department of Cell Biology at Vanderbilt University Medical and Professor of Cell Biology and Pathology. Phi Kappa Phi honor society, Alpha Omega Alpha honor society. He also received the Merrell Award for Research in Pathology while in medical school. A Diplomat of the American Board of Pathology, received a Research Career Development Award from the National Institutes of Health, the Ester Langer Award for Meritorious Cancer Research from the University of Chicago. Outstanding Investigator Award from the National Cancer Institute, Outstanding Alumnus Award from Cumberland College. A member of the American Association for Cancer Research, the European Association for Cancer Research, the American Society for Cell Biology, the American Association for the Advancement of Science, the Tissue Culture Association, the American Association of Pathologists, and the United States and Canadian Academy of Pathologists. Member and then Chairman of the Chemical Pathology Study Section of the National Institutes of Health. A member of the Scientific Advisory Board of the Division of Cancer Biology and Diagnosis of the National Cancer Institute. A member of the Board of Directors of the American Association for Cancer Research. He is the author or co-author of 125 papers in research journals. Co-edited two books on cancer research and growth factors. He is an editor of the *Journal of Cellular Physiology*, and Associate Editor of *Cancer Research, Carcinogenesis, Oncogene Research,* and *Molecular Carcinogenesis.* Member of the editorial board of the *Journal of Cellular Biochemistry, The International Journal of Cancer, Laboratory Investigation and Molecular Endocrinology.* He has given over 100 invited lectures on his research at various meeting and universities in the United States, Europe and Japan.

John R. Jones graduated from Pleasant View High School as valedictorian of his class in 1950. He graduated from Cumberland in 1952, University of Kentucky in 1954, and was a graduate from the University of Louisville Medical School in 1957. He interned at Lackland Air Force Base in San Antonio, TX, continued medical training in Rantrol, Illinois Air Force Base, and did his residency at Vanderbilt Hospital in Nashville, TN in Orthopedic Surgery.

Jones worked in private practice in Nashville, served as assistant professor of orthopedic surgery at Vanderbilt University Hospital, and was a member of the Biology Department and team physician at Cumberland. He was a member of the American Academy of Orthopedic Surgeons, the American Medical Association, and the Tennessee Walking Horse Breeder Exhibitor Association. In 1993, he retired as Chief of Staff at the Baptist Regional Medical Center in Corbin, KY. Jones passed away in 1994 at the age of 60.

Glen R. Baker, Jr. Born: Corbin, Kentucky. Married, Gail Annett Landsverk. 5 Children: Melissa, Andrew Patrick, Sara Beth, Alison, John Edward. Cumberland College, Williamsburg, Kentucky 1960-1964, University of Louisville School of Medicine, University of Louisville School of Medicine & Affiliated Hospitals. Mayo Graduate School, Mayo Clinic, Fellowship in Internal Medicine. Fellowship in Department of Respiratory and Environmental Diseases, University of Louisville School of Medicine & Affiliated Hospitals. Internal Medicine, Pulmonary Diseases, American College Chest Physicians Kentucky State Board of Health. Whitley County Medical Society, Kentucky Medical Association, American Medical Association, Kentucky Thoracic Society, American College of Physicians, American Thoracic Society, American College of Chest Physicians, Mayo Alumni Association (Founding Member), Brothers Mayo Society. Private Practice, Corbin, Ky. Consultative Pulmonary Disease & Internal Medicine, Director, Respiratory Care Services, Baptist Regional Medical Center, Corbin, Ky. Chief of Medicine, Baptist Regional Medical Center, Corbin, Ky. Medical Examiner. CSX Railroad Retirement Board. Medical Examiner, U.S. Department of Labor, Determinations of Pulmonary Disorders. Medical Examiner for various insurance companies. Quality Assurance Committee, Executive Committee, Pharmaceutical & Therapeutical Committee. Outstanding Alumnus, Cumberland College, 1976. Class Agent, Cumberland College Alumni Association.

Ralph Myers Denham. Born in Hazard, Kentucky. One son: Ernest Wilder Denham. Grades 1-5:

Cumberland College Primary Department. Grades 6-12: Williamsburg Graded School and High School. Graduated, Cumberland Junior College. University of Kentucky, B.S., Vanderbilt University, School of Medicine – M.D., Henry Ford Hospital, Detroit, Michigan: Intern, Resident and Fellow in Cardiology. U.S. Army Medical Corps, Captain. Henry Ford Hospital: Member of Staff. Private practice in Cardiology, Louisville, Kentucky 1951 until retirement 1985. Clinical Professor-emeritus of Medicine (Cardiology) University of Louisville, School of Medicine. President- Kentucky Heart Association. Governor for Kentucky, American College of Cardiology. President, Kentucky Baptist Hospital. President, Methodist Evangelical Hospital. Certified American Board of Internal Medicine; Certified in Cardiovascular Disease; Ralph M. Denham Annual Lectureship in Cardiology - Louisville, Kentucky; Ralph M. Denham Achievement Award, Williamsburg Kiwanis Club; Doctor of Humane Letters, Cumberland College; Deacon, Jeffersontown Christian Church. Phi Beta Kappa. Alumni Board of Directors, Kentuckiana Chapter of Alumni. Assisted in fund raising projects of the college.

JoAnne Sexton earned an associate's degree from Cumberland in 1946. She went on to receive her bachelor's degree from the University of Kentucky and an M.D. from the University of Louisville. After completing medical school and pediatric training in Louisville, Dr. Sexton went to Houston where she spent nearly 4 years in pediatric neurology fellowship. She then returned to Kentucky and for eight years worked in Maternal and Child Health in the State Health Department. While there she developed a team of doctors, nurses, EEG technicians, psychologists, and nutritionists. Sexton

41

and her team went to 25 counties from one end of the state to the other evaluating children with suspected neurological problems. Through this program Dr. Sexton's team discovered that many children who were failing in school and were suspected of being mentally retarded were not retarded at all, but were failing because of poor attendance, cultural deprivation or other problems. She worked in Hazard, Lynchburg, and Nashville. The last eight years of her practice were spent at Meharry Medical College in Nashville – a job that was very rewarding to Dr. Sexton, and where she saw patients and taught medical students.

Eddie Steely Perkins graduated Cumberland College in 1985 with a Bachelor of Science in biology. Following employment with a major pharmaceutical company he attended medical school and was graduated from the University of Health Sciences in Kansas City, Missouri. He completed a transitional year in family medicine and then a four year residency in obstetrics and gynecology through Ohio University. He is a board certified obstetrician and gynecologist and has extensive laparoscopic surgical experience. Dr. Perkins has served as Dean and Program Director of Cumberlands' School of Physician Assistant Studies and now as Vice President for Medical Services at Cumberlands.

Martha Charlene Hill Robinson, M.D. Parents: Lillian and Charlie Hill, three sisters, one brother. Married to Jimmy Don Robinson. Williamsburg Cumberland College, Williamsburg, Ky. June 1958 to August 1959; Georgetown College; Cumberland College, Williamsburg, Ky. June 1960 to May 1961; Bachelor of Science/Chemistry/Biology/Pre-med; First four year Cumberland graduate to go to medical school; University of Kentucky Medical Center, Received M.D. in June 1968. Interned at Greenville General Hospital, Greenville, South Carolina. Solo

Family Practice, Ballard County Health Clinic, Barlow, Ky. Coroner of Ballard County, Ky. First woman coroner to be elected and serve in Kentucky. Owned and operated Eagle Rest Plantation, Kevil, Ky. Livestock farm with international reputation, especially known for jack stock which are marketed worldwide. Member of KMA, Ballard and Graves

County Medical Association and Board of Health, March of Dimes – Past Chairman of Purchase Area, Medical Advisory Board, Distinguished Volunteer Award. Organized first bike-a-thon in nation, subsequently made two movies promoting bike-a-thon for March of Dimes. Member of Church of Christ. Emblem Business Professional Woman's Club of Mayfield, Woman of the Year – Mayfield Woman's Club. Chairman of Civics Improvement Project of Kentucky to institute crisis line. Kentucky State Emergency Planning Committee and Steering Committee for Kentucky Mother and Child Health. Major role in promoting child abuse programs in Kentucky. Purchase District Fair Board, Kentucky State Fair Special Events (donkey and mule show), Ballard County Fair – Chairman of Jack and Jennett show, parade, and mule race. United Way – Board member of Graves County. Distinguished Southerners, Who's Who Among Colleges and Universities, and Business Professionals. Cumberland College Board of Directors, Cumberland College Scholarship for Nursing Schools. Class Agent.

Lee Durham, a native of Williamsburg, KY, earned

a bachelor's degree in biology from Cumberland in 1965. He received his M.D. at the University Of Louisville College Of Medicine, and interned at Mound Park Hospital in St. Petersburg, FL. He began his practice in Corbin, KY and also practiced at Jellico Hospital in Jellico, TN. He has been employed as a family physician at Williamsburg Family Medicine and currently at Highland Park Primary Care in

Williamsburg, KY. His special interests include aviation development in Whitley County and horse breeding.

Casey Patrick grew up in Williamsburg, Kentucky. He was a recipient of the James H. Taylor II Memorial Scholarship, a four year member of the

football team and graduated from Cumberland in 2000. Following his undergraduate studies, Casey attended the University Of Kentucky College Of Medicine and graduated in 2004. In 2007, he completed residency training in Emergency Medicine at Indiana University. He has worked in multiple emergency departments in both Indiana and Texas. Currently, Dr. Patrick is the Associate Medical Director of the Conroe Regional Medical Center Emergency Department in Conroe, Texas where he and his three children reside.

His current volunteer activities are focused on the need for increased awareness of the importance of organ donation education. Casey's mother, Norma Patrick, served as a professor of education at Cumberland from 1985-2011, who passed away in April 2012 while awaiting a liver transplant. Casey and his brother, Jason, started a charitable organization, The Red Boot Foundation, with the goal of raising funds and awareness of the dire need for organ donors in the US. In April 2013, the Inaugural Red Boot Run was held on Cumberlands' campus and over $10,000 was raised. $5,000 was donated to the Norma B. Patrick Endowed Scholarship Fund, the income from which will be used to assist a single mother planning to pursue a degree in the education field and living in the southeastern Kentucky area.

Michael D. Hayre earned a B.S. from Cumberland in 1974 and a D.V.M. from Tuskegee University, Tuskegee Institute. Hayre began his professional career in the U.S. Army as the Chief of Veterinary Services for the 3rd U.S. Infantry Caisson, headquartered at Arlington National Cemetery. From there he served a tour of duty in the Republic of Korea and returned to complete a residency in comparative medicine at the Walter Reed Army Institute of Research. He completed residency

training in 1986 and was elected a Diplomat of the American College of Laboratory Animal Medicine in 1987. After leaving the military in 1988 with the

rank of major, Hayre became the Assistant Director of the Laboratory Animal Resources Center of the Rockefeller University in New York City. He was named Director in 1991. In June of 1999, Hayre became Vice President, Comparative Medicine at **St. Jude Children's Research Hospital** in Memphis, TN.

In addition to his responsibilities at St. Jude, Hayre also served on the boards of several corporations and nonprofit organizations. He served as Chairman of the Board of Americans for Medical Progress (AMP) from 1997 to 2001. In August 2001, Hayre was hit by a vehicle while jogging near his home and passed away in the hospital the next day at age of 49. AMP established the Michael D. Hayre Fellowship in Public Outreach in 2008 to honor his memory and to continue the advocacy he so faithfully pursued in service to medicine and science.

Anthony Johnson attended Cumberland until 1989. He went on to attend the University of Louisville,

earning his Doctor of Dental Medicine degree in 1993 and his Doctor of Medicine degree in 1997. He became board-certified in Oral and Maxillofacial Surgery in 2004 and is also a diplomat of the American Dental Society of Anesthesiology. Dr. Johnson has been in practice in Mooresville, North Carolina since 2000. He served as a chief of Oral and Maxillofacial Surgery at Carolinas Medical Center in Charlotte, North Carolina from 2004-2006. In May 2005, he opened his own private practice. Dr. Johnson has devoted his professional career to all aspects of oral and maxillofacial surgery.

Terrell Mays earned an associate's degree from Cumberland in 1957 and completed medical school at the University of Louisville. During the Vietnam

War, he served active duty in South Vietnam with the 2nd Battalion 138 Artillery, a National Guard unit. His work was primarily with the American soldiers, but he also worked with Vietnamese patients in the Hue Provincial Hospital through MEDCAP (Medical Civic Action Program).

Mays was in private practice for 25 years in  Elizabethtown, KY. He also served on the faculty of the University of Louisville School of Medicine. A member of the Hardin-LaRue Medical Society and the American Medical Association, he wrote articles in the Kentucky Journal and other medical publications. Dr. Mays and his wife, Gail, generously supported Cumberland until his passing in 1996 at the age of 59. Gail continues to support her husband's alma mater.

Lewis W. Cornelius, a native of Whitley County, KY, attended Williamsburg City School from first through twelfth grade and graduated from Cumberland in 1969. Lewis and his wife, **Wanda (Begley) Cornelius**, a 1971 alumna were married in 1969. He was a Captain in the USAF and served

 from 1969-1973. Cornelius graduated from University of Kentucky Medical School in 1979 and completed his residency in family practice and OBGYN in Savannah, GA from 1979-1984. Lewis and Wanda moved to Campbellsville, KY in 1985 where Lewis had his OBGYN practice. They returned to Whitley County in 2003. Currently, Lewis is working as an Emergency Room Physician. He spends his spare time writing gospel songs that Wanda sings and records. They feel this is their mission to spread God's word in music and song. Lewis also loves photographing and identifying native plants and birds. He and Wanda have three children and seven grandchildren.

James P. Moss was raised in Williamsburg and attended Cumberlands in 1961 before enrolling at

UK. He was graduated from University of Louisville Medical School in1966. He is the great-grandson of Dr. E. S. Moss - founder and first chairman of the Board of Trustees of Williamsburg Institute.

Dr. Moss has left a substantial mark on the field of  medicine, including the invention of the Moss T-tube, the creation and evaluation of post-graduate surgical education programs, and the establishment of an in-house education resource center. Moss was the first surgeon in the English-speaking world to remove a gallstone left behind at surgery without having to have a second operation.

Dr. Moss returned to Williamsburg and to Cumberlands in the fall of 2013 to teach in the Physician Association Program.

Although not a Cumberlands alumnus, **William E. Moss** was also raised in Williamsburg and was graduated from University of Louisville School of Medicine in 1972. He and his brother, Dr. James Moss, were both also inducted to the Williamsburg Hall of Honor. Dr. William E. Moss lives in Louisville, KY with his wife Susan B. Moss.

Carolyn Barnwell Petrey, a native of Middlesboro, Kentucky, was graduated from Cumberlands in 1971 with a major in chemistry. She did post graduate work in chemistry at Florida Atlantic University before enrolling at Oklahoma State University

 College of Osteopathic Medicine. She is board certified by the American Osteopathic Board of Family Practice.

Dr. Petrey has been a physician at Family Practice Clinic in Lawrenceville, GA since completing her postgraduate studies. She has served as the President of the Georgia Osteopathic Medical Association and was named Physician of the Year in 2000.

Dr. Petrey is on staff at Eastside Medical Center in Snellville, GA and DeKalb Medical Center in Decatur, Georgia. She serves as clinical professor at the Philadelphia College of Osteopathic Medicine and Pikeville College of Osteopathic Medicine. She has trained medical students and interns through her practice. Dr. Petrey also serves as Senior Aviation Medical Examiner for the FAA and as a delegate to the American Osteopathic Association House of Delegates. She volunteers with the area schools, Special Olympics, and the Boys and Girls Club. Dr. Petrey has served on Cumberlands' Alumni Board of Directors and currently serves on the University's Board of Trustees. She is married to Dr. **Dallas Petrey** and is the mother of one daughter.

Dallas E. Petrey, a native of Williamsburg, Kentucky, entered the pre-pharmacy curriculum at Cumberland in 1967. He enrolled at Mercer University School of Pharmacy in Atlanta, Georgia in 1968. Following pharmacy school, Dallas practiced pharmacy in Clewiston, Florida and Madisonville, Kentucky and maintained membership of the Georgia, Kentucky, Florida and American Pharmaceutical Associations.

In 1977, he entered the West Virginia School of Osteopathic Medicine at Lewisburg, West Virginia and graduated in 1981. He completed his post graduate medical training at Oklahoma Osteopathic Hospital in Tulsa, Oklahoma and is board certified in family practice medicine.

Dr. Petrey practiced in Tucker, Georgia with hospital affiliations at

Northlake Regional Medical Center in Tucker, Georgia and DeKalb Medical Center in Decatur, Georgia. In addition, Dr. Petrey was a clinical professor at West Virginia School of Osteopathic Medicine and Oklahoma State University College of Osteopathic Medicine. Dr. Petrey represents Georgia as a delegate at the American Osteopathic Association House of Delegates. Dr. Petrey presently serves on the Board of Trustees of the University of the Cumberlands.

Dr. Petrey is married to Dr. **Carolyn Petrey** and is the father of four daughters.

As a non-traditional student, Dr. **Susan Hawkins** graduated from Cumberland College in 1987 with her B.S. in Biology. In 1991, she graduated from the University of Louisville with her M.D. in Pediatrics and completed her residency at the University of Louisville's Kosair Children's Hospital. She achieved this goal amid the stress of having a husband who risked his life each day as a Kentucky State Law Enforcement Officer, a son who was serving our country in the Persian Gulf, a teenager and twin daughters in school. Dr. Hawkins is currently practicing pediatric medicine in Greenville, Kentucky.

Jack Heneisen. Father: Thomas Clarence Heneisen. Mother: Florence Ruth Heneisen. Wife: Connie Barrett Heneisen. Children: David Keith, Kendra Dawn, Nicholas Barnett. B.S. Memphis State University. Physics, M.S. plus 30 hours Clemson University. Physics, M.D. University of Kentucky. Family Practice residency – Memorial Medical Center. Fellow of American Academy of Family Practice. Director and owner of Family Health &

Birth Center, Chief of Staff Effingham County Hospital, Medical Director Tidelands Mental Health Service, Industrial Physician Ft. Howard Paper Company, Student preceptor Program – Emory University, Morehouse University. Board of Directors Latch Key Program, Delegate of the Congress of Georgia Academy of Family Practice, Founder and Chairman of the Board Effingham Community Cardiovascular Council Georgia Medical Society, American Medical Association, Sigma Xi. Chairman of Physics Department – 1973-1976. Student at Cumberland College – Pre-engineering – 1966-1968.

Meet a few of our Dentists

As a local boy from Williamsburg, Cumberland College was a part of **Sam Ballou's** life from youth. Ballou enrolled at Cumberland in the fall of 1951.

He was active in basketball and softball intramurals, played on the varsity baseball team, helped start a Science Club of which he was the first President and served as President of the Student Body. Ballou graduated from Cumberland in 1953 with an associate's degree. He earned his B.S. from Eastern Kentucky University in 1954 and his D.M.D at the University of Louisville Dental in 1958. While at Louisville Dental School, Ballou met and married Peggy Beams of Hazard, a dental hygiene student. They have three children, two of whom began their education at Cumberland and seven grandchildren. The Ballous moved to Corbin in May 1958, to work in the dental practice of his uncle, Dr. O.L. Ballou. Sam practiced dentistry from 1958 until 1998, retiring after arthritis in his hands and back made it increasingly difficult to work. He and his wife continued to fill in for their daughters and son-in-law, Dr. Keith Gibson, who had joined the practice in 1990.

Ballou was also active in his community; in the recreational area he was on the original group that began a golf and country club, served as a little league baseball coach, played and coached a church softball team, and helped organize a Christian Bass Club. He became concerned that the city schools in the 50's had less than 40% high school graduates attend college so he served a term on the city school board and helped push for a policy that did not allow extracurricular participation unless a C average was maintained. Ballou served as a trustee at Cumberland for decades and was chairman when Dr. Taylor was appointed President. He was an active member of the Corbin Lions Club for over 35 years serving in all of the offices of the club. Ballous served as a Deacon and Adult Sunday School teacher in Central Baptist Church. He and his wife each served as Volunteer Overseas Missionaries.

Byron M. Owens was graduated from Cumberland in 1962 with a Bachelor of Arts degree in biology and a minor in chemistry. Owens completed his D.M.D. at the University of Kentucky - College of Dentistry. Originally from Brodhead, KY, Owens now resides in Somerset, KY and is a self-employed dentist, with a career spanning more than 45 years. Since graduating, he has also gone on to participate in numerous organizations, serving in various leadership positions. These organizations include Fellow – University of Kentucky, the KY Dental Association, the American Dental Association, as well as the U.S. Navy where he served as a Lieutenant in the Dental Corps. Owens was also the past president of the Kiwanis Club in Somerset, KY

and the South Central Dental Society of KY. He has previously served on the board of First Farmers Bank, as the advisory director of Union Planters Bank, a member of the Somerset Jaycees and as the chairman of the board of directors to the Regional Mental Health Association.

John David Mountjoy, a 1975 graduate, **Michael R. Smith**, a 1978 graduate, and **John A. Jeffries**, a 1977 graduate, are three of Williamsburg's dentists who began their careers at Cumberlands.

Dr. David Ison holds a bachelor's degree from

Cumberland College with a Major in Psychology and Biology, and a Minor in Chemistry. He is a 1983 graduate of the University of Kentucky College of Dentistry, in Lexington, Kentucky. He also earned a master's degree in administrative social work from the University of Kentucky, and a master's equivalency in anatomical science.

Dr. Ison is on staff through the Department of Surgery at Georgetown Community Hospital,

Frankfort Regional Medical Center, and New Horizons Medical Center in Owenton, Kentucky where he has served as Chief of Surgery for the last four years. He is a member of the Special Care Dentistry Association and the American Association of Hospital Dentists. Dr. Ison is licensed by the Kentucky Board of Dentistry to provide I.V. Conscious Sedation in his office and in the hospital.

Dr. James E. Croley, Jr., D.D.S.
Married Lonnie Sue Croley. Children: Dr. James E. Croley, III, M.D.; Jennifer Lou Croley; Tasha

 Lefevers. Graduated from Pineville High School, Cumberland College (1943), Berea College and the University of Missouri. Korean War – Marine Officer Training – Paris Island, South Carolina – 1st Lt. Dental practice in

Pineville, Kentucky. President of Pineville Jr.

Chamber of Commerce. Chairman, Pine Mountain State Park Development Committee. Mayor of Pineville, Kentucky. Advisory Board for the Union College Environmental Education Center. Kentucky Colonel. Chairman of the Kentucky Mountain Theatre, Inc. Practiced dentistry in Harlan. Deacon, First Baptist Church, Pineville, Kentucky. Served as President of Southeastern District Dental Society. Selected as one of Kentucky's Three Outstanding Young Men by the Kentucky Junior Chamber of Commerce. Selected as "Man of the Year" for the city of Pineville. Appointed by Governor Bert T. Combs to the Advisory Board of the Kentucky Tourist and Travel Commission. Honorary Colonel in the Kentucky State Police. Listed in the Marquis Who's Who in Kentucky, Who's Who in South and Southwest and Who's Who in the United States. Listed in Kentucky Lives. Member of Kentucky Mountain Theater, Inc. – Produced the world famous outdoor drama "Book of Job" at Pine Mountain State Park. Member of Southeastern Kentucky District Dental Society, State Dental Association and American Dental Association. Outstanding Alumnus Award – Cumberland College. Appointed Supt. of Sunday School – First Baptist Church, Pineville, KY. Served on the Cumberland College Board of Trustees. President of Cumberland College Alumni Association.

Meet a few of our Pharmacists

David Nickell Huff was graduated from Cumberland College with a B.S. in 1953 and a graduate of

University of Kentucky Pharmacy School. While attending Cumberland, Dave was a member of the basketball team and received the scholastic award for athletics; was named Outstanding Athlete and Mr. Cumberland College.

During Huff's career he was president and owner of Huff Drug Company in Corbin and Hazard. He served as Vice President of the Executive Board of Directors of First National Bank in Corbin and also a member of the Bank of Columbia (Kentucky). He was a member of the Board of the Baptist Regional Medical Center and served as Treasurer of Cumberland River Medical Health Board. Dave was also on the Advisory Board at Whitaker Bank in Corbin.

Currently, Huff serves as Trustee at UC. He is also a member and past Deacon at the First Baptist Church in Corbin.

Huff is married to Patricia Ann Farmer Huff. The couple has three children: Shanna Huff Elliott, James David Huff and Rex Nickell Huff, six grandchildren and one great granddaughter.

Maryam Tabatabai came to Cumberland after attending Oneida Baptist Institute. After graduating from Cumberland in 1994 with a degree in biology (minor in chemistry), Maryam graduated from Shenandoah University School of Pharmacy in 2000.

While at Cumberland Dr. Tabatabai was involved in various clubs and organizations: President of the Medical Careers Club, member of the American Chemical Society, member of the Environmental Awareness Committee, involved in theatre productions, the women's tennis team and Campus Activities Board.

She now resides in Berryville, Virginia. Dr. Tabatabai is the Director for Drug Information at Magellan Health Services where she provides leadership across a spectrum of clinical initiatives, such as overseeing, developing and maintaining Therapeutic Class Reviews and the clinical writing team. She serves as Chair for the Drug Policy Development Committee - a clinical think-tank and action committee – and the Drug Availability Surveillance Committee, as well as the clinical coordinator for manufacturer relations and clinical presentations.

Dallas E. Petrey (see Meet a few of our Doctors)

Roger Powers and his brother **Jonathan** own and operate a pharmacy in downtown Williamsburg. Roger Powers is a 1980 Cumberland graduate.

Meet a few of our Radio and TV Personalities/Entertainers

In 1980, **Bill Bryant** was hired as the first TV-3 anchor to deliver local news to Williamsburg each

weekday night. Viewer response throughout the small mountain community was excellent. Soon the staff was able to bring in notable political figures as weekly guests, which helped ratings. One of the highlights of the first year was the station's coverage of the 1979 Kentucky governor's race which featured several interviews with candidates and live coverage of election returns in November. TV-3 was purchased by Cumberland in 1989. Known today as UCTV-19 it continues to grow and evolve just as it did when it began to blossom in 1980. Dedicated students and staff help make the TV station one of the most successful unique programs on campus.

Bryant traces his journalism roots to the 5th grade when he and some classmates printed up a newspaper and sold it on the streets of his hometown of Williamsburg. Bill got into radio by the time he was 15 and also played basketball, ran track and served as class president. He attended Cumberland before earning his degree in broadcasting and political science from Eastern Kentucky University. It was after his junior year at Eastern that Bill did an internship at WKYT.

He is now the longest serving male news anchor in Lexington television history and is the host of "Kentucky Newsmakers" on which he has interviewed virtually every important Kentucky political and business leader of the last quarter century. After nearly three decades at the station his energy and enthusiasm are on display every day as he co-anchors "27 News First This Morning" 5 to 7 a.m., the "Fox 56 Morning Edition" for WDKY, "27 News First Midmorning" at 10 a.m. and "27 News First at Noon".

Between newscasts, Bill is a strong editorial voice in the newsroom, serving as managing editor. He has also previously filled in as acting news director, in charge of news operation for several months. He

loves political reporting and presents a daily "Political Notebook" on the 5:30 p.m. newscast. Bill also serves as political analyst on election nights and is a frequent fill-in host of KET's statewide program "Comment on Kentucky."

Hayes McMakin, a 1966 graduate, served the US Navy before beginning his career in communications. He worked at WLEX TV and owned and operated Gateway Radio Works in Mt. Sterling, KY.

Stanley Lovett enrolled at Cumberland in 1961. He participated in various sports and became enamored with radio broadcasting. Stan started working for the local radio station WEZJ in Williamsburg while attending Cumberland. He did play-by-play covering

the local high school team. He also worked as News Director and D.J. He took a class in journalism and became the Sports Editor for the Cumberland College newspaper, The Echo. Stan was elected President of the Town and Commuting Students during his sophomore year and Vice President of the

SGA during his junior year. Stan graduated from Cumberland in 1965 and married **Roberta Noe Lovett** whom he met at Cumberland. They have two daughters and three grandchildren. Lovett taught at Whitley City Elementary in McCreary County, Kentucky, before moving in 1967 to Lexington, Kentucky to teach at Picadome Elementary. He retired in 1992. While teaching, Stan continued his love for broadcasting doing local sports for TV and radio stations in Lexington. In 1991, Stan returned to Williamsburg to broadcast Williamsburg High School football, basketball, Union College Basketball, University of the Cumberlands baseball, and numerous Whitley County games as well as district tournament and regional games for WEZJ radio station. In 2002, he was elected to the Williamsburg Hall of Fame for broadcasting Williamsburg games. He has served and attended Centenary United Methodist Church in Lexington for over forty years.

David Paul Estes was graduated from Cumberland in 1990. Estes has been the Voice of the Patriots since 1988. He has broadcast over 225 Cumberlands football games and over 800 Cumberlands basketball games. Estes served for six years as the Victory Sports Network Columnist and National Rater for NAIA Men's Basketball. He also served as the play by play voice for NAIA National Basketball Tournament video feeds for two years. In 2004, 2006 and 2009, Estes was named the MSC Media Person of the Year as voted on by Conference Sports Information Directors. He was nominated in 2006 for the AP Kentucky Sport Caster of the Year Award. For seven years, Estes was a member of the University of the Cumberlands Alumni Board of Directors, serving as both Secretary and President. He was a founding member of the Cumberlands Alumni Association Athletic Hall of Fame Committee, served on the committee from 1997-2004, and was inducted into the Athletic Hall of Fame for broadcasting in 2012. Estes is the owner and operator of Whitley Broadcasting Company Inc., which owns local radio stations EZ Country 104.3 and We Rock 102.7. He is the head coach of the Whitley County Middle School girl's basketball team. Estes and his wife, Stacey, reside in Williamsburg, Kentucky and have three children, Abbey, Jackson and Grayson.

Paul Estes, a 1950 graduate of Pleasant View High School, joined the Air Force serving his country during the Korean Conflict from 1950 through 1954, spending much of that time at Alaskan outposts. After leaving the Air Force in 1954, Paul attended Cumberland College in 1954 and 1955 and the University of Kentucky in 1956. In 1957, Paul began a 15-year career at United Air Lines.

Estes moved his family to Whitley County in 1972 and, along with his wife Theresa, purchased a local

Montgomery Ward catalog store. Soon thereafter they added Estes Furniture Sales. In 1977, Estes was appointed mayor of Williamsburg and was later twice elected mayor. During his tenure, he helped the city improve its financial condition and helped lead the city out of the worst flood of record. Other accomplishments included the construction of a new water plant, new recreation facilities, and greater quality of life for all Williamsburg citizens. He has since served six terms as a Williamsburg City councilman. In 2004 after the resignation of Williamsburg's mayor, he was asked to again assume the duties of mayor for several months until a new mayor could be elected. When his council term expired in 2006, he had served the City of Williamsburg for over 21 years.

In 1980, the Estes family purchased radio station WEZJ-AM. At the time, it was Williamsburg's only radio station. In 1990, the FCC granted them their second radio station, WEZJ-FM. In 1997, they purchased WEKX-FM. They also owned and operated local television cable channel 3 for nine years before it was acquired by Cumberland College and became what we now know as TV 19.

Estes served as a member and chairman of the board of directors of the Bank of Williamsburg for 20 years. He currently serves as a member of the Advisory Board of Directors for Community Trust Bank. He has served as chair of the Cumberland College Board of Trustees and currently is a member of the Board having served since 1976. He is a deacon and trustee of the First Baptist Church of Williamsburg, past president of the Williamsburg Chamber of Commerce, a past president of the Williamsburg Rotary Club, a founding member of the Williamsburg Old Fashion Trading Days, past chairman of the Williamsburg Whitley Industrial Foundation, a past member of the Cumberland Valley Development Board, and a past member of the Bell Whitley Community Action Agency.

Paul and his wife, Theresa, have two children and four grandchildren. Their daughter, Paula, is married to UC Faculty member Dennis Trickett and her daughter, Allison Adair, is enrolled in a doctoral program at UK. Their son, David Estes, is married to Stacey Prewitt and they have three children, Abigale

Estates and twins, Jackson Paul and Grayson Taylor, who are students in the Whitley County School System.

Brandon Hensley, 2010, hails from small community of Wallins Creek located in Harlan County, KY, where he attended high school at James A. Cawood High School and college at Southeast Community College. Before arriving to Williamsburg, he held several jobs that paved the way to the University of the Cumberlands. Most notably getting his start in radio at 105.1 WTUK-FM in Harlan in 2001, before moving on to television in 2005. Hensley worked at WYMT-TV in Hazard, KY primarily as Sports Director and Sports Anchor. He anchored and produced Kentucky Broadcasting Association award winning shows such as Sports Overtime, Sports Overtime Saturday Night, The WYMT Pigskin Preview Show, The WYMT Roundball Preview Show, and the Road to Rupp.

In January of 2008, after exploring several opportunities, Hensley sought a change from television. After several meetings with the Sports Information Department, Jennifer Wake-Floyd, he enrolled at the University of the Cumberlands to finish up his undergrad degree. Hensley was awarded a position on the student staff where he broadened his skills in story writing, radio broadcasting, and eventually video editing. In December of 2010, Hensley earned a Bachelor of Science in Communications and was hired as a full-time employee at the University as the Multimedia Video & Sports Radio/Video Coordinator. He specializes in highlight videos for all of Cumberlands' athletics, as well as, doing radio play-by-play for a variety of UC Sports (Football, Women's Basketball, Men's Basketball, Baseball, and Softball).

The past six years, he has provided play-by-play for over three hundred radio/video broadcasts. Hensley was instrumental in helping implement video shooting/editing/video streaming in the Sports Information Department (Now Multimedia & Athletic Services Department). Since 2009, over four hundred videos have been released, highlighting the student athletes and faculty/staff of the University of

the Cumberlands. In the last three years, over a hundred live athletic event video streams have taken place, giving the Patriot students athletes a chance to have their games, matches, and meets shown worldwide. UC Coaches have reported that the video aspect has aided in recruiting and retention for their respective student athletes.

At Homecoming in 2013 Hensley was recognized by Cumberlands with the Young Alumni Award.

Marvin Edward West, enrolled at Cumberland as an elementary education major, but changed to speech and theater communication his senior year and

graduated in 1990.

West credits his love for the arts, especially music, to his Cumberland music teacher, Donna Colegrove. He was an active member of the Cumberland College Choral, Show Choir and Madrigal. He was also in several drama productions.

Upon graduating, Marvin was employed by Hershend Family Entertainment (Dollywood) in the award winning Entertainment Division.

West's movie debut was in 2007. Between 2007 and 2011, he appeared in several acclaimed stage roles for which he won the Best Lead Actor in a Musical Award, Ebenezer Scrooge in A Christmas Carol, and Best Director Award for "Steel Magnolias."

In 2011, West landed his first nationwide theatrical release movie role in "Joyful Noise", followed by "The Three Stooges" and released his first CD. He has also had several guest starring roles.

West currently teaches special education and drama at Sevierville Intermediate School in Sevierville, TN and portrays Sheriff Roscoe P. Coletrane in the popular tourist attraction, Hazard County Hoedown at the Smith Family Dinner Theater in Pigeon Forge, TN.

Meet a few of our Engineers

Donald Reid Ellison attended Cumberland in 1947. He also attended Wayne University and graduated from the University of Alabama in 1952 with a degree in electrical engineering. Ellison owned and operated Groundhogs, Inc., a construction company in Birmingham and was a member of various engineering societies, including holding his professional engineering license in Alabama, Tennessee and Kentucky. He was an honorably discharged US Navy veteran of WWII and a Major of the US Air Force Reserves. Ellison was a lifetime member of the VFW and American Legion. He was Quartermaster of the V.F.W. #3167 of Williamsburg. Ellison was a member of the board of trustees and an instructor in the school of mining at Cumberland.

Robert Kenneth Jones arrived on the Cumberland College campus in the fall of 1949. While a student in Dr. **J. T. Vallandingham**'s math class, Robert met **Phyllis Ann Hall,** '51, with whom he soon fell in love and later married.

In 1955, Jones enrolled at University of Kentucky's Engineering School where he studied electrical engineering. The Jones family moved to Baltimore, Maryland where Robert took a position with the Martin Company. He pursued and completed his master's degree while there, and the family grew to four children.

In 1960, the family moved to Lexington, Kentucky where Robert began his successful career with International Business Machines and was selected an IBM Outstanding Manager in 1967.

In 1970, Robert was transferred to Austin, Texas, where he spent the remaining 17 years of his career with IBM until his retirement in 1987. Phyllis was a successful business teacher and office coordinator in Texas. She, too, retired in 1987.

Robert was diagnosed with Parkinson's disease in 2001 and passed away in 2009 from complications associated with the disease.

Meet a few of our Entrepreneurs

William Reed "Bill" Bryant was graduated from Cumberland in 1962 with a double major in English and business. Bryant went on to teach business in the

Whitley County School system until his retirement in 1992. Bill and his wife, **Nancy Dale Bryant** (who also attended Cumberland) have three children who have attended Cumberland. He also has three sisters, a son-in-law and a daughter-in-law who are graduates of Cumberland.

Bill and Nancy started the successful Ken-Ten Advertising business in 1973, featuring imprinted business gift items. They are still active in this business, which is the oldest business in Williamsburg still being operated by the very same people who organized it.

In April, 2013, Bryant was appointed President of the Creech-Boswell Club, a club for alums who were graduated 50+ years ago and who possess golden memories of Cumberland College.

H. Ray Hammons graduated in 1990 from Cumberland with a B.S. in business administration and computer information systems (CIS). He earned

a three year Reserve Officer Training Corp (ROTC) scholarship and received a minor in military science.

After Cumberland, Hammons moved to Louisville where he began working for Capital Holding Incorporated as a financial analyst. He continued his education at Webster University and in 1992 completed a Master of Arts in Finance. In 1994, he earned a Master in Business Administration also from

Webster. Currently, he is studying at Harvard and at The London Business School.

Hammons worked as a financial analyst with Humana, Incorporated and later he signed on with the global accounting firms of Ernst & Young, with Price Waterhouse and with Ejiva, Incorporated before venturing out on his own. In 2001 he founded of HRH Capital, LLC, a holding company, and in 2002, purchased Roller Die and Forming and Hammons became the company President of HRH Capital which purchased Kentucky Industrial Coating and HRH Realty in 2004. Today, HRH Capital is a diversified holding company displaying stubbornness for success with Hammons as its CEO.

Hammons was inducted into Cumberlands Alumni Hall of Honor in 2010 as Alumnus of the Year.

Mary Farler Rutledge. Widow of Lt. Col. Clyde E.

Prewitt (Class of '52). Mother of three children, Theresa, Mark and Will. Presently the wife of Charles C. Rutledge, M.D. Mother of three step-children. Attended Cumberland College, Graduated in 1956. Attended Hazard Community College in field of Data Processing. Lived abroad. Traveled extensively. Worked as Legal Secretary. Worked in field of Interior Design. Operated furniture store and gourmet dining room. Worked as an office manager and bookkeeper. Member of First Baptist Church of Hazard. Chosen "Woman of the Year" by Beta Sigma Phi. Active in many community and charitable affairs. Chosen as "Student of the Month." Vice President of Baptist Student Union. Was member of choir and many campus activities. Served on the Alumni Board for 4 years, 1 year as president. Was honored as "Alumna of the Year." Served on Board as Member-at-large.

Keith Gannon and Georgetta Gannon - Dr. Keith Gannon graduated from Cumberland College in 1985 with a B.S. in Chemistry and Mathematics. He graduated *magma cum laude* and received the Presidential Scholar Award for honors research he completed.

Dr. Gannon provides leadership to a number of charitable, educational and trade groups including serving as a trustee for the University of Kentucky, an Advisory Board member to the Morehead State University at Mount Sterling Campus and as a trustee for the University of the Cumberlands. Dr. and Mrs. Gannon, '85, have also set up the Gannon Endowment Scholarship Fund for students at the University of the Cumberlands.

Dr. Gannon is the CEO of Boneal Inc. in Menifee County, Kentucky. Prior to taking the helm at Boneal, Dr. Gannon worked as a research scientist while managing polymer labs for BASF Corporation in North Carolina. During this period, Dr. Gannon also served as an adjunct professor of chemistry at the University of North Carolina, Asheville, where he taught senior-level chemistry classes. Dr. Gannon graduated from Vanderbilt University with a Ph.D. Keith and his wife, **Georgetta Gannon**, a CPA who serves as Boneal's CFO, reside in Mount Sterling, Kentucky.

Georgetta (Hollon) Gannon graduated from Cumberland College in 1985 with a B.S. in Accounting and Mathematics. She graduated *summa cum laude* and received the Gorman Jones Award of Leadership.

Georgetta and her husband, Dr. Keith Gannon, '85, set up the Gannon Endowment Scholarship Fund for students at the University of the Cumberlands. They also serve as trustees for the University of the Cumberlands.

Georgetta is a Certified Public Accountant and is a partner in Boneal, Inc, a prime-contracting manufacturer for government agencies and industry. She has been a member of the Boneal Management Team since 1992. Mrs. Gannon serves on the Boneal

Board of Directors and is Chief Financial Officer. Prior to joining Boneal, Mrs. Gannon spent 10 years in the public accounting field. She served as an auditor for the Nashville, TN, public accounting firm of Kraft Brothers, Eastmann, Patton and Herald and the Asheville, NC, firm of Johnson, Price and Sprinkle before forming her own firm in 1990.

Georgetta and Dr. **Keith Gannon** reside in Mount Sterling, Kentucky.

Mahan Siler. Executive Food Broker and Bean Packer. "Cumberland College has contributed greatly to the cultural and economic welfare of the Appalachian region. I know of no school that gets as much per dollar expended as does Cumberland."

Ronald Leon Glass. Born December 17, 1946 in Louisville, Kentucky. Married to Phyllis L. Turner Glass. Two sons, Ronald L. Glass, Jr. and Kevin S. Glass. Lincoln High School – Graduated.

Cumberland College – B.S. degree. President of Glass Natural Resources, Inc., President of Glass Brothers' Associates, and an Account Executive of Merrill Lynch Pierce Fenner and Smith, Inc. Member of the Engineering Club, Cumberland College. Active in the Old Kentucky Home Council on Boy Scouts, Member of the Louisville Jaycees. An active participant in track and field events at Cumberland College. Worked as a Director of the Student Interest Association, served as Consultant to the President of Cumberland College on student involvement, Advisor to the Student Government, member of the Alpha Pi Omega and the Engineering Club. Co-Captain of the track team in his junior and senior years. Class Agent and Member of the Kentuckiana Alumni Chapter. In 1980, Ronald was alerted to the fact that he had leukemia, and stood a slight chance of surviving. Against all odds and given a short span of time, he continued to demonstrate through his Philosophy of Life: "That one can achieve whatever one wants out of life, as long as one has determination." Ronald L. Glass died on October 28, 1985.

Clyde Edward Faulkner, a native of Williamsburg, KY, graduated from Cumberland College in 1951. He was the owner of Faulkner's Inc. of Jackson, AL for over 40 years and partner of Faulkner-Taylor Furniture Store with his brothers; Vernon and Harold Faulkner. Clyde passed away on April 13, 2005.

Nick Greiwe of Goshen, Ohio, was graduated from Cumberland College in 1974. He also graduated from the Louisiana State University School of Banking of the South in 1984.

Nick has served 30-plus year in community banking in Southeastern Kentucky, with 13 years at the Bank of Williamsburg as Executive Vice President and Security Officer. He was the first Project Manager opening operations for SI International at the Kentucky Consular Center in Williamsburg, Kentucky – a Department of State owned facility dealing with immigration. Nick was later named as Project Manager for SI International at the Corbin Production Facility which is responsible for the printing of Visa cards for foreign visitors and Green Card recipients. He is currently employed as Vice President for Hometown Bank at the London, Kentucky office.

Greiwe presently serves as Board Member and Treasurer of The Cumberland River Mental Health Mental Retardation Corporation and a member of the Corbin Varsity Club Board, as well as service on Cumberlands Alumni Board of Directors.

He and his wife, Debbie (Carroll), have two children, Becky and Scott.

Paul P. Steely graduated from Cumberland in 1949 with an A.A. in Elementary Education. He met his wife **Stella (Davidson) Steely**, a 1950 alumnus, at Cumberland. He also graduated from Union College in 1953 with his Bachelor of Science. Steely earned his Master of Arts, Rank I and Certificate in Education from Eastern Kentucky University in 1964 and 1969. He was a teacher and administrator in the Whitley County school system for 30 years, and is an active member of the Kentucky Teachers Retirement System. Steely was a partner with his son at Paul Steely Ford, Inc. in Williamsburg, KY for 30 years. Paul and Stella are blessed with two sons, Paul D.

Steely, a 1976 alumnus, and Samuel Steely, a 1978 alumnus. Mr. & Mrs. Steely are active members of Main Street Baptist Church. Steely has shown his support and dedication to Cumberland serving as a current Trustee, a member and President of the Alumni Board of Directors, as President of Creech Boswell Club and through financial gifts. He has served on the Kentucky Baptist Convention Executive Board for several years; active with the Shriners and a 60 year member of the Williamsburg Masonic Lodge. Steely was inducted in Cumberlands Alumni Hall of Honor in 1996.

Ted R. "Teddy" Byrd was born in Williamsburg,

Kentucky to Clarence and Ruth Byrd. He attended school at Williamsburg and after graduation enrolled at Cumberland, where he majored in art education and minored in biology.

In May 1966, Byrd married the former, Lois "Cookie" Hendrickson, a union that has been blessed with three daughters, Carolyn, Tracee and Kelley, (all three are graduates of Cumberlands) four grandsons, Corey,

Zackerey, Joey and Louey along with two granddaughters, Kristin and Kacey.

Byrd finished his degree in 1970, graduating with *cum laude* honors. The Byrds moved to Virginia, where Teddy taught for three years, only to return to be closer to family. One year later, the brothers partnered with their parents to start the family business, Byrd Glass Company. The men worked with their father while their mother served as the business secretary.

Teddy states, "From getting our degrees here (at Cumberlands) to being our biggest customer, University of the Cumberlands has been a large part of our lives."

Byrd is an ardent supporter of Cumberlands Athletics, attending as many home basketball and football games as his schedule will allow. "He has touched this campus from pillar to post," said Dave Bergman. "He has been a strong supporter of Cumberlands athletics, both as an Indian and as a Patriot.

In 2010, Byrd was inducted into Cumberlands Alumni Hall of Honor for Alumni Appreciation.

Eric Brant Poore earned a bachelor's degree in political science and computer information systems from Cumberland in 1994. He is the founder and CEO of Information Capture Solutions, LLC (ICS),

languages, quicker o learn

ng of have ll pass

ICS

which provides customers technology for categorizing, capturing, and extracting their vital business data into usable pieces of information. Integrating hardware and software applications into a tightly integrated data capture workflow process allows customers to access necessary data more efficiently.

ICS employs several Cumberlands alumni, several of whom have played key roles in the growth and success of the company according to Poore.

Poore resides in Williamsburg, KY with his wife Jennifer, their daughter and three sons.

Wallace Boyd was born on October 28, 1909. When

he was only 9 years old, his father, a lawyer in Williamsburg, passed away suddenly at age 50. When he was 11 years old he started working in the backroom of the great A&P Tea Company in Williamsburg, weighing beans and doing odd jobs. To help support the family, he took on various other jobs which included jerking sodas, carrying milk, firing furnaces and raising gardens and mowing lawns. When he was older, he sold some of the only inheritance he had, some wild land in the flat woods of Whitley County to pay his tuition to Cumberland Junior College. At the time Cumberland was only 2 years and Wallace graduated amidst holding several jobs to help the family. The next few years he worked in the mines in Harlan and Bell County and did very well before deciding on a career in the National Guard. Unfortunately, after he had sold his business, he was turned down at a routine physical because of high blood pressure. With a military career an impossibility and no job waiting at home, Wallace, 6 months later, called Dick Stout, also from Williamsburg, and asked him to go into the grocery business with him. The one store in Clinton grew to 2 stores in due time. After the war, however, they decided to relocate in either Lexington, Ky., or Kingsport. His brother-in-law, Eugene Siler, Sr., advised him to go to Kingsport which was "one of the most progressive cities in the south". They came to Kingsport in 1946 and began Oakwood Markets, Inc. which is still run today by the family. Wallace is survived by his wife, the former Nettie Lewis Jones, daughter of Professor Gorman Jones, a professor and founder of Cumberland College. He is also survived by his three children, Mary Alice, Ann, and Wally, and also six grandchildren. Through his life he was extremely active in civic and church affairs as well as other benevolent causes. He valued education highly, and sent many kids through many schools, including several at Cumberland. He was proud of Cumberland and the opportunities it had given him as a young man, and was pleased to be able to give something back to her for future generations.

Arthur A. Dale. Born at Packard, Kentucky. Graduated from Williamsburg High School,

graduated from Cumberland College – A.A. Degree, Pollitte Real Estate, Harlan, Ky. as broker owner of the company. Worked for Standard Oil Co., Commission Agent for Standard Oil in Harlan. Member and past president of Harlan Lions Club. Deacon, Harlan Baptist Church. Member of Gideons, International. Chairman of Faith Fund. Member of Board of Directors of Cumberland College. Student, member of basketball team. Member of Alumni Association, Former member of Board of Directors. Attended the Madrigal Dinner at Christmas for many years. Class agent.

Charles E. Reed received a B.S. Degree in Psychology from Cumberland College in May 1975. Prior to joining ARCO, Charles was recruited by Bethlehem Steel Corporation to work in their Mining Division's Industrial Relations Group in Pennsylvania. In October 1980, Charles joined ARCO Coal Company in Denver as an Employee Relations Representative. In June 1982, he was transferred to ARCO Metals in Wisconsin as the

Employee Relations Manager for General Casting Corporation. He was transferred to ARCO Oil and Gas, Employee Relations Department, in Dallas in March 1983, as an Employee Relations Generalist. He assumed the responsibilities as the Director of College Recruiting in September 1983. In January 1985, Charles served as the Employment and Recruitment Manager for ARCO Resources Administration. In August 1985, Charles served as the Manager, Employment for ARCO Oil and Gas Company. In April 1986, Charles served as the Manager of College Recruitment and Relations for ARCO Oil and Gas Company. Since June 1987, Charles has served as Director, Employee Relations for ARCO Oil and Gas Company in Midland, Texas. He is co-founder and

first President of Cumberland College's Black Students' Union, has been listed in "Who's Who in American Colleges and Universities" as an athlete and as a student in 1972 and 1975, "T.J. Roberts Most Outstanding Campus Leadership Award" in 1975, "Who's Who is Business and Industry" in 1981, Outstanding Alumni Award- Cumberland College in 1979, Alumni Board of Directors, Cumberland College, and IROADS/ Dallas Business Coordinator of the Year in 1984. He serves as a member of the nominating committee for the Southwestern Placement Association, a member of Texas A&M Placement Advisory Board, and Chairman of Region V Advisory Board for the National Society of Black Engineers. In March 1987, Charles received the National Society of Black Engineers Award of Appreciation given to one individual nationally for outstanding contribution to the organization.

Ray Lipps, Founder and president of Esquire Galleries, a company that sells art at auctions throughout the U.S., Ray Lipps has been one of Cumberlands' most dedicated alumni. He has never missed a Homecoming since arriving on campus. He has been an avid supporter of the athletic programs, attending hundreds of events including many national tournament games.

In 1981, Lipps founded Esquire Enterprises and in 1985 he started Esquire Galleries in Powell, Tennessee. Early on Lipps participated in approximately 200-225 auctions annually. Today, the company sells at auction, 2,500 pieces of framed art, framed documents, framed antique documents and framed artifacts each month throughout the

eastern United States.

One of the founders of Cumberlands' Athletic Hall of Fame, he instituted both the alumni homecoming auction to support scholarships and the Athletic Hall of Fame auction. He has also donated much of the framed artwork seen in campus buildings, for a total contribution in excess of $350,000.

A native of London, Ky. Lipps was a student leader at Cumberland College who has continued to be active in many businesses, political and civic organizations. He served on the Cumberlands Alumni Association Board of Directors for more than 20 years in several leadership roles, including three terms as president. Inducted into Cumberlands' Hall of Honor in 1990, he received the J.M. Boswell Outstanding Alumni Award in 1999 and an honorary Doctorate of Fine Arts from Cumberland in 2011. Also in 2007, the University named a classroom in the Hutton School of Business the Ray Lipps Room. He is a member of the Farragut Lions Club.

Lipps and his wife, **Patricia Skeen Artman Lipps**, reside in Knoxville, Tennessee and are active members of Powell Presbyterian Church. Two brothers - his twin, Ralph (of London) and Abner (of Frankfort) - also graduated from Cumberlands. As a result of the Lipps brothers' love of Cumberlands, the campus, the faculty, the staff and students have received immeasurable support from Ray Lipps and his brothers.

At Homecoming in 2013, Cumberlands Alumni Hall of Honor was named for and dedicated as the Ray Lipps Alumni Hall of Honor.

Ray's wife, **Patricia Skeen Artman Lipps,** although not a Cumberlands graduate, is a member of the Cumberlands family as well, and was named an Honorary Alumnus at the 2013 Homecoming celebration.

In May 1999, Pat met Ray Lipps, a 1970 alumnus of University of the Cumberlands. They were married on the Millennium at 12:01. They traveled to Alaska on a church mission trip for their honeymoon in the summer following their marriage. They have traveled extensively in numerous states; Ray calls

their trips vacations and Pat calls them business trips. Together they have three children and eleven grandchildren. Dr. Michael Artman of Apex, North Carolina, Jan Artman LaPrade of Charlottesville, Virginia, and Denise Bender Sesler, a 1989 Cumberland alumna.

Pat became partners with Ray in business, Esquire Galleries located in Powell, Tennessee. The Lipps participate in numerous auctions annually and sell at auction, 2,500 pieces of framed art, framed documents, framed antique documents and framed artifacts each month throughout the eastern United States. They are active

members at Powell Presbyterian Church and the Farragut Lions Club. Pat shares Ray's passion to support University of the Cumberlands.

Bill Roark, a native of Leslie County, is co-founder and CEO of Torch Technologies, Inc. in Huntsville, Alabama. Torch provides aerospace and engineering services primarily to Department of Defense (DOD) agencies.

Under Roark's leadership, Torch has been named one of the Top 100 Fastest Growing Companies in America by Entrepreneur Magazine. The company has twice received the Better Business Bureau Torch Award for outstanding business ethics and has been recognized as the Huntsville Chamber of Commerce Small Business of the Year.

Roark credits much of the company's success to the employees who not only work there but also own the company. Roark believes that Cumberland laid a good foundation for his successful career. Roark earned a Bachelor of Science in mathematics and a minor in physics, and then went on to earn a master's degree in physics from the University of Kentucky.

At Cumberlands, Roark met his wife **Brenda Napier Roark, '81.** The Roarks have two daughters.

Arloe W. Mayne. Born in Whitley County,

Kentucky. Married Virginia C. Mayne. Four sons: Arloe Wesley, Jr., Leroy, Larry Lee, and Fred Hollis. Graduated from Cumberland College, University of Kentucky, College of Law. General practice of law. Board of Trustees of the Greater Ashland Area Cultural and Economic Development Foundations, Inc. Member of Ashland's Senior Management Committee, Chairman of the Board of Directors of Ashland Oil Canada Ltd, Member of the Board of Directors of Oil Insurance Limited.

58

Member of the American Bar Association, Kentucky Bar Association and Boyd County Bar Association. Served two terms as President of the Boyd County Bar Association. Member of the American Petroleum Institute's General Committee on Law. Member of the Legal Committee, Manufacturing Chemical Association. Member of the University of Kentucky Fellows, Member of the University of Kentucky Development Council.

Lloyd Abdoo, 1980, is a native of Fleming Neon in Letcher County, Kentucky. Abdoo earned a Bachelor of Science degree from Cumberland. His studies included a degree in Public Services Administration with an area of concentration in business administration and accounting.

While working at the Holiday Inn in Williamsburg, Lloyd began a lifelong dedication of support of Cumberland College. He provided lunch to Cumberland professors, Nell Moore and Richard Fuson, among others affiliated with the faculty and staff on a regular basis. As a student, he helped many fellow classmates by employing them in hospitality positions. For nearly half a century he has hired Cumberland graduates. Many of the alumni still hold high positions in the hospitality industry around the country. Lloyd has been a Cumberlands' ambassador in many ways, the least of them being a recruiter of prospective students.

Abdoo is a seasoned hotel developer, owner and operator with over 45 years of experience in all phases of hotel operations, food and beverage operations, and property management. Proficient in  innovative and comprehensive approaches to administrative management, finance, sales & marketing, leadership, preventative maintenance, security, human resources, rooms management and food & beverages with a reputation for integrity among customers and associates. To his business success, Lloyd has received numerous honors and awards in the hospitality and food & beverage business.

Lloyd has been married to his wife, Teresa, since 1971. They have two sons, Jonathan and Steven. Cumberlands recognized Abdoo at Homecoming 2013 as Alumnus of the Year.

Donald A. Swanson. Born February 26, 1924 to Adolph and Marie Swanson, youngest of six children. Married Mary Elizabeth Hughes August 8, 1953 – two sons: Craig and Steven. Attended Cumberland 1942-43 – called to service February 1943.

 Graduated University of Michigan B.S. Pharmacy – graduate courses Columbia and Virginia business schools. Retired as Vice-President Sales Parke-Davis 1986 after 36 years of service. Rha Chi Honor Society (Pharmacy), N.A.R.D. (National Assoc. of Retail Druggists). Arkansas Traveler, former member Board of Governors U. of Michigan College of Pharmacy. Honorary Doctor's Degree in Science Cumberland College. Gave commencement address to 1985 Cumberland graduates.

David Lawrence Jones was born in Chicago, Illinois and lived most of his early life in Louisville, Kentucky. In 1976, he received a basketball scholarship to Cumberland where he attended school for three years. Upon leaving Cumberland, Jones moved to Jacksonville, Florida where he obtained a Transportation degree. Jones gained valuable experience by working as a Transportation Terminal Manager in Montgomery, Alabama and Hattiesburg, Mississippi, and then moved to Knoxville, Tennessee, where he and his family currently reside. Over the past three and a half decades, Jones has formed and managed many successful transportation and service-related businesses in Tennessee and Kentucky, and continues to explore business opportunities in the transportation and  containerization industries.

In 2008, after a long relationship with Toyota Tsusho America, a subsidiary of Toyota, Jones sold his transportation company to the Japanese company where he is a minority stockholder, and continues to serve as President and Chief Operating Officer of the company.

In 2011, Jones was inducted into Cumberlands' as Alumnus of the Year. Jones is married to his high school sweetheart, the former Lisa Grantz of Louisville, Kentucky. They have two children.

C. W. Mayes, Jr., a 1971 graduate, served as mayor of Norris, Tennessee at the early age of 27. C. W. Mayes, Jr., founded Drives & Conveyors, Inc. in 1976 as a specialty lubrication business. From the initial two-man operation in Corbin, Kentucky, the company grew into a 20 employee team with a second location in Norton, Virginia, a sales office in Andersonville, Tennessee, and over 21,000 square feet of combined warehouse space.

Over the years, Drives & Conveyors, Inc. evolved and expanded its range of expertise with the goal of providing the best products and services to the industries in our region. They achieved this goal and are now the leading independently owned power transmission and material handling company in our market area.

Don Adkins and wife, **Janice Childers Adkins**, both 1966 graduates, are active members of the First Baptist Church in Williamsburg. They have owned numerous businesses in Williamsburg and served on various Boards. Currently they are owners of Ex-Cell-O Casket Company. Janice retired from teaching at Williamsburg Independent Schools. The Adkins are the parents of two sons, Tim and David, and one daughter, Sandy (deceased).

William Anthony "Tony" Wilburn of Pulaski County, Kentucky, was recruited by Cumberland College basketball coach, Paul Falin, and accepted a  varsity scholarship to play for the Indians. Wilburn earned varsity honors all four years and was graduated from Cumberland in 1979 with a Bachelor of Science degree in accounting and business administration. He later earned his Certified Public Accountant degree and practiced as a CPA for

twenty years. In 2002, when Wilburn learned Cumberland Security Bank was up for sale, he purchased it and has served as its President since taking ownership. In 1982, Wilburn and his brother, Doug, became joint partners in D. W. Wilburn Construction, Woodstock Holding Company and other businesses. Wilburn states, "I was blessed to attend Cumberland College and obtain an education. I was blessed then and continue to be so." Wilburn continues to apply his steady work ethic in all of life's dealings. In 2011, he was inducted into Cumberlands Alumni Hall of Honor as the Distinguished Alumnus Award Recipient. Wilburn is married to the former Sherry Vaught and they have two children, both of whom work at Cumberland Security Bank of Somerset.

John Bill Keck was graduated in 1962, the first in his family to ever attend college. Following college he served in the military for a number of years before coming back home where he taught school for a while. He decided that teaching was not what he wanted to do for the rest of his life so he became a door to door salesman selling encyclopedias. He then signed up with super salesman Zig Ziglar and sold cookware door to door. As soon as he had the money  set aside, he purchased a coal mines for $55,000 and worked every moment to pay his bill. But coal mining was not his future and he eventually sold the mines for $1.3 million. The gentleman who bought the mines knew nothing of mining so he gave Mr. Keck 20% of the mine to operate it for him. Keck ran the mines for a number of years but eventually sold his share to expand his construction company. His company has built schools, banks, motels and other businesses and he personally owns over 150 pieces of real estate.

Jack Isaacs graduated from Cumberland in 1955. He earned a B.S. from Union College in 1956, an M.S. from Eastern Kentucky University in 1958, and also studied at George Peabody College and the University of Kentucky. Isaacs began his career in his hometown of Lynch, KY serving as teacher, director of pupil personnel and principal. Concern about his five children growing up in a depressed economy caused Isaacs to move the family to Lexington, where he served as principal and director of pupil personnel until retirement. He was named NCCJ Administrator of the year 1969-70 Fayette County. He served three terms as president of the

Central Kentucky Secondary Principals' Association, and served on the Board of Directors of the Kentucky Association of Secondary Principals and the Kentucky Association of Pupil Personnel Workers. He has also served as a member of Central KY Council Peace and Justice, Cumberlands' Board of Visitors, and Phi Delta Kappa. Isaacs and his wife, Fay, reside in Lexington, Kentucky.

Judy Sizemore Rose, born in Clay County, Kentucky to Frank and Nancy Sizemore. Rose attended Cumberland College and was a recipient of the Ruby G. Archer Scholastic Scholarship and was graduated from Cumberland in 1958 with a degree in music. She completed further studies at the University of Kentucky and Eastern Kentucky University and received an Honorary Doctorate degree from University of the Cumberlands in 1985.

Dr. Rose has taught at Clay County High School; owner and operator of a supermarket; assisted in

operations of family owned coal companies; owner and operator of art galleries in Tennessee and Georgia; owner and president of Cumberland Valley Insurance Agency; Vice President of Tri-State Realty Company; President of J. Rose, Inc.; major stockholder in banks in Central and Eastern Kentucky.

Dr. Rose has extensive public service to her credit which includes serving as Trustee for University of the Cumberlands and Alumni Board Member; various service on numerous committees include: Lexington Dream Factory – Board of Governors. Ky. Supreme Court and Court of Appeals – Judiciary Nominating Community. Cardinal Hill Hospital – Vice Chairman, Board of Directors. McDowell Cancer Network – Board of Directors. American Heart Association – Board of Directors. Kentucky Mountain Laurel Festival – Board of Directors. KET – Advisory Committee; KET – 1987 Study Commission Adult Education Chairperson; Forward in the Fifth. Board of Directors; Scott Rose Foundation – Founder and Board Member. Southern Baptist Theological Seminary Foundation – Board of Directors. Kentucky Easter Seal Society – Secretary, Board of Directors. National Federation of Republican Women. Manchester Women's Club (Outstanding Member – 1975). University of Kentucky Women's Club. Kentucky Colonels. Selected for Who's Who in South and Southwest. "The profession to which I have devoted the most time and of which I am most proud is that of wife and mother."

As a result of her service to others, Dr. Rose has received numerous awards and recognitions include: 100 Alumni Award and Servant Leadership Award from University of the Cumberlands; Outstanding Philanthropist Award from National Association of C & J; The National Easter Seals Society Volunteer of the Year Award, First Faith & Vision Award from Lexington Christian Academy, to name a few. Dr. Rose was married to the late James L. Rose. She is the mother of three children, grandmother to eleven and great grandmother of seven.

She is very active in her church and choir at Immanuel Baptist Church in Lexington, and she has performed as Vocalist throughout the United States.

R. Bruce Kirby, an entrepreneur, is a mountain boy who has stayed close to his roots. A native of Harlan County, Kentucky, he is the **great nephew of former**

Cumberland College president, Lloyd Creech (1925 -1946). Kirby attended Harlan County schools and was graduated from Cumberland in 1964. His wife, the former Jacqueline Dunaway, is a 1963 Cumberland graduate and is also from Cumberland, Kentucky.

The Kirby's have fond memories of their college days and are supporters of the college and recently purchased a stone for Dr. Creech's grave indicting the years he was president of the college so it will be documented for the years to come.

61

He is owner and president of Kirby Properties, Incorporated. A faithful member of Corinth Baptist Church, London, where he is active in Sunday School, Triple L, Operation Christmas Child and the Christian Shelter for the Homeless to name a few.

Cort Dondero attended Cumberland in the fall of 1969 and spring of 1970 and was a member of the golf team. Currently, Dondero is the Chief Operating Officer at Panadero Aggregates, the holding company for Bluegrass Materials. Bluegrass Materials is an aggregates and concrete block producer that owns and operates seven quarries and two block plants in the state of Kentucky. Dondero is also on the Board of Directors of the publicly traded, Gencor Industries, Inc., and the leading manufacturer of asphalt plants, soil remediation plants, combustion systems and screening equipment for the road and highway construction industry. Previously, Dondero was Vice President of Quality Assurance for Ryder Transportation Group.

Due to Dondero's reputation of being able to reduce operating costs without displacing employees, several large corporations were interested in utilizing his business model. As a result, he founded the consulting firm, Dondero & Associates. The mission of Dondero & Associates was to assist organizations seeking to improve their long-term competitive position. On September 19, 2011, students, faculty, and staff at The Hutton School of Business welcomed Dondero to the University campus. Students from the undergraduate business program and the Master of Business Administration program had the opportunity to hear Dondero speak on various subjects including how to market your MBA degree. Dondero spoke briefly on a variety of subjects including interview tactics, appropriate dress, and resume techniques.

Lillian Galloway. Grew up in Vicco, Ky. in a family of six children. Attended Dilce Combs High School, Perry County, Ky., Cumberland College, Eastern Kentucky State University, University of Louisville, University of Cincinnati. Founder and president of Cincinnati Model Agency International. Galloway is also founder and president of the Lillian Galloway

Modeling Academy, founded in 1971, and the Children's Model Agency, founded in 1985. Additionally, she has established student model boards which serve many specialty shops throughout the tri-state area of Kentucky, Ohio and Indiana. In 1976 Cincinnati Model Agency International and Lillian Galloway Modeling Academy were named in the International Blue Ribbon Model Agency and School. Galloway was named 1986 Woman of Achievement by Executive Women International. An Outstanding Alumna of Cumberland College, Galloway has received many such honors over the years. She was named Outstanding Business Woman by the Advertisers Club of Cincinnati and has also been recognized as one of the Top Five Business Women in Cincinnati and one of the Top Ten Business Women of Washington, D.C. Galloway has served as president of the Cumberland College Alumni Board and of the Modeling Association of America International, New York City. She has

served on several program committees and has been chairman of three International Models Conventions, held annually at the Waldorf Astoria in New York. Having majored in music education at Cumberland, Galloway remains involved in education. She works closely with high school counselors, not only advising girls who are interested in modeling but, also working with girls who have drug or family problems or who want to improve themselves in general. Galloway credits her success to her happy family life and her understanding husband, Tom Galloway. They have three sons, David, Scott, and Donald. Board of Directors, President of Alumni Association, Cincinnati Chapter Task Force, Outstanding Alumna Award.

Robert M. "Mike" Duncan was born in Oneida, Tennessee and grew up in his family's home in McCreary County, Kentucky. He attended nearby Cumberland College and graduated with a BA in history in 1971. Thereafter, he enrolled in the University of Kentucky - College of Law. Upon graduation, he returned to Appalachia, practiced law part-time and joined the Inez Deposit Bank. After two years, Mike became the youngest bank CEO in Kentucky.

Duncan has developed a strong and diverse management background with business, non-profit, and government organizations. He complemented his  legal education with attending the Harvard Business School executive education program and by taking on a full-time, yearlong assignment at the White House through the President's Commission on Executive Exchange. After a fruitful year working in the White House Office of Public Liaison, Mike returned to Inez with a renewed commitment to his eastern Kentucky community.

Mike has served as board chairman of a state university and a private college. He was a Trustee of the Christian Appalachian Project, the 15th largest private social services agency in America. In addition, he devotes much of his time to promoting regional cooperation and has developed a reputation of bringing diverse groups together. During one project, Mike led the effort to develop a strip-mined site into an industrial park bringing hundreds of new jobs of the area with a federal prison and other employers. His public service has been recognized with several distinctions, including honorary degrees from the College of the Ozarks, Cumberland College, and Morehead State University. His student-mentoring program, in its 36th year, has been featured on CBS Sunday Morning and in *The Los Angeles Times*.

Numerous officials have called on Mike to serve at various levels of government. In 2003, Kentucky Governor Fletcher asked Mike to chair his Transition Team where he directed over 500 volunteers in the most comprehensive reorganization of state government in three decades. President George W. Bush appointed Duncan to the President's Commission on White House Fellowships and nominated him to the Tennessee Valley Authority Board, a position to which he was unanimously confirmed by the United States Senate in March 2006.

In January 2007, Duncan was elected as the 60th Chairman of the Republican National Committee. As Chairman, he raised an unprecedented $428 million dollars, grew the donor base to 1.8 million – more donors than at any time in RNC history, and presided over the exceedingly successful 2008 Republican National Convention in Minneapolis-St. Paul. After completing his service as Chairman of the RNC, the TVA Board of Directors elected him in February 2009 to lead as Chairman of the Board. He served as Chairman of TVA from 2009-2010.

The Duncan family is the principal owner of a community bank with five offices in eastern Kentucky. Chairman Duncan has served as President of the Kentucky Bankers Association and as a Director of the Cleveland Federal Reserve Bank Cincinnati Branch.

Duncan was selected as President and CEO of the American Coalition for Clean Coal Electricity in August 2013 to represent the interest of coal companies, railroads and electric utilities. He has received honorary degrees from University of the Cumberlands, College of the Ozarks, and from Morehead State University.

Mike and his wife, Joanne, are 1974 graduates of the University of Kentucky - College of Law. They live in Inez, Kentucky, and have one son, Rob, an Assistant US Attorney in Lexington, Kentucky, who is married to Valerie Ridder of Springfield, Missouri. They have two grandchildren, Taylor and Olivia.

Edgar Croley. A native of Whitley County, Ky.

Attended Williamsburg Elementary School. Graduated from Saxton High School, Cumberland College, Naval Reserve Officers School at North Western University. Businessman. Enlisted in the Navy stationed at Great Lakes Navy Training Station, when Pearl Harbor was attacked. Served at the Navy Reserve Officer School at Notre Dame University. Served the remainder of the war aboard a High Speed Minescraper in the North Atlantic & the South Pacific. Three major invasions: Linquian Gulf in Philippines, Saigon – Tinniaw & Iowa Jima. Local businessman in Williamsburg: Gasoline stations, motel and real estate investments. Bank director. Received a commission as a Lt. in the Navy Reserves. A member and deacon of First Baptist Church. Sunday School Teacher. Sunday School

Superintendent. Chairman of the Board of Deacons. Assistant Church Moderator. Played two years with Cumberland's basketball team. Served one term on the Alumni Board. Attended most of the home college basketball and football games. Traveled twice to Kansas City to see Cumberland play in NAIA Tournament. Class Agent.

Eugene Adkins Lovett. Born, Williamsburg,

Kentucky. Married, Virginia Johnson. Children, Stanley Lovett and Troy Lovett. Cumberland College, University of Kentucky. Was employed by First National Bank, Williamsburg. the Prudential Insurance Company, Renfro Supply Company, and Bank of Williamsburg. Owner and manager of Lovett's Variety Store. Now Retired. Perfect Attendance at the Rotary Club. Whitley County Veterans, Member of the United Methodist Church. Received Certificate of Appreciation from Whitley Co. Veterans. Was instrumental in formulating and helping develop the Urban Renewal Project in the early 60's. Wrote the book *The History of Williamsburg.* Commissioned a Kentucky Colonel by Governor Louis B. Nunn.

Sandra Faulkner Brown, a 1953 Cumberland graduate and her husband, **Robert L. Brown, Jr.** were born and raised in Whitley County. Sandra

spent her working days as a teacher and accountant. Robert retired from the Air Force after a 27 year career, and he and Sandra owned and operated several businesses including Brown Chevrolet, Brown Motor Company and Williamsburg Motel. Mr. Brown also served as president of Williamsburg's Farmers National Bank.

Meet a few of our Architects

John Maudlin-Jeronimo graduated from Cumberland in 1967 with a bachelor's degree in mathematics and history. He did graduate studies in education and engineering science at the University of South Florida; earned a Bachelor of Architecture degree and a master's in urban planning from the University of Miami. Jeronimo also earned a certificate in the Management Development Program at Harvard University Graduate School of Education and a finance and administration certificate from the American Society of Association Executives.

Jeronimo has worked for the planning departments in Miami Beach and Miramar, FL, and Annapolis, Maryland. As the city's architect/urban designer in Annapolis, he had enforcement responsibility for the city's historic district ordinances and provided professional support to the Historic District Commission. A Certified Association Executive, Jeronimo spent close to two decades in senior management positions.

During his sixteen years as Executive Director of the National Architectural Accrediting Board, he provided technical assistance and advice and counsel on the development of more than thirty new schools and programs in architecture in the United States. He served as a consultant to Canadian Architectural Certification Board assisting in the development of an architectural accreditation system in Canada. As a United Nations supported consultant to the People's Republic of China he helped establish a national system of quality assurance in higher education. He has given numerous lectures, authored countless publications, and served as a member of committees/boards. From 2004 until his retirement, Jeronimo served as Associate Dean for External Affairs at the University of Maryland School of Architecture, Planning and Preservation.

Donald B. Shelton, a native of Whitley County, earned an associate's degree from Cumberland in 1953. Shelton also earned the Bachelor of Science

degree in Civil Engineering and Master of Science degree in Structural Engineering from the University of Kentucky. Prior to the establishment of his own firm, Shelton was associated with several engineering and architectural firms in Lexington. Donald B. Shelton, Architect-Engineer and Associates, located in Lexington, have completed projects ranging over two-thirds of the state of Kentucky, many in the Corbin-Williamsburg area.

Nicholas Joel Buccalo attended Cumberlands in 1979. He received his undergraduate degree from The Ohio State University before enrolling at the Harvard University Graduate School of design where he received the master's of architecture. He specializes in architecture, architectural design and rendering. In 1993 he established Simple Twig Renderings and has won numerous architecture awards and honors.

James Ford was born in Louisville, KY; his family

moved near Somerset, KY in 1930. His first job was as a Louisville Courier-Journal newspaper boy. As a teenager, he earned the Eagle Award in Boy Scouts. Ford graduated from Somerset High School in 1944 and joined the Navy, serving in the Naval Ammunitions Department in Indiana. After his discharge, he returned home to study engineering at Cumberland, graduating with an associate's degree in 1948. He later earned his B.A. in architecture in 1951 at the Alabama Polytechnic Institute (now Auburn University).

Six months after graduation, Ford married his wife, Doris, while working at an architectural firm in Birmingham, AL, where he drew plans for a variety of buildings, residences, apartments, churches, institutes, and industrial buildings. He, Doris, and their three children moved back to Kentucky in 1970 where he began working with the Lake Cumberland Area Development District. Ford applied his gifts and talents to assist area cities and counties to work together developing comprehensive plans, including the community efforts in rebuilding Mannsville, KY after the devastating 1974 tornado attack. In 1985, he and his family moved to Georgetown, KY, where he worked for a number of architectural firms providing services to Frankfort, Louisville, Lexington and Cincinnati. In 2002, he retired to take care of Doris who was experiencing health issues, until her passing in 2012.

Ford is also a co-founder of the Scott County Habitat for Humanity, which has significantly contributed to the community area with 24 homes built thus far in "Habitat Village," (seven other homes on individual lot), and the expanding self-supporting ReStore Thrift Store.

Harry L. Siler graduated from Cumberland in 1960.

 He went on to the School of Architecture at the University of Kentucky and was among its first six graduates in 1964. Siler worked for Eero Saarinen Associates as an architect in New Haven, Connecticut on several projects, including Connecticut Wesleyan's Creative Arts Center and the New York City Metropolitan Museum of Art. In

1969 he moved to Washington D.C. to begin teaching architecture and there joined the Potomac Group to work with the National Park Service as a client on the construction documents and exhibit design for the proposed Jefferson National Expansion Memorial beneath the Gateway Arch in St. Louis.

Siler established his own Washington architectural practice and again worked with the National Park Service to design the Orientation Center within the National Military Park in Gettysburg, and in Washington, D.C. worked with the National Park Service to design the Bicentennial Information Center. His architectural practice included numerous Washington area residential renovation projects adapting existing structures for private clients. All the while he continued to teach at Howard University's School of Architecture in Washington.

Siler retired to Williamsburg, only to leave again to serve as a United States Peace Corps Volunteer in South African from 2001 to 2003. Now in full retirement, Siler came home to Williamsburg in 2003.

Meet a few of our Attorneys, Legislators

Meriel D. Harris, a native of Somerset, Kentucky, was graduated from Cumberland College in 1933.

He later attended Western Kentucky University, the University of Kentucky, and Northwestern University where he earned his Juris Doctor Degree in law. Mr. Harris has served as a practicing attorney in Somerset from 1951 to the present.

Hubert F. White, a native of Williamsburg, attended Cumberland College from 1921 to 1923, where he served as captain of both the football and basketball teams. He graduated with an Associate of Arts

degree and enrolled at the University of Kentucky in 1923, where he completed his undergraduate degree in 1925 and graduated from law school in 1927. He practiced law in Harlan and Middlesboro for 55 years and served as the city attorney for Middlesboro for a total of 30 years. White served as mayor of Middlesboro from 1958 to 1962. He was married to the former Fay Cawood for 60 years.

During the 2011 Founders' Day convocation, University of the Cumberlands posthumously honored with the Distinguished Alumni Award and induction into the Alumni Hall of Honor. His sons, Robert and Frank accepted the award on behalf of their father.

William Gullett graduated Cumberlands cum laude in 1971 with a degree in history. Gullett graduated UK College of Law in 1977.

Bill is a member of Frost Brown Todd, LLC and has represented industrial Fortune 500 companies and closely held corporations. His practice areas include construction law; corporate/business; energy, natural resources and utilities; international services group;

lending and commercial services; and mergers and acquisitions.

Prior to joining Frost Brown Todd, he served as in-house counsel for Ashland Oil, Inc. (now Ashland Inc.), Ashland Coal, Inc. and the LTV Corporation. Bill continues to represent and actively work with businesses of all sizes. Gullett currently serves on University of the Cumberlands' Board of Trustees.

Gullett is married to alumnus, **Jenny Hall Gullett,** 1973, and they have one son, Jonathan

Phillip M. Armstrong. One daughter, Katie, and one son, Phillip, Jr. Cumberland College – B.S.;

University of the Kentucky – Juris Doctor. Senior Counsel, Pulp and Paper Division of Georgia-Pacific Corporation. Law Clerk, Research Assistant, Legal Officer, Georgia-Pacific Corporation Assistant to Division Counsel, Division Counsel, Senior Counsel. Licensed in Kentucky and Georgia. American Bar Association, Kentucky Bar Association, Georgia Bar Association, Atlanta Bar Association. College and Law School – Dean's List, J.T. Vallandingham Honor Society, Who's Who in American Colleges and Universities, Student Government Association, Student Life Committee, Class President, Distinguished Military Graduate, Phi Delta Phi Legal Fraternity. Phi Alpha Theta Historical Society, Junior Achievement, Army Commendation Medal, Kentucky Law Alumni Association, Corporate Counsel Association of Greater Atlanta. President, Cumberland College Alumni Association. Georgia Chapter Task Force.

Class Agent, Cumberland College Alumni Association.

Thomas "Tom" Lee Jensen was graduated from Cumberland in 1972 and went on to attend law school at Northern Kentucky University, Chase College of Law. Jensen graduated from law school in 1978 and opened his practice in London, KY, where he has a successful practice with three other partners in the firm of Jensen, Cessna, Benge, and Webster. During his tenure at Cumberland, Jensen became interested in politics after being recruited to get involved with the college's Republican Club. He has been chairman of the Laurel County Republican Party, chairman of the 5th Congressional District Republican Party, and chairman of the State of Kentucky Republican Party. He has also held a

number of political positions, including nearly every leadership position in the State Republican party. In 1985, Jensen was elected as state representative and served two years. In addition, he served as legal counsel to the House of Representatives before being elected again to the House of Representatives where he served as minority floor leader. In 2003, Jensen was inducted into the Republican 5th District Hall of Fame for his work and dedication to the Republican Party. Jensen and his wife, **Nannette Curry Jensen**, 1974, have two daughters and two grandchildren.

Maurice Byrd is a 1974 alumnus of Cumberland. A

graduate of the University of Kentucky School of Law, he has attained a broad range of legal experiences from law firms to corporate legal departments.

Byrd, a native of Harlan, KY, now lives in Atlanta, GA, where he is rearing his daughter, Jada Simone. While at Cumberland, he distinguished himself, as both an athlete and student, becoming an All American and being inducted into the Athletic

Hall of Fame in 1999. He has served on the UC Board of Trustees and actively recruited more than twenty students, fulfilling his goal to remain personally involved and to provide African American students with an opportunity for a UC education.

Jerry D. Bryant. Born in McCreary County. Married to Glenna Mattingly (Cumberland '69). Has 3 children: Laura, Jennifer, and Jeremy. Graduated McCreary County High School. B.S., Cumberland College, (high honors). Indiana University School of Law, Doctor of Jurisprudence. Attorney in

Wilmington, Ohio. Licensed to practice in Ohio, Kentucky, and Florida. Former Wilmington, Ohio Municipal Court Judge. Admitted to practice before the United States Supreme Court. Member of American, Ohio, Kentucky, and Florida Bar Associations, American and Ohio Trial Lawyers Association, Ohio Committee on Ethics, Past President Clinton County Bar Association, Clinton County Board of Elections, Former Chairman of the Board of Pound Puppies, Inc., Special Counsel to Ohio Attorney General, Visiting Assistant Professor of Law, Wilmington College. Graduate of Cumberland 1969, served on Board of Directors of Cumberland College Alumni Association. Received Outstanding Alumni Award 1979, Chapter Task Force in Central Ohio, Class Agent.

James W. Bowling. Senior partner of Vernis & Bowling, P.A., alternates living and working between his homes in the Florida Keys and in Fisher Island, Florida, and his offices along the South East Coast of Florida. Born in Corbin, Kentucky to a railroad

family. After service in the military during the Korean War, he returned to Cumberland College, where he graduated in 1958. Afterward, attended the University of Kentucky, where he graduated with a Bachelors Science Degree in Marketing and Advertising.

Migrated to South Florida in 1960 where, after working for seven years as an Insurance Adjustor, he attended Law School at the University of Miami. He graduated in 1970 with a Juris Doctorate Degree in Law. Shortly thereafter he and Frank C. Vernis, Jr., founded the law firm known today as Vernis And Bowling, P.A., which now has four offices along the South East Coast of Florida and one office in New Orleans, Louisiana. Specializes in insurance matters for corporate clients. His specialty is in insurance, and law firm management and client relationships. Jim has a long history of Financial Support of Cumberland College. Class Agent for the Alumni Association.

Tommy Warren Butler. Married Nancy Tombras Butler. Sons: John and Tom. Daughter: Lucy.

Graduated Cumberland Junior College, 1951 (Bachelor of Science) Business Administration, University of Tennessee. U.S. Army – Korea, 1954-56. J.D., University of Tennessee School of Law. Attorney, Senior Partner in Firm of Butler, Vines, Babb & Threadgill, Knoxville, Tennessee. 11 Member Law Firm in General Practice of Law. Member of Knoxville Bar Association, Tennessee Bar Association, and American Bar Association. Arbitrator, Federal Mediation and Conciliation Service (Inactive). Past President of Cumberland College Alumni Association on two separate occasions. Served on various Alumni Boards. Speaker on Cumberland College campus.

Frances Jones Mills. Gray, Kentucky. Graduate of Cumberland College, Williamsburg, Kentucky,

Attended Eastern Kentucky University, Richmond, Kentucky, Attended Union College, Barbourville, Kentucky. Kentucky State Treasurer, Kentucky Secretary of State, Kentucky State Treasurer, Kentucky Clerk, Court of Appeals, Kentucky House of Representative, Director of Women's Activities for Kentucky Division of Civil Defense (Author of National Award winning publication "What Would You Do?"), Public School Teacher, Medical Assistant. National Association of State Treasurers, Past Vice-President Southern Region. National Association of Appellate Court Clerks, Past President and Co-Founder. National Association of Secretaries of State, Past Program Chair and Past Member of Executive Board. Kentucky Federation of Business and Professional Women, Kentucky Mountain Laurel Festival Board Member, Cumberland College Development Committee, Order of Eastern Star – White Shrine, Century Club, National Kidney Foundation of Kentucky, Past Honorary Board Member, Gray Baptist Church. Who's Who in Kentucky, Who's Who in American Women, Personalities of the South, Who's Who in American Politics, International Platform Association, Distinguished Woman of Knox County (one of eight), Woman of Achievement, Tri-County Business and Professional Women. Southeastern Kentucky's Outstanding Woman of the Year, Outstanding Alumna of the Year, Cumberland College. 1983 Public Service Award, Kentucky Federation Business and Professional Women.

Edwin R. Denney. Born at Monticello, Wayne

County, Kentucky, March 8, 1904. Completed grade and high school at Monticello. Attended Cumberland College in 1923 and Eastern State Teachers College at Richmond, Kentucky, for one year. Employed by Southeastern Coal Company as a high school principal for two years and also was the principal of a new high school for two years at Horse Branch, Ohio County. Graduated with A.B. degree from University of Kentucky and was granted his L.L.B. degree from the law school in 1932, and upon his graduation was granted the Order of the Coif. He formed a law partnership with Mr. C.C. Williams of Mt. Vernon, Kentucky, and in 1943 was elected from Rockcastle County to serve in the Kentucky Legislature and was elected Minority Floor Leader during the session. Was appointed Circuit Judge of the 28th Judicial District, Rockcastle, Pulaski, Wayne and Clinton Counties, to succeed John Sherman Cooper who was elected to the United States Senate.

On the expiration of his term as Circuit Judge, he returned to his law practice at Mt. Vernon. In 1951 he was elected President of the Alumni Association of the University of Kentucky, and in 1953 **President Eisenhower appointed him United States Attorney for the Eastern District of Kentucky**, acceptance of which required him to move to Lexington. He resigned in 1955 to **run for Governor**. The son of the late Joseph R. Denney and Hattie Lovelace Denney. His two older brothers, Fred R. Denney of West Liberty and Perk E. Denney of Monticello have passed away. Married to Elinor Kundert, formerly of South Dakota and graduate of Berea College. Two children: Suzanne Denney Carmichael of Washington D.C. and Joseph E. Denney of Burnsville, North Carolina. Also blessed with five grandchildren. In college he was a member of Sigma Chi social fraternity and a member of Phi Alpha Delta legal fraternity. He was a member of Calvary Baptist Church, Lexington, Lexington Kiwanis Club, and a Mason. In later years his L.L.B. degree was exchanged to that of J.D., Doctor of Jurisprudence. Until his retirement, he practiced law at Lexington and was granted an honorary degree, that of Doctor of Humanities by Cumberland College in 1985. He is a member of the Idle Hour Country Club, an active member of the Lafferty Society, and a member of the Fellows Club of the University of Kentucky. Judge Denney passed away on June 22, 1986.

Theodore W. Clarke. Born in Lothair, Kentucky.

Married to Ms. Gwendolyn R. Tramel. Three Children: Kenneth T. (Graduate Cumberland College), Rebecca S. George, Karen D. Blackburn. Two grandchildren. Hazard City Schools, Hazard High School, Cumberland College, University of Kentucky, Degree granted Arts-Law. Post Graduate work – University of Kentucky Law School. August 1942 – February 1946 separated 1st Lt. AUS (Med Adm Corps). October 1948 – March 1966 United States Air Force. Retired 31 March 1966 – Lt./Col. USAF (Med Serv. Corps). Awards and Decorations: American Defense Medal, European Theater of Operations (ETO) w/ 5 Battle Stars, ETO Victory Medal. U.S. Civil Service, Charleston AFB, South Carolina. 1968-1977 Retired GS 12. Class Agent for Class of 1941.

Robert Michael Duncan (See Meet a few of our Entrepreneurs)

Charles Siler served the Kentucky House of Representatives from 1985 until 1990 and from 1995 until his retirement in 2010. Siler earned an associate's degree from Cumberland in 1950, a bachelor's degree from the University of Maryland in 1960, and a master's degree in public relations from the University of Wisconsin-Madison in 1964. He served in the United States Army from 1947-1972

and was inducted into the Infantry OCS Hall of Fame in 1998. He previously served as Chief Operating Officer for the Adantz Mental Health District; Finance Chair of the Veterans Nursing Homes of Kentucky; Regional Representative - Baptist Hospitals of Kentucky; Secretary/Treasurer, Whitley County Farm Bureau; President, Whitley County Cattleman's Association and President, Whitley County Bass Club.

Harry "Gippy" Graham was born in 1929 at the start of the Great Depression. He says he was 10 before he even saw a basketball - but his first encounter hooked him on the sport and eventually led to scholarships, which enabled him to go to college at Cumberland and Georgetown.

Graham was the first of his family to attend college and received his associate's degree from Cumberland in 1950. During his Cumberland days, he worked and played basketball. His first season, Cumberland won the Southeastern Junior College Championship. Later, while a Georgetown student, Graham was named an all-Kentucky Intercollegiate Athletic Conference player.

Graham earned a bachelor's degree from Georgetown College and served in the United States Air Force. He then taught and coached at Georgetown while he completed his master's degree from the University of Kentucky.

His varied career has included teaching and coaching at both the secondary and college levels and serving as associate superintendent in the Office of Adult and Community Education of the Kentucky Department of Education. He also has served as administrative assistant to the commissioner of the Kentucky Department of Highways, as the state representative for Franklin County and as Mayor of the City of Frankfort. In 2010, Graham was inducted into Cumberlands Alumni Hall of Honor as Distinguished Alumnus.

Rick G. Nelson, a native of Middlesboro, KY, graduated from Cumberland with a B.S. in 1976 and earned an M.A. from Eastern Kentucky University in 1988. While at Cumberland, he served as Manager

of the baseball team under Coach Walter Mathis. In 1976, Nelson began his teaching career in the Bell County School System. He also served as a coach for girl's high school softball from 1990-1998. In 2000, Nelson was elected Kentucky State Representative for District 87, which includes Bell County and part of Harlan County, and has served for the past 13 years. Nelson is also a member of Gideons International, Kentucky Education Association and National Rifle Association.

Roger C. Noe, a 14-year veteran of the Kentucky House of Representatives, served for seven years as that Chamber's Chair of the Education Committee. The Harlan Democrat, who represented Kentucky 88th House District, also served on the influential House Appropriations and Revenue Committee, Budget Review Subcommittee on Education, and was a member of the Legislature's Task Force on School Reform.

Currently a professor of psychology at Southeast Kentucky Community and Technical College where he has been employed for some 40 years – Noe stepped down as the institution's Dean of Academic

Affairs in 2004 to return to teaching. He received a M.A. from Eastern Kentucky University (EKU) after completing his undergraduate work at University of the Cumberlands (UC) and holds a Doctorate in education from University of Kentucky in Policy Studies and Evaluation. He studied State and Local Government Policy at the John F. Kennedy School of Government at Harvard University in 1986 and has published scholarly articles in such journals as the *Progress of Education*, *The Journal of Education Finance*, and the *Yale Law and Policy Review*.

Noe's honors include receiving outstanding and distinguished alumnus awards from both UC (1986) and EKU (1988). He is a 1988 Charter Inductee to

the Hall of Honor at UC and in 1989 was inducted into the Political Science Society as an honored member at EKU. He was named as one of Kentucky's Outstanding Young Men by the Kentucky Jaycees in 1980.

One of his legislative projects – The Parent and Child Education Program – was recognized by the Ford Foundation as one of the nation's ten best "Innovations in State and Local Government." In addition, he was recognized as one of the Top 10 Legislators in the Kentucky General Assembly in 1990 by the *Lexington Herald Leader*. Noe has stayed active in his community – serving as a member of the Harlan Independent School Board; coached basketball and baseball for the Cawood Ledford Boy's and Girl's Club and was recognized by that organization with its "Volunteer of the Year Award" in 2005 for his extensive involvement with the area's young people. In addition, he has served as an assistant coach of the Harlan Lady Dragon's Softball team for the past 4 years.

Dr. Noe has served higher education in his role of Professor, Division Chair, Chair of Faculty, Dean of Academic Affairs (Provost) at Southeast Kentucky Community and Technical College and Interim President at both Ashland Community and Technical College and Maysville Community and Technical College.

Willard Marion Hamblin. Born in Gatliff, Kentucky. Married, Virginia Nichols Hamblin. Children – Pierce Willard Hamblin and Cynthia Margaret Hamblin.  Cumberland College, University of Louisville – Law Degree. Practicing Attorney in Lexington, Kentucky. Manager of the Sub-Regional Veterans Administration Office. Author of the book, *Hamblin Family*, a genealogical book of his family. He also wrote and published 'Tall Tales With a Down Home Touch.' Served in the Army. Army rank of Major, recipient of the Silver Star for heroism, the Bronze Star for bravery, the Purple Heart for wounds received in combat, and the American Theatre, European Theater, and African Theatre Medals. Member of the Retired Officers Committee for Kentucky, Tennessee, Ohio and West Virginia. A charter member of Spindletop Hall, University of Kentucky Club, Retired Officers Association, American Legion Post #313, Lexington Lodge #1, Free and Accepted Masons. Member of the American Bar Association, the Kentucky Bar Association, and the Fayette County Bar Association.

Dewayne Bunch was a 1992 graduate of Cumberland. He began teaching at Whitley County  School system immediately after graduation and taught there for 17 years. In November 2010 he was elected as Kentucky State Representative for the 82nd district. Bunch retired from the National Guard in 2008 after a 23 year career including two deployments where he earned numerous honors and recognitions including the Bronze Star.

Bunch passed away in 2012 from an injury sustained in 2011 at the high school while breaking up a fight.

Regina Petrey Bunch is a 1995 Cumberland  graduate and a seventh grade teacher in the Whitley County School system. Her husband, Dewayne Bunch, was critically injured while breaking up a student fight at the high school where he had taught and had to resign his seat in the House of Representatives. Regina Bunch was the only candidate from either party to seek his seat in a special election. She served the remaining year of her husband's two-year term and then ran for and was elected to the office.

Edward Moss Gatliff. In the center of the court house square, front side, is a pretentious native stone marker bearing this inscription: "This tablet is placed here by the people of the Ninth District, led by citizens of Whitley County, in honor of Edward Moss Gatliff, member of the Kentucky State Highway Commission who by his rare leadership and distinguished success in building highways has won the lasting gratitude of his people. May 21, 1935."

 Edward Moss Gatliff was the son of Dr. Ancil Gatliff and Florida Moss Gatliff. Edward was graduated from Williamsburg Institute in 1907. As a student, he left a legacy as editor of *The Eglantine* yearbook and Senior Class President. He also played football and baseball all four years, during which time he was captain of the football team in 1903 and manager in 1905. Following graduation, he served as head baseball coach for several years primarily during the transition from Williamsburg Institute to Cumberland College years.

Gatliff attended the University of Virginia, University of Michigan, and Columbia University. He was vice-president of High Splint Coal Company, U.S. Assistant District Attorney from 1917-21, State Highway Commissioner from 1932-36, and a member of the State Central Committee for the Democratic Party. He was the outstanding leader of his party in the ninth district and throughout the state for many years.

Gatliff was a member of the Sons of the American Revolution, Zeta Psi Fraternity, and of the Pendennis Club of Louisville. He was a Mason and a member of the Baptist Church. Gatliff was married to the former Beverly Davidson of Greensboro, Georgia.

As chairman of the War Bond Committee in World War II, Gatliff received for Whitley County a citation of achievement for exceeding the quota on each of the seven drives. Throughout the years, he served on numerous committees, giving unreservedly of his time for the betterment of the community. He was instrumental in helping many young people through college and untiring in his efforts to procure positions for worthy young men and women. (Renfro Revelations June 1946 Vol. III No. 6.) Cumberland College records indicate Gatliff served the last year of his life as a Trustee in 1949.

Albert Robinson began his career in the Kentucky Assembly as a state representative where he served from 1972 until 1984, and again from 1987 to 1988.

As a non-traditional student, Robinson graduated from Cumberland in 1980.

He was first elected to serve in the State Senate from 1994 to 2004, then again from 2013 to present representing the 21st District. He is a member of the Banking and Insurance Committee, the State and Local Government Committee, the Transportation Committee, and the Veterans, Military Affairs and Public Protection Committee.

Robinson also is a self-employed real estate broker, auctioneer, farmer and founder of the Robinson Sausage Company. He is a member of the Pentecostal Church and a 33rd degree Mason. Currently, he lives in the community of Viva, in Laurel County, with his wife Lucille. They have three children, five grandchildren, and one great grandchild.

Meet a few of our College Presidents

While we embrace many students from the most humble of circumstances, we also have the bright and the beautiful. Then, too, I must confess among others how proud I am of the Cumberland graduates who have gone on to such stellar careers as college and/or university presidents.

William A. McCall. Born in Wellsville, Tenn. A.A.L., Cumberland College; Bachelor of Arts, Lincoln Memorial University; Teachers College, Columbia University. Member of the faculty at

Columbia Teachers College at the age of twenty-four. He taught during the summers and during sabbaticals at the University of North Carolina. George Peabody College, the University of California, Auburn University, the Chinese National

University of Peking, Peking Teachers College, the Peking Christian University, and University of Miami in Florida. Goodwill Ambassador to China in 1923. He helped revise and modernize the Chinese educational system. Publications: "*How to Measure in Education*," "*How to Experiment in Education*," and "*The McCall Speller*." Co-author of McCall-Crabb *Standard Test Lessons in Reading.* Dr. McCall was survived by his wife, Gretchen McCall, a scholar and an outstanding teacher in her own right.

James Lloyd Creech. A native of Harlan County, Kentucky. Williamsburg Institute, University of Michigan Law School, Kentucky Bar, B.S. Degree

from Columbia University, Harvard Graduate School of Education and Columbia University. Teacher in rural schools of Kentucky, teacher in the Barbourville Institute. Member of the faculty of Cumberland College. Honorary

Doctorate from Georgetown College. Member of the faculty of Cumberland College, Treasurer of the class

of 1907; vice-president of his graduating class; member of the Literary Society, glee club, oratorical association, served as dean of the teachers' department and as superintendent of the grades, President of Cumberland College. Listed among the education and psychology faculty. The years served by Dr. Creech as president of Cumberland College were difficult years, for it was during the time that this great nation faced an economic depression and the Second World War. It was through the tight-fisted integrity of President Creech that the College was kept alive with the momentum it needed to survive.

Betty L. Siegel. Married to Dr. Joel H. Siegel. Has two sons, David and Michael. Florida State University – Ph.D., University of North Carolina at Chapel Hill – M.Ed., Wake Forest University – B.A., Cumberland College – associate degree (1950). President – Kennesaw College. Dean of the

School of Education and Psychology and Professor of Psychology at Western Carolina University in Cullowhee, NC. Served as the Dean of Academic Affairs for Continuing Education, as Professor of Psychological Foundations in the College of Education, and as an associate in the Institute for the Development of Human Resources at the University of Florida. Taught at Indiana University and at Lenoir-Rhyne College in Hickory, NC. Dr. Siegel holds the distinction of being the first woman to head an institution in the 35-unit University System of Georgia and the longest serving woman president of a public university in the nation while leading Kennesaw State from 1981-2006. Honorary Doctorates from Cumberland College and Miami University in Ohio. A nationally known lecturer and speaker, has delivered over fifty papers, served as a consultant in over 200 school systems, been keynote speaker at seven international associations, fifty

74

national associations, and over 250 regional and state conferences, has delivered over 175 addresses to business, professional, governmental and civic groups in 49 states, Puerto Rico, and four foreign countries. Who's Who in American Education, World Who's Who of Women, Leaders in Education, Dictionary of International Biography, and Who's Who Among of American Women. The first woman named to the Board of Directors of Atlanta Gas Light Co., and Equifax, Inc. Board of Directors of Atlanta Chamber of Commerce, Vice President of Area Councils for the Chamber, served on the Board of Trustees of Leadership Atlanta, Inc., a sponsor for the Marietta Arts Council and the Atlanta Women's Network, a member of the Cobb Landmark Society and the Georgia Executive Women's Network, named an International Business Fellow. Active on the Governor's Commission of the Job Training Partnership Act. Appointed to the Governor's Commission on Growth Strategies. Served on the Board of Directors of the Cobb Chamber of Commerce, member of the Communications Committee, served on the Executive Council, and Vice President of Community Dev. Board of Directors of the American Association of State Colleges and Universities, the American Council of Ed., Southeast Regional Advisory Board of the Institute for Internal Ed., President of the Southern Council of Teachers Ed., The National Commission of Programs & Projects of the American Association of Colleges of Teacher Ed. Member of the Executive Council of Teacher Ed. Council of State Colleges & Univ. Named to the Executive Committee of the National Association for Intercollegiate Athletics, co-founder & co-director of the International Alliance for Invitational Education. Georgia Chapter Task Force, Alumni Board of Directors, Outstanding Alumna Award, Campus Speaker for Cumberland College. She has been recognized for many outstanding awards: Distinguished Teacher of the Year, University of Florida (1969), University of the Cumberlands Hall of Honor (1988), Cobb County, Georgia Citizen of the Year (1996), Georgia Woman of the Year by the Georgia Commission on Women (1997), OAK Award (Outstanding Alumni of Kentucky (1998), Junior Achievement Business Hall of Fame (1999), Cobb County Who's Who and Most Influential Atlantians (multiple years), 100 Most Influential Georgians (nine different times), Women in Business Lifetime Achievement Award, Peabody Award from the School of Education at the University of North Carolina at Chapel Hill, honorary member of the Kappa Delta Epsilon Professional Education Fraternity. Currently, Dr. Siegel serves as President Emeritus at Kennesaw State University and holds the Betty L. Siegel Endowed Chair of

Leadership, Ethics, and Character at Kennesaw State. Dr. Siegel is the co-founder of the International Alliance for Invitational Education

Arliss Roaden was graduated from Cumberland in 1949. He received an A.B. from Carson Newman College and master's and doctorate degrees in Educational Administration from the University of  Tennessee. Roaden served as a professor, dean of the graduate school and Vice Provost for Research at the Ohio State University. He was president of Tennessee Technological University for eleven years and retired after ten years of service to the Tennessee State Higher Education Executive Officer's post with the Higher Education Commission.

His career afforded him the opportunity to author, co-author or edit five books and to publish numerous research reports, articles in professional journals and chapters in books. Roaden received a number of commendations for his service in the field of education, including one from the Tennessee Legislature and the Governor and the Tennessee Board of Regents authorizing the naming of the Student Center at Tennessee Technological University, "The Arliss L. Roaden University Center." He has received additional honors and has been recognized by numerous organizations and foundations for his profound community service work. Dr. Roaden and his wife Mary Etta, are the proud parents of two daughters and four grandchildren. They reside in Brentwood, Tennessee.

Vivian Bowling Blevins is the third and youngest daughter of Caleb Powers Bowling and Opal Moore Adams. Her brother, William Bowling, attended Cumberland from 1959-1960 as did her sister, Frances Turner, who attended Cumberland from 1954-1956.

Dr. Blevins was graduated from Cumberland College with an associate's degree in 1958 and from the Management Institute, Harvard University. She received her M.A. at EKU, her B.Ed. at University of Toledo, and earned her Ph.D. from The Ohio State University.

Currently Dr. Blevins is on the faculty at Edison State Community College; serves as Consultant for Major Telecom Companies through the Training Solutions Group, Inc.; is a Columnist for *Harlan Daily Enterprise* and *Middlesboro Daily News*; is a Producer for Veterans' Voices, Cable Channel 5, and is a free-lance writer.

She is past Chancellor of St. Louis Community College District and Rancho Santiago Community College District; past President at Lee College in Texas and Southeast Kentucky Community and Technical College.

Dr. Blevins has held some extensive leadership roles at local, state and national levels in higher education particularly to bring opportunities to the disenfranchised. Selected honors of which she is most proud include: Cumberland College Alumni Association Hall of Honor; Woodward (Ohio) High School Hall of Fame; recipient of NAACP's Barbara Jordan Award; California Latina Leadership Network Madrina Award; Kentucky Colonel UMWA recipient; Texas Woman of the Year Award; Honorary Degrees from Urbana University and Lee College; Urbana University Distinguished Faculty Award; and recipient of the 105th Congress' Congressional Record Tribute by California U.S. Representative Loretta Sanchez.

She is married to **Jack W. Blevins**, a Cumberland College student (1956-58) and they have two sons, Jack Lance Blevins and Quentin Moore Blevins.

Basil Manly Parks, Colonel, United States Army, was born on May 2, 1888 and died on 2 May 1954. He served in both World War I and World War II and was the brother of Floyd L. Parks, General, United States Army. He is buried near his brother and his nephew, Basil Manly Parks II, Colonel, United States Army, in Section 30 of Arlington National Cemetery.

Cratis Williams. Special Assistant to the Chancellor, Professor Emeritus of English, and for sixteen years was Dean of the Graduate School at Appalachian State University, Boone, North Carolina. He was a nationally known authority on the cultural heritage of the southern mountains. A mountaineer himself, Dr. Williams grew up near

Blaine in Lawrence County in the Big Sandy Valley, referred to frequently as "Kentucky's last frontier." Mostly of Scotch-Irish origin, he is a descendant of

Indian fighters, "long hunters", veterans of the American Revolution, Tories escaped to the backwoods, refugees from the Whiskey Rebellion, and Kentucky mountain feudists. He thinks of himself as a "complete mountaineer." His master's thesis, written on the ballads and songs of Eastern Kentucky, was used extensively by Malcolm Laws in his revised edition of *National American Balladry*. His dissertation, called by a writer for the *Journal of American Folklore*, "the most comprehensive and valuable current work on Southern Highland literature," was written on the Southern Mountaineer in fact and fiction. The product of eight years of research and writing, the 1600-page document, which examines the social and cultural history of mountaineers and evaluates the vast body of fiction written about them, earned a citation for distinguished scholarship from the Board of Regents of New York University. Dr. Williams attended Cumberland College at Williamsburg, Kentucky and held the B.A. and the M.A. degrees from the University of Kentucky and the Ph.D. degree from New York University. He joined the faculty of Appalachian State University in 1942, and was Dean of the Graduate School there from 1958 to 1975. A past member of the editorial boards of *Mountain Life and Work*, *The Appalachian South*, and *North Carolina Folklore*, Dr. Williams has contributed to these publications as well as to *Kentucky Folklore Record*, *Journal of American Folklore*, *Shenandoah*, *Appalachian Faculty Publications*, *Appalachian Heritage*, *Appalachian Journal*, and a number of educational journals. In addition to his responsibilities at Appalachian State University, Dr. Williams served on the Planning and Policies Committee of the Council of Graduate Schools in the United States, was for ten years one of three consultants to the Committee on Graduate Studies of the American Association of State Colleges and Universities, and was a member of the Executive Committee of the Council of Southern Graduate Schools. In 1972, Dr. Williams was the recipient of the annual award of the Western North Carolina Historical Association in recognition of his contributions to scholarship on the history and folk traditions of Appalachia. He received the O. Max Gardner Award for distinguished contributions to the welfare of the human race in 1973. In 1975 he was a recipient of the Brown-Hudson Award of the North Carolina Folklore Society, which recognized him as "Master Folklorist of Appalachia." He was awarded the Doctor of Humane Letters degree from Berea College in 1977, and in May, 1980, he received Berea College's Special W.D. Weatherford Award for published work that in a significant way furthers understanding of Appalachian people. Dr. Williams was Acting Vice Chancellor for Academic Affairs at Appalachian State University from January to August 1974, and Acting Chancellor from March to September, 1975. He retired on July 1, 1976, after 46 years as teacher and administrator, but continued at Appalachian State University on a part-time basis as Special Assistant to the Chancellor. Dr. Williams is listed in *Who's Who in America*, *Who's Who in Education*, *Directory of American Scholars*, and Lawless' *100 American Folk Song Singers*. He passed away May 10, 1985.

Dr. Roger Noe (See Meet a few of our Attorneys, Legislators)

Michael B. Colegrove was born in Point Pleasant, West Virginia. He attended the public schools of Mason County, West Virginia, graduating from Point Pleasant High School in 1967. Colegrove earned his Bachelor of Science Degree from Cumberland College, graduating in 1971. He completed his Master of Arts degree at Eastern Kentucky University in 1973, and earned the Doctor of Philosophy Degree from George Peabody College of Vanderbilt University in 1981.

Colegrove has been actively involved in teaching and administration since his graduation from Cumberland College. He currently serves as Vice President for Student Services, Professor of Education and Director of Leadership Studies at the University of the Cumberlands. Colegrove has served at Cumberland in various capacities for forty years. He served for two years (1987-1989) as President of Hargrave Military Academy.

He served as a member of the U. S. Army Reserve for 30 years and retired at the rank of Colonel. He commanded units at all levels. His final assignment was with the U. S. Army War College as a staff instructor.

Actively involved in his community and church, he serves as a member of the board of directors of the Michael H. Minger Foundation, the Southern Kentucky Chamber of Commerce, the area chapter of the American Red Cross, the Cumberland River Comprehensive Care Center and the Williamsburg/Whitley County Airport Board. He has served as a director of Dayspring Healthcare System, Inc., the American Cancer Society and the American Heart Association.

He is past president of the Williamsburg Independent School PTA and the Williamsburg Kiwanis Club. He served as Lt. Governor for Region 6 Kentucky - Tennessee Kiwanis in 2000. He currently serves First Baptist Church of Williamsburg as a Deacon and Sunday School Teacher.

Colegrove and his wife **Donna Foley Colegrove**, 1971, reside in Williamsburg. Donna is a retired music teacher. The Colegroves have one daughter, Kimberly who is married to Matt Joyce (Class of 2000). Matt and Kimberly have two sons, Jackson and William.

A favorite memory of Cumberland College: "My fondest memory of Cumberland College is the opportunity to meet Donna Foley. We met during our freshmen year and our love grew on the CC campus! We are extremely happy growing older together!

Robert M. "Mike" Duncan (See Meet a few of our Entrepreneurs)

James Harold Taylor (See About the Author)

A. J. Meadors (See The Opening)

A. S. Petrey (See The Opening)

Meet a few of our College/University Administrators/Staff

Terry Phillip Dixon was graduated from Cumberland in 1968 with a B.S. in biology and

chemistry. While attending Cumberland, he ran cross country in his freshman year and was on the judo team for four years. Dixon served as the student coach under Dr. O. J. Helvey for the judo team, taught judo courses and led the first Cumberland judo team to the National Intercollegiate Judo Tournament. Dixon won the Southern States Judo Championship for the lightweight division and second place for the overall weight division, being beat out by a fellow team member.

After graduating from Cumberland, Dixon earned an MSE from Illinois State University and an Ed.D. at the University of Nebraska-Lincoln. In 1997, Dixon was named to the Cumberland College Alumni Hall of Honor. From 2004 – 2010 he served on the Cumberland Alumni Association Board of Directors serving as board member, president elect, president, past president and secretary.

His education career has spanned 45 years. Dixon has served as an elementary and high school teacher, a baseball and basketball coach. He served as Provost for the American InterContinental University; Provost and Acting President for Clarkson College; Vice President for Academic Affairs and Acting President for University of Central Texas; Vice President for Academic Affairs at Troy State University; Associate Provost for Troy University; Dean of Students, Division Chair Education, Physical Education and Dance at Tarkio College; and Provost and Chief Academic and Student Services Officer at Columbia Southern University.

Dixon is a higher education consultant and nationally recognized speaker on a variety of topics including the future of higher education, adult education, online education, career planning, faculty development and regional and professional accreditation. He is a poet, playwright, researcher and author of a variety of journals, publications, research and projects.

Dixon and his wife, **Evelyn Bowman Dixon**, 1968, served as host for the 50th Anniversary of the Civil Rights Reporters as they toured Civil Rights sites throughout Central Alabama. They were among the small group that hosted Rosa Parks and the Dr. Martin Luther King family through the Rosa Parks Museum before the official museum opening.

John Heneisen graduated from Cumberland in 1965 with a B.S. in biology and was selected as Outstanding Leader of the graduating class. While at Cumberland, John was on the Judicial Branch of the Student Government Association and served as President 1964-65. He was also in the Biology Club. John has also served on Cumberlands Alumni Board of Directors and was President from 1976-1977.

Heneisen received his master's in student personnel administration from Indiana University and his Doctorate of Education from the University of Cincinnati. Heneisen returned briefly to Cumberland and taught both education and psychology classes. He also worked in various offices on campus. In 1970, he became the Assistant Financial Director and Director of the Student Work Program at Southern Illinois. He then worked at Berea College, first as Director of Financial Aid, and from 1975-1984 as the Associate Dean of Labor and Financial Aid. In 1984, Heneisen became the first Dean of Work at Berry College in Rome, GA.

Heneisen is married to **Martha Cobb Heneisen**, a 1966 alumna, they have two children.

Walter E. Watson. A native of Jefferson County, Kentucky. Graduated from Cumberland College in 1922. He is also a graduate of Columbia University and received the Ph.D. in Psychology from the University of Kentucky. In 1965 he served as Academic Dean of Midway College in Midway, Kentucky. Prior to his tenure at Midway, Dr. Watson served as Director of Corrections, as Chairman of the

State Board of Examiners in Psychology, as President of the Kentucky Mental Hygiene Association and as acting Director or Commissioner of numerous state government agencies including the State Parole Board, the Kentucky Division of Corrections, the Division of Probation and Parole and as President of Central States Corrections Association. He is a former professor at the University of Kentucky, Eastern Kentucky University and Cumberland College. Dr. Watson served as a Class Agent for the Alumni Association. He passed away on February 17, 1986. He is survived by his widow, Lela and his son, Walter E. Watson, III.

E.E. Sheils. Married – Mildred Stephens Sheils.

Children: One daughter: Margaret Sheils, three stepsons: Dr. Charles Stephens, Henry Stephens and Mark Stephens. Graduated from Thomas R. Brown High School, Catlettsburg, Ky. – 1927, Cumberland Jr. College – 1930, Union College – 1933, Degrees B.S., Ed., Additional graduate study U.K. Membership Ky. Assoc. of College Registrars & Adm. Officers. American Assoc. of College Registrars and Adm. Officers. 1944, Bursar and Teacher, 1950 Registrar and Dir. Of Admissions, Advisor to students under G.I. Bill, International Students for Cumberland College.

Joseph E. Early, Sr., a native of Williamsburg, graduated from Cumberland with an associate's degree in 1959 and a bachelor's degree in 1963. His mother was an elementary school supervisor who came to Cumberland while he was a student. As a matter of fact, Early's mother taught his wife, **Phyllis Stephens Early**, 1963 alumna, while she was a student. Early attended graduate school at the University of Tennessee and then went on to earn a doctorate in mathematics and education. Following graduation, Early and his wife moved to Mt. Sterling, KY and he taught math in a variety of grade levels. They returned to Williamsburg in 1969, after a visit

from Early's mentor and former Cumberland math professor, Dr. J.T. Vallandingham. The return to Williamsburg was originally meant to be temporary,

a 4 year stay. Upon retirement in 2002, however, Dr. Early had been employed at Cumberland for 33 years, 21 of those years as Vice President of Academic Affairs.

In addition to his dedication to Cumberland, Dr. Early has served as chairman of the Kentucky Professional Standards Board and in several different capacities for the Southern Association of Colleges and Schools (SACS), which is an 11 state accrediting agency. He was honored as the 2011 Meritorious Award Recipient at the SACSCOC Annual Meeting in Orlando, FL.

Wheeler Conover, a native of Manchester, KY, graduated from Cumberland in 1987 with a major in chemistry and a minor in mathematics. While at Cumberland, he did undergraduate research on the viscosities of polyimides and polyamides, polymers

that were the backbone of parts used by NASA for the Space Shuttle. He was also the male recipient of the T. J. Roberts Campus Leadership Award given at graduation. Conover has followed a path of both science and academics since then. He earned an M.S. in chemistry from the University of Tennessee and a Ph.D. in radiochemistry from the University of Cincinnati in 1996. He received the Science Alliance Assistantship Award at the University of Tennessee in 1987 and the National Institute of Staff and Organizational Development Teaching Award at Southeast Community College in 1999 and 2003. Following graduation, he returned to southeastern Kentucky and accepted a tenure-track position as a chemistry professor at what was then Southeast Community College. In 2005, Conover became Provost and Chief Academic Officer of what is now Southeast Kentucky Community and Technical College in Cumberland, KY, following Cumberland alumni Vivian Blevins and Roger Noe as occupants of that office. During his tenure he has worked to keep science education at the forefront in Kentucky, serving on a peer review team that shaped the new Next Generation Science Standards for K-12 among other activities. In his tenure as Provost, Southeast was named by the Aspen Institute as one of the Top 10 Community Colleges in the nation. He has also served as a competition judge for the Chemistry Department Science Olympiad, the very competition that drew Conover to Cumberland in the first place and on the Alumni Association Board of Directors for five years, with two terms as board secretary.

Howard R. Boozer. Birthplace: Monterey, Kentucky. Wife: Frances Kintner Boozer. Children: Four grown daughters. Cumberland (Junior) College – Diploma. Howard College, Birmingham, Alabama. A.B. Washington University, St. Louis, Mo. – B.S., M.A.Ed., Ph.D. Baptist College at Charleston –

LL.D. Executive Director, South Carolina Commission on Higher Education. Director, Educational Development Administration, RCA Corp., Cherry Hill, N.J. Adjunct Professor of Education, Duke University, Durham N.C. Vice President, Regional Education Laboratory for the Carolinas and Virginia. Director of Higher Education & Assistant Director N.C. Board of Higher Ed. Staff Associate, American Council on Education, Washington D.C. Instructor in Education Webster College, Webster Grove, MO. English & Social Studies Teacher, Webster Grove Junior High School. Assistant Personnel Director, Mall Tool Company, Chicago, Ill. Graduate Student, Washington University. Active Duty, U.S. Navy. American Association for Higher Education, International Association of Torch Clubs, Newcomen Society of North America, Phi Delta Kappa, Kappa Delta Pi, Gorman Jones Scholarship, (Cumberland College). Citation for service to Public & Private Higher Education in North Carolina from the Council on Christian Higher Education, N.C. Baptist State Convention. Resolution in Recognition of Contributions through Research and Service to Higher Education in North Carolina, Adopted by the North Carolina Board of Higher Education. Distinguished Citizens Award from North Carolina Governor, Dan K. Moore. President, Alumni Association, Cumberland College. Doctor of Laws Degree, Baptist College at Charleston, S.C., Who's Who in America, Who's Who in the South and Southwest, Who's Who in Health Care, Who's Who in American Education. Member Carolina Chapter of Alumni, Class Agent, Member Development Board, Outstanding Alumni Award – Cumberland College.

Jana Bailey moved to Williamsburg in 1974 after

marrying **Micaiah Bailey**, a 1970 alumnus and professor of business administration and accounting at University of the Cumberlands from 1973 to present. Bailey has a B.S. in Accounting from Union College and an M.A.Ed. with a strong emphasis in business education, economic management and accounting from Cumberland College (1984). Upon completing her degree in accounting in June 1975, she joined the Cumberland College business office staff as a loan officer. In 1977, she was promoted to Comptroller, serving in this position until 2003 at which time she was promoted to Executive Director of Finance. In 2006 until the present, she serves as the Vice President of Finance.

Bailey and her husband have served the University for 40 years. They have one son who is an engineer and currently lives in Maryland.

Stephen James Allen was graduated from Cumberland in 1991 with a B.S. in business administration. Allen first began working for Cumberlands as a work-study student in the Admissions Office. Upon graduation, he accepted a position as an admissions counselor and worked for nearly two years recruiting students. He then left Cumberlands and accepted a position as a loan officer at a local bank. Allen remained in banking until 1996, before returning to the college as an admissions counselor and then as a records manager. His next assignment was the position of Director of Human Resources. He served in this position until accepting the Director of Student Financial Planning position.

Allen currently serves as Vice President for Student Financial Planning. He is married to his high school sweetheart, **Dawn Malugin Allen**, a 1993 alumna, and they have two children, Kyler and Mallory. He and his family have served on several mission trips, including a trip to Haiti in the summer of 2012. Allen is also actively involved in Main Street Baptist Church of Williamsburg, where he serves on various committees and as a Trustee.

Richard "Rick" Fleenor, 1985, earned the Bachelor of Science, Business Administration in May 1985, the Master of Arts in Christian Education in

December 1991from The Southern Baptist Theological Seminary, Louisville, KY and the Doctor of Education, Leadership in May 2002 from The Southern Baptist Theological Seminary, Louisville, KY.

Rick initially came to Cumberlands as an undergraduate student

from his hometown in West Carrollton, Ohio. After graduating from college, he served churches in Columbus and Carlisle, Ohio, and in Lawrenceburg, Kentucky. Rick returned to Cumberland in 1991 and has served in a variety of roles at the university while also being actively involved as a member and assisting the staff at Main Street Baptist Church in Williamsburg. He currently serves as an assistant to the President for the university, with responsibilities in Church Relations and International Relations, and as Dean of the Chapel. Rick and his wife, **Martha Ragan Fleenor**, 1983, are the parents of one son, Cory.

Chris Ferguson earned his bachelor's degree in physical education and health from Cumberland in 1981. He was a four-year basketball letterman, earning a pair of letters each at Central Wesleyan College in South Carolina and Cumberland while helping both squads to NAIA National Tournament appearances. Ferguson is well respected in the coaching fraternity. His strengths lie in his on-the-

floor coaching abilities and his recruiting prowess. His energy and enthusiasm on the court is infectious, keeping pace with today's youth.

Ferguson began his coaching career in 1982 as an assistant head coach. He earned his first collegiate position in 1986 at UNC-Asheville, serving a one-year stint before moving north to Appalachian State. From 1987 to 1991, he worked as an assistant coach and helped lead

the Mountaineers to upper division finishes in the Southern Conference his final three seasons before his appointment at Virginia Tech. He spent six years on staff at Virginia Tech from 1991 to 1997. While in Blacksburg, he helped guide the Hokies to 63 victories in his last three seasons, including a 23-6 mark in 1995-96 which earned Virginia Tech an NCAA Tournament appearance. A year earlier, the Hokies produced a school-record 25 wins and an NIT title. Ferguson began eight-year tenure with the Tennessee Volunteers in the 1997-98. Ferguson was promoted to associate head coach in 2003. In his eight seasons in Knoxville, Ferguson helped lead the Vols to an impressive run of six consecutive postseason appearances, including four-consecutive NCAA Tournament appearances. Tennessee advanced to the second round in 1999 before earning a Sweet 16 berth the following season. In all, Tennessee captured two Southeastern Conference Eastern Division titles and one overall SEC championship during his stay. While with the Vols, Ferguson was also credited with recruiting and coaching 11 different players who made All-SEC, three All-Americans, two SEC Players of the Year, four McDonald's All-Americans, four NBA players and a lottery pick. Ferguson joined the East Carolina University staff in 2005 and was promoted to associate head coach of the Pirates before going to Oklahoma State prior to the 2007-08 season. He was instrumental in Oklahoma State's return to the NCAA Tournament in 2009 and 2010. Ferguson played an integral part in signing one of the top recruiting classes in the country in 2009, ranking as high as No. 4 according to *HoopScoopOnline.com*. He also recruited current Cowboy Marcus Smart, a McDonald's All-American.

Jennifer Wake-Floyd, a 1997 graduate with a B.S. in biology, began her career at Cumberlands in 1999 as an Athletic Trainer and adjunct faculty member after receiving her M.A. in Athletic Training from West Virginia University in Morgantown, WV. In 2001 she assumed the position of Sports Information Director while still continuing to work part-time as an Athletic Trainer.

In 2011 the offices of Public Information and Sports Information were combined to form the Multimedia and Athletic Services Office with Ms. Floyd as Director. This office, including six full-time staff and around 50 student employees, covers all publicity including radio, television, internet, and print coverage for 23 athletic teams and the university family in general; athletic team statistics; campus photography, video and audio; social media; layout and design of publications; and news releases. In addition, Ms. Floyd has led the Multimedia and Athletic Services staff and students along with other university students in numerous charitable activities including food drives, Barefoot for Bare Feet, Trunk or Treat, Children's Gift Day and Essential Boxes.

Ms. Floyd and daughter, Sydnee Elizabeth, reside in Williamsburg.

Linda Carter received her B.S. from Cumberlands in 1972, her M.Ed. from University of Georgia and her M.A. from Eastern Kentucky University. She

serves at Cumberlands as assistant professor of education and Dean of Student Life.

She has been recognized by the College Personnel Association of Kentucky with the Outstanding Achievement Award. This award recognizes special individuals who have made an impact on the field of student services. Ms. Carter, a veteran in the field, has devoted a life of service to the University of the Cumberlands.

Charles Dupier, III, 1996, was graduated with a B.S. in computer information systems. In 2010 he

earned his MBA from Cumberlands. Mr. Dupier's working career includes auditor at the Cumberland Inn, followed by being named Director Institutional Research and special projects and then as Registrar.

In his spare time, Dupier enjoys playing the piano.

He has a reputation of being a wizard with computers and is an accomplished carpenter. He is also an avid fisherman and takes to the lakes any time he can.

Chuck is married to **Georgia Jo Dupier**, Bursar. Mrs. Dupier is a 1996 Cumberland graduate with a B.S. in business administration. In 2009 she received her MBA from Cumberlands.

Donnie Grimes, 1989, earned his Bachelor of Science degree in Mathematics from UC and his master's degree in Computer Science from the University of Tennessee.

Since beginning employment at UC, Grimes has been the Director of Information Technology, a professor in the Information Systems Department, the Campus Network Director and Vice President of Information Services. He oversees and creates all data related technology including web servers, iLearn, MyUC student portal, network infrastructure (wired and wireless), ERP system, and internet technology and its safety.

In his years at UC, Grimes has won numerous awards and accolades for his service and the work he provides the University. In the last few years alone he has earned awards for "Best Online Service," "Most Successful Infrastructure Project," "Best New Campus Application," "Most Innovative Use of Technology for Instructional Purposes," and "Best Student Online Service."

Donnie is married to **Kellye Jamison Grimes**, 1998, and they have one daughter, Hailey.

Pearl Baker, 1968, was raised in Harlan County in a family of seven children. At Cumberland she

majored in elementary education. After graduation she continued her education at Eastern Kentucky University, receiving a master's of education degree.

She currently serves as Cumberlands' Human Resources Director. Previously she worked in the Registrar's Office, in the Bursar's Office, and in the National Defense Student Loan Office.

Actively involved in supporting breast cancer research, she works diligently during UC's Relay for Life events to raise money.

Ms. Baker has one son, Roger, of Miami, Florida.

John Marc Hensley is an alumnus with a B.S. in General Studies, Political Science and Religion. As a

non-traditional student, Mr. Hensley learned how to juggle a job and family responsibilities with his school work. Prior to returning to Cumberland to complete his degree in 2005, he worked numerous jobs including Minister of Music, owner/operator L. A. Shell Mart; manager/salesman for

Corbin Alternator and Special Assistant to Whitley County Judge Executive.

Following his graduation, Mr. Hensley was employed by the University as Director of Mountain Outreach. He continued his education at Cumberlands while serving as Mountain Outreach Director and in 2012 he earned the M.S. degree in Christian Studies.

Marc and his wife, **Wanda Meyers Hensley**, a 1986 graduate, are the parents of two daughters, Leslie and Jenna.

Erica Harris is a 1984 alumnus with a B.S. in Business Administration. Since graduation, Mrs. Harris has worked in the University's Admissions Office. She was named Director of Admissions in 1993.

Erica is married to **John Harris**, 1984, a teacher at Williamsburg Independent Schools. They have three children, Tyler, Katelyn and Haley.

Debbie Harp is a 1979 graduate of Cumberlands

with a major in Sociology. She earned her M.A. in Counseling and Student Personnel from Eastern Kentucky University.

She currently serves as Director of Career Services; Leadership and Community Services and Mentoring Program.

Carolyn Reaves is a 1974 graduate of Cumberlands. She earned her M.A. from Union College and her Ed.D. from Cumberlands. Dr. Reaves is Director of the Academic Resource Center and adjunct faculty member. She and her husband Rev. Anthony Reaves have two adult daughters.

David Bergman was born in Georgetown, KY to Jim and Betty S. Bergman Later the family with four children moved to Alice Lloyd College in Pippa Passes so both private and public schools influenced Bergman's formative years while growing up on the campuses of Georgetown College and Alice Lloyd College. The cultures of Central and Eastern KY were instrumental in his decision to remain in the state. Bergman enrolled at University of the Cumberlands and was elected SGA President during the school's yearlong Centennial Celebration. The impact of this milestone event left impressions that would shape his decision to return following graduation in 1989. He gained valuable sales experience in Lexington, KY before returning to Cumberlands as Assistant to the President for

Development in 1990. While developing friendships and raising funds for scholarships and various projects, Bergman has traveled much of the United States.

 He earned a Master of Arts in Philanthropy and Development from Saint Mary's University of Minnesota. In 2006, Bergman was appointed Alumni Director and shares time between development and alumni work. As Chairman of the UC Athletic Hall of Fame and the Executive Director of the Alumni Board of Directors, new programs and events have been developed under his tenure. Bergman received a surprise induction into the UC Alumni Hall of Honor in 2012.

The father of two, Bergman is a member of First Baptist Church of Williamsburg, Kiwanis Club of Williamsburg, and Kentucky Mountain Laurel Festival Board of Directors. His Kiwanis service includes one term as President, Board Member, founder and co-chair of the Kiwanis Cruise for Kids event, and participation in projects such as the Repair Affair, Relay for Life, Whitley County Pride Clean-up. Recognitions include induction into the Kiwanis International Leadership Society and Kiwanian of the Year for Kentucky-Tennessee Division 6. His partnership with city and tourism officials has led to the development of new playground equipment at Briar Creek Park and City Park along with a new Williamsburg-Kiwanis Skate Park.

Kyle Gilbert attended Cumberlands from 1974 to 1975 before transferring to Eastern Kentucky University to earn an associate's degree in juvenile corrections and a bachelor's degree in public administration. Following graduation he worked for Storm Security and SECURO before returning to Cumberlands to manage the bookstore from 1985-1987.

From 1987 until 1999 he worked as manager of Sentinel Office Products before coming back to Cumberlands to take the position previously held by his father, Doyle Gilbert, as director of property management and bookstore manager. In 2007, Kyle was named Vice President of Support Operations.

Meet a few of our Ph.D.'s

Here a distinction is made between reality and theory, real thing and theory, facts and concepts. Here faculty provide research opportunities on genuine research projects.

Wheeler Conover (See Meet a few of our College/University Administrators/Staff)

Anne Victoria "Annie" Saylor came to Cumberland  after winning the 1969 math contest held on campus and receiving a math scholarship. Saylor was graduated in 1972 with a degree in Mathematics.

After earning her doctorate at UK, Saylor moved to Huntsville, Alabama to teach. Four years later, she helped to found Simulation Technologies, Inc. Dr. Saylor serves as the executive vice president of Simulation Technologies, Inc., which provides radar and infrared simulations and systems engineering services to the U.S. Department of Defense as a small business prime contractor and subcontractor.

Dr. Saylor's parents and extended family still live in Harlan County, KY, and she credits her success to her upbringing.

Sara Ash was graduated from Cumberland with a  B.S. in biology in 1993. At Texas A&M University, she studied Wildlife and Fisheries Sciences, earning an M.S. in 1995 and a Ph.D. in 2001.

In January 2000, while a graduate teaching assistant at Texas A&M University, Dr. Ash was presented with the Vice Chancellor's Award for Excellence in Graduate

Teaching in the College of Agriculture and Life Sciences. She was also designated Outstanding Doctoral Student in Wildlife and Fisheries Sciences. She returned to Cumberland College in 2000, joining the faculty as a Wildlife Biologist.

In 2011, Dr. Ash was elected President-Elect of the Kentucky chapter of The Wildlife Society at the annual meeting, which includes serving as President-Elect for two years, then President for two years, then as a member of the executive committee for two years. Dr. Ash continues active research in the areas of wildlife ecology and behavior. Most recently, she has been studying the behavior and ecological impact of feral and urban stray cats.

Jeroline Baker, a native of Paris, KY, graduated from Cumberland in 1952. She went on to earn a  bachelor's degree at Georgetown College, a master's degree from the University of Kentucky, and a Ph.D. in Education from North Texas State University. Baker taught in the Lexington City Schools for five years. She was the elementary director and kindergarten teacher at Immanuel Baptist Church in Paducah for three years and a professor at Southwestern Theological Seminary in Fort Worth Texas for 27 years. She was a volunteer at the Kentucky History Center and an active member of Crestwood Baptist Church in Frankfort, Kentucky. Dr. Baker was inducted into Cumberlands Alumni Hall of Honor in 1991. Dr. Baker passed away on November 5, 2007.

Alex G. Cummins arrived at Cumberland in the fall of 1963 from Harlan, Kentucky. He received a four-year scholarship to Cumberland from Pearl Gatliff Perkins and Una Gatliff Mahan. He also paid for part of his room and board by working in the Dining Hall and serving as an assistant to Professor P.R. Jones,

Chemistry Department Chair.

While at Cumberland, Cummins initially pursued two major programs: chemistry and music. In his junior year, he switched his major to history. After graduating from Cumberland in 1968, Cummins worked at Sears-Roebuck and pursued graduate work in history at the University of Kentucky. Oline Carmical, '66, fellow Harlanite and Cumberland alumnus, was Cummins' classmate in graduate school. His time in Lexington was cut short when he was drafted into the U.S. Army. Cummins' scores on the Army foreign-language aptitude test resulted in his being sent to Monterey, California to learn Russian at the Defense Language Institute (DLI). While there, he studied with peers drafted from graduate programs in major universities such as Harvard, Yale, Indiana, Chicago, Texas, and Minnesota. After completing the one-year Russian course at DLI, he was assigned to the Army Security Agency and sent to West Berlin, Germany, where he worked as a linguist on the Soviet target.

After the end of his enlistment in the Army in 1972, Cummins reentered the graduate-history program at the University of Kentucky where he received the M.A. in European History. The National Security Agency (NSA) hired him in 1975 and he moved to Maryland, where the NSA is located. Cummins' career at NSA, which lasted until 2002, consisted of using Russian to determine Soviet economic and industrial performance, especially in the development and production of weapon systems. He served on numerous committees in the Intelligence Community that included the Central Intelligence Agency, State Department, and Defense Intelligence Agency. He also served on a special team for the Strategic Defense Initiative. As the Soviet Union dissolved in 1991, he pursued other opportunities which included Visiting Professor to the Air Force Academy, professor at the Defense Intelligence College, which awarded advanced degrees to Intelligence professionals, and manager of NSA's extensive foreign-language testing program and foreign-language training. While at NSA, Cummins earned the Ph.D. in Russian-Soviet history from the University of Maryland.

Since retiring, Cummins has embarked on a second career as author and teacher. He is an adjunct professor of history at Flagler College in Saint Augustine. In the 1990s, he became editor of *Documents of Soviet History*, a volume of which is published every two years.

Aaron Nathanial "Nathan" Coleman graduated from Cumberland in 2001 with a B.S. degree in history. During his tenure at the University Nathan was President of the Student Government

Association from 1999-2001 – the first student in Cumberlands' history to serve four straight semesters as President. He continued his studies at the University of Louisville where he obtained his M.A. degree in history in 2003. While at both the Cumberlands and Louisville, he was active in Phi Alpha Theta, the national honor society in history, serving as president of both school's chapters. He obtained his Ph.D. in early American history from the University of Kentucky in 2008. From 2008 to 2013 he was the Assistant Professor of History at Kentucky Christian University. Nathan is currently an Associate Professor of Education and History at University of the Cumberlands.

Nathan has published actively in leading journals in history and has presented papers at a number of conferences and symposiums. He is married to **Emily Lumsden Coleman**, 2001, and they have two children, Alex and Lorelei. Emily serves currently as Cumberlands Student Success Coordinator.

Thomas Brooks Frazier is a native of Evarts,

Kentucky, and earned a B.A. in English and history from Cumberland College in 1969, an M.A. in English from Eastern Kentucky University in 1976 and D.A. in English from Middle Tennessee State University in 1994. Upon his honorable discharge from the US Air

Force, Dr. Frazier came to Cumberland College as Director of Promotions and Part-Time English Instructor. In 1985 and 1990, Dr. Frazier was awarded James Still Fellowships for Advanced Studies at the University of Kentucky. In 1987, the Cumberland College faculty designated him Honored Professor, and in 2004 recent alumni voted him the J. B. Fuqua Excellence in Teaching Award. While pursuing his doctorate, Dr. Frazier was awarded doctoral fellowships at Middle Tennessee State University and, in 1996 Evarts High School named him to its Alumni Hall of Honor. For several summers Dr. Frazier taught in University of the Cumberlands London Summer Program at Imperial College. Dr. Frazier has published poetry, fiction, and nonfiction in various journals, magazines and reference publications. He has spoken at numerous gatherings on popular culture and literature, most significantly on Ernest Hemingway's poetry at the International Hemingway Conference in Paris and on Steinbeck's translation of Malory's *Le Morte D'Arthur* at Oxford University. Currently, Dr. Frazier serves as a Professor of English and the Chair of the Department of English and Foreign Languages at Cumberlands.

Todd M. Hamilton grew up in Franklin, Ohio.

While at Cumberland, he was in the first marching band and traveled with the speech and debate club. In the summer of 1989, he was selected as one of twelve students in the nation to attend the Summer School in Nuclear Chemistry at San Jose State University. He was a Presidential Scholar and completed a B.S. in Chemistry in 1990. He earned his **master's in nuclear chemistry at the University of California at Berkeley in 1992 and completed a Ph.D. in physical chemistry at Indiana University** in 1996.

Dr. Hamilton served as assistant and associate professor of Chemistry for seven years at Adrian College in Adrian, Michigan. He also served as Chair of the Chemistry Department for four years. In 2005, he went to Georgetown College where he currently serves as Professor and Chair of Chemistry. Dr. Hamilton has published 45 research papers, pedagogical articles, and general letters. He met his wife, **Lisa Burns Hamilton**, 1991, at Cumberland. They met on the viaduct and enjoyed going on many walks across campus and married in June 1991. Lisa

is a U.S. history and AP U.S. history teacher at Scott County High School. They have one daughter and one son.

Thomas E. Hays grew up in Williamsburg, Kentucky. He graduated from Cumberland with a B.S. in Mathematics and Education. He taught mathematics and American History for four years at Williamsburg High School. He received a National Defense Education Act fellowship to pursue graduate studies at the University of Tennessee-Knoxville and earned a doctorate in mathematics. Hays joined the

faculty at **The Ohio State University at Newark** (OSUN) and taught there for forty years, retiring at the end of June 2012. While Hays published several articles, his primary focus has been teaching mathematics courses for prospective elementary teachers.

Dr. Hays and his wife, **Joan Bradford Hays**, 1969, have served in several volunteer positions in their local church and at the district level, as teachers, administrators, in-service leaders, and in out-reach service to their local members. They have five children and fourteen grandchildren.

Kasee Clifton Laster, the daughter of two alumni, graduated in 1990 with a bachelor's degree in English and accounting. During her time at Cumberland, she received a Campus Service Award, served as assistant editor of the student newspaper and as a student government senator, and was a member of the English honor society and business

Club. Laster received her Ph.D. in 1999 from the University of Georgia with a specialty in British literature. From 1996-1999, she served as an instructor in the University of Georgia's English Department and Assistant Director of UGA at Oxford, one of UGA's largest study abroad programs and one of only three year-round programs operated by US universities in Oxford (the only such by a public institution.

Laster was employed as an Assistant Professor of English at Ashland University in Ashland, Ohio from 1999-2002 and Department Chair of Humanities (comprising English and three foreign languages) at Shorter College in Rome, Georgia from 2002-2005. Since 2005, she has served as the Director of Education Abroad at the University of Georgia, overseeing 100 faculty-led study abroad programs and 50 reciprocal exchanges, representing every continent of the world and dozens of subjects and majors; UGA is consistently ranked in the top twenty nationally in the number of students who study abroad annually.

Laster has taught British literature from all periods seventeenth through the twentieth centuries, as well as composition/rhetoric and business communications. She regularly presents on topics related to study abroad management, academic quality, and health and safety, while keeping up with her original discipline as a regular reviewer for *XVIII: New Perspectives on the Eighteenth Century*, the journal of the Association of International Educators and of Phi Beta Delta, a society of international scholars.

Her husband, **Jonathan Eugene Laster**, a 1991 alumnus of Cumberland, opened the Laster Law Firm in 2012, specializing in all types of real estate transactions. The couple has two daughters and resides in Oconee County, Georgia. They are members of Athens First Methodist Church.

Charles E. McFarland, originally from LaFollette, Tennessee, Dr. McFarland graduated from

Cumberland in 1962 with a degree in elementary education, received his master's degree from the University of Alabama and his doctorate from Florida State. He taught special education, was a former principal of Silver Sands School, **started the third existing Special Olympics chapter in the U.S.** and the first in the state of Florida, and served as the Special Olympics coordinator for over 40 years in

Okaloosa County, located in Fort Walton Beach, Florida.

McFarland read a 1969 article about a Special Olympics event being held in Columbia, SC. McFarland and three colleagues received permission from the school board to work with 20 students from Silver Sands to participate in the South Carolina sectional games in June of 1969. These first steps taken over 40 years ago changed special education and the Special Olympics in Florida and throughout the entire country. The development of this program accelerated the following year when McFarland and his colleagues applied to the Kennedy Foundation and received the charter which enabled them to host the first State Games of Florida.

Working as the Director of Exception Education, McFarland discovered that physical education teachers were not very educated on how to work with special needs students and that special education teachers did not know much about sports. In an effort to solve this problem, Okaloosa County was the first in Florida to offer a certified in-service for physical education and special education teachers in 1972.

In 1977 McFarland submitted a paper on the topic of the comprehensive screening program for handicapped conditions to the first World Congress on Future Education at University of Stirling, Scotland, which led to an invitation and acceptance to be on an International panel at the conference. He was nominated by Heisman Trophy winner, Danny Wuerffel, and received the President's Call to Service Award from the President's Council on Service and Civic Participation, which honor was introduced by the Honorable Jeff Miller of Florida into the Congressional Record.

At McFarland's retirement ceremony, he was bestowed the title of County Coordinator Emeritus and Father of Florida Special Olympics.

Charles "Chuck" Lawless, Jr. currently serves as Professor of Evangelism and Missions and Dean of Graduate Studies at Southeastern Seminary, in addition to serving as Global Theological Education Consultant

for the International Mission Board. He previously served as a Vice President for Global Theological Advance for the IMB. Prior to that, he was dean of the Billy Graham School of Missions and Evangelism at Southern Seminary in Louisville, Kentucky, where he also served as Vice President for Academic Programming and as the Director of Professional Doctoral Studies.

Dr. Lawless served as pastor of two Ohio churches prior to joining the Southern Seminary faculty in 1996. He received a B.S. degree from Cumberland (now University of the Cumberlands) and M.Div. and Ph.D. degrees from Southern Seminary. He and his wife, Pam, reside in Wake Forest, North Carolina.

He is the author of eight works, including *Membership Matters, Spiritual Warfare, Discipled Warriors, Putting on the Armor, Serving in Your Church Prayer Ministry,* and *Mentor.* He has contributed articles to denominational periodicals, written Sunday School curriculum for LifeWay, and led conferences on spiritual warfare, healthy church growth, leadership, evangelism and discipleship, and prayer.

Aaron D. Purcell, a native of Brodhead, Kentucky,

earned his undergraduate degree at Cumberland in 1994, and he earned a master's degree in history from the University of Louisville, a master's of library science degree focused in archives and records management from the University of Maryland, College Park, and a Ph.D. in history from the University of Tennessee.

Purcell is Professor and Director of Special Collections at Virginia Tech, in Blacksburg, Virginia. He previously served as University Archivist at the University of Tennessee and held positions at the National Library of Medicine and the National Archives and Records Administration in Washington, D.C.

Purcell's interest in research, archives, and primary sources began while a student at Cumberland. Since the mid-1990s Purcell has focused on research, writing, and publishing. In addition to three books,

he has written twenty articles in history, archives, and library journals and is currently working on three book-length projects. He also serves as editor of *The Journal of East Tennessee History*.

Jolly Kay Sharp graduated from Cumberland College in 1974 with a B.A. in English. In 1988, she earned an M.A. in English from Wright State University, and was invited to return to Cumberland as a member of the faculty in 1991. In 2008, Dr. Sharp completed the requirements for her Ph.D. in English from Middle Tennessee State University, where she specialized in the works of Flannery O'Connor. Dr. Sharp has been frequently recognized for outstanding achievement in teaching. The University of the Cumberlands Student Government Association has twice recognized her, designating her Honored Professor in 1996 and 2000. She received

the J. B. Fuqua Excellence in Teaching Award in 2001 and 2003. In 2007, Dr. Sharp received the Excellence in Teaching Award from Cumberlands. She was named Teacher Who Made a Difference Award by the University Of Kentucky College Of Education, having been nominated by a former UC student. In 2011, Mercer University Press published Dr. Sharp's book "*Between the House and the Chicken Yard: The Masks of Flannery O'Connor.*"

Oline Carmical, a native of Evarts, Kentucky,

graduated from Cumberland College in 1966 with a B.A. in history. Eight years later, after earning both an M.A. and a Ph.D. in history from the University of Kentucky, he was invited to return to Cumberland College as a member of the faculty. In 1984, as the recipient of the prestigious James Still Fellowship, he completed post-doctoral study at the University of Kentucky.

Dr. Carmical specializes in United States constitutional and legal history, British North American colonial history, and pre-19th century west European expansion and government. He is a member of the American Historical Association, the Southern Historical Association, and the Organization of American Historians.

For students engaged in research, Dr. Carmical's office is frequently a first stop. Within the History and Political Science department, **he is referred to as the "library man," in recognition of his encyclopedic knowledge of works published in all areas of history and political science.**

Oline is married to **Shirley Rhymer Carmical** 1984. The Carmicals have one daughter, Veronica Carmical ('95) who teaches Family and Consumer Science at Whitley County High School.

Eric Wake was born and raised in Louisville, Kentucky. Wake, a 1965 alumnus and professor and chair of the History and Political Science Department and has taught at Cumberlands since 1967. After his graduation from Cumberland, Dr. Wake earned an M.A. in history from Texas Christian University, returning to Cumberlands as a faculty member shortly afterwards. He continued his studies at Texas Christian University and was awarded a Ph.D. in Early Modern Europe in 1973. Dr. Wake currently serves on the National Advisory Committee for Phi Alpha Theta, the international honor society in history, and several other committees for Phi Alpha Theta. For many years, Dr. Wake served **as faculty**

advisor for Upsilon-Upsilon, the college's award-winning chapter of Phi Alpha Theta. Founded in 1974, the Upsilon-Upsilon chapter of Phi Alpha Theta holds the distinction of being both the oldest and the most frequently honored society at University of the Cumberlands. As one of the most active organizations on campus, Upsilon-Upsilon sponsors a popular lecture series, fundraisers, social events, and publishes the scholarly journal, *The Upsilonian*. The chapter has been **named "Best Chapter" for schools with fewer than 3000 students for the past 35 years.** Dr. Wake is an active member of the American Historical Society, the Southern Historical Society, and the Kentucky Association of Teachers of

History for which he has served as president for two years.

His major publications include *What God Has Done: Main Street Baptist Church, 1906-2006* (2006) and his most recent *A City Set on a Hill Cannot Be Hidden, A History of University of the Cumberlands on the Occasion of Its 125th Year: The Past 25 Years* (2013). He has also written several articles.

He is married to **Sue Wake**, a 1970 Cumberland graduate who serves as Cumberlands Vice President for Institutional Advancement, and they have two daughters, Kimberly and Jennifer.

James E. Gover studied pre-engineering at Cumberlands in 1959 and earned his B.S. in electrical engineering at the University of Kentucky and his M.S. in electrical engineering and Ph.D. in nuclear engineering from the University of New Mexico. Gover retired from Sandia National Laboratories after thirty-five years. He was awarded IEEE-Fellow for his work on radiation effects.

From 1998 until 2012, Gover served as professor of electrical engineering at Kettering University in Michigan. He is now Professor Emeritus at Kettering, but remains active in hybrid vehicle education for IEEE. He also worked in public policy research and served as science advisor to Senator Pete Domenici, the House of Representative Science Committee, Senator Bill Roth, the Department of Energy and the Department of Commerce as an IEEE Congressional Fellow and IEEE Competitiveness Fellow. IEEE-USA awarded him its Citation of Honor for his policy research. He currently researches and writes about job creation, innovation and competitiveness for IEEE policy committees.

Gover credits much of his professional success to the education foundation he received at Cumberland College. **"Were it not for Cumberland, I would**

likely have been another casualty of inadequate high school preparation," he notes.

The author of numerous articles in distinguished publications and a well-known and respected presenter and speaker, Gover returned to campus in 2006 and 2007 to speak to physics classes about nuclear power. "I hope to

90

help promote Cumberland as a university that prepares graduates for a career in engineering and science."

Dr. and Mrs. Gover have two daughters and two granddaughters and attend Calvary Chapel Church in Albuquerque, New Mexico.

Ronnie Day was born near London, Kentucky, and educated in the public schools at Bush, Kentucky. He received a B.A. degree with a major in history from Cumberland in 1963 and M.A. and Ph.D. degrees from Texas Christian University in 1965 and 1971, respectively. In 1968 Day joined the Department of History, East Tennessee State University, as assistant professor and retired in 2005 with the rank of Professor Emeritus. During his

tenure, he served as department chair for eleven years. His research interest is World War II in the South Pacific and he has published one book, several scholarly articles, photographic essays on battle sites and wrecks and served as consultant for television documentaries on the wrecks in the Solomon Sea.

Dr. Day lives in Johnson City, Tennessee where he continues work on the history of the war in the Solomon Islands.

Howard Partin was born July 7, 1923, at Bond, Ky. He was the son of Pearl and Maggie Partin, and was

mostly reared in Bell County. On February 21, 1942, Howard was married to Altha Murray. To this union was born four children: Ronald Partin, Janice (Partin) McPhetridge, Barbara (Partin) Reed, Shirley

(Partin) Grant. Howard was a veteran of World War II. He was ordained into the Baptist ministry on July 18, 1954 and pastored six different churches in Laurel County, where he lived with his family. He received his bachelor's degree from Cumberland College, Williamsburg, KY in 1961 and his master's degree from University of North Carolina, Chapel

Hill, NC in 1964. He taught high school at Hazel Green in Laurel County for seven years, before going to teach at Cumberland College. He received his doctorate degree from Ohio State University, Columbus, Ohio in 1977. He majored in biology. His minor, chemistry. He taught biology courses including many of the courses required for nursing students, for more than 15 years at Cumberland College. At one time he was head of the college's biology department. He resigned because of ill health. He was a strong teacher, a man of good character, a valuable asset to the college. He died of cancer on September 13, 1984.

Bill R. Booth, an internationally recognized scholar and lecturer, entered Cumberland College in the fall of 1953. In his words, "The experience of being at Cumberland College confirmed my values and gave me the academic foundation and direction that has guided me throughout my career." Booth graduated with an associate's degree from Cumberland in 1955. He earned a bachelor's degree from Eastern Kentucky University in 1960, a master's degree in 1963, and an Ed.S. at Peabody-Vanderbilt University in 1965. For three years he served as an Assistant Professor of Art at Wisconsin State University-Oshkosh before earning his Ph.D. in art history from the University of Georgia in 1970. Booth also taught in Kentucky public schools for seven years, had a Graduate Teaching Assistantship at Peabody-Vanderbilt and two years as a Doctoral Teaching Fellowship at UGA. After completing his doctorate, Booth became Head of the Department of Art and Director of the Claypool-Young Art Gallery at Morehead State University. During his tenure at MSU, he was a full professor and retired as Professor Emeritus of Art in 1998. Booth continued to teach part time for four more years at MSU before his full retirement in 2002. His teaching career spanned 43 years with over 25,000 students.

Booth also taught in China on three occasions. His experience visiting the cities and learning to appreciate the culture, history and art prompted him to begin a study of the First Emperor of China, Qin Shi Huang Di. His tomb in Xian, Shaanxi Province was the burial place for the Emperor and is guarded by 7,000 life-size terra-cotta warriors, chariots and a variety of weapons. After visiting the tomb, Booth, who had always been fascinated by Archeology, began the 2000 Exhibition entitled: "Imperial China: The Art of the Horse in Chinese History." The exhibition spanned the period from 1,000 B.C. to 2,000 A.D. with over 140 items of art and history from Chinese museums. It was an enormous success attracting visitors from all 50 states and 13 foreign countries to the International Museum of the Horse in Lexington, KY. Booth began the process in 1990 and worked ten years on the exhibition which attracted over 240,000 visitors and provided almost three million dollars of revenue to the museum. Catalogs from this exhibition were sold at the Metropolitan Museum of Art in New York City, The San Francisco Museum of Asian Art and at book stores around the country. Booth made 45 trips to China from 1980 until 2012. He also served for ten years as an Advisor to the Director to the National Palace Museum in Taipei, Taiwan.

Booth and his wife of 49 years enjoy traveling to countries and meeting people from all over the world. They have one son, Dr. Eric C. Booth, who teaches at Southeastern University in Louisiana.

Carl Thomas Cloer, Jr. was born in 1945 to an Appalachian sawmill family. He was graduated from Cumberland College with a B.S. in education; earned his M.Ed. from Clemson University and a Ph.D. from the University of South Carolina. Dr. Cloer is **Professor Emeritus at Furman University.**

Dr. Cloer is widely published having over 100

publications to his credit, including books, tests, instructional reading materials, computer software, journal articles, and numerous articles about the Appalachian mountaineer. During his tenure at Furman University (1974-2004) Dr. Cloer presented over 150 workshops related to literacy. He has also presented over 100 papers at local, state, national, and international levels. Dr. Cloer has been a featured speaker at the 9th World Congress on Reading in Dublin, Ireland, and at the European Reading Conference. He also presented at the World Congress on Reading in Buenos Aires, Argentina.

At Furman, Dr. Cloer was awarded the Meritorious Teaching Award (1988) and the Meritorious Advising Award (2003). Dr. Cloer was selected as **the first 1988 recipient of South Carolina Governor's Professor of the Year Award, being chosen by the Governor and the South Carolina Commission on Higher Education.** He received the 1993 and 2001 Outstanding Article Award from the Journal of Reading Education for his research publications co-authored with Furman undergraduate research assistants. Dr. Cloer has served as an officer, member of the Board of Directors, and on the Editorial Board for the American Reading Forum. A scholarship fund has been established at Furman University with Dr. Cloer's name attached "In appreciation for the guidance and concern for Furman students."

At Cumberland, Tom and his wife, **Elaine Kowalski Cloer**, 1967, from New York, met as Appalachian volunteers, working with literacy in the one-room schoolhouses of the Kentucky mountains. They have two children, a son, Tom III, who graduated cum laude from Furman in 1991; and a daughter, Shana, who received her bachelor's and master's degrees with honors in sociology from Clemson. They have four grandchildren, Brandon Thomas Cloer, Dylan Ossielee Cloer, Ryan Jones Cloer, and Harvest Wolf Newton.

James Meeks, a Harlan County native, was graduated from Cumberland College in 1962. He earned his M.S. at Purdue University in 1965 and Ph.D. at Louisiana State University in 1974. He has further studies at Purdue University, Argonne National Laboratory, Virginia Tech, Murray State, Southern Illinois and University of Kentucky.

Meeks joined the Cumberland faculty in 1964 and was head of the Chemistry Department from 1967-1978. He served as chairman of the Department of Chemistry at Murray State from 1978 to 1982. He also served as the professor of physics and lecturer of chemistry and bio chemistry at Southern Illinois University and the Program Coordinator of Physical Sciences at Paducah Community College. Meeks is a former chairman of both the Kentucky Lake Section of the

American Chemical Society and the Chemistry Division of the Kentucky Academy of Science.

Meeks was very active in Cumberlands' Amateur Radio Club. Dr. Meeks and his wife, **Peggy Taylor Meeks**, 1963, reside in Elizabethtown, Ky.

Anna Mary Creekmore grew up in the 1930's in a coal mining area in central Kentucky. Her Mother, who attended Cumberland and was an elementary school teacher in McCreary County, passed away when she was six; her father, a high school graduate of Cumberland Academy, worked as a taxi driver, a small time farmer and a country store owner. Creekmore's interest in clothing design began at an early age by cutting and shaping crude dresses for her dolls from her Dad's worn out shirts.
Creekmore received her diploma in provisional elementary studies and earned her Teaching Certificate from Cumberland in 1940. In 1945, she  studied home economics at the University of Tennessee and earned a B.S. with majors in textiles and clothing and vocational education. She earned her master's degree from the University of Tennessee in 1950 after studying textiles and clothing and related art. In 1963, Creekmore completed her Ph.D. in Clothing from Pennsylvania State University earning minors in psychology & sociology. She was one of the early researchers in the field of clothing and textiles when few Ph.D. programs existed and the social-psychological content was being formed.

Creekmore began her professional experience as an elementary school teacher from 1940-1943 in McCreary County. She then worked in clothing retail sales from 1945-1947 gaining firsthand experience with consumers. From 1948-1949 she returned to McCreary County as the vocational home economics teacher. She later taught clothing design and construction at the University of Miami, Iowa State University, Oregon State University, Michigan State University, the University of Tennessee, University of British Columbia, Vancouver, Canada and the University of New Brunswick in Fredericton, Canada.

At Michigan State in the late 1970s, after a discussion with a colleague of a possible change in her pattern-making course, Creekmore reorganized the approach, content, illustrative materials, and schedule for the course. This approach was later adopted by a former colleague to develop computerized instructions for designing garment patterns. Her course on the history of western dress led to her investigation in 1972 of the then current styles of clothing being worn in capital cities around the world. During a sabbatical year Creekmore traveled in Africa, the Middle East, and Europe, documenting clothing styles trends. The information collected resulted in a presentation at the American Home Economics Association meeting in Atlantic City, NJ in June 1973.

While traveling, Creekmore spent much of her time in museums, studying and photographing clothing and accessories in paintings, tapestries, ancient artifacts as well as actual garments and textiles when exhibited. Her interest in the basic raw materials for clothing led to a unique course in historic textiles at Michigan State University. Her research resulted in a 332 page book, printed in 1982. Much of her lecture material came from information she gathered from her travels and research studies.

Creekmore retired in 1984 but continued sharing her knowledge and research, traveling as far as Seoul, S. Korea for presentations.

Thomas Croxton graduated from Cumberland in 1976 with a B.S. in mathematics. He is the Chief of the Airway Biology and Disease Branch, one of three branches in the Division of Lung Diseases. This branch supports research and research training in chronic obstructive pulmonary disease, asthma, cystic fibrosis, bronchiolitis, lung imaging, and airway function in health and disease.

Matt Rasure grew up in Evansville, Indiana and was the first of his family to attend college. Rasure was graduated from Cumberland in 2004 with a B.A. in mathematics and minors in physics and biblical languages. He graduated from Princeton Theological Seminary in 2007 with a M.Div. and also received the David S. Weadon Award for Excellence in Sacred Music. He then studied for two years at the Hebrew University of Jerusalem.
Rasure then **enrolled in the Department of Near Eastern Languages and Civilizations at Harvard**

University for his Ph.D. At Harvard, he taught courses in Hebrew Bible and Semitic Philology, and served as an editorial assistant for Hebrew Bible submissions at the Harvard Theological Review. He twice won the Harvard University Certificate of Distinction in Teaching.

Additionally, Rasure completed the ordination process with the American Baptist Churches of Massachusetts. His wife, Rachael Pettengill-Rasure, is an ordinand in the Episcopal Diocese of Massachusetts and serves as the Protestant chaplain at Tufts University.

Paul Chitwood, a Jellico, Tennessee native, is a 1992 Cumberland graduate where he received his bachelor's with a major in Religion and a minor in Biblical language. Chitwood is married to **Michelle Elaine Herron Chitwood**, a 1993 Cumberlands

graduate and they have three children. He has served on the UC Board of Trustees. Dr. Chitwood provides leadership for the Kentucky Baptist Convention as Executive Director. He has served as pastor of First Baptist Church, Mt. Washington; First Baptist Church of Somerset (1999-2003), First Baptist Church of Owenton (1995-99), and South Fork Baptist Church in Owenton (1993-95). He also served as KBC president (2005-06); KBC first vice president (2003-04); president of the Kentucky Baptist Convention Pastors' Conference (2002); chairman of the board for the International Mission Board of the Southern Baptist Convention from (2008-10); trustee and former adjunct professor of missions and evangelism at University of the Cumberlands; former assistant professor of evangelism and church growth at Southern Baptist Theological Seminary in Louisville.

The time Chitwood spent studying at and working with Cumberlands greatly prepared him for his leadership position with KBC. "As a student at UC, I gained a foundation of knowledge that has served me well in all of life's endeavors and prepared me for my seminary studies," Chitwood explained. "As a trustee at UC, I have gained insight into the relationship between the KBC and her partnering institutions as well as learning great leadership lessons from observing Dr. Taylor and his staff."

John E. Sasser, a 1968 alumnus of Cumberland, has been employed as a professor of mathematics at five different universities in the United States and Europe. He also serves as an Educational Consultant, both in the United States and abroad, primarily in the areas of mathematics and mathematics technological applications. He is the author of several books and published articles.

Dr. Sasser graduated *summa cum laude* from the University of Maryland; holds two master's degrees and the doctorate from the University of Southern California.

In 1991 Dr. Sasser received the Outstanding Achievement Award to Kentucky Education and in 1992 was commissioned as a member of the Governor's Advisory Committee on Federal Funding by the Governor of the Commonwealth of Kentucky. Professor Sasser is a member of several associations and in 1995, he was inducted into the International Eurasian Academy of Sciences.

During 1998, Dr. Sasser lived in Saudi Arabia and traveled throughout the Middle East researching a book, published in 2000, entitled: *The Islamic Connection*, showing the influence Islam has had on the Moslem contribution to mathematics.

Joseph Everett Early, Jr., is the son of Dr. Joe

Early, Sr., former Vice President for Academic Affairs at Cumberland. He graduated from Cumberland with a bachelor's degree in 1993. In 1997, he earned his Master of Divinity degree from Midwestern Baptist Theology Seminary in Kansas City, MO, where he also served as an adjunct professor. He received his Ph.D. from Southwestern Baptist Theological Seminary in Fort Worth, TX in 2002 and worked as a teaching assistant there. Early also served as Visiting Assistant Professor of religion at Baylor University

94

and from 2004-2009 taught at Cumberlands. Since 2009, he has served as Assistant Professor of theology at Campbellsville University and was awarded the Servant Leadership Award in 2012. Early is the author of several articles and books which focus on Baptist history and influence. He has also given several presentations and frequently speaks at historical conferences across the United States.

Virginia Young is a graduate of Williamsburg High School. She earned a bachelor's degree in mathematics from Cumberland in 1981 and a Ph.D. in mathematics from the University of Virginia in 1984. From 1986 to 1990, Dr. Young taught in the math department at Cumberland. She was named a Fellow of the Society of Actuaries (FSA) in 1992. She was appointed Nesbitt Chair of Actuarial Mathematics in August 2003 at the University of Michigan and currently resides in Ann Arbor, Michigan.

William "Bill" Henard, a 1977 alumnus of Cumberland, has received a B.A. degree in religion. He serves as senior pastor of Porter Memorial Baptist Church in Lexington, Kentucky since 1999. Prior to moving to Lexington, Henard served as pastor to several different churches throughout the South, including Alabama, Texas and Tennessee. He has served as president of the Kentucky Baptist Convention, first vice president of the Southern Baptist Convention, and an assistant professor of Evangelism and Church Growth at Southern Baptist Theological Seminary. Dr. Henard also holds degrees from Southwestern Baptist Theological Seminary and Southern Baptist Theological Seminary (Ph.D.).

A former president of the Kentucky Baptist Pastors' Conference, Dr. Henard served three times as chairman of the KBC Mission Board's administrative committee. He also has served on the KBC Committee of Nominations, Cooperative Program Research Committee, and as chairman of LifeWay Christian Resources' Board of Trustees. Dr. Henard and his wife, **Judy (Patterson) Henard**, a 1977 Cumberland alumna, have three children and two grandchildren. On September 15, during the first joint Convocation of 2008-09, Dr. Henard received the Honorary Doctor of Laws Degree from the University of the Cumberlands.

James Manning, 1981, has been a member of the University's faculty since 1987. Following his graduation from Cumberlands, Dr. Manning earned his Ph.D. in Physics from UK. On campus he sponsors the Society of Physics Students and the physics and mathematics honor societies.

As a member and officer of the Lion's Club, he helps to prepare Christmas food baskets; conducts fundraising auctions to provide eye care and glasses

for those in need; and helps prepare food-filled backpacks for school children to enjoy on weekends. A member and deacon of Central Baptist Church in Corbin, he oversees the church library and assists with sound and video during services.

James is married to **Tammy Manning** who also attended Cumberlands and they have two sons, Andrew and Matthew.

Jonathan Ramey chose Cumberland College, his hometown college, as the best place to begin his

higher education in mathematics, earning a B.A. in 1987. He continued his education at Vanderbilt University, earning an M.A. in Mathematics in 1989. He joined the Cumberland College faculty in 1991 while pursuing a Ph.D. at Vanderbilt, which he completed in 1994. In 2013, he was named head of the math department at Cumberlands.

Dr. Ramey is a member of the Mathematical Association of America, the American Mathematical Society, and Kappa Mu Epsilon, the mathematics honor society. He is an avid photographer and can be found taking photos of most activities on campus.

William Baylor Wilder, a native of Whitley County,

KY, graduated from Cumberland in 1939. He also earned degrees from Western Kentucky University and Purdue University, where he received a doctorate in plant breeding and genetics. Wilder began his career as a professor of biology at Cumberland and went on to be named the first head of the department when the college gained its four year status, a position he held until his retirement in 1985. In 1995, he was inducted into Cumberlands Alumni Hall of Honor. Wilder was married to Hazel Wilder. Following Hazel's passing, Wilder later married Alice Johnson Wilder who had three children.

Julie Lay-Choo Tan came to University of the Cumberlands from Selangor, Malaysia as a student.

She completed her B.S. in Chemistry in 1987 before attending the University of Tennessee-Knoxville where she earned a Ph.D. in Organic Chemistry, Dr. Tan returned to Cumberlands as a member of the faculty and now heads the Chemistry Department. She is a member of the American Chemical Society (ACS) Division of Organic Chemistry and Chemical Education, and serves as faculty director of the department's Alchemist Club.

Dr. Tan is married to **Chin Teck Tan**, 1987, (see Meet a few of our college/University Administrators/Staff) and they have two sons, William and Christian.

Meet a few of our College Professors

John Thompson "J. T." Vallandingham was graduated in 1911 from Georgetown College with a major in mathematics, and in 1912 he served as teacher and principal of the Brookville High School. In 1913 Dr. Vallandingham came to Cumberland College to teach for one semester, but stayed in the College's employment until his retirement. His duties at Cumberland also included responsibilities in the treasurer's office as a keeper and collector of students' accounts and dean of men.

He took graduate studies at Ypsilanti State College in Michigan, the University of Chicago, and the University of Kentucky. In 1956 he received the honorary Doctor of Laws degree from Georgetown College, and in 1969 he received an honorary degree from Cumberland College. In 1964 he was honored by having the Scholastic Honor Society at Cumberland College named for him.

Dr. Vallandingham served in both World War I and World War II. He became a First Lieutenant of the Field Artillery. During World War II he served as a Major.

In 1928 Professor Vallandingham married one of his former students Virginia Jones, the daughter of Professor and Mrs. Gorman Jones. One daughter was born to the union.

Dr. Vallandingham was an active member of the First Baptist Church of Williamsburg where he taught Sunday School and served as a deacon and deacon emeritus. He also held a 29-year perfect attendance record at the Williamsburg Rotary Club.

Merita Thompson, the first in her family to attend

college, graduated from Cumberland College in 1965 with a double major in health and physical education and a minor in biology. While at Cumberland, Dr. Thompson was involved in the Baptist Student Union, Intramurals, and the Student Government Association. Since graduating, she has continued to serve Cumberland as a member of the Board of Visitors. She earned a Master of Science degree in 1966 from the University of Tennessee and a doctorate of health education in 1972 from the University of Alabama. She began her career as a teaching assistant at the University of Tennessee in 1965. From 1965 to 1971 she served as an assistant professor of health at Pikeville College, followed by one year as a teaching assistant at the University of Alabama. In 1972, she became a professor of health education at Eastern Kentucky University in Richmond, KY. Throughout her career at EKU, Thompson received numerous awards and professional achievements, including being the first woman to receive the stated prestigious Acorn Award in 1995 and becoming a faculty regent of the EKU Board of Regents. She was inducted into Cumberlands Alumni Hall of Honor in 1996. Merita was married to the late Dr. Kelly Thompson, also an EKU professor, and has one son.

Eleanor Mitts Behrmann, a native of Williamstown (Grant County)

Kentucky, graduated from Cumberland College in 1936. She majored in chemistry, receiving a B.S. (1938) and M.S. (1939) from the University of Kentucky and a Ph.D. degree in organic chemistry at Iowa State University in Ames, Iowa (1943). During World War II, she conducted research in plastics at Shell Development Company in California, followed by two years (1947-1948) in a joint teaching and research appointment at Radcliffe College/Harvard University in Cambridge, Massachusetts. After eight years in the role of mother/homemaker, she returned to teaching chemistry at the University of Cincinnati. She retired in 1982 as Associate Professor, Emerita. She is married to Robert Behrmann, a retired businessman. The Buhrmann's have a son, Michael (a George Mason University Professor), and a daughter, Ann (a pediatrician in Madison, Wisconsin). Dr. Behrmann was a member of Cumberland's Alumni Board from 1985-1988 and served as President of the Alumni Association from 1986-1987. She was honored as an "Outstanding Alumnus" of Cumberland College in 1975.

James Boyd Scearce, Jr. Father: James Boyd Scearce. Mother: Lizzie McCoy Scearce. Sales Associate, Century 21, Johnny Cobb Realty, Statesboro, Georgia. Bagdad High School. Attended Cumberland College 1932-34 and Eastern Kentucky State Teachers College, graduating with a B.S. degree. Received the M.A. degree from Eastern. Did graduate work at New York University, University of Kentucky, and The University of Southern Mississippi. Teacher of general science, biology, and physics. Basketball coach, Jenkins High School. Director of physical education and athletics and baseball and basketball coach, Norman Junior College. Director of Physical Training and Athletics, North Georgia College. Served in the U.S. Navy. Director of Athletics and teacher of education and physical education, was a baseball and basketball coach, Cumberland College 1946-47. Chairman Division of Health and Physical Education, Director of Athletics and Head Basketball Coach, Associate Professor of Health Education, and Head Basketball Coach, Georgia Southern College, Retired in 1980. GEA, NEA, GAHPER, AAHPER, BCAA, Kappa Delta Pi, professional organizations. Jr. Chamber of Commerce, Lions Club, Chamber of Commerce, Rotary Club, Statesboro Board of Realtors, and Century 21 Investment Society. Class Agent. College Basketball Coach of the Year in Georgia, 1956-58-59-64-65-66. Kentucky Colonel. Inducted into Helms Athletic Foundation Hall of Fame. Selected to coach NAIA All-Star team on 47 day tour of the Far East. Appointed Commissioner of the South Atlantic Conference, NCAA Division II. Elected to Eastern Kentucky University's 100 outstanding alumni. Received Cumberland College Outstanding Award, 1985. Inducted into State of Georgia Sports Hall of Fame.

Besse Mahan Rose. Besse Mahan Rose (1889-1963), the daughter of Ben and Margaret Early Rose of Williamsburg, was graduated from the Williamsburg Institute in 1909 and from Georgetown College in 1912. Her first teaching assignment at the Institute was in the grade school. She later taught in high school, then in the College. She served as principal of the grade school and of the high school and also held the titles of registrar and head of the

English department during her tenure. After coming to the Institute, Miss Rose earned her master's degree from Columbia University and did further work at the University of Wisconsin and George Peabody College. In 1956 the yearbook was dedicated to Miss Rose with these words: "During her years here, she has patiently taught the fundamentals of English, given us a clearer understanding of literature, guided us in our dramatic club productions and conversed with us about the colorful background of Cumberland."

John Lloyd Wilson served in Europe during World War II receiving the Bronze Star and retiring as a Major from the United States Army Reserve. He graduated from Cumberland with an associate's degree in 1947 and went on to earn five more degrees, a B.S., M.B.A., L.L.B. and L.L.M. Wilson taught at Cumberland from 1956 to 1969 and again in the late 1980s. He served as the Head of the Commerce and Economics Department and as a Professor of Business Administration. Wilson also practiced law in Monticello, Williamsburg and Bowling Green and taught at Western Kentucky University and Mississippi College of Law.

Harold Hubbard attended Oneida Institute and then Clay County High School. He graduated from Berea College with a B.S. in Business Administration in 1958 and then went on to earn an M.B.A. from the University of Kentucky in 1960. In 1972, he completed requirements to become a Certified Public Accountant. With the exception of four years, 1962-

1966, Hubbard has been employed with the Cumberlands since 1960. Although not a Cumberlands alumnus, Hubbard received the Honorary Alumnus Award in 2008, the 21st Century Leadership Award in 2009, and was inducted into the Athletic Hall of Fame in 2011 for his outstanding devotion to Cumberland.

Harold has served UC in many capacities: as professor and acting chair of the Business Department, as sponsor of both Phi Beta Lambda and Students in Free Enterprise and on various committees, including the Alumni Athletic Hall of Fame Committee since its inception in 1996. Hubbard also began working closely with the NAIA in 1974 and served as Eligibility Chair for the Kentucky Intercollegiate Athletic Conference, Mid-South Conference, NAIA District 32, Region XI and the Association of Independent Institutions. He also served on the NAIA National Eligibility Committee and the Constitution and By-Laws Committee since its inception in 1996. The NAIA announced Hubbard as one of the 2011-2012 inductees into the Hall of Fame.

Hubbard is well known in the local business community, sitting on the boards of the Williamsburg National Bank, Forcht National Bank NA, and the Whitley County Communities for Children and serving as an advisory board member for Professional Home Health.

Ann Renfro Shelley earned her A.A. degree from Cumberland College in 1939, her A.B. degree from Union College, and her master's degree from George

Peabody College for Teachers. Her first teaching experience was at the Williamsburg City School. Mrs. Shelley was employed at Cumberland College as head of the education department for 30 years (1955-1985) and worked with over seven thousand students. In 1959-60, she developed the college student teaching program and became the first director of student teaching. The organization closest to her heart was the A.R. Evans Chapter of the Student National Education Association that she organized when she came to Cumberland in 1955. She had the honor of serving as advisor for the N.E.A. longer than any other person at any other chapter in the state of Kentucky. Mrs. Shelley was inducted into Cumberlands Alumni Hall of Honor in 1989.

Dennis Trickett graduated from Cumberland in 1979 with a B.S. in psychology. In 1981, he earned an M.A. in religion education from New Orleans Baptist Theological Seminary, followed by an Ed.D. in

psychology and counseling in 1986. Prior to his returning to Cumberland in 1997 as a member of the faculty, Dr. Trickett spent ten years as a therapist and Director of Substance Abuse Prevention at the Cumberland River Comprehensive Care Center. He is a member of the Society for Teaching of Psychology, the American Counseling Association, and the International Association of Marriage and

Family Counselors. He also lends his professional expertise to the Whitley County Board of Education as a consultant.

At Cumberland, Dr. Trickett is Professor and Department Chair of Psychology for undergraduate studies, professor in the Master of Arts in Professional Counseling program. He was selected as the 2011-12 male recipient of the Honored Professor Award by the Student Government Association.

He is married to **Paula Estes Trickett**, a 1982 alumnus (See Meet a few of our Superintendents).

Chester A. Nevels was the son of John M. Nevels

and Louisa Hughes Nevels of McCreary County, Ky. He grew up and attended school in the same county. He continued his education at Cumberland College and received an Associate of Arts Degree. In 1955, he was drafted into the United States Armed forces and served

with the 8th Army in Japan. After being discharged from the armed services, he furthered his education at Eastern Kentucky University and received a Bachelor of Science Degree. Later he obtained his master of mathematics degree from the University of Tennessee. With this degree, he procured a position as Associate Professor of Mathematics at Cumberland College. He retired from this position in 1984, after 20 years as an educator. During his career, Mr. Nevels was a member of the National Council of Teachers of Mathematics and of the Mathematics Association of America. He was also named an Outstanding Educator of America and an Outstanding Man of America. While at Cumberland College, he directed the Cumberland College math contest and was a faculty adviser to the math club. He passed away on August 27, 1985.

Vaughn Hatcher is a 1975 alumnus of Cumberland. He is married to **Verna McNeil Hatcher**, a 1980 graduate. After graduating from New Orleans Baptist Theological Seminary in 1976, Hatcher taught religion and physical education at Cumberland for 27 years and was active in high school and KIAC sports officiating. Since his retirement in 2003,

Hatcher enjoys time with his family and caring for the horses on his farm. From 1990 until May, 2009 he served as Worship Leader at Calvary Baptist Church in Corbin, Kentucky.

In 2008, Hatcher was inducted into Cumberlands Alumni Hall of Honor for Alumni Appreciation.

Albert Robinson Evans. Albert Robinson Evans was asked to serve as acting president following the

resignation of Dr. Wood on March 29, 1919. Professor Albert Robinson Evans (1880-1957) was another of Cumberland's Phi Beta Kappa scholars. The son of James George and Sarah Miracle Evans, he was raised in Knox County, Kentucky, and

attended the Williamsburg Institute, being graduated from the Collegiate Department in 1905. Evans then taught at the Institute for a few months before entering Brown University. In 1908 he was graduated from Brown University, and returned to the Williamsburg Institute where he remained except for a few years until his retirement in 1955. Evans did additional work at the University of Chicago and received his Master of Arts degree from the University of Kentucky. Professor Evans at times taught Latin and philosophy, but his main interests

were in the area of education and social science. He was considered an excellent teacher. Sometime in the early part of 1914, Evans was approached about considering the principalship of the Jellico, Tennessee high school. The trustees of the College got word concerning this offer and called a meeting of the Board because the "inducements being offered were rather attractive." According to the Board's *Minutes*, May 11, 1914, the trustees acted immediately "to affect an agreement whereby he remains as teacher in the Cumberland College." The agreement was reached and the *Cumberland College Monthly*, June 1914, reported "Professor Evans has been offered the principalship of the Jellico High School, but has decided to remain with us. Everyone here is highly gratified at his decision." Evans, however, did not confine himself to the College. He was active at the First Baptist Church, teaching the Florida Moss Gatliff Sunday School class and serving as chairman of the Deacons. He was also a member of the Williamsburg City Council. A.R. Evans and his wife Mabel Carrie Gatliff were the parents of two daughters, Helen and Virginia. Professor Evans served as acting president from March 29, 1919 until May 26, 1921, but he continued to serve the College as a teacher until his retirement in June 1955. He passed away on September 28, 1957.

Liz Young Krause was born in Sparks, George and

attended Poplar Creek High School in Williamsburg. She received a scholarship in chemistry at Cumberland College and was graduated in 1945. Krause then earned a **B.S. in nursing from Johns Hopkins University** and her master's degree in nursing from Wayne State University.

She was a professor in B.S. nursing program for Hope-Calvin College and for Ferris State University.

Krause's honors, awards and recognitions include: Woman of the Year, Business and Professional Women's organization of Allegan County, Michigan; candidate for Outstanding Public Health Nurse of the Year for her work in starting a Scoliosis Back Screening Program in the Allegan County Schools; charter member of Allegan County on Child Abuse and Neglect Council; honored for outstanding contribution to child health. She has served in the Michigan Nurses Association and as Chairman of General Duty Nurse State Committee for 8 years; charter member of Wings of Hope Hospice; charter member of Kids Hope Organization; Chairman, Ladies Allegan County Republican Organization for 4 years, and Chairman of Allegan County Medicare and Social Services Board for 20 years.

She has served as Class Agent for the Cumberland College Alumni Association. She remains active in her church and community and the County Republican Party. Krause and her husband, Lewis, have three children, Bob, Konrad, and Karen, and they have ten grandchildren and 3 great-grandchildren.

Charles D. Barnes. Married to **Shelva Dean Mabes Barnes**, 1956 alum. Two Sons: David, Greg.

Member East Baptist Church, downtown Louisville, 33 years. Deacon 31 years. Treasurer 6 years. Also served as Sunday School Superintendent, Department Superintendent, and teacher. Trustee; chaired various committees. Lay Speaker in Longrun Baptist Association, Southern Indiana, and other Kentucky churches and meetings. Chairman of Public Relations Committee 1975-76, Finance Committee 1977-82: Member of Long Run Priorities Committee 1981-82: Moderator of the Association 1983: Member of Administrative Committee 1983-86, Personnel Committee 1986, East Baptist Center Committee 1986, Inner City Task Force. Chairman of Long Range Planning Committee 1984-85. Executive Board of KBC 1981-83. Chairman of Finance Committee of Executive Board 1981-83. First Vice President KBC 1983-84. Member of Administrative Committee of Executive Board 1982-83. Planned Growth in Giving Task Force 1985-86. Trustee, Cumberland College 1969-77; 1979-86. Chairman of Board of Trustees of Cumberland College 1979 & 1980. Director of Kentucky Baptist Foundation 1987. Graduate of Oneida Baptist Institute, Cumberland Jr. College 1955, University of Louisville (BSC in Accounting & Finance), University of Louisville (MBA), University of Kentucky School of Banking; Stonier Graduate School of Banking Rutgers University. Executive

Vice President of First Kentucky National Corporation & First National Bank of Louisville; Director of First Kentucky Trust and National Processing Company. Chairman, Director, and Trustee of Kentucky Independent College Fund. Mayor, City of River Bluff, Oldham County, Kentucky. Southern Baptist Seminary Foundation Trustee, 1986. Past-President of Louisville Chapter of American Marketing Association. Lecturer at University of Louisville for 11 years. Active in numerous other business, civic, and church related affairs.

Maurice Byrd (See Meet a few of our Attorneys, Legislators)

Paul Estes (See Radio and TV Personalities)

William Gullett (See Meet a few of our Attorneys, Legislators)

Billy Grey Hurt. Married **Scharlyene Harbison Hurt**, 1952 alum. Children: Billy Grey Hurt, Jr., Robert Hal Hurt, Mark Harbison Hurt. Hazel High

School – Graduated, Cumberland College – A.A. Degree, Union University – B.A. Degree, Southern Baptist Theological Seminary – M. Div. Degree – Ph.D. Degree. Pastor – First Baptist Church, Frankfort, Immanuel Baptist Church, Paducah, First Baptist Church, Independence, Missouri, First Baptist Church, Benton, Scott's Grover Baptist Church, Murray, Bethel Baptist Church Humboldt, TN. Industrial Engineer, Proctor & Gamble Defense Corporation – Milan, TN. Has been Visiting Professor: Georgetown College and Cumberland College. Has had various articles published. Adjunct Professor: SBTS. Who's Who in Religion, Personalities of the South, The Director of Distinguished Americans. Served on several committees for South Baptist Convention and Kentucky Baptist Convention. Served as Chairman for Franklin Baptist Association, Past President – Frankfort/Franklin County Ministerial Association, Trustee – Campbellsville College. West Union and Blood River Association, Paducah, KY and Independence, MO. Board of Benton Municipal Hospital, KY Social Service Advisory Committee.

101

Human Rights Committee, Fair Housing Commission, Jennie Lund School of Practical Nursing Advisory Board, Board of Planned Parenthood, Honorary Board of Directors, New Independent Medical Center, Rotary International, Head Start Grant Police Council, Chamber of Commerce, Paducah, Board of Directors, Renaissance House, Bluegrass Area Dev. District Council, United Way of Frankfort, Chaplain Kentucky General Assembly, Board of Regents, Murray State University. Trustee- Cumberland College. Visiting Professor: Religious Emphasis Week, Cumberland College, Campus Speaker, Central Kentucky Chapter Member.

Chin Teck Tan, 1987, received a B.S. in business and data processing systems from the University of the Cumberlands, his M.B.A. from Tennessee Technological University, and Ed.D. degree from the University of the Cumberlands. Tan is a member of the Kentucky Economic Association, the Institute for Management Accountants, and the Academy for Business Administration. Dr. Tan is an associate professor of Business at Cumberlands.

Having come to Cumberlands from Klang, Malaysia, Tan enjoys recruiting international students for the men and women's tennis teams which he coaches. He has led several tennis teams to NAIA finals and has been named Coach of the Year four times throughout his career. He coached the Malaysian National Tennis Team in 1999.

Dr. Tan is married to **Julie Lay-Choo Tan,** 1987, (see Meet a few of our Ph.D.'s) and they have two sons, William and Christian.

B.J. Temple is a 2001 graduate with a B.S. in Movement and Leisure Studies. He received the master's degree in sport science with an emphasis in sport coaching from the United States Sports Academy in Daphne, Alabama and in 2013 he earned an Ed.D. in Educational Leadership from Cumberlands.

Dr. Temple teaches in the Movement and Leisure Studies department and he works as assistant track coach at the University of the Cumberlands. Dr.

Temple has been a part of Cumberland's Track and Cross Country program since the fall of 1998. During

his first year, he was a member of the third place cross country team at the NAIA National Championships. The following season he joined the coaching staff as a student assistant and moved into a full-time position in the spring of 2001. He has proven to be successful as an assistant coach having coached his student-athletes to 56 All-American honors and 11 National Titles.

Coach Temple hails from upstate New York and currently lives in Williamsburg, with his wife **Jamey Hill Temple**, 2003, and their two children, Jadon and Chloe.

E. Jane Carter earned her first degree in 1975 in the area of Music Education. In 1980, she earned an M.B.A. in Marketing from the University of Kentucky, and has since completed further study at

West Georgia College, the University of Tennessee-Chattanooga, and the Philanthropy Tax Institute.

Ms. Carter currently holds the rank of associate professor of business administration. She is a member of the American Marketing Association, Delta Kappa Gamma Society International, the Kentucky Council for Economic Education, and serves as Vice Chair of the Board of Directors for Kentucky Highlands Investment Corporation.

102

Meet a few of our Superintendents

Lonnie R. Anderson, a native of Williamsburg, KY, graduated from Cumberland in 1975. During his years as a student, he participated in the work-study program as an assistant in the Public Relations Department where he took photographs and wrote articles. He was also involved in the Student Government Association and the Young Republican Club.

Anderson's educational career began in Whitley County as a teacher and as the gifted and talented program coordinator. He also served as athletic director, food service director, Chapter I and public relations coordinator, before being named superintendent of Whitley County Schools in 1991. At that time, the Whitley County district was under state management and ranked last among Kentucky's 176 public school districts. In 1999, Whitley County was one of the top districts in the state in terms of academic improvement. Under Anderson's leadership, the school system made numerous improvements both within and outside the educational community. His numerous accomplishments included the coordination of a school facility modernization program that included the construction of three new elementary schools, science wing addition, library and kitchen at the high school, renovation of middle school, the establishment of Rockholds Opportunity School, 12 room addition and cafeteria expansion to Whitley Central Elementary, and the renovation of three existing elementary schools.

Anderson has served as president of the Upper Cumberland Association of Superintendents and a member of the Board of Directors of Family Medicine Centers' Rural Health Program; Board of Directors, Jellico Community Hospital; Board of Directors (advisory), Union Planters Bank, Corbin, KY; Board of Directors for the Center for Rural Development, Somerset, KY; K.A.S.A. – Kentucky Association of School Administrators; Board of Directors, Bell Whitley Community Services Agency; Member Advisory Board, Whitley County Adolescent Health Clinic; Chairman-Kentucky Educational Development Corporation; Vice President-Council for Better Education; Chairman-

U.N.I.T.E Board of Directors. In 2000, he was named the recipient of the F.L. Dupree Award for exemplary contributions to education by a superintendent and received the Kentucky School Board Association Kids First Advocacy award in 2005. Anderson retired from his educational leadership duties in 2010 with the districts test scores resulting in a top 10% ranking in the State. He is now owner of a local real estate company and pharmacy. Lonnie is married to **Glinda Morgan Anderson**, a 1970 graduate.

Before enrolling at Cumberland, **David Denton**

served in the United States Air Force for four years. He earned his associate's degree from Cumberland in 1958 and was inducted into the Alumni Hall of Honor in 1989. Denton also received a B.A. at Lenoir Ryhne College, an M.A. at San Francisco Valley State College and California State University-Northridge, an Honorary Doctorate from Western Maryland College and a certificate of teaching from North Carolina School for the Deaf.

Denton is the retired Superintendent of Maryland Schools for the Deaf in Frederick and Columbia, Maryland. He developed a model statewide program for the education of deaf children. He helped establish the teacher development program in the area of deafness which has been honored by the National Association of the Deaf. Denton has also implemented recent knowledge on language development and learning in deaf children in a statewide pre-school program and in parent education classes. He served as president-elect of the Council of Organizations Serving the Deaf.

Denton is the author of numerous articles for professional journals and a frequent panelist and speaker on education for the deaf. He has written two books, one about his career in Deaf Education and the other is a collection of stories. He was the resident storyteller at Fontana Village Resort in the Smokey Mountains in 2006.

Denton is married to Peggy and they have two children, David Jr. and Mary. They currently reside in Walkersville, Maryland.

Herb Steely, a native of Louisville, Illinois, moved to Williamsburg with his family in 1913. He attended both Cumberland College and the University of Kentucky and received his master's degree from Eastern Kentucky University. While still a high school student, he played basketball for Cumberland. His interest in sports led him to a coaching position with the Williamsburg School system. While coaching the 1944-45 basketball team, he set a record with a 26-5 season. In 1955, he was also assistant football coach and a charter member of the Optimist Club. Steely worked with the Williamsburg School System for 29 years, during which he held four different positions, coach, teacher, principal and school superintendent. He held the superintendent position for 14 years from 1962 to 1976.

Conley Lee Manning of Pine Knot, Kentucky, was graduated from Cumberland in 1954 with an associate's degree. He also attended Newport News Ship Building and Dry Dock Company – Apprentice School and later received his B.S. from Eastern Kentucky State Teachers College and Rank 1 from Eastern Kentucky University.

Manning served in the US Army and has served at various levels of education for the last 56 years which include: Assistant Professor at Midway College; Supervisor of student teachers in the Lake Cumberland area; Teacher/Coach- Federal Coordinator - McCreary County High School; as Superintendent of the McCreary County School System, Somerset Independent School System and as Interim superintendent for both Mercer and Russell County School Systems; Director, Division of Program Development and Health and Physical Education Consultant, Kentucky Department of Education; Instructor for Graduate Classes for EKU and Cumberland; Kentucky Department of Education Trainer-Evaluation for School Administrators.

In 1961, Manning was selected as Kentucky Jaycees' Outstanding Young Man of Kentucky and as

Kentucky Superintendent of the Year in 1990 and again in 1995. He received the F.L. Dupree Award; the award for Outstanding Jaycee in McCreary County; "Excellence in Teaching" award; EKU Centennial Award; Distinguish Service Award - Kentucky Association for Health, Physical Education and Recreation, Kentucky Association for Health, Physical Education; Kentucky. Manning served as the Department of Education's Liaison with the Kentucky High School Athletic Association for 11 years, as well as President State Service Council, Kentucky Red Cross and a member of Pulaski County Red Cross Chapter.

Manning has been a Sunday School Teacher for 54 years and is a member and Deacon at First Baptist Church-Somerset. Further, he has served as a member of various local and state civic educational organizations, Kentucky Historical Society, Kentucky School Superintendents' Association, Kentucky Association of School Administrators, Lake Cumberland Superintendents' Council, Somerset Kiwanis Club. Cumberland College Alumni President, Eastern Kentucky University Alumni President, Eastern Kentucky State Teachers' College Alumni 2nd Vice President, ASA Assistant State Commissioner (softball), McCreary County Library Board Secretary, McCreary County Jaycee Board of Directors, President, McCreary County Educational Association, Member of NEA/KEA, Kentucky Association for Health, Physical Education, and Recreation, Kentucky Association for Educational Supervisors, Member of the Kentucky High School Athletic Association's Board of Control, Class Agent, Alumni Board of Directors.

Manning is married to Sandra Ann (Lindsay) and the couple has two children, Stuart Douglas Manning and Jennifer Lee Manning, both of whom are Cumberland graduates.

Dennis Byrd is a 1962 graduate of Williamsburg

Independent School District and a 1967 graduate of Cumberland. He began his teaching and coaching career at Evarts High School in Harlan County. After one year, Dennis returned to WHS as a teacher and coach. While at Williamsburg, he

was Head Boys and Girls Basketball Coach and Assistant Coach for the Football Team. In 1977, Dennis started a new career in banking as Vice President and Branch Manager of First Federal Saving Bank. He later worked at Williamsburg National Bank, now Forcht Bank, and served on the bank board. During his banking years, he became a Certified General Real Estate Appraiser and continued in that profession after his banking days. Dennis and his wife, Lezlee Jo, also built and owned the Dairy Queen Restaurant in Williamsburg, as well as, Byrd Apartments. Dennis continued his education by attending the University of Wisconsin Graduate School of Banking and received a master's degree, Rank 1, and superintendent degrees from Eastern Kentucky University. Dennis became Superintendent of the Williamsburg Independent School District in 2002 and continues to serve in that position. In the past ten years, Williamsburg Independent has seen a growth in students and expansion in the campus. The newest additions include a 20,000 square foot addition to the present building and acquiring a baseball field. Land expansion has tripled and constant improvements are being made throughout the campus.

Jesse B. Mountjoy - After World War II and a tour of duty in the U.S. Navy, Jesse B. Mountjoy, of Danville, enrolled in 1947 at Cumberlands.

Mountjoy played basketball and enjoyed the business

classes. This led to his decision to become a teacher. He met **Marcella Faulkner**, a piano instructor at the college. J.B. and Marcella married in 1948 and he graduated in 1950. He had started operating a small restaurant which was a popular place with students, the Campus Grill, on Main Street.

Mountjoy earned a bachelor's degree in business administration from Union College in 1952 before beginning his teaching career at Jellico High School in Tennessee. He was hired by the Williamsburg Independent School in 1955 where he taught, served as basketball coach and assistant coach in all other sports. Later, he was promoted to head coach of all sports. Eventually, he became assistant principal and then Superintendent in 1976.

The Williamsburg Independent School badly needed a new facility and Mountjoy began to pursue that project. Land was purchased, state permission granted and partial funding was secured. A new school was built on Main Street and the older building sold to the college. Mountjoy stayed 32 years at Williamsburg Independent School and retired in 1987. The gymnasium is named in his honor.

Mountjoy was a charter member of the Williamsburg Optimist Club for 25 years and member of the First Baptist Church for 51 years. He has been a member of the Williamsburg Kiwanis Club and active in the Sons of the American Revolution, President of the Captain Charles Gatliff Chapter.

A native of Clay County, KY, **Reecia Isom Samples**

has dedicated her career to serving the educational needs of children in her home area. Samples earned a Bachelor of Science in business administration from Cumberland in 1978, followed by a master's degree in education from Union College. She then received her Rank-1 certification at Eastern Kentucky University, and later, her superintendent certification from Cumberland. "I sort of ended up where I began, at the University of the Cumberlands. Her career began in career development, and she taught computers, data processing and programming at Clay County High School. In 1995, she was appointed district coordinator, and later became an instructional supervisor. Named assistant superintendent in May 2009, Samples became superintendent of Clay County Schools in July 2009. Reecia is married to **Roger Samples**, a 1977 Cumberland alumnus and retired teacher.

Paula Estes Trickett graduated *summa cum laude* in 1982 with a major in mathematics and accounting, receiving the Gorman Jones Leadership Award at graduation.

While at Cumberland, Trickett was active in Student Government, serving as Student Government Vice-President her senior year and also serving as editor of the student produced newspaper, *The Observer*. She was also inducted into the J.T. Vallandingham Honor Society.

After graduation, Trickett began working for Jerrico, Inc. in Lexington KY as an accountant in their systems purchasing department. At 22, she became the youngest person to ever be promoted to

Accounting Supervisor at Jerrico. In 1985, she moved back to Williamsburg to become Senior Accountant at her alma mater until 1991 when she made a career change to the education field.

Trickett began teaching mathematics at Whitley County High School in 1991. She earned an M.A. in Mathematics Education from Cumberland in 1995 and a Rank I from Union College in Instructional Leadership in 1996. In 1996, she left the classroom to become Assistant Principal of Whitley County High School and in 1998 she also assumed the responsibilities of Secondary Curriculum Coordinator.

In 2007, Trickett was promoted to Director of District-Wide Services and Title I Director. In 2009, she was promoted to Assistant Superintendent and in 2010 she was named Deputy Superintendent and Treasurer of the Whitley County School District.

Paula lives in Williamsburg with her husband Dr. **Dennis Trickett**, 1979 alumnus and current UC Professor. She is a mother, stepmother and a grandmother.

Colonel **E.T. Mackey**, native of Meadow Creek, Whitley County, Kentucky, served as superintendent of public schools of Williamsburg in the late 'thirties and early 'forties. He was a noted citizen of Williamsburg and a popular school administrator. Mackey Avenue bears his name. He assisted in the formation of the National Guard in Whitley County and served in both World War I and II. He made a career out of the Army. He died in the Walter Reed Hospital in 1954 and was buried in Arlington National Cemetery.

Meet a few of our Principals

Carolyn Murray Falin graduated from Lee County High School in Beattyville, KY in 1961. She

attended one year at Lees Junior College and graduated from Cumberland College in 1968. Throughout her college career, she was able to attend college only one year full time. She furthered her education at Eastern Kentucky University, earning a master's degree in business education and physical education in 1972 and Professional Certification (Rank I) in school administration/supervision in 1983.

Throughout her career, Carolyn remained dedicated to students and the betterment of education. At Cumberland, she served in a variety of positions, including secretary to the Registrar, secretary to the Director of Financial Aid, Instructor of the Evening Business Program and College Coordinator and Instructor of Business Education Courses. In addition to her service at Cumberland, Carolyn spent nearly three decades in the Whitley County School System. She was an Instructor of Business Education and Computer Science, Vocational Department Chair and Business Department Chair at Whitley County High School for twenty three years. She served two years as District Technology Coordinator and Assistant Principal/Athletic Director at Whitley County High School, followed by two years as Principal of Whitley County Middle School. From 2002 – 2012, Carolyn traveled to Tier 3 Districts and Schools as an Educational Consultant, Leadership Assessment Auditor and Target Assistant Coach for the Kentucky Department of Education. Carolyn and her husband, **Paul Falin**, '68, are retired and reside in Corbin, KY. On September 1, 2012, they celebrated their 50th wedding anniversary. Carolyn and Paul were inducted into Cumberlands Alumni Hall of Honor in 2012 for Alumni Appreciation.
Falin was appointed to serve as 2013-2014 State President of the Kentucky Retired Teachers Association. From 2013 through 2015 she will serve as Regent of the William Whitley Chapter of the National Society of the Daughters of the American Revolution.

Richard Prewitt came to Cumberland from Boston, Massachusetts and was graduated from Cumberland

in 1980 with a degree in biology and health. Through additional study he earned certifications in Elementary, Middle, and High School Principalship, Director of Pupil Personnel, Supervision, and Superintendency. He is also a licensed EMT.

Prewitt has been a high school basketball, baseball, and football coach and a teacher of middle and high school science and health. He served 15 years as Principal of Whitley County Middle School and then as Principal of Corbin Educational Center.

Prewitt has served as President of Cumberlands Alumni Association; President of the Kentucky Middle School Association and Chairman of Whitley County Tourism Board. He is very active in his association with the National Guard Kentucky-Tennessee Border Bowl Committee.

Prewitt married **Nina Hicks Prewitt**, '80, from Harlan, Kentucky. They have two children and one grandson.

Jack Isaacs (See Meet a few of our Entrepreneurs)

Jerry Hodges attended Cumberland from 1967–1971, where he played basketball and baseball for all

four years. He graduated in 1971 with a degree in history and government. He received his M.A. and Rank 1 from Union College. While at Cumberland Jerry was named all-conference in basketball and became a member of the 1000 Point Club with his 1365 total points scored.

Upon his graduation from Cumberland in 1971, Jerry was named Head Basketball and Baseball coach at Whitley County High School and taught Social Studies. In 1986 he moved to Williamsburg High school and taught Social Studies and served as principal from 1991-1999. During his tenure as Williamsburg principal, Jerry was named 1995 Kentucky Principal of the Year and was honored by the Milken Foundation with the prestigious National Educator Award.

Jerry is a past member and president of the Alumni Board of Directors and received an Outstanding Alumni Award.

He is married to **Brenda Stephens Hodges**, 1971, and they have two sons, Jason (Stephanie) and Craig (Kayla) and have one grandson, Wyatt.

Meet a few of our Educators

David Atwood of Lilburn, Georgia, David, is the son of Richard and Judy Atwood. His sister, Katie, '10,

is also an alumna of the University of the Cumberlands. Atwood states, "I came to Cumberland because I knew that God was calling me to this university to pursue His calling on my life, which is teaching."

While a student at Cumberland, Atwood was involved in BCM, Appalachian Ministries, and the Chamber Choir. Upon receiving his bachelor's degree in 2007, Atwood was awarded the Algernon Sydney Sullivan Award and the Top Middle School Education Major Award. He was also named Outstanding Male Graduate 2007 and Who's Who Among College Students. In 2009, Atwood earned his M.A. degree from Cumberland. He was inducted into Cumberlands Alumni Hall of Honor as the Young Alumnus of the Year in 2010.

At Cumberlands Atwood met the former **Magan Hess**, '06, from Somerset, Kentucky while on a mission trip to Cincinnati. They married in 2007 and now reside in Williamsburg. Atwood currently teaches seventh grade math at Whitley County Middle School while Magan works for Cumberlands' Baptist Campus Ministries, serving as Director of Appalachian Ministries. David is a regular volunteer for the program. They have one son, Benjamin David.

Carolyn Olive Siler of Williamsburg was the daughter of Eugene and Lowell Jones Siler and the granddaughter of Gorman Jones, Professor of French, Greek, and History and Acting President (1911-12) and Adam Troy Siler, Trustee (1901-1953). She earned an associate's degree from Cumberland in 1953 and a B.S. and M.S. from the University of Kentucky. She was married to **Harold A. Browning, Jr.**, who also graduated from Cumberland in 1948.

Harold's parents, the owners of Williamsburg's weekly newspaper, were always interested in Cumberland and its scholastic endeavors. Harold was a very accomplished journalist, having graduated from Transylvania University before entering the Graduate School of Journalism of Columbia University. His career included being telegraph editor of the Lexington Leader and later being Assistant City Editor of the Louisville Times.

Carolyn chose teaching for her life's work. She taught Choral Music, Spanish and language arts to both elementary and middle-school students. Locations of Siler's teaching tenure included Kingsport, TN, Lexington, KY, and for many years at Anchorage Independent School, Anchorage, KY. Her years of teaching totaled 52, and recently Anchorage School honored Siler by naming its auditorium for her. Siler was inducted into Cumberlands Alumni Hall of Honor in 1993.

Richard "Dick" Koeniger, 1967, was born in Cincinnati, Ohio the son of Elmo and Grace Koeniger. He was graduated from Greenhills High School in 1959. Koeniger entered military service

with the U.S. Navy after realizing college enrollment options were financially unattainable. Serving aboard on the USS Rich, a Navy destroyer in the Atlantic Fleet, Koeniger remained connected with former Greenhills High classmates, Bob and John Hollingsworth. These contacts provide his pathway of opportunity to enroll at Cumberland College. His first year of his college expenses came from savings made in the Navy.

His second year at Cumberland, Koeniger was encouraged to continue pre-medical study at Eastern Kentucky State College. Financial difficulties forced him to drop out of EKSC his senior year and he worked as an over-the-road truck driver for McLean Trucking Company, to save for further studies. In 1966, he wrote a letter to Dr. **James Boswell** asking for advice and the response came with news of a new G.I. Bill he qualified for and accepted as means to return to Cumberland. Koeniger completed his degree at Cumberland College with majors in biology, chemistry, and education. He began a teaching career in the fall of 1967 at Colerain Junior High School near Cincinnati.

Koeniger enjoyed a 35 year teaching career before retiring in 2003. His career included coaching football for 30 years and five years serving as high school principal at North College Hill High School, near Cincinnati. His post graduate studies include George Peabody College of Vanderbilt University, University of Cincinnati, and Xavier University. He is a graduate of the Ohio Peace Officer's Training, served as a Park Ranger, and Special Deputy Sheriff for Hamilton County, Ohio, and has a long career with the Colerain Township Department of Fire and EMS, where he continues to serve in an administrative capacity. He is a Training Officer for a volunteer fire department that services Indiana where he owns property. Among his service affiliations, Koeniger has twice served as President of Cumberlands' Alumni Board of Directors, a function he continues to enjoy with lifetime Board Member Emeritus distinction. His marriage resulted with the adoption of son, John Warren Koeniger. An unfortunate and unexpected event took the life of John in 2011.

Currently, Dick's greatest joys include sharing with and assisting Amish friends in Indiana, enjoying the laughter and joys of their children, and his time serving and sharing with his "brothers" in the fire service. Koeniger has spent the last six years hiking the Appalachian Trail, a journey beginning in Georgia and ending in Maine.

Koeniger was recognized at Homecoming 2013, with the Cumberlands Alumni Appreciation Award.

Anna Lucille Cottrell Faulkner graduated from

Cumberland in 1950. She taught for three years in a one-room school in Harlan County. She was married and moved to Dayton. The remainder of her 30 years teaching was spent in Dayton, Ohio, city schools, the last 22 years being in kindergarten. Mrs. Cottrell was graduated from the University of Dayton in 1966.

Throughout her career, Mrs. Cottrell was actively involved in missionary work. She served as Missionary Education Director for Ohio Women of the Church of God and went on mission trips to Mexico. She served as the teacher or director of Vacation Bible Schools for more than 30 years. Mrs. Cottrell also served as secretary of the Central Ohio Cumberland College Alumni Chapter, a group she helped to organize and was inducted in Cumberlands Alumni Hall of Honor in 1990. One of Mrs. Cottrell's life philosophies was to look at everything as an opportunity for God, instead of an obligation. Mrs. Cottrell passed away on November 7, 1997.

Maureen "Cookie" Thompson Henson was raised in Manchester, Kentucky and graduated from Clay County High in 1970. She enrolled at Cumberland where she became the school's first African-American cheerleader. In 1974, Henson received a Bachelor of Science Degree in Health and Physical Education. She later received her Master of Arts in Education and Rank 1 from Union College.

In 1976, Henson began a 33 1/2 year career with the Clay County Board of Education, teaching health, physical education, science and biology. During Henson's career, she was active as the girls' softball coach, Beta Club sponsor, cheerleader coach, and Pep Club sponsor. She was also involved as a teacher in the Teacher/Buddy program, the school's Transformation Team, and as a member of the school's Home Economics Advisory Committee. In 2003, she was nominated to the African American Leadership Summit and was named Clay County's Fiscal Court Woman of the Year in 2009.

Since her retirement in 2010, Henson has remained active and currently serves on the University of the Cumberlands Board of Trustees and Alumni Board of Directors, the Clay County Board of Education School Board, and the Kentucky Education Association's Retired Board of Directors. She is also the Legislative Liaison to the KSBA.

She is married to McCoy Henson and they have one child, McKeshea.

Jean Angel Freeman, a native of Williamsburg, KY, graduated from Williamsburg High School before enrolling at Cumberland. She graduated with an associate's degree from Cumberland in 1946. Freeman participated in Sunbeams at First Baptist Church of Williamsburg, where she first heard and learned "Jesus Loves Me." This early influence gave her a life filled with singing, most of it in church choirs. She recently retired from the adult choir of Severus Valley Baptist Church, Elizabethtown, where for 43 years she was a faithful member.

Jean and her husband, Norman were married in 1958 and they celebrated 55 years of marriage in 2013. After marrying, they lived wherever Norman's profession took them. Lawton, Oklahoma, and Lexington consumed several years when the offer arrived to move to Elizabethtown, KY, where they have lived for 45 years. After 30 years of teaching in elementary schools, Jean retired. Since 1983, Jean and Norman have traveled the world, spending time in 75 foreign countries and flying on 45 different airlines. They are also avid members of the Garden Club of Elizabethtown. Jean has recently finished writing a book "Celebrating 40 years of Gardening" which marked the clubs fortieth birthday in 2012.

Freeman's role models were her sisters, Gertrude (Angel) Dale, '32, and Sylvia Angel, '36. Gertrude served as librarian at Cumberland from 1943-48 at Cumberland and from 1964-72 at Southeast Community College in Cumberland, Kentucky. Her husband, Arthur Dale, '48, was a trustee of the school from 1969-78 and generously donated the Angel-Dale House, which now houses Baptist Campus Ministries. Sylvia was a part of Cumberland's staff from 1956-81 serving in a variety of positions including Librarian, Associate Librarian, Director of Placement, Curriculum Lab and Learning Materials Center.

Lois Ellison Goldsmith, a native of Williamsburg, KY and daughter of the late Dr. C.G. and Rachel Mahan Ellison, graduated from Cumberland in 1925. She was also a graduate of the Cincinnati Conservatory of Music. During the war, she worked for the American Red Cross. Goldsmith was inducted into Cumberlands Alumni Hall of Honor in 1995.

Kenneth Howard's mother discovered he was visually handicapped when he began to walk. He attended Magoffin Baptist Institute before enrolling at Cumberland. He completed the two-year program at Cumberland in 1959 and then attended the University of Kentucky. He returned to Cumberland

and earned his education degree in 1961. This is when he met and married his wife, **Marlene Wells Howard**. Kenneth and Marlene taught in Ohio public schools until Kenneth decided to enter George Peabody College in Nashville to study the education of the visually impaired. He taught in Owensboro during the school year and attended Peabody in the summers until 1966 then Kenneth started teaching the sixth grade at the Kentucky School for the Blind until his death in 1990. Kenneth Howard was posthumously inducted into the Alumni Hall of Honor in 1992 for his service in educating blind students.

William R. "Bill" Lyttle was graduated from Clay County High School before earning a B.S. degree in

Business Commerce with a minor in English from Cumberland in 1975. Lyttle went on to attend Union College where he earned an M.A. in Education in 1979. He has been teaching at Clay County High School for over three decades. Bill and his wife Donna Spurlock Lyttle of Manchester were married in 1991. They have 3 children and 4 grandchildren.

Lyttle has been the recipient of several awards during his lifetime and teaching career and in 2002; he was nominated and received an Outstanding Educator Award for the Governor's Scholars Program 9. He was a Charter member of Future Business Leaders of America at Clay County High School. He served as Writing Cluster Leader for Clay County High School for 18 years. He is the Chief Ticket Manager for Clay County High School and Elementary Football.

Lyttle served several years on the Alumni Board of Directors at the University of the Cumberlands, serving as its President from 2008-2009. He is currently on the Board of Visitors at the University of the Cumberlands and strives to recruit students for the University of the Cumberlands. He was inducted into University of the Cumberlands' Alumni Hall of Honor in October, 2013.

Anna Frances Parker Rutherford of Barbourville, Kentucky, was graduated in 1946 with a degree in Math.

After teaching math for seven years in the Cincinnati area, Mrs. Rutherford received a science and math scholarship to the University of Virginia, where she met her husband and they were blessed with a daughter. Only a few years later, Mrs. Rutherford's husband passed away and Mrs. Rutherford moved to Tennessee, near her family, realizing their support could help her as she raised her daughter. She began her 20-year career, training student teachers for the University of Tennessee, and met her second husband.

Mrs. Rutherford is a shining example of what Cumberlands hopes all students will become once they leave campus. Not only has she accomplished much professionally but she also has worked just as hard at being a good mother, neighbor and friend. She is the epitome of a gentle southern lady.

Mrs. Rutherford has also been faithful in her financial support to Cumberlands.

Harrison Allison born 1917, West Liberty, Kentucky. Married. Children: Dr. James L. Allison, Mrs. Anita L. Charles, Mrs. Nancy A. Zarcynski, Ms. Sandra Elizabeth Allison, Mrs. Olivia Sue Johnson. He served public schools of Kentucky and Fork Union Military Academy. Graduate of Cumberland College and Georgetown College, University of Alabama – M.S.. Additional study – Morehead State, Transylvania, University of Kentucky, LSU. National Science Foundation Summer Institutes: Indiana University, University of North Carolina &

Kansas State College of Pittsburg. Chemical Warfare School US Army – Replacement Center Officers' course, Command and Staff course. US Army Infantry School – Basic and Advanced Officers courses. Member Presbyterian Church. Served as Deacon, Elder and Sunday School Teacher. Headed Departments of Science and Criminal Justice.

Retired May 14, 1988, after 38 years of service. Served one term as Chairman, Perry Co. Alabama Republican Committee. Substitute teacher, Public Schools, Carter Co. Kentucky. US Army Lt. and Captain – retired. Products Engineer, Sylvania Electric Products Inc. Marion Military Institute and Marion Police Department – Identification and Training Commander. Division of Chemical Education – American Chemical Society, Chemistry in the two year College – one year Regional Vice-Chairman. Life Member, International Association of Chiefs of Police, International Association for Identification, Alabama Peace Officers Association. Fellow American Institution of Chemists Fellow, American Association of Criminology. Life member-Retired, Officers Association. Life Member, Disabled American Veterans. "Professor of the Year" by Board of Trustees, Marion Military Institute. "Who's Who in Alabama," "Who's Who in the South and Southwest," Personalities of the South. Contemporary Author. Class Agent for Cumberland College Alumni Association.

Fred Anness was graduated from Cumberland

College in 1970 with a B.S. in history; attended University of Dayton – Transportation Specialist, and received his M.A. from Xavier University in 1978. He taught at Little Miami local Schools System and since 1978 Anness has been Regional Coordinator for the Rider Safety Program of Ohio which includes 88 school districts.

Anness served as board member of Lebanon Nazarene Church, the Ohio Speaker Bureau; Ohio Association of Administrators – Pupil Transportation (OAAPT) and National Association of Pupil Transportation (NAPT); as Commissioner of Morrow Athletic Association. He served on the Cumberland Alumni Board from 1985-1988. In 2013 the "Fred Anness Ohio On Bus Instructor Award" was established in Fred's honor to be awarded annually by OAAPT.

Anness and his wife, Candy, have one son, Brandon (Misty) and two grandsons (Cameron and Drew).

Vivian McClure Johnston. Married, has three children and three grandchildren. Cumberland Junior College, University of Kentucky – A.B. – M.A. Domestic Engineer. Taught high school Math in Kentucky. Taught in New York and Delaware. PTA's Girl and Cub Scouts, Church Schools, Literacy Volunteers, Historical groups, escorting our children to their many and various activities. Member of the A.A.U.W., D.A.R., The Mayflower Society, University of Kentucky and Cumberland College Alumni and several Historical Family Associations.

Lela Dodson. Father: Joie Dodson; Mother: Lizzie Dodson; Sisters: Ruby Bell and Velda Roberts. Elementary and High School – Wayne County. Cumberland College 1956, BA Georgetown College, M.S. Indiana University. First grade teacher at North Vernon Elementary. First Baptist Church, National

Education Association, Indiana State Teachers Association, Jennings County Classroom Teachers Association, Delta Kappa Gamma Society International, Muscatatuck Board of Realtors, National Association of Realtors, 1971 Outstanding Young Women of America. Worked with

a committee to get an active alumni group established in southern Indiana.

Jo Florence Cordell was graduated from Cumberland with an A.A. in English in 1954; she earned a B.S. from Eastern Kentucky University and her M.A., ED.S. from Union College. Mrs. Cordell was a teacher of English and later Guidance Counselor at Williamsburg High School. She is a member of Delta Kappa Gamma; Phi Delta Kappa; Kentucky Association Counselors; Upper Cumberland Association Counseling and Development; Kentucky Association College Admissions Counselors; Kentucky Association School Administrators; selected as Outstanding

Young Women of the South; Who's Who in American Colleges and Universities; Named Outstanding Teacher for 2 years, and as Cumberland College Outstanding Alumni- 1986. She has published articles in Church Recreation Magazine of Southern Baptist Convention.

She has also served as UC Alumni Board Member and Alumni Fund Raising Committee Member; UC Board of Trustees from 1995–2002. She has also served as Director of Adult IV Sunday School Department, First Baptist Church.

Jo Florence is married to **Otis W. Cordell**, 1961, and they have two sons.

V. Troy Lovett was graduated from Cumberland with a BA in math in 1969; he continued his graduate work at Eastern Kentucky University and earned his Rank II at Western Kentucky University.

Lovett's mathematics teaching career spans over 31 years at Fern Creek High School in Louisville. He was elected to the Fern Creek High School Hall of Fame in 2000. He was also involved in many school activities while at Fern Creek High School. He has been an adjunct

professor of mathematics at Indiana University Southeast-Perdue from 1998 to present date.

Lovett's connections to the Williamsburg and Southeast Kentucky area go back seven generations. His grandmother's uncle was Admiral Charles Blakely ('03). His mother, Virginia Johnson Lovett, taught English at Cumberlands for over 30 years. His father, Eugene Lovett ('31) was inducted into the 1988 Cumberland Hall of Honor and his brother, Stan, has served as a local radio sports announcer for a number of years.

Lovett is a member of Christ United Methodist Church in Louisville and has served as a lay delegate; on the Pastor-Parish Committee and on the District Superintendent's Committee. He was Pianist for Vesper and Early Service from 1980-2010. He is the author of 10 books including: *The Life of Dr. Fred Roth*; *A Remembrance of the Corbin Softball League from 1966-1969*" as well as several books based on his personal journals from1960s and 70s. In addition, he has written a number of articles including articles on Dr. James M. Boswell and on Dr. J. T. Vallandingham.

Lovett is married to **Karen Kidd Lovett**, 1971, and they have two children, Peter and Jeannie.

Marcella Faulkner Mountjoy, daughter of John Wesley and Stella Renfro Faulkner, was graduated from Cumberland College in 1943 with an associate degree. Marcella earned her B.A. from Vanderbilt University, M.A. from Eastern Kentucky University and Rank I from Union College. She has retired from teaching science at Williamsburg High School and also taught courses at Cumberlands, as well as instructor in piano.

Marcella is a member of First Baptist Church, Williamsburg, Kentucky.; Daughters of the American Revolution; Pi Beta Phi sorority; Delta Kappa Gamma Society; Williamsburg Women's Club; Cumberland College Lyric Theatre Board; Williamsburg City Council; Highland Cemetery Board; Whitley County Emergency Planning Committee; Cumberland College Centennial Committee. She has received the Woman of Achievement Award in 1978, by Williamsburg Business and Professional Woman's Club; Outstanding Teacher (twice) from Williamsburg Independent School, and was elected Mayor pro tem by the Williamsburg City Council in 1987 and elected as Mayor of the City of Williamsburg from 1990 – 1994.

She is the wife of **J. B. Mountjoy** (Class of 1950) and their children are Michael B. Mountjoy (Carolyn), Marcella "Marcy" Mountjoy, Dr. John B. Mountjoy (Teri) and she has six grandchildren: Bart, Emily, Meredith, Jessica, John and Matthew.

Doris J. Spafford. Born in Chicago, Illinois. Cornell Elementary, Hirsch High School, Cumberland Junior College, Carroll College – B.S., Eastern Kentucky University – Rank I. Teacher, Williamsburg City School. Triangle Industries, Chicago, IL; Prairie Farm High School, Prairie Farm, Wisc.; Crete-Monee Unite – Crete, IL; Taught Adult Classes in Computer at Williamsburg; Taught Adult Modern Math at Crete and Williamsburg. Math Department Chairman; Member of First Christian

Church, London, Kentucky; Sang in choir. Member of Alumni Board of Directors, Homecoming Committee, Alumni Board of Directors, Class Agent. "She is a great inspiration to our alumni association," reported Director of Alumni Affairs, Brian Shoemaker. "She is one of the most loyal alums I have ever met."

Martha Hall Victor was born in Washington County, Kentucky. After a year at Georgetown College, she entered Cumberland at the same time as her sister, Annabel Hall, in 1924. Following graduation from Cumberland in 1926, she taught for two years at Mackville High School which is now part of the Washington County School System. She received her B.S. degree from the University of Kentucky and taught junior high English in Erlanger, Kentucky, for eight years. Victor returned to Cumberland for a year to take the head resident position in Johnson Hall but ultimately spent the majority of her teaching career, 30 years, at Beechwood School in Fort Mitchell, Kentucky. She retired in 1970 after 41 years of teaching. Victor was inducted into Cumberlands Alumni Hall of Honor in 1992.

Vernon West was born at Kay Jay, Ky. in Knox County October 24, 1938. Vernon attended Knox Central High School in Barbourville Ky. where he

graduated in 1959. Vernon worked afternoons at West Chevron service station to earn his spending money. Vernon married Helen Perry January 11, 1960. Vernon and Helen had two sons, Vernon Jr. and Michael West, who attended Cumberland College. Vernon served his country in the U.S. Army from 1961-1963, where he was promoted to a Sgt. E5 rank. Vernon entered Cumberland College in the fall of 1964 and graduated in 1968, with a major in history and political science. He was active in the International Relations and Young Democrats clubs. After graduating from Cumberland, Vernon was employed by the Knox County Economic Council as an Education Coordinator. Shortly after he advanced to Assistant Director of that program. In 1971, Vernon West was elected Director of Bell-Whitley Community Action Agency. He was especially interested in the Head Start program. Vernon was influential in establishing numerous Head Start Centers in Bell and Whitley Counties. Unfortunately on July 15, 1974 Vernon died as a result of a tonsillectomy. Vernon's dedication to the underprivileged will long be remembered by many people in Knox, Bell and Whitley Counties and throughout Kentucky.

Wayne F. Whitmer. University of Cincinnati – Ed.D. , Ed.M.; Xavier University – Ed.M.; Cumberland College – B.S. born in Buffalo, NY, raised in Salamanca, NY., to Gaithel and Robert J. Whitmer. Coordinator of the microcomputer lab, information lab, and the keyboarding room. College representative on Screening Committee for Teacher Education, on the Library Subscription/Membership Committee, and on the Academic Council. National Business Teachers Association, Tennessee Business Education Association, Society of Data Educators, Delta Pi Epsilon, Kappa Delta Pi, and Phi Delta Kappa. Consultant and volunteer for the Director of Tourist Commission, Clarksville – Montgomery County. Served on the College of Business Library

Committee, AACSB Committee, Tenure, Promotion, and Retention Committee and the committee to review the Student Evaluation of Instruction instrument. Served on evaluation team for Vocational-Technical Education, Metro-Nashville. Organized the first post-secondary Office Education Association (TOEC) chapter in the state of Tennessee. Past advisor for APSU'S TOEC chapter. Division coordinator for the M-4 TOEC Competitive Events and for the TOEC Office Leadership Conference. Assisted chairpersons of various committees at the Post-Secondary OEA National Leadership Conference held in Nashville. Coordinated and judged the Typing I & II contests at the Secondary OEA National Leadership Conference. Served as Tennessee representative for the Post-

Secondary Division on the Office Education Association Classroom Educators Advisory Committee (CEAC). Edited regional, state, and national tests in accounting and typewriting. Served on the University's SACS Self-Study.

Ohio Business Teachers Association: Member of the Executive Board, Professional Development Committee, Awards Committee for Business Teacher and for Business Educator of the Year. Chairperson of the South-Western Ohio Education Association. Member of the Executive Board, Kappa Delta Pi. Chairperson of the National Leadership Conference Exhibition, Office Education Association. Member of the Screening Committee and a judge for Miss Ohio Office Education Association's Queen Contest, Ohio State Fair. Visiting Lecturer, College of Education, University of Cincinnati. Served two years on the Alumni Association Board of Directors. Received Outstanding Alumnus Award, 1982.

Roddy Harrison. Roddy Harrison is the son of the late Roger E. Harrison, Sr. of Jamestown, TN and the late Phyllis Harrison of Williamsburg, KY. He is a 1978 graduate of Williamsburg High School and a 1983 graduate of Cumberland College. Continuing his education, Harrison received an M.A. from Cumberland and a Rank I from Union College in Barbourville, KY. He is married to Maria Bryant Harrison, a 1987 alumnus, and they have one daughter, Mandy.

Harrison retired in 2011 after teaching middle school science for 27 years in the Williamsburg City School System. In addition to teaching, Harrison also served 11 years as Assistant Baseball Coach, 16 Years as Assistant Football Coach, 17 years as a Williamsburg Little League Baseball Coach, and 15 years on the WHS Alumni Board of Directors. He was inducted into the WHS Hall of Fame in 2011.

Throughout his professional career, Harrison has served his town and community in a variety of leadership positions. For more than 10 years, Harrison was the Williamsburg City Pool Manager. He served on the Williamsburg City Council from 1993 to 2004, when he became the Mayor of the City of Williamsburg. From 2004 to present, Harrison has also served on the Bell-Whitley Board of Directors, Whitley County Board of Health, Refuge Ridge Board of Directors, and Cumberland Valley ADD Board of Directors. He has been involved with the Kentucky League of Cities as a member (2007-2009), on the Executive Board (2009-present), and as Second Vice-President (October 2013-present).

Meet a few of our other Faithful Friends

Edna Jones Nicholson was a native of Williamsburg and the daughter of Mr. and Mrs. George Jones. Her

parents were active in the Williamsburg community and were faithful church members. Mrs. Nicholson made her home in Lexington, North Carolina where her husband, O.T. Nicholson, was an outstanding businessman. The Nicholson-Jones

Residence Hall, formerly known as the Sophomore Dormitory, was dedicated February 19, 1982.

Mary Doyle Johnson of Mason County, Kentucky, was graduated from Cumberland College in 1948 and earned additional credits at University of Kentucky and University of Louisville.

Ms. Johnson retired from Fansteel/VRWesson in Lexington, Kentucky, following 35 years of employment as an Executive Secretary.

Past activities for Ms. Johnson include her association with Pilot Club International; the Kentucky Genealogical Society's Board of Directors; volunteer at Kentucky Department of Libraries and Archives; The Arthritis Foundation -

serving on the Board of Directors; newly chartered Faber-Wells Chapter, National Society of Daughters of the Union; Cumberland College Alumni Association President for two terms, as well as service on Nominating Committee and Awards Committee.

Johnson is currently volunteering at local offices of Hospice of the Bluegrass and Alzheimer's Association. She continues her member in Pilot Club of Lexington and University of the Cumberlands and University of Kentucky Alumni Associations.

Ethel Miracle Burrier attended Western Kentucky University, Marshall College and graduated from Cumberland with an Associate of Arts in 1928. While attending Cumberland, Mrs. Burrier participated on the Academic Team and Baptist Student Union. Mrs. Burrier maintained her contact with and support of her alma mater until her passing in 2004. In 1975, she retired from the staff at the University of Kentucky following 25 years of dedicated and loyal service. Mrs. Burrier was inducted into Cumberlands Alumni Hall of Honor in 1995, a recognition she was extremely proud of, according to her children.

Frances Begley Morris, 1953, was born in Pineville, KY, the youngest of six children born to George and

Gertrude Partin Begley. She graduated from Cumberland with an associate's degree in June 1953 at the age of nineteen. She went on to receive a bachelor's degree from Eastern Kentucky University in 1960 and a master's degree from Union College in 1969. Only two months after her

graduation from Cumberland, Morris began her teaching career in August 1953. During her first year of teaching, she had grades three through five in a three room school. The schools consolidated after a few years. Morris taught at Buckeye Elementary in Bell County, KY for thirty years until her retirement in 1983. In 2012, Frances made a generous gift to the

University in memory of her sister, 1950 alumna **Sue Begley Stooksbury,** 1950, who passed away in 2010. The magnanimous gift was given because Morris said her sister "loved this school (Cumberland College)." After being graduated from Cumberland, Bobbie "Sue" went on to work at and retire

from Martin Marietta Energy Systems, Inc. in Oak Ridge, TN. She lived in nearby Clinton for more than 50 years before her passing.

At Homecoming in 2013, Mrs. Morris was recognized by Cumberlands as Alumnae of the Year.

Millard R. Francis, a native of Somerset, KY, attended Cumberland from 1953 until 1955; earned a B.S. from the University of Kentucky in 1957 and a M.S. from Butler University in 1960. While at Cumberland, Francis was involved in the Baptist Student Union, Athletic training, Intramurals and SGA. He was also the editor of the yearbook and writer of the Echo newspaper. Francis retired from General Motors Corporation. Currently he resides in Indianapolis, IN with his wife, **Norma Lee Tackett Francis**, a 1955 alumna.

Howard M. Stephens spent two years serving his country during World War II in both the Army and the Navy. He spent the next six years recovering

from injuries sustained during the war. In 1953, Stephens earned his GED and decided to attend Cumberland where he received an associate's degree in business administration. Stephens gives credit for his desire to attend college to his late brother, Professor Sydney Stephens, Jr., who retired from Cumberland and Eastern Kentucky University's math departments. Stephens also earned a bachelor's degree in Biology in Wildlife Management from Eastern Kentucky University. He is a Retired Wildlife Biologist. Stephens served on Cumberlands' Development Board and was inducted into the Alumni Hall of Honor in 1993, and received an honorary Doctor of Laws degree from the University of the Cumberlands in 2006.

Jerry W. Croley, 1978, Jerry Croley is a lifelong resident of Williamsburg. Jerry was graduated from Tennessee Military Institute in Sweetwater, Tennessee. He was graduated from Cumberland in 1978, having earned a degree in History, Political Science with a minor in Biology. Later, he graduated from the Kentucky School of Mortuary Science in Louisville, Kentucky.

Professionally, Jerry has been serving the Williamsburg and Whitley County community for

over 50 years alongside his mother, Edna Early, and son, Andy Croley. Jerry has been a coach with the Little League programs in the Williamsburg and Whitley County area for over 40 years. He has selflessly dedicated both his time and financial resources to the success of Williamsburg Little League coaching baseball, football and basketball in the Little League, Senior League and High School League divisions. Over the last 10 years, he has enjoyed coaching his baseball travel team (The Undertakers), who recently qualified for the USSSAA World Series. Jerry has provided his team with an indoor batting cage where they have the

opportunity to practice year round.

Jerry is married to Ola Terrell Croley of Williamsburg and they have two sons Paul Croley and Andy Croley. Jerry has two grandchildren, which he enjoys spending time with them. Jerry is a member of Calvary Baptist Church in Williamsburg.

At Homecoming 2013, Jerry Croley was recognized with Cumberlands Alumni Service Award.

Joseph Craig King, Jr., was graduated from Williamsburg High School, class of 1940, and enrolled at Cumberland College in the Fall of 1940. He completed one semester prior to being inducted into the U.S. Army where he served until September 1945. Mr. King then studied engineering at the University of Oklahoma and the University of Kentucky where he graduated in 1950 with a B.S. in Commerce (Industrial Administration).

Mr. King was employed by the Henry Vogt Machine Company in Louisville, Kentucky for 32 years, serving as sales engineer for the Valve & Fittings Division and as Manager of purchasing for all four divisions of the company. He considers the highlight of his career being featured on the April 2, 1970 cover of PURCHASING, a magazine with worldwide distribution published by the Conover-Mast Publishing Company.

Mr. King married Jane Hibbard at the Clovis, New Mexico Army Air Base on February 21, 1944 and they have eight children. One, Richard, graduated from Cumberland College in 1971.

Meet a few of our Fundraisers

Arthur "Topper" Criscillis, Ed.D, serves as a Managing Partner of Alexander Hass. Arthur brings over 25 years of development and nonprofit experience to the firm.  Arthur moved from advancement work for colleges and universities into consulting for the opportunity to work with and for a wide variety of colleges, universities, and independent schools. Prior to joining Alexander Hass, Arthur led the advancement programs for Purdue University College of Science, Rhodes College and Centre College. At Purdue, he provided the leadership for the College of Science in the University's $1.3 billion Capital Campaign. Arthur was Dean of Planning and Development at Rhodes College in Memphis, Tennessee where his leadership during the College's 150th Anniversary Campaign garnered $152 million against its goal of $120 million and increased its unrestricted annual fund from $1.9 million to $2.9 million, with 50 percent alumni participation. He was instrumental in Rhodes' securing a $35 million gift in April 2001 – its largest ever. At Centre College, Arthur was the chief advancement officer. He planned and directed the silent phase of a $60 million campaign, securing $42 million for a campaign that ultimately raised $72 million. He also led the effort to increase leadership annual giving to the College which saw a 150 percent increase in two years. Alumni participation exceeded 60 percent in each of his years at Centre.

In his consulting work, Arthur has served a wide range of higher education clients, including the University of Tennessee, Kansas State University, Auburn University, Florida State University, Georgia State University, Florida Atlantic University, The University of Tampa, Harvey Mudd College, Berea College, West Virginia Wesleyan College, Furman University, and Young Harris College, to name a few. He has helped clients with campaigns as large as $1 billion and as small as $5 million. Arthur also specializes in training volunteers, academic leaders and development staff for major gift solicitations.

Consistently garnering the highest accolades for his speaking, including the CASE Crystal Apple Award, Arthur has chaired the CASE Conference on Major Gift Solicitation six times and the CASE Conference on Successful Annual Giving Strategies two times. He has also served as faculty for the CASE Summer Institute on Educational fundraising.

Arthur earned his doctoral degree in higher education from Vanderbilt University and holds the Master of Divinity degree from Southwestern Baptist Theological. He graduated from Cumberland in 1976 and served at various positions in the college and community including assistant director of admissions, director of admissions, instructor of religion, dean of admissions, assistant to the president for development, Williamsburg Independent School Board member, and deacon of Williamsburg First Baptist Church and a member of the Leadership Tri-County Board of Directors.

Martha Crume Ash was graduated from Cumberland in 1944 and went on to obtain an AB from Georgetown College in 1946. She served as a member of Cumberland's Alumni Board from 1995-1998 and has been a financial supporter of the school. Ash was a Communications Specialist and Corporate Fundraiser before retiring.

Meet a few of our Librarians/Curators

Gertrude Angel Dale was married to **Arthur A. Dale**. She attended Cumberland College's Model

School in 3rd, 4th, & 5th grades, graduated from Williamsburg High School, Cumberland College – A.A. Degree, Eastern Kentucky University – B.S. Degree, George Peabody College for Teachers – B.S. in L.S. Degree, and M.A. in L.S. Degree. Librarian and teacher in Whitley County, Williamsburg High School, Middlesboro High School, Cumberland College, Harlan County Schools, UK Southeast Community College. Taught as part time faculty, Real Estate Courses. Licensed Real Estate Sales Associate with Pollitte Real Estate, Harlan. Licensed Real Estate broker with Pollitte Real Estate. Pollitte Real Estate, Principal Broker. Member of Harlan Woman's Club, Delta Kappa Gamma, National Teacher's Sorority, Harlan Baptist Church, Sunday School Teacher for Adult Class, Member of Harlan Chapter, American Red Cross. President of Harlan Appalachian Regional Hospital Auxiliary, member of Harlan Appalachian Advisory Board, Council of Volunteer Services for the State of Kentucky, Kentucky Hospital Association, Council, member of Advisory Board, University of Kentucky, Southeast Community College, Harlan County Tax Evaluation Board, member of Glory Singers, Harlan Baptist Church, Rural Development Committee for Harlan County & Treasurer.

Sylvia Marcia Angel whose paternal and maternal ancestors were of the Angel family were in Whitley County from Pioneer Days. Paternal families were Angel, Taylor, Smith, Meadors and others from the upper Jellico Creek area. Maternal families were Hayes, Bishop, Underwood and others from the Rockholds area. Father, Milford L. Angel, Sr. and mother, Stella Alice Hayes Angel, lived in Williamsburg, 1227 Pelham Street. This was her home place for seventy years. Sylvia was born there and this was her home address all her life time. Sylvia entered Cumberland's Model School, Roburn

Hall, in first grade in September 1921. In third grade she transferred to Williamsburg City Schools. Graduated from Williamsburg High School in 1932. Graduated from Cumberland College in 1936.

Graduated from Eastern Kentucky University in 1946. Attended University of Kentucky Library School. 1933-34 Worked as sales lady in clothing store. 1937-1954 Taught in Whitley County Schools and Williamsburg City Schools. 1954-1981 Cumberland College: Librarian, Placement Director, Librarian of Curriculum Materials Center. 1981 Retired. 1984 Deceased. Member of First Baptist Church, Williamsburg, Ky. Member and Leader of Joie B. Mahan Circle and WMU for many years. Member and President of Williamsburg Business and Professional Club. Member of Delta Kappa Gamma Teachers Sorority. Class Agent for Alumni Association of Cumberland College.

Laura Vinson Northrup, a 1990 graduate, worked

after graduation at Fuqua Gardens in Atlanta. Dr. & Mrs. Fuqua were wonderful supporters of the University. Northrup is currently employed as Master birder and slide curator at the Atlanta Audubon Society.

Meet a few of our Publishers

Don W. Estep, a native of Corbin, KY, and his wife Judy Holman Estep were married in June, 1964 and they have three daughters; Angela Thompson, Ashley Estep and Amber Estep-Adams and three grandchildren, Blake, Adelyn and Polly. He is a  1957 Graduate of Corbin High School and earned a BA Degree from the University of Kentucky in 1961. Estep was a radio sports announcer for 30 years, which included broadcasting the games for Cumberland College. He worked at WCTT in Corbin from 1961 to 1970 and was the Mental Health Educator for the Cumberland River Comprehensive Care Center from 1970 to 1977. He became Advertising Director for the Corbin Times Tribune in 1977, and then moved to the London Sentinel-Echo in the same position in 1980. In 1987, he started working with Terry Forcht as publisher of the Whitley Republican and in the same year started a new newspaper called Corbin! This Week. The two papers were merged in 1992 and it is now called the News Journal. Estep has been publisher and part-owner of this newspaper for 26 years which has won numerous awards from the Kentucky Press Association. He served as a Trustee for the University of the Cumberlands for 19 years, is a past president of the Corbin Lions Club, chairman of the Corbin Tourism Commission, served on the Board of Directors of the Southern Kentucky Chamber of Commerce and served on the Board of Directors of the Kentucky Press Association. He is a member of Central Baptist Church where he has served as chairman of the Deacons and Television Director. Estep was inducted into the Corbin High School Redhound Hall of Fame in 1993, received the Community Service Award in 2004 for his contributions to the City of Corbin, and is recipient of an Honorary Alumnus award from Cumberland College.

Oscar Combs began covering UK basketball and  football in 1964, first as sports editor of The Hazard Herald and later with the East Kentucky Voice. In 1976, Combs launched *The Cats' Pause*, the first independent college sports weekly of its kind, of which there are more than fifty-two today. Combs sold the publication in 1997. In 2002, he was inducted into the Kentucky Journalism Hall of Fame. According to Combs, his career began in grade school when he delivered the *Hazard Herald*. After attending Cumberland College he again worked *The Hazard Herald*. In 1968, both *The Lexington Leader* and *The Courier Journal* talked to him about jobs with the CJ offering him a sports position. He turned that offer down after learning he would have to pay $22 a month for a parking space in a nearby parking garage next to the CJ building.

Then in September of 1969, he went to work for Newspapers Inc. (now Landmark Newspapers) as the editor/publisher of *The East Kentucky Voice*, a new semi-weekly newspaper started in competition with *The Hazard Herald*. In 1970, he purchased *The Tri-City News* in Cumberland and two years later he resigned the Hazard position to devote full-time to the Cumberland paper. His resignation was counter-offered with a proposal to purchase *The East Kentucky Voice* and six months later sold *The Tri-City News* and moved to Lexington on Memorial Day, 1976, to start *The Cats' Pause*.

Meet a few of our Relations Representatives

Laura Sue Gaines '86, credits her success to President Jim Taylor, '68, who helped her obtain a scholarship to Cumberland, and to Dr. John Broome,

who encouraged her to give up 46 college-credit hours, earned at Carson-Newman College as a home economics major, to become a business administration major. Her brothers, Michael Winhold, '84, and William Joseph Winhold and her sister, Michelle (Shelly) Rose Hopkins all attended Cumberland College, as did her first husband, Mitch Gaines, '86, and their daughter, Courtney Nichole Gaines-Bowlds.

As a full-time, married student and mother of a two-year-old, working two jobs and singing in her church choir, Laura had little time for extra-curricular activities. After graduation from Cumberland she earned a master's degree from Tennessee Technological University and worked as field representative for U.S. Congressman Bart Gordon. She is now the vice president of government affairs for Solutions Through Innovative (STI) Technologies, Inc. The recipient of numerous awards for outstanding scholarship and leadership, she is pursuing a doctorate in international business at Johns Hopkins University.

David B. Rhodes graduated from Cumberland in 1980 with a Bachelor of Science in business administration. Since graduating, he has been employed by The Walker Company of Kentucky, Inc. in Mt. Sterling, KY and is currently the Director of Sales and Marketing. Rhodes has served as Past Chairman of the Board, Kentuckiana Association of Builders and Contractors. He also served on the University of the Cumberlands Alumni Board as both member and president.

Jerry Andrew Rickett is a 1972 alumnus. He received a B.S. degree in geography/geology from Cumberland and went on to receive an M.S., M.A., from Eastern Kentucky University. He has been involved in economic development since his graduation, working for The Kentucky River Area Development District in Hazard, Kentucky, as a physical planner; as the chief physical planner for the Cumberland Valley Area Development District in London, Kentucky; and as Marketing Manager for Kentucky Highlands Investment Corporation in London, Kentucky until 1988 when he was elected as President and CEO and still serves in that position.

Under his leadership, Kentucky Highlands has been recognized as one of the nation's leading rural economic development organizations. It has been involved in the genesis of many rural development programs and policies which have been expanded to other regions in the United States.

Rickett is a member of the Advisory Committee of the Federal Home Loan Bank of Cincinnati and has served with various civic and community organizations. Rickett has also received several awards and honors (most notable was the 1996 Governor's Economic Development Leadership Award). He is invited to speak at many conferences, including being invited to the White House to share the podium with the President and Vice President. He also served on a committee to develop recommendations on how to best create and manage a Kentucky venture capital fund.

Rickett met his wife **Elaine Taylor Rickett**, a 1972 alumna, while both were attending Cumberland. They have two children.

Allen E. Robbins is a life-long resident of Sevier County, Tennessee. A graduate of Sevier County High School in 1985, Robbins went on to earn a Bachelor of Science Degree in Business Administration from Cumberland in 1990. At

Cumberland, Allen was a member of the first football team in 1985. His 1988 football team recorded the first 10-0 undefeated regular season in the fourth season, a first nationally at any level of play. The team earned the first post season game. He was a three year letterman earning Honorable Mention and Second Team All-Conference honors in 1988 and 1989.

In 1991, Robbins began his career with Sevier County Electric System, a Tennessee Valley Authority electric power distributor. From 1996-2003, he was the Programs Administrator, coordinating all phases of the marketing of electric services within the Tennessee Valley Authority's Energy Right Program. He served on the Green Power Switch development team and was honored to speak at the National Press Club in Washington D.C. on April 19, 2000, representing the Tennessee Valley's 158 power distributors and presented the new Green Energy initiative as only one of three accredited Green Power products in the Nation. In 2004, the Sevier County Electric System Board of Directors elected Robbins to his current position of Secretary and Treasurer.

Allen was a volunteer football coach at the middle school and high school levels for 18 years. He served two terms, 2010-2011 and 2012-2013, as Chairman of the Sevierville Chamber of Commerce Board of Directors and is the current President of the Sevier County High School Quarterback Club. Robbins is a member of Richardson Cove Baptist Church and teaches the Senior Adult Sunday school class, better known as the Chum Class.

Robbins was elected to serve one term on the University of the Cumberlands Alumni Board of Directors (2008-2011). He was elected by the Board to serve on the Executive Committee (2011-2014) including President in 2012-2013.

He is married to the former Jachar Lyons and they have three children, Jacob (20) a current student/athlete at University of the Cumberlands, Dexter (18) a student/athlete at Liberty University, and Sierra (12) a concert band member at Sevierville Middle School.

Jo Nell Maynard Mullins graduated from Cumberland in 1998 with a major in biology and a minor in chemistry. She went on to receive a master's degree in environmental health from East Tennessee State University. Jo Nell currently is the Headquarters Quality Assurance (QA) Director at CDM Federal Programs Corporation (CDM Smith). She is responsible for the overall management of the CDM Smith QA program which allows her to be a quality manager for several U.S. federal projects and includes traveling to offices nationwide as an environmental consultant.

In 2008, she was named an "Emerging Leader," one of eighty individuals from among 4,500 employees worldwide to receive this honor. She is a certified quality auditor through the American Society of Quality. She is also a certified Nuclear Quality Assurance Lead Auditor as well as an International Organization for Standardization 14001 Qualified

Lead Auditor for Environmental Management Systems. A native of Pikeville, Kentucky, and oldest child of Rodney and Barbara Maynard, Jo Nell attributes her successes in life to how she was raised and the opportunity her parents gave her by attending Cumberland College. Jo Nell resides in Andersonville, Tennessee along with her husband Scottie (Assistant to President Taylor) and son Andrew.

Meet a few of our Health Professionals

Abner J. Lipps graduated with a bachelor's degree

from Cumberland in 1970. He holds a master's degree from Union. He spent his career of over thirty years at Bluegrass West Comprehensive Center as a social worker doing alcohol and drug abuse counseling. Lipps also served as an instructor for traffic school and became the general manager of the state program.

Ralph Lipps earned a Bachelor of Science in Biology and Chemistry from Cumberland in 1970 and a master's degree from Union College. He did post-graduate work at Eastern Kentucky University, Union College, University of Tennessee and Syracuse University.

Three days after graduating from Cumberland, Lipps began working at Cumberland River Comprehensive Care Center in Corbin, KY. He helped to establish the first programs for developmentally disabled adults and children in Laurel and Rockcastle Counties. Later, he worked with the Kentucky Infant and Preschool Program in Laurel County. In the early 1970s, Lipps was a case worker and director of a developmental disabilities program in Tennessee. He returned to Kentucky in 1974 as director of the Laurel County Child Development Program and then as personnel director and human resources director. Lipps was appointed executive director of Cumberland River Regional Mental Health/Mental Retardation Board Inc., a position he held for ten years before retiring in 1999. Since retirement, Lipps has served one term as president (2003-04) and two terms as member (1999-2002 and 2005-08) of Cumberlands Alumni Board of Directors.

Ella Mae Lentz Shearon, a native of Harlan, KY

and a coal miner's daughter, earned an associate's degree from Cumberland in 1952. Ella Mae taught psychology and English at Cumberland from 1961-62. She was the great-niece of former Cumberland President, Dr. Lloyd Creech (1925-45) and sister of Dr. Betty (Lentz) Siegel, a 1950 alumna and President Emeritus of Kennesaw University in Marietta, GA. Shearon became the Founder and Director of the Institute of Psychodrama in Cologne, Germany and Virginia Beach, VA.

Roger D. Baker born in Berea, KY. The first of four children to attend Cumberland and the first in the family to complete college. One son, Roger Warren.

B.S. Cumberland, Williamsburg, KY. M.A. Union College, Ed.D. Nova University. Additional: Ohio State University. Assistant Executive Director of ARC/Marion, Ocala, Florida. Member Marion County Schools Advisory Board for Health Occupations, Board of Florida Diagnostic and Learning Resource Center, Florida Association of Behavior Analysis, Ocala-Marion County Chamber of Commerce (Education). Part-time instructor for Central Florida Community College. Member of North Central Florida Health Planning Council. Eight publications, including: Four in journals, two in ERIC (U.S. Government), one by National Professional Organization. Kiwanis Service Award 1986, HOSA Service Award 1987, Service to community letter from County Commission 1987. Employee 1969-81 of Cumberland College. Florida Chapter Task Force.

Meet a few of our Authors (Writers)

Cratis Williams (See Meet a few of our College Presidents)

James Thomas Cotton Noe taught at Williamsburg Institute in Kentucky in 1893 before marrying Williamsburg native Sidney Stanfill in 1894. Noe practiced law in Springfield, Kentucky from 1894 to 1898. He gave up the practice of law to resume his

studies at the University of Chicago in 1899. He then returned to teaching in Hartsville, Tennessee; Pineville, Kentucky and Lincoln Memorial University and in 1908 became an assistant professor of education at the University of Kentucky. He was on the faculty of the College of Education for nearly thirty years and was head department from 1912 until his retirement in 1934. Noe was Kentucky's first poet laureate, an honorary title he held from 1926 until his death in 1953. Noe published eight volumes of poetry before his death in Beverly Hills, California by 1953.

Lois Carter Kelly grew up in the R. C. Tway coal

mining camp of Harlan County, Kentucky. She met **Charles Kelly** on Cumberland's campus in 1948, and in September, 2013, they celebrated their 60th anniversary. Kelly dedicated herself to a teaching career spanning from 1950 to 1989. She started teaching at Wallins Creek School in Harlan County, Kentucky then taught in North Carolina, Wisconsin, and Georgia, having been named Teacher of the Year four different times. She taught at the Georgia Governor's Scholars Program during four separate summers. Lois enjoyed storytelling and attended the National Storyteller Convention in Jacksboro,

Tennessee. She serves as an elder in the Presbyterian Church. She authored a book in 2006, *Charity's Children, The Tway It Was*, about her Carter family growing up in Harlan County, Kentucky.

Kentucky author, **James Still**, was named honorary alumnus of Cumberland in 1977. Still was chosen for his *Telling the Story of Appalachia and It's People* through his numerous short stories, poems and novels. His sensitive portrayals of mountain life led many to regard him as Appalachia's foremost

literary artist. Still, Kentucky's poet laureate in 1995 and 1996 was an Alabama native, which surprised Kentuckians learning about his work for the first time. His life and work were so deeply rooted in Knott County that it seemed as if he had lived there forever. After high school, he

went to Lincoln Memorial University in Harrogate, Tenn., where he worked as a janitor in the library while earning a bachelor's degree. Still also earned a bachelor's degree in library science from the University of Illinois at Urbana - Champaign and a master's degree in English at Vanderbilt University. He worked as a librarian at Hindman Settlement School, traveling Knott County delivering books to remote one-room schools. The first three years he worked for room and board only. During this time Still's poems and short stories began appearing in magazines throughout the country. He supplemented his income with $2 and $3 payments by sending poems to magazines. In addition to selling an occasional poem or story, Still supported himself by growing and preserving most of his own food. He also taught at Morehead State University, Berea College and Ohio University. Until his health declined, Still spent much of the last two decades of his life traveling to schools in Appalachia, reading and talking to children. Some of his works included: *The Hounds on the Mountain*; *On Troublesome Creek; Way Down Yonder on Troublesome Creek; The Wolfpen Rusties; Sporty Creek and Jack and the Wonder Beans*. *Jack and the Wonder Beans*, an Appalachian version of Jack and the Beanstalk, was chosen by the New York Times as one of the nine best illustrated children's book for 1977.

Tom Siler is an alumnus of Cumberlands who worked as the sports editor for the *Knoxville New Sentinel*. According to a story in *Tennessee Towns: From Adams to Yorkville* (Knoxville, Tennessee: East Tennessee Historical Society, 1985, p. 44.) Jack Howard of Scripps-Howard newspapers received a letter from the College asking for money. He asked Siler if he knew anything about the College, and Siler responded that yes he had even attended the College. Since that time Mr. Howard has supported the College.

Rayford Watts was born in Kentucky but grew up in Indiana where his father was employed. Rayford enrolled at Cumberland in1958 after a good friend told him about the college. He decided to major in English after taking a course from Professor Carnes. He met **June Queener**, his future wife, at Cumberland. Today their daughter is an English professor at South College in Knoxville. She also teaches creative writing at the University of Tennessee. They have two grandsons.

Following graduation, Rayford taught English for forty-two years and has been a potter for forty years.

He and June continue to operate Paint Creek Pottery near Williamsburg. In October of 2009, Rayford began writing and recording songs, ably assisted by Virgil Bowlin, his good friend, guitar teacher, recording engineer and another Cumberland alumnus. To date, Virgil and Rayford have completed seventeen albums with more to come in the future.

Howard Wasdin attended Cumberland College from 1980-1981 before joining the Navy. He later became a Navy S.E.A.L. where he gained extensive medical training and first hand medical experience. He also earned a Silver Star and went on to be awarded the Purple Heart before his medical retirement in 1995. Wasdin was responsible for training the U.S. Security Team which provided for the security of the 1996 Olympics in Atlanta, GA.

While a Navy S.E.A.L. Dr. Wasdin was shot multiple and sustained injuries. He eventually visited a Chiropractor to help alleviate his pain. Wasdin decided to return to college and earned a Bachelor of Science in biology from Life University, Marietta, GA in 2007. He went on to earn his Doctor of Chiropractic from Life University in 2009. He now finds great rewards from seeing patients get relief from pain and increasing his or her level of wellness.

In 2011, Wasdin published a book titled: *Seal Team Six,* filled with stories about his time in the Navy as a TEAM SIX Navy S.E.A.L. The book topped the New York Times best seller list. Wasdin has also published various articles.

Christopher Helvey, 73, is the son of O.J. and Marjorie Helvey, two of Cumberlands long-time faculty members. Chris grew up in Williamsburg and was graduated from Cumberlands with majors in history and political science. Helvey's short stories and poems have appeared in numerous magazines and journals, including *Kentucky Monthly, Idiolect,*

Kudzu, Nougat, The Chaffin Journal, Ace Weekly, Kentucky Blue, Modern Mountain Magazine, Best New Writing, New Southerner, Solstice, Bayou, Dos Passos Review, and *Minnetonka Review*. His chapbook *On the Boulevard* was released in 2011 by Finishing Line Press. His novel *Whose Name I Do Not Know* is slated for release in 2013 by Hopewell Press. He attended graduate school at Spalding University and received his MFA in Writing. He currently serves as a writing coach and as editor of *Trajectory Journal.* Helvey lives and writes in Frankfort, Kentucky with his wife Gina.

Jolina Miller, '08, was recognized at the 2008 Commencement as the Berger Foundation Outstanding Female Graduate. She was born in the heart of Amish country, Lancaster County, Pennsylvania, but moved to the hills of Tennessee with her family when she was only three years old.

126

Jolina came to Cumberlands from Greenbrier, TN where she helped her family at their Amish Country Store to display and sell fruits and vegetables. As she manned her post, she would write stories in a journal thus developing her love for the written word.

At UC, Jolina double majored in Communication Arts and English with an emphasis on creative

 writing. Her sophomore year, Jolina took a creative fiction class under the guidance of Nancy Jensen and wrote a short story loosely based on her waitressing experiences at a schoolhouse cafeteria located in the rural town where she'd grown up. "Secrets at the Thresherman Show" won UC's first creative writing award and fostered Jolina's confidence to write about what she knew.

Two more years of solid instruction from the professors in both the English and Communication Arts Departments helped streamline Jolina's writing. She continued working with the student newspaper, and loved the staff there, but felt herself steering away from journalism and embracing creative writing instead. She became a student editor on the literary journal, *Pensworth*, took another creative writing class with Nancy Jensen, and began to think that perhaps storytelling was what she was always meant to do.

After being graduated Jolina was married and moved to East Tennessee where she worked and wrote and became a mother. Jolina published several short stories before deciding that she was ready to write a novel, and she chose a topic with which she was very familiar – the Mennonites. The novel titled *The Outcast* is a modern day tale of *The Scarlet Letter* with a more personal involvement by the reader.

Her next book, *The Midwife*, will be released in the summer of 2014.

Meet a few of our Ministers

Daniel W. Carroll was born Detroit, Michigan. Married, one daughter and one stepson.

Williamsburg High School, Cumberland College, Episcopal Seminary, Berkeley Divinity School at Yale. Assistant at St. Bartholomew Episcopal Church in North Augusta, SC. Air Corps in Albany, GA. ASTP at University of Pittsburgh. Served Christ Episcopal Church, Cordela, GA & Augusta, GA. Patient Representative in the Emergency department of University Hospital, August, GA. Volunteer Chaplain in University Hospital and both VA Hospitals in Augusta. Sunday School teacher and Choir member in First Baptist Church. National Honor Society's highest honor: the Berkeley Cross. Named Chaplain of the Year. Class Agent for Cumberland College Alumni Association.

Harold Dean Haun, a native of Knoxville, Tennessee, graduated from Cumberland College with a Bachelor of Arts in Religion and Pastoral Counseling in 1977. He went on to earn a Master of Divinity with preaching emphasis from Southwestern Baptist Theological Seminary in 1981 and a Doctor of Ministries, Expository Preaching, from Trinity Theological Seminary in 1998. In 2011, Haun was inducted into Cumberlands' Alumni Hall of Honor for Religious Service.

Dr. Haun has been serving as full-time pastor since 1979, at churches in Texas, Florida, Tennessee and Georgia. Currently, Haun is the Senior Pastor at First Baptist Church in Morristown, TN, where he has been serving since November 2007. Throughout his ministry, Dr. Haun has served on numerous committees and participated in several missions, including the International Mission Board of the Southern Baptist Convention.

Haun is also extremely active in ministry to Israel where he is a member of the Board for the Olive Tree Foundation, founder of Harvest of Israel and a member of the Board of Advisors for the International Christian Embassy in Jerusalem. Additionally, he has led numerous tours to Israel and has participated in mission trips to Russia, South America, Africa, Europe, the Middle-East, Alaska and Canada. Haun is currently serving as the 2012-2013 Tennessee Baptist Convention President.

John "Scott" Brady is the eldest son of a career Air Force enlisted man. Having lived in various locations around the United States and in Europe,

home is "everywhere and nowhere." Brady came to personal faith in Jesus Christ while participating in youth activities when his family was stationed in Berlin, Germany. He attended all four years of high school at Berlin American High School and graduated first in his class. Having received a "full ride" military scholarship, Brady's plans included a career in the Air Force. Sensing God's call in another direction, he gave up his plans for a military career and instead pursued study at Cumberland. Formative extracurricular experiences included serving with Love-In-Action, Mountain Outreach, Baptist Student Union, and serving as both Student Government Vice President and President. Following graduation from Cumberland in 1995, Scott worked for his alma mater for two years while discerning and resisting the call to pastoral ministry. Surrendering to the call to ministry, Brady was invited to attend the **Princeton Theological Seminary** where he received the Master of Divinity degree. His extracurricular experiences at Princeton included serving as the Interim Baptist Chaplain to Princeton University and planting a thriving and growing church in Medford, NJ. After graduating from Princeton and being assured that the church would continue in his absence, Brady accepted an invitation to teach religion classes at Cumberland for the Spring Semester in 2001. He then served in the Admissions Office at Cumberland until receiving an appointment to serve as the Associate Pastor of the

First United Methodist Church in Sevierville, TN. Brady is currently an Elder in Full Connection in the Holston Conference of the United Methodist Church and is serving as lead pastor of Piney Flats United Methodist Church. He is married to **Elizabeth Alexander Brady**, a 1995 alumna of Cumberland and recipient of the Doctor of Jurisprudence degree. Scott and Beth have four children: Jonathan (16), Emily (15), Katie Grace (11), and Rylee (9).

Robert Williams South graduated from Cumberland in 1935 with an associate's degree and from Wake Forest College in 1937 with a bachelor's degree. He also graduated from the Episcopal Theological Seminary in Alexandria, VA, and the chaplain's school at the North Carolina Baptist Hospital in Winston-Salem. Prior to being in the ministry, Rev. South was a chemist and spent some time in technical sales with the American Cyanamid Company of Wayne, NJ. Reverend South served in six churches in North Carolina, four in Georgia and two in Vermont. He organized a chaplain's program at Beaufort Count Hospital and served as its director, was a lecturer for the nurses' in-service training program at the hospital, and served as acting Rector of St. Mary's Church in Northfield, VT during the summers. He also held a private pilot's license and was the Chaplain-Captain in the USAF department of the Civil Air Patrol. *Bashin' Bob Clarke & Other Tales of Heartache and Hunger Creek*, a book based on Rev. South's experiences preaching in small, southern towns in Georgia and North Carolina was published in the fall of 2000. Rev. South and his wife, Margaret, were married 62 years before his passing on December 28, 2000.

Billy Mitchell, a 1955 graduate, is a long-time resident of Williamsburg and pastor of Briar Creek Baptist Church in Williamsburg.

Tony Clifford Merida, a native of Barbourville, came to Cumberland on a baseball scholarship and graduated in 2000 with a degree in health education. In his sophomore year he surrendered his life to Christ. Following graduation he received a Presidential Scholarship to New Orleans Baptist Theological Seminary where he earned a Master of Divinity in Biblical studies and a Master of Theology and went on to earn a Ph.D. in preaching, with an emphasis in theology. While at New Orleans he served as senior pastor of his first church, Kenner Baptist in New Orleans.

Shortly after receiving his doctorate, Merida was offered the position of dean of the chapel at NOBTS. He taught at the seminary, where he had been an

adjunct instructor while a doctoral candidate. Merida has also taught at international seminaries, such as

Kiev Theological Seminary in Ukraine. In 2009, Merida and his wife Kimberly adopted siblings from Ukraine: James, Angela, Jana and Victoria. He accepted the position of interim pastor at Temple Baptist Church in Hattiesburg, Mississippi, where he eventually became teaching pastor of a congregation of approximately 2,500 members.

Merida is the Lead Pastor of Imago Dei Church, Raleigh, NC and serves as Associate Professor of Preaching at Southeastern Baptist Theological Seminary. He travels all over the world speaking at various events to various groups, including student camps & conferences, orphan care events, and pastor's conferences.

Richard Harris, a native of Somerset, KY, graduated from Cumberland College in 1970. During his time at Cumberland, he was involved in the

Baptist Student Union, basketball and the Student Government Association, of which he was President. He earned an M.A. from Eastern Kentucky University in 1971, a Master of Divinity from Southwestern Baptist Theological Seminary in 1973 and a Doctorate of Ministry from Southwestern Baptist Theological Seminary in 1976. He was pastor of Maxey Baptist Church, Paris, TX from 1973-1977 and Burgin Baptist Church, Burgin, KY from 1977-1981. From 1981-82 he served as the Associate Director of the Mass Evangelism for the Home Mission Board (HMB), and in 1983 was named Director of Mass Evangelism for the HMB, Atlanta, GA. He was a workshop leader for the Billy Graham International Conference for Itinerant Evangelists in Amsterdam in 1983, 1986, and 2000, which he led until 1977. He then led the Church Plantings Group as Vice President for NAMB from 1997 until 2007. He is the author of numerous books and articles on evangelism and church planting. Dr.

Harris retired as Vice President of the Sending Missionaries Group for the North American Mission Board (NAMB) after 30 years of service with NAMB and its predecessor, the Home Mission Board. During his last two years at NAMB he served as interim president for 13 months. In 1987, Dr. Harris received Cumberland's Outstanding Alumnus Award. He has served as a guest speaker for the master's in Christian Studies program that is available online through University of the Cumberlands. Also, he had led 26 interim pastorates. Dr. Harris and his wife, **Nancy Metcalf Harris**, '71, currently reside in Alpharetta, Georgia, and they have two sons, Brad (an Oral and Maxillofacial Surgeon) and Aaron (an Attorney) and five grandchildren.

Don Mantooth (See National Television)

Paul Chitwood (See Meet a few of our Ph.D.'s)

Bill Henard (See Meet a few of our Ph.D.'s)

Billy Hurt (See Meet a few of our College Professors)

Jerry D. Lowrie was graduated from Cumberland College, Carson-Newman College and Southwestern Baptist Theological Seminary. He has served in churches in Kentucky, Mississippi, Texas, Ohio, and

Tennessee before coming to Main Street Baptist Church in March, 1977, serving for 25 years. Under his leadership, the church began a radio, TV, senior adult, van, Deacon, watch care, and homebound ministries. Additional staff was added to the church as needs arose. The sanctuary was remodeled. An educational wing was added and additional properties for future expansion and parking were purchased. Approximately one million dollars was raised toward a new sanctuary. The church became a leader in the Kentucky Baptist Convention in missions giving. The church, at his retirement, established the Dr. Jerry D. Lowrie Endowed Scholarship Fund at Cumberland College. He has served eight churches as interim pastor since retiring in 2002.

Dr. Lowrie's denominational service includes: Executive Board Member of Kentucky Baptist Convention, State Convention of Ohio Baptist and

Tennessee Baptist Convention; served and chaired several committees of the state conventions; member of the Credential Committee of Southern Baptist Convention; teacher of seminary extension classes in Ohio, Tennessee, and Kentucky.

He served as pastor, counselor and friend to countless Cumberland students, staff and faculty. He was inducted into the Association Hall of Honor in1988; received an Honorary Doctor of Divinity degree in1990; served as Alumni Board President from 1990-1991 and as an adjunct professor. Dr. Lowrie is married to **Arvilla Mays Lowrie**, 1981, and they have two sons, Derrick (Yvonne), Kevin (Tammy) and Deborah (John) and six grandchildren, Jessica, Jacob, Caleb, Christopher, Chase and Miriam.

Bill Messer attended Knox Central High School in Barbourville, Kentucky and was graduated from Cumberland College in 1968 with a BA in history. Messer attended New Orleans Baptist Theological Seminary; was the recipient of the J. Wash Watts Old Testament and Hebrew Scholarship, and earned his Doctor of Ministry degree from Southern Seminary in 1991. Messer served as Pastor at First Baptist Church, Ashland, Kentucky.

While attending Cumberland Messer served as president of College Baptist Student Union, as president of College Student Government, and he received a track scholarship. Messer received a Senior Faculty Leadership Award. Messer has also served as moderator for the Anderson Baptist Association; president - Anderson County Ministerial Association; Executive Board of Kentucky Baptist Convention; Chairman, Foreign Mission Committee; Committee on Committees – KBC; Church Council and Advisory Boards at Cumberland and Campbellsville College; Administrative Committee – KBC; Chairman of Missions Committee - KBC. He was selected by Foreign Mission Board and Argentine Baptist Mission to preach and teach in Argentina, 1982. He was also selected by Home Mission Board to preach in Nova Scotia in 1987. In 1988 Messer was elected to Kentucky Baptist

Pastor's Conference, and in 1989, Messer was elected as President of Kentucky Baptist Convention. He has served on short-term mission assignments to Brazil, Taiwan, and Siberia Russia. He has also served as Transitional Pastor in three churches in North and South Carolina. Messer has also served as president - Ashland Area Ministerial Association; served on the first College Advisory Board; Chapel Speaker, and participated in Senior Salute Day. Messer has been the sponsor for Cumberland College youth teams and special groups in church services. He received an Honorary Doctorate from University of the Cumberlands in 1991.

Messer and his wife, **Sharon Kilgore Messer**, 1968, have three children: Rebecca, Michael and Rachael and grandparents of seven grandchildren.

Donnie Bruce Patrick, 1992, is a native of Williamsburg, where he met and married the former Debbie Jo Combs. His parents are Donnie L. Patrick

and Susan Conley. He has a rich family heritage involving the University of the Cumberlands, including one of the key persons of its inception, Reverend A.S. Petrey. Donnie graduated from Williamsburg Independent School in 1987, the University of the Cumberlands in 1992, and completed his post graduate work with a Master of Divinity from Southwestern Baptist Theological Seminary in Fort Worth, Texas. Currently, he is in the writing phase toward earning his doctorate from the Southern Baptist Theological Seminary in Louisville, Kentucky.

Donnie became a Christ follower in his mid-twenties. Upon receiving Christ, God placed within him a great passion to help fulfill the Great Commission. He has preached, cultivated disciples, and trained pastors in various parts of the world. He has also led others to participate in the far reaching Great Commission efforts of the Cooperative Program. Donnie has been used of God to foster new Great Commission initiatives and missions in Kentucky, Texas, and globally. The most recent mission endeavors being a Hispanic church plant, a South Asia partnership locally and internationally and the formation of a

gospel centered needs based ministry used of God to touch the lives of thousands known as Mission Crestwood. He has served on various community leadership boards and committees throughout his ministry.

Donnie formerly served as a mission's pastor at Mission Arlington and Community Fellowship, a mission of Travis Avenue Baptist Church in Texas. He served as senior pastor at First Baptist Church, Paintsville Kentucky for ten years before being called to Crestwood Baptist Church, Oldham County Kentucky in 2008. Donnie and Debbie have two daughters, Hannah and Grace.

Patrick was recognized at Homecoming 2013 by Cumberlands when he received the Alumni Religious Service Award.

Robert C. Jones, a native of Corbin, KY and current resident of Louisville, KY, earned an associate's

degree from Cumberland in 1950. He also received B.A. from Georgetown and a B.D. from Southern Baptist Theological Seminary. Jones grew up believing you could not quit school until you finished college. While at Cumberland, he participated in the BSU council and college choir, serving as president.

Jones was the Director of Missions for the Kentucky Baptist Convention and as Director of the Direct Missions Department – totaling twenty years' service. He served seven years as Mountain Missions Director and four and a half years as Associational Director of Missions in Pike Association. He also held pastorates in Bowling Green, Beattyville, Petersburg, West Virginia, and Stephensport, Kentucky. Jones served as Chairman of Task Force to develop a three-year partnership between Kentucky Baptist Convention and Kenya. He participated in mission trips to Alaska, Kenya, Brazil, Russia, Greece, and Poland. He was a member of Board of Directors and Treasurer of the Knox County, Kentucky Genealogical Society; oversaw construction of a multi-purpose building at the Freeda Harris Baptist Center at Lookout, Kentucky; and volunteered with Kentucky Baptist Disaster Relief.

Jones also served six years on Board of Overseers, Boyce Bible School, Southern Baptist Theological Seminary and was a member of Cumberlands Alumni Board. In 1976, he was honored as the Cumberland College Outstanding Alumnus. As Class Agent, Jones periodically produced a newsletter to maintain contact among the Class of 1950.

Elmer West graduated from Cumberland in 1941, and from the University of Richmond, Virginia in1943, before earning a Bachelor of Divinity from Colgate Rochester Divinity School. West received a Doctor of Divinity at University of Richmond in 1957. He pastored churches in New York, North Carolina and Virginia. West served on the staff of both the Christian Life Commission and the Foreign Mission Board of the Southern Baptist Convention, before those agencies were reorganized. He has written articles for numerous Baptist periodicals and theological journals concerning social, family and world missionary issues and has addressed 15 state Baptist conventions in annual session. West has also lectured at numerous colleges, universities, and seminaries, as well as at interracial and family life conferences. He has traveled in more than 60 countries and supervised the enlistment of and the appointment of over 1,300 new missionaries. He was a leader in developing a formal orientation program for new missionaries and in expanding the types of missionary service. West served on the original Board of Trustees of the Baptist Theological Seminary of Richmond and was an incorporator of the school. He has served several additional terms as trustee as well. He and his wife, Betsy, have been directly involved in the growth and development of BTSR throughout its history. At a special service, Elmer and Betsy were recognized as "parents of the seminary. The seminary's Board of Trustees, in an unprecedented move, named Elmer as Honorary Life Trustee, the first to receive that honor. West was recognized as an Outstanding Alumnus of Cumberland College in 1987, and received a Doctor of Laws in 1990. In 2012 he was given a Doctor of Divinity degree by Baptist Theological Seminary of Richmond.

Clara Higgins Reed graduated from Cumberland in 1975 with a degree in sociology. She earned a M.A. from the University of Pittsburgh in 1978, and also received a Master of Divinity in 1987 with a Doctorate of Divinity in 1992 from Southern Methodist University. Reed is an Elder in the United Methodist Church, where she served as District Superintendent of the Metro District, North Texas Conference in Dallas, TX. As District Superintendent, she is responsible for 260 pastors and

80 churches. She is currently pastor of Spring Valley United Methodist Church, a 1400 member congregation in Dallas, Texas. Clara is married to her high school sweetheart, **Charles Reed**, a 1975 alumnus of Cumberland. They have one child and one grandchild.

Jerry Hayner. Senior Minister, Forest Hills Baptist Church, Raleigh, North Carolina. Cumberland College (AA), Georgetown College (BA), Southern Baptist Theological Seminary (M. Div.), Southern Baptist Theological Seminary (D. Min.). Wife: Karen Kay. Children: Kelli Dawn, Jerry Todd. Frequent speaker at Southern Baptist conference

centers. Author of six books. Member of Raleigh Civitan Club. Past member of Southern Baptist Theological Seminary Trustee Board. Past member of Alumni Board, Cumberland College. Recipient of Outstanding Alumnus Award, Cumberland College. Outstanding Young Men of America, 1968. Honorary Kentucky Colonel. Outstanding Personalities of the South, 1969.

Sharon Taylor Finch, a native of LaFollette, Tennessee and **Robert C. Finch**, a native of Rochester, New York met on the University of the Cumberlands campus in the fall of 1974. The Cumberland programs and educational training set these two alumni on a path of

132

service to God, country, and community. Sharon became a Christian at the age of eight and surrendered to full-time Christian service at the age of twelve. Bob became a Christian at the age of nineteen while in the Air Force and surrendered to full-time Christian service during his freshman year at Cumberland.

The Finches were graduated from Cumberland in 1977; Sharon earned a teaching certificate in art education. Bob earned *cum laude* honors and a degree in history. Bob enlisted in the United States Air Force in 1971 and upon graduation from Cumberland he was commissioned a 2nd Lieutenant. He served in North Carolina, South Carolina, The Netherlands, and Italy. He retired from the Kentucky Air National Guard in 1996 with a rank of Major.

Since graduation Bob has served as youth minister, pastor, in Kentucky, Vermont and New York; a North American Missionary, bi-vocation pastor, bereavement counselor, director of missions, and UNITE Chairman in Pike County, Kentucky. Sharon has been a school teacher, led many women's retreats and women's bible studies, a teacher in VBS, Sunday school and AWANA. She served with Bob as a Home Missionary in Vermont, and a home-school teacher for 10 years.

They have one son, Charles Aaron, a 2003 Cumberland alumnus. Bob and Sharon were inducted into Cumberlands' Hall of Honor for Religious Service in 2007.

Floyd Price came to Cumberlands from Covington,

Kentucky. In 1967 he earned his B.A. in English. Dr. Price served as Assistant to President Boswell in 1967. He continued his education and received his M. Div. and D. Min degrees from Southern Seminary in Louisville. Price pastored churches in

Kentucky, Indiana and Tennessee and served as a voluntary missionary for two years while serving in the U.S. Air Force in the Philippine Islands. He has been involved in numerous associational offices and denominational activities, most notably as President of the Kentucky Baptist Convention, 1996-1997, and as a Trustee of Cumberlands, 1982-1990. In 1998, Dr. Price received an honorary doctorate of laws degree from Cumberland. Currently, Dr. Price is the Director of Senior Adults at First Baptist in Richmond, Kentucky.

R. B. Hooks, Jr. is the son of R. B., Sr., and Katherine Koon Hooks, one of four children – Carter, Frances, and Monita – and grew up in Louisville, Kentucky. RB is married to **Bobbye Jo Sawyer**, 1951. Four children: Stephen Carter, Lisa Michele Young, RB, III, and Mark Price. RB's service to churches began early in life. At thirteen, he answered the call to the ministry. At nineteen, he became the pastor of Union Missionary Baptist Church in Butler County, Kentucky. RB served as a youth minister to the mountain people while he attended Cumberland College. He served as Assistant Pastor at Franklin Street Baptist Church, Louisville, Ky., after his Cumberland College days and while he attended the

University of Louisville. Service to other churches followed. These included Salem Baptist Church, Butler County; Smiths Grove Baptist Church, Warren County; Arcade Baptist Church, Jefferson County; Providence Knob Baptist Church, Warren County (17 ½ years); Sandy Creek Baptist Church, Butler County. He was twice recognized as the Kentucky Rural Pastor of the Year by *Progressive Farmer* magazine and as such was selected to attend a special session at Emory University. A Kentucky Colonel and received an award for outstanding service from the Governor. Served as Sunday School director. State approved member of a Sunday School Assist Team. Served as a Commissioner of the State Historical Commission. Served as President of the Bowling Green Education Association, delegate to KEA. He helped to develop a history curriculum for KET. Co-authored a paper presented at the Southern Sociological Society meeting in New Orleans. A member and an officer of the Lions Club.

133

Ronald Wayne Griffin, 1975, is an Episcopal Priest and rector at St.Timothys Episcopal Church in Mountain View CA. Rev. Griffin's first career was as a business executive in Nashville where he started and grew music companies. He drifted  toward a life in ministry after moving with his family to Colorado and starting a program for young adults. He said he believes that community outreach is a critical component of the spiritual life of the church. Rev. Griffin said he is a strategic planner who believes it's important to draw input from those with other life experiences.

Meet a few of our Missionaries

Mike Wilson (See National Television)

Howard Atkinson and Libby Sweet Atkinson arrived at Cumberland in the fall of 1967 where they met and later were married on December 20, 1969.

While attending Cumberland, Howard accepted his first pastorate at Carpenter Baptist Church in eastern Whitley County. From 1969 to 1971 he led the rural church until the time of his graduation from Cumberland with a B.A. in religion. The experience provided many lessons and set the foundation for what was to come in their ministry together.

From 1971-1973 Howard was pastor at Paint Lick Baptist Church in Warsaw, Kentucky, where they learned the importance of pastoral ministry to families. From 1973-1976 Howard was Ministry of Education at Bethlehem Baptist Church in Louisville. From 1977-1979 Howard was Senior Pastor at Calvary Baptist Church in Colorado Springs, Colorado, their first rebuilding experience. From 1981-1999 Howard was a Church Planter and Evangelist in Colombia where he served as Pastor in Bogota, which later became the strongest Baptist church in central Colombia and an outreach center. From 1999 –2004 Atkinson was strategy coordinator in eastern Cuba where they evangelized the Cubans. From February 2008 to October 2008 he served as Vice President of Strategic Alliances for Conexión 10/40. From December 2008 to the present Howard has served as Director of Missions for West Union Baptist Association.

For over forty years, Reverend and Mrs. Atkinson have faithfully served God's people from Carpenter to Cuba. They were inducted into Cumberlands Alumni Hall of Honor for Religious Service in 2010.

Ethel Rebecca Harmon was born at Rye, Whitley County, Kentucky, July 20, 1905. Graduated from

Cumberland College 1932, A.A. degree, and from Georgetown College in 1937, B.A. degree. She graduated from the Women's Missionary Training School, Louisville, M.R.E. degree, 1938. She taught public school in Whitley County and Highsplint, Kentucky. Ms. Harmon was appointed a missionary May 11, 1938 by the Foreign Mission Board of the Southern Baptist Convention. She served first as a

teacher, Elam Memorial School, Shaki, Nigeria, 1938-1939; director, Sunday Schools and Vacation Schools for Nigeria, beginning in 1938; director, Baptist Training Union of Nigeria, 1940-41, 1944-47; teacher, Baptist College, Iwo, 1940, 1945. She served in other missionary activities until her retirement in 1971.

Benjamin Pleasant Roach. Benjamin Pleasant Roach was graduated in 1899 from the Williamsburg

Institute and from Southern Baptist Theological Seminary in 1903. In 1904 Roach was appointed as the missionary to China, and he and his bride Laureola Lloyd Roach went to China where he served for fifteen years. Mrs. Roach died in 1918 and shortly thereafter Roach retired. After returning to the United States, Roach pastured several churches. In 1948 he married Virginia Cox and took over the family business, the Bank and Trust Company of Jonesboro, Tennessee. Mr. Roach passed away in 1961.

Marshall Phillips of Shelby County, Kentucky, was graduated from Cumberland College in 1954. He earned his B.A. from Georgetown College in history; his Master of Divinity is from Southern Baptist Seminary. He has served numerous churches, including First Baptist Church, Pruden, Tennessee;

Highland Baptist Church – Shelbyville, Kentucky; Woodland Baptist Church – Middletown, Kentucky;

and various interim pastorates. Phillips served as Field evangelist in Kisumu, Kenya, Nairobi, Kenya and Mombasa, Kenya and he also conducted community centers in both Nairobi and Mombasa and his missionary career was concluded while assigned to the Baptist Seminary of East Africa, located in Arusha, Tanzania. He served as Director of the Department of Camps and Assemblies for the Kentucky Baptist Convention, together with being the manager of Cedarmore Baptist Assembly at Bagdad, Kentucky. Phillips speaks Swahili fluently. For a time Phillips taught both beginner and advanced Swahili at the University of Louisville.

Phillips served on various committees of the Kentucky Baptist Convention. He was a member of the Kenya Partnership Committee which set up and supervised the three year partnership with Kenya and he conducted the orientation for almost 800 Kentucky Baptist volunteers. He is a member of Kentuckiana Alumni Chapter. He has served as Cumberland Class Agent and has been a campus speaker.

Since retirement, he has been part of a team that set up a partnership with Brazil and the Kentucky Baptist Convention and did most of the volunteer orientation. He has also published a book, *He Leadeth Me*, an autobiography and has experienced a great deal of adventures and work in East Africa.

Lonnie Riley, 1980, and his wife, Belinda, minister and reside in the Lynch, Kentucky area. They have three children and six grandchildren. Lonnie and Belinda Riley are the co-directors of the Meridzo Center, Inc. in Lynch, Kentucky. They are frequent speakers at men's, women's, state, evangelism and prayer conferences, revivals, and many other events. Recently, they have gone to many countries sharing the message of faith and hope in Jesus Christ.

The Rileys have served as college administrators, pastored large and small churches, as well as served as denominational servants in the Ohio Convention of Baptists and many other Kingdom causes. Both were

recognized by the North American Mission Board as "Missionaries of the Year" in 2004 for the United States and Canada. Their ministry, the Meridzo Center, Inc., is a multi-faceted ministry with a wide scope of Service and Evangelism ministries including Solomon's Porch Retreat Center; Christian Community Center, a church for local people and visiting teams to worship and minister; Shekinah Village, youth camp and retreat center; The Chapel at Lake Cumberland Resort; Calvary Campus in Letcher County; and Meridzo's Maytown Center.

Rose Marlowe, a graduate of the class of 1912, was appointed as a missionary to China in 1921. After

the Communist takeover of China, Miss Marlowe was transferred to Japan where she lived until her retirement in 1956. During World War II, Miss Marlowe spent several months in an internment camp and a month on a prison ship. After her return to the United States, Miss Marlowe lived in Louisville where she continued her missionary work though retired. She passed away in 1980.

Meet our KBC Presidents

Green Clay Smith (See The Beginning). Smith served as Moderator of the General Association of Baptists in Kentucky in 1879-87.

W. H. Felix served as a member of the Institute's Board of Trustees, 1902-1912. Felix pastored the

First Baptist Church of Lexington 1863-1869 and again 1887-1898. He served as Moderator of the General Association of Baptists in Kentucky in 1894, 1897-98, 1900, 1903-04.

In 1906 Felix Hall was built to accommodate about 90 boys. The name of the dormitory

was later changed to Mahan Hall. The plaque displayed in the foyer of the building notes that Dr. Felix was "a friend and honored member of the Board, a wise counselor, a generous contributor to the endowment, and a loyal supporter of the cause."[34]

Ancil Gatliff (See The Beginning). Gatliff served as Moderator of the General Association of Baptists in Kentucky in 1915-1916.

Charles William Elsey, although not an alumnus, Elsey did serve as the college's president. Elsey was born in Laurel County, Kentucky and grew up in

Lexington. A graduate of Southern Seminary, he held pastorates in Lexington and Cynthiana before coming to Williamsburg in 1921 to serve as President of the College. Elsey's time at Cumberland was spent trying to raise the funds with which to pay the students who worked to help maintain the buildings

and assist in the dining hall and kitchen. Also during Elsey's presidency Cumberland Normal School was granted approval by the State Department of Education and students who completed this course of study were granted certificates to teach without having to take an examination. Coincidentally it was

during Elsey's tenure that Cumberlands began offering courses in religious culture. These courses were aimed at preparing the students with intelligent and sympathetic understanding for leadership in the local churches and in their life's work. Elsey resigned as Cumberland's president effective 1 June 1, 1925.

Elsey served as Moderator of the General Association of Baptists in Kentucky in 1939-40.

A.T. Siler (See Coal). Siler served as Moderator of the General Association of Baptists in Kentucky in 1944-45.

Eugene Siler, Sr., (See Meet a few of our Judges, Legislators, Justices and Congressmen). Siler served as Moderator of the General Association of Baptists in Kentucky in 1953-54.

Bill Messer (See Meet a few of our Ministers). Messer served as President of the Kentucky Baptist Convention in 1990.

Robert Browning is not an alumnus of this institution, but he did serve as a member of the Board of Trustees, 1986-1993; 1995-1998. Browning served as President of the Kentucky Baptist Convention in 1994.

Floyd Price (See Meet a few of our Ministers). Price served as President of the Kentucky Baptist Convention in 1997.

Charles D. Barnes (See Meet a few of our College Professors). Barnes served as President of the Kentucky Baptist Convention in 1999.

Eugene Siler, Jr. (See Meet a few of our Judges, Legislators, Justices and a Congressman). Siler served as President of the Kentucky Baptist Convention in 2004.

Paul Chitwood (See Meet a few of our Ph.D.'s). Chitwood served as President of the Kentucky Baptist Convention in 2006.

Bill Henard (See Meet a few of our Ph.D.'s). Henard served as President of the Kentucky Baptist Convention in 2008.

Meet a few of our Musicians

The year was 1984. It really wasn't George Orwellian, but it was a gratifying year. George Herbert Walker Bush was being inaugurated as President of The United States. All national networks where carrying this inaugural ceremony. I had just turned on the television. There in front of my eyes was Senator Wendell Ford from Owensboro, Kentucky, who was clearly in charge of this inaugural ceremony. In a moment the camera panned to *David Davies*, a Cumberland alumnus, who was directing the world renowned Harlan Boys Choir, this time without their silver incandescent coal miners' hats. I beamed with pride. What a year!

Then, too, we are delighted to have the talents of Rayford Watts who writes the words and Virgil Bowling who puts those words to music one can only describe as traditional Appalachian music. Two songs readily come to mind when I think of Rayford and Virgil: *Cable up Our Hollar, Walmart in Heaven.*

Virgil Bowlin is a talented instrumentalist and vocalist from Williamsburg. He earned a B.A. in music from Cumberland in 1997. Virgil grew up in a musical family, The Bowlin Family, which performed at churches, civic groups and the Kentucky Baptist Convention. After college, he was hired by the legendary bluegrass music artist Larry Sparks. With Sparks, Virgil performed nationally and abroad at venues like the Ryman Auditorium in Nashville, TN and the National 4th of July Celebration in Washington D.C. Virgil sings and plays many instruments including the mandolin, guitar, banjo, fiddle, lap dulcimer, bass fiddle, and others. Virgil is a self-employed professional musician. He teaches music lessons, runs a recording studio, Peerless Studios, and tunes pianos. His band, Virgil Bowlin and Peerless Mountain, performs a mixture of traditional Appalachian, bluegrass, folk, and gospel music. Virgil lives near London KY with his wife, Angie, and five children.

Virgil has written the music to accompany the words, written by **Rayford Watts**, to a song commemorating our University's 125th Anniversary. It was first performed at the theatre's presentation of "Shining our Light," the 125th Anniversary play written by faculty member, **Kim Miller**.

Wanda F. Begley Cornelius, a native of Harlan County, moved to Whitley County with her family in 1957. She graduated from Whitley County High School in 1967, earned her B.A. in Education from Cumberland in 1971, and received a master's in education in 1995. Wanda married **Dr. Lewis W. Cornelius**, a 1969 alumnus, in 1969. She taught at Eagle Elementary in Honey Bee, KY from 1973-75. In 1975, Wanda and Lewis moved to Lexington, KY and Lewis completed medical school at the University of Kentucky. They moved to Savannah, GA from 1979-84 while Lewis completed his residency in family practice and OBGYN. In 1985, they moved to Campbellsville, KY, where Lewis had

his OBGYN practice and Wanda was a stay-at-home mom to their three children. She served on the Taylor County School Board for ten years, ran for Lt. Governor in 1999, and held positions as Taylor County Republican Party Committee Chair, Vice Chair and Treasurer of the Women's Republican Party. Wanda and Lewis moved back to Whitley County in 2003. Lewis writes gospel songs which Wanda sings and records. She travels to different churches to sing and feels that this is now her time and mission in life to spread God's word in song and music.

David L. Davies, a native of Harlan, KY, graduated from Cumberland in 1955 with an associate's degree in music and in 1983 with a Bachelor of Arts in music.

Davies worked in the Harlan County and City School Systems for over four decades, teaching English and coaching the junior high school football and basketball teams. In 1965 he founded the Harlan

Boys Choir, which achieved international recognition at the International Youth Music Festival in Graz, Austria, and along with only two other choirs in the competition received a superior rating. Other prestigious performances included Ottawa, Norfolk, Virginia, California, **the presidential inauguration of President George H. Bush in 1989 and the inauguration of Kentucky governor, Ernie Fletcher.** Davies was named Outstanding Young Man of the Year and Harlan Countian of the Year in 1972. In 1976 he was honored with Cumberland's Outstanding Alumnus Award for his service to God, nation, community and his alma mater. Since his graduation from Cumberland, Davies has been active in the Alumni Association, serving as President from 1978-79. Davies was named Kentucky Teacher of the Year in 1978 - the first man to receive the award in the state of Kentucky. He received the Robert K. Barr Choral Excellence Award in 2007 and retired in 2009 after 51 years of classroom teaching and 44 years of directing the Harlan Boys Choir.

Richard R. "Dick" Tunney graduated from Cumberland College in 1978 with a Bachelor of Music Education degree. Dick and his wife,

Melodie, are long-time Christian musicians and songwriters. Their musical offerings, both written and recorded, have been honored with 10 Dove Awards (the Gospel Music Association's highest honor) and nearly 30 Dove nominations. Their song "How Excellent Is Thy Name," co-written with Paul Smith and recorded by Larnelle Harris, won a prestigious Grammy Award. More than 150 of their songs have been recorded and appear in numerous print publications including several church hymnals. Dick and Mel have also

shared the platform with some of Christ music's most significant and historic artists. Tunney has spent more than two decades seated behind the grand piano accompanying many of the most significant artists in contemporary Christian music. His early years of musical ministry included time with the pioneering Christian group, TRUTH, five years of touring with the award-winning group, The Imperials, and four years as pianist and musical director for Sandi Patty. He also acted as musical director and/or conductor for the highly successful Young Messiah Tours as well as numerous television shows and specials.

In the early 1990s Dick and Mel were launched into a solo ministry and spent more than a decade traveling upwards of 40 weekends per year to local churches. Currently Dick is serving as pianist and Musical Director for well-known Christian artist Steve Green as well as Musical Director for the "God of All Glory Tour", a multi-artist tour of Legacy artists. His name appears as producer on more than 90 recording projects ranging from independent Christian artists to children's projects animated television specials.

The Tunneys have served as guest speakers for the master's in Christian Studies program that is available online through University of the Cumberlands. The Tunneys currently reside in Franklin, Tennessee, and have two married daughters and three grandchildren.

Jean Ritchie Pickow, born in Viper, Kentucky.

Married to George Pickow. Viper High School, Cumberland College, and the University of Kentucky. Renowned Appalachian folk song singer, recommended for the prestigious Acorn Award given by the state for stellar accomplishments and all of whom received the award from the various Governors of Kentucky. First Social work position was with the Henry Street Settlement on New York City's Lower East Side, taught Kentucky songs and games to the children. First book, *Singing Family of the Cumberlands*, published in 1955, was widely reviewed as an American Classic. Other books followed. Concerts, festival appearances, television and radio shows, and recording contracts. As a Folklorist, she has represented her country at international folk conferences, at Expo in Canada, at the Folklife Festival in Washington, D.C., at the Cultural Olympics in Mexico. One of the seven original directors of the Newport Folk Festival, she served a term on the folklore panel of the National Endowment for the Arts. Has been a visiting professor at many major universities. President of Geordie Music Publishing Company, vice-president of Greenhays Recordings, and a partner in Folklife Productions, in New York. The University of Kentucky Founders Day Award and a place in their Hall of Distinguished Alumni, the Phi Beta Kappa Certificate of Honor, Honorary Doctor of Letters degree from the University of Kentucky, was the recipient of the 1984 Milner Award from the Kentucky Arts Council as Outstanding Kentucky Artist of the Year. Ritchie Family Week was declared, and Jean accepted Proclamations from the City of Lexington, Kentucky. The State of Kentucky, the National Congress, together with a capitol flag and a letter from the President, honoring her and her family's contribution to music. Her book, Celebration of Life, won a national prize upon publication. Her album, "None But One", received the Rolling Stone Critic's Award as Best Folk Album, and a similar Melody Maker Award for that year in England.

Karin Erlandsson Pelfrey was born and raised Northern Sweden. Karin's independence and a

strong desire to serve God led her, at age 17, to join Youth with a Mission in Scotland. It was during her time in Scotland that Karin met former University of Cumberlands Board Member, Dr. Jerry Burgess, and his wife Janie. Jerry and Janie brought Karin to Whitley City for a visit and, after six months, enrolled her at the University. Karin graduated with honors in 1989 with Bachelor of Science degrees in Elementary Education and Vocal Performance. Karin received her master's degree in middle school teaching at Eastern Kentucky in 1994.

In 1988, Karin married Larry Pelfrey and moved to Berea, Kentucky where they have since resided. In 1993 they welcomed their son Charles Benjamin Pelfrey. Ben is currently following his mother's footsteps and serving as a missionary in Northern Ohio through Campus Outreach. Karin taught fifth grade in Madison County for ten years before deciding to become a stay-home mom. Karin continues to sing in churches, at college functions, and special events. Her desire is to serve the Lord in this way for the years to come.

Paul Pace, 1990, grew up on a farm near Cattletsburg, Kentucky, in the same area that spawned Ricky Skaggs, Keith Whitley, the Judds, Loretta Lynn, Patty Loveless, Dwight Yoakam and Billy Ray Cyrus. In support of his musical ambition,

Pace's mother enrolled him in piano lessons when he was in the second grade. His parents got him a guitar when he was in junior high school. In high school, he wanted to play in bands so he started playing the guitar more and singing more. Although his was a minority opinion in high school, Pace says he never wavered in his love for country music. Pace planned to go to college and major in agriculture, but he changed his mind at the last minute. He enrolled at Cumberland College and studied music there for six years. Urged on by Judy Jennings, then the general manager of radio station WTCR in Ashland, Kentucky, Pace entered the local division of the True Value Country Showdown in 1991 and won. Then he competed at the state level and won there as well. Emboldened by his success, he began commuting to Nashville. Jennings introduced him to the legendary Jack McFadden, who was so impressed by Pace's powerful voice and stage charisma that he offered to manage him. McFadden had become famous managing Buck Owens and, years later, Keith Whitley and Lorrie Morgan. Unfortunately for Pace, McFadden was also handling another newcomer at the time, Billy Ray Cyrus. When "Achy Breaky Heart" broke the following year and McFadden found himself riding a superstar, Pace knew it was time to move on. By this point, Pace had become a formidable songwriter. To develop that talent and pursue a recording career, he relocated to Nashville in 1995. Since then, local gigs, songwriting sessions and an occasional show "back home" have kept him busy.

Meet a few of our Olympic Contenders

Edward "Eddie" J. Liddie of Bronx, New York, was graduated from Cumberland College in 1983 with a B.S. in Movement and Leisure Studies. Prior to his graduation from Cumberland in 1983, Liddie distinguished himself as a two time NCJA All-American. He consistently performed as an outstanding competitor in local, state, national, and international judo arenas. Liddie holds the record for winning the most medals in judo during the annual Olympic Festivals from 1978 until 1991. Liddie earned a spot on the United States Olympic Judo Team and was the first American to win an Olympic Medal in judo for those games, as he captured the Bronze Medal in the 1984 International Olympic Games. He later competed in the World Judo Championships and placed fifth in both the 1988 and 1989 tournaments and seventh in 1991. He was also named as an alternate for the 1992 Olympic Judo Team. Liddie was on the 1979-1983 Cumberland College All-American Team. He was inducted into Cumberlands Athletic Hall of Fame in 1999.

Liddie's career highlights include: 2013 Paralympic Coach of the Year USA Judo and in the top three finalists USOC; 202 USA Judo Coach of the Year; 1996 and 1998 USA Judo Developmental Coach of the Year. Liddie has served as a Coach for the National Judo Institute, as Assistant Coach for the 1996 Women's Olympic Judo Team, as Head Coach for the 1997 U.S. World Judo Team, as Head Coach of the Resident Judo Team at the U.S. Olympic Training Center. He was selected as the Judo Coach for the 2000 Olympic Games which were held in Sidney, Australia.

Eddie and his wife Tammie are the proud parents of two girls and one son. The family resides in Colorado Springs, Colorado, and each family member participates in the sport of judo.

Leo White, Jr. graduated from Cumberland in 1980 earning his bachelor of Science degree in business administration with a minor in military science. As a student athlete at Cumberland, White repeatedly distinguished himself as a Kentucky State Judo Champion and a NCJA Champion. He won a

Bronze Medal in the 1979 Pan American Games and a Gold Medal in the 1980 Pan American Championships. Each year during his college career, White was named as an NCJA All American. After college, White continued his judo interests while serving in the United States Army. He received numerous awards including the 1983 U.S. Military Athlete of the Year and Army Athlete of the Year

awards. That same year, he was inducted into the Judo Black Belt Hall of Fame. White's further career highlights include being the only U.S. judo athlete to win a Senior National Championship in each of the last 3 decades. He is also a 6 time U.S. Olympic Festival Championship, 4 times U.S. International Invitational Champion, 4 times World Military Champion, and a 2 time member of the U.S. Olympic Judo Team. He has served on the Athlete's Advisory Council to the United States Olympic Committee and as a member of the U.S. Olympic Committee Board of Directors since 1992. His successes in judo have earned him invitations to the White House, where he's met President Clinton, both Bushes, and legendary entertainer Johnny Carson, among others. White was also invited to the White House once again following the 2008 Olympic Games

Tocarra Montgomery was graduated from University of the Cumberlands in 2007 with a Bachelor's degree in elementary education in 2007. While at Cumberlands she was a member of the women's wrestling team and was an Olympic contender in the 2004 Games held in Athens, Greece where she placed seventh.

Zafer Roback came to Cumberland in 1963 with knowledge of Judo and Karate which he learned while serving in the US Army in South Korea. Zafer wanted to teach Judo and Karate at Cumberland

College with the desire to put Cumberland on the map as a power-house of the art, Judo. Dr. O. J. Helvey was one of Zafer's first students. Judo became a very popular sport at Cumberland. After he graduated from Cumberland with a B.S. degree, Dr. Helvey continued the GREAT tradition established by Roback, who provided the inspiration and groundwork for what became one of the finest Judo programs in the world. The Judo program produced several Olympians and an Olympic Medalist.

Following his graduation in 1965, Roback taught and coached Judo and Karate at the University of Tennessee for eleven years. As Cumberlands' Judo teams progressed, they achieved national recognition as the team won more than fifteen Midwest Collegiate Judo Championships and three National Championships. The women's Judo team won four National Championships. Along with the championships, the Judo members participated in World Games and The Pan American Games. Four of the Cumberland College Judo Team members were members of the U.S. Olympic teams in 1984, 1988, and 1992. Throughout the history of Cumberland College Judo, Roback remained an avid supporter. In furthering his individual interest in sports, he was an eight-time participant in the Senior Olympic Games, accumulating about forty medals in the process.

Zafer is "the Father of Judo" at Cumberland College. He plays racquetball twice a week and works out at a local health club. He has been in the real estate business for thirty-five years in Knoxville, Tennessee.

Meet a few of our Government Related Alumni

One of my first jobs at Cumberlands was in the area of student recruitment, and I will never forget recruiting a young man from Eastern Tennessee, *Robert Michael Duncan*. Mike, as we at Cumberland know him, became chief liaison for President George W. Bush and went on to become National Chairman of the Republican Party. While Mike was serving as chief liaison my wife, Dinah, and I took our son to Washington, D.C. for a tour of The White House. This will always be a very precious moment to us and will continue to be remembered as a special time we had with our son before his passing. While in the Indian Treaty Room that evening with Mike we were looking down through the windows into The White House and we saw a young and attractive African American Lady named Condoleezza Rice standing before General Norman Schwarzkopf, Jr., reading. I asked Mike what was going on. He explained that Rice was a foremost interpreter of intercepted Russian communiques and that in all likelihood she was interpreting an intercepted message on Russian troop movements. Remember this was before Regan said: "Mr. Gorbachev, tear down this wall," and this was before the communist party largely disintegrated. Also this was years before Condoleezza Rice became a nationally known figure.

Later Mike Duncan along with Karl Rove would be on campus to deliver a nonpartisan speech about being all you can be, encouraging words for our students and sponsored by the Forcht Group of Kentucky Center for Excellence in Leadership. Other lecturers in this Series include: Roy Moore, Zell Miller, Stephen Covey, Ben Stein, Mike Huckabee, Rudy Giuliani and Charles Krauthammer.

Then again, I remember watching over national television Cumberland alumnus **Nelda Barton-Collings** hammering the Republican Convention to order over several four year terms as she served as National Secretary of the Republican Party from Eisenhower through the Bush administration.

To be fair and balanced I should also mention we've had President Jimmy Carter on campus who has great appreciation for our house building program in Appalachia as well as native Kentuckian Helen Thomas. We've hosted almost all of the Kentucky Governors, Senators and Congressmen over the past four decades including those currently in office: Kentucky Senator Rand Paul of the Tea Party, Republican Senator and Senate Majority Leader Mitch McConnell, and our beloved Congressman Hal Rogers, now head of the Congressional Appropriations Committee.

I then think of the state of Kentucky which at one time or another was administered in part by Cumberland alumni including **Bert Combs** as Governor, **Pleas Jones** as Chief Justice of the State Supreme Court and **Frances Jones Mills** who served for years alternately as Treasurer or as Secretary of State, not to mention the large number of alumni who've served and continue to serve in prominent positions in our state legislature.

Bill Nighbert attended Cumberland prior to beginning several local businesses. He served as mayor for the City of Williamsburg for three terms. He also served as Whitley County treasurer and

Williamsburg City administrator for four years. In addition, he served as district chairman of the Cumberland Valley Area Development District, former past president of the Kentucky League of

Cities (KLC), former board member of the Kentucky Appalachian Commission (KAC) and he is a 2002 Inductee of the Williamsburg High School Hall of Fame.

Nighbert was a key civic activist in Williamsburg, coaching Little League, small-business owner, booster club president, church member and bank board member.

Nighbert answered the call to be a part of state government when he served on behalf of Governor Ernie Fletcher as Deputy Commissioner for the Governor's Office for Local Government (GOLD). In 2004 he was appointed by Governor Fletcher and Transportation Cabinet Secretary Maxwell C. Bailey to serve as Commissioner for the Department of Intergovernmental Programs. The Department of Intergovernmental Programs, formerly the Division of Rural and Municipal Aid, is responsible for managing the Rural and Secondary Roads Program and the Transportation Enhancement Program. In March 2005 Governor Fletcher named Nighbert as acting Secretary for the Transportation Cabinet. In November 2005 Fletcher announced that Nighbert was given a full appointment as Secretary of the Transportation Cabinet.

Henry Dale Hall graduated from Cumberland in 1974 with a major in biology and a minor in chemistry. He worked for the United States government for 34 years, the last 30 with the U.S. Fish and Wildlife Service, where, nominated by President George W. Bush, he served as director from 2005 until his retirement in 2008.

Hall defines education as "learning how to apply things that are important and relevant to everyday life," and believes that Cumberland was instrumental in helping him attain success.

After four years in the Air Force, Hall came to Cumberlands and graduated 27 months after his discharge from service. He said that his Cumberland experience prepared him for the demands of a professional life and the schedules and deadlines of the work place.

Hall, who grew up in Harlan County, now resides in Springfield, Virginia. He and his wife, Sarah, have three children.

Alex G. Cummins (See Meet a few of our Ph.D.'s)

Cloyd McDowell, a native of Harlan County, entered Cumberland in 1929, and finished the spring of 1931. Following graduation, he taught one year in Harlan County before entering Morehead College, where, after attending school in the spring and summer and teaching in the fall, he earned his A.B. in economics and sociology, and a minor in history.

McDowell held numerous governmental and industry-wide positions including Assistant Secretary and Labor Commissioner of the Operators' Association of the Williamson Field, Williamson, WV; President, National Independent Coal Operators Association and President, Kentucky Independent Coal Producers. He became secretary of the Harlan County Coal Operators Association in 1957, and president in 1958. He remained president until his resignation on January 1, 1979. From 1968 to 1972 he served on Secretary Rogers' C.B. Morton's Committee on Coal Mine Safety Research. Starting in 1974, he served on a MSHA committee to promulgate safety rules for underground miners. He was involved in the passing of the 1969 Federal Coal Mine-Health and Safety Act, the passing of a law that set up 100 Safety Analysts in 1978, and the first recipient of the Conservation Award from the Department of Natural Resources. From 1981 until the early 1990s, McDowell served as the Director of Cumberlands associate's degree in Mining Technology program.

Nelda Ann Lambert Barton-Collings, born in Providence, KY. Married to Harold Bryan Barton, M.D., three sons, two daughters. Graduate of Providence High School. Attended Western Kentucky University, Graduate, Norton Memorial

Infirmary School of Medical Tech. Attended Cumberland College. Long-term Care Continuing Education. Health Care Executive. President and Chairman of Board of the Following: Health Systems, Inc., Corbin, Barton & Associates, Inc., Corbin, Hazard Nursing Home, Inc., Hazard, Williamsburg Nursing Home, Inc., Knott County Nursing Home Inc., Key Distributing Inc., The Whitley Whiz, Registered Medical Technologist, Licensed Nursing Home Administratrix. Chairman of Board and Organizer, Tri-County National Bank, President, Tri-County Bancorp Inc. Executive Committee & Director, Greensburg Deposit Bank. Chairman Green County Bancorp, Inc. Board Director, Leadership Kentucky, Kentucky Chamber of Commerce. Advisory Council, Forward in the Fifth Education Committee. Vice-President, Southeastern Kentucky Rehabilitation Committee. Member, Business and Professional Women's Club. Parliamentarian, Kentucky Mothers Association. Charter Member, Women's Forum of Kentucky. Board Member, Federal Council on Aging. Member, American College of Nursing Home Administrators. American and Kentucky Health Care Association. Auxiliary to Kentucky Medical Association. UK Center on Aging Foundation. Vice-Chairman, Republican National Committee, Republican National Committeewoman for Kentucky. National Republican Institute for International Affairs. Speaker, Republican National Convention. Co-Chair of Kentucky Reagan-Bush Campaign, Bush Campaign National Advisory Council. John Sherman Cooper Distinguished Service Award, KY. Young Republicans Fed., Honorary Mother of KY Award, KY Mother's Association, KY Woman of Achievement Award, KY Business & Professional Women, Better Life Award, KY Association of Health Care Facilities Recognition Award, Joint Republican Leadership of the U.S. Congress, Bluegrass Council Boy Scout Thank You Award, Mayor of Corbin Proclaimed "Nelda Barton Day," 10-22-73, The Dwight David Eisenhower Award, KY Colonel, Corbin Colonel &

TN Colonel, Indiana Sagamore of the Wabash, KY Republican Woman of the Year, KFRW Tribute to Women Award, P.T.A. Life Membership, Academic Scholarship to Western KY University. Valedictorian, Providence High School. Member, First Christian Church. Member, Cumberland College Development Committee. Campus Speaker.

Jeemes L. Akers retired in August 2013 after more than twenty years of exciting and rewarding U.S.

government service, including approximately fifteen years with the U.S. Central Intelligence Agency where he became an accomplished analyst assessing a broad array of Southeast Asian and Middle Eastern security, cyber, terrorism, and proliferation issues. He traveled extensively in Asia, Europe and Oceania, was deployed to various stations abroad, and prepared analytical reports and briefings for U.S. senior officials and foreign partners on a number of security-related issues. Akers received a number of exceptional performance awards and other special recognitions for his Agency-related activities.

Prior to joining the CIA, Akers spent several years as a college instructor at Alice Lloyd College where he taught various history and philosophy courses, ran the public relations office and helped with fundraising efforts. In 1984—at the request of Alice Lloyd College president, Dr. Jerry Davis, Akers became the founding Director of the June Buchanan School, a private, co-educational college preparatory school co-located on the college campus. He returned to lead the school from 1994-1998.

Akers studied law at Salmon P. Chase College of Law, Northern Kentucky University, receiving his J.D. in 1990 and was admitted to the Kentucky Bar the same year. He briefly worked as an attorney for a prestigious law firm in Hazard, Kentucky, before going to Washington to work for the Agency.

Akers is a Vietnam veteran, enlisting in the U.S. Air Force in 1971 and trained as a Chinese Mandarin linguist; he was awarded the Air Medal as a crew member for intelligence-related combat sorties in Southeast Asia.

In retirement, Akers plans to spend more time with his wife, Imogene, two daughters and two grandchildren. Other "bucket list" items include: a return to the college classroom, travel, expanding his artwork business, writing additional Christian fiction novels, spending more time in the garden and participation in a variety of ministry opportunities.

At Homecoming in 2013, Akers was recognized by Cumberlands as an Inspirational Alumnus.

Colonel **Carlos R. Glover** was raised in Williamsburg, KY, and graduated from Williamsburg High School. He earned his bachelor's degree in

health services from Cumberland and his master's degree in public administration from Shippensburg University. He was commissioned in 1978 as a Second Lieutenant in the Infantry from the ROTC program. He has served in a multitude of positions throughout his 30 year career and his tours of duty include: The 7th Infantry Division, Fort Ord, California, numerous assignments with the U.S. Army Infantry School, Fort Benning, Georgia, two tours with the 101st Airborne Division, Fort Campbell, Kentucky, MacDill Air Force Base, Tampa, Florida, 25th Infantry Division, Schofield Barracks, Hawaii, Joint Readiness Training Center, Fort Polk, Louisiana, and Fort Jackson, South Carolina. His last assignment was Fort Monroe, Virginia where he was Commander of The Army's Junior ROTC program for 7 years. He retired from there in June 2008.

Colonel Glover's military schools include the Infantry Officer Basic and Advanced Courses, U.S. Army Airborne and Ranger School, Infantry Mortar Platoon Leader Course, Jungle Warfare School, Air Assault Course, Armed Forces Staff College, Australian Command and General Staff College, and the U.S. Army War College. Colonel Glover is married to the former Susan F. Wilson and they have four children, Ryan, Bryan, Ashley, and Jessica, and one granddaughter, Casey Jane.

John McCauley earned a bachelor's degree in business administration, with an emphasis in economics and management from Cumberland in

1981. He went on to complete graduate work at Kentucky State University and the University of Louisville. McCauley served as the managing member of JWM Consulting Service for seven years. He has served as director of the Division of Pesticide Regulation in the Kentucky Department of Agriculture; on the governor's Commission on Literacy; in the Kentucky Labor Cabinet; in the Kentucky General Assembly; and on the staff of former U.S. Senator Walter D. Huddleston. In 2010, McCauley was named to serve as Kentucky State Executive Director for the Farm Service Agency at the USDA.

Frances Jones Mills. (See Meet a few of our Attorneys/Legislators)

From The Hills to Harvard

From the beginning, students educated at Cumberland have been successful as they have gone from Cumberland to graduate and professional schools across this country and around the world. When asked these students will tell you that the education they received served as a solid foundation for their graduate studies and that they were as well prepared, if not better prepared, than anyone else in their classroom.

John Paul Maggard earned his associate's degree in 1941 for studies in Teacher Education and Allied Health. While at Cumberland, he participated in the College Choir and worked several jobs such as carrying mail, sweeping floors, and firing furnaces to help pay his tuition. At the age of 19, Maggard became Principle at Grassy Gap, where he taught the upper elementary grades in a two-room log schoolhouse. When WWII started, he joined the military along with some of his students. Following his time in the military, Maggard went back to school studying one year at Harvard Graduate School of Business. He earned his A.B. from the University of Kentucky and his M.B.A. from the University of Alabama received his Ph.D. from the University of North Carolina. From 1956 until his retirement in 1984, Maggard taught at Miami University.

As the Founder and Chairman of the "Laws Hall and Associates," Maggard setup advertising contracts with major U.S. companies creating real world advertising experiences for his students. In their senior year, students would compete in groups, by creating advertising campaigns, with the winning group's campaign being used by the representing company. Among the companies participation in the program were: Marathon Oil, Smucker Company, Husman Potato Chips, Goodyear Tire & Rubber Co., Avon Products, Kings Island Amusement Company, Borden's, Wendy's, Mead Corporation, Armco Inc., Huffy Bicycle, Success Magazine, and Pantone Inc.

In 1976, Maggard was selected by the American Assembly of Collegiate Schools of Business to receive the annual nationwide Western Electric Award for innovative undergraduate teaching. In addition, he received several awards from Miami University. On his retirement, Maggard received a commendation from the 115th assembly of the Ohio Senate in recognition for his life's work as a teacher and his contribution to society. Maggard was also the recipient of the Outstanding Cumberland College Alumni Award in 1985.

Matt Rasure (See Meet a few of our Ph.D.'s)

Leslie Boozer graduated from Cumberland in 1996 and with a double major in business administration and history/political science. She earned her J.D.

from the University Of Cincinnati School Of Law. After practicing law for a few years, she felt led to a career of public service. She then moved to Los Angeles and became a teacher at a high need school to try to make a difference and improve the lives of disadvantaged children through the education system. As a public school educator, she encountered numerous challenges that needed sustainable, systematic solutions. Through active involvement on several school councils and committees, she quickly became conscious of her desire to enact long lasting and widespread change. Realizing she needed additional skills and knowledge, Boozer applied to the doctoral program at Harvard and was accepted into one of Harvard's most prestigious programs, the Zuckerman Fellowship. This is a cross-disciplinary, co-curricular program that assists in the preparation of students for public service. Sponsored by Mortimer Zuckerman, editor-in-chief of U.S. News and World Report, the program selects twenty-five students with a professional degree to learn from top leaders in a variety of industries, including business, government, education, and healthcare. Boozer was one of six doctoral students in the Urban Superintendent's Program at Harvard University's Graduate School of Education. Currently, she is the Chief of Schools for the North/Northwest Side High School in Chicago, IL. She now serves as Superintendent of Fontana Unified School District, the twelfth largest school district in California.

Laura Sue Gaines (See Meet a few of our Relations Representatives)

147

Gorman Jones Roberts graduated from Cumberland in 1942. Roberts also received a B.S. from Northwestern University in 1947 and an M.B.A. from Harvard University in 1949. He served as a trustee of Cumberland (1956-1979), trustee of Southern Seminary, and Chairman of the Southern Baptist Foundation in Nashville, TN. Roberts retired as the Executive Vice President of Hilliard Lyons Inc.

Todd M. Hamilton (See Meet a few of our Ph.D.'s)

H. Ray Hammons (See Meet a few of our Entrepreneurs)

Virginia Young (See Meet a few of our Ph.D.'s)

Andrew Lynch graduated from Whitley County High School in 2004 and earned his bachelor's degree in Chemical Engineering from the University of Kentucky in 2008. In 2011 Lynch completed coursework on entrepreneurship at Cumberlands. During his senior year of undergraduate work, Lynch was awarded one of the nation's 45 prestigious Gates Cambridge Scholarships to pursue his graduate studies at Cambridge University in England. Lynch was UK's first student to be awarded a Gates Cambridge Scholarship since the program began in 2001. He joined 44 other scholars selected from an applicant pool of 635 students studying subjects in the arts, science, humanities, social science, technology and medicine. This was the fifth national scholarship honor in less than a year bestowed upon Lynch and made him the only individual to receive all five of these particular national scholarships — the Astronaut, Beckman, Gates Cambridge, Goldwater and Udall.

The 4.0 student was also accepted into the NASA Undergraduate Student Research Program where he performed biochemical research at Los Alamos National Laboratory. Building on this work, Lynch conducted research at UK, presenting his findings at conferences around the country and in Europe. As a sophomore, after studying abroad in Malaysia with the Border Green Energy Team gave Lynch the opportunity to install solar and micro hydroelectric stations in Thailand while researching the Thai government's rural solar energy initiative. Based on this work, Lynch authored a study which was published by the International Solar Energy Society. Continuing to pursue his interest in science and technology policy, Lynch's senior thesis as a fellow at the UK Gaines Center for the Humanities analyzed the regulatory implications of mountaintop removal coal mining in Appalachia. With his work at Cambridge as a foundation, he hopes to one day find solutions to environmental and public health problems facing communities in Kentucky and around the world.

Meet our Michelangelo

At Cumberland, **Jerry "Wayne" Taylor** pursued a concentration in art with enough education courses to allow him to teach. Taylor was graduated in 1972 with a Bachelor of Science in art.

Growing up in the small town of Waynesville, Ohio,  Jerry Wayne Taylor had no idea that one day he would play a great role in the transformation of his alma mater into a remarkably beautiful, renowned university. Nor did he know that one day another Taylor, Dr. James Taylor, president of Cumberland College, would dub him "The Michelangelo of Cumberland College", because of the remarkable, meaningful showpieces he has created on campus.

While at Cumberland he met and married **Mimi Sadler**, '72. Recognizing both Taylor's talent and the married student's need for a little extra cash, Jim Taylor, who was then in the development office, hired Taylor to draw illustrations and cartoons for Cumberland Today and to use his calligraphy skills to create certificates of appreciation for various individuals.

Taylor taught in public schools in Ohio's Kettering City Schools, where he worked for 33 years, the last 20 in administration.

In the early 90's, Taylor received a phone call from Dr. Taylor asking him to paint a mural in the dome. So began the first of three mural projects inside the domes of buildings on the campus of University of the Cumberlands.

Taylor designed the mural at the Cumberland Inn to feature twelve angels engaged in a variety of activities, representing children whose brief lives brought great joy to their parents and whose loss brought equally great sorrow.

The dome in the fine arts building again shows angels representing children whose lives had been all too brief. While the angels in the Inn are engaged in more general or abstract activities, those in the dome of the Grace Crum Rollins building represent the fine arts activities slated to take place in the building. Taylor chose to divide the dome into four quarters to depict four artistic pursuits; visual arts, music, drama, and dance.

The third mural project is in the dome of the Correll Science Complex. It depicts eleven constellations. All three murals have one thing in common, a Pegasus, which is the symbol of James Taylor II.

Meet our Potter

Rayford Watts was born in Kentucky but grew up in Indiana where his father was employed.

Watts enrolled at Cumberland in 1958 after a good friend told him about the college. He decided to major in English after taking a course from Professor Carnes. He met **June Queener**, 1961, his future wife, at Cumberland. Today their daughter is an English professor at South College in Knoxville. She also teaches creative writing at the University of Tennessee. They have two grandsons.

Following graduation, Watts taught English for forty-two years and has been a potter for forty years. He and June continue to operate Paint Creek Pottery near Williamsburg. In October of 2009, Watts began writing and recording songs, ably assisted by Virgil Bowlin, his good friend, guitar teacher, recording engineer and another Cumberland alumnus. To date, Bowlin and Watts have completed seventeen albums with more to come in the future.

The Potter's Wheel

I took a piece of potter's clay
And gently fashioned it one day,
And as my fingers pressed it still,
It moved and yielded to my will.
I came again when days were past;
The bit of clay was hard at last;
The form I gave it still it bore,
But I could change that form no more.

I took a piece of living clay
And gently formed day by day;
And molded with my power and art,
A young child's soft and yielding heart.
I came again when days were gone;
It was a man I looked upon.
He still that first impression wore,
And I could change it never more.
--Author unknown

Meet our Mountain Outreach Founders

Two students, **David Emmert** and **Robert Day**, began what is now known as Mountain Outreach. Here's the story of the founding of that program. The program idea originated in the summer of 1982 when one of my Appalachian students decided to show a friend through our mountains. This young man's friend was from a middle class family and had simply never seen truly poverty-stricken households. He was shocked as they passed one tar paper shack after another and realized that many of them had no running water, no electricity, and no proper sanitation.

The boys began by repairing a house for an old man with a mentally retarded son. They cut weeds and removed trash from around the house and began to try to patch the cracks and holes in the roof, walls and floor where the wind, rain, and snow would enter. They quickly realized that the house was almost impossible to simply "patch up." It was too far gone.

The boys then did something that perhaps only young people with boundless energy and innocence of practical problems could do -- they decided to build a new house.

Though neither had any experience in construction they begged, scrounged, and salvaged materials. Word of their project traveled fast on campus and pretty soon the two boys had twenty other students who could help work on weekends, evenings, and sometimes weekdays on the project.

They learned by their mistakes, got help from Cumberland College staff and local builders, and made up for their lack of knowledge with pure hard work and determination. To give you an idea of the problems they faced there wasn't even a road to the building site, let alone any electricity there. All tools had to be hand operated; every piece of building material from lumber to cement had to be carried to the site. One by one the heavy cinder blocks for the foundation were lugged by relays of kids across a field and through the woods from the nearby dirt road.

As Thanksgiving came and went the weather turned colder. The kids would huddle around a fire trying to keep warm while they ate bologna sandwiches for lunch.

By Christmas the house was almost finished but not yet ready to move into, and work stopped for two weeks while most of the students went home. It was then that tragedy struck. The kids had patched the old house as best they could and had cut enough wood to keep his stove going.

But when the students returned after Christmas, they found the old man dying. Here's how they described the scene. "The fire had gone out and Lee was lying on his bed under a blanket, shivering. I tried to take his shoes off, but he said he was afraid something would fall off."

When they finally did get his shoes off, his feet were black from frostbite. "We were never able to find out whether the fire had gone out while he was asleep or whether he simply became too weak to get up and put on more wood."

The boys called an ambulance knowing that the situation was desperate. By the time they got the old man down the mountain and to the hospital he was weaker still. He died in the hospital of complications resulting from severe frostbite, hypothermia, and the loss of his feet.

Naturally, the students were deeply affected by Mr. LeForce's death but they vowed to continue their work.

As of this writing 143 homes have been built and hundreds of handicap ramps built, roofs patched, clothing has been distributed, wells dug etc. How did we ever build 143 homes? Well, we built the first one, and that was the turning point.

David Emmert was graduated from Cumberland in 1985 and was a co-founder of Mountain Outreach when it started in 1982. His wife, **Pam Schume Emmert**, a 1985 alumna, designed Mountain Outreach's original logo. Emmert was inducted into Cumberlands Alumni Hall of Honor in 1994. He  received his master's from New Orleans Baptist Theological Seminary and completed two years of doctoral studies at United Theological Seminary in Dayton, OH. He has served as minister of youth at University Baptist Church in Thibodaux, LA; a Foreign Mission Board journeyman in Zambia and as summer resident director of the journeyman program for the Foreign Mission Board. He also served as Pastor of First Baptist Church, Lobelville, TN; director of the Theological Education, Baptist Mission of Ethiopia, affiliated with the Foreign Mission Board of the Southern Baptist Convention; and Associate Pastor of Outreach at Pleasant Valley Baptist Church in Kansas City, MO. Currently, he is the Senior Pastor at Celebration Baptist Church in Tallahassee, FL where he and Pam reside with their children.

 **Reverend Robert Day**. Day received a master's of social work degree and a certificate in theology from The Southern Baptist Theological Seminary, Louisville, after graduating from Cumberland College in 1985. While in Louisville, he served on the staff at Baptist Tabernacle, working with inner city youth. From Louisville, he and his wife Karen, moved to Alaska where he worked for the State's Division of Family and Youth Services as an Intake Investigator - investigating reports of child abuse and neglect. At the same time he served as Associate Pastor of the First Baptist Church of Anchorage. In July of 1990 he accepted the call to serve as Pastor of the First Baptist Church in the Southeast Island community of Ketchikan, AK. After serving in Ketchikan four years, Day accepted the position of pastor at the Alliance Bible Church in Anchorage. Day and his wife **Karen Haynes Day**, '85, have four children. He was inducted into Cumberlands Alumni Hall of Honor in 1994.

125 Alumni Careers Categories

ACCOUNTING, BOOKKEEPING, CONTROLLER, CPA ASSISTANT

Annabel Hall 1927
Ethel M. Burrier 1928
Charles L. Higginbotham 1938
Frances Mahalia York 1938
Vasco Truman Lawson 1939
Alma Pitts Whiteman 1939
Joyce Marie Stephenson 1940
A. T. Hensley 1941
Nora D. Roberts 1942
June Eastin Withington 1942
Arizona Stanfield 1944
Robert E. Lee Jr. 1945
Harvey Lee West 1947
Mary Lou Brown 1948
Velma Jean Clark 1948
Dessie Gladys Cupp 1948
Billy C. Ball 1949
John M. Cross 1949
Geneva Green Ambrose 1950
Roberta Meadows 1951
Charlene Sergent 1951
Donald T. Thompson 1951
Bertie Mildred Terry 1952
Sandra F. Brown 1953
John C. Drake 1954
Paul Richard Lovett 1955
Ernestine Partin 1955
Floyd Scott 1955
Charles E. Zumwalt 1955
Thomas J. Cunningham 1956
Bobbie Franklin 1956
Clyde Henegar 1956
Jay T. Meredith 1956
Robert F. Sawyer 1956
Rosa Lee Slusher 1957
Roy C. Wainscott 1957
Loel Gray Broyles 1959
Harold D. Bible 1962
Omer Champion 1962
Peggy Ann Owens 1962
Wendell Ball 1963
Jimmy C. Rogers 1963
James B. Taylor 1963
Garvy P. Croley 1964
Mary L. Davis 1964
James Robert Kahl 1964
Leland L. Roaden 1964
Brenda Steely 1964
Larry Joe Willis 1966
Marcella C. Catron 1967
Carrie Lee Kincaid 1967
Donald G. Lloyd 1967
Elaine Norman 1967
Forest Cecil Shepherd 1967
Charles T. Beckett 1968
Jerry H. Harris 1968
Clarence R. Pryor 1968
Judson Scott 1968
Richard L. Wilson 1968
Andrew M. Adams 1969
Daniel L. Bell 1969
Imogene Brown 1969
Billy F. Burgess 1969
Lyle B. Hammons 1969

Jack Short 1969
Brenda S. Smith 1969
Kenneth K. Kelly 1970
Carol Jean Perry 1970
Ancil Collett 1971
Regina Farley 1971
Judy C. Arnett 1972
Kenneth Wayne Bryant 1972
Wanda Lee Cole 1972
David Ray Setzer 1972
Richard Darrel Sweets 1972
Sheila K. Welch 1972
Marilyn Belcher 1973
Zono Jane Howard 1973
Charles Allen Keck 1973
John F. Eastham Jr. 1974
Irvin E. Huffman 1974
Seiji Kato 1974
Elena D. Moore 1974
Bob R. Shoemaker 1974
James T. Woodward Sr. 1974
Henrriann Gaddis Black 1975
Gary Dean Caldwell 1975
Deborah A. VanLennep 1975
Delores Wagers 1975
Marsha Gay Abel 1976
John Wayne Alton 1976
Sharon Rose Dees 1976
Gladys Ann Faulkner 1976
Donna Kay Guilkey 1976
Thomas M. Tye 1976
Faye Wasson 1976
Catherine Marie Donchatz 1977
Barry Alan Mitchell 1977
Nancy Leigh Anderson 1978
Bruce E. Fitch 1978
Carl Gay Jr. 1978
Myra J. Grayson 1978
Rhonda Marie Keeton 1978
Carrie Leonda Matthews 1978
Glenda G. Powell 1978
Mary Lynn Snyder 1978
Sandy K. Wyatt 1978
David Murray Bemiss 1979
Kimberly O. Combs 1979
Barry Dee Daulton CPA 1979
Della M. Morrow 1979
William A. Wilburn 1979
Michael J. Witt 1979
Patricia K. Bassett 1980
Wilma Sue Greer 1980
Terry M. House 1980
James E. Marlow 1980
Terry Hobert Oliver 1980
Dale Roger Shultz 1980
Robert M. Snider Jr. 1980
Donald Edward Watkins 1980
Robert C. Wilson 1980
Laurie Marie Adkins 1981
Ayen Alem T. Berhanu 1981
David Gordon Boyd 1981
Jon F. Caudle Jr. 1981
Marc W. Chambers 1981
Karen Lynn Fischer 1981

Glen Ray Hall 1981
Pamela Kay Jones 1981
Marianne Nichols 1981
James Kevin Powell 1981
Kimberly Hope Sergent 1981
Ralph Wesley Stephens 1981
Merrie L. Stephens 1981
Patricia Jo Weaver 1981
Roger West 1981
Robyn L. Cain 1982
Kimberly Ann Cloyd 1982
Sherry Lynn Dobbs 1982
Cathy Ann Evans 1982
Debra Lynn Freeman 1982
William John Graw Jr. 1982
Michael Eddy Haggard 1982
Kenneth Hudson 1982
Mary Maxine Hutton 1982
Janice Ann Manning 1982
Patricia Ann Price 1982
Tabb Bahner 1983
Linda Sue Glancy 1983
Michael Mills 1983
Leslie Susan Roberts 1983
Deborah A. Sams 1983
Agnes Orena Sweeney 1983
Andrea Chlea Bowers 1984
Lisa Nell Cavanaugh 1984
Randy Couch 1984
Esther Marie Dunsil 1984
Steven Ray Hoblit 1984
Edythe F. Hoblit 1984
Teresa Ann Lewis 1984
Michael David Lewis 1984
Rosella Hubbard Shafer 1984
Steve T. Ware 1984
Rebecca Susan Young 1984
Craig S. Daniel 1985
Deana R. Desmond 1985
Georgetta H. Gannon 1985
Diana Sue Greer 1985
James William Head 1985
Amanda D. Herrell 1985
Raymond Earl McGhee 1985
Esther Lucille Peace 1985
Jon E. Stewart 1985
Sandra L. Wilson 1985
Wanda Fay Davis 1986
Kimberly M. Durst 1986
Cleta Sharon Gross 1986
Dega A. F. Hersi 1986
William Michael Hurd 1986
Dorothy Alice Cecil 1987
Donald R. Jones 1987
Anthony A. Kern CPA 1987
Julie Laurie 1987
James C. McDowell Jr. 1987
Wonda Faye Morgan 1987
Douglas F. Parker 1987
Beverly J. Wallace 1987
Beverly J. Wallace 1987
Grover Carey Wilson 1987
Patricia A. Burton 1988
Joni L. Keith 1988

Sandra Lee Martin 1988
Angela Kay Mitchell 1988
Barsha Ann Goins Rogers 1988
Margueritte Louise Williams 1988
Rhonda M. Black 1989
Gerald Wayne Calia 1989
Pauline M. Eldridge 1989
Kevin M. Gibbs 1989
Burley McFarland 1989
Elbert Edwin Phillips 1989
Judy E. Poynter 1989
Darla Rene' Rea 1989
Lewis Franklin Rhodus 1989
Carol Angela Bailey 1990
Phillip Estil Collins 1990
Teresa Lynn Hicks 1990
James David Higginbotham 1990
James Smith Lawson III 1990
Debra Ann Raines 1990
Anne Elizabeth Sawyer 1990
Robyn Elizabeth Flynn 1991
Gina Renee' Hamlin 1991
Connie Lynn Hill 1991
Patricia Jo Mullins 1991
Robin Renee Smith 1991
Shirley Ann Storms 1991
Melissa Kay Peterman Bishop 1992
Cynthia Dawn Brackett 1992
Candy Rechelle Culpepper 1992

Alicia Gaye Logan 1992
Dennis Bryan Miller Jr. 1992
Vickie Lynn Croley 1993
Kyle Russell Foster 1993
Bobby Kidd 1993
Rhonda Lynn Mayne 1993
Patreana Louise Shepherd 1993
Stephanie Gay Skelton 1993
Jami Lynn Vallandingham-Hoskins 1993
Tizita Ephrem 1994
Kaleen Annette Fearing 1997
Glenda Annette Grant 1997
Kelly Ann Miller 1997
Lina Bell 1999
Glenn Edward McGuire Jr. 1999
Arden Elizabeth Turner 1999
Melissa Anne Ferguson 2000
Bradley Justin Weihe 2000
Marcia Lynn Adams 2001
Alicia Lyn Crane 2001
Kristen Marie Cruse 2001
Ericka Taylor Dimichino 2001
Nicole Ruth Gordon 2001
Thomas John Hammontree 2001
Laura Jane Ward 2001
Christy Nicole Barton 2002
Amanda Jean Ellis 2002
Autumn Marie Huskins 2002

Mindy Darlyn Nance-Cox 2002
Kevin Thomas Goodman 2003
Chris Everett Mitchell 2003
Sara Kathryn Mitchell 2003
William Wesley Scott Hicks 2004
Star Leta Johnson 2005
Katherine Elizabeth Ramey 2005
Jacob Alan Sumner 2005
Melanie Rose Draper 2006
Linda Hacker Lawson 2007
Brian Patrick Chaney 2008
Cathy Ann Evans 2008
Amanda Blair Farris 2008
Brian Patrick Chaney 2009
Joshua Wayne Dillman 2009
Amanda Blair Farris 2009
Sarah Elizabeth Grizzell 2009
Alicia Renee Hasty 2009
Dana Davenport Hurd 2009
Pamela Kay Jones 2009
Jessica Nicole Leonard 2009
Christopher Nathaniel Bingham 2010
Amanda Jean Ellis 2010
Marvin Kelly Harness 2010
Wonda Faye Morgan 2011
Joshua Wayne Dillman 2012
Kyle Russell Foster 2012

ADMINISTRATOR, ASSISTANT

Walter Howell Reed 1927
Earl C. Roberts 1940
E. T. Henry 1948
Thomas A. Harris 1949
Claudette Holladay 1956
Cade D. Sexton 1956
Ova D. Pittman 1965
James Darrell Watson 1966
Larry Bowman 1967
Leland Wayne Henegar 1968
Ray D. Petree 1968
David L. Altenburg 1969
Larry Ray Davis 1969
Clarke David Higgins 1969
Larry L. Redwine 1969
James Smith Lawson 1970
Curtis A. Shaw 1970
Larry A. Brock 1972
Marla K. McCleskey 1975
Kenneth Lowell Smith 1975
William D. Kremer 1977

Linda Morgan Young 1977
Larry R. Van Hoose 1977
Volena Adelle LeTourneau 1978
Mary Jane Wilson 1979
Julia Rose Singleton 1980
Kimberly Erin White 1981
Glenn McKiddy 1982
Wilma Jean Nelson 1982
Louise Reda Smothers 1982
Gail Timperio 1982
Cecelia Genia Hoffman 1983
Erin Colleen Wade 1983
Barry William Blacey 1984
Michele Lee Mahoney 1984
Lora McClain Patterson 1986
Everett Benjamin Bays 1987
Chamunorwa Henry Chiromo 1987
Roger Dean Cornett 1987
Janice S. Jaynes 1988
Craig Armishaw 1989
Malissa Blair 1989

Rhonda Leah Shoemaker 1989
Tammy Marie Capps 1991
Cynthia Ann Dehner 1991
Laura Jean Imhof 1991
Barry Wayne Hickey 1995
Molly Virginia Oxendine 1996
Michael Maria-Lyne Richardson 1997
Joy Johnson Hewett 1998
Philip Wayne Ritchey 1998
Amanda Louise Kelly 2001
Michael Allen Taylor 2003
Marsha Danielle Marcum 2004
Joshua Edward Cravins 2006
Kimberly Tracy Morgan 2006
Brandy Nicole Leitner 2007
Christie Dawn VanNorstran 2008
Barry Wayne Hickey 2009
Kimberly Elizabeth Hay 2010
Mary Carolyn Taylor 2010
Kari-Anne Pettit 2012
Michael Allen Taylor 2012

AGRICULTURE RANCHING, FARMER

Charles Cecil Stallings 1927
Ned C. Stewart 1943
Orman Reid Burton 1947
John A. Rickett 1948
Thomas C. Quarles 1949
Odell Gilreath 1950
Jack Sawyer 1951
Delbert Denney 1953
Wilbert B. Siler 1956
Samuel D. Perry 1959
David Goodman 1962

Gary Wayne Anderson 1964
Willard Sammy Hill 1964
Edward Clark Ralls 1966
Norman Ray McRay 1967
Earl Reed Jr. 1967
Charles Warren Lakes 1968
Gary L. Chitwood 1970
John W. Scoville 1970
Jack Ronald Corder 1971
William F. Cooper 1974
Esther Mason 1974

Jesse Everett Moberly 1974
Elizabeth B. Hooks 1981
Christopher Stacy McKeehan 1990
Sharon Marie Brillhart 2001
Janice Marie Musick 2003
Brandon Kyle Moehling 2006
Matthew Dylan Holt 2009

ANALYST

Howard C. Murray 1931
Nicky Moore 1960
Michael Louis Meyer 1974
Richard Stephens 1974
William Melton Charles 1975
Jordan Christopher Neel 1977
Arlene Elizabeth Armeli 1979
Margaret E. Wetherell 1979
Donald Edward Ballou 1980
Jeffrey L. Connor 1981
Anselmo Ornelas 1982

Carrie Vernia Dawson-Brown 1983
Marvin Brown 1984
Douglas Keith Blankenship 1985
Melinda Bennett 1986
Harold Lynn Jones 1986
Laura Ann Allinder 1988
Jeffery Wayne Caudill 1989
Michael Wayne Couch 1989
Susan Elizabeth Brockway 1991
Karen Denise Riel 1991
Laura Deanne Ormes 1992

Kim Kinser 1994
Steve Lamar Imel 1996
William Travis Baker 1997
Merritt Wilbert Reece IV 2000
Brooke Ashton Smith 2001
Jennifer Lynn Ruark 2002
Jessica Lynne Holbrook 2005
Timothy Craig Wylie 2009
Brandon Lee Yancey 2009

ARCHITECT, ARCHITECTURE URBAN PLANNING

James E. Ford 1948
Donald B. Shelton1953
Charles M. Porter 1955
Harry L. Siler 1959

John M. Maudlin-Jeronimo 1967
Ernest Layne Newsome 1969
Nicholas Joel Buccalo 1979
Roger Stephen Greene 1982

Arthur David Nichols 1986
Jared Franklin Tackett 2006

ART, ARTISTIC PROFESSION, ARTS FINE, ARTS PERFORMING, ARTS CREATIVE

Bonnie L. Langdon 1933
Charles Harrison Jones 1935
Lillian Moss Slight Trust 1938
Dottie Velma Smith 1950
Donald R. Runyon 1959
Sandra Ann Harris 1965
Robert Charles Young 1965
David Ray Farmer 1969
Janet F. Schnauber 1969
Linda Margaret Thatcher 1969
Suda F. Tuggle 1969
Vicki Sue Kuhn 1972
Charlotte T. Griffin 1974
Kenneth Prater 1974

Charles D. Worley 1974
Susan Thiel 1975
Nancy Jean Brining 1976
Bob E. Shelley 1976
Margaret Lee Sykora 1976
Elizabeth Anne Stevens 1977
Judy Rose Langford 1978
Richard R. Tunney 1978
Patricia Gail Clayton 1979
Susan Smith Bunch 1981
Jacqualeen Sellards 1981
John Pierre Lemaire 1982
Christopher Thomas Wolfer 1983
Edward Dennis Davenport 1987

Marlon G. Hurst 1990
Barbara Ann Willingham 1990
Jacquelyn Lee Borgeson 1992
Barbara Ann Willingham 1994
Shane Eric Caudill 1995
Jason Wayne Day 1998
Emily Jean Kraus 1998
Jennifer Marie Loveday 1998
Thomas Allen Hall 2003
Tabitha Rebecca Cuomo 2004
Shelly Danielle Sexton 2009
Erin Jessica Hammond 2012

ATHLETIC TRAINER

William Neal Quinn 1981
Pamela Ann Fitzgerald 1982

Shelly Lynn Blackburn 1997
Brina Kylene Strebeck 2002

Sabrina Stephens Pletz 2003

AVIATION AEROSPACE

John William Carson 1939
Bettie B. Wood 1941
John P. Moore 1953
Ted Garrison 1956

Gary M. O'Hara 1958
Milburn Hugh White 1959
David L. Lefevers 1963
Robert D. Messer 1964

Michael Douglas Carrigan 1971
Steve A. Reeves 1982
Bart Shannon Harter 1992
Michael Mark Sztanyo 1997

BANK RELATED

Clarence Cecil Shepherd 1926
Dempsey Ballou 1930
Willnetta Ruth Coates 1941
Lola Mary Wright 1942
Lillian L. Sullivan 1943
Delsie Horne 1948
Margaret Jean Owens 1950
Harold R. Bell 1951

Ralph Edwin Buchanan 1951
John H. Brown 1953
Kenneth L. Meadors 1953
Betty Jewell Hinton 1955
Lillian Joan Stacy 1956
Dennis R. Roberts 1958
Joyce Day 1959
Gorman Berry Croley 1960

Esley Ann Brennenstuhl 1962
Joyce E. Freeman 1962
Roberta Lovett 1965
Joyce Sue Watson 1968
Robert E. Harris 1969
Georgia Y. Noble 1969
Anna Mae Stigall 1969
Paul Edward Taylor 1969

Donnie L. Patrick 1971
Wallace Warfield 1971
Michael Carlos Bastin 1972
John Edward Lawson 1972
Michael D. Smith 1973
Randell Keith Day 1974
Gary W. Horne 1974
Julie A. Mallory-Yowell 1974
Linda J. Miracle 1974
Kenneth W. Cobb 1975
Linda Alice Roach 1975
Phillip B. Bramlett 1976
Elaine Braden 1979
Debbie Felts 1979
David L. Brown 1980
Barbara C. Grimsley 1980
Janet Lynn Neal 1980
Abbie Joyce Birchfield 1981
Frances Fuson 1981
Lisa Marie Jodlowski 1981
David M. Sullivan 1981
Gary Wayne Wagoner 1981
Joann Carol Dotson 1982
Joye B. Hunt 1982
Gregory Scott Russell 1982
Mary Betty Stivers 1982
Billie Lynne Begluitti 1983
Daylene J. Hensley 1983
Diane McClary 1983
Michael Thomas Blount 1984
Mary Lee Brock 1984
Sherry H. Bryant 1984
Donna B. Felts 1984
Lori Ellen Hampton 1984
Guy R. Jones 1984
Gordon Wade Kidd 1984

Teresa Wicker 1984
Shon D. Bearup 1985
Janet Leigh Sandlin 1985
Wayne W. Wollen 1985
Arlene C. Cottongim 1986
Duane Scott Flora 1986
Sherry Kay Housley 1986
Barry Scott Adams 1987
Judy Gail Faulkner 1987
Joseph G. Richards II 1987
Senait Berhe 1988
Jerry Radford Llewellyn Jr. 1989
Connie Michelle Cain 1990
David Kelly Garmon 1990
Teresa Lynn Hofstatter 1990
Michele L. Broxterman 1991
Scott John Burleigh 1991
William Barrett Cosby 1991
Jeffery Glenn Steely 1991
Krystal Schorre Floyd 1992
Loren Michelle Rose 1992
Michael Dale Sharpe 1993
Barbara Arlene Logan 1994
Candy Leeann Holbrook 1995
Kimberly Ann Hunt 1995
Donald Scott Collins 1996
Natalie Jeanette McGary 1996
William Michael Jarboe 1997
Nancy Jill Phillips 1998
Jonathan Calvin Williams 1998
Randle Everett Bargo 1999
Jessica Amber Bruner 1999
Kimberly Dionne Harris 1999
Jeffrey Chad Howard 1999
Shawn Everett King 1999
Robert Lewis VanLeer Jr. 1999

Cynthia Denise Jett 2000
Lewis Aaron Madron 2000
Allison Barnes Mull 2000
Robin Jane Sammons 2000
Russell Allen Upchurch 2000
Hong Kathy Zhang 2000
Eldon Townsley Jr. 2002
Cara Therese Wills 2002
Lindsey Joy Helveston 2003
Michael Owen Taylor 2003
Kelli Rae Carr 2004
Christopher Matthew Lundin 2004
Joseph Albert Salvato 2004
Jessica Leigh Tomi 2004
Nancy Ruth Abbott 2005
Dorian Wade Asher 2005
Anna Meadors Baird 2005
David Adeyemi Morris 2005
Evan Dana Akins 2006
Landen Earl O'Banion 2006
Heather Nichole Wilkes 2006
Pamela Michele Bunch 2007
Willard Kelland Ball 2008
Stanley Keith Jones 2008
Willard Kelland Ball 2009
Amy Danielle Blankenship 2009
Sherry Lynn Green 2009
Gina LaChale Marcum 2009
Brandi Cheri Mullis 2009
Rusty Wayne Ray 2009
Liberty Cabe Roberts 2009
Regina K. Smith 2010
Desaray Raven Wilson 2010
Rebecca A. Thompson 2012

BEAUTICIAN, FASHION BEAUTY

Attie F. Campbell 1970
Glenda L. Grigsby 1971
Linda S. Maloy 1971
Danna L. Nassida 1976

Jean A. Stephens 1977
Julie Lyons 1979
Dean Mark Stooksbury 1980
Lori Sue Haynes 1981

Timothy Lowe 1984
Julie Ann Hagenbart 1999

BROKER MANAGER, BROKERAGE SECURITY INVESTOR

Clayton Wendell Blanton 1959
Marilyn Brown Cundiff 1979
Timothy R. Guthrie 1989

Thomas Wayne Black 1991
Carrie Sue Mullens 1995
Jonathan Scott Minner 1997

Brandon Mulford Marsh 2002

BUILDING CONTRACTOR, CARPENTER, CONSTRUCTION CONTRACTING, CONTRACTOR, PLUMBER

Maynard E. Langdon 1950
Gerald Leigh 1950
Bill R. Booth 1955
Robert L. Teague 1955
Edward W. Haverly 1956
William Kent Howard 1957
Charles Kidd 1957
Arvil C. Mays 1958
Ernest L. Reynolds 1959

James H. Sutton 1960
John Bill Keck 1962
Leslie Franklin Gooch 1963
Glenn E. Worley 1964
Julian R. Harris 1965
Diamond Salmons 1967
Joe Kelly Asher 1968
Jerry Wayne Browning 1968
Bob W. Sparks 1969
Jerry Wayne Blair 1970

Ancil G. Cox 1970
Dennis Kearns 1970
Charles Lewis 1970
Richard Lee Gibbs 1972
Wayne Cooper 1973
Randall Warren Faulkner 1973
Terry Wayne Miracle 1973
Dennis Gorden Pate 1973
Darrell Lynn Gross 1974
Teddy Dwight Damewood 1975

Kenny M. Nantz 1976
Vernon Hoskins 1977
Brenda Kay Abner 1978
Danny Gimbel 1979
David Bruce Rhodes 1980
Russell Wayne Steele 1980
David Jonathan Wilson 1980
James Ed Kicklighter 1984
Ronald K. Pulley 1985
Shig O'Hara 1986
Timothy Lynn Cross 1987

William Jeffrey Davis 1988
Brian E. Grable 1988
Glen E. Mullennix 1988
Franklin Keith Brown 1989
Robert Anthony Oliver 1992
David Wayne Shirah 1993
Darren Lloyd Poore 1994
David Scott Shepherd 1994
Arthur Freeman Buis III 1995
Walter Winn Davis Jr. 1995
George Stephen Tuggle II 1998

John Anthony Jones 2000
Juston Lynn Cox 2002
David Thomas Destefano 2003
Jeremy Michael Prater 2003
Thomas Kyle Cato 2005
Aaron Logan Ellis 2005
James Weston Mullins 2005
Todd Michael Allen 2006
Aaron Elroy Gilpin 2010

BUSINESS ENTREPRENEUR, OWNER, BUSINESS PERSON, CEO, IMPORT/EXPORT

Catherine Elizabeth Gillis 1927
Don R. Smith 1932
Verlin Blankenship 1935
Charles D. Brown 1936
William Edwin Alcorn 1937
Gloria Carrel 1947
Jack B. Galbreath 1947
Dorothy B. Faulkner 1948
Betty Fish Smith 1948
Paul P. Steely 1949
Leland R. Crabtree 1950
George E. Faulkner 1950
Charles Eugene Watson 1950
Hildrige M. Bunch 1951
Jack S. Strange 1951
Roy Baker 1952
Norma Clark 1952
Kizzie S. Owens 1952
Betty Carol Broyles 1953
Don J. Conatser 1953
Nita J. Ewing-Thomas 1953
Joe C. Perkins 1954
William G. Ray 1954
Sterling Baird 1955
Harold Dennis Gross 1955
Shirley J. Kilgore 1955
Mary S. Smith 1956
Mary Ann Dodson 1957
Joseph H. Surgener 1957
Rondall Joe Sutton 1957
Charles Cornett 1958
Shirlie Elliott 1958
Dennis A. Spaulding 1958
James Harold Bailey 1959
Jessie Lee Baird 1959
Donald Ray Greene Sr. 1959
William E. Smith 1959
Thomas Creech 1960
Patty C. Ross 1960
Carolyn A. Taylor 1960
Vernon Baker 1962
Peggy B. Grabeel 1962
Donald Lee Grabeel 1962
Wilford L. Johnson 1962
Charles M. Miller 1962
Robert Leon Miracle 1962
Howard Edwin Shelton 1962
William Wade Slusher 1962
Dolores June Watts 1962
Richard Brashear 1963
Myrna Loy Combs 1963
Betty J. Fischer 1963
A. Bruce Rose 1963
Sandra J. Bourbeau 1964

Barbara Joe Colter 1964
Sam E. Hill 1964
Chester Benny Smith 1964
Rudean Adams 1965
Caner Patton Cornett 1965
Donald E. Ray 1965
Bob Roark 1965
Sandra Kay Brans 1966
John M. France 1966
Brenda Henson 1966
Janis Carol Herndon 1966
Hays McMakin 1966
Arville G. Phillips 1966
Jerry L. Poynter 1966
Pamela Chloe Cannon 1967
Shirley Combs 1967
Paul Clark Combs 1967
James Philip Kincaid 1967
Kyle Wayne Riner 1967
Jerry W. Stewart 1967
Linda Jean Bryan 1968
Lonnie C. Ellis 1968
Susan Safford 1968
Harold R. Smith 1968
Adney C. Taylor Jr. 1968
Roger D. Baker 1969
Garry Critt Ball Sr. 1969
Sharlene Brady 1969
Richard E. DeMarco 1969
Charles W. Heinzelman 1969
David Neil Keithley 1969
E. T. Stamey Jr. 1969
Ray Lipps 1970
Robert Wayne Malicote 1970
James A. Smith 1970
Peter Francis York 1970
Joe Virgil Bailey Jr. 1971
Larry Bundy 1971
Judith Ann Hause 1971
Garry Lynn Henson 1971
Gary J. Strayer 1971
Steven Joseph Arnold 1972
Patricia Crist 1972
Leon Justice 1972
Richard L. Kagy 1972
Dan Lawson 1972
Gordon R. Loomis 1972
C. Wesley Morgan 1972
David R. Owens 1972
Patricia D. Walker 1972
Boyd Dean House 1973
Berneda Buell 1974
Dorothy Marie Goodwin 1974
David Y. Higgins 1974

Jack R. Trammell 1974
Von Dale Allen 1975
Frank Bizjack 1975   •
Penelope Maria Davis 1975
Robert A. Kellough 1975
Stephen D. Logan 1975
James Philip Majors 1975
William E. Nevin 1975
Charles E. Reed 1975
Hershel Collett 1976
Ashley A. Parker 1976
Rick L. Pickett 1976
Danny Wayne Marcum 1977
Bernard Joshua Johnson 1978
Max C. Phelps 1978
William Arnold Deaton 1979
John Michael Gallen 1979
Douglas James George 1979
Robin Gail Haines 1979
Thomas Lamb 1979
Connie M. Riddle 1979
Ed A. Skaggs 1979
Jeri West 1979
Donald Wayne Burdine 1980
Won G. Chu 1980
Kathleen L. Martin 1980
Tanya L. Patrick 1980
Bobby Joe Petrey 1980
Larry Ray Witt 1980
Lucille Bowling Carloftis 1981
Nina Daniel 1981
Sonja K. Dittrich 1981
John Warren McCauley 1981
Gary D. Neal 1981
James Anthony Powers 1981
Christopher L. Seale 1981
Lura Louise Janbakhsh 1982
Paul Douglas Scheuer 1982
Barry Keith Woodlee 1982
Mitchell Ben Harmon 1983
Connie H. Kerns 1983
Kerry C. Phelps 1983
Roger Wayne Wattenbarger 1983
Robert Dewayne Anderson 1984
Steven Wade Canada 1984
Christina Finley 1984
Jeanna Renee Hall 1984
Lesly Rayna Terry 1984
Margaret Ann Wollen 1984
Elizabeth J. Adkins 1985
Drucilla P. Aubrey 1985
Gordon Lee Miller 1985
Judge K. Burns 1986
Glenn Warren Caudill 1986

Melody Lynn Hall 1986
Randolph Scott Roark 1986
John S. Saba 1986
Danny E. Hall 1987
Michael W. Ray 1987
Walter Brian Thornton 1987
Claudia Marie Bojantchev 1988
Patricia Carole Curry 1988
Anthony L. Bell 1989
Marvin Junie Hemphill 1989
Kathy Jane McCoy 1989
Kimberly L. McKinney 1990
Michael Wayne Yeazel 1990
Richard Bates 1991
William McKinley Bryant 1991
George Lloyd Potter 1991

Jennifer A. Boren 1992
Bradley Dale Greer 1992
Timmy Dean Hill 1992
Richard Darrin Spencer 1992
Daniel Lee Callahan 1993
Gary Sean Elliott 1993
David Todd Hurst 1993
Bobby Kidd 1993
Coleen Shay Hewitt 1994
Daphne Renee Loze 1994
Charles William Allen 1995
Solomon Mullins Jr. 1995
Eric Gerald Smith 1995
Marcy Rochelle Freeburg 1996
Michael Alan Griebe 1996
Robin Allison High 1997

Julie A. Jordan 1997
Stephen Paul McLeod 1998
Wendy Lynn McHolan 1999
John Christopher Baird 2001
Kyle Douglas Bargo 2002
Julie Ann Hesson 2003
Michael Carl Jones 2003
Phillip Heath Payne 2005
John Alexander Tyler 2005
Todd Irvine Petzold 2006
Donna Karen Allen 2007
Amber Leigh Malicote 2007
Stephen Marcus Reddy 2007
Steven Lynn Cole 2009

CASHIER

Jeane Elizabeth Raby 1974
Tina Maria Howard 1988
Peggy Suzanne Estes 1995

Marjorie Faye Frazier 1998
Shannon Amanda Parker 2000
Rebecca Marie Rains 2006

Seth Nathanael Ellis 2010
Scarlett Faith Thomas 2010
Scarlett Faith Thomas 2011

CHEMIST

Charles J. Barton 1930
William Woodrow Ayers 1934
Roy Hobbs 1955
James Parker Brown Jr. 1968
Burchen D. Helton 1968
Gary W. Parks 1971

Roger Wayne Roark 1972
Dennis Blaine Steely 1977
Richard L. Shields 1980
Kimberly Susan Hanzelka 1982
Gerald L. Hitch 1982
James D. Stout 1982

Deborah Kay Bailey 1983
Karolyn S. Nelson 1991
Misti Lea Jones 1996
Gregory Keith White 1998
Anderson Lloyd Chinn 2000
Hannah Renee Lane 2005

CHILD CARE

Clelie Bourne 1977
Margaret Ruth Couch 1978
Charlotte Dupier 1980
Juanita Arlene Johnson 1980
Deborah Lynn Atkinson 1984
Deborah Lynn Atkinson 1988

Ann Marie Hundley 1992
Larina Lynn Wagers 1995
Heather Lee Price 1998
Sarah Maxine Russell 1999
Leanne Ray Brackey 2001
Julie Allison Smith 2001

Nicole Marie Jones 2003
Rebecca Mae Barkley 2007
Nicole Marie Jones 2008

CHIROPRACTOR

Rodger Farragher 1976
Jeannie L. Terrell 1977

Steven Karl Newton 1980
Otis Brandon Forrester 2000

CHURCH EDUCATION DIRECTOR, CHURCH RELATED, YOUTH MINISTER, CHURCH RELATED MINISTRY CHILDHOOD EDUCATION

Louis B. Cochran 1929
Della R. Andrew 1975
David L. Burt 1976
Susan Thompson 1976
William Frank Thompson 1977
Cheryl Lynn Deal 1979

Willis Bennie Bush 1980
Stephen Earl Ellis 1981
Kristina Beth Barker 1994
Abigail Elizabeth Wilder 2000
Toney Edward Cooksey Jr. 2003
Charles Ryan Sumner 2003

Alice Boechat Lemos Tremaine 2003
Andrew Michael Mahan 2004
Susanne Elizabeth Pederson 2008
Anthony David Jolly 2009

CLERK CLERICAL, DOCUMENT EXAMINER

Lexie Huffaker 1939

Imogene Schoch 1952

Gail Sharon Roark 1958

Carolyn Sue King 1962
Joanne Maggard 1964
Betty Kade Gamblin 1967
James B. Prewitt 1967
Fred H. Thomas 1967
Harvey Smith Duncan Jr. 1970
Steve Rodeheffer 1970
Sandra Louise Dickhaus 1971
Robert E. Rudd 1971

Susan M. Moses 1975
Donnie Lowell Partin 1978
Tom Rains 1979
Ralph D. Roaden Jr. 1979
Kimberly Charlene Gilbert 1982
Teresa Ann Black 1984
Philip Taylor Keith 1985
R. Barry Minton 1986
Rick L. Russell Jr. 1987

Margaret Renee Smith 1988
Kim Kathleen Higgins 1991
Zachary Kenton Lynch 2004
Jennifer G. Daugherty 2006
Joshua Wade Davidson 2009
Chasity Jo Gambrell 2010
Heather Raschelle Henson 2010
Jamie Nicole Rhodes 2010
Jacqueline Sue Shelley 2010

COACHING, ASSISTANT COACH

Kenneth Earl Hicks 1965
Gordon Dale Bocock 1967
Chris J. Ferguson 1981
Rhonda Lynn Broyles 1983
Leroy Ryals 1989
Jeffrey Thomas Renshaw 1990
Jeffrey Thomas Renshaw 1991
Lars Goran Andersson 1994
Vicki Ellen Helton-LeMaster 1994
Melissa Elayne Irvin 1995
Jerry Patrick Herron Jr. 1996

Jerry Patrick Herron Jr. 2003
Edward Mahan Jr. 2003
Andrew S. Medders 2004
Brian Nicklas Rosario 2005
Ryan J. Baily 2006
Jerrod Michael Martin 2006
Brent Michael Vernon 2006
Beth Ann Wooley 2006
Sabrina Arlene McCullough 2007
Wilkennthsner Prophete 2007
Melissa Elayne Irvin 2008

Nicholas Ryan Philpot 2008
Sacha Maria Santimano 2008
Bradley Dwight Shelton 2008
Brent Michael Vernon 2008
Gary Wayne Rach 2009
Shane Hamilton Anglin 2010
Elizabeth Ashley Butt 2010
Shane Hamilton Anglin 2011
Wilkennthsner Prophete 2012
Beth Ann Wooley 2012

COLLEGE PRESIDENT, COLLEGE RELATED

Lillian Beatrice Simms 1929
Alan C. LeForce 1965
Pearl Jean Baker 1968
Jerry C. Davis 1968
Micaiah Bailey 1970
Linda C. Sutton 1974
Terry H. Stigall 1975
Belinda L. Morgan 1976
Betsy A. Gray 1982
Patsy Lynn Cross 1983
Jana Kay Bailey 1984
James Edward Moore 1984
Bill E. Rains 1984
Bill E. Rains 1987
Carla Sue Rawlings 1989
Walter Scott Bryant 1990
Myrin Montell Roberts 1990
Trent Richard Grider 1991
Crystal Gail Broyles 1992
Brenda Gwen O'Dell 1992

David Duane Close 1993
Brett Patrick Crowley 1993
Corey Terrell Holliday Sr. 1993
Laura Jeanette Smith 1993
Daniel Stephen Fields 1995
Gina Lori Bowlin 1998
Johnny Chris Hill 1999
Jeffery Douglas Mills 2000
Elizabeth Ann Booker 2001
Sara Beth Mahan 2001
William J. Temple 2001
Timothy Edward Wolz 2002
Edward Mahan Jr. 2003
Mindy Erin Rector 2003
John Marc Hensley 2005
Erin Lee Stockdale 2005
Tanya Rene Gilmore 2006
Roy Matthew Rhymer 2007
Christopher Wayne Sexton 2007
Jonathan Andrew Fister 2008

Tanya Rene Gilmore 2008
Tonya Gail Maynard 2008
Kellene Joy Turner 2008
Angela Lee Asher 2009
Stephanie Renea Bowlin 2009
Sarah Elizabeth Hammond 2009
Boyd Anthony Kidd 2009
Tatsuro Kusunoki 2009
Randle Lee Teague 2009
Tanya Rene Gilmore 2010
Elizabeth Ann Booker 2011
Tonya Gail Maynard 2011
Sherry E. Roaden 2011
Gina Lori Bowlin 2012
Heather LeAnn Cole 2012
John Marc Hensley 2012
Roy Matthew Rhymer 2012
Paul Edward Stepp 2012

COMPUTER HIGH TECHNOLOGY, COMPUTER PROGRAMMER, SYSTEMS COMPUTER RELATED, SOFTWARE DEVELOPER

Cordelia Y. Strange 1931
Leona Irene Valentour 1941
Betty Walker 1951
Robert Earl Bartley 1952
Mary Eva Wright 1957
Donald Irvin Carnes 1959
Charles Truman McCracken 1960
Marvin Lawrence Gilreath 1962
Link D. Johnson 1962
Thomas L. Karsner 1963
Chester R. Lilly Jr. 1965
Frances Ann Toig 1965
Sonny Dion Boring 1966
Curtis Thomas Gross 1967

L. Cathern Bailey 1969
Donna S. Jones 1970
Shirley F. Noble 1970
Carol Janet Noonan 1970
Charles Wesley Perkins 1970
David E. Randall 1970
James Eugene Fellers 1971
Carlotta Travis Bartleman 1972
James Michael Rouse 1973
William Glenn Beil 1974
Gary Wayne Clements 1974
Jack Milton Preston 1975
F. Joseph Miller 1976
Dan Edgar Egner 1977

Rebecca Shields 1977
Stephen M. Gifford 1978
David Allen Reynolds 1978
Ginger Wilburn 1978
Robert Lawrence Harris 1979
Jack Stephens 1979
Jeffery L. Siler 1980
Alan Leon Patterson 1981
Paul Norman Williams 1981
Jeffrey Croley 1982
Eileen B. Lad 1982
Kyle Robert Theriot 1982
David Boyd Stephens 1983
Randal Wayne Adkins 1984

Donna Marie Brewer 1984
Deborah Maria McChargue 1984
Douglas E. Nelson 1984
Bonnie Lynn Partin 1984
Jeffrey Keith Wilder 1984
Steven R. Hall 1985
William Knuckles 1985
Kenneth B. Roaden Jr. 1985
Terry L. Singley 1985
Francis M. Trammell 1985
Ermias Tsehay 1985
Cynthia B. Wulfekamp 1985
Sara H. Miller 1986
Martha Elizabeth O'Hara 1986
Warren Louis Sippel Jr. 1986
Mark Edward White 1986
Jamie M. Bennett 1987
Donny Dewaine Bolton 1987
Kathy Carolene Kirkland 1987
Angela Hutsell Kress 1987
Nabil Saba 1987
David Wayne Cloud 1988
James E. Huddleston 1988
Robert Emerson Smith 1989
Fernie Day Williams III 1989
Ronald Eugene Brown Jr. 1990
Jerry Allen Conner II 1990
Timothy Lee Cox 1990
Helen Darge 1990
Rae Jeanne Doerman 1990
Maude Melissa Freeman 1990
Rebecca S. Hackler 1990
Charles Edward Hight 1990
Jesse Clayborn Meece 1990
Rula Saleem Saba 1990
Mark Aaron Terry 1990

Lance Lamar Treadway 1990
Jonah May Jr. 1991
Ronald William Herren 1992
Larry Nolan Kendrick II 1992
Lisa Denise Miracle 1992
Carson Leonard Hall 1993
Brian Michael Kearns 1993
Tammy Renae Meadors 1993
Jon David Spurlock 1993
Steven Mark King 1994
Gary Anthony LeMaster 1994
Chad Matthew Wick 1994
Jeffrey Leon Yount 1994
Kevin Wayne Becknell 1995
Melissa Lynn Hamblin 1995
Jason Eric Christman 1996
Amy Louise Cooke 1996
Barry Edward French 1996
Jennifer Nicole Reeder 1997
Lesley Jo Swann 1997
Brian Scott Anderson 1998
Robert Michael Brooks 1998
Duane Scott Grimes 1998
Michelle Rhea Gulyas 1998
Kyle Jason McCowan 1998
Christopher Lee Stephenson 1998
Janice Kimberly Vann 1998
Kevin Michael Whitten 1998
Jeremie Scott Woodall 1998
Travis Lee Adkins 1999
Gary Lee Goins 1999
Roger Dale Hensley 1999
David James Marble 1999
Carl Daniel Middleton 1999
Jeffery Matthew Miracle 1999
Paul Joseph Robinson 1999

Timothy Lawrence Sowers 1999
Chin Guan Tan 1999
Jiandong Jim Fan 2000
Velma LaVonne Hampton 2000
James Randall Miles 2000
Dante Lamont Sweatt 2000
Jason Mark Van Dyke 2000
Alexander Cox 2001
Virgie Gail Parnell 2001
Denis Brent Prewitt 2001
Ron Travis Profitt 2001
Eric Lee Ritchie 2001
Sarah Elizabeth Wiley 2001
Kara Faye Bradley 2002
Jason Thomas Burton 2002
David Clark Dennis 2002
Kevin Scott Lee 2002
Thomas Shellie Bayne 2003
Joy Kathryn Spencer 2003
Jonathan Ray Bright 2004
Jonathan Michael Patton 2004
Jamie Leann Rowe 2004
Jordan Joseph Britton 2005
Jessica Renee Shearer 2005
Martin Lee Goley 2007
Tammy Kay Lanham 2007
Michael Scott Farwell 2008
Natasha Nicole Owens 2008
Michael Anthony Patterson 2008
Dustin Hamilton Sansale 2008
Travis Lee Adkins 2010
Mark Aaron Terry 2010
Kevin Scott Lee 2011
Michael Anthony Patterson 2011

CONSULTANT

William Jasper McCreary 1939
Harold E. Eagle 1955
Joseph E. Early Sr 1959
Taylor N. Hollin 1960
Robert Lee Byrd 1961
Joseph E. Early Sr. 1963
Larry Kirk Helton 1966
Charlotte Ballou 1968
Brenda L. Odor 1969
Harry L. Turner 1969
Susanne C. Fortune 1971
Robert Paul Duff 1974
Ralph T. Maynard 1974
Nick Hanna 1975

Douglas Glen James 1975
Theresa Ann Thomas 1975
Max C. Phelps 1978
James Wayne Seivers 1979
Art Keith Guyton 1980
Phillip E. Applegate 1981
Allen Ray Watts 1981
Donna Kaye Wind 1982
Stephanie Ann Adams DO 1983
John Charles Taylor 1983
Randel M. Bonham 1986
Debra Lynn Hall 1988
Steven Andrew Sheffield 1988
Amon Wesley Couch 1991

Stephanie Christine Lindemann 1991
S. Andrew Stallworth 1991
Kristina Hall Whitesell 1992
Amon Wesley Couch 1995
Joseph Lou Deater 1995
Jill Kendra Arvanitis 1997
Derek James Orf 2001
Stella E. Delph 2006
Deborah Kay Lawson 2009
Mary Ruth Meadows 2009
Amon Wesley Couch 2012

COORDINATOR, VOCATIONAL COORDINATOR

Joanne L. Watts 1954
John Ed Craynon 1963
Danny A. Davis 1970
Warren E. Heatherly 1971
Glynna Jayne Brown 1972
Barbara Hubbard 1972
Crit King Jr. 1972
Patricia Gale Cooper 1973
Arthur R. Boebinger 1974

Sharon L. Britton 1975
Marbeth Sue Carmack 1977
Linda Lee Gritton 1977
William S. Sergent III 1978
Terry Ann Womack 1978
Debra Kaye Bostic 1981
Dedra Anne DeBerry 1981
Kathy Renae Stephens 1981
Paula Denise Hetzel 1985

Calvin D. Perry 1985
Chad Edward Joyce 1986
Karen Kay Kowa 1987
Diana Dugan Warmoth 1987
Connie Jo Barnett 1990
Greta Melissa Wright 1990
Cheri Lynn Dobbs 1991
Joy Lynn Langdon 1992
Lisa Nicole Allen 1994

Kimberly Dawn Richardson 1998
David Michael Baker 1999
Emily Marie Eskridge 2001
Kurt Clark Brockman 2003

Jennifer Dawn Edwards 2003
Samuel James Lufi 2003
Cynthia Dawn Major Bleier 2003
Jamey Leann Temple 2003

Chassidy Ann Turner 2006
Veronica Joyce House 2007

CORPORATE PRESIDENT, CORPORATE MANAGEMENT, CHAIRPERSON

Cloyd D. McDowell 1931
Clarence B. Brown 1937
Philip R. Torres 1937
Edgar Croley 1939
Claude M. Brown Jr. 1949
Tom C. Brown 1951
Jack R. Sellars 1952
Joel H. Safriet 1954
Charles D. Barnes 1955
Charles R. Dozier 1955
Edward L. Helton 1955
Oren L. Collins 1956
Geraldine Green 1956
J. W. Tyree 1957
Ercill Ray Hunt 1958
Dale Guy Simpson 1959
Janet Laval Slay 1959
Kenneth Roger Foster 1961
Donald Gene Dobson 1963
Glover Fugate 1963
Dennis G. Lay 1963
Alvin E. Hickey 1964
Paul Eugene Gipson Jr. 1965
Robert A. Ohler 1966

Thomas Potter 1966
Dennis Wayne Byrd 1967
Patricia A. Perry 1967
Charles W. Axten 1968
Ronald Edward Reinstedler 1968
C. Howell Wilson 1968
David L. Childs 1969
Clifford Edvan McNeeley Jr. 1969
Ronald Lynn Patrick 1969
Ralph D. Shope 1969
Gary I. Conley 1970
Cort Joseph Dondero 1970
Holbert E. Hodges Jr. 1970
Larry Thomas Enscore 1971
Gary T. Hampton 1971
C. W. Mayes 1971
Glenda Price 1972
Jerry A. Rickett 1972
Terry Ray Sowder 1972
Jack L. Coffey 1973
Stephen Randall Widner 1973
Thomas Joseph Cooney 1974
Nick F. Greiwe 1974
David Wayne Keen 1974

Dan R. Brock 1976
Joel Preston Yaden 1976
Marc C. Ames 1978
Kevin Browning Castleberry 1978
Debbie Ann Flynn 1978
Steve Howard 1978
Al J. Lang 1978
Tom W. Lovett 1978
Marvin C. Baker 1979
Tammy L. McCall 1979
Edward J. Scala 1979
Mary E. Bowman 1980
Jim A. Gardner 1981
Robert Glen Graves 1981
Gary E. Tillman 1981
Keith A. Kinder 1982
Barbara M. Neubert 1985
Stephen Russell Jones 1986
Ronald Alan Coppock 1987
Norvan C. Blakley II 1989
Alexander Michael Martinez 1998
Hugh Edward Unger III 2002
Eric Lewis Greer 2010

COUNSELING, COUNSELOR, GUIDANCE COUNSELOR

Ross Chasteen 1932
Irene H. Holbrook 1941
Eunice D. Howerton 1948
Marjorie S. Walden 1951
Gail Owens 1954
Anna Spurlock 1954
Clive White Jr. 1955
Orville Cupp 1958
Patricia Ann Herr 1959
Billy L. Jett 1959
Bobby D. Hatcher 1961
Fred W. Robbins 1961
Mary Louise Elizabeth Angel Ph.D. 1962
Charles Richard Creech 1962
Norman W. Ferguson 1962
Carolyn S. Smith 1962
Henry Freeman Thompson 1962
Lois West Harris 1963
Robert Hollingsworth 1963
James F. Perkins 1964
Wallace Franklin Pursiful 1964
Larry Thomas 1964
James Darrell Brashear 1965
William J. Lee 1965
James Edward Stewart 1965
Sara K. Caudill 1966
Connie S. Hatcher 1966
Roger G. Hollars 1966
Kenneth Roger Johnson 1966
David Jones 1966

Roy L. Miller II 1966
Sondra Owens 1966
Gary Q. Teague 1966
Frank B. Abdoo 1967
Linda Charlene Flowers 1967
Joe E. Rains 1967
Sharon R. Davies 1968
Donna Kay Paul 1968
Lowell David Ball 1969
Linda E. Barlow 1969
Judy Carolyn Cook 1969
Jerry Walter Potinsky 1969
Mary Susan Flynn 1970
Margie Lee Hampton 1970
Gail E. Krahenbuhl 1970
Anita Mullins 1970
Larry W. Parman 1970
Jerold Gary Cordell 1971
Lillian Ruth Emory 1971
Janie H. Ledbetter 1971
Ronnie Mayne 1971
Christine M. Moore 1971
Marilyn Evans 1972
Hettie Viola Lyttle 1972
Kenneth Wesley Roark 1972
Jennings Asher Roberts 1972
Patricia Sue Bailey 1973
Judy G. Biechler 1973
William R. Harpool 1973
Kathy Lynn Harris 1973
Charles Leroy Cox 1974

Umbelina R. Jalowski 1974
Joan Marler 1974
Ken Carvalho 1975
Martha Chambers 1975
Steve Craig Karnehm 1975
Jerry R. Moses 1975
Gary B. Taylor 1975
David R. Webster 1975
Earl Black 1976
Larry Douglas Heaton 1976
Derryl Renee King 1976
Jeanne W. Carson 1978
Elizabeth Greer Cunningham 1978
Randell G. Touchatt 1978
Douglas Lynn Vicars 1978
Phillip C. Colton 1979
David Wayne Dryden 1979
Laurie P. Martishius 1979
Dale Vaughn Whitaker 1979
Gary M. Collins 1980
Carolyn C. Dryden 1980
Michael Eugene Martin 1980
David A. Mullins 1980
Jo Ann Sharpe 1980
Valerie W. Ward 1980
Linda Bailey 1981
Karen Rose Collins 1981
Revel Dawson III 1981
Kathy L. Oller 1981
Anita Gale Prater 1981
Thomas E. Siler 1981

Maurine N. Triplett 1981
Colleen F. Terry 1982
Kathy Malcolm Hall 1983
Gracie Mae Lay 1983
Pamela Ruth McGeorge 1983
Deborah Gail Thompson 1983
Joseph Smith Arnold 1984
Tekaligne Berhanu 1984
Paul D. McNeil 1984
Phillip Steven Fann 1985
Charles D. Jones 1985
Alan Bernard Buchanan 1986
Barbara Lynn Lawson 1986
Drew Preston 1986
Steven Drew Preston 1986
Twyla Susan Hammons 1987
Alice Lucille Smith 1987
Cindy Rae Dillman 1988
Sandra Lee Dodson 1988
Darla Christine Crawford 1989
Clinton E. Hammack 1990
Cheryl A. Looney 1990
Brenda Sue Rose 1990
Stanley E. Taylor 1990
Deborah R. Wesley 1990
Thomas E. Siler 1991
Katrina M. Vaughn 1991

Matthew Douglas Geyer PsyD 1992
Donald Brooke Jones 1992
Timothy Jay Todd 1992
Regina Lee Bond 1993
Susan E. Bugh 1993
Chad Eric Sage 1993
Dorcas Fay Buhl 1994
Linette Kay McPhetridge 1994
Jennifer Grace Mullins 1995
Timothy Ray Stockton 1995
Wesley Alan Denham 1996
Shelby Dean Greene 1996
John Anthony Messer 1996
Russell Edward Carr 1997
Jo Ann Foster 1997
Emily Ruth Byrd 1998
Richard Lee Clark 1998
Rachel Ann Day 1998
Shauna Kaye McCullough-Dilworth 1998
Brian L. Fuston 1999
Retha Howard 1999
Lila Lynn Martin 1999
Heather Michele Owsley 1999
Chasity Lee Prewitt 1999
April Lynn Vermillion 1999
Amy Janette Foulkes 2000

Heather Evelyn Miles 2000
Andrew Land Cooper 2001
Amber Kay Earle 2001
Emily Elizabeth Van Dyke 2001
Katherine Jo Lackner 2002
Jenny Joanne Remack 2002
Michelle Elizabeth Henson 2003
Christopher Glenn Hoover 2003
Candace Nicole Kitts 2003
Deborah Ray McChesney 2003
Tiffany Lynn McCoy 2003
Uteaka Denise Knapp 2004
Jonathan Hampton Pinnick 2004
Rachel Theresa Tharp 2004
Christopher Kyle Kersey 2005
Erin Leigh Lanter 2005
Nicole Suzanne Powers 2005
Larissa Hope Roark 2005
Anna Marie Trautwein 2005
Lisa Joy Van Berkel 2005
LeNita Sheryl White 2005
Abbie Nicole Wilson 2005
Jennifer Leigh Lyon 2006
Katie Ann Barnes 2007
Tammy Jo Morgan 2007
Daniel Wesley Lowe 2008
Anna Marie Trautwein 2011

COURT RELATED, JUDICIARY

Jack D. Duncan 1950
Ronald Blaine Stewart 1953
Carolyn P. Mize 1962
Jerry D. Winchester 1963
William Frank Archer 1964

Buzz Carloftis 1973
Gail W. Watkins 1980
Patsy Roberts 1982
Tim Joseph Ballou 1983
Jeffrey Thomas Burdette JD 1986

Sherry Lynne Ausmus 1988
Patricia Ann Halcomb 1989
Marvin Lanell Shelton 1996
Christina Lynn Bright 1999

DATA PROCESSING

Ebert Keith Warren Jr. 1964
Patricia Sue Ray 1965
Alan Ray Tackett 1968
Michael W. Kellett 1974
Robert Queener 1977
Richard Chadwell Privette 1978

Shelly Delanea Griffith 1979
Debbie Moon 1979
Patricia Lynn Fox 1980
Rhonda Lou Bowling 1984
Alan Keith Bruce 1986
John William Engle 1986

Barbara E. Sears 1987
Robin D. Smith 1987
Barbara Lynn Abner 1988
Jamie Lee Bryant 1989
Mark Dewayne Irvin 1990
Michael Edward Combs 1991

DENTISTRY, DENTAL ASSISTANT

O. L. Ballou 1932
Charles C. Lowery 1938
Franklin Davis Jr. 1942
James E. Croley Jr. 1943
Henry H. Davis Jr. 1943
Ben Casey Sharp USN Ret. 1943
Clifton Raymond Smith 1943
Charles M. Smith 1943
Sam D. Ballou 1953
Elbert L. Ballou DMD 1955
Benny J. Wilson DMD 1961
Robert S. Adkins 1962
Byron Morris Owens DMD 1962
Susan S. Lee DMD 1965
Norma Jean Mink 1965
William B. Galbreath 1967

Robert L. Ballou 1968
John M. Patierno 1969
James Frank Shaw 1969
David E. Ison DMD 1972
Brendon Berg 1975
Henry Dale Coffey 1975
John David Mountjoy 1975
L. B. Moses 1976
John A. Jeffries 1977
James Dwight Williamson 1977
James Francis Cleary III 1978
Dennis K. Baird 1980
Steven L. Haines 1980
Anna Marie Rehrman 1981
Keith & Susan Gibson 1984
Susan B. Gibson 1984

Kimberly Yvette Whaley 1984
Glen Denham Anderson 1990
Michael Christopher Herren 1991
Adam K. Rich 1993
Calley Jo Perry 1994
Tonya Lynn Harmon 1995
Bradley Ray Harmon 1995
Jeffery Allen Townsley 1997
Darrin Ray Combs 1998
Jason Otto Gambrel DDS 1998
Rebecca Lynn Baker-Sams DMD 1999
James Donald Cooper II 2000
Caroline Faith Brown 2001
Amy Lee Welch 2008

DIRECTOR

Tallu Fish Scott 1946
Marjorie A. Barrett 1953
Margie T. Chellew 1954
James Arthur Hackney 1954
Joyce Vinson 1956
Rodney D. Van Zandt 1957
William G. Mullins Sr. 1959
Brenda S. Taylor 1960
Caleb Stephens 1964
Jerry W. Bruce 1965
Paul E. Cox 1965
Billy Ray Eversole 1965
Joyce S. Hewell 1965
Dickie J. Bruce 1966
Roy Dennis Burchwell 1968
Jimmy Ray Webb 1968
L. Michael Chaney 1969
Brenda Sue Charny 1969
David John Ellis 1969
Reuben E. Sawyers 1969
Diana L. Vandy 1969
Robert O. New 1970
Charles R. White 1970
Barbara Alice Childers 1971
Penny Maretta Ann Robinson 1971
Robert Alan Walker 1971
John Dennis Aldridge 1972
Carolyn Carson 1972
Joy Michelle Cupp 1972
Harold Edwin Givens 1972
Sharon Diane Dean 1974

Dianne R. Wolfe 1974
Deborah Jean Parker 1975
James E. Prim 1975
Monty Lee Salyer 1975
James R. Bradfield 1976
Larry Dodson Brown 1976
Gail DeLeon 1976
Joseph Daniel Jones 1976
Jeffrey Allen Royalty 1976
Bobby Karl Taylor 1976
Robert Charles Finch 1977
Mesrak Gessesse 1977
Grover Cleveland Harrison 1977
Pamela Sue Hodge 1978
Robert Stephen Jones 1978
Thomas Ray Smith 1978
Barbara Kay Moore 1979
Tammy Elaine Woody 1979
Donna L. Jarvis-Miller 1980
Bruce Allen Ellis 1981
Michael Anthony Jarrett 1981
Ellen Gail Phillips 1982
Sherry Lynne Creekmore 1983
David Lynn Gibbs 1984
Paul Jackson 1984
Timothy David Leach 1984
Matthew E. White 1984
Raymond Curtis Smith 1985
Kidest Mimi Hailegiorghis 1986
Jeff Hiett 1986
Rebecca Sue Shorrosh 1986

David K. Steele 1986
John R. Mitchell 1987
Kelly Lamont Raglin 1987
Christy Louise Sayres 1987
Georgina Lynn White 1987
Phillip Raymond Brewer 1988
Starla J. Hutson 1988
Charles Lavon Graves 1989
Kenneth Allan Channels 1990
Donna Rea Cooper 1990
Kime Sue Harris 1990
Amanda Golden Evans 1991
Mark E. Hensley 1991
Hoover K. Lee 1991
Tamara Lynn Stewart 1991
Derek Charles Plant 1994
Christopher Phillip Rood 1994
Lisa Lynn Sweatt 1996
Erica Lynn Wilson 1996
Christen Tomlinson Logue 1997
Jason H. Padgett 1997
Robert Michael Brooks 1998
Cheryl Jean Harvey 1999
Kimberly Lynn Fields 2001
Lynn Axten 2002
Beau Jason Canada 2002
Karen Virginia Morgan 2003
Daniel Edward Roberts 2003
Theresa Graceann Rhea 2008
John Henry Begley 2009
William Christopher Brewer 2009

EDUCATION ADMINISTRATION

Jean Lee Lanter 1923
Edward E. Sheils 1930
Elmer James Maggard 1931
Amy J. Cox 1933
Zola B. Rice 1933
W. R. Duerson 1934
Martin Lee Ellison 1934
Fred D. Trammell 1934
Clyde E. Rodgers 1935
Ray Fritts 1936
Jessica Floyd 1937
Loma J. Taylor 1937
Carl Oswald Adkins 1938
John F. Campbell 1938
Paul E. Carter 1938
Thelma Elizabeth Jones 1938
Edward C. Murray 1938
Waldo W. Smith 1938
Alice K. Hill 1939
Archie B. Hill 1941
Arnold F. Payne 1941
Edith Evans Bradford 1942
Alfred Garred West 1942
Ruby C. Stephens-Keeton 1943
Bertha B. Snowden 1944
John C. Alexander 1946
Clyde E. Hill 1946
Elmer Smith 1946
Jack W. Murphy 1947
Athalee A. Turner 1947

Ralph Campbell 1948
Vernon Wesley Evans 1948
Leland Lloyd Goodin 1948
Edgar A. Kidd 1948
Jackson Lance Partin 1948
Johnnie Arvil Perry 1948
Betty L. Taylor 1948
Jack Foley 1949
James Clyde Petrey 1949
Suzanne Quarles 1949
Arliss L. Roaden 1949
John Paul Young 1949
Mary Faulkner 1950
Denzil Othel King 1950
J. B. Mountjoy 1950
Betty L. Siegel 1950
Ruth Ann Spitler 1950
Russell E. Bridges 1951
JoAnn Chitwood 1951
LaVerne L. Jones 1951
Kenneth Ray Jones 1951
Bessie S. Lloyd 1951
Nevada Ann Partin 1951
Imogene Ramsey 1951
J. Baxter Hamblin 1952
Flora Mae Hicks 1952
Carlos Frank Lester 1952
Ike M. Slusher Jr. 1952
John Franklin Stringer 1952
Luster L. Strunk 1952

Eddie Brown 1953
James L. Davis Jr. 1953
William Curtis Foutch 1953
Joe C. Holcomb 1953
Joyce S. Majonos 1953
Ethel Eastridge 1954
Billie Sue Hood 1954
Conley L. Manning 1954
John Mays 1954
John D. Warren 1954
Betty Witt 1954
Arlis Chapman 1955
Jack Isaacs 1955
Sarah Monita H. Laws 1955
Peggy B. Park 1955
Lloyd Smith 1955
Orland Hoskins 1956
Pearl Ray Lefevers 1956
Dolores F. Morris 1956
James D. Turpin Ph.D. 1956
Willard L. White 1956
Dewey W. Bradley 1957
Dacker Combs 1957
Clarence T. Scott 1957
Robert G. Fox 1958
H. Keith Lawson 1958
Harold Lee Patterson 1958
J. C. Hensley 1959
Johnny Robert Mayne 1959
Donnie Ray Rains 1959

163

Anna Lee Shirmohammad 1959
Phillip R. Carter 1960
James Harve Hampton 1960
Ralph Madison Mays 1960
Charlene Witt 1960
William Franklin Baker 1961
Kenneth Ray Baker 1961
Lela N. Brooks 1961
Odus Tyler Cheek 1961
Roland Stewart Cornett 1961
Lyna Jo Cornett 1961
Charles Dixon 1961
Henry D. Howard 1961
Clarence W. Jarboe Ph.D. 1961
William E. Mayne 1961
Joan K. Miracle 1961
Bobby Ray Morris 1961
Irene Peace 1961
Jerry R. Ratliff 1961
Clancy H. Roth 1961
William R. Sullivan 1961
Jerry W. Thompson 1961
Phillip G. Catron 1962
Harry V. Dinsmore 1962
Jerry R. Fee 1962
Jeanette Fritz 1962
George Folton McFarland 1962
Charlie Edmunson McFarland 1962
Gerry Gregory Mills 1962
Charles Edward Moore 1962
Joseph Howard Pierce 1962
Gene Sell 1962
Edward Lea Smith 1962
Eugene Stagnolia 1962
Anna Laura Wegener 1962
J. C. Wilder 1962
Mitchell Lee Barrett 1963
Frankie Blakley 1963
Jennings Edward Byrd 1963
Anna M. Cole 1963
Roy Lee Croley 1963
Ray Dixon 1963
James Winston Fields 1963
Sheila Hollin 1963
Wesley Ray Jones 1963
Kenneth Ray Jordan 1963
Burlie Gene King 1963
Opal Miller 1963
Henry Morgan 1963
Mary E. Reed 1963
Arlene Rhodes 1963
Kale Saylor 1963
Ernest Lee Siler 1963
Gerald K. West 1963
Don Edward Wilson 1963
James W. Wright 1963
Phillip R. Baker 1964
Sallie Ginger Brashear 1964
Gertrude Bridges 1964
Charles Hubert Cameron 1964
James H. Daniels 1964
James Edward Davis 1964
Gwendolyn Noertker Fleissner 1964
Evelyn June Frady 1964
James L. Harbuck III 1964
John Robert Haynes 1964
Richard C. Hensley 1964
Coleman House 1964
Kenneth Gene Johnson 1964
Robert Samuel Lawson 1964

Larry Dee Lewis 1964
John M. Lowe 1964
Lewis Carl Madron 1964
Herman Moore 1964
Reba Jewell Osborne 1964
Bobby Curtis Rice 1964
Robert Lynn Rose 1964
Lola Deane Smith 1964
Benjamin Edward Taylor 1964
Martha E. Thornton 1964
Wendell H. Wilson 1964
Gerald K. Wilson 1964
Brenda W. Bedford 1965
Robert E. Blair 1965
Thomas Michael Bowdon 1965
Nancy Kay Bowling 1965
Earl Eugene Brown 1965
James Bush Cole Ph.D. 1965
Anna Louise Edwards 1965
Janelle R. Esch 1965
John Robert Heneisen 1965
Cecil Hoskins 1965
Susan Rosemary Huff 1965
Denver Jackson 1965
Ronald Franklin Jones 1965
Bertha Lou Lay 1965
De Alvin Martin 1965
Ronald D. Murphy 1965
Wade Slusher 1965
Elmer A. Sparks 1965
Arnold Wilbert Swain 1965
Bige R. Warren 1965
Jimmy Wilson 1965
Dickie J. Bruce 1966
Nan Rose Collins 1966
Donnie Collins 1966
Larry R. Compton 1966
Bessie Couch 1966
James Harbour Grogan 1966
Thomas E. Henegar 1966
Owen Hensley 1966
John B. Hornsby 1966
Larry C. Ison 1966
Sue Carrol Jacobs 1966
W. Lester Shelley 1966
Omus Shepherd 1966
Jerry Lynn Stout 1966
George Edward Walker 1966
James Darrell Watson 1966
Shelby Gene Watts 1966
Charles Kenny Cooper 1967
Clayton Douglas Cornett 1967
Joe Wayne McKnight 1967
Chester B. Osborne 1967
Kenneth Wayne Rickett 1967
Jimmy W. Roark 1967
Thomas J. Sizemore 1967
William Henry Smith 1967
Glenn Steely 1967
James A. Sutton Jr. 1967
Albert N. Webb 1967
Douglas Whitaker 1967
Robert Louis Anderson 1968
Jerry W. Bond 1968
James Ernest Boothe 1968
Nedra Brown 1968
Donald K. Byrd 1968
David Lee Chitwood 1968
Drucilla Clark 1968
Caleb Collins 1968

Jerry Wayne Cox 1968
Glenn Carter Crocker Jr. 1968
Terry Phillip Dixon EdD 1968
Dennie Clarence Gaw 1968
Charles M. Glanzer 1968
Richard Wayne Hamlin 1968
Kenneth Maynard Head 1968
Edwin Holbrook 1968
Betty Lou Huff 1968
Damon Huff 1968
Larry Edward McKeehan 1968
Jerry W. Minor 1968
Lloyd E. Nowlin 1968
Margaret G. Sizemore 1968
Bobby Wendell Slusher 1968
Roy Eugene Smith Jr. 1968
Earl Smith 1968
Sandra Ruth Stanley 1968
Garrett Wesley Swain 1968
Dinah L. Taylor 1968
James H. Taylor 1968
David M. Thompson 1968
Robert Allen Bell 1969
Betty Lou Bond 1969
Linda K. Brown 1969
Eugene Burnett 1969
Green Odell Calihan 1969
Charles Ray Campbell 1969
Anna Massey Collins 1969
Enoch Foutch 1969
Yvonne W. Gilliam 1969
Lynn Glanzer 1969
Gary Hackler 1969
Curt Hall 1969
Gerald Wayne Hammons 1969
William Darrell Hansel 1969
David M. Heath 1969
Donald Ray Hensley 1969
Angelo Kidd 1969
Homer Lawson 1969
Dennis Conley Minton 1969
Maudie Murphy 1969
Robert L. Roszell 1969
Fred Sagester 1969
Robert Franklin Smith 1969
James K. Sowder 1969
Pauline Adkins 1970
Phyllis Louise Amick 1970
Fred Anness 1970
Randell B. Baker 1970
Ronald Lee Branscom 1970
Allan Ray Chapman 1970
Patrick Sullivan Clore 1970
Harve J. Couch 1970
Sue P. Gambrel 1970
John Stanley Jones Jr. 1970
Raymond Frederick Kahre 1970
George Glen Karsner 1970
Jerry L. Lewis 1970
David W. Lewis 1970
Conley Manning 1970
Ricky D. McCrary 1970
Paul David Meadors 1970
Wallace Reed Napier 1970
Gene F. Owens 1970
Barbara D. Payne 1970
John R. Robinette 1970
Billy Harold Stout 1970
Elizabeth Sue Wake 1970
Larry E. Warren 1970

Charles D. White 1970
Lynnda J. Williams 1970
Russell Coy Alley 1971
Randall Delbert Baker 1971
Frank Wayne Baker 1971
Joie Bukowski 1971
Gary A. Bumgardner 1971
Marie Chadwell 1971
Michael W. Champion 1971
Michael Bruce Colegrove 1971
Wanda Faye Cornelius 1971
Penny Cox 1971
Larry Wayne Cox 1971
Ernest Lee DeBord 1971
Wallace Michael Denny 1971
Lawrence Lee Geise 1971
Elizabeth Ann Gray 1971
George Thomas Grove 1971
Gary A. Hensley 1971
Jerry Lee Hodges 1971
June B. Lominac 1971
Fred Marion 1971
Jane Sharp Morrow 1971
David E. Neuner 1971
Homer Radford Jr. 1971
Clayton W. Ray 1971
David R. Shepherd 1971
Kereath B. Smith 1971
Jack Lynn Stanfill 1971
Johnny L. Strunk 1971
Fletcher W. Tidwell 1971
Roger W. Walden 1971
Morris Dale Yates 1971
John Marion Ashurst 1972
Carl Emitt Baird 1972
Jerrie J. Bolton 1972
Janet Wiley Brashear 1972
Robert Lee Brewer 1972
Michael Wayne Burchfield 1972
Harold Ace Combs 1972
James Michael Davis Ret. 1972
Donald R. Douglas 1972
Bonita Duncan 1972
Larry Elliott 1972
Kenneth Ray Gann 1972
Tommy Giles 1972
Robert Glenn Greene 1972
Gwindlen Kay Hammons 1972
Darlene Hart 1972
Patricia Ann Howard 1972
Frank L. Jones 1972
Randy Gene Martin 1972
Kenneth L. McIntosh 1972
Marshall David Merris 1972
David V. Rains 1972
Vena Sue Raleigh 1972
Charles Henry Roberts 1972
Eddie L. Saylor 1972
Gary Smith 1972
David Lee West 1972
Woodrow Wilson Woods 1972
David Martin Wright 1972
William Otis Belcher 1973
Walter R. Benge 1973
Harry Lenn Chitwood 1973
Calvin Douglas Crawford 1973
Billie Walters Ferguson 1973
Connie Sue Lester 1973
Esther Marple 1973
Robert R. Massengill 1973

Wanda F. Moore 1973
Jimmy Morgan 1973
Shirley Louise Nelson 1973
Janice F. Reid 1973
Joe Robbins 1973
Yvonne Smith 1973
Robert H. Spacey 1973
Patricia Smith Stonecipher 1973
Raymond Sine Vater 1973
Robert V. Wagoner EdD 1973
Michael Lewis Deaton 1974
Ann Marie Longworth 1974
Andy McKamey 1974
John Phillip Nelson 1974
Charles M. Rice 1974
Kimber Lee Simonson 1974
Floyd Clarence Stroud 1974
Dawna Leigh Wilson 1974
Lonnie Ray Anderson 1975
Donald Ray Branim 1975
Kent J. Chapman 1975
Curtis Wayne Chitwood 1975
Roger D. Durham 1975
Richard Earl Grimsley 1975
Dwight S. Hoskins 1975
Mike Jones 1975
Michael Jay Jones 1975
Sandra Kay Lowery 1975
Tommy McKinney 1975
Patrick Montenegro 1975
Gary Layne Perkins 1975
Michael David White 1975
Hanna Broyles 1976
Cecil Ray Combs 1976
Doris Marie Cooper 1976
Debra Ann Desser 1976
Gilbert Michael Lay 1976
Ardith Wayne Napier 1976
David Lee Perkins 1976
Kenneth Powell 1976
Marilyn Radford 1976
Larry J. Robbins 1976
Rhonda Michelle Seger 1976
Thomas L. Shelley 1976
Jack Dean Sherman Jr. 1976
Sharon K. Valentine 1976
Pamela Jean Davis 1977
Steven Lee Hardock 1977
Schyler Jones Jr. 1977
Lonnie Morris 1977
Marna Lynn Roselle 1977
David Allison Woods 1977
Cynthia A. Durham 1978
Deborah A. Kelly-Hoehn 1978
Anita Lucille Lewis 1978
Karen Lynn McKinney 1978
James Clem 1979
Mary Lynn Coalson 1979
Barbara Jean Cox 1979
Kyle Denise Godfrey 1979
Stephen Ralph Hampton 1979
Debbie M. Harp 1979
James Clarence Harville Jr. 1979
Kimberly Jo Mantooth 1979
Olivia G. Minton 1979
Harvey Allen Pensol 1979
Kimberly L. Simpson 1979
Dennis Jackie Smith 1979
Carl V. Coalson Jr. 1980
James Douglas Frazier 1980

Shirley Phillips 1980
Richard E. Prewitt 1980
John Lee Robbins 1980
Mary Agnes Steely 1980
Scott Kelly Teague 1980
Sue Weedman 1980
Connie McDonald Brookins 1981
Patsy Bryant 1981
Sandra Gail Cox 1981
Dwight Edward Creech 1981
Elmer E. Hall 1981
William Daniel Jones 1981
Jimmi Susan McIntosh 1981
James Thomas Arnold 1982
Beverly C. Browning 1982
Paula Kaye Goodin 1982
Penny L. Hammons 1982
Loretta Jones 1982
Laura Jean Keown 1982
Emily Jeanette Meadors 1982
Robert Larry Taylor 1982
Paula Jean Trickett 1982
Connie Sue Belcher 1983
Bruce Kenyon Lay 1983
John Robert Taylor 1983
Mark Britton Bailey 1984
Carolyn L. Combs 1984
Joy Lee Comingore 1984
Wanda Renee Diamond 1984
Erica Ann Harris 1984
Alberta King 1984
Glen A. Miller 1984
Kathy Ward 1984
Richard A. Fleenor 1985
Charles Edward Lawless Jr. 1985
Timothy W. Moore 1985
Harold Dean Shotwell 1985
Robert Larry Taylor 1985
Gary Allen Meade 1986
Elaine Starr Ozment 1986
James Edwin Paul 1986
Lloyd Smith 1986
Norma Jean Thomas 1986
Edwin Wheeler Conover 1987
Ronald Alan Coppock 1987
Julena Edwards 1987
Donna Sue Longino 1987
Rhonda Petrey'Collins 1987
Betsy Rae E. Rains 1987
Charlotte Rhodes 1987
Connie Sue Belcher 1988
Anita Jo Davenport 1988
Lillian Carrie Norris 1988
Catherine Rene Rice 1988
Terry Alan Sweet 1988
Dinah L. Taylor 1988
Ray M. Ball 1989
Ergun Mehmet Caner 1989
Thomas Virgil Hoggard 1989
James Darrell Lacey 1989
Betsy Rae E. Rains 1989
Dorothy Jane Bays 1990
Molly Geneva Jones 1990
Kasee C. Laster 1990
George Scott McClanahan 1990
Deborah R. Wesley 1990
Amon Wesley Couch 1991
David Wayne Cummins 1991
Melissa Lynn Mee 1991
Timothy W. Moore 1991

Robin Lynn Pittman 1991
Charlotte Rhodes 1991
Paula Dianne Rickett 1991
Don Raymond Skipper Jr. 1991
Terry Alan Sweet 1991
Scott Kelly Teague 1991
Vincent Deon Henley 1992
Linda Lawson Reynolds 1992
B. Kevin Maples 1993
Rebecca Rae Price 1993
Shelia Fay Woodward 1993
Guy Robert Crubaugh 1994
Jenny Ann Sweet 1994
Paula Jean Trickett 1994
Harry Dale Winkler 1994
Amon Wesley Couch 1995
Dwight Edward Creech 1995
Marcee Renee Leach 1995
Douglas Lee Oak 1995

Elizabeth Nicole Branch 1996
Georgia Jo Dupier 1996
Charles Mayer Dupier III 1996
Lisa Maria Perry 1996
Rebecca Rae Price 1996
Larry Clinton Brown 1997
Harold Dean Shotwell 1997
Kelly Anne Stinnett 1997
Jennifer Lynn Wake-Floyd 1997
Jane M. Chandler 1998
Amy Leigh Greene 1998
Christopher Alan King 1998
Story Anne Stringer 1998
Raymond Russell Clere 1999
Shane Derek Goad 1999
Marcee Renee Leach 1999
Jason T. Mitchell 1999
Harry Dale Winkler 1999
Carla Renee Kersey 2000

Nicole Renee Bull-Eguez 2001
Omari H. Gletten 2001
Connie Lynn Sulfridge 2001
Tyrhon Renard Crawford 2002
Jimmy Allen Kidd 2002
Stacy Dittrich Mahler 2002
Kelley Anne Wood 2002
Paul Warren Baker 2003
Schyler Jones Jr. 2005
Holly Brooke Valentine 2005
Tonya Ann Frazier 2008
Brenda Sue Helton 2008
Georgia Jo Dupier 2009
Charles Mayer Dupier III 2010
Dennis Jackie Smith 2011
Daniel Butler Carney 2012
Amon Wesley Couch 2012

EDUCATION COORDINATOR, DEAN

Linda L. Carter 1972
Shanda M. Perkins 1974

Evelyn J. Hall 1981
Leslie Anne Boozer 1996

Ginger E. Leach 2001
Lucy Jennifer Fultz 2002

EDUCATION RELATED, SCHOOL RELATED

James C. Beavers 1957
Carl Ray Baldwin 1958
Anna Bowlin 1963
Curtis Edwin Skiles 1965
Wesley Bowlin 1967
Betsy Brentwood Pearce 1967
Donald Hatfield 1968
Jimmie Dale Murray 1968
George J.P. Sweeney 1969
Donna Sue Sonnenberg 1973
Kenneth C. Fread 1974
Curtis M. Baker 1975
Cy Nicholas Aures 1979
Carylon Marie Burdine 1982
Robyn Elizabeth Arnold 1986
Anita Lynn Spangler 1986
Edith S. Collett 1987
Carl Ray Baldwin 1988
Susan Faye Warmoth 1989
Sharon Faye Foley 1991

Cecilia Rose Prater 1992
Lansford Hobert Lay Jr. 1993
Jill Elizabeth Rainey 1993
Cathy A. Hoskins Chaffman 1994
Jennifer Rebecca Flores 1997
Tonya Diane Watkins 1997
Lansford Hobert Lay Jr. 1999
Sonya Michelle Breedlove 2000
Anna Lori Hollen 2001
Anna Lori Hollen 2001
Susanna R. Kendrick 2001
Curtis Moore Storm 2001
Jennifer Lynn Brown 2003
Stephanie Therese Moore 2003
Lori Elizabeth Barton 2004
Jessica Arlene Bertucci 2004
Karen Sonia Hensen 2006
Gretchen Rose Phelps 2006
Jessica Arlene Bertucci 2008
Joshua Ronnie Bowman 2008

Benji Carla Burchett 2008
Jami Lynn Benning 2009
Candy Lynn Curnutt 2009
Veronica Ashley Hoskins 2009
Sherry Lee King 2009
Amy Jo Scott 2009
Beverly Eileen Yancey 2009
Joshua Ronnie Bowman 2010
Melissa Dawn Jordan 2010
Lori Elizabeth Barton 2011
Sonya Michelle Breedlove 2011
Cathy A. Hoskins Chaffman 2011
Lisa Jo Caudill 2012
Shanna Lynn Hamm 2012
Anna Lori Hollen 2012
Anna Lori Hollen 2012
Lansford Hobert Lay Jr. 2012
Jennifer Elizabeth Perkins 2012

EDUCATION STUDENT AFFAIRS

Olan James Barton 1938
Lorraine Nance 1955
Myrna C. McGlamery 1959
Ann Hope Hollars 1966
Christine Cooper 1969
Susan Drucilla Ireland 1976
Carl B. Kidd 1976
Gloria Faye Blankenship 1978
Linda Mattingly 1978

Robin C. Prewitt 1982
Colleen Marie Dalga 1984
Dianne Noel Gallant 1985
Susan G. Burnett 1986
Karen Perry 1987
Lisa Michelle Lewis 1988
Sherry Denise Kelly 1992
John Dean Lavey 1992
Cynthia Elizabeth Downey 1994

Sherry Denise Kelly 1995
Christy Lynn Widener 1997
Tammy Lynn Stephens 1998
Jeffrey Scott Vincent 1998
Jessica Ruth Digh 2000
Jeremiah Everett Tudor 2003
Ashlee Lachele Alcorn 2005

ELECTRIC COMPANY RELATED, ELECTRICIAN

Robert Gene Petrey 1950
Ralph E. Arnett 1952
Lowell Bray 1956

Danny T. Gambrel 1968
Jerry L. Asher 1971
Clyde Warren Cooper 1973

James Perry Hampton 1980
Susan M. Elliott 1989
Clyde Warren Cooper 1992

ENERGY RESOURCES OIL GAS, OIL RELATED

Edna Belle Floyd 1946
Raymond A. Huffaker 1949
Douglas Hunter Ashby 1955
Darwin Dwight Carnes 1972
Clyde Vance 1973

Timothy Ray Reed 1979
Donald I. Curry 1980
Bishara S. Shorrosh 1986
Brian Lewis Vincent 2000
Reggie Jay Tipton 2002

James Brandon Creekmore 2005
Robert Lewis Allen 2008
William Franklin Lethcoe III 2008
Teresa Marlene Abbott 2009
Robert Lewis Allen 2012

ENGINEER, CIVIL ENGINEER, ENGINEER (TECHNICAL), ELECTRICAL ENGINEER, SYSTEM ENGINEER, ENGINERING

Milford Leandor Angel 1937
Alex H. Anderson Jr. 1940
Eugene Samuel Cantrall 1940
Paul Smith Croley 1940
Hubert Hall 1941
James Addie Shearer 1941
John J. Blankenship 1943
Paul Eugene Martin 1943
Arnold A. Murphy 1943
Evelyn Barnett 1946
Eugene M. West 1946
Donald R. Ellison 1947
John S. Taylor 1947
Sterling H. Bunch 1948
Frank W. Caddell 1948
Billy F. Caudill 1948
John D. Eastin 1948
Jesse Gibbs 1948
Austin Eugene Hickey 1948
Paul Ray Campbell 1950
Arnold Eugene Smith 1950
B. H. Evans 1951
Gerald Fee Gravett 1951
Gene E. Howard 1951
Robert K. Jones 1951
Lowell V. Poling 1951
Charles Albert Cornelius 1952
Arnold Birchel Magee 1952
Homer Dale Blythe 1953
Robert Brockman 1953
Richard Boyatt Jr. 1954
Charles Edward Broyles 1954
Bert Cox Jr. 1954
Frank D. Crabtree 1954
Joseph Lee Dykes 1954
Ray Harrison Thurmond 1954
Charles E. Croley 1955
Robert E. Frye 1955
Russell L. Ingram 1955
William Goble Jones 1955
Joseph Edward Scalf 1955
James Herbert Smith 1955
Lowell C. Strunk 1955
William E. Lane 1956
Kenneth A. Pennycuff 1956
Raymond Hoskins 1957
David Waide Hughes 1957

Doyle E. Buhl 1958
Cecil V. Cornett Jr. 1958
Jack W. McCowan 1958
Louis K. Bertram 1959
Mel C. Bunch 1959
Ortis Ronald Burns 1959
Emil De Vane Chapman 1959
Bobby F. Creekmore 1959
Roy E. Gilburth 1959
Darie F. Kmieciak 1959
Paul K. Roberts 1959
Edward H. Adams 1960
Carl R. Chambers 1960
Dale R. Logan 1960
Daniel K. Miller 1960
Fred P. Francis Sr. 1961
William A. Payne 1962
Joseph Miller 1963
Edward Francis Mize 1963
Byron B. Palmer 1964
Alvin Smith 1964
Jerry L. Lane 1967
Dana L. Ramey 1967
Jerry Wayne Campbell 1968
Phyllis Johnson-Ervin 1968
Glennis Earl Broyles 1969
Leamon Perry 1969
Earl H. Reed Jr. 1969
Curtis Neal Wilcox 1969
Walter Lee Cobb 1970
Jesse L. Blake 1971
Paul Edward Fields 1971
Timothy B. Henderlight 1971
Mark Steven Hoffman 1972
Annie Victoria Saylor 1972
Charles Mike Kirby 1973
James Arthur Powers 1973
Arthur E. Alvis Jr. 1974
Michael B. Gill 1974
William L. Turnbow 1974
Lonnie R. Warren 1974
Roger D. Wilson 1974
Kenneth G. Couch 1975
Ronald Wayne Garland 1975
Bradley J. Judge 1975
Tracy L. Shannon 1975
Ramona C. Sumner 1975

Steven Allen King 1976
Larry R. Dickson 1978
Herbert A. Sons Jr. 1978
John W. Brown 1979
Ralph C. Pemberton 1979
Michael Lee Bassett 1980
Gregory Keith Powell 1980
Michael Dobson 1981
Randall Dobson 1981
Kenneth John Moore 1981
Neal Christopher Peck 1981
William J. Griffith 1982
John W. Ledington 1982
Robert Elliott Campbell 1983
Edward L. Oller 1983
Bobby Bruce Anderson 1984
Bradley A. Daniels 1984
Lyle Lee Lankford 1984
Gary Minton 1984
Marty Joe Partin 1984
Billy Kendall Whittington 1984
Kelemwa Hailegiorghis 1985
Michael Calebs 1986
Harold Wayne Carter 1986
Timothy Edward Dorsey 1986
Christine R. Johnson 1987
Jeffrey A. Lucas 1987
Harold Cecil Raines Jr. 1987
Teresa Carol McKinley 1988
Russell Jennings Blakley 1989
Bryan Scott Istre 1990
Ralph Konrad McWilliams 1990
Julie McNeil Worthington 1990
Julie McNeil Worthington 1990
Josie Cassandra Clark 1994
James Larry Byers 1995
Fukare Aklilu Yimtatu 1995
Eric Alan Thornsbury 1996
Sherri Michelle Chappell 1997
Michael M. Cash 1998
Edward Leon Hardy 1998
Michael Brian Tolliver 1999
David Bruce Blakeman 2001
James Micheal Jamison 2002
Anthony Lampson Laschon 2003
Daniel Edwin Masten 2004
Walter Chris Harp 2005

Walter Chris Harp 2009
Robert Edward Hutton 2010

Joshua Adam Frosch 2011

ENTERTAINMENT

James Lynn Singleton 1970
Rory Dexter Alexander 1981
William R. White 1984
Joseph L. Kent 1987

David R. Dampier 1988
Anthony Maurice Luewellyn 1992
Jeffrey Scott Smith 1995
Jennifer Marie Loveday 1998

Michael Allen Taylor 2003
Michael Allen Taylor 2012

ENTREPRENEUR

Paul King 1952
Lanny Myers 1964
Sharon T. Sims 1967

Darrell L. Shirley 1978
Michael James Powers 1987
David Alan Skinner 1990

Michelle Ann Skaggs 1992
Tonya Lynn Cloe 1998
Michael James Powers 2009

ENVIRONMENTAL SCIENCE, ENVIRONMENTALIST, CONSERVATIONIST

Howard M. Stephens 1954
Richard C Rookard 1963
Kenneth S. Cress 1964
Jesse David Wilson 1964
James Donald May 1965
David Joe Depew 1971
Alan L. Kreps 1971
Linda S. Holmes 1973
Samuel William Avery Jr. 1974

Dennis Arnold Borden 1974
Michael T. Matthews 1975
Carson J. Payne 1975
Larry Garrison 1979
Jacqueline Fran Metcalfe 1981
Timothy Elmon Wright 1990
Russell Kenyon Danser III 1991
Tony Don White 1991
Charles Curtis Palmer 1996

Jason Wayne Bolton 1997
Christopher A. Rhorer 1998
Thomas Tyler Barbour 1999
Daniel Joseph Emmons 2000
James Alexander Majors 2000
Kyle Browning Hazlett 2001
Michelle Suzanne Baker 2006

FIELD REPRESENTATIVE, FIELD INSPECTOR

Jewell Emery Farris 1937
Phyllis Bowling 1948
Charles E. Marlow 1949
John B. Shoemaker 1952
David Greenwood Ridner 1963
Arlin David Prewitt 1964
Jerry Douglas Harville 1965
Walter Stewart Taylor 1965
Lonnie E. Wilson 1969

Robert L. Cheek 1970
Gary J. Lawson 1970
Ronald W. Bundy 1972
Fred A. Hoskins 1972
Danny Carmon Campbell 1973
Jackie Duane Champion 1977
John W. Mooneyham 1980
Cheryl Katrina Wheeler 1980
Sherry Lee Applegate 1983

Jamie W. Vermillion 1984
James Earl Koogler 1986
Caroline Barnes-Weygandt 1987
Karen Wyrick 1989
Amy Elizabeth Hamilton 1991
Anthony Eugene Irvin 1998

FINANCIAL ADVISOR, FINANCIAL ANALYST, FINANCIAL CONSULTANT, FINANCIAL SERVICES, TAX CONSULTANT

Everette F. Wilson 1922
Roy E. Stewart 1949
Vernon Wesley Thomas 1949
Joel W. Howard 1958
Reecie Stagnolia Jr. 1962
Judith Slone 1964
Hugh C. Spradlin 1964
Billy Wayne Whittaker 1965
Robert M. Wormsley 1965
Roger C. Smith 1967
James Dennis Monhollen 1969
Gary W. Derringer 1970
Stephen H. Nickerson 1972
Dale Daniel Walker 1972
Patricia D. Walker 1972
Randall L. Osborn 1973
Jay Dudley Wilson 1973

Richard D. Clark 1977
James Forrest Hough 1977
Kim Bang Le 1979
Rick Stephen Brewer 1980
Sherri A. Siler 1980
Brenda Sue Silvestri 1980
Amanda Stone Yntema 1980
Michael E. Pickern 1981
Ramona L. Seale 1981
Brenda L. McDaniel 1982
Tammy Cheryl Matney 1983
Lolita Leena Wilson 1985
Donna D. Brewer 1986
Karen J. Patton 1986
Bruce B. Sahli 1986
Michael Joe Parker 1987
Amy Lynn Huss 1988

Brian Scott Oakley 1988
William Garrett White 1988
Lisa Gates-Kovinchick 1989
Susan Faye Warmoth 1989
Kathy Ann Keith 1990
David Brian Sexton 1990
Heidi N. Hall 1991
Kevin Blaine Widener 1991
Steven McIntyre 1992
Romel Tassew 1992
Cameron Mark Bowman 1993
Sandra Dee Cullins 1993
Charles F. Layman 1994
Ying Wang 1994
Elizabeth Brady 1995
Stefanie Ann Gallagher 1996
Fady Dabbah Issac 1996

Joseph McKinley Woods 1996
Anthony Keith 1997
Andy Chuen-Keong Khoo 1997
Kevin Blaine Widener 1997
Travis J. Wortinger 1997
Susan Christina Bradley 1998
Tammy Cheryl Matney 1998

Karen Gail Powell 1998
Nedrah Carrie Stagner 1998
Stephen Wesley Hatfield 2000
Christy Lee Rose 2002
Hugh Edward Unger III 2002
Joshua James Wilcox 2002
Heather Elaine Hart 2004

Wai Kin Khoong 2005
Linda Ruvarashe Chiromo 2006
Shawna Jo Lundin 2006
Rhonda Kay Hatfield 2008
Andrew Christopher Johnson 2010

FIREFIGHTER

Raymond L. Dean 1968
Curtiss Glenn Herd 2004

Ernest Gregory Spreitzer 2005
Cecil Todd Hollen 2006

FUNDRAISING

Bill F. Freeman 1949
Arthur L. Criscillis 1976

David Bergman 1989
Jeffrey (Jeff) Lynn Steely 1990

Dianne Marie Reach 1992

FUNERAL SERVICES, MORTICIAN

Ralph W. Jeffers 1956
R. Don Adkins 1966
Raymond Willis Adams 1972

Gary Lynn Harp 1980
Crayton Greer Ellison 1981
Larry Stephen Lisenbee 1983

Regina S. Paul 1993
Christopher Wayne Orr 1999

GEOLOGISTS

Donald C. Haney 1956
David K. Morris 1975

John Randolph Walter 1975
Oscar Barton Davidson 1976

Stephen Jerry Patrick 1982

GOVERNMENT RELATED

Mildred Oaks Barringer 1932
Chester F. Coffey 1936
George Edgar Everly 1937
A. Y. Morgan 1937
Earl Raymond Sutton 1937
Clarence Arthur Cornelius 1938
Anna Lee Young 1941
Samuel T. Vanover 1942
Tip Edward Cobb 1948
Ernest E. Bunch 1949
Clifford P. Jones 1949
Lois M. Thwaite 1949
Christine Vincent 1949
Charles H. Crowe 1950
Charles Lewis Siler 1950
Norman Lee Stephens 1950
Clyde Newman Rains 1952
Howard Dykes 1953
Bradley D. Hamblin 1954
Dwight Martin Hendrix 1954
Eddie C. Lovelace 1954
Lawrence Reeves 1955
Chandler P. Strunk 1955
Jo Elizabeth Dulworth 1956
Howard Dean King 1956
Lillus C. Campbell 1957
Carl E. Campbell 1957
Gene R. Graves 1957
Ralph D. Roaden 1957
Joseph W. Alfred Jr. 1958

Winslow Baker 1959
Russell Giles Bell 1959
Joyce Ann Clark 1960
James Ellis Wallace 1961
Jerry Franklin Taylor 1962
Jerry Lee Connell 1963
Carolyn M. Green 1963
Jimmy Arnold Stephens 1963
Charles Richard Jody 1964
Bruce Phillip McCutchen 1964
Frank E. Cameron 1965
John Greene 1965
Jimmie R. Mosley 1965
Norman W. Brown 1966
William C. Henning 1966
Lana Sue Witt 1966
Gary L. Scalf 1967
Jewel Lee Vanderhoef 1967
Janet S. Hollingsworth 1968
Larry Gale Price 1968
Elsie Mae Smith 1968
Clayton W. Gibson 1969
Edward E. Hummel 1969
Larry R. Patrick 1970
Kyle L. Privett 1970
Orin Bruce Wells 1970
Evelyn Carol Blair 1971
William Dester Lay 1971
Winston K. New 1971
James Robert Cooper 1972

Judy Ann Parsons 1972
Jimmy Russel Powers 1972
James L. Segda 1972
Phyllis Irene Bingham 1973
Thomas E. Buckley 1973
Gary Morgan Faulkner 1973
Jack Dean Gray 1973
Willis Clayton Hubbs 1973
Charles G. Woodall 1973
Raymond Calvin Braden 1974
Henry Dale Hall 1974
Gene Allen Hancock Jr. 1974
Leslie C. Mayfield 1974
Andrew David Meadors 1974
Clifford Ray Moses 1974
Stephen B. Mays 1975
Jo Moran 1975
Eileen Holderfield 1976
William J. Peeler 1976
Kenneth R. Satterfield 1976
Forrest G. Smith 1976
Don Ray Stricklin 1977
Gary W. Barton 1978
Katherine Farler 1978
Samuel Benjamin Gilbert 1978
Frederic D. Hall 1978
Lawrence Devoe Harris 1978
Jeffrey L. Jagnow 1978
Donald Carl Meadors 1978
Gregory S. Rose 1978

Charles Curtis Siler 1978
Philip L. Webber 1978
Donna Fay Blevens 1979
Darrell Hollis Holcomb 1979
Bruce Allen Laine 1979
Lawrence Edward Anderson 1980
David L. Buck 1980
Larry Roger Chandler 1980
Affell Grier 1980
Deborah G. Hill 1980
Walter Petrule 1980
Patricia Anne Smith 1980
Donnie L. Adkins 1981
Jeffrey L. Connor 1981
Deborah Kay Eubank 1981
Colan J. Harrell 1981
Thresa Marcel Jagnow 1981
June Terrell Parker 1981
Bob Proud 1981
Helen Rae George 1982
Timothy Wayne Gray 1982
Sheila S. Owens 1982
Roger E. Prewitt 1982
Kris Oscar Ringgold 1982
Jennifer M. Tindle 1982
Marcella Bowling 1983
Edward J. Liddie 1983
Willie B. Randolph 1983
Mary Ann Young 1983
David Cecil Bowman 1984
Ruth A. Combs 1984
Clifford Earl Curington 1984
Kimberly Lynn Girdner 1984
Aunderia Jevonna Jones 1984
Jeffrey Todd Parker 1984
Rondal Ray Sears 1984
Billy J. Terry 1984

Suzanne W. Underwood 1984
Allen Ramsey 1985
Ramona H. Smith 1985
Laura Sue Gaines 1986
Richard Kevin Hall 1986
Larry Earl King 1986
Nelson Eddie Miller 1986
Vicki Eileen Sawyers 1986
Melissa Kaye Smith 1986
Rosa L. Combs 1987
Joyce Faye Parker 1987
Janine K. Shackelford 1987
Leila Wauita West 1987
Ivonne E. Bazerman PsyD 1988
Alan Scott Hampton 1988
Kevin Ray Jones 1988
Dorotha M. Weber 1988
Stephen B. Clay 1989
Kristin Jo Moses Rains 1990
Jerome Rutherford 1990
Pamela Crabtree Schneider 1990
Ruth Ann Flynn 1991
Charles L. Croley 1992
Leigh Morris-Greer 1992
Stacy Ann Craig 1993
Felicia Yvonne Patterson 1993
Jan Marie Seratte 1993
Otis Dwayne Mills 1994
Michelle Lee Taylor 1994
Russell Shannon Thomas 1994
Vance Livingston Avera 1995
Desta Anne Cogan Schwendau 1995
Shannon Lee Varney 1995
Stephen Corneal Fuller 1996
Michael Lee Jones 1996
Amy Renee Abbott 1997
Tony Ray Brady 1997

Daniel Scott Connell 1997
Bradley Stafford Redmond 1997
Robert Wayne Warfield 1997
Sarah Elizabeth Boettner 1998
Lara Christine Brewer 1998
Elizabeth Anna May Duff 1998
Kevin Daniel Grace 1998
Deidre Gay Jewell 1998
Travis James Masters 1998
Albert Wayne Secrest 1999
Michael Lee Smith 1999
Melissa Dawn Ashley 2000
Misty Michelle Rutherford 2000
Laura Ellen Wilford 2000
Sherman Robert Partin 2001
Ambres Kevin Rader 2001
Adam Kyle Schaffner 2001
Wendy Lynnette Harris 2002
Alvin Bernard Lewis Jr. 2002
Selma Eleanor Alves 2003
Steven Andre Newell 2003
Leslie Nicole Fields 2004
Stephanie Lauren Paul 2004
Amy Rebecca Stroud 2004
Jennifer Renee Turner 2004
William DeVito Wagner 2004
Ronald R. Moses 2005
David Tyler Mullins 2005
Betty Jean Croley 2007
Mikeal Curtis Brooks 2008
Kelly Renee Vaught 2008
Jessica Rae Davis 2009
Andy Jack Decker 2009
Letitia G. Rudder 2009
Mason Craig Sutton 2009
Jonathan Scott Noel 2010
Mason Craig Sutton 2010

GRAPHIC DESIGN, GRAPHICS OPERATOR, ADVERTISING

William Reed Bryant 1962
Barbara S. Newman 1973
Latrescia G. Goss 1976
Nathan Melvin Bryson 1980
Charles Frank Hicks 1980

Anita Sue Dunn 1987
Tracey Martin Hamilton 1990
Eric Jason Dishon 1996
Michael Jay Roddy 1998
Adam Christopher Stille 2001

Brandon Shaun Fields 2002
Addie Mikella Chmura 2003
Kari Lynn James 2004
Adrian G. Fields II 2008

HOMEMAKING

Ruby A. Hibbs Ball 1922
Dorothy E. Black 1923
Elizabeth Hummel 1923
Irene S. Hubbard 1924
Bess Estes Lloyd 1924
Cora J. Ellison 1925
Lillian H. Perkins 1925
Neva Dishman 1926
Kathryn G. Alsover 1928
Jane Jack Carpenter 1928
Edythe N. Melton 1928
Katherine D. McBeath 1929
Mildred E. Bean 1930
Helen Marie Anderson 1931
Golda S. Moss 1932
Jane W. Welch 1932
Nettie Francis Keisling 1933
Nannie I. Wyatt 1933
Helen T. Adams 1934

Marie B. Ainsworth 1934
Jane K. Crume 1934
Hazel H. Edwards 1934
Betty W. O'Hara 1935
Delphia Jean Singleton 1935
Elizabeth Ralston Arbuckle 1936
Irma Butcosk 1936
Nora Alzena Gold 1936
Lois G. King 1936
Virginia Rose Trammell 1936
Lorena Craiger 1937
Johnie W. Hill 1937
June Pepper 1937
Alma D. Roberts 1937
Mary Willy Veach 1937
Cathlyn Cheely 1938
Doris Inez Corder 1939
Joyce Carson 1940
James Benjamin McCarty 1940

Sam Boyd Neely 1940
Charlsie T. Bradford 1941
Marjorie Wender Callaway 1941
Aileen H. Campbell 1941
Mary V. Thomas 1941
Georgie Levena Tweedy 1941
Marguerite B. Fish 1942
Frances Stambaugh 1942
Doris J. Alford 1943
Blondell Blankenship 1943
Frances S. Huggins 1943
Emma P. Kuhn 1943
Jo Camille Stanley 1943
Bessie Bowling 1944
Imogene W. Murphy 1945
Mary Snow Brandon 1946
Katherine Elizabeth Denney 1946
Martha Eberhard 1946
Wilma H. Kelley 1946

Florence Imogene Brown 1947
Kitty Lee East Renfro 1947
Mary M. Ellison-Collins 1947
Marcia Imogene Siler 1947
Barbara J. Whalen 1947
Dorothy White 1947
Wilma Lee Bristow 1948
Helen Louise Cobb 1948
Virginia Criscillis 1948
Nancy P. Daffron 1948
Peggy Davies 1948
Bess W. Davis 1948
Ruby Earls 1948
Wilma Faulkner 1948
Mary Allison Hammond 1948
Naomi Harp 1948
Janie Evelyn Hill 1948
Alma Ruth Nelson 1948
Doris Pierce 1948
Frieda H. Rickett 1948
Mary Lena Shaw 1948
Iva Lillian Ward 1948
Patsy A. White 1948
Diadenna Woods 1948
Clara E. Atkins 1949
Barbara Davis 1949
Eunice O. Faulkner 1949
N. Maxine Gibson 1949
Ella Mae Gregory 1949
Virginia J. Logan 1949
Axie Belle Matthis 1949
Louise Quarles 1949
Vivien R. Cooke 1950
Thressa Harris 1950
Marjorie L. Hart 1950
Betty Jane Hines 1950
Alfred F. Miller Jr. 1950
Angelena Sears 1950
Jenny Perkins Smiddy 1950
Lena Lay 1951
Anna S. Raines 1951
Mary Elizabeth Waters 1951
Barbara Wilson 1951
Lois F. Collins 1952
Ruth H. Patrick 1952
Sandra Swinehart 1952
Ruth Baker 1953
Freda D. Bartley 1953
Mary Ann Haigis 1953
Dorothy Lockman 1953
Margie Mayne 1953
Carolyn A. Stewart 1953
Biddie Williamson 1953
Gloria Sue Perkins 1954
Christine B. Stephens 1954
Margaret S. Wright 1954
Edith A. Bogaard 1955
Shirley R. Davenport 1955
Rosella B. Dixon 1955
Patricia A. Waddle 1955
Nina Brooks 1956
Jackie Croley 1956
Joyce Yvonne Dolen 1956
Janice L. Estep 1956
Susan T. Faulkner 1956
Irene S. Harris 1956
Jacquelin Jordan 1956
Iona Faye Lovett 1956
Virginia Ann Williams 1956
Wilma C. Couch 1957

Nancy L. Siereveld 1957
Linda C. Slusher 1957
Carolyn Jean Bennett 1958
Barbara L. Hundley 1958
Eloise Meadows Mayne 1958
Patty Pennington 1958
Donna Reece 1958
Margaret Maxine Sorg 1958
Betty Lou Bukovitz 1959
Hester Hamblin 1959
Mamie L. Heit 1959
Beverly A. Kantor 1959
Margie Ellen Keith 1959
Wanda Faye Keith 1959
Nellie L. Maddle 1959
Janet Jeanette Powers 1959
Jo Eileen Rains 1959
Bette S. Rios 1959
Delores Clark 1960
Bonnie Jean Goodfellow 1960
Janice Hopkins 1960
Ella Joan Partin 1960
Marilyn Dye 1961
Eva Allen Hendrickson 1961
Doris Jean Hucaby 1961
J. Ann Owens 1961
Betty Robbins 1961
Christine Chalek 1962
Margaret June Hopkins 1962
Doris Martin 1962
Jane Delano Plumlee 1962
Martha O. Stagnolia 1962
Judith E. Carter 1963
Jackie Childress 1963
Wanda Downey 1963
Joann Gambrell 1963
Larry W. Hammon 1963
Dorothy J. Hooker 1963
Jacqueline Kirby 1963
Shirley Joann Witt 1963
Phyllis A. Hopper 1964
Ruth A. Litton 1964
Margaret J. Longstreth 1964
Mary A. McKnight 1964
Mary Nancy Myers 1964
Rita Rose 1964
Ruth Thompson 1964
Beatrice Hail Carlier 1965
Betty S. Eddy 1965
Helen Janeway 1965
Frankie Woolum LeMaster 1965
Judith Lynn Lilly 1965
Anna K. Smith 1965
Phyllis Carol McSpadden 1966
Genive Phillips 1966
Lois Faye Rice 1966
Patricia H. Brown 1967
Wanda Minner 1967
Christy D. Siler 1967
Patricia Williams 1967
Barbara Bramlet 1968
Joanne Broughton 1968
Shirley A. Curd 1968
Elaine Kidd 1968
Norma Jeanne Pryor 1968
Judith Ann Sitterson 1968
Brenda L. Vaughn 1968
Brenda Sharon Wombles 1968
Sara Kaye Zurawick 1968
Janet Mae Begley 1969

Frieda B. Chapman 1969
Nancy Long 1969
Janice Miller 1969
Ella L. Smith 1969
Linda Jo Sullivan 1969
Charlene Beshears 1970
Rebecca Hicks 1970
Brenda L. Meadors 1970
Sandra K. Smith 1970
Brenda Gay Eversole 1971
Nancy Lee Harris 1971
Lois Madge McClain 1971
Wanda Lou Woods 1971
Anne Melanie Drake 1972
Donna Hubble 1972
Deanna P. Meadors 1972
Helen Elaine Rickett 1972
Deborah Y. Boston 1973
Beverly Ann DeMoss 1973
Karen Sue Hackworth 1973
Robyn Hammock 1973
Bonnie Carol Hooper 1973
Delia J. Reagan 1973
Cynthia Ann MacLellan 1974
Debra Marie Stewart 1974
Pamela Ann Tirey 1974
Regina Lefevers Warren 1974
Gail Brock 1975
Nancy Elizabeth Chapman 1975
Deborah Carol Dobson 1975
Debra Loree Ehrhard 1975
Phyllis Ann Fannon 1975
Lillian Ann House 1975
Debby C. Carter 1976
Vicki Lynn Gilbert 1976
Terry Holden 1976
Gene Ann Liechty 1976
Sharlotte J. Powell 1976
Cathy Susan Barnett 1977
Wanda Faye Carter 1977
Deborah Condley 1977
Elisabeth Ann Gatewood 1977
Gail June Beebe 1978
Kathy Dawn Durrett 1978
Claudia P. Long 1978
Anita Patton 1978
Kathy Ann Petrey 1978
Norma Jennifer Sykes 1978
Shelia Ann Cauley 1979
Sheryl Kay Cross 1979
Sandy Jo Davis 1979
Connie Sue Jones 1979
Nancy K. Okruhlica 1979
Debra Lynn Peterson 1979
Teresa Van Hook 1979
Beverly A. Whiteside 1979
Mary Jane Wilson 1979
Kathy Lynne Capps 1980
Glenda Dawn Gunter 1980
Katrina Marie Hyde 1980
Vicki Lynne Johnson 1980
Kathy Iona Karr 1980
Darlene Beulah Lawson 1980
Pamela Lay 1980
Cynthia Lou Orsborne 1980
Lola May Paul 1980
Brenda N. Roark 1980
Nancy Lynn Young 1980
Gloria Donna Bowling 1981
Karen Marie Douglas 1981

Helen Arvilla Lowrie 1981
Tina Mae Roberts 1981
Marlene Lucille Shealy 1981
Gail Evon Wheat 1981
Jolene D. Burgdorf 1982
Janice L. Dobson 1982
Carol A. Douglas 1982
Kristiann L. Farenholtz 1982
Kayla L. Gibson 1982
Donna C. Stanifer 1982
S. Elizabeth Correll 1983
Darlene S. Cox 1983
Cheryl Lea Frazier 1983
Kathy Renee German M.D. 1983
Janice L. Joseph 1983
Penny D. Monroe 1983
Patricia Ann Thomas 1983
Lena L. Whittington 1983
Pamela S. Caldwell 1984
Shirley R. Carmical 1984
Catherine Smith Finley 1984
Angela Beth Johnson 1984
Kathy Ann Kennett 1984
Robin P. Minton 1984
Connie Jane Perkins 1984
Rhonda Maria Reynolds 1984
Ginger Sharon Saylor 1984
Ruth Susan Schick 1984
Catherine Marie Tarrant 1984
Charlotte L. Mauk 1985
Robin Lee Williams 1985
Myong-Cha Croley 1986
Vickie Lynn Dubberly 1986
Heather Melinda Hammiel 1986
Flora Marie Stone 1986
Tammy L. Gates Agdeppa 1987
Kristy N. Bartley 1987
Kathy Jonathan Bloom 1987
Stella L. Brock 1987
Kim Combs 1987
Bonita S. Mathews Robinson 1987
Ethel Lee Starkey 1987
Rena A. Tumbleson 1987
Luann Marie Anderson 1988
Jill DeBusk Blevins 1988
Karen D. Graves 1988
Lori Kathleen Hoffman 1988
Cynthia Sue Moll 1988
Linda V. Prewitt 1988

Gwendolyn R. Cloutier 1989
Sherry Lynn Mitchum 1989
Edith Minva Smith 1989
Kimberly J. Bates 1990
Tracy Lea Keller 1990
Julie A. Monestel 1990
Samantha Katherine Schuhmann 1990
Janice Lee Walker 1990
Alicia Michelle DeBolt 1991
Tama Michelle Fortner 1991
Lisa Gail Hamilton 1991
Sarah Lynn Tirey 1991
Kimberly Geraldine Waegaert 1991
Linda Carol Bowden 1992
Jody Lynn Harris 1992
Julie S. Hill 1992
Tracy Dawn Knight 1992
Jennifer Kersey Michna 1992
Jami Westerfield Parsley 1992
Jamie Lynn Selter 1992
Melissa Suzanne Keck 1993
Jackie Gwyn Kilbourne 1993
Allison Kay Deater 1994
Kimberly Elaine Farthing 1994
Cynthia Ann Johnson 1994
Marki Ann Osborn 1994
Elizabeth Lee Schmidt 1994
Kathrine Lynn Bradford-Brown 1995
Anita Lynn Brady 1995
Lacey Elizabeth Keigley 1995
Georgia Marie Krakora 1995
Angela Jan McKiddy 1995
Elizabeth Ann Murphy 1995
Michelle Renae Parker 1995
Gretchen Beth Phelps 1995
Shannon Raye Conty 1996
Carla Linn Earley 1996
Danielle Lynne Gross 1996
Amy Nicole Liddle 1996
Karyn Elizabeth Talley 1996
Tammy Lynn Taylor 1996
Tina Michelle Burriss 1997
Wendy M. Heintz 1997
Tammy Lynn King 1997
Sharla Kaye Martinez 1997
Heather Marie Morris 1997
Lana Ruth Ogle 1997
Aubrey Noel O'Reilly 1997
Heather Colleen Steele 1997

Salena Pepper Wilson 1997
Vicky Marie Bates 1998
Suzanna Carol Cupp 1998
Lisa Marie Greene 1998
Christiane Leigh Herndon 1998
Jennifer Kay Meador 1998
Elizabeth Lorraine Messick 1998
Winifred Ruth Moran 1998
Laura Katherine Sheridan 1998
Tara Kathleen Thomas 1998
April Michelle Wetherill 1998
Janie Lynne Bicknell 1999
Irena Viacheslavona Forquer 1999
Jamie Renee Hansen 1999
Tara Lynn Jones 1999
Jerri Christina Kramer 1999
Lorri Jo Pilcher 1999
Dana Rachelle Presley 1999
Amy Rebecca Provance 1999
Sarah Maxine Russell 1999
Caroline Campbell Scott 1999
Margo Lea Wheeler 1999
Bridgett Annette Blakeman 2000
Kelly Jo Hogue 2000
Janet Lynn Jones 2000
Melanie Beth Roden 2000
Tara Amy Bunch 2001
Carrie Leigh Cabell 2001
Jamie Renee Hansen 2001
Susanna R. Kendrick 2001
Kristina Ruth Morgan 2001
Amy Michelle Wills 2001
Krista A. Woodyard 2001
Julie Marie Bowden 2002
Lindsay Christine Carter 2002
Malissa Dawn Mahan 2002
Luann Marie Anderson 2003
Amber Nichole Meadors 2003
Rebecca Ann Measel 2003
Amy Melissa Tucker 2003
April LeDawn Wyatt 2003
Jessica Lauren Anderson 2004
Christina Marie Elkins 2004
Kristin Dawn McCleese 2004
Claudia R. Males 2005
Carol Kieffer Tudor 2005
Lola May Paul 2009
Marianne Yancey 2009

INSPECTOR

Clifford M. Perkins 1950
Albert R. Jones 1959
Douglas M. Farris 1963
Mary Louise Reid 1963
Coleman Lewis England 1965
Earl Moses 1969

Jacob Scholl 1970
Billie J. Carey 1975
Kevin L. Ringley 1975
Joan Rene Norvell 1977
Eric Hazen Kimball 1978
Aubra Arnold Petrey 1979

Laura G. Newell 1980
Michelle Anice Kellogg 1983
Darren C. Lee 1986
Laura G. Newell 1994
Steven Dean Wolf 2009

INSURANCE, CLAIMS ADJUSTOR

Clarence Greene 1936
J. L. Finley 1939
Frank B. Fitzgerald 1948

Claude C. Costigan 1949
James Kenneth Anders 1950
Anna Ray Combs 1952

Ernestine Wilson 1953
John W. Grubbs 1955
James E. Branam 1957

Ferrell Henegar 1957
Roy Eugene Henry 1958
Lawrence Jerome Taylor 1958
Robert Tyrone Bentley 1959
Elmer Day 1960
Franklin D. Tolliver 1961
Jim Wilder 1961
Billy J. Fox 1962
Ronald A. Browning 1963
Raymond McDonald 1963
Sam J. Watts 1963
Vernon L. Gilreath 1964
Lloyd D. Emert 1965
Kay Norman 1965
Marvin Everett Deaton 1966
Jackie Lee Sears 1966
Charles Allen Webb 1966
Mike Leak 1967
James H. Linville 1967
Larry R. Boyd 1968
Eldon Asher Jr. 1969
Huey L. Cornelius 1969
Ralph William Cromer 1969
Bobby W. Caudill 1970
Ray E. Cole 1970
Gary K. Elliott 1970
Thomas Harold Elsea 1971
Dennis A. Faulkner 1971
Mark Stephens 1971
Barbara Strayer 1971
David M. Aldridge 1972
Allen R. Blevins 1972
James Edward Prewitt 1972

Norbert Lewis Skees 1972
Thomas Lee Freeman 1973
James Larry Goins 1973
Randall Hillman 1973
Ronald L. Osborne 1973
Gary Green 1974
Glenn Michael Howard 1974
Donald K. Nicholson 1975
Eddy Delon Siler 1975
Tony Hampton 1976
Greg K. Sutton 1977
Belinda Delvoyia Branch 1979
Clayton George Hill 1979
Janet L. Smith 1979
John J. Walker 1979
Bradley N. Delaney 1980
John Oliver Smith II 1980
Taylor K. Hignite 1981
Roger Dale Stanifer 1982
Larry Dean Jones 1983
Joe Randy Blount 1984
E. Kim Norvell 1984
Karen G. Scudder 1984
Suzanne W. Underwood 1984
Michael A. Winhold 1984
Anthony Lavonne Taylor LUTCF 1985
Elizabeth Ann Clark 1986
James Glen Curry 1986
Alice Chapman 1987
John Timothy Engel 1987
Jeffrey Charles Clark 1988
Tim H. Mills 1988
Bethani Anne Carnes 1989

Jeff Alan Seltzer 1990
Emily Ellen Byers 1991
Michele L. Hayden 1991
Gregory William Boggs 1992
Heather Annette Fox 1992
Traci Lynn Life 1992
Mark Edwin Anderson 1993
Susan Leslie Henry 1994
Michael Patrick Hansel 1995
George Grady Wilson IV 1995
Marjorie Jeanice Shans 1996
Jennifer Renee Chumley 1997
Stacey Michelle Smith 1997
Kendall Stephen Bradley 1998
Clifton Wade Lunsford 1998
Ella Jo Brown-Issifi 1999
Jennifer Lynn Martin 1999
Anthony Gabriel Steele Jr. 1999
Jonathan Samuel Childers 2000
Melanie Beth Roden 2000
Brent Alan Turner 2000
Michelle Anne Sanford 2001
Kurt Clark Brockman 2003
Andrea Renee Hall 2003
Daniel Adam Jones 2003
Matthew Bradley Sims 2004
Larry VaShone Hay 2006
Rachel Darlene Liford 2006
Leslie Allyson Wells 2006
Jennifer Renee Chumley 2009
Steven Dean Wolf 2009

INTERIOR DECORATOR DESIGN, INTERIOR DECORATOR

Beverly Butcher Webb 1949
Margaret Kolligian 1950
Marielyn R. Hardin 1959
Patricia Eleanor Smith 1960

Jacquelyn S. Regan 1961
Phyllis Morgan 1966
Joyzette Fields 1968
Carl Lewis Capo 1985

Gloria Denise Cornett 1991
Josephine Lean Looi Khoo-Smith 1994
Heather Jo Burkhart 2003

INTERNET SERVICES DEVELOPMENT

Jeffrey J. Bartholomew 1979
Donald Kevin Grimes 1989
Theresea Lynelle Harris 1991

Christine Marie James 1991
Dena Laschele Carter 1997
Forrest Paul Bates 1999

Kenya Danielle Dossett 2009
Travis Eugene Coleman Jr. 2010

LABORER, MAINTENANCE

Clyde E. McNeil 1928
Opsie P. Hale 1938
Charles Arthur Mays 1950
Arnold Mays 1950
Ruth Ann Blair 1951
Bill Botkins 1951
Elbert Caddell 1951
James Vernon Enix 1951
Roy Jarvis 1951
Edward Stanley Teague 1953
Burlyn G. Calder 1956
Robert S. Bukovitz 1957
Horace David Rader 1958

James L. Weldon 1959
Jerry Wayne Hammons 1960
Freddie Marie Saylor 1960
Donald Leon Collett 1962
John Leslie Gibbs Jr. 1962
Anna Louise Runyon 1963
Donald F. Garland 1964
Palmer Adams 1966
Lewis W. Helton 1967
Hubert Manson Sluss 1967
Thomas Wayne Allen 1969
Daniel Lee Dunaway 1969
Jerry Clem 1970

Larry Shelley 1970
J. Andrea Webster 1970
David W. Berryhill 1971
Lee A. Marsili 1971
J B Blair 1972
Mitchell Turner 1972
Jerry Delbert York 1972
Charles Edward French 1973
Kenneth Demby Sharp 1973
Dora Mobley 1974
Paul Joseph Kaeser 1975
Robert Joseph Kleather 1975
Henry Albert McCleskey 1975

Oliver Lee Taylor 1975
Herbert B. Waldleitner 1975
Wayne Creekmore 1976
Kathy Sue Champlin 1977
Mark Eugene Trickett 1977
Patricia A. Bales 1978
Wayne Alan Campbell 1978
Patrick E. Pace 1978
Ronnie E. Johnson 1979
Charles Ralph Blakley 1980

Margaret Elizabeth Campbell 1980
Gerald John Taylor 1981
Benjamin Franklin Atchley Jr. 1982
Terry Lee Green 1982
Timothy Clark Phillips 1983
Murton Lynn Wilson 1983
Billy Mounce 1986
Donald Raymond Witt II 1988
David Eugene Jarboe Jr. 1989
Gregory Scott Lucous 1989

Lenell Jackson 1990
Ira Allen Amburgey 1993
Edward Scott Curtis 1996
Dale Byron Davis 2000
Thomas Christopher Dool 2001
Michael Casey Scott 2002
Bonnie L. Glenn 2008
Travis William Madison 2010
Dale Byron Davis 2012

LAND SURVEYOR

James Daniel Dean 1962
Wimer B. Jones 1962

Robert Ralph Moses 2007
Robert Blake Germaine 2009

Robert Ralph Moses 2009

LANDSCAPING

James Stephen Wiley 1981

David Mark Schwab 1999

James Stephen Wiley 2004

\

LAW ENFORCEMENT, SECURITY GUARD

Meriel D. Harris 1933
Walter H. Muth 1955
Donnie L. Bennett 1959
Larry Lewis 1968
Norma Lee Walker 1969
James Freddy Yaden 1969
Philip K. Wilson 1970
Patricia Jeanne Meredith 1972
Earl Edwin Nicholson 1972
David Allen Hoffman 1974
John Ricky Dye 1975
Michael Eaton 1975
Vernon L. Huff 1975
Tony Wardlow 1977
L. Ruth White 1977

Stephen T. Banks 1978
Jerry Wayne Huffman 1978
Maurice Elmer House 1979
Jody Judson Adams 1980
Norma B. Sizemore 1980
Rick J. Williams 1981
Timothy C. Gregory 1982
Judy L. Yonce 1982
Kenneth E Ely 1985
David Lennon 1985
Charles D. Steely 1985
Wanda J. Frederick 1987
Barry Kevin Knuckles 1987
Walter Meachum 1987
Lynn Ellen Gibson 1990

Michael D. Royer 1991
Andrew Ottmon Abbott 1994
Brian F. Key 1996
Barry Thomas Pickett II 2002
Brad Steven Hawkins 2003
Michael Robert Redfern 2003
Elizabeth Rose Wilson 2003
James Brandon Creekmore 2005
James David Gay Jr. 2006
Matthew Jason Bryant 2007
Shaun Michael Faulkner 2007
Adam Stanley Garrett 2007
Gloria B. Inman 2007

LAW, LEGAL SERVICES, LAWYER, LEGAL ASSISTANT, PATENT COUNSEL

M. Jack See 1926
Joseph King Beasley 1932
Glenn W. Denham 1937
George W. Hatfield 1941
Lura Elizabeth Ethridge 1942
John L. Wilson 1947
Nixon Curtis Duncan 1948
Imogene C. Brown 1951
Tom Warren Butler 1951
John H. Isert III 1952
A. D. Petrey 1952
Philip R. Morgan 1956
James Wallace Bowling 1958
Charles Bruce Pemberton 1958
Delmer Ray Smith 1958
Gayle G. Huff 1960
William R. Elam 1964
L. Wayne White 1964
Marva Melinda Gay 1965
Mary Elizabeth Wickline 1967
Aaron L. Wright 1967

Richard G. Warren 1968
John Green Arnett Jr. 1969
Barbara A. Bale 1969
Jerry Doyle Bryant 1969
Sondra Elaine Davis 1969
Corbet Hensley 1969
Ralph E. Lynch 1969
Jeemes Lee Akers 1970
Phillip M. Armstrong 1970
Marcus M. Burgher III 1970
Larry W. Davis 1970
Audra Lee Gipson 1970
George Brent Cox 1971
William Charles Gullett 1971
Douglas D. Wilson 1971
Sherman E. Fetterman 1972
Thomas Lee Jensen 1972
Patricia Elaine Patrick 1972
Ronald Dean Stewart 1972
Pamela L. Bennett 1973
Barbara Ann Carnes 1973

Ronald W. Bunch 1974
Maurice S. Byrd 1974
Mary Lynne Walters 1974
Dennis S. Risch 1975
James E. Hibbard 1976
Dennis Wayne Mattingly 1976
Ronald Douglas Williamson 1976
David Howard 1978
Kathy Parrott 1978
Gregory Dee Rawlings 1978
Regina Sheehan 1978
Pamela Kay Clay 1979
Heather Lane 1981
Belinda Mae Taylor 1981
Fred F. White 1981
Edward Adair 1982
H. Brent Brennenstuhl 1982
Brett D. Davis 1982
Karla Nadine Grant 1982
Chris W. Keegan 1983
Judy Lynn Thacker 1983

174

Kelly L. Wylie Chesnut 1983
Pamela A. Beck 1984
Rebecca S. Byrd 1984
Thomas Robert Wyvill 1986
Ric T. Edwards 1987
Melissa A. Stewart 1987
Steven Jarvis Moore 1988
Clarence W. Westerfield 1988
Deborah Campbell Myers 1989
Tina Louise Nunley 1989
Lisa A. Porter 1989
Lisa Ann Copeland 1990
Michael David Lyons 1990
Timothy Paul Webb 1990
Donald Andrew Wood 1990

Tracie Malinda Boyd 1991
Jonathan Eugene Laster 1991
Cheryl Adel Meyer 1991
Jeff E. Forsell 1992
Danny Ray Glover Jr. 1992
Sara Elizabeth Godby 1992
Jill Ann Lance 1992
Stacy Ann Craig 1993
William Ray Adkins 1996
Robert Ernest Stephens Jr. 1996
Lisa Ann Woods 1996
Jeffrey Daniel Holloway 1997
Jacquelin M. Brown 1998
Timmy G. Robinson 1998
Jackie Lynn Steele 1998

William Allen Backer 1999
Jason Paul Price 1999
Larry Cleveland Jones 2000
Jeffrey Keith Hill 2001
Clay Brent Wortham 2001
Tracy Elizabeth Fields 2002
Mark Adrian Hall 2003
Phillip Michael Vogelsang 2003
Andrew Nicholas Wilson 2003
Summer Destine Rogers 2004
David Thomas Vance 2009
Robert Byron McKeehan 2010
Summer Destine Rogers 2011

LIBRARIAN LIBRARY SCIENCE, LIBRARY MEDIA SPECIALIST

Margarette B. Register 1934
Patricia C. Ballard 1935
Edith Waldroup Withers 1939
Kathleen Parker Heck 1943
Joanna Chelf 1946
Wilma Creekmore 1948
Madge S. Fisher 1949
Rea Perkins Smart 1949
Artie Lavena Centers 1950
Katherine R. Buck 1952
Louise S. Lester 1952
Norma Kelley 1953
Barbara Morrow 1953
Lula M. West 1953
Verna Lee Bruce 1955
Frances H. Catlett 1955
Glennis Hensley 1956
Shirley L. Haney 1957
Carolene Coy 1958
Helen Elaine Hurd 1958
Audrey Charlene Mauk 1958
Linda Brashear 1959
Joyce H. Freeman 1959

Wilma C. Adams 1962
Patricia Sampson Faulkner 1962
Drucilla Hembree 1962
Kathleen Norris Pennington 1962
Mae Sibert 1962
Elmer Clay Smith 1962
Anna Joyce McKeehan 1963
Bonnie Morgan 1963
Clara T. Morgan 1963
Carol F. Brown 1964
Naomi Jean Craig 1964
Binnie N. Faulkner 1964
Janet Maiden 1964
Patsy M. Bunch 1965
Dianna A. Wilson 1965
Susie Shaw Henson 1966
Sandra Sue Johnson 1967
Maureen McRay 1967
Maxine Carr 1968
Jonathon B. Castle 1968
Nancy Fletcher 1968
Suzanne Lennon Gieszl 1968
Mary Faye Roark 1968

Joe D. Smith 1968
Maudie Elizabeth VanBever 1968
Carrie Lou Farmer 1969
Donna M. Hackman 1969
Gail R. Harris 1970
Essie K. Lewis 1970
Sandra K. Miller 1970
Mary Jane Morrow 1970
Linda Sandlin 1970
Brenda Sue Guinn 1971
Brenda Kaye Hodge 1971
Sandra K. Bill 1972
Sonja D. Lawson 1972
Jean N. Lillie 1973
Norma Jean Turner 1973
Ovelyn B. White 1973
Timothy Joe Edwards 1975
Kathie L. Farmer 1975
Janice Eva Sue Marlow 1975
Robert Keith Schrum 1975
Katherine Alice Tulissi 1975
Robert Bruce Williams 1975

MANAGEMENT, ASSISTANT MANAGEMENT

Gladys Carter 1921
Edward Arkley Davis 1933
Elijah Keith 1941
Margaret C. Crook 1942
Joseph Craig King 1942
Mary Virginia Baldock 1943
Arnetta W. Fallis 1945
Ann W. Stout 1945
Rosalee L. Centers 1946
Edwin M. Kidd 1947
Gene L. Strunk 1948
Harold E. Dupuy 1949
Jack L. Harris 1949
Dorothy D. Liles 1949
Georgia Renfro 1949
John L. Turnblazer 1949
Charles Burbage 1950
James Earl Hensley 1950
Dewey R. Jones 1950
Margaret Joanne Richards 1950
Roger M. Solheim 1950

Charles D. Young 1950
Lowell C. Frazier 1951
Kenneth L. Hackler 1951
Jack D. Jones 1951
James A. Marsee 1951
Grace Mays 1951
Harold Nevels 1952
General Bernard Williams 1952
Doyle Louis Davenport 1953
Earl D. Freeman 1953
A. L. White 1954
Leland Leslie Bingham 1955
William Robert Campbell 1955
Charles Harold Johnston 1955
Earnest Ray Parker 1955
Carl E. Price 1955
Billy C. Broughton 1956
Eugene Browning 1956
Wade Gordon 1956
Willard L. Hamblin 1956
Richard D. Harris 1956

Herbert C. Housley 1956
Virgil L. King 1956
Ronald F. Reid Sr. 1956
Mary Carolyn Rutledge 1956
Jack Richard Stearns 1956
June Wilder 1956
Jayne Adams 1957
Arnold Jake Bennett 1957
Mary C. Broyles 1957
Cecil England 1957
Donald Roark 1957
Ann Gail Van Zandt 1957
Charles Thomas Warren 1957
Carl O. Abner 1958
Michael Hastings 1958
J. Ronald Lawson 1958
Tommy May 1958
Donald R. Partin 1958
Shelby Jean Pruitt 1958
Alene Faye Roe 1958
Jerry Swim 1958

Doyle Russell Hale 1959
Orban Ison 1959
George P. Rains 1959
Johnny Delmar Cuel 1960
Robert Lee Madon 1960
Ted Emery Potter 1960
Charles Marshall Robinson 1960
Anna Mae Amburgy 1961
Pleas David Jones Jr. 1961
Edgar Franklin Jones 1961
Lawrence Albert Thornton 1961
Meredith L. Bastin 1962
Charles M. Bishop 1962
Laura Frances Bridgeman 1962
Lydia Belle Harris 1962
Ronnie Jack Kitts 1962
Stanley R. Stokes 1962
Lillian M. Bowles 1963
Brenda Joyce Chinn 1963
Bill Crook 1963
Larry Edward Hutson 1963
Jennifer Jones 1963
Donald Ray Broughton 1964
Lynne Ann Fontaine 1964
Wanda Sue Harkins 1964
Lucille W. Light 1964
Jesse James Nave 1964
Catherine Queener 1964
Carl Randal Brown 1965
James S. Grayson 1965
Glennis Edward Grayson 1965
Jim McKnight 1965
H. Kermit Wagers 1965
Donald Bruce Ward 1965
Bill W. Sharp 1966
Elmer Wombles 1966
Joe M. Brown 1967
Jerry W. Cornett 1967
Tom M. Pendergrass 1967
Michael A. Phillips 1967
Bobby E. Ross 1967
Henry W. Bussey III 1968
Jo Ann Castle 1968
Paul E. Haynes Jr. 1968
Judy Diane Sizemore 1968
David G. Starker 1968
Gary Lee Cromer 1969
David L. Fuson 1969
John Gary Goodman 1969
Harold Gary Jackson 1969
Peter Stuart McComb 1969
James W. Rogers 1969
Walter Don Smith 1969
Gary Ray Welch 1969
Gerard B. Bordes 1970
Denny Wayne Bowman 1970
Evelyn Brown 1970
Jerald Lee Cassidy 1970
Curtis Cole 1970
Anne Jones Cox 1970
Howard Lee Elliott 1970
Jackie Sue Freeman 1970
Vickie L. Hammer 1970
Carl Edwin Hicks Jr. 1970
Dennis R. Leger 1970
Jay H. Long 1970
Randall Wayne Rowe 1970
Marvin Douglas Shepherd 1970
Carl V. Stanifer 1970
Gary E. Wright 1970

James Howard Amos 1971
Sharron Bryant 1971
Richard A. King 1971
Gary D. Miracle 1971
Larry Edward Steadman 1971
Charles E. Vires 1971
Joe Edward Caldwell 1972
Dorothy Campbell 1972
Clinton D. Campbell 1972
Beth G. Clifton 1972
James Robert Cooper 1972
Donovan F. Daulton 1972
Donald L. Disney 1972
Jerry W. Jones 1972
Stephen H. Pettit 1972
John Wilson Stansberry 1972
Morris L. Stephens USCG Ret. 1972
Axie Faulkner 1973
Lon E. Head 1973
Terry H. Henderson 1973
Darlene Rebecca Lara 1973
Carl Orlee Napier 1973
Rodney E. Nickell 1973
Roy Howard Price 1973
Charles L. Teague Jr. 1973
Harold Terry 1973
Arlin L. Yeager 1973
Judy Diane Bell Ridenour 1974
Barry Gess Cole 1974
Randall Durham 1974
Danny Ray Harrell 1974
Morris Reginald Jordan Jr. 1974
Carl Otis Noe 1974
Steve J. Oakman 1974
Charles Polly 1974
M. Marita Rice 1974
Douglas Singleton 1974
Molly Stevens 1974
Jerry N. Wilhoite 1974
Arlene Emily Barton 1975
James Kevin Booth 1975
James Randall Burns 1975
Charles Calvin Burton 1975
Sharla A. Busch 1975
Steven V. Bush 1975
Larry Allen Freeman 1975
Nick Hanna 1975
Wesley C. Lovitt Jr. 1975
Brenda Gail Ramsey 1975
Charles Thomas Rose 1975
Katherine Alice Tulissi 1975
Rex David Wilson 1975
Kim Donald Anderson 1976
David Edward Baker II 1976
Glenn L. Jacobs 1976
William Harvey Johnson 1976
Jerry Glenn Richardson 1976
J. Michael Stone 1976
John Marshall Townsend 1976
G. Roger Whitaker 1976
Alfred Brooks Apple 1977
Kevin T. Collins 1977
Karen Sue Crockett 1977
Roy Edward Ingram 1977
William Hodge Mason Jr. 1977
Nancy Y. Sargent 1977
Kathy Gayl Sharp 1977
Debbie Anders 1978
Twila R. Barnett 1978
Thomas D. Davidson Jr. 1978

Donald Gordon Davis 1978
Billie Jean Hamilton 1978
Jo Elizabeth Kinchington 1978
Loretta Lewis-Golden 1978
Ritchie Lewis Longworth 1978
Lance D. Marshall 1978
Gregory S. Pierson 1978
Anthony Clifton Deal 1979
Frank Richard Hall Jr. 1979
Sherri K. Macko 1979
David A. Prewitt 1979
J. Stephen Sproles 1979
Cathy B. Stout 1979
Julie Kathleen Thompson 1979
Clarence Wayne Ware 1979
Mark Douglas Wilson 1979
Thomas David Broyles 1980
Glenn Michael Burgett 1980
Keith Boyd Collins 1980
Darrell Wayne Fincher 1980
Debra Gail Haggard 1980
William D. Hendricks 1980
Delphos J. Howard 1980
Richard Alan Mack 1980
Michael Keith Roberts 1980
Mary Ann Strausbaugh 1980
Derrell Lee Wilson 1980
Sandra K. Biddinger 1981
Linda D. Blair 1981
Charles William Browning 1981
Rodney Endmon Bunch 1981
Connie D. Bush 1981
Donnie Ray Cox 1981
Evelyn J. Hall 1981
William Russell Hardin Jr. 1981
Douglas Dean Hawkins 1981
Harold Gary Jackson 1981
Jane Reeves 1981
Linda Sue Roach 1981
James Darryl Smith 1981
Jessie Lee Smith 1981
Janice E. Bryant 1982
Jean Marie Carpenter 1982
David Michael Combs 1982
Joseph Matthew Glogoza 1982
Janet Leigh Kitts 1982
Alfred Mitchell Lewis 1982
Karen Sue Martin 1982
Lucian G. Muncy 1982
William Roark 1982
Donnie Senters 1982
Tammy F. Turner 1982
Craig Warren Velte 1982
Samuel David Ballou 1983
James D. Botner 1983
Charles E. Correll Jr. 1983
Sandy Jo Goins 1983
Janis L. Harris 1983
Beth Anne Hobson 1983
William Ralph Lewis 1983
Kissick B. Lindsay 1983
June A. Miller 1983
Donald Wayne Stewart 1983
Heron G. Sullivan 1983
Genise Thomas-Bradshaw 1983
Brian G. Cline 1984
Pamela Ann Godby 1984
Kevin W. Kearns 1984
David L. Lewis 1984
Steven Joe Massengill 1984

Lisa Ann Pflueger 1984
Chooi Khim Tan 1984
David Wayne Witt 1984
Mark Todd Adams 1985
Betty Anne Barton Collett 1985
Diana Jean Bybee 1985
Elizabeth Ann Hacker 1985
Jerry Lynn Hopkins 1985
Connie Lynne Hughes 1985
Pamela M. Jackson 1985
James Cody Johnson 1985
Donald R. Keene II 1985
James Michael Smith 1985
Marlynn Kay Soliwoda 1985
Soloman Yonas 1985
Stephen Scott Burton 1986
Lisa Annette Johnson 1986
Claudia Kay Manning 1986
John McCoy 1986
Lisa B. Nantz 1986
Barry Lee Perry 1986
Margaret A. Smith 1986
Paul Milner Tarrant 1986
Stephanie J. Wilson 1986
Gary W. Brewer 1987
Shannon G. Cox 1987
Mary Ellen Creekmore 1987
Marvin Cress Jr. 1987
Delbert Mitchel Goodin 1987
Regina Hammons 1987
Susan C. Hawkins 1987
Jeffery Todd Haysley 1987
David S. Hopper 1987
Tim L. Keith 1987
Gina Renee Kirker 1987
Verlin Glenn Roberts 1987
Rhonda Lynn Rose 1987
Melanie D. Taylor 1987
Lisa A. Westerfield 1987
Darryl Rufus Wilson 1987
Rick Edward Centers 1988
Camron Clyde Davenport 1988
Frank N. Fee 1988
Garrett Dewayne Gregory 1988
Kimberly Sue Hensley-Vance 1988
Richard Kevin Meuth 1988
Glenn D. Miller 1988
Nontasorn Neal Ploadpliew 1988
Stephen Robert Robinson 1988
Mark C. Taylor 1988
Glenda J. Bennett 1989
Todd Lee Bibler 1989
James J. Cain 1989
Rhonda Sue Campbell 1989
Steve Lee Collins 1989
Lisa Marie Mitchell-Anderton 1989
Seble Nebiyeloul 1989
Lisa Joyce Sample-Brown 1989
David A. Taylor 1989
Richard J. Thompson 1989
Senedu Agonafer 1990
Richard Brian Beamer 1990
Diana Jean Bybee 1990
Timothy DeBolt 1990
Maria A. Hagan 1990
Cathy Ann Hoffman 1990
Diana L. Hooker 1990
Mark Edward Justice 1990
Robert William Ostendorf 1990
Donna Sue Pilkey 1990

Eric Rodney Reihing Jr. 1990
George Michael Rhodes 1990
Lee Ann Rinck 1990
Jeffrey Alan Sharpe 1990
Michael Todd Steely 1990
Michael Darren Tirey 1990
Timothy John Wheeler 1990
Christine Bernice Anderson 1991
Jano Jonie Childers 1991
Warren Dewayne Coleman 1991
Lloyd Scott DeGonia 1991
Richard L. McCoy 1991
Walter Laverne Mehlenbacher Jr. 1991
Gregory C. Slade 1991
Tommy Edward Sullivan 1991
Carol Ann Christenson 1992
Virginia Mecheal Collins-Freeman 1992
Edward James Mears 1992
Michael Dennis Neal 1992
Nathan Burnham Sanders 1992
Cecil Jeffery Lee Taylor 1992
Joseph Vance Williams 1992
Thomas Jeffrey Williams 1992
Thomas Edwin Cox 1993
Paul Douglas Goforth 1993
Michelle Hope Johnson 1993
Charles William Lester 1993
Krista Lynn Mullins 1993
Dwayne Steven Steely 1993
Timothy R. Sweet 1993
Kelley Bolen Collier 1994
Michael Chad Conty 1994
Wendy Taylor Ennis 1994
Stephen Lloyd Hall 1994
Deborah Anne Paul 1994
Charles Monty Sears 1994
Geneva Mae Witt 1994
Valerie Lynn Clark 1995
Lisa Marie Weiss 1995
Gwendolyn Marie Willis 1995
Kristina Diane Kitzmiller 1996
Teresa Lynne Adams 1997
Dawn Marie Broyles 1997
William Ryan Fitzwater 1997
Laura G. Garlich 1997
Sharon Brooks Kidd 1997
Jason Ralph Lipps 1997
Jason Ralph Lipps 1997
Kimberly D. Lunsford 1997
Kelly Jo Oldaker 1997
Hal Lawrence Bennett 1998
Charles Jason Kramer 1998
Ryan Matthew Schneeman 1998
Alecia Daphene Stephens 1998
Steven Zachary Allen 1999
Chad Micheal Benoit 1999
Jason Binder 1999
Clark Barnette Bugg 1999
Regina Lynn Callihan-May 1999
Scott Daniel Carlisle 1999
Ronald Matthew Forquer 1999
Allison Leigh Lay 1999
Steven Lee Means 1999
Juanita Leigh-Anne Miracle 1999
Joseph David Mouser 1999
James Philip Pilcher 1999
Travis Allen Bell 2000
Travis Richard Brabb 2000
Franklin E. Brillhart 2000
Todd Daniel Davis 2000

Jennifer Anne Hale 2000
Monica Gwen Haydon 2000
Joseph Shane Hinkle 2000
Casey Ray Hutchens 2000
Jason Matthew Roesch 2000
Keeli Jane Stone 2000
Gareth Dennis Wilford 2000
Jeremy Nathan Bryant 2001
Crestene Lee Dietrich 2001
Therese Marie Grieco 2001
Tim J. Kelly 2001
Estella Sue Phillips 2001
Johnathan Charles Porter 2001
Jesse Lee Terrell 2001
Travis Wayne Wills 2001
Timothy Paul Wyatt 2001
Tracy Lynn Bryson 2002
Robert C. Cornelius 2002
Shane Ethan King 2002
Rebecca Kathleen LaVoie 2002
Stephen Mark Madrid 2002
Matthew Paul Nash 2002
Kristin A. Riggs 2002
Robert Alan Walker II 2002
James Randall Young 2002
Glen Eric Bolton 2003
Aaron Daniel Drake 2003
Corey Wayne Floyd 2003
Dale Robert Huffman 2003
Rebecca Lynn Jones 2003
Jamie Christopher McCleese 2003
Misty Mae Poynter 2003
David Bradford-Ross Shotwell 2003
Binnie Lynn Hatmaker 2004
Christopher Matthew Lundin 2004
Melinda Dawn Mann 2004
Jason Lee Swanson 2004
Douglas Aaron Brock 2005
Peggy Gail Byrd 2005
Lauren Michelle Cosentino 2005
Barbara Sue Duncan 2005
Sara Elizabeth Hawkins 2005
Joshua Ray Peek 2005
Rebecca Ann Schoolcraft Flinchum
2005
Alan Brian Sutton 2005
Holly Brooke Valentine 2005
Michael Wayne Ward 2005
Brandon Edward Ward 2005
Harlan Lindsey Winston II 2005
Michael Wayne Delph 2006
Martha Hubbard 2006
Marianne Elizabeth Trimble 2006
Kimberly Erin Catoe 2007
Jonathan Charles Meadors 2007
Heather Lynn Moehling 2007
Anna Lindsay Moehling 2007
James Hugh Sibert 2007
Timothy Marshall Thoreson 2007
Christopher Lynn Wood 2007
Ronald Eugene Yancey 2007
Daniel Lee Burns 2008
Clinton Charles Masters 2008
Robert Kade Moehling 2008
Andrew Michael Morrison 2008
Amanda Gayle O'Banion 2008
Sandra Kay Terry 2008
Stacy Lynn Calvert 2009
Andrew Craig Denton 2009
Brittni Ann Dozier-Tuttle 2009

177

Katie Jo Eviston 2009
Michael Edward Gregory 2009
Mary Alice Kelly 2009
Trevor Warren Laughlin 2009
Brian Neal Sutton 2009

William Andrew Townsend 2009
Amanda Gayle O'Banion 2010
Ashley Candace Sizemore 2010
Wilma Gayle Troxell 2010
Amanda Louise Young 2010

Brittni Ann Dozier-Tuttle 2011
Allison Leigh Lay 2011
Richard Alan Mack 2011
Estella Sue Phillips 2011
Wilma Gayle Troxell 2011

MANUFACTURER, MANUFACTURING

William Paul Feltner Sr. 1950
Harry Elliott Davenport 1954
James B. Ginn 1956
Travis W. Welch 1956
Joy M. McCormick 1957
Martha J. Miller 1957
Jerry W. Hummel 1958
Zelia Rose Willis 1958
John W. Butler 1959
James Robert Byrd 1962

Theodore Wayne Koch 1964
Ernie L. Hobbs 1967
Michael W. Thompson 1967
Keith B. Vaughan 1967
Jerry W. Pease 1968
James C. Howard 1969
Robert Glenn Shelton 1975
Helen H. Taylor 1975
Harold Lewis Davis 1978
Sam K. Steely 1978

Mark Alan Walls 1978
Anthony R. Bryant 1980
Wilda Dean Worley 1980
Douglas Lee Fletcher 1981
Susan K. Taylor 1981
Douglas Eugene Tucker 1984
Robert Glenn Shelton 1997
Andy Jack Decker 2009

MARKETING

Raymond Arthur Partin 1959
Sandra Smith Ellsworth 1963
Paula Jean Hammons-Allen 1975
Gary Dean Howard 1975
Linda S. Tate 1978
Joseph M. Yonce 1979
Joy H. Marini 1981
Steven Paul McCoy 1981
George H. Cespedes 1982
Penni B. Neikirk 1983
Lydia Jill Higgins 1984

Ruhi Bedi 1985
Charles E. Travis II 1988
Janelle Maria Cavendish-McCarty 1989
Laura B. Mize 1990
Candace Hope Williams 1991
Angela Leigh Weigel 1992
Rachel Lynn Gustwiller 1997
Erin Elizabeth Wysocarski 1997
Bradley Scott Parham 1999
Michael Paul Quillen 1999
Erica Marie Hansen 2001

Allene Bellolivia Hayes 2002
Joshua Daniel Benton 2004
Michael J. Humphries 2004
Brittany Paige Christerson 2005
Daisuke Hirata 2005
Dedra Burke Duty 2006
Misty Lynn Blevins 2007
Matthew Joel McDowell 2008
Brittany Paige Christerson 2011

MATHEMATICS STATISTICS

Philip W. Brashear 1960
Virgie Thomas 1965

John Estep Sasser 1968
Kathy Elizabeth Rush 1986

Aric Daniel Schadler 2001

MAYOR

Jonathan G. Booher 1934
Harry G. Graham 1950

Michael W. Bryant Sr. 1969
Roger Elvis Harrison 1984

Roger Elvis Harrison 1989

MEDICAL ADMINISTRATION, MEDICAL ASSISTANT, MEDICAL RELATED, EMERGENCY MEDICAL TECHNOLOGIST

Hester Priscilla Pritchett 1947
Carl C. Johnson 1950
Gillis A. Clawson 1951
Ella Mae Shearon 1952
Louise B. Tipton 1954
Bill J. Eaton 1956
Henry P. Stephens 1956
Janice H. Kelly 1958
Marcus G. Yancey 1959
Garnell Blanton 1960
Ralph E. Hopkins 1960
Clarence Louis Bates 1962
Phillip Vaughn Akers 1963

Margaret Sue Barr 1964
Della S. Marshall 1965
Martin A. Pemberton Jr. 1965
Robert D. Slone 1966
James Roland Cetone 1969
Nancye E. Davis 1969
Joan Hays 1969
Billy Wayne Short 1969
Ralph Lipps 1970
Gary Dale Parker 1972
Paula Nee Thullen - Osborn 1973
Paul Eugene Barnes 1974
Kay W. Howard 1974

William R. Provence 1974
Richard Bryan Stokes 1974
Iva B. Griggs 1975
Earlane Cox 1976
Thomas Clark Heaberlin 1976
Sharon Ann Lowe 1976
Charles Thomas Snapp 1976
Kathryn J. Sullivan 1977
Bill Ray Young 1977
Lynette Cosby 1978
Susan Faith Frazier 1979
Paul Curtis Henson 1979
Pamela Teresa Dallas 1980

Cheryl J. Davis 1980
Beth O. Holthusen 1980
Karon Sue Clark 1981
Donna M. Clinkenbeard 1981
Saundra Gale Duncan 1981
Kimberly Edith Mullins 1981
Patricia Karen Renfro 1981
Kenneth Earl Riggsby 1981
Diane Lynn Roberts 1981
Hermina J. Robinson 1981
Donna J. Russell 1981
Noella M. Deaton 1982
Brenda Gayle Wilson 1982
Robert Klotzle 1983
David Schaufuss 1983
Anna L. Spencer 1983
Teresa Jane Mays 1984
Cheryl Anne Ringley 1984
Margaret Ann Wollen 1984
Nola A. Wyatt 1984
Kenneth R. Foster II 1985
Kenneth J. Reed 1985
Paul James Walker 1985
Jennifer Gail Wyatt 1985
Elizabeth Jackson 1986
Jane Elizabeth Murphy 1986
Diana Dugan Warmoth 1987
Paul Edward Cordell 1988
David Scott Cornett 1988
Rodney Brian Richardson 1988

George G. Shackleford 1988
Kari Kristine Ward 1988
Charles A. Dille IV 1989
Kimberly RayDen Wake 1989
Mark A. Hensley 1990
Donna Lynn Loveday 1990
Paul David Moyer 1990
Lee Rachelle Richardson 1990
Russell Dean Barker 1991
April D. Smith 1991
Wesley Kent Griebel 1992
David Lee Owens 1992
Gary James Strunk 1992
Donald Mark Walker 1992
Michael John Young 1992
Tonya Dee Arning 1993
Craig Meyer Cain 1993
Mark Allen Dye 1993
Christopher Brad Evans 1993
Lee Williams Richardson 1993
Lisa Renee Strunk 1993
Shannon Ruth Ball 1994
Terry Thomas Carr 1994
Gary Bradley Hall 1994
Gary Bradley Hall 1994
Kimberly Dawn Elliott 1995
Jason Elliott Thompson 1995
Kelly M. Goodin 1996
Jennifer Ann Ronniger 1996
Tracey Anne Schneeman 1996

Jacquelin M. Brown 1998
Carmen Marie Elliott 1998
Kellye Michelle Grimes 1998
Richard Marden 1999
Joseph Richard Martin 1999
Jennifer Rose Taylor 1999
Donita Raye Poynter 2000
Holly Renea Chitwood 2001
Shawna Marie Gilbert 2001
Jasie Kathryn Logsdon 2001
Nathan Andrew Riner 2002
Jonathon Darren Murray 2003
Megan Lanea French 2004
Deborah Ann Southerland 2004
Marsee Anne Huffman 2005
David Alan Powers 2005
Trisha Jean Price 2005
Laura Elizabeth Cornelius 2006
Noel Alexander Zvonar 2006
Jerrod Cameron Johnson 2007
Elizabeth Marie Johnson 2007
Jessica Amber Yeager 2007
Staci Cheri Case 2008
Megan Marie Magallon 2008
Noella M. Deaton 2009
Matthew Scott Jones 2010
Mark Edward Steely 2010
John Lee Mitchell 2012

MEDICAL TECHNOLOGIST

Elizabeth Austin 1937
Freda Y. Blakey 1939
Maureen E. McKinney 1941
Kathleen Scott 1942
Geraldine Bird 1943
Eloise Brown 1944
Loraine C. Burst 1945
Christine R. Fletcher 1945
Genevieve Alexander 1946
Margaret Johnson 1946
Nell C. Roach 1947
Sarah Alyne Taylor 1947
George E. Moses 1948
Waunita Kearney 1949
Gloria H. Monday 1949
Anne S. Clark 1950
Joann Coffman 1950
Edna Rose Walker 1950
Mary Lou Baker 1951
Wanda L. Bryant 1951
Phyllis J. Gaddy 1951
Peggy K. White 1951
Bette Bellamy 1952
Faye C. Henegar 1952
Peggy Ann Hodges 1952
Christine Whitehead 1952
Joyce Sue Cox 1953
Wilma B. Prewitt 1953
Jo Ann Safriet Harman 1954
Irene B. Denny 1955
Norma Lee Francis 1955
Peggy Lou Inks 1955
Norma Jean Bray 1956

Betty Lou Hutson 1956
Elsie Steele 1956
Betty J. Wood 1956
Marjorie A. Grout 1957
Martha Lee Ravenna 1957
Ted N. Stokes 1957
Carol Sue Collinsworth 1958
Connie M. Murphy 1958
June B. Russell 1958
Patricia Ann Douglas 1959
Lee Linville 1961
Jerry Wayne Ison 1962
Hettie Lou Pennington 1963
Barbara Faye Shedd 1963
Phillip E. Dixon 1964
Alice Alvena Hill 1965
Billy Sharian Hutt 1965
Elizabeth L. Johnson 1966
Elizabeth Hale 1967
Jean E. Wiggins 1967
Tommy K. Peercy 1969
Robert D. Moore ACA 1970
Cecilia Elizabeth Fohl 1972
Kenneth C. Hopper 1972
Cynthia Emily Griffith 1974
Brenda J. Darling 1975
Jo Ann Duncan 1975
Harold Bryan Barton 1977
James Mahan Renfro Jr. 1977
Leila D. Cromer 1978
Virginia Susan Bickers 1979
Judith Ann Collins 1979
Larry Gene Grant 1979
Cynthia J. Applegate 1980

Sharon Rose Coverdale 1980
Tim Daubenmire 1980
Janie B. Bridges 1981
Deanna J. Moore 1981
Connie Lynn Clark 1982
Janice Elaine Foley 1982
Tobitha M. Hainesworth 1982
Deborah Peace 1982
Robert Garland Carnes 1983
Janet B. Fields 1983
Terri Renee Woodward 1983
Paula Jean Lacefield 1984
Beverly Joyce McGowen 1984
Debra K. Moore 1984
Johnny L. Thomas 1984
Jolene Michele Goins 1985
Alice Ann Hardwick 1985
Melanie Aulds White 1985
Shawn A. Keegan 1986
Sonja Denise Kindig 1986
Leslie Karen Brewer 1987
Penny Ailene Madden 1987
Jay Andrew Weisenberger 1987
Kimberly Ann Wyatt 1987
Mark Shawn Orsborn 1989
Donald Andrew Greene 1991
Carl Lorenzo Croon 1992
Ambryn Kay Laubenstein 1995
Jillyne Sue Wisdom 1996
Brian Christopher Goelz 1999
John Eric Whitson 2003
Amanda Jo Clamme 2004
Andrea Carol Leach Hall 2005
Jolene Nichole Rethwisch 2005

MENTAL HEALTH, MENTAL HEALTH TECHNICIAN, PSYCHIATRIST, PSYCHOLOGIST

Genevieve D. Kohn 1943
Reba Moore 1964
Robert George Farrell 1981
Jeffrey L. Hicks Ph.D. 1982
Tracy Lynn Bryson 2002
Fred K. Campbell 2002

Jessica Page Canada 2004
Crystal Michelle Pace 2004
Amanda Lynn Coy 2007
Shannon Marie Gray 2007
James Hadren Worley Jr. 2007
Illyssa Marie Russell 2008

Amanda Lynn Coy 2009
Carletta Estelle Creekmore 2009
Russell David Maynard 2009
Shannon Marie Gray 2011
Carletta Estelle Creekmore 2012

MILITARY, ADJUTANT (MILITARY ASST), SERVICE RELATED ARMY, ETC.

Leslie W. Bailey 1937
John Baker 1937
George F. Carroll 1940
Theodore W. Clarke 1941
Curtis F. Martin 1941
Clifford C. Slaton USAF Ret. 1942
Dorothy Frances Kline 1948
Daymond E. Helton USAF Ret. 1949
Thomas Edward Arthur 1951
Harvey L. Wallace USAF Ret. 1952
Boyce Dean King 1953
Leonard Alfred Evans 1956
Gayle L. Hamblin 1957
John Edward Clinton USMC Ret. 1958
James Eldon Thomas 1958
Thomas E. Gillis 1962
Donnie L. Martin 1962
Nancy Faye Irene Stormer 1962
Eugene B. Davis USN Ret. 1963
George Gurley 1966
Robert Wayne Anderson 1969
Polly Hall 1969
Robert Donald Young 1969
Jim H. Siler 1970
Kenneth Theodore Clarke 1972
John Michael Sutherland 1972
Dreama F. Fumia 1974
John Elmer Noe 1974
Richard Mark Nixon USMC Ret. 1975
Marcia Patrao 1975
Jonathan Chuma Ikerionwu 1976
Kenneth McKiddy 1976
Alice Ruth Darnell 1977
Jimmy R. Barton 1978
Gabriel R. Collett 1978
Kenneth Stewart Dowd 1979
Robert Lee Hagan 1979
John D. Knox 1979
Dennis W. McMillen 1979
Daniel Quance 1979
Terry Lee Whiteside 1979
Frank Alphus Martin III 1980
Michael K. Lane Jr. 1981
Theodore James Merriss 1981

Deborah Karen Nonnemaker 1981
Thomas Wayne Cox 1982
Marcia Ann Hamblin 1982
Sandra Kay Merriss 1982
Linda Catharine Aberdeen 1983
Darryl Wayne Hensley 1983
Robert Paul Kennett 1983
Kevin Shackleford 1983
David A. Hammiel USAF 1984
David A. Hammiel USAF 1984
Thomas Edward McMillan 1984
Kenneth Grant Moody 1984
Paul D. Patterson Jr. 1984
Joseph Lance Smith 1984
James Baker Smith 1984
Mark E. Stephens 1984
Allison Sue Bowman 1985
William Moss Cox III 1985
Robert Fitzgerald Duke 1985
Alex E. Hill 1985
Norman Spears 1985
Kimberly Jo Clowser 1986
Christopher V. Herndon 1986
Martin Claye Ledington 1986
Stephen A. Robinson 1986
Ronald Rowland Robinson 1986
Brian Curry 1989
Thomas Andrew Deakins 1989
David Michael Farley 1989
Claude E. Hoffman 1989
Cassandra F. Maxwell 1989
Lance Cody Patterson 1989
Daphany Lynn Prewitt 1989
James Edward Scalf 1989
Danny Carl Howard 1990
Stephen C. Sears 1990
Kelvin Wayne Mauk USAF 1991
Brent Ashley McKinney 1991
Charles S. Paul 1991
John Edward Smith Jr. 1991
Charles R. Carter 1992
Anna Lisa Chappell 1992
Jeffery Lewis Holland 1992
David Allen Holt 1992

Kenneth Mitchell Knight 1992
Tewanna Katrina Moss 1993
Leslie Dean Begley 1994
Raymond Alan Slusher 1994
Raymond Alan Slusher 1994
Gary Lee Davis Jr. 1995
Julie Marie Francis 1995
Melita Beth Mullins 1995
Dale Edward Taylor 1995
Jeffrey Scott Harris 1997
Jeffrey Scott Harris 1997
Vinson Bryan Morris 1997
David Allen Mundrick Jr. 1997
David Allen Mundrick Jr. 1997
Peter & Hope Pohl 1998
James Matthew Smith USAR 1998
James Matthew Smith USAR 1998
Carl Wesley Pagles 1999
Joseph Eugene Tarry IV 1999
David Gregory Brumlow 2000
David Caleb Bingham 2001
Robert Eugene Certain Jr. 2001
Matthew Scott Holbrook USAR 2002
Issa Marie Alvarez 2004
Matthew Adam Halligan USMC 2004
Monica Carol Hardin 2004
Brian Edward Livingston USAF 2004
Jason Floyd Wood 2004
Kiara Teresa Baugh 2005
Barron Neal Davis 2005
Timothy Dale Dowd 2005
Mandy Lee Pursley 2005
Kendall Louis Brown 2006
Christopher Lloyd Browning 2006
Colin Michael Corrigan 2006
Kenneth James Smith 2006
Marc Thomas Leng 2007
Joel Hobson Taylor 2007
Andrew George Gebert 2008
Peter George Wooden 2008
Sharon Kay McDonald 2009
Clint Jerry Moore 2009

MINING TECHNOLOGY

Homer Cobb 1952
Claude West 1969

Eddy Ray Brittain 1973
Johnny M. Newport 1976
Keith Root 1976

Randall Partin 1978
Calvin E. Riddle 1982
Lester Scott Cox 1988

MINISTRY, PASTOR, CLERGY

Robert H. Stephens 1930
Louise M Bowers 1931
George Grubbs 1935
Robert W. South 1935
Daniel W. Carroll 1936
Clive Smith 1936
William Jackson Johnson 1940
Elmer S. West Jr. 1941
H. Marlowe Link 1948
Raymond M. White 1948
Green Ellis 1949
Paul J. Godsey 1949
Burney Manning 1950
Robert Earl Moses 1950
Sylvia P. Pollard 1950
Willie Paul Shoupe 1950
Will T. Bowlin 1951
Orville D. Hickey 1951
R. B. Hooks Jr. 1951
Billy Grey Hurt 1951
Wayne O. Markham 1951
Mae E. Miller 1951
Robert D. Hopkins 1953
Lenwood N. Nichols 1954
Marshall Phillips 1954
John P. Weaver 1954
Ledies Bargo 1955
Ray Cummins 1955
Thomas D. Davidson Sr. 1955
Marshall N. Eastham 1955
Fred B. Hill 1955
Bill Mitchell 1955
Eugene Reynolds 1955
Franklin & Lola Woods 1955
Troy A. Christopher 1956
Richard A. DeBell 1956
H.G. Pratt 1956
Archie C. Brock 1957
Jerry D. Hayner 1957
Earl J. Hopkins 1957
John N. Meadows 1957
Thomas G. Younger 1957
Ben A. Baird 1958
Jesse Buell 1958
Richard Dendler 1958
Wilmer Glenn Edwards 1958
Jerry D. Lowrie 1958
Gordon Ewing Price 1958
W. Wayne Price 1958
Dennis A. Spaulding 1958
Leslie W. Baker 1959
Coy Elmo Brewer 1959
Kendall Hatton 1961
Gary K. Sharp 1961
Edsel Lee West 1961
James Garland Bridges 1962
Allen F. Harrod 1962
John Calvin Hornsby 1962
Joseph M. Slade Jr. 1962
William Robert Cobb 1963
Chester P. Culver 1963
Ralph Nolan Hopkins 1963
Kenneth R. Leach 1963
Robey A. Walters 1963
Arthur A. Wilson 1963
David Douglas Aker 1964

Bill Collett 1964
Robert A. Finley 1964
William M. Thomas 1964
Eleazer Benenhaley 1965
Earl R. Jackson 1965
Janus Eugene Jones 1965
Ernest Mitchell Harris 1966
Marion Martin 1966
Sam B. Smith 1966
Joe E. Burton 1967
Robert D. Mantooth 1967
Floyd D. Price 1967
Roger Darrell Williams 1967
James Houston Clark 1968
Roy S. Faulkner 1968
Robert L. Hedrick 1968
Calvin Durand Hibbard 1968
Bill Messer 1968
E. Linville Miller 1968
James Clayton Allen 1969
Michael W. Bryant Sr. 1969
Bradford Howard Coffey 1969
Ronald W. Lee 1969
Phillip W. McClendon 1969
Larry Sears Nichols 1969
Larry W. Stewart 1969
Donald R. Yeager 1969
Anthony B. Carson 1970
Everette Walter Eads 1970
Stephen E. Earle 1970
Richard H. Harris 1970
Leonard Samuel Markham 1970
Ronnie Crit Mitchell 1970
John C. Vaughn 1970
Edna Mae Wagers 1970
William E. Willard 1970
Ted C. Avant 1971
Ronald L. Chastain 1971
Joseph Mixon Cowart 1971
Richard E. Hill Sr. 1971
James Elmer Holloway 1971
Karen Gale Lovett 1971
William E. Owens Sr. 1971
Charles E. Webster 1971
Bob Bausum 1972
Cyrus William Bush 1972
Gayle L. Clifton 1972
Charles Kimp Coffman 1972
C. Kenny Cooper 1972
Ruby Couch 1972
Jerry Merridieth Easley 1972
Victor L. Edwards 1972
Donald Joe Kannady 1972
Donald G. McGuire 1972
Dennis A. Meyer 1972
Glenn Noe 1972
Philip Daniel Ronk 1972
Gary Allen Rose 1972
Ronald Wagers 1972
John P. Wesley 1972
Isaiah W. Cotton 1973
James Larry Hannah Sr. 1973
David L. Hughes 1973
John William Keith 1973
Donald David Martin 1973
Bobby Joe Rouse 1973

James Edward Taylor 1973
Curtis James Wagers 1973
W. Carl Zinn 1973
Steve Fegenbush 1974
Anthony Gerrard Givens 1974
Johnny M. Jervis Jr. 1974
Kenneth Wayne Marler 1974
Sharon Diane Mitchell 1974
John Carl Moore 1974
Paul Edward Tirey 1974
Terry Yeager 1974
William Ray Campbell 1975
James Ledford Cox Jr. 1975
Kenneth Lyle Faught 1975
Ronald Wayne Griffin 1975
Bobby Ray Hallmark 1975
George Irvin Hensley 1975
Pam Huffman 1975
Ronald Ralph Huffman 1975
Mark Orr Johnson 1975
Carlos King 1975
Danny Mullins 1975
Ricky D. Pelfrey 1975
Clara M. Reed 1975
Terry W. Sharp 1975
Don F. Smith 1975
H. Craig Smith 1975
David Malcom Thomas 1975
George Edward Thompson 1975
Daniel Wilkerson 1975
Stephen Wayne Alford 1976
Ron Dale Andrew 1976
David L. Burt 1976
James Edward Carpenter 1976
William Ronald Cathers 1976
Richard Steven Copenhaver 1976
Daryl Kim Cox 1976
Sam Ray Davenport 1976
Michael Franklin Gibson 1976
Larry W. Huff 1976
Timothy Jerome Johnson Sr. 1976
Ernest Lemoine Laughner 1976
Roger Douglas Martin 1976
Robert Joseph Mobley 1976
Terry Zane Murphy 1976
George Lee Naylor 1976
Billy D. Reynolds 1976
Leonard Charles Robinson 1976
James H. Shemwell 1976
Rick Shoemaker 1976
Charles R. Shonkwiler 1976
James E. Simpson 1976
Angia Kay Snyder 1976
Thomas J. Sparks 1976
Dennis Randall Tate 1976
Doug White 1976
John Douglas White 1976
Kenneth Ray Whitehouse 1976
Willie E. Ailstock III 1977
Harold Fred Black 1977
Glenda Cox 1977
Harold Dean Haun 1977
William David Henard III 1977
Johnnie L. Holloway 1977
Taylor Hooker 1977
Steven Adrian Jett 1977

Mark Andrew Keith 1977
David Michael Lee 1977
James Lowe 1977
Drew Martin 1977
Michael G. McCoy 1977
Charles Wayne Myers 1977
Barry L. Roberts 1977
Allen Lee Shouse 1977
Michael Thomas Smith 1977
Carl H. Young 1977
Donald Morrow Black 1978
Philip Michael Campbell 1978
Victor Babatunde Dada 1978
Daniel Wade Davis 1978
Michael Wayne Hail 1978
Jewell Edward Hail Jr. 1978
Robert M. Hanson 1978
Richard V. Holden 1978
David Edmond Hyde 1978
Gary Leonard Kasey 1978
Michael Glen Long 1978
Jerry H. Mantooth 1978
William Robert Miller 1978
Evelyn Ruth Miller 1978
David S. Mosley 1978
James Ernest Murray Jr. 1978
Wendle Shane Nickell 1978
Larry W. Riley 1978
Charles Bailey Scrivener 1978
Richard Spencer 1978
Jerry L. Tooley 1978
Bernard Lee Toppings 1978
Kenneth Ora Willoughby 1978
Kemp Edward Wynn 1978
Richard Allen Adams 1979
Robert Lee Barnes 1979
Terry W. Broyles 1979
Michael Caudill 1979
Bruce Douglas Couch 1979
Herbert Kenneth Dick 1979
Scott W. Ferry 1979
Duane A. Floro 1979
Rick Martin Frazier 1979
Barbara June Gregory 1979
Russell Gross 1979
Rodney Keith Hale 1979
Clayton Hanshaw 1979
Mitchell Houston Jones 1979
Edward Ray Lafferty 1979
John Nunley 1979
Donald Glen Petree 1979
Floyd A. Powell 1979
Robert Charles Rice 1979
Brian Lee Shoemaker 1979
Jerry Wayne Stanfield 1979
David Thomas Bickers 1980
William Daniel Blair 1980
Floyd Blake Jr. 1980
Joseph Edward Burt 1980
Carter H. Corbrey III 1980
Barry Wayne Draper 1980
Daniel Lee Ferguson 1980
Curtis H. Fox Sr. 1980
Darlene E. Frazier 1980
Steve Hogg 1980
Jeffrey R. Houghton 1980
Timothy David Maynard 1980
Randall Clayton Millwood 1980
Ralph Douglas Neal 1980
Berrimond Scott Pond 1980

Anthony Wayne Richmond 1980
Lonnie Riley 1980
John Douglas Stutz 1980
Jerry Eugene Waugh 1980
Carl Prentice Williams 1980
Mary E. Wright 1980
Donald Ray Wuerzer Jr. 1980
Patricia A. Baldwin 1981
Joseph Kie Bowman 1981
D. Terrell Bradley 1981
Jimmy Grant Caywood 1981
Ronald V. Chambers 1981
Mark Vincent Douglas 1981
J. Jonathan Gardner 1981
William Ray Gott 1981
Kenneth Earl Harp 1981
Vernon K. Holden Jr. 1981
David E. Meadows 1981
David Roscoe Moss 1981
Vincent Paul 1981
Earl Lester Quick 1981
Patricia Carol Quick 1981
Larry R. Sizemore 1981
David P. Soden 1981
David Milton Trimble 1981
Roger Lynn Webb 1981
Mark Randall Carmack 1982
David Charles Cheek 1982
H. Joel Dick 1982
Ronald Ray Dingus Jr. 1982
Michael Robert Duncan 1982
Michael R. Frazier 1982
Mary Beth Hammett 1982
Larry Curtis Harmon 1982
James Roy Hume DMin 1982
Michael Alan Jones 1982
Gary Lee Lambert 1982
Edith Allene Little 1982
Mark Derrick Partin 1982
William M. Pearson 1982
Franklin Dwight Smith 1982
James Phillip Taylor 1982
Denvil Taylor Jr. 1982
D. R. Vencil 1982
Terri Carver Adams 1983
David Allen Cooper 1983
James Elliott 1983
Charles Gary Kirby 1983
Lequine Lee Lambert 1983
Timothy Britt Martin 1983
Stephen Len Nichols 1983
Jimmy Scott Orrick 1983
Elmer Lloyd Alder Jr. 1984
Jerry T. Browning 1984
Joy L. Cox 1984
Robert Jay Day 1984
Martin Louis Fischer 1984
Jackie Hendricks 1984
Lewis A. Jennings 1984
Donald L. Jones 1984
Joseph Thomas Lewis 1984
Donald Dwayne Lynch 1984
Jimmie Dale McKinney 1984
Rose E. Shelton Ph.D. 1984
Bruce E. Treon 1984
Roy T. Walker 1984
John D. Combs 1985
Roland Eugene Cornett 1985
David Goodwin Emmert 1985
Michael Edward Monroe 1985

Wayne Edwin Phillips 1985
David Kentner Popham 1985
Kenneth Darrel Schick 1985
H. Steven Scudder 1985
Shaun S. Shorrosh 1985
John Roger Stanley 1985
D. R. Vencil 1985
Jeff Scott Whitehouse 1985
Tom A. Wicker 1985
Vola W. Brown 1986
William Langford 1986
John Thomas Patterson 1986
Todd Ronald Stewart 1986
Edwin T. Adkins 1987
Jerry Douglas Adkins 1987
Robert Eugene Burnett 1987
Daniel Edward Flynn 1987
Rose M. Istre 1987
Timothy Joseph Kraynak 1987
Timothy A. Morris 1987
Leonard A. Steuwe Jr. 1987
Timothy Wayne Thompson 1987
Steven Neal Davidson 1988
Charles Edward Higgins Jr. 1988
Roy H. McNiel 1988
Wesley Paul 1988
Mary Lee Shelley 1988
Stephen L. Whitaker 1988
Richard Eric Bowden 1989
Michelle Elaine Cloud 1989
Peter John Coleman 1989
Daryl C. Cornett 1989
Randall Scott Edwards 1989
Keenan Todd Franklin 1989
Jeffrey Lynn Perkins 1989
Terry Allen Roberts 1989
Luther Todd Allen 1990
Virgil R. Grant 1990
Kevin D. Hampton 1990
Kevin W. Roach 1990
Wesley Glenn Brockway 1991
Richard Preston Burns 1991
Margaret Feltner 1991
Matthew K. Robbins 1991
Troy D. Shelton 1991
Christopher Shawn Watson 1991
Hiram Wesly Williamson 1991
Shannon Ray Back 1992
Roddy Gene Bracken 1992
Paul Harrison Chitwood 1992
Terre' A. Jasper 1992
John Kenneth Jordan 1992
Donna Sue Kidd 1992
Robert Wesley Roy Jr. 1992
Edward Lee Barnes 1993
Kelvin Mandel Blackshear 1993
Nicholas Theodore Osborn 1993
James Landon Stewart 1993
Nathan Everett Ward 1993
Daniel Keith West 1993
William Bradley Clark Jr. 1994
Douglas William Grote 1994
David Ray Hewitt 1994
Albert Wayne Jones 1994
Sarah Catherine Sleet 1994
Stewart Smith 1994
Chad Douglas Blevins 1995
John Scott Brady 1995
Richie Alan Cheek 1995
Paul Gregory Cornelius 1995

Shawn Wesley Finch 1995
Logan Blaine Murphy IV 1995
Kevin Michael Parker 1995
Christopher Donald Talley 1995
Amy Denise Wilhelmus 1995
Robert Anthony Adams 1996
Joe Williams Allen Jr. 1996
Jason Matthew Pierce 1996
Timothy Gronendyke 1997
Darrel Andrew Rewis 1997
Lesley Jo Swann 1997
Ryan Philip Tucker 1997
Benjamin Mark Beaudoin 1998
Nathan Michael Howard 1998
Jerry Daniel Kemper 1998
Justin Carl Murphy 1998
Matthew Clay Norton 1998
Stephen H. Ambrose 1999
Karen Lee Broyles 1999
Joseph Michael Dodridge 1999
Scott Aaron Ogle 1999
Robert Anthony Pursley 1999
Donald George Settles 1999
Galen Matthew Combs 2000

David Alan Hockney Jr. 2000
Aaron Denny Hogue 2000
Johnny B. Lewis 2000
Matthew O. McKee 2000
Tony Clifford Merida Ph.D. 2000
Ryan Nathan Stelk 2000
Jamie Dean Woodyard 2000
Michael Dan Cabell 2001
Lori Lunsford 2001
Joy Susanne Schadler 2001
Matthew J. Walton 2001
Thomas J. Wright 2001
Heather Marie Cheney 2002
Jonathan Michael Eskridge 2002
Roger Kevin Floyd 2002
Matthew A. Howe 2002
Emily Christine Pepper 2002
David Alan Riggs 2002
Jack Wendall Willis II 2002
Timothy Paul Farmer 2003
Scott Allan Gilbert 2003
Michael David Jones 2003
Matthew Thomas McKay 2003
Brandon Lee Moore 2003

Gordon Dale Prather Jr. 2003
Charles Ryan Sumner 2003
Joseph Paul Thomas 2003
James Brandon Elkins 2004
Elley Pittard Fisk 2004
Andrew Michael Mahan 2004
Daniel Scott McKee 2004
Daniel Allen Plemons 2004
David Michael Reed 2004
David Michael Reed 2004
Sarah Courtney Hodges 2005
Christina Madelyn Newby 2005
James Floyd Wilson 2005
Janet Lee Jones Brown 2006
Christopher Douglas Neal 2007
David Kelley Baldridge 2009
Gregory Edward Bruce 2009
Sean Patrick Hendy 2009
Ronald Lee Watkins 2009
Forrest James Coleman 2010
Ronald Lee Watkins 2010
Gregory Edward Bruce 2011

MISSIONARY

Gifford Walters 1924
Elizabeth Y. Evans 1942
Horace David Coppedge III 1969
Cora Elizabeth Atkinson 1970
Howard Gene Atkinson 1971
Gerald L. Rice 1972
Teresa Rice 1973

Robert Leon Green 1975
Susan Thompson 1976
Sharon Diane Finch 1977
William Frank Thompson 1977
Frederick Louis Heineman 1981
Bobby R. Blevins 1983
Oliver Clay Hawkins Jr. 1987

Oakie Lea Blevins 1989
Gregory Allen Phillips 1989
Cheri Beth Floyd 1991
Todd Ryan Hughes 1997
Sarah Brooke Pounds 2000
Joshua Josiah Pollitt 2008

MUSICIAN, SINGER

Jean Ritchie 1944
Jack Wade Scalf 1962
Johnny C. Chadwell 1977
Elizabeth C. Griffin 1982

Lynn M. Slaughter 1982
Marvin Edward West 1990
Robin Gadd 2008
Simon Wesley Louallen 2009

Lynn M. Slaughter 2009
Robin Gadd 2011

NURSE, NURSE PRACTITIONER, NURSE AID

Hazel C. Ellis 1930
Margaret B. Lewis 1931
Faye E. Willis 1931
Margaret Marsh Smith 1938
Virginia W. Casey 1942
Liz Young Krause 1945
Sarah L. Moore 1946
Bonnie Ruth Bishop 1952
Rhoda Ann Guenthner 1953
Nancy J. Scroggins 1953
Alva Flynn Breeding 1954
Selmalou Bryant 1955
Barbara Jane Meeks 1955
Doris Jean Wilham 1955
Billy J. Hampton 1959
Clarice Anita Wilson 1959
Ralph Judd Alford 1960
Betty Sue Watson 1960
Frances Y. Hughes 1962
Dortha P. Hatmaker 1965
Martha Ann Heneisen 1966

Jack C. Lane 1966
Nancy Beth Baksa 1968
Shirley Davis 1968
Elaine Lipps 1968
Patricia Barton 1970
Karen Lieane Rotz 1971
Jane M. Buckner 1972
Corinne Teresa Hudson 1972
Norman D. Bentley 1973
Geneva D. Rollins 1973
Lynne Sennett 1974
Marjorie J. Worley 1974
Barbara Root Bargo 1975
Velma Bowling 1975
Von Leon Bullock 1975
Janice Sue Dalton 1975
Evelyne P. Dupier 1975
Richard A. Gibson 1975
Vickie Hollen 1975
Pamela Jo Johnston 1975
Hazel B. Lawler 1975

Henrietta P. Miracle 1975
Teri C. Mountjoy 1975
Elizabeth A. Neal 1975
Mary M. Pennington 1975
Jayola R. Saylor 1975
Deborah Sue Shelley 1975
Karen C. Stephens 1975
Connie F. Warner 1975
Nancy Wilkinson 1975
Everett Eugene Wyatt 1975
Glenn Adkins 1976
Wookena Lynne Alder 1976
Carl A. Burroughs 1976
Lou Ella Cole 1976
Lois Ann Davis 1976
Martha Rebecca Garrison 1976
Jeanette Harrison 1976
Donna Lynn Hickman 1976
Dee Joiner 1976
Lena Ruth Meadors 1976
Carolyn J. Meeds 1976

Deane Nelson 1976
Rebecca M. Owens 1976
Beulah Abner Penn 1976
Sherry Lynn Robbins 1976
Lillian E. Sparks 1976
Kimiko Stallings 1976
Roberta J. Ward 1976
Martha Sue Wilcox 1976
Lydia Zimmerman 1976
Ramona Jill Booth 1977
Ramona Jill Booth 1977
Gary Wayne Brown 1977
Barbara Caroline Coston 1977
Joanna Lynne Cox 1977
Rhonda Kay Foley 1977
Shirley Ann France 1977
Pamela Dolen Guy 1977
Mary Lou Hutson 1977
Helen Sue Jones 1977
Dawn Jones-Baer 1977
Katherine Elaine Kaufling 1977
Pamela Jo Maynard 1977
Sandra Lynn Nickell 1977
Sandra Brooks Payne 1977
Barbara J. Peterson 1977
Vivian Anderson 1978
Debbie Lynn Baker 1978
Muriel Kathline Barnhill 1978
Mary Ann Blevins 1978
Kathy Rose Burdette 1978
Claudia G. Caines 1978
Carlene Hasting 1978
Donna Sue Rhodes 1978
Vivian Ruth Scharf 1978
Kathy L. Bellamy 1979
Velma Margaret Cardwell 1979
Gladys Hart Cornn 1979
Terri Lyn Elliott 1979
Cheryl Rae Graham 1979
Tina Gross 1979
Kimberly A. Hempleman 1979
Lauren K. Hester 1979
Carol Jean Hitch 1979
Marletta Kay Lawson 1979
Lori L. Lowmaster 1979
Brenda L. Mack 1979
Anna Jean Mahan 1979
Glenda Sue Martin 1979
Elizabeth B. Riley 1979
Wanda M. Siler 1979
Pamela Diane Sizemore 1979
Janet Leigh Smith 1979
Lisa Stewart 1979
Ruth Lorene Wilson 1979

Patsy M. Adams 1980
Donna Jane Bennett 1980
Charlene Brown 1980
Dianna L. Davis 1980
Lisa Nell Davis 1980
Katherine Jeanette Ferguson 1980
Sandra Greear 1980
Linda Lou Greene 1980
Colleen M. Greenwell 1980
Linda Gail Grumblatt 1980
Elizabeth C. Harp 1980
Mary J. Higgins 1980
Terri Lynn Moore 1980
Susannah Janelle Mullally 1980
Patricia Jacoba Nies 1980
Tammy Y. Prewitt 1980
Patricia Spears 1980
Martha Ann Steele 1980
Marcia Gayle Stout 1980
Lisa Morgan Trujillo 1980
Anna A. Tucker 1980
Deborah Sue Wilson 1980
Illana B. Wines 1980
Mary Magdalene Baker 1981
Patsy Ann Bunch 1981
Bridgett Janell Chaudry 1981
John David Drazdik 1981
Danny Feltner 1981
Deborah Ellen Foster 1981
Deborah Ellen Foster 1981
Patsy J. Lawson 1981
Retta Sue Lee 1981
Sandra Jo Maner 1981
Sherrie Lynn Mays 1981
Autumn Elaine Mays 1981
Judy Ann McKiddy 1981
Suzette Marie Mills 1981
Dianne L. Napier 1981
Pamela Sue Painter 1981
Carla Ann Pasqualini 1981
Carolyn Sue Peace 1981
Rhonda Rae Pfoff 1981
Kristi Kai Simms 1981
Sandra Carolyn Young 1981
Valerie Gayle Allen 1982
Jean Barton 1982
Margaret Ann Carnes 1982
Renee Susan Church 1982
Cynthia Marlene Harris 1982
Natalie B. Matthews 1982
Frankie Daniel Miller 1982
Nancy Audrey Mullins 1982
Tammy Woodby 1982
Deborah L. Baker 1983

Sandra Faye Bays 1983
Marcia Gail Bogue 1983
Kenneth Wade Cornett 1983
Sherri Ann Davison 1983
David Brian Grinstead 1983
Victoria L. Hubbard 1983
Mark Roberts 1983
Teresa Ann Russell 1983
Ronda Denise Sharp 1983
Laurie Lynn Tucker 1983
Ginny Paulette Volkman 1983
Gwendolyn Diane York 1983
Vicki Lee Bell 1984
Ruby (Mickey) M. Clifton 1984
Benita Ruth Jackson 1984
Terry Marie Moore 1984
William R. Kinney 1985
Martha Louise Blansette 1986
John Paul Eversole 1986
Laurie Orr 1986
Gwendolyn C. Rickett 1987
Teresa Lynn Burns 1988
Samantha Kay Cooper 1988
William Cody Martin 1988
Alice J. Harp 1989
Kimberly Ann Reynard 1990
Karen Lynn Shoop 1990
Cheryl Laurayne Dodd 1991
Amy Carolyn Neer 1991
Karen Michelle Wilson 1991
Mae B. Odgen 1992
Anthony Glenn Dillander 1994
Ethel Jane Leach 1994
Joseph Cass Paul 1994
Christine Ann Oliphant 1995
Cheryl Lynn Gebbie 1996
Linda Carolyn Hale 1997
Tracy Michelle Kramer 1998
Alicia Jean Cottrell 2000
Carla Michelle Jarboe 2000
Christina Gail Scott 2000
Christy Suzanne Brush 2001
Erica Dawn Joyner 2001
Jodi Nicole Rominger 2001
Maggie Elaine Robinson 2002
Randy Terry 2002
Janet Ayers 2006
Rachel Megan Elbon 2006
Christen Michelle Von Hertsenberg 2006
Alice Faye Anderson 2007
Janet Ayers 2009
Jodie Elizabeth Quillen 2010
Rachel Elizabeth Harp 2012

NUTRITION, MEDICAL HEALTH SERVICES

Jimmy M. Kamso-Pratt MD, Ph.D. 1975
Maxine Lora Mullennix 1983
Charlene Hawkins 1984

Deborah Dell Tidrick 1994
Jerry Wayne Barker 1996
Sheila Rae Noe 2002
Jaime Susan France 2003

Amy Lynn Hicks 2003
Ashley Dawn Clark 2008
Sarah Patricia Lovitt 2008
John Henry Begley 2009

OFFICE MANAGER, OFFICE WORKER

Rae C. Pond 1979
Edna M. Moses 1998

Brenna Dolores Smith 1999
Jerri Susanne Carroll 2001

Karen Lynn Paul 2002
Sara Eliza Kroetsch 2004

Emily Shawn Benton 2005   Mirissa Kay Nicole Cumpston 2012

OPERATOR

Bertha Sue Faulkner 1968   Jonathan Cole McKeehan 1980   Mark Douglas Caldwell 1991
George Robert Morgan 1971   Gary Lee Hollis 1984   Jacqueline Ann Campbell 1993
Patricia Ann Foley 1976   Jay L. Whirley 1986   Jarrod Lynn Johnson 2009

PARK RANGER

Conley Edmon Blevins 1961   James Edward Arnold 1974   Danny Emery Brown 1975
Renn C. Strunk 1967   Darryl Dean Bingham 1974   John David Young Jr. 2002

PATHOLOGIST

Wanda A. Freeman 1961   Kimberly Jo Turner 1987   Kristy Michelle Bolen 2001
Johnny Roger Brown 1971   Amy Williams 1991   Amy Marie Ritchie 2001
Janice Pauline Crick 1979   Erica Lynn Wilson 1996   Candice Hart Coleman 2002
Patricia Parkey 1983   Aleme Assefa 1997   Teresa Kay Lawson 2006
Michelle H. Ledger 1984   Trent Anderson Hayes 1997
Scarlet W. Henderson 1986   Virginia Louise Mills 1997

PERSONAL SERVICES

Herbert (Jerry) G. Taylor 1958   Dwight Lemore Haun 1982   Jennifer Lee Endicott 1996
Bonnie Lee McCullah 1961   Susan Zorn 1983   Jason R. Moody 2003
David C. Gay 1973   Vickie Leech Kelly 1994

PERSONNEL HUMAN RESOURCES

Millard R. Francis 1955   Scott Michael Murphy 1977   Belinda Lee Lonergan 1994
John D. Staley Jr. 1961   Edwin D. Langford 1979   Lisa Marie Weiss 1995
John David Damron 1962   Laura Gayle Terrell 1979   Heather Marie Scott 1996
Lester Joe Belcher 1967   Sandy K. Glick Lenk 1982   Wendy M. Heintz 1997
Helen P. Rector 1968   Robin Lynn Croley 1983   Jennifer Kay Meador 1998
Joyce E. Proffitt 1970   S. Dawn Moreland 1985   Brandon Lee Pettit 1998
Michael Charles Dougherty 1971   Vicki Renee Blair 1986   Christopher D. Jones 1999
Clayton Woods 1972   Darin Robert Steely 1989   Rebecca Louise Lindeman 1999
Albert Earl Chitwood Jr. 1974   Gregory Scott Nunnelley 1991   Meredith Elise Sizemore 2000
Nannette E. Jensen 1974   Tammy Jolene Varble 1991   Jennifer Kaye Barry 2001
Michael S. Scales 1974   Maria Aileen Hooks 1992   Timothy Wayne Phipps 2001
Thomas Champe Greis Jr. 1975   David Todd Hurst 1993   Joni Marie Bingham 2002

PHARMACIST, PHARMACOLOGY, PHARMACY TECHNOLOGIST

Manuel P. Romero 1939   Glenn G. Sasser 1964   John Shell 1973
Donald T. Rollins 1953   James Edward Walden 1964   Gary M. Briggs 1974
Joe Hurst 1954   Fred Cox 1965   Mark Eugene Goodan 1974
Donald Stanfill 1954   E. H. Creekmore 1965   Catina L. Cain 1976
Floyd T. Curd 1955   Alton Wilson 1965   Teresa Adell Brown 1980
Ronald M. Rains 1955   Terry L. Disney 1966   Pamela Jo Mellott 1980
Victor E. Pettit 1956   Dallas and Carolyn Petrey 1968   Roger L. Powers 1980
Sue Garner Sims 1958   R. Bruce Yandell 1969   Patricia L. Carr 1981
Jimmie W. Lockhart 1959   Gene C. Farley 1970   Gail Jean Lunsford 1981
Jerry L. Marcum 1959   Kenneth Ray Shaw Jr. 1970   William Alan Shepherd 1983
Bernard Moore 1959   Dalton Trent Walters 1970   Sherry Lynn Rains 1984
Donald Ray Hamlin 1960   Robert Edward Croley 1972   Darrell Craig Mack 1985
William Edward Entrekin 1964   Cordell K. Brown 1973   John Tipton McNiel Jr. 1987
B. R. Minnich Jr. 1964   Steve Leeds 1973   Craig D. Vermillion 1989

Paul Frederick Wolfe 1990
Donald Lynn Branam 1993
Karen Dismukes Maples 1993
Donna R. Majewski 1994
Christina A. Darden 1998
Sarah Jane Raines 1998
Toshia Rae Reid 1998

Matthew Clinton Fields 2000
Jessica Nicole Wilson 2004
Brittany Lachelle O'Neal 2005
Ciera Danielle Swords 2008
Jeffery Erik Cloud 2009
Victor Joseph Gregory 2009
Christina Danielle Hayes 2009

Jennifer Leeann Mooneyham 2009
Jefferson Lee Davis 2010
Jennifer Yvonne Price 2010
Jordan Cox Smith 2010
Stacy Michelle Starrett 2010
David Bruce Phillips 2012

PHOTOGRAPHER

M. Chandler Scifres 1935
Charles E. Kelly 1950

William Vincent Cox 1983
Tyne Elaine Lyle 2006

PHYSICIAN, SURGEON, PEDIATRICIAN, GYNECOLOGIST, OPTOMETRIST

Charles G. Baker 1924
Reuben N. Lawson 1927
Robert E. Lawson 1935
Ralph M. Denham 1936
Doris V. Spegal 1937
Orville Leo Meadors 1940
Charles Luther Roach 1940
Charles E. Freeman 1942
John Woodrow Simmons 1943
Benjamin R. Baker 1944
John D. Hummel Jr. 1944
Leo Randall Taylor 1944
Jo Anne Sexton M.D. 1946
Jo Anne Sexton M.D. 1946
Hoover A. Perry 1948
Chloe Chitwood 1949
Norman L. Renfro 1949
Paul Ray Smith 1949
James B. Cox 1950
John R. Jones 1951
Frank H. Catron Sr. 1953
Wallace B. Sullivan 1953
Don R. Stephens 1954
Truman R. Perry 1955
Paul C. Powers 1955
Charles L. Stephens 1955
Ruth Demetral 1956
George Greene Ellis 1956
Terrell D. Mays 1957
Gary S. Sowder 1959
M. Charlene Robinson 1960
Donald Lee Evans 1961
Wanda A. Freeman 1961
Gerald Ray Roberts 1962
Glen R. Baker Jr. 1964
Lee Gatliff Durham 1965
M. Ruth Perry 1965
Michael C. Bilinsky 1968
Jack D. Heneisen 1968
Lewis Wayne Cornelius 1969
Jack L. Hollins M.D. 1969
Fred M. Southard 1970
Johnny Roger Brown 1971

Paul W. King 1971
Michael D. Perkins 1971
Carolyn B. Petrey 1971
James Everett Croley III 1972
Charles Grant Dye 1972
Bernard Charles Moses 1972
C. Ray Young 1972
Johnny James Lipps 1973
Nancy Katheryn West 1973
Don V. Bryson 1974
Daniel David Sennett 1975
Larry E. Taylor 1975
Arlene Yvonne Alsgaard 1976
Linda Ford Gooch 1976
Larry Helveston 1976
William Dwayne Sizemore 1976
James Cauley 1977
Nola R. Ball 1978
James Edward Brennan 1978
Michael Abiodun Ibrahim 1978
Janice Pauline Crick 1979
Kimberly Cornelius 1980
Richard H. Mays 1980
Michael Ostapchuk 1980
Donna Yvonne Morhous 1982
Patricia Parkey 1983
Anthony C. Adams 1984
Michelle H. Ledger 1984
Michael Loren Clark 1985
Cheryl Cole 1985
Jackie D. Maxey 1985
Eddie Steely Perkins 1985
Scarlet W. Henderson 1986
John Curtis Mobley 1986
Robert Michael Derr 1987
Larry Travis Lay 1987
Kimberly Jo Turner 1987
John Anthony Johnson 1989
Robert Francis Monestel 1991
Steven Edward Morton 1991
William Partin 1991
Amy Williams 1991
Jared Kevin Wilson 1991

David Michael Lefler Jr. 1992
Brian Douglas Looney 1992
Suzanne Michelle Morton 1993
Lynn Ellen Engle-LaNeve 1994
Jill Cox Browning 1995
Elizabeth Anne Butcher 1995
Eric Ronald Mullins 1995
Thomas Lewis Wheeler II 1995
Erica Lynn Wilson 1996
Marty Allen 1997
Aleme Assefa 1997
Trent Anderson Hayes 1997
Virginia Louise Mills 1997
Donnie Wayne Bunch 1998
Stanley Robert Daniel M.D. 1998
Bradley Paul Gipson 1998
Ty Owen Hanson 1998
Joshua Eric Nichols 1998
Michael William Presley 1998
Paul Thomas Provance 1998
Jarred Jeremy Thomas 1998
Christopher William Edwards 1999
Kelvin Dale Perry 1999
Danny Eugene Yarger 1999
William David Arnold 2000
Jennifer Rice Howell 2000
Casey Brock Patrick 2000
Kristy Michelle Bolen 2001
Annie Josephine Cruz 2001
Travis Daniel Gilbert 2001
Miranda Gray M.D. 2001
Dusty Allen Moses 2001
Amy Marie Ritchie 2001
Rachel Ezell Bevins 2002
Candice Hart Coleman 2002
Charles Christian Key 2002
Jason Edward Goodman 2003
David Michael Hesson M.D. 2003
Cassandra Hope Nida 2003
Brent Joseph Morris M.D. 2004
Grover Chase Wilson 2004
DeAnna Marie Ball 2006
Teresa Kay Lawson 2006

PHYSICIST

Charlie Gibbs 1951
Ray Darwin Foley 1965

Candace Ruth Perry 1999
Simeon Phillip Hodges III 2000

PILOT, FLIGHT ATTENDANT

Roger D. Chambers 1970
Michael B. Powers 1972
Anthony J. White 1975

Joseph D. Hicks 1979
Daphne J. Graves 1981
Guy Kent Franklin 1990

Brian David Hudson 1995
Christopher James King 1995

PLACEMENT SPECIALIST

Julia L. Satterwhite 1937
Stephen Henry Lawson 1971

David Lee Crocker 1972
Theron L. Rowe 1988

Janet Elaine Ball 1990

PRINCIPAL, ASSISTANT PRINCIPAL

Frank Binford 1936
H J Litton 1947
Warren Glen Anderson 1953
Louis Gaines Steely 1954
William Augustus Lee 1962
Elsie E. Crabtree 1963
Robert Estes Sharp Jr. 1964
Naaman L. Cox 1965
Randall Eugene Denton 1969
James Richard Tucker 1969
Edward Lee Fields 1971
Joe Eddie Ledington 1971
Fred J. Nuss 1971
Mary Ann Robbins 1971
Johnny T. Smith 1972
Harry Lenn Chitwood 1973
Charles Hubert Minks 1973
William F. Steiner 1973
Lonnie David Couch 1974
Bonnie Lue Satterfield 1975
Eugene Hensley 1976

Derryl Renee King 1976
Geraldine R. Phillips 1976
Lee Charlene Hensley 1978
Gary Patton 1978
Leonard Aaron Greear 1980
Charles Edward Newton 1980
Donald Douglas Doan 1981
Michael J. Harris 1982
Margaret Sue Adkins 1983
Ramona Gail Davis 1983
Chester Ray Simpson 1983
Shawn David Robinson 1986
Winona L. Griggs 1988
Gregory Kirk Huff 1989
Donna J. Taylor 1989
Susan A. Brock 1990
Ron J. Treadway 1990
Susan A. Brock 1991
Donna J. Taylor 1991
Margaret Sue Adkins 1992
Lansford Hobert Lay Jr. 1993

Rachele Denean Rice 1994
Donna Sue Singley 1994
Sheila Rae Hobbs 1996
Lorraine Sue Stivers 1996
James Randall Durham Jr. 1998
Robi W. Votel 1998
Malinda Sue Brooks 1999
Lansford Hobert Lay Jr. 1999
Rachele Denean Rice 1999
Jason Wayne Creekmore 2000
Joseph Robert Ellison III 2001
Joseph Robert Ellison III 2001
Conley Travis Wilder 2002
Jason Wayne Creekmore 2003
Jason Craig Faulkner 2005
James Adam Brehm 2009
Rachel Ann Joiner 2009
Jason Wayne Creekmore 2011
Donna Sue Singley 2011
Lansford Hobert Lay Jr. 2012

PRODUCTION PLANNER

Dennis Dale Pruitt 1976
Hans Nathaniel Wortman 1989

Jason Hunter Hernandez 1997
Gabriel Shawn Crutchfield 2004

PROFESSIONAL SPORTS, SPORTS

Leon Silas Scearse 1957
Bill Carlyle 1960
Jack Douglas Froman 1972
Jerry Allen Stephens 1973
Brian D. Waddell 1975
James Elwood Dees 1977
James Earl Crawford 1981
Michael Wesley Heise 1984
Fred Lynn Gillum 1987
Richard Lee Stansbury 1989
Lamont J. Pennick 1991
Michelle Williams Pray 1991

James R. Ball 1993
Michelle Williams Pray 1993
Christopher Gilbert Anderson 1994
Rachelle Lanea Stebe 1994
Steven William Cummings 1996
Jeremy Allen Markham 1996
Jennifer Lynn Wake-Floyd 1997
Eddie Lee Lynch 3rd 1998
Jeremy Allen Markham 1999
Kevin P. Wardlaw 1999
Shawn Robin Berner 2000
Michael Shawn Rymer 2000

Kara Lindsay Clemenz 2002
Randall Jay Greer 2002
Randall Jay Greer 2002
Mark Alexander Vernon 2002
Kristopher Thomas Strebeck 2003
Glen Robert Bates 2004
Danika Jill Cox 2004
Jeremy Robert Stephenson 2005
Matthew Tyrus York 2005
Pierre Semoine Darden 2007
Mark Alexander Vernon 2008

PROFESSORS

Virginia W. Brumbach 1942
Roberta H. Hall 1944
Jess R. White 1948
Walter L. Helton 1951

Will Estil Waters 1952
Harold L. Moses 1956
Vivian B. Blevins 1958
James Edwin Gover 1959

Ronnie Day 1963
John P. Hollingsworth 1963
Linda N. Iams 1963
James Lee Cox Jr. 1964

Oline Carmical Jr. 1966
Bill D. Janeway 1966
Alex G. Cummins Jr. 1968
Gary Ronald Jones 1968
Thomas Brooks Frazier 1969
Fred Sagester 1969
Wayne F. Whitmer 1969
Mary Lou Beasley 1970
Suzanne Harris 1970
Doris Elaine Chitwood 1971
Kenneth LeRoy Beckett 1972
Gary Pate 1972
Chester Ballard 1973
Edna Jane Carter 1975

Ben Edmonds 1975
Steven Adrian Jett 1977
Geraldine Allen 1978
John Casey Carroll 1978
Karen L. Carey 1979
Dennis Jackie Smith 1979
James Ora Manning 1981
Virginia Ruth Young 1981
Elijah Buell Jr. 1982
Peggy Dianne Partin 1982
James Elliott 1983
Essam Sima'an Ackleh Ph.D. 1986
Thomas N. Hall 1986
James Richard Tarrant III 1986

Kenneth Stephen Sims 1987
Julie Lay-Choo Tan 1987
Chin Teck Tan 1987
Todd Matthew Hamilton Ph.D. 1990
Geraldine Allen 1992
Ava Marie Allison 1994
Nicole Lynn Moore 1997
Jennifer Anne Simpson 2000
Cristy Lynn Hall 2001
Ava Marie Allison 2008
Charles Christopher Browning 2009
Dennis Jackie Smith 2011
Chin Teck Tan 2011
Jennifer Anne Simpson 2012

PUBLIC RELATIONS

Frankie H. Jordan 1950
Donald Ray Miracle 1969
Carol Ann Shields 1969
Glena L. Buchanan 1970
Everett James White 1970

M. Lincoln Patrick 1971
David Elliott Ford 1980
Linda Gail Terry 1983
Peggy Jayne Jones 1986
Susan J. Mitchell 1988

Laura Vinson Northrop 1990
Jeffrey Scott Meadors 1996
Catherine Elizabeth Mack 2006

PUBLIC SERVICE

James Albert Jones 1947
Gilbert E. Bryant 1951
Amon Edward Blevins 1955
James Hillard Sutton 1958
Hershel Anthony Gaw Jr. 1959
Martha Elaine Crase 1965
Richard Lee Frederick 1965
Michael Grant Summers 1967
Donald W. Falin 1969
Ernest Ray Rudder 1969
William R. Holleran 1972
John Wesley Doughman 1976
John Davis Long 1979
Yvonne Combs 1980

Jon Christopher Haney 1981
Elva Lee Jones 1981
Bill David Orsborne 1981
Dusty Joe Allen 1983
Stephanie W. Gover 1989
Lawrence Oliver Twitty 1989
Orrin Scott Hamilton 1991
E. Cameron Hudson 1991
Lester Donald Crosswhite Jr. 1992
Anthony J. Pray 1992
Bradley Marcus Scott 1993
Lonnie G. Alsip 1994
Rebecca R. Lee 1994
Patrick Michael Gallagher 1996

Anthony Michael Scott 1996
Katherine Loraine Bryant 1998
Christiane Leigh Herndon 1998
John Robert Reichenbacker 1998
George Gregory Rehberg V 1999
Emily Jean Judd 2000
Robert Edward Adams 2001
Roderique Ivan-Collins McClain 2001
Gregory Alan Argo 2002
Ryan David McElfresh 2002
Tyson Everett Lawson 2003
Kelly Michelle Foreman 2004
Calvin Mitchell Townsend Jr. 2004

PUBLISHING

Louise B. Hatmaker 1943
Dorman E. Cordell 1950
Jerry P. Marcum 1970
Kathryn Marie Storrie 1971
Donald Kash Cable 1979

Glenda Kay Streib 1979
Eugene M. Waddle 1981
Heather Ann Kalista 1990
Edith (Edie) Schmidt 1990
J. Travis Rhoden 1994

Toby Lynn Ashbaugh 1995
Sarah Smurr 1996
Nicole Marie Ackley 1997
Andrea B. Emerson 1997

PURCHASING

Louise Newby 1951
Jimmy Lynn Carrier 1969
John Jefferson Milam 1969
Dewey Michael Williams 1971
William Morris Patterson 1972

Douglas Wright 1972
Dianna Carol McKeehan 1975
Fred Sutton 1983
Lori A. Bidwell 1986
Allen Shepherd 1986

Glenn Edward Bloomer 1987
Kimberly Ann Teague 2008
Kimberly Ann Teague 2012

RAILROAD, LOCOMOTIVE ENGINEER

James Lester Clark 1950
Earl M. Davenport 1953
Carlus Hundley 1958

J. B. Curd Jr. 1962
Wiley Brown 1964
T. R. Lawson 1964

Clifton A. Robinson 1972
Joseph Daniel Kuhn 1975
Billy Harrison Brafford 1979

Shaun Michael Francisco 1989   Hiram Coffer Begley III 2005   Charles E. Allen 2007

REAL ESTATE

Sarah W. Almgren 1922
Myra B. Cralle 1925
James B. Scearce Jr. 1934
Ernest E. Stephens 1936
Charles Hubbell Swearingen 1940
Arthur & Gertrude Dale 1948
Wanda D. Jones 1949
Peggy W. Miller 1950
John Wesley Stott 1950
Chester Boyd King 1951
Glenn R. Freeman 1952
Pauline W. Brown 1955
Philip M. Smith 1955
Shirley D. Tiller 1956
Bonnie Mitchell 1957
Pat D. Layton 1958
Lola M. Miles 1958
Boyce J. Holt 1962
Jenny H. Cain 1964
Virgil C. Clark Jr. 1965
John Richard Cornett 1965

Zafer Roback 1965
Charles G. Baute 1967
Norman Ray McRay 1967
Rosalita Wright 1967
Robert F. Amburgy 1969
Earl C. Brady 1969
Norma Elizabeth Frost 1970
Susan Lee Hodges 1970
Charles David Elkins 1972
Maurice K. Smith 1972
David Robert Longmire 1973
Charles Edward Robbins 1973
Marvin Eugene Hurst 1974
Dennis Ray Wright 1974
Dennis Alan Wood 1975
Donna S. Abner 1976
Emma J. Williams 1976
Thomas J. Flynn 1977
Kim Douglas 1979
Richard L. Kinyon 1980
Ricky Edward Emert 1981

James Glynn Butler 1985
Ricky Aldon Wiggington 1985
Sharon L. McGee 1986
Kimberly Ann Farr 1987
David L. Powell 1988
Danny Paul Bush 1989
Daniel K. Rawlings IV 1990
Stuart C. Robinson 1990
Michelle Lynn Gregory 1992
Cecil Jeffery Lee Taylor 1992
Carla Wright 1992
James Brent Gregory 1994
Phyllis Ann Desmond 1995
Amy Louise Cooke 1996
Terri L. Rose 1996
Conner W. Cornett 1999
Christopher D. Jones 1999
Charles Matthew Ford 2001
David Alexander Shanks 2001
Weston Asher Woodford 2001
Joshua Andrew Maples 2003

RECEPTIONIST, SECRETARY, ADMINISTRATIVE CLERICAL SECRETARIAL

Louise R. Howard 1933
Lena H. Hill 1934
Ivory Ethel Davis 1936
Roberta Maffia 1940
Betty L. Cardwell 1943
Genevieve L. Tabor 1943
Alma I. Early 1947
Lucretia S. Gates 1947
Rosella L. Henson 1948
Mary Doyle Johnson 1948
Dalphene M. Coolidge 1949
Flora Elizabeth Prewitt 1949
Eileen Phillips 1950
Betty Lou Abbott 1951
Norma Jean Barton 1951
Una Lee Lanter 1953
Terry Cummins 1955
Barbara J. Davidson 1955
Eila Jane Gessells 1956
Nancy Annette Ross 1956
Lois F. Bowling 1957
Carolyn L. Price 1958
Janice H. Patterson 1959
Joyce B. Schaefer 1959
Lana S. Hammond 1960
Betty Sue Wright 1960
Jerry Ann Abbott 1962
Emma Kate Alder 1962
Manuel Amburgey 1962
Betty J. Broyles 1962
Emily Jean Hale 1962
Lloyd John Heisler 1962
Otis E. Meadors 1962
Betty Estes Arnold 1963
Sarah D. Fredericks 1963
Nancy E. Philpot 1963
Wilma Jo Watson 1963
William David Taylor 1964
Sandra Gayle Ward 1965

Phyllis E. Bruce 1966
Sue Ann Vaughan 1966
Patsy Jane White 1966
Polly S. Clark 1967
Elaine Frances Cloer 1967
Dorothy Lee Gaw 1967
Lynda Ann Roszell 1967
Joyce F. Kemmery 1968
Edra Caroline Rice 1968
Brance E. Steely Jr. 1969
Sandra L. Leichman 1970
Wayne Hackworth 1971
Linda Jackson 1971
Janis Marie Glenn 1972
Rhonda Kay Goad 1972
Sandra Kay Kelly 1973
Dianna Carpenter 1975
Nancy Lynne Coates 1975
Sherry Jane Roe 1975
Melanie Majors 1976
Karen Lynn Harp 1977
Jane F. Deaton 1978
Cheryl Ann McCoy 1978
Ramona J. Thomas 1978
Connie Ann Finch 1979
Kristie Lynn Lyons 1979
Pamelia A. Perkins 1979
Karen Ann Rice 1979
David Lee Ammerman 1980
Tammy Lou Ekrut 1980
Laura D. Hartwell 1980
Adele E. Millwood 1980
Sibyl Lynne Stricklin 1980
Vickie L. Bennett 1981
Paulleta Dick 1981
Linda Marie Phillips 1981
Sherry Diane Stephens 1981
Jana Swanner Tindle 1981
Elizabeth Vickers 1981

Karen Annette Davis 1982
David Estill Duvall 1982
June Gayle Galloway 1982
Donna Marsee Perkins 1982
Susan Elaine Case 1983
Delora Elaine Copher 1983
Delora Elaine Copher 1983
Joann Baker 1984
Pamela Cook 1984
Lisa L. Hill 1984
Lynnelle Anne Combs 1985
Tammy Michelle Cornelius 1985
Sarah Kate Jackson 1985
Elizabeth K. Saylor 1985
Christina L. Vincent 1985
Laura R. Bowling 1986
Deborah A. Hardin 1986
Wanda Lynn Hensley 1986
Mary Ellen Jennings 1986
Mary Ann Monhollen 1986
Glenda Lou Santiago 1986
Kerrie Ellen Shahan 1986
Pearlie L. Wingeier 1986
Teresa Lynn Davis 1987
Sherry Lee Jones 1987
Shelleigh Lynn Broome Moses 1987
Amy B. Neal 1987
Anita Lynn Wells 1987
Mary Charles Coy 1988
Rodney Wayne Johnson 1988
Anita Kaye Meuth 1988
Teresa Sue Riley 1988
Kelly Kathleen Ferguson 1989
Karen Elaine McCollum 1989
Susan Michelle Smith 1989
Larry J. Starkey 1989
Katherine L. Farmer 1990
Pearlie L. Wingeier 1990
Lois Michelle Tinch 1991

Angelica Lynn Wanner 1991
Cynthia Lynn Cornett 1992
Wendy Elise Dyke 1992
Deborah G. Rich 1992
Mary Meshelle Clark-Banschbach 1993
Constance Jean Close 1993
Mark A. Fryer 1993
Cheryl Lynn Lee 1993
Angelia Marie Roaden 1993
Margaret Shannon Tuggle 1993
Angela Kay Snyder 1994
Jennifer Dawn Atkins 1995
DeVona Marie Kelley 1996
Christi Lee Porter 1996
Stephanie Rose Sims 1996
Agnes Beatrice Brown-Oliphant 1998
Cheryl Berniece Tarter 1998
Jenna Rose Sherman 1999

Christina May Cecil 2000
Brandy Jenise Kinser 2000
Keeli Jane Stone 2000
Sara Beth Davis 2001
Jamie LeAnn Goodwin 2001
Morgan Nichole Lewis 2001
Michelle Renae Bernard 2002
Bianica Celeste Stephens 2002
Jessica Lynn Kidd 2003
Craig Brandon Lewis 2003
Amber Michelle Marie McKiddy 2003
Barbara Jane Broadwell 2005
Jessica Lynn Bullock 2005
Jennifer Alissa Gilbert 2005
Belinda Joy Honeycutt 2005
Lindsey Rene Hufford 2005
Billie Jo Sumpter 2005
Laura Brittany Hadley 2006

Barbara Jean Owens 2006
Nancy Pauline Perkins 2006
Susan Elizabeth Felts 2007
Amber Leigh Malicote 2007
Linda Marie Mathias 2007
Gail Lynn Teague 2007
Edwina Ann Chaney 2008
Lisa Ann Kidd 2008
Crystal Rae McKiddy 2008
Courtney Rae Wesley 2008
Samantha Jean Gilreath 2009
Regina L. Kennedy 2009
Madeline Denise Rains 2009
Amanda Lee Warford 2009
Peggy Rose Cook 2010
Shelley Dawn Reynolds 2010
Susan Elizabeth Felts 2011

RECREATION LEISURE SERVICES

Bobby J. Davenport 1958
Darlene Couch Walker 1976
David Thomas Parker 1981
Cheryl Lynn Clarkston 1983
Cynthia Emrich 1986
Lawrence Thompson 1986

Barbara A. Spratling 1990
Maria L. Kuster 1995
Ronnie Chad Shirley 1996
Jamey Michael Short 2002
Crystal Andrea Cowden 2004
Steven Thomas Kissinger 2005

Kristi Jo Wright 2005
Charle Cherie Delph 2008
Steven Thomas Kissinger 2011
Jamey Michael Short 2012

RELATIONS REPRESENTATIVE

Bill D. Edwards 1955
Frank A. Burns 1963
Robert Leon Green 1975

Jonathan Michael Moody 1987
Angela Cooper Moses 1997
Gail Eileen Rector 1997

David Paul Collett Jr. 2002
Jocelyn M. McBride 2002
Elizabeth Suzanne Swanson 2004

RESEARCH DEVELOPMENT, METHODS PROCEDURES ANALYST

Leroy Voris 1925
Lee Norman Lawson 1936
Charles B. Estep 1942
Albert Ray Mullins 1958
Charles Edwin Hammons 1963
John Robert Howard 1965
Emma Jean Anthony 1967
Denny Elisha Daugherty 1968
George Stephen Tuggle Sr. 1969
Jack C. Murley Jr. 1970
Jimmie Neal Short 1971
Russell R. Waesche 1971
Sherry Lynne Wright 1972
Deborah M. Ringley 1975

John Edmund Aull 1976
Philip James Davis Ph.D. 1976
Bruce E. Suttle 1976
Jerry M. Parks 1977
Linda M. Thornton 1980
Bobby Ray Cloud 1981
Lisa Kay Jackson 1984
Fenton Dorian Williams 1984
Bobby Ray Cloud 1985
Paul Donald Estes Jr. 1986
Shawn Adam DeWeese 1989
Cynthia Dianne Peel 1989
Burton Lyle Wilson 1990
Kimberly Jo Jeskie 1991

Niki Anissa Braggs 1995
Dawn Louise Anderson 1998
Jessica Allen Ramsey 1998
Brian David Smith 1998
Hui Koon Khor 1999
Deena Lynn Salenbien 1999
Margo Lea Wheeler 1999
Barry Matthew Joyce 2000
Stephen Paul Wargacki 2000
Ahmad Rashad Broadnax 2002
Whitney Allyn Swan 2003
James Thomas 2004

RESTAURANT RELATED, CHEF, HOTEL RESTAURANT CATERER

Emerson Carroll Woods 1974
Ollie Naomi Bunch 1975
Mohamed Eid Armeli 1979
Reggie Glen Finley 1982
James David Disney 1986
Terry E. Leigh 1986
Brenda Carol Warren 1989

Melissa Faye Crosswhite 1992
Joe Alan Lowery 1992
Theron Hardin Mack 1996
Shawn Paul Hornaday 2001
Mindy Darlyn Nance-Cox 2002
Rebecca Ariane McKinney 2004
Jeanne Marie Waters 2004

Angela Devona Perry 2005
Toni Marie Cornelius 2006
Jill Marie Hughes 2007
James Hugh Sibert 2007
Amye Lee Song Daniels 2008
Tessa Nicole Jones 2009
Jeanne Marie Waters 2009

RETAIL, SALES

William C. Carter 1939
Fannie Harrison 1941
Atrel S. Cole 1948
Patricia S. Estes 1948
James Warming 1951
Eugene E. Croley 1953
Doris Aileen Gilbert 1954
Barbara Sharp 1955
Paul Estes 1956
Willard D. Siler 1956
Retha Jane Davis 1957
Joy M. McCormick 1957
Johnny J. Reeves 1957
Shirley Gaffney Scully 1958
Coleman E. Smith 1959
Lester Cornett 1960
Ray B. Wireman 1960
Lon Wilson 1961
Mildred Adams 1962
William David Back 1962
Phillip Brenton Cocks 1962
Donald R. Douglas 1962
Julian G. McGinley 1962
Jack E. Sterling 1962
Bill M. Davis 1963
Frank Josef Gieszl 1963
Rondal Glenn Prewitt 1963
Mary Ann Stewart 1963
Robert L. Creech 1964
William Henry Cardwell 1965
Rose E. Hopper 1966
Reva Kay Zevenbergen 1966
Glenn Taylor 1967
Leslie H. Warren 1967
Elman Blair 1968
Carl Hoskins 1968
Sharon Ann Messer 1968
James Clayton Foley 1969
Gregory V. Hawks 1969
Harvey C. Hubbard 1969
Ronald Floyd Meadors 1969
Lynda S. Nowlin 1969
David Styer 1969
Linda Margaret Thatcher 1969
Henry W. Bialczak 1970
Gary Woodrow Elliott 1970
Ray W. Kelly 1970
Frank A. Roberts 1971
Patricia Sue Blue 1972
Ronnie Lee Eaton 1972
Ronald Ford 1972
Charles W. Hatmaker 1972
William L. Frazier 1973
Diana Faye Hamilton 1973
Cleta Gaye McCowan 1973
Randall J. Bowman 1974
Lee Jacob Graefe Jr. 1974
Berry Eugene Riley 1975
Charlene Bryson 1976
Paul David Steely 1976
John Bill Gibbs 1977
Donna D. Goodman 1977

Gloria Dean Ruberry 1977
Timothy Van Campbell 1978
Akbar Malik Sheikh 1978
Terry Lee Calico 1979
Billy Lee Hincher 1979
John Timothy Meney 1979
Christopher Craig Carden 1980
Jeffrey Wayne Davis 1980
Lee E. Blasingame 1981
Anna Faye Brock 1981
Wendy G. Bunch 1981
Kimberly Hope Sergent 1981
Timothy Karmout 1982
Jerry Duane Rose 1982
Roxanna Schrader 1982
Savannah Brafford 1983
Steven Craig Siler 1984
Cynthia Gayer 1985
Patrick Thomas Blackburn 1986
Charles Henry Cooper III 1986
Ted Elbert Hodge 1986
Karen J. Patton 1986
Kelli Sue Pettigrew 1986
Christopher Wayne Watkins 1986
James A. Taylor 1987
Jenna L. Arvin 1988
Gary A. Averill 1988
Deron Scott McIntosh 1988
Robin Elaine Smith 1988
Richard J. Thompson 1989
Jim Kelly Wasson 1989
April Lee Brinks-Bailey 1990
David B. Carmichael 1990
Regina B. Dodson 1990
Stephen R. Hall 1990
Melinda Renee House 1990
Kara Ann Fulkerson 1992
Ernest White 1992
Jeffrey Paul Wollam 1992
B. Keith Brashear 1993
James Brian Dupier 1993
Lisa Katrena Hoehn 1993
Chad Alan Sanders 1993
Jeffrey Alan Barker 1994
Karen Elizabeth Mitchell 1994
Bethely Dawn Morton 1994
Michelle L. Wagers 1994
April Marie Williams 1994
Kristin Elaine Grogan 1995
Kristie Lynn Spencer 1995
Gwendolyn Marie Willis 1995
Laura Katherine Hagen 1996
Charles E. Spencer Jr. 1996
Kimberly Ann Wheatley 1996
Rodger Miles Oliver 1997
Katina Owens 1997
Stephen Daniel Brown 1998
Morgan David Chapman 1998
Jeffrey David Fowler 1998
Jasper Benjamin Van Nes 1998
Donald Dean Wright 1998
Brent Anthony Canady 1999

Justin Wade Chaniott 1999
Micah Shawn Davies 1999
Emily Elaine Lucas 1999
Stephenie Ellen Reynolds 1999
Brian Keith Risner 1999
Kelli Lyn Shook 1999
Shannon Marie Evans-Harrington 2000
Shannon Marie Evans-Harrington 2000
Matthew Clinton Fields 2000
Lance Christopher Smith 2000
Lisa Dotson 2001
Kristopher David Fields 2001
David Alan Ginter 2001
Keith Anthony Hamm 2001
Amanda Louise Kelly 2001
Deana Nicole Norman 2001
Jeffrey Hunt Owens 2001
Julie Lynn Rea 2001
John Arthur VanHoose 2001
Jason Bennett Vanhoose 2001
Darius W. Ward II 2001
Jeremy Wallace Haile 2002
Charles Lee Hall 2002
Jott Dwayne Harris 2002
Stephanie Lynn Mahler 2002
Robert Joseph Melton 2002
Joshua A. Moses 2002
Craig Matthew Murdock 2002
Randel Joseph Hambrick 2003
Travis Paul King 2003
Jonathon Randall Lee 2003
Erin Elizabeth Murdock 2003
Elizabeth Rose Wilson 2003
Derrick Dewayne Douglas 2004
Megan Kaye Freeman 2004
Adam Lee McChesney 2004
Alisha Ann Nash 2004
Monica Charis Hoegsted 2005
Ryan Keck Norvell 2005
John Harold Settle 2006
Austyn Jade Slone 2006
Marie Lois Spradlin 2006
Susan Marie Benning 2007
Lindsay Blair Lowe 2007
Carson Edward Payne 2007
Elaine Michele Perkins 2007
Charles Russell Sewell 2007
Alicia Danielle Wolfe 2007
Alonda Marie Cornett 2008
Jolina Joy Petersheim 2008
Jack Creed Rogers 2008
Christopher Scott Skaggs 2008
Shannon Patricia Tolson 2008
Josie Caroline Tyree 2008
Shawn Patrick Boyle 2009
Melody Hope Farwell 2009
Gary Stuart Sharp 2009
Donald Anthony Shouse 2009
James Edward White II 2009
Rachel Elizabeth Worley 2009
Hong Zhou 2009
Megan Renee Hensley 2010

RETIRED

Lela W. Pope 1918

Ethel F. Prewitt 1920

Gladys H. Cotton 1923

Ralph M. Alexander 1924
Everett Bowman Lanter 1924
Edith Long Monson 1924
Eubie E. Tiller 1924
Charles G. Calloway 1925
Alton B. White 1925
R. Ronald Connelly 1926
Dora Inas Lamb 1926
Mack Roberts 1926
Nell E. Davis 1927
Rubye McNamara 1927
Harold Irvin Moon 1928
William Mounce 1928
Kathryn Parker 1928
John McKinley Raines Sr. 1928
A. Glenn Broyles 1929
Ethel Denny Crawley 1929
Silas B. Dishman 1929
A. B. Morgan 1929
William H. Riley 1929
Vivian A. Robbins 1929
Lester C. Root 1929
Elizabeth Ashley 1930
John H. Bailey 1930
Mary J. Gatliff 1930
Maurice Gatliff 1930
Clifford Lowe 1930
Nell Sandusky 1930
Letha T. Sutton 1930
Joseph M. Alsip 1931
Nettie Ethel Coleman 1931
Irene D. Cunningham 1931
Lula Carr Davenport 1931
Homer B. Davis 1931
Elizabeth Gillis 1931
H. Lloyd Goodlett 1931
Mary L. Mahan 1931
Agnes Montgomery 1931
Eva Smith 1931
Gertrude Dale 1932
Gayle M. Denny 1932
Ethel Harmon 1932
Grace Johnson 1932
John F. Thomas Jr. 1932
James Robert Allen 1933
Ernest G. Butts 1933
William Clay Crume 1933
Louise Curtis 1933
Harry Gant Hatler 1933
John Norman Keith 1933
Flossie Meadors 1933
Pearl C. Powell 1933
John O. Roaden 1933
Francis Edmund Shearer 1933
Howard Shoemaker 1933
Leetta Sutton 1933
Frances Wynn Woods 1933
Verna Y. Barefoot 1934
Mary C. Galbraith 1934
Anna Lee Greene 1934
Grace M. Jondo 1934
Sara B. McGibney 1934
Willard O. Cooper 1935
Effie Marie Creekmore 1935
Pauline Deeken 1935
William E. Guyn 1935
George F. Jarboe 1935
Stella Mae Meece 1935
Horace V. Payne 1935
Martha Collette Phillips 1935

Evelyn Bertram Rector 1935
Joseph J. Romero 1935
Dora Sharpe 1935
Paul Clarence Shoemaker 1935
Rosalie White 1935
Helen Whitehead 1935
John M. Blevins 1936
Dallas Siler 1936
Edward P. Smith Private Foundation 1936
Thomas W. Stanfield 1936
Evelyn Tuggle 1936
Jack Oakley Whitehead 1936
James Oliver Gant 1937
Lillian McDermott 1937
Mildred Y. Rigsby 1937
Winifred T. Royalty 1937
Jack T. Sutherland 1937
Virgil Woods 1937
Violet Peterson Bell 1938
Elsie Freeman 1938
Thomas R. Fritts 1938
Edna E. Robinson 1938
S. Jones Tallent 1938
Ruth H. Tarkington 1938
Claude Ezra Butler 1939
Dick Creekmore 1939
Ethel S. Crook 1939
Gertrude E. Early 1939
Zella Ann Freiberg 1939
Helen Joyce Seeley 1939
Ann R. Shelley 1939
Charles E. Stamper 1939
Lorine Trosper 1939
Raymond S. Wells 1939
William Baylor Wilder 1939
Conda Baird 1940
Mary Blanche Corder 1940
James Robert Davis 1940
Joe Davis 1940
James E. Douglas 1940
Walter W. Jones 1940
Gladys Yvonne Kief 1940
Thelma Mae Larrison 1940
Willard S. Mitchell 1940
Ruth Everly Nuckols 1940
Sanders W. Petrey 1940
Gladys K. Raggio 1940
Rowena B. Sears 1940
Retha Thomas 1940
William Jenkins Turnblazer 1940
H. R. White Jr. 1940
Larry Wilson 1940
Irene Campbell 1941
Paul Adrian Criscillis 1941
James Merle Howard 1941
Lana J. Moyer 1941
Oleta Bernice Naylor 1941
Eula Sears 1941
Kathleen Sharpe 1941
Thelma Shearer 1941
Pauline Suiter 1941
Lois Swartz 1941
Howard R. Boozer 1942
William Buhl Jr. 1942
E. N. Campbell 1942
Bernard R. Crouch 1942
Enoch Clyde Ellis 1942
Pauline F. Faulkner 1942
Kathleen Jarboe 1942

Charles R. Jarboe Jr. 1942
Mary Josephine Johnson 1942
Virginia Puckett 1942
Gorman J. Roberts 1942
Gladys Sulfredge 1942
Joseph B. Warfield 1942
Dorcas M. Watson 1942
Stellian Virgil Anderson 1943
Margaret Louise Bartley 1943
Mary Eugenia Campbell 1943
Margaret H. Dempster 1943
Thomasine Hailey 1943
Hoyt Glenn Hickey 1943
Lois B. Houser 1943
Dorcas Kretzinger 1943
Mary Belle Porter 1943
John Pershing Stanley 1943
Donald A. Swanson 1943
Anna Lee Watts 1943
Wanda L. Wilmoth 1943
Amanda Estepp Coffey 1944
Opal P. Croley 1944
Stella H. Day 1944
Edward A. Fish 1944
Harold Lewis Gant 1944
L. Howard Gordon 1944
Eudora J. Schafer 1944
Clinton C. Taylor 1944
Marie Bennett 1945
Helen C. Hamblin 1945
Margrie Alean Justice 1945
Louise Miriam Ward 1945
Iva Dean Bird 1946
Elsie Y. Fields 1946
Florine Hamblin 1946
Beaulah Rose 1946
Anna P. Rutherford 1946
Mary Lou Salyer 1946
Ben Smith 1946
Rosella S. Smith 1946
Joyce C. Strunk 1946
Gloe L. Bertram 1947
Thomas Edward Davis 1947
B. Harry McKeehan 1947
Paula Patton 1947
Ora Moss Smith 1947
John T. Sowders 1947
Garrett Teague Jr. 1947
Artie Marie Vahldiek 1947
Shafter Watts 1947
Robert L. Allen 1948
Edmund C. Asher 1948
Randall Barker 1948
Benjamin H. Carr Jr. 1948
Marvin Raymond Clark 1948
Jack Davis 1948
Lawrence W. Gregory Jr. 1948
Robert Curtis Hayes 1948
Robert E. Loper 1948
Clarence Isham Lovitt 1948
Andy Meadows 1948
Ruth Louise Moyers 1948
Pete A. Parks 1948
James Matt Payne 1948
Eugene Russell Rollins 1948
Jack Roundtree 1948
Henry C. Sawyers 1948
Carolyn Siler 1948
Charles E. Story 1948
Loran H. Strunk 1948

Ralph Greene Sullivan 1948
Hallice F. Upchurch Sr. 1948
George S. Walker 1948
J. T. Back 1949
Andrew J. Crawford 1949
Suzanne M. Dehm 1949
Virgil E. Harmon Jr. 1949
Paul Mauney 1949
Orie Perkins 1949
Hershel C. Reeves 1949
Lois Jean Smith 1949
Glenn A. Stephens 1949
Willard Ray Thomas 1949
Wilma Jean Trotto 1949
Betty S. Webb 1949
Earl Armes 1950
Wyoma Cymbal 1950
William E. Davies 1950
Ralph C. Eaton 1950
Joyce Ruth Fowler 1950
Anna Ruth Howd 1950
Randolph Jarvis 1950
Homer E. Jones 1950
Juanita Jones 1950
Robert C. Jones 1950
Lois Carter Kelly 1950
Marcella Logan 1950
Geneva R. McKee 1950
Roy Daniel Mitchell 1950
Norma June Moses 1950
Guin Renshaw 1950
Ramona Hurt Simpson 1950
Doris Jean Spafford 1950
Sydney Stephens Jr. 1950
Everett Truman Strunk 1950
Earl G. Watson 1950
Ida Elizabeth Wilson 1950
Luther Gerald Wyrick 1950
Edgar Allen 1951
Albert L. Bryant 1951
Billy J. Cawood 1951
Clyde Edward Faulkner 1951
James Hill Jr. 1951
Leonard R. McFarland 1951
Cora Rains 1951
William S. Smith 1951
Clyde Cooper 1952
Sallie P. D'Haillecourt 1952
Carter K. Hooks 1952
Arthur Jeffries Jr. 1952
Patricia Ann Lovitt 1952
Jackie M. Mace 1952
Bernice B. Meyers 1952
Nora Siler Simpson 1952
Glenn Taylor 1952
Anna Lou Weiskittel 1952
Corean Wells 1952
Joseph Charlie White 1952
Jack Bell 1953
Carolyn Yvonne Bell 1953
Betty Ruth Cox 1953
Elizabeth P. Edwards 1953
Donald Hart 1953
David N. Huff 1953
Ernest D. Payne 1953
Micki T. Yeary 1953
Bill R. Broyles 1954
Harvey R. Cantrell 1954
James R. Clem 1954
Robert Scogin 1954

Patricia Ruth Smith 1954
Donald Thomas 1954
Doris L. Wood 1954
Phyllis C. Wright 1954
Norma Sue Ballou 1955
Paul W. Beasley 1955
Johnny Doyle Cox 1955
Andrew Denny Jr. 1955
Lillian C. Galloway 1955
Harold E. Gordon 1955
Billy R. Gordon 1955
George B. Haley 1955
Vivian Lois Hamilton 1955
Patricia Jean Hill 1955
Betty Faye Kitchen 1955
Donna M. Lisenbee 1955
Rondal L. Salley 1955
Donald L. Tower 1955
Patricia A. White 1955
Jill Bailey 1956
Shelva D. Barnes 1956
Damon Brown 1956
Jack Clifford 1956
Robert W. Coker 1956
Emily Copenhaver 1956
Peggy Lou Flanigan 1956
Edgar H. Shoupe 1956
Betty Jo Smith 1956
Ann H. Smith 1956
Carolyn F. Tiller 1956
David Zane Anderson 1957
Evelyn Angel 1957
S. James Costigan 1957
Roy Lee Cox 1957
Mary Jo Delligatti 1957
Silas Goodin 1957
Dorothy J. Leckey-Blanton 1957
Francis W. Logan 1957
Paul Robbins 1957
Abe Slusher Jr. 1957
Pat Sutton 1957
Lendon Welch 1957
Don J. Apking 1958
Robert N. Ashby Jr. 1958
Coye Lee Bailey 1958
Donna S. Brown 1958
Clarence Henry Davis 1958
Billy Ray Duncan 1958
Jo Anne Gregory 1958
Peggy Lynne Hopper 1958
Charles Lamb 1958
Vester Mahan 1958
John H. Stidham 1958
Roger L. Trussell 1958
Norma Katherine Adams 1959
Sue C. Apking 1959
Archie H. Bays 1959
Bert Boggs 1959
Robert S. Bryant 1959
John Lee Crockett 1959
Joan Davis 1959
Clarence Marvin Goodin 1959
Jean Henry 1959
George S. Hunt 1959
Betty H. Miller 1959
Roman Strunk 1959
Opal A. Young 1959
Rodney B. Curd 1960
Wayne S. Heatherly 1960
Herman Stanley Ratliff 1960

Charles Artis Jr. 1961
Fred H. Baird USAF Ret. 1961
Benny Jerrell Collier 1961
Otis W. Cordell 1961
Helen Cross 1961
Arthur Heth 1961
Kenneth A. Hill 1961
Roy Eugene Jones 1961
Elvis Dean Kidd 1961
Bobby R. May 1961
Linda Cox Miller 1961
Wendall Tolly Mitchell 1961
Clyde Edward Neff 1961
Joe Frank Patrick 1961
David R. Sawyer EdD 1961
Almereen Tower 1961
Charlene D. Baker 1962
Louetta Adams Clemons 1962
Helen C. Crabtree 1962
Ann W. Culver 1962
George Croley Davis Sr. 1962
Parcel Flannery 1962
Billy J. Grabeel 1962
Nonnie Lou Hamlin 1962
George A. Helton 1962
Tommy J. Howard 1962
Reba June Jackson 1962
Jeanne A. Jackson 1962
Phyllis H. Lathrop 1962
Dolores Lawson 1962
Patsy Faye Mullins 1962
Paul G. Noe 1962
Rina Kay Pyles 1962
Lana Lewis Santavicca 1962
Patricia Ann Teague 1962
Mabel D. Ward 1962
Louvenia D. Wilson 1962
Peggy C. Brock 1963
Ronald Edward Campbell 1963
Shanda Clark 1963
Ida L. Crase 1963
Joyce F. Curd 1963
Lorene B. Davenport 1963
Phyllis Ann Early 1963
Russell M. Franklin 1963
L. H. Gaddis Jr. 1963
Arvele Grubb 1963
William Hubert Hammons 1963
Jonia Marie Hensley 1963
Stella B. Jefferis 1963
Jerry Paul Lawson 1963
Ralph Souleyret Jr. 1963
Mary Juanita Stallard 1963
James Tuggle Sr. 1963
Ronnie J. Wilson 1963
Lucy Fern Woods 1963
James David Bowman 1964
Edgar Blaine Bryant 1964
Eula Faye Campbell 1964
Minnie Chambers 1964
Carmen Davidson 1964
Henrietta S. Duke 1964
Chester MacArthur Gibson 1964
Elsie Lee Hill 1964
Charles Richard Hoskins 1964
Ernest J. Hughes 1964
John C. Miracle 1964
Lena L. Parker 1964
Lawrence David Rhodes 1964
Jack W. Sheffield 1964

LeRoy Stallard 1964
Ronald Henry Steele 1964
Ebert Keith Warren Jr. 1964
Janice Caudill Wolod 1964
Horace L. Wright Jr. 1964
Glen Lee Bertram 1965
Oscar Combs 1965
Patricia Louise Crider 1965
Sandra Faye Daniel 1965
James Wayne Dunn 1965
Paul Falin 1965
Jack Agee Faulkner 1965
Vanbert L Frazier 1965
Beulah Mae Gray 1965
Adna Jean Howard 1965
Burchell J. Martin 1965
Joyce McCormack 1965
Shirley A. Mikel 1965
Epp Osborne 1965
William Lowell Ray 1965
Michael Y. Walters 1965
Doris F. Bishop 1966
Lela Frances Daniels 1966
Jo Ann Gander 1966
Ann M. Hoffelder 1966
Jack C. Lane 1966
Helen F. Miller 1966
Robert M. Moser 1966
Iva Darlene Osborne 1966
Jessie Pauline Philpot 1966
V. L. Stonecipher 1966
Bernard Watts 1966
Eileen B. Baird 1967
Margaret Bowling 1967
John Eugene Clifton 1967
Shirie J. Cottongim 1967
Arline P. Crouch 1967
Grace Franks 1967
Kenneth Ray Harp 1967
William John Higgins 1967
William R. Hinton 1967
Loraine Hodges 1967
Jesse E. Kidd 1967
Richard F. Koeniger 1967
Wayne Leitch 1967
Larry Eugene Mills 1967
Miriam W. Oglesby 1967

Lucy V. Smith 1967
Hiram Bowling 1968
Vada Clark 1968
Naomi Crabtree 1968
Carolyn Sue Falin 1968
Janice Foley 1968
Arlis Leroy Gilbert 1968
Dorothy Hamblin 1968
Judson Spencer Harmon Jr. 1968
Ralph W. Hodge 1968
Ina Fae Kenney 1968
Linda J. Lyles 1968
Dian S. Lynch 1968
Barry Donald Pencek 1968
James Douglas Sharp 1968
Jerry L. Abbott 1969
Joe W. Allen 1969
Ronald G. Baker 1969
Glenna Jean Bryant 1969
Earl Clemons Bundy 1969
Max K. Hetzel 1969
Darlene Hibbard 1969
William Farmer Higginbotham Jr. 1969
Dianne Logsdon 1969
Phyllis O. Malcomb 1969
Charles Glenn Nolan 1969
Robert C. Perrone 1969
Richard H. Poe 1969
Henry Coy Powell 1969
Maedean Sumner 1969
Carl Emerson Wilson 1969
Lee A. Bishop 1970
Theresa W. Bolton 1970
Betty Ruth Brock 1970
Clarence Nelson Curtis Jr. 1970
Phyllis Ann Huff 1970
Michael L. Mace 1970
William H. Ott 1970
Arlo C. Sharp Jr. 1970
JoAnne A. Thomas 1970
Michael James Gregory 1971
Ramona B. Harp 1971
Cinda Lavenne Jones 1971
Vicki Marie Kinsel 1971
James M. Lankster 1971
Kathy Sue Long 1971
William Ray Moore 1971

Linda J. Sharp 1971
Anna K. Six 1971
Bobby W. Terrell 1971
Carl J. Brooks 1972
William Edward Cook 1972
David Lawrence Cornett 1972
Mary Ellen Kelley 1972
William E. Pyle 1972
Jo Ann Siler 1972
Gordon Lee Beil 1973
Carolyn Sue Elliott 1973
Zella Jane Goodin 1973
Donald William Humble 1973
Larry C. Nidiffer 1973
John William Thomas 1973
Gary Lynn Hammonds 1974
Patricia Jill Johnson 1974
Morris Acey Lefevers 1974
Karen E. Lofquist 1974
Chuck Fletcher 1975
Agnes Karen Melton 1975
Ricky Gene Nelson 1976
Janice A. Stewart 1976
Barbara Ann Daniels 1977
James Michael Smith 1977
Larry R. Van Hoose 1977
Linda Sue Barnett 1978
Nelda Ann Barton-Collings 1978
Carlos Ray Glover 1978
Grover C. Lynch 1978
Steve J. Mondl 1978
Deborah A. Denney 1979
Karin Lynn Edgington 1979
Helen Fay Scott 1979
Margaret E. Davis 1980
Kimberly G. Jelle Jones 1980
Linda Morin 1981
Patricia Ann Swain 1981
Kime Espich Murphy 1982
Mary Lou Schick 1982
Homer Howard Gibson 1983
Vicki K. Ross 1984
Janice Gates 1985
Alvin Arthur Gates 1987
Vicki K. Ross 1988
JoAnne A. Thomas 1993

SCIENCE

Eleanor M. Behrmann 1936
Lucille A. Viator 1944
Evelyn E. Watson 1946
Leonard Pierce Jr. 1947
Billy Ray Neely 1964
Chester Odell Goins 1966
James H. Denny 1967
Carlton Leroy Cantrell 1970
Michael Woods 1980
Rebekah E. Woods 1980

Cheryl Gresham Roberts 1983
Patricia L. Jackson Ph.D. 1985
Merenda 'Susie' Jones-Brier 1986
Beth A. Pyles 1989
Anissa Caroline Machal-Kelley 1990
Rigat Abraha 1992
James Lacey Shelley 1994
Charles Christopher Waits 1994
Mark Alan Nevitt 1996
Bridget Michele Graves 1998

Heather Marie Curry 1999
Aime Dawn Powers 2001
Autumn Suzanne Carter 2002
Sarah Marie Hayes 2003
Joseph Patrick McDaniel 2004
Justin William Waters 2005
Justin Ronald Gadd 2009
Christina Marie Perkins 2009

SELF EMPLOYED

Rhoda Hamlin 1935
Robert Estes Sharp Sr. 1937
Bill Bristow 1948
Kenneth Bunch 1948

Glenos Cox 1948
James E. Wyatt 1948
Betty Greene Nichols 1949
John E. Renfro 1949

James W. Boyer 1950
Isham McKinley Sharpe 1951
Janet Spicer 1951
Yvonne B. Hurst 1953

E. David Wilson 1953
Bobbie Jean West 1954
Arlis Bailey Faulkner 1955
Stanley Earl Steely 1955
Charlene Ann Williams 1955
Lloyd Burton Hacker 1956
Zee Faulkner Kurfees 1956
Harold Cecil Raines Sr. 1956
Barbara P. Runager 1956
James Allen Brown 1957
Jeanette B. Gilbert 1957
Marjorie A. Grout 1957
H. Ray Ledbetter 1957
Joseph Donald Faulkner 1958
June Edna Byrd 1959
George T. Cox 1959
Jerwyn D. Jones 1959
Ryland Hugh Lovett 1959
Judith Kaye Rice 1959
Shirley A. Planet 1960
Willard Bingham 1961
Billy Gordon Brown 1961
Harry B. Pruden III 1961
Richard Ellis Shepherd 1961
Gary L. Gatliff 1962
Bruce Miracle 1962
Ronald Oaks 1962
Phil A. Brennenstuhl 1963
Betty Rose Brock Gibson Comer 1963
Louise Hacker 1963
Ruth M. Osborne 1963
Betty Pearl Bryant 1964
Thelma J. Gregory 1964
R. Bruce Kirby 1964
Fred Longmire 1964
Charles P. Peace 1964
Donald L. Price 1964
M. Jeree Creech 1965
J. Kay Hamlin 1965
Janice Marie Southall 1965
Ned S. Tramell 1965
Terry R. Byrd 1966
Barry D. Enlow 1967
James Bowling 1967
Jackie Lee Dunaway 1967

Billie Jean Poynter 1967
Irene Saylor 1967
Nelson Sizemore 1968
Jim H. Brennenstuhl 1969
Stella Eleschia Cummins 1969
Warren E. Gagner Jr. 1969
Jeffrey Clinton Hammer 1969
James C. Richardson 1969
David Maurice Tribell 1969
Teddy Ray Byrd 1970
Jack L. Crabtree 1970
John R. Davis 1970
Janet Link Harris 1970
Larry Edgar Harris 1970
David L. Helton 1970
Carson H. Hounshell 1970
Earl L. Johnson 1970
Bruce Wayne Lominac 1970
Marcus Edward Brock 1971
Gary Wayne Cupp 1971
Robert Michael Forester 1971
J. Michael Giorgio 1971
James E. Napier 1971
Luping Pell 1971
Frank R. Queener 1971
Tom D. Watkins 1971
Larry E. Bayless 1972
Gary L. Branam 1972
Marvin Calvin Hughett 1972
Linda Dianne King 1972
Jimmy F. Watkins 1972
Dianne Ola Hill 1973
Joseph Rick McReynolds 1973
Henry F. Flythe 1974
Roy Blane Helton 1974
Jerry Thomas Hammons 1975
Carl Eric Humphrey 1975
Gorman Stanley Jones 1975
Roger Eric Thomasson 1975
Darrell Ray Vanover 1975
Randy Allen Blair 1976
Timothy Gerard Desser 1976
Tim W. Lovett 1978
Nancy Bankston 1979
David K. Fee 1979

Robert Reid Kimball 1979
Joseph Dennis Scherzinger 1979
Grace Ann Eckert-Delpero 1980
Albert L. Robinson 1980
Al Arnett 1981
Delbert W. Johnson 1981
Alex Kirk Painter 1981
Billy Sizemore 1981
Marvin Butch Housman 1982
Regina Sue Seals 1982
Orgus Craig Seals 1982
Johannesburg C. E. Boulware 1983
Brent Pier Freeman 1983
H. Rodney VanHoose 1983
Charles R. Barrowman Jr. 1984
Angela Payne Childers 1984
Rex Huff 1984
Beverly B. Lucas 1984
Donna L. Shannon 1984
Carlton Jerome Powers 1985
Jasper Douglas Smith 1985
Curtis L. Hopkins 1986
Juder Stidham III 1986
Sharon L. Asher 1987
Kathy Byrd 1987
Ralph Eugene Chambers 1987
Joe Keith Jones 1989
Jon E. Smitley 1989
Tama Michelle Fortner 1991
Carla Suzanne Crowell 1992
Donna Sue Singley 1994
Richard Dean Hoffman 1996
Randall Eric Deaton 1998
Julie Anna Sears 1999
Brian Michael Whitaker 1999
Aaron Todd Scott 2000
Jessica Moneen McDonald 2005
Betty Jean Croley 2007
Virginia Lee Hamblin 2007
Linda Rae Burcham 2009
Tammy Marie Siler 2009
Jeremy Fishback 2010
Shane Conley Furlong 2010
Donna Sue Singley 2011

SERVICE REPRESENTATIVE

Barbara Jo Manning 1957
Danny Paul Johnson 1971
Jerry Wayne Lankster 1974

Thomas Sterling Adams 1980
Kimberly A. House 1980
Victoria J. Trammell 1984

Betty E. Daniel 1986
Kimberly Joanano Rains 1990
Cynthia Renee Thomason 1990

SOCIAL SCIENCE

Jennifer Susan Berven 1992
Catherine L. Branham 1979

Kimberly Dawn Cox 2001
Paola Veronica Negro-Boling 2002

SOCIAL WORK

Enoch Stafford Cody 1938
Frances Jones Mills 1940
Stephen Kelemen 1948
Robert L. Jones Jr. 1950
Jack Taylor Parrent 1950
Anna Jane Wallace 1952

Stonney Ray Lane 1957
Loten Ben West 1963
Homer E. Conlin 1964
Dan Cupps 1968
Shafter Jackson 1968
David Ray Ayers 1969

Donna Clore 1969
James Wayne Jones 1969
William Kenneth Clendaniel 1970
James Albert Hackler 1970
Dennis Prewitt 1970
Larry Joel Freeman 1971

Anna Lee Mayne 1972
Stephen G. Bowen 1973
Robert D. Stallard 1973
James Keith Johnson 1974
Sarah J. Ballard 1975
Denny Allen 1976
David Neal Clinkenbeard 1979
Roger D. Ownby 1982
Michael Edward Earley 1983
Mark Johnson 1983
Marcia Elaine Claiborne 1984

Dennis Wayne Patterson 1986
Dennis Wayne Patterson 1986
Alfred Collett 1987
Sidney William Johnston 1987
Tammy M. Pennington 1987
E. Austin Price 1988
Mark Alan Barrett 1991
Cynthia Ann Dehner 1991
Sherita Ann Holder 1993
Melissa Dawn Boaz 1995
Regina Gail Bunch 1995

Patricia Carol Ganzy 1999
Jamie Kay Goins 1999
Nathan Lee Hale 2000
Erin Margaret Schaffner 2004
Ryan Ernest Creech 2007
Jacob Ryan Hanley 2008
Janet Elaine Griffith 2009
Wilma B. Haar 2009
Brenda L. Lundbloom 2010

STATE RELATED

Enoch Stafford Cody 1938
Frances Jones Mills 1940
Stephen Kelemen 1948
Robert L. Jones Jr. 1950
Jack Taylor Parrent 1950
Anna Jane Wallace 1952
Stonney Ray Lane 1957
Loten Ben West 1963
Homer E. Conlin 1964
Dan Cupps 1968
Shafter Jackson 1968
David Ray Ayers 1969
Donna Clore 1969
James Wayne Jones 1969
William Kenneth Clendaniel 1970
James Albert Hackler 1970
Dennis Prewitt 1970

Larry Joel Freeman 1971
Anna Lee Mayne 1972
Stephen G. Bowen 1973
Robert D. Stallard 1973
James Keith Johnson 1974
Sarah J. Ballard 1975
Denny Allen 1976
David Neal Clinkenbeard 1979
Roger D. Ownby 1982
Michael Edward Earley 1983
Mark Johnson 1983
Marcia Elaine Claiborne 1984
Dennis Wayne Patterson 1986
Dennis Wayne Patterson 1986
Alfred Collett 1987
Sidney William Johnston 1987
Tammy M. Pennington 1987

E. Austin Price 1988
Mark Alan Barrett 1991
Cynthia Ann Dehner 1991
Sherita Ann Holder 1993
Melissa Dawn Boaz 1995
Regina Gail Bunch 1995
Patricia Carol Ganzy 1999
Jamie Kay Goins 1999
Nathan Lee Hale 2000
Erin Margaret Schaffner 2004
Ryan Ernest Creech 2007
Jacob Ryan Hanley 2008
Janet Elaine Griffith 2009
Wilma B. Haar 2009
Brenda L. Lundbloom 2010

STUDENT

Mattie Dewese 1956
Daniel R. Mitchell 1961
Mary Yvonne Jones 1966
Rebecca Elizabeth Steely 1967
Jacqueline McClendon 1968
Guindal Carlos Croley 1972
Elizabeth Ann Kennedy 1972
Thomas Reed Maggard 1974
Lora Lee Randolph 1975
Linda Rains 1976
Vickie Elaine Bramlett 1979
Annette L. Campbell 1981
Patrick T. Herlihy 1982
Stephanie Ann Adams DO 1983
Dawn Marie Webster 1983
Joseph A. Correll 1984
Penny R. Doan 1984
Michael D. Melson 1984
Basil Said Shorrosh 1984
Charles David Sulfredge 1984
MeLessa June Ellis 1985
Mona Shorrosh 1985
Steven Saunders Dean 1986
Robin Eileen Malone 1986
Sherry Lynn Baker 1988
Todd William Golden 1988
Jason Michael Hurst 1989

John Christopher Poirier 1989
Jo Ann Stanfill 1989
Timi Deann Tucker 1989
Charles Phillip Deusner 1990
Jeffrey Driggs 1990
Thomas Reed Maggard 1990
Michael Ward Minton 1990
Brian Forest Varble 1990
Brian E. Chastain 1991
Shannon L. Sexton 1991
Roger Alan Smith 1991
William Lloyd Stevens 1991
Sonia G. Stevens 1991
Melanie Jackson 1993
Timothy Wayne Estes 1995
Jeffery Allen Townsley 1997
Jonathan P. Gibson 1999
Bradley Grant Collins M.D. 2000
Leslie Ann Croley 2000
Benjamin Eric Neptun 2000
Jennifer Studdard 2001
LeeAnn Michelle Cox 2002
Anna Corrie Lufi 2002
Elizabeth Jayne Bass 2003
Heather Lynn Burns 2003
Rebecca Jane Powell 2003
Rosemary Calia Schenck 2003

Nina Lois Shotwell 2003
Amy Jackson 2004
Matthew Robert Rasure 2004
Erica Lynn Breitenbach 2005
Jamison Joan Bridewell 2005
Eleshia Gail Caldwell 2005
Tiffany Danielle Coffman 2005
Dawn Marie Georgalas 2005
Jessica Lynne Holbrook 2005
Kourtney Cornell Howard 2005
Justin Lee Nierengarten 2005
Qiana Michelle Rains 2005
Jamie Nicole Ratliff 2005
Ashlee Dehnae Smith 2005
Christina Ann Winebrenner 2005
Angela Renee Calchera 2006
Keysha Gayle Hammons 2006
Christopher James Mills 2006
Amanda Webb Carter 2007
Jessica Ann Francisco 2007
Tori Nicole Thoreson 2007
Meggy Elizabeth Cooper 2008
Michael Joshua Rudolph 2008
Lisa Ann West 2008
Paul Andrew Wilkes 2008
Marcus Lee Bradbury 2009
Lauren Michelle Howe 2009

SUPERINTENDENT, ASSISTANT SUPERINTENDENT

David Morris Denton 1958
Walter R. Smith 1961
Jay Roger Keck 1962
Roger C. Hornsby 1970
Alva Darryl Wilder 1970
Bert Minton 1972
Douglas Clifford Adams 1973
Ora Cobb Jr. 1973
Douglas Dobson 1973

Ben Edmonds 1975
Clara M. Reed 1975
Jesse Phillip McCall 1979
Timothy G. Moore 1979
John Mark Reed 1980
Paula Jean Trickett 1982
Gary R. Tripp 1985
Scott Layman Paul 1989
Rhonda Lynn Bunch 1990

Amon Wesley Couch 1991
Scott Layman Paul 1992
Paula Jean Trickett 1994
Amon Wesley Couch 1995
Aaron Dwight Anderson 1997
Aaron Dwight Anderson 1999
Aaron Dwight Anderson 2011
Amon Wesley Couch 2012

SUPERVISOR

Gene E. Mauney 1948
Thomas E. Simpson 1950
Elizabeth B. Thompson 1950
Robert K. Angel 1951
Lida Lee Minton 1952
Truletta Jones 1955
Daisy Alene Powers 1955
Tommie Lou Burns 1956
Franklin D. Earle 1956
Billy G. Ralston 1958
Enoch Jerome Gibbs 1960
Gene A. Peavley 1960
Dewey Charles Brock 1962
William David Perry 1962
Clay Vandergriff 1962
Avery Franklin Barnett 1963
Benjamin F. Meney 1965
Phillip Brown 1966
Jimmy Lyttle 1966
Eugene Philpot 1967
Pete Melzoni 1968
Della Arlene Miller 1968
Leon Douglas Davis 1969
Carlson C. Lewis 1969

Jeffrey R. Smith 1970
Alan Saunders Threlkeld 1970
Larry Jack Hurt 1971
Donna Rae Ison 1972
Robert William Ruskaup 1972
James Emmett Ashlock 1973
Randall Wade Carrier 1973
Doug Fortune 1974
Steven Dale Thompson 1974
Alice Theresa Kilgallon 1975
Clarence Ernest Miracle 1975
Paul R. Owens 1976
Jerry W. Powers 1976
Clifford L. Keith 1977
David Peter Sykes 1977
Cloyd Edwin Webb 1977
Brenda K. Dotson 1978
Patsy Smith 1978
Manus Wright 1978
Margaret L. Young 1978
Bruce Wayne Atwood 1979
Steven D. Windle 1979
Thomas L. Harp 1980
Thomas J. Clouse II 1982

Lynette Sue Gross 1982
Amey Jane Geoghagan 1983
Timothy Good 1983
Robert E. Prewitt 1983
Dan F. Ridenour 1983
Chris Delaney Vermillion 1984
Brenda Gregory 1985
Sylvia Ann Beasley 1987
Farhad Forohar 1988
Laura Beth Gregory 1988
Paul E. Brewer Jr. 1989
Angela C. Hogg 1990
Melissa G. Keith 1990
Woubayehu Ketema 1990
Chris L. Sears 1990
Jack LaRue Wright 1990
Melissa Ann Byrum 1992
Nathan Langdon 1993
Jerome Hawthorne 1994
Karen Gayle West 1994
Bryan Darrell Oliphant 1995
Daniel Richard Blevins 1998

TEACHER

Josephine E. Quarles 1922
Lucy R. Dillion 1923
Lessley Colson 1925
Lois E. Goldsmith 1925
Ethel F. Hoskins 1925
Flora Lee Steely 1925
Martha H. Victor 1926
Annie Lou Herrell 1927
Ruby M. Proctor 1927
Sue Ross 1927
Thelma Elizabeth Aleo 1928
Loel Jean Barberick 1928
Ruby C. Becknell 1929
Dorothy W. Hoag 1929
Eula D. Howard 1929
Nancy Marie Jones 1929
Edith E. Moore 1929
Buena V. Riley 1929
Charlotte Royalty 1929
Robert E. Wiley 1929
Grace J. Champion 1930
Alice Clark 1930
Hillis E. Foree 1930
Jo S. Furgason 1930
Mossie E. Gay 1930
Elizabeth M. Insko 1930

Chester Arthur Insko 1930
Euna A. Jones 1930
Hubert Mattingly 1930
Hallie B. Shewmaker 1930
Douglas Terry 1930
Stella Wilder 1930
Georgie C. Adkins 1931
Julia B. Cooper 1931
Georgia McHatton Edwards 1932
Margaret Jean Harrell 1932
Virginia Mays 1932
Mildred K. McKinley 1932
Rena W. Mounce 1932
Lillian S. Smith 1932
Orena C. Whitlock 1932
Floy B. Bogie 1933
Beulah Bridges 1933
Anna Brittain 1933
Ittylene Virginia Cordell 1933
Mary E. Hamm 1933
Vivian Johnston 1933
Raymond Lovett 1933
Dimple E. McAnelly 1933
Thelma Rodgers 1933
Roger Bruce Stephens 1933
Virgina E. Sundheimer 1933

Roy G. Teague 1933
Bessie Trammell 1933
Lloyd Wilson 1933
Alta S. Bean 1934
Alma B. Bickford 1934
Grace H. Kilgore 1934
Pauline D. Markel 1934
Lillie L. Pedigo 1934
Madeline B. Phipps 1934
Emma Olive Sharp 1934
Roxie S. Smith 1934
Margaret Vermillion 1934
Hazel Bowling 1935
Mary E. Disney 1935
Rubye H. Early 1935
Chester G. Farmer 1935
Kathryn Smith Hayes 1935
Robert Leon Hayes 1935
Pearl Hensley 1935
Jane Johnson 1935
Lela Leach 1935
Daphine Sullivan 1935
Roxie Elizabeth Zecchini 1935
Flossie R. Angel 1936
John G. Arnett Sr. 1936
Gladys T. Bordes 1936

Grace Brock 1936
Dixie Durham 1936
Evelyn Ely 1936
Ed D. Graves 1936
Thelma Jean C. Greene 1936
Lucy A. Hopkins 1936
Alma D. Jenkins 1936
Joyce R. Logan 1936
Lola Frances McKee 1936
Blanche D. Mitchell 1936
Alza Walker 1936
Fred Walters 1936
Edna Lee Wilson 1936
Nancy B. Witt 1936
Harrison C. Allison 1937
Dessie J. Barton 1937
Jean Ragan Colbert 1937
Mary Lewis Denney 1937
Hobart C. Eaton 1937
James Albert Elmore 1937
Marie J. Hill 1937
Raymond Kirby 1937
Mildred Conatser Nichols 1937
Jennie W. Smith 1937
Gladys Steely 1937
Roberta Steinhauser 1937
Nell C. Stickley 1937
Helen B. Warden 1937
Sara Lois Wilcher 1937
Una Janice Wooton 1937
Velma Baldwin 1938
Ruth Evelyn Ball 1938
Jemmie D. Batchellor 1938
Ruth Brewer 1938
Thelma C. Brown 1938
Ola G. Cody 1938
Aileen Dye 1938
Lavanor S. Faulkner 1938
Pearl B. Forth 1938
Betty E. Galloway 1938
Christine Grigsby 1938
Dorthie Anne Hall 1938
Begie E. Hatmaker 1938
Thelma Hayes Herrin 1938
Billy Laub 1938
Annie Joe Lewis 1938
Virginia O. Linkenhoker 1938
Josephine B. Petrey 1938
Edna Marie Prater 1938
Marion A. Richardson 1938
Maxine M. Sanders 1938
Ruth Ellen Scott 1938
Cynthia Sexton 1938
Francis Asbury Stephens 1938
Joie Tucker 1938
Clara Arnett 1939
Lois Ball 1939
Oda W. Catron 1939
Elma L. Cayton 1939
William G. Cooper 1939
Glenna Alma Craig 1939
Ova J. Girtman 1939
Nell Clara Henderlight 1939
Marcella Lindsay 1939
Ollie M. McHargue 1939
Christine Proctor 1939
Dorothy W. Roberts 1939
Bonnie Rutherford 1939
Nadine M. Siler 1939
Ruth Marie Vermillion 1939

Beulah Belle Back 1940
Anna G. Ball 1940
Christine L. Blevins 1940
Thelma Coffman 1940
Imogene D. Cornett 1940
Anna Mary Creekmore Ph.D. 1940
Diana M. Faulkner 1940
Mable Feltner 1940
Virginia C. Foster 1940
Vena Alberta Jones 1940
Mary E. Morrison 1940
Alma L. Parker 1940
Margaret M. Pierce 1940
Gladys E. Pinney 1940
Ida R. Powers 1940
Mildred Smith 1940
Eva K. Stokes 1940
Rae Taylor 1940
Geneva Thomas 1940
Elizabeth S. VanPelt 1940
Dora Edna Carman 1941
Henry George Davidson Jr. 1941
James H. Denney 1941
Marjorie K. Goff 1941
Geneva Hacker 1941
Genevieve S. Horne 1941
Ruth H. Johnston 1941
William W. Kilgore Jr. 1941
John Paul Maggard 1941
Sarah S. Martin 1941
Kathleen J. McCreary 1941
Marcella Faulkner Mountjoy 1941
Eula Mae Roaden 1941
Mary Dee Steely 1941
William R. Walton 1941
Dessie Florence Young 1941
Sara D. Abitanta 1942
Martha Alsip 1942
Gladys Lorraine Brown 1942
Mary Rebecca Burton 1942
Jessie Marie Carroll 1942
Mary Dale Freeman 1942
Mae C. Hipps 1942
Marcia Bryant Prather 1942
Maude S. Randall 1942
Helen Estepp Riddle 1942
Josephine L. Vaughn 1942
Ethel Emily Warfield 1942
Mary Frances Wills 1942
Jimmie Mullis Wissing 1942
Joie Rose Womack 1942
Bradley C. Baker 1943
Bernice B. Phelps 1943
Etherage Shadoan 1943
Ella Joann Stewart 1943
Marie P. Weaver 1943
Della Asher 1944
Lena P. Brewer 1944
Zella C. Campbell 1944
Dorothy L. Carr 1944
Mollie Jewell Corder 1944
Bernice Ann Cox 1944
Rufus V. Halcomb 1944
Euna Leach 1944
Cleda Lee 1944
Norma Shirley Martin 1944
Irene Owens 1944
Opal Partin 1944
Ollie Evelyn Smith 1944
Mary Lou Smith 1944

Sylvia Jones Taylor 1944
Fannie White 1944
Virginia L. Allen 1945
Mary Virginia Bowlin 1945
Vivian Delph 1945
Alma Jean Heaton 1945
Winifred Pearl Hornstein 1945
Audrey R. Hudson 1945
Imogene C. Owens 1945
Ella Mae Shelburne 1945
Maude H. Skinner 1945
Billie Bryant Brafford 1946
Mossie Slaton Bunch 1946
Pauline M. Cox 1946
Jean A. Freeman 1946
Edwina C. Gibson 1946
Carmaine Hall 1946
Joyce Jones Holbrook 1946
Glenna C. Jackson 1946
Nellie Mae Langley 1946
Bernice L. Lenz 1946
Velma Lindsey 1946
Martha Begley Lovett 1946
Marjorie Mae Partin 1946
Helen B. White 1946
A. Claudine Wyrick 1946
Doris M. Croley 1947
Kathleen N. Foxx 1947
Edna Holland 1947
George Issac Large 1947
Hazel Lovett 1947
Newton Lovitt Jr. 1947
Virgellen B. Lovitt 1947
John G. McAllister 1947
Pauline Brown 1948
Marilyn R. Bunch 1948
James M. Carter 1948
Sheila M. Denney 1948
Opal Faulkner 1948
June M. Gilbreath 1948
Russell Edward Gilreath 1948
Maurice Ray Gover 1948
Inez G. Jones 1948
Mary Joseph 1948
Virginia Langley 1948
Vesta Jean Lenhart 1948
Jeanette Looney 1948
Eleanor L. Martin 1948
Pearl S. McCarty 1948
Burniedean R. Siler 1948
James Smiddy 1948
Eugene Emerson Steely 1948
Susan Dolores Sutton 1948
Margaret Anne Thomas 1948
Martha Lee Anthony 1949
Mollie B. Baker 1949
Shirley T. Barker 1949
Hobert Bird 1949
Randal Y. Bishop 1949
Marjorie Blankenship 1949
George Albert Chandler 1949
Anna Baker Cormier 1949
Reva S. Draughn 1949
E. Aileen Florence 1949
Christine B. Godsey 1949
Ida Mae M. Judy 1949
Lenwood Lay 1949
Luther Clyde Lay 1949
Thelma Ruth Leigh 1949
Neva Sue Litton 1949

John Hicks Murrell 1949
Geneva Stout 1949
Elmer Ball 1950
Thelma Lawson Chinn 1950
Dora Lorene Cockrum 1950
Howard Corder 1950
Anna L. Cottrell 1950
Zana Casey Coyle 1950
Norris Clinton Delph 1950
Marie Janette Donan 1950
Ethel C. Donohew 1950
William Lewis Gooch 1950
Junella Margaret Hamblin 1950
Betty Lou Hill 1950
Garnett Beach Jones 1950
Mildred Kennedy 1950
Jimmie F. Lane 1950
Katherine Lewis Langford 1950
Phyllis L. Lay 1950
Richard T. Lyons 1950
Theda J. Marlow 1950
Donna M. Martin 1950
Lola Matthews 1950
Eloise S. Mitchell 1950
Mossie Neale 1950
Pearl Janet Rains 1950
Beulah I. Reineke 1950
Lillie Renshaw 1950
Walter K. Reynolds 1950
Rebecca Faye Shoupe 1950
Enoch Hubert Siler 1950
Florence V. Smith 1950
Stella D. Steely 1950
Marilyn Taylor Teague 1950
Audrey Daphian Watson 1950
Marion June Webber 1950
William H. Welch 1950
Charles W. Williams 1950
Carol M. Yunker 1950
Harold A. Browning, Jr. 1951
Gorman Bruce 1951
Howard Chitwood 1951
Salome S. Coleman 1951
Volena Craft 1951
Lena E. Douglas 1951
Roger Duncan 1951
Phyllis Chatfield England 1951
Andy R. Evans 1951
Norma Jean Feltner 1951
Donnie S. Flynn 1951
Carl R. Flynn 1951
Marie B. Frazier 1951
Betty J. Gault 1951
Margaret J. Hendrix 1951
Bobbie Jo Hooks 1951
Mildred A. Humphries 1951
Phyllis A. Jones 1951
Lawrence H. Langford 1951
Dorothy Mays 1951
Earl New 1951
Donald K. Queener 1951
Mary Nancy Redder 1951
Ethel F. Richardson 1951
Barbara J. Roberts 1951
James H. Robertson 1951
James Earl Scott 1951
Rachel Mahan Shoemaker 1951
Charlene Stephens 1951
Jerry Strange 1951
Raymond Hargus Taylor 1951

Patsy Dean Teague 1951
Julie Jackson Templeton 1951
Thelma D. Ward 1951
Darrel W. Wininger 1951
Agatha W. Young 1951
Jacqueline C. Adams 1952
Priscilla J. Anderson 1952
Jeroline Ann Baker 1952
Shirley Bruce 1952
Ella Mae Bruce 1952
Ivan G. Bunch 1952
Anna Ruth Correll 1952
Anna Jo Creech 1952
Betty Daniel 1952
Elizabeth Daniel 1952
Charles N. Haney 1952
Rollie J. Harp 1952
Agnes M. Hendren 1952
G. B. Hendrickson 1952
Ray Humble 1952
Scharlyene Hurt 1952
June E. Kudla 1952
Anis Mahan 1952
Betty Lou Martin 1952
Vernon Northfleet Martin Ph.D. 1952
John Partin Jr. 1952
Pearl J. Petrey 1952
Joan P. Rillo 1952
Helen W. Ross 1952
Hazel H. Shaw 1952
Margaret Alice Slusher 1952
Wilma Ruth Strunk 1952
Katherine M. Strunk 1952
James W. Taylor Jr. 1952
Lonnie E. Watters 1952
Ruth L. Webb 1952
Sylvia Arnett 1953
Jeweldene Baker 1953
Marie Brown 1953
Eleanor S. Buhl 1953
Mary Elizabeth Carter 1953
Anna Mae Cody 1953
Martha Dossett 1953
Elizabeth Ann Foley 1953
Lois Foutch 1953
Wallace M. Gosser 1953
Betty Frances Halbrook 1953
Libby W. Jones 1953
R. Howard Jones 1953
Mary S. Mann 1953
Frances Begley Morris 1953
Mac Dwight Morrow 1953
Marguerite Murphy 1953
Bill J. Pfoff 1953
Marjorie Pilman 1953
Sara Katherine Scent 1953
Yvonne B Shoemaker 1953
John Raphael Skeese 1953
Launa Tiller 1953
Jane M. Wilson 1953
Norma Joyce Bardill 1954
Cleta Ruth Broyles 1954
Lane Gray Broyles 1954
Jo Florence Cordell 1954
Mary Ann Dykes 1954
Glenda Fackler 1954
Rosetta Hall 1954
Betty S. Jones 1954
Wanda L. Kidd 1954
Laura Helen Larck 1954

Imogene M. Mays 1954
L. B. Oliver 1954
C. Sue Phelps 1954
Arizona Reeder 1954
Mary Rose Reynolds 1954
Mary C. Savage 1954
June Frances Sawyer 1954
Paula Scott 1954
Sybil Sullivan Walker 1954
Jack Wilder 1954
Leon Wilson 1954
Anna Jean Wood 1954
Vernon Byrd 1955
Marlene V. Callanan 1955
Henry Ford Cornett 1955
David L. Davies 1955
Alma Jean DeBell 1955
Betty S. Hammett 1955
Mary Maud Hiestand 1955
Martha E. Highland 1955
Verna Katherine Hill 1955
Aline Hoffman 1955
Lena Rue Hutton 1955
Nancy Carrigan Isaacs 1955
Norma Jean King 1955
Gladys Lay 1955
Etta Mae Lester 1955
Vester L. Lewis 1955
Mary Alice Lundy 1955
Vera Massengale 1955
Genevieve Steely McGregor 1955
Dallas Messer 1955
Peggy M. Metcalf 1955
Ronald C. Mitchell 1955
Bennie Mullins 1955
Mary Ann O'Brien 1955
James T. Ohler 1955
Lynette D. Polson 1955
Barbara Ann Scott 1955
Lonzo Calvin Staley 1955
John Wetzel Strunk 1955
Betty Joy Sutton 1955
Clyde H. Tiller 1955
Carol Ann Trussell 1955
Rhoda Lue Webb 1955
Kathleen Johnson Werner 1955
Gladys Mae Alsip 1956
David Bilbrey 1956
Mary Caroline Bowlin 1956
Don Dreyfus Brashear 1956
Jonah Carpenter 1956
Harold Glenn Clarkston 1956
Lela Mae Crowe 1956
Shirley J. Daunhauer 1956
Charles Kenneth Hatfield 1956
Willie P. Isaacs 1956
Carrol Dean Kidd 1956
Kathleen Lawson 1956
Phyllis Gail Lawson 1956
Shirley Jean LeForce 1956
Andrew Jackson McIntyre 1956
Pauline C. Morrison 1956
Joyce Mullins 1956
Arnold Rose 1956
Jerry A. Shackelford 1956
Parker Slaven 1956
Loretta Brewer Smith 1956
Norman G. Strunk 1956
Gayle Lenore Taylor 1956
Robert L. Taylor 1956

Robert Ray Tomlinson 1956
Betty L. Turpin 1956
Irene M. Upchurch 1956
Alma L. Walker 1956
James H. Washam 1956
Georgia Wilder 1956
Jane Zoochi 1956
Robert E. Arnett 1957
Sally Ada Brock 1957
Clevis Don Carter 1957
Magdalene Carver 1957
Ray Marion Chapman 1957
George Couch 1957
Mary Rosaleen Crane 1957
Robert E. Dizney 1957
Winfred M. Douglas 1957
Shirley Anne Elliott 1957
Henry Julius Garrison 1957
Patricia C. Goggins 1957
Patty Golden 1957
Patricia A. Higgs 1957
Marcena M. Hill 1957
Jan A. Jackson 1957
Perna Ruth Leach 1957
Harold K. Lester 1957
Wilma June Miller 1957
Orena Morgan 1957
Barbara Sue Morris 1957
Louise T. Nichols 1957
Evelyn G. Norman 1957
V. Janet O'Leary 1957
Joyce Ann Rains 1957
Sally R. Rhodes 1957
Margaret J. Shackelford 1957
Charlotte Welch 1957
Shirley Furnish Whitehead 1957
Betty Lois Williams 1957
Judge S. Wilson 1957
Charlotte Sue Biondo 1958
Phyllis M. Blaylock 1958
Cilla S. Boggs 1958
Bertie J. Bostic 1958
Lillias Yvonne Byrd 1958
Nancy Ruth Clark 1958
Peggy Jane Clark 1958
Harold Cornett 1958
Doris Jean Correll 1958
John C. Fletcher 1958
Joyce Wanda Fulkerson 1958
Frances M. Hall 1958
Elizabeth Wassum Hall 1958
Lewis Douglas Harp 1958
Patricia H. Hayden 1958
Imogene Henegar 1958
Winston L. Jackson 1958
Phyllis Annette Jett 1958
Martha Lynn King 1958
Catherine G. Mayes 1958
Luster C. Patterson 1958
Lona Ann Prichard 1958
William Bryant Roark 1958
Sylvia Lou Robinson 1958
Norma Scalf 1958
Pat J. Schrader 1958
Mary Carroll Smith 1958
Joyce Stacy 1958
Sue Carol Tomlin 1958
Betty H. Webster 1958
Paul E. White 1958
Joyce B. Wong 1958

Betty Mavin Banks 1959
Henry Babe Barton 1959
Jessie Lee Carpenter 1959
Betty Sue Christman 1959
Edith J. Davis 1959
Shirley Aretta Edwards 1959
Julia Freeman 1959
Josh Ralph Howard 1959
Kenneth C. Jones 1959
Margaret Ann Lewis 1959
Betty Jo Lucas 1959
Bertie Mills 1959
Reba Jane Mounce 1959
Harriett D. Ray 1959
V. Ellouise Shepherd 1959
Gwendolyn A. Amburgy 1960
Jack W. Bailey 1960
Robert B. Cain 1960
Nancy Baker Cooper 1960
Mary George DeVary 1960
Patricia Kathryn Frakes 1960
Harriet J. Johnson 1960
Loretta Faye Lyttle 1960
A. B. Moore 1960
Jeanette Christine Sutton 1960
Jack Asbury 1961
Velma Ball 1961
Ronald Marvin Banks 1961
Peggy Bates 1961
Eula Edith Boring 1961
Annis M. Bowlin 1961
Patricia Brown 1961
Lula Jane Bush 1961
James M. Buttram 1961
Randall Byrd 1961
Ethel Carnes 1961
Evelyn Cox 1961
Edna Cross 1961
Gene R. Daugherty 1961
Roberta Evans 1961
Agnes Foster 1961
John A. Gilliam 1961
Nadene Heth 1961
G. Irene Hill 1961
Marlene W. Howard 1961
Kenneth Howard 1961
Larry Irwin 1961
Evelyn W. Jeffers 1961
Mary Elizabeth Johnson 1961
Paul K. Jones 1961
Anita Louise Keeton 1961
John R. Keeton 1961
Pete Killgore 1961
Nancy M. Kirk 1961
Norma E. Lawson 1961
Ilas Lawson 1961
Ronda S. Leffew 1961
Judith Ann Lezotte 1961
Wilma E. Mayne 1961
Patricia Mae McGowan 1961
Robert Lee Merritt 1961
Dale Martin Metcalfe 1961
Wilma June Miller 1961
Janet Sue Miracle 1961
Rose Yvonne Noe 1961
Brenda Rose Orme 1961
Sarah Elizabeth Paley 1961
Mary Evelyn Partin 1961
Horace Partin 1961
Shelby Pennington 1961

Clayton Dillard Perry 1961
Brenda Rains 1961
Barbara Eileen Ramsey 1961
Georgia P. Robinson 1961
Gladys Shepherd 1961
Virginia P. Shepherd 1961
Margaret Hazel Siler 1961
Jaola G. Siler 1961
Pauline T. Simpson 1961
Betty June Smith 1961
Carl Thornton 1961
Alice Adelaide Toole 1961
Mildred Troxel 1961
Martin Eugene Wheeler 1961
Barbara Wilder 1961
Dollie R. Williams 1961
Lon Wilson 1961
Hilda Mae Angell 1962
Thelma Sue Bach 1962
Ledford A. Baird 1962
Chastine Baker 1962
Idela Barnett 1962
Dorcas E. Benge 1962
Mary Ann Bingham 1962
Don Bingham 1962
Ernest Blair 1962
Conrad Wayne Bowling 1962
Iva Louise Branson 1962
Doris Canady 1962
Hascue Carter 1962
Nancy Olive Cathcart 1962
Sarah E. Combs 1962
Rita Charlene Cox 1962
Pauline Cox 1962
Ada Opal Creech 1962
Anne Criscillis 1962
Merrill J. Davies 1962
James C. Eaton 1962
Betty W. Elmore 1962
Rita M. Gibson 1962
Amanda Lorene Goodin 1962
James Carl Gordon 1962
Mearl Halcomb 1962
Eula Faye Hall 1962
Marvis Lynn Hall 1962
Carol Jean Hammons 1962
Joyce Harrod 1962
Harold Dean Hart 1962
Angie Hodge 1962
Brenda Joyce Hollingsworth 1962
Harold Jack Holt 1962
Spurgeon Holt 1962
Edna I. Hoover 1962
Karen C. Hubbs 1962
Glen W. Johnson 1962
Louis F. Jones 1962
Gloria Jean Karr 1962
Peggy Joyce Keith 1962
Flora M. Kelly 1962
Elvena A. Kidd 1962
Ira C. King 1962
Helen S. Klingler 1962
Bill Lambdin 1962
Mary Edith Land 1962
Bessie Jane Lawson 1962
Eula Lee 1962
Betty S. Lusby 1962
Edward Mahan 1962
Mabel Nadine Manus 1962
Chester Maupin 1962

Fayrene J. Meadors 1962
Charity Ann Metcalfe 1962
Dorothy M. Morris 1962
Shirley Norman 1962
Jeanette T. Petrey 1962
Phyllis Pryor 1962
Diana Rose 1962
Ralph Edward Ross 1962
James Wilbur Sawyer 1962
Ruth C. Sharp 1962
James E. Shepherd 1962
Bessie E. Siler 1962
Hester S. Smith 1962
Anita Stamper 1962
Nancy A. Stout 1962
Letha Taylor 1962
Mary Tharpe 1962
Kenneth Turner 1962
Wanda B. Twyford 1962
Elsie Roberta Walden 1962
George Wendell Waldroup 1962
Clara M. Waldroup 1962
Jack Ward 1962
Cassie J. Williams 1962
Betty J. Wilson 1962
Robert Zane Abbott 1963
Faye Lorene Adams 1963
Linda Agee 1963
Charlotte Atchison 1963
Mary Baker 1963
Frances C. Ball 1963
Caroline N. Ball 1963
Rella F. Banks 1963
Imogene S. Barnes 1963
Arlie O. Barnes 1963
Gwenave Edwina Bell 1963
Herman Blair 1963
John H. Brewer 1963
Mary Ann Brewster 1963
Barbara Sue Brown 1963
William Hobert Brown 1963
Orlis L. Burton 1963
Kyle R. Carmony 1963
Robert Lynn Cathcart 1963
Dorcas Catron 1963
Clifton Ray Centers 1963
LeeElla Chenoweth 1963
Irene Clawson 1963
Irma Sue Clifton 1963
Pat D. Cobb 1963
Alma Conken 1963
Inez Ruth Cox 1963
Rodney Lee Croley 1963
Barbara J. Curd 1963
Boyd Edward Daniels 1963
Jean C. Davis 1963
John E. Faulkner 1963
Alma Ruth Faulkner 1963
L. Kathy Kathleen Flowers 1963
Dickey D. France 1963
Eunice S. Garrison 1963
Jim E. Gilreath 1963
Wallace Winston Goins 1963
Gladys D. Grever 1963
Cora Frances Hacker 1963
Delores Hall 1963
Betty Catherine Hamblin 1963
Pauline Hammons 1963
Sharon Hart 1963
Thomas Eugene Hays 1963

Norma Kelly Henegar 1963
Katherine Anna Hill 1963
Martin Edward Hill 1963
Clayborne R. Holmes 1963
Patricia Lou Hopkins 1963
Monte S. Hounchell 1963
Romie D. House 1963
Billy Norris Hubbs 1963
G. Len Hughes 1963
Barbara Ann Hummell 1963
Clarence R. Hunter 1963
Sandra P. Jackson 1963
Gladys H. Jones 1963
Larry A. Jordan 1963
Anetha Joyce King 1963
Elizabeth Ann Kuenzli 1963
Mildred Lake 1963
Mary Ann Lang 1963
Lois Jean Langdon 1963
Suevella Lawson 1963
Patricia Anne Lawson 1963
Ronna Gail Lester 1963
Mildred Doreen Mauney 1963
Phyllis Merryman 1963
Edith Ann Miller 1963
Lillian Moore 1963
Bonnie P. Noplis 1963
Lowell G. Osborne 1963
Herbert G. Partin 1963
Anna Mae Patrick 1963
Glenn Edward Peace 1963
Mary Catron Perkins 1963
Neva Phillips 1963
Herbert N. Proffitt 1963
Mitzi Lou Reeves 1963
Charlene S. Rex 1963
Robert L. Reynolds 1963
Sandra M. Rhoads 1963
Edna S. Riley 1963
Edna Sue Roark 1963
Kitty Faye Robbins 1963
Wanda Roberts 1963
Ralph Robinson 1963
Barbara Ann Rosenbaum 1963
June Ross 1963
Rebecca W. Rudolph 1963
Geneva Bruce Sasher 1963
Gwendolyn Sharp 1963
Mary Sharon Shelton 1963
Barbara F. Sizemore 1963
James E. Smith 1963
Mary Sue Smith-Locke 1963
Walter M. Steely 1963
Anna Joyce Teague 1963
Carol Teague 1963
Hazel K. Teague 1963
Lucille Trammell 1963
Silas Griffin Trammell 1963
Doris Q. Triplett 1963
Leora Vandergriff 1963
Willie Jean Vaughn 1963
Ruth Wallace 1963
Wilma Jo Watson 1963
Edgar Clay Watson 1963
Rayford Watts 1963
Charles M. Wells 1963
Alice Faye Wilder 1963
Lavonne Wilson 1963
John Dee Wilson 1963
Orvetta M. Wilson 1963

Linda Sims Wright 1963
Linda Holmes Anderson 1964
Bonita Asher 1964
Effie Mae Ball 1964
Particia Sue Barnes 1964
Charles Riddle Beaty II 1964
Mary Ann Bertram 1964
James David Bishop 1964
Alfreda Boggs 1964
Paul Bond 1964
Eddie Wayne Boyd 1964
Merlin Bradley 1964
Dora Fields Brashear 1964
Wayne E. Brock 1964
Nora Lee Brooks 1964
Rose C. Brown 1964
Billy Joe Brown 1964
Royce Darrell Burton 1964
Shirley Campbell 1964
Leslie Philip Carnahan 1964
Alvin Ray Carr 1964
Betty Casada 1964
Virginia Juanitta Casada 1964
Uma Ann Clark 1964
David Collins 1964
Bretta Conley 1964
Vivian L. Cooper 1964
Helen Marie Cox 1964
Jerome Cox 1964
Betty H. Creech 1964
Noel Gene Davidson 1964
Joyce C. Davis 1964
Bobby Ray Davis 1964
Jimmy B. Delk 1964
George Dudley Donaldson 1964
James Michael Downey 1964
Opal M. Duncan 1964
Faye C. Eaton 1964
Judy Faye Engle 1964
Glenda Sue Gieszl 1964
Nelda Jean Gilreath 1964
Sue Etta Godman 1964
Albert Lee Goforth 1964
Lena Gordon 1964
Charlotte June Graves 1964
Margaret Griffith 1964
Alice Rhea Gross 1964
Edsel Ford Hacker 1964
Edward E. Ham USN Ret. 1964
Joe F. Hatfield 1964
Jana Sue Hill 1964
Anne B. Hill 1964
Joyce M. Hill 1964
Janie Hines 1964
Helen Hollingsworth 1964
Carole A. Hommel 1964
Barbara Faye Hopkins 1964
Norma Jean Hoskins 1964
Michael Ray Howard 1964
Maxine S. Hubbs 1964
Doyle Keith Karr 1964
Jerry Ronald Kersey 1964
Donald Kuracka 1964
Wanda Joyce Lake 1964
Sierra Langley 1964
Linda Lou Lanham 1964
Phyllis A. Lay 1964
Kathleen Elizabeth Lay 1964
Beulah H. Lewis 1964
Margaret H. Lovitt 1964

Cora Ellen Mathis 1964
Everett Eugene McFarland 1964
Martha Jane McIntyre 1964
Arthur Elbert McKeehan 1964
Nora Morgan 1964
Lois Morgan 1964
Victor Lewis Morris 1964
Clifford Ray Morris 1964
Reba Doris Morse 1964
Mary Kathryn Kirby Moss 1964
Helen Frances Nicely 1964
Joyce Ann Parker 1964
Virginia Ruth Peace 1964
Barbara Ann Philpot 1964
Helen Phipps 1964
Marilyn June Phukan 1964
Wilma Colene Ponder 1964
Ben Carl Powell 1964
Alvis Mitchell Privett 1964
Mary Rose Pursiful 1964
Barbara F. Reed 1964
Frank Allen Reed 1964
Cenia Evelyn Reeves 1964
Edna L. Rice 1964
Lucille H. Ringley 1964
Mary Lillian Rivers 1964
Bonnie C. Sears 1964
Lee Edd Sears 1964
Robert Clement Shelley 1964
Joyce A. Siler 1964
Gardner Slone Jr. 1964
Carlos Edward Slusher 1964
Lenora F. Slusher 1964
Carl Robert Smith 1964
Barbara Kay Smith 1964
Martha Sparkman 1964
Donald Strunk 1964
Linda Lou Turner 1964
Barbara M. Vowell 1964
Janice Walters 1964
Arthur Darwin Walters 1964
Nancy A. Watts 1964
Lucille Webb 1964
Patsy Sue Wells 1964
Juanita S. Williamson 1964
Gwendolyn J. Wilson 1964
Carl M. Woods 1964
Pauline Wyatt 1964
Betty D. York 1964
Gloria Jean Younce 1964
Jean R. Abbott 1965
Carol Jean Arthur 1965
Lila Asher 1965
Jimmie Bain 1965
Kathlyn Baker 1965
Arthur Thomas Baker 1965
Betty Janice Baldwin 1965
Janice Barton 1965
Charlotte Louise Bays 1965
Robert Verlin Beckner 1965
Susan Katherine Begley 1965
Sonney B. Begley 1965
Iris Verna Black 1965
Richard Kent Black 1965
Donny H. Blankenship 1965
Janis Bowling 1965
Sylvia Bowling 1965
Levi Bowling 1965
Beatrice Brashear 1965
Florence Beatrice Breniser 1965

Ella Cordelia Bryant 1965
Thelma S. Buell 1965
Bobby Lee Carnes 1965
Yvonne B. Clark 1965
James Arthur Cobb 1965
Edna M. Cox 1965
Henry Damewood 1965
Sandra A. Davenport 1965
Jerry Wayne Dixon 1965
Carol Dobson 1965
Nancy Jo Dossett 1965
Betty Carolyn Dunn 1965
Gary Fairchild 1965
Jewell Foley 1965
Edna Frost 1965
Asenath Fuson 1965
Patricia Ann Goins 1965
Reed Roberts Gregory 1965
Elizabeth A. Hall 1965
Sandra J. Harbuck 1965
Linda Faye Hawkins 1965
Shirley Maxine Helton 1965
Betty Jo Helton 1965
Mary Kay Hibbard 1965
Jerome Hill 1965
Gerald Foster Hill 1965
Roy G. Houser 1965
Carnie Lee Hughes 1965
James H. Hughett 1965
Emily Sue Hutchison 1965
Brenda J. Jody 1965
Daniel Edward Jody 1965
Cassandra Lee Jones 1965
Anna Elizabeth Jones 1965
Thomas Joe Kilgore 1965
Doris Satterfield Lawson 1965
Harry Lee 1965
Elizabeth Griffith Lewallen 1965
Brenda Kay Lewis 1965
Erma Lee Libbee 1965
Herman Ray Long 1965
Stanley Lovett 1965
Ralph Eugene Lyons 1965
John S. Maggard 1965
Robert Rosslyn Mercer 1965
Lee Owen Mills 1965
Claudette Miracle 1965
Jack Allen Moore 1965
Everett Morgan 1965
Berlin Morgan 1965
Karen Daphane Murphy 1965
Martha C. Nantz 1965
Phyllis Jeannette Neal 1965
Barbara Okumura 1965
Johnny Edgar Partin 1965
Helen Sue Paul 1965
Robert Franklin Petrey 1965
Rochelle Phillips 1965
Darla Pool 1965
Sandra Mae Proctor 1965
Gordon Harvey Queen 1965
Rosella Reynolds 1965
Flora Richmond 1965
Franklin D. Rowland 1965
Margaret Janice Scalf 1965
Albert W. Scalf 1965
Violet Schmidt 1965
Joseph Mack Sharp 1965
Alvin D. Sharpe 1965
Wilbur G. Shoun 1965

Melanie Kay Skiles 1965
Richard Vaughn Smith 1965
Hughie Roosevelt Smith 1965
Donald Eugene Smith 1965
Edith Bernice Spangler 1965
Sandra Sue Stacy 1965
James Harold Stanley 1965
Paul Eugene Stewart 1965
James Nathan Stone 1965
Norman B. Sweat 1965
Fannie Elaine Taylor 1965
Wendell Earl Taylor 1965
Thelma L. Terry 1965
Merita L. Thompson 1965
Carolyn Underwood 1965
Bobby R. Underwood 1965
Sue Davis Vaughan 1965
Eric L. Wake 1965
Dorothy L. Walden 1965
Faye Rains Warfield 1965
Robert William Watkins 1965
Alice Fae Weiland 1965
Michael L. Wilson 1965
Janice L. Adkins 1966
Archie Lee Anderson Jr. 1966
Roger Alan Asher 1966
James M. Atkins 1966
Virginia M. Badida 1966
Faye W. Begley 1966
Coleen Binning 1966
Freda C. Blansett 1966
Joyce C. Bowling 1966
Harold Morsene Bradford 1966
Larry Joe Brewer 1966
Margaret H. Brock 1966
Evalee Brodbent 1966
Unis Mae Broyles 1966
Gary Arnold Bruce 1966
Rubye Olivia Brummett 1966
Wanda Faye Buhel 1966
James Bruce Bullen 1966
Neal Burton 1966
Betty Gayle Calloway 1966
Maude Campbell 1966
Peggy Charlene Centers 1966
Anita Faye Childers 1966
Katherine Childs 1966
Juliet W. Clark 1966
Janice Holman Closs 1966
Alfred Cobb 1966
Judy E. Cobb 1966
Emil Arthur Cook 1966
Howard B. Cox 1966
Johnny Lynn Davis 1966
Cynthia Lou Deaderick 1966
Judy L. Dean 1966
Sillisene Drew 1966
Ernestine Duval 1966
Thomas N. Duval 1966
Tommy Ray Faulkner 1966
Julius Fey 1966
Betty Joyce Fisher 1966
Judy A. Ford 1966
Ernie E. Fuller 1966
Leroy Gordon 1966
William Carl Green 1966
Linda M. Griffith 1966
Flossie C. Grigsby 1966
Alma Jean Harrison 1966
Charlotte R. Helton 1966

Harold Hoskins 1966
Joyce C. Hunley 1966
Barbara Sue Ison 1966
John Thomas Janeway 1966
Betty Lou Johnson 1966
Curtis Keeton 1966
Lillie Mae Kinder 1966
Linda Joyce Kirk 1966
Elsie B. Koger 1966
Thelma Irene Leforce 1966
Boyce N. Lester 1966
John D. Love 1966
Alberta M. Masters 1966
Mildred Ann McClary 1966
Linda S. Melhorn 1966
Dorothy C. Miller 1966
Glenna F. Mofield 1966
Oona Lee Moler 1966
Roger Dwain Morris 1966
Sandra Mullins 1966
Linda Lou Phillips 1966
Ruth Ann Phillips 1966
Royce Leon Rains 1966
Larry Roscoe Ramey 1966
Carolyn Ann Roback 1966
Helen K. Robbins 1966
Ronald W. Rose 1966
Lois Ann Sharpe 1966
Lowry Sibert 1966
Earl Sizemore 1966
Mary Etta Smith 1966
Elijah R. Smith 1966
Mary Frances Steely 1966
Dallas B. Steely 1966
Mary Ruth Stephens 1966
Mildred O. Storm 1966
Mildred Strunk 1966
Rosemary Taylor 1966
Daniel S. Thomas 1966
Russel Wayne Thompson 1966
Jo Ann Uptmor 1966
Yvonne Vanlandingham 1966
Imogene B. Vann 1966
Glenna S. Walters 1966
Gary Wendell Warrix 1966
Deborah June Weaver 1966
Jewel Webb 1966
Wanda Christine Wilder 1966
Gary Douglas Williams 1966
William Woodville Williamson 1966
Herman Caroll Wilson 1966
Charles Edward Wilson 1966
Carl Henry Yahnig 1966
Kenneth Ray Adams 1967
Glenn A. Adams 1967
Lillian Berdie Mae Althouse 1967
Bertha Jo Anderson 1967
Geraldine Anderson 1967
Vera Arvin 1967
John Wayne Badida 1967
Patricia Dawn Ball 1967
Glenn L. Bennett 1967
Mary Linda Blanton 1967
Joyce Christine Bowlin 1967
Alene P. Bowling 1967
Richard Pratt Bowling 1967
Betty Louise Bowman 1967
Tom Frank Brewer 1967
Mossie Brock 1967
Barbara Jo Brown 1967

Clyde Jerome Brummett 1967
Patricia White Burton 1967
Doris Caldwell 1967
Betty Jane Z. Chitwood 1967
Robert Wayne Clark 1967
Jenny Ruth Clifton 1967
C. Tom Cloer Jr., Ph.D. 1967
Evelyn C. Cobb 1967
Joyce Ann Compton 1967
Robert Otis Correll 1967
Kenneth J. Cottongim 1967
Margaret F. Davis 1967
Paul Dixon 1967
Jimmy Joe Dunaway 1967
Geneva Mae Duncil 1967
J. C. Engle 1967
David Lee Fairchild 1967
William Edward Fannin 1967
Roger Wayne Faulkner 1967
Brenda Faye Fowler 1967
Sam J. France 1967
Sally Manning Frazier 1967
Shirley Ann Fugate 1967
Gwen Renfro Goode 1967
Loyd H. Gordon 1967
Thelma Ellen Green 1967
Wilburn Lonnie Grimes 1967
Judith Ann Grove 1967
Walter Pearl Hacker 1967
Bobbie June Heath 1967
Sandra Helton 1967
Vivian E. Henegar 1967
Jeanette Hensley 1967
John Marvin Hoffman 1967
Idella Hubbard 1967
George W. Ingram 1967
Mitzi Johnson 1967
Henrietta Elisabeth Krey 1967
Rebecca Anne Lawson 1967
Shelby L. Lewis 1967
Lou Malicoat 1967
Danny Lee McAlarnis 1967
Campbell B. McIntyre 1967
Ernestine McIntyre 1967
Doris Meadors 1967
Donna Tresa Moses 1967
Larry J. Mynatt 1967
Doyle Edward Nevels 1967
Lois Darleen Nolan 1967
Gary Russell Owens 1967
Glenda Sue Painter 1967
Linda J. Parris 1967
Brenda Patrick 1967
Janna Lou Perkins 1967
Betty Lou Perkins 1967
Melva Kaye Phelps 1967
Sharon L. Piepmeyer 1967
Mary Reba Price 1967
Ruth Susan Purdom 1967
Pamela Kay Pursifull 1967
Rachel Richardson 1967
Mary Agnes Roberts 1967
Joanne Robinette 1967
Orville Ray Robinson 1967
Laura Jane Rodarte 1967
Earl M. Rodgers 1967
Janet L. Schehr 1967
Naomi Ruth Sears 1967
Carolyn S. Sewalls 1967
Wanda Shelley 1967

Maureen Shepherd 1967
Lena Mae Short 1967
Virginia Lee Smith 1967
Edith Darlene Smith 1967
Bruce Harold Smith 1967
Sonny L. Snellings 1967
Joyce Sue Steely 1967
Glennis M. Steely 1967
Edna Pearl Stephens 1967
Nancy S. Sutton 1967
Thermon W. Taylor 1967
Shirley R. Thompson 1967
Ida M. Tidwell 1967
Larry Eugene Tucker 1967
Joan G. Webb 1967
Phyllis Fayetta Whitaker 1967
Fernie Day Williams Jr. 1967
Lucy Cline Wilson 1967
Larry A. Wingfeld 1967
Kelly Baker 1968
Mary Sue Barnes 1968
Betty Sue Barnes 1968
Jane Bevers 1968
Terry Bird 1968
Kenneth W. Bird 1968
Teresa Pauline Blankenship 1968
Billie Sue Boothe 1968
Bob Bowlin 1968
Arcelia D. Bowman 1968
Lois P. Bowman 1968
Wanda Lee Bowman 1968
James Sechrert Bowman 1968
Jean Carol Breeding 1968
Elsie Mae Brown 1968
John Wesley Bruce 1968
Genny Bryant 1968
Bonnie Burns 1968
Patricia Hicks Carr 1968
Joy Constance Carrier 1968
Barbara Jean Carrigan 1968
Robert D. Caudill 1968
Albert L. Charny Jr. 1968
Ronald A. Cinnamon 1968
Millard Couch 1968
Linda Curry 1968
Evelyn Dixon 1968
Dennis M. Doan 1968
Rodney L. Dunham 1968
Sherry Lorene Eley 1968
Janet Kay Fairchild 1968
Margaret E. Faulkner 1968
Margaret Ann Faulkner 1968
Doris Jean Ferguson 1968
Betty Faye Floyd 1968
Richard Wayne Foley 1968
Julia Alice Foley 1968
Jimmy D. Garland 1968
Therman Gibson 1968
Janice M. Gilbert 1968
Carolyn Ruth Gregory 1968
Lois Faye Grimes 1968
Sharon Lynn Hale 1968
Sue E. Hall 1968
Pauline Hensley Harber 1968
James Malcolm Higgins 1968
Wanda Hudson 1968
Myona Sue Hutson 1968
Vernon Jackson 1968
Wanda J. Jeffries 1968
Garry Morris Jervis 1968

Byron P. Jody 1968
Jewell J. Johnson 1968
Roger Charles Johnson 1968
Brenda Lou Keith 1968
Mary Keith 1968
Harold Nelson Kennedy 1968
J. C. King 1968
Jay Kolb 1968
Stella Mae Lamblin 1968
Joyce Ruth Lawson 1968
Jacquelyn W. Lee 1968
Mildred S. Leger 1968
Margie Lingenfelter 1968
Marie S. Logan 1968
Janice Massey 1968
Curtis Wayne Massey 1968
Jane A. McFarland 1968
Audra Cathern McGeorge 1968
Jon Colin McKeehan 1968
Helen E. Mills 1968
Michael C. Mills 1968
Alfredia Morris 1968
Aretta Moses 1968
Charlene Nixon 1968
Bonnie Juanita Overton 1968
Marcella Owens 1968
Sharon Kenoa Parrott 1968
Kenneth E. Patrick 1968
Garry Michael Paul 1968
Nora Marie Pendergrass 1968
Toby Ann Poore 1968
Robert Posey 1968
William N. Proctor 1968
Norma Jeanne Pryor 1968
Barbara G. Reeves 1968
Herman Harold Rhodes 1968
Janet S. Roundtree 1968
Doug Safford 1968
Kenneth Marion Sandusky 1968
Arthur Leman Saylor 1968
Phyllis D. Schnacke 1968
Roda Charlotte Schumann 1968
Bruce Edwin Sexton 1968
Betty Ruth Sharp 1968
Sandra A. Shelton 1968
Bobbie Sue Shoun 1968
Earl Wayne Siler 1968
Patricia Ann Smith 1968
Mickey Anne Smith 1968
Donna L. Smith 1968
Hollis Roger Smith 1968
William J. Stadtlander 1968
Darlene Taylor 1968
Bob Craig Teague 1968
Walter Doug Trammell 1968
Juanita Lee Troutman 1968
Charlene W. Vonderschmidt 1968
George Clayton Warren 1968
Joyce Ann Watson 1968
Bobbie Weatherly 1968
Paula Sue White 1968
Bonnie L. Wilder 1968
Patricia Ann Wilkins 1968
Roberta R. Williams 1968
Jennie Lee Wilson 1968
Mary Elizabeth Wilson 1968
Jerry Lee Woods 1968
Dallas W. Anderson 1969
Joann Barton 1969
Patricia Ann Bingham 1969

Nancy Katherine Bird 1969
Phyllis Bishop 1969
David Raymond Blackburn 1969
Robert M. Bradford 1969
Billy R. Brewer 1969
Carol Joan Brown 1969
Joe Clinton Broyles 1969
Marion Clyde Burchette 1969
Dorothy Eva Burress 1969
Steven Carter Byrd 1969
Ruby H. Cain 1969
Phyllis C. Callaway 1969
William Lloyd Campbell 1969
Carolyn Canada 1969
Terri Rae Capek 1969
Theresa Ann Carnes 1969
Karen King Carnes 1969
Karen King Carnes 1969
Micheal Angelo Caruso 1969
Janice Ann Chaney 1969
Martha Pearl Cheek 1969
Walter Jennings Combs 1969
James Robert Combs 1969
Clarence R. Conley 1969
Charles Robert Conley 1969
Larry Wayne Cordell 1969
Harry Cordell 1969
Glenn Douglas Correll 1969
Kerry Mason Cowan 1969
Gary Thomas Cummins 1969
Judy Alene Curtis 1969
Cecil Deel 1969
Deanne Denny 1969
Michael Dixon 1969
William Lee Edwards 1969
Alta Kathleen Elliott 1969
Richard Michael Ellis 1969
Luther C. Ellis 1969
Joanne Ferguson 1969
Bonnie Lou Frazier 1969
Gilbert Gladwell 1969
James Lee Goodan 1969
Janice Goss 1969
Anna Sue Greenwell 1969
Alice Gregory 1969
Wanda Faye Griffith 1969
Eva Dairlene Grubb 1969
Bobbie Haggard 1969
Emma Joyce Hall 1969
Bob George Hamblin 1969
Judy Lynne Hardin 1969
Joe Earl Helton 1969
Rita Hensley 1969
Arretta Fern Hice 1969
Pansy Hill 1969
Lige Glyn Hubbard 1969
Mary Humphrey 1969
James Hurst 1969
Deborah Kay Hurt 1969
Richard Wayne Hurt 1969
Della Ingram 1969
Howard Larry Jackson 1969
Loyd V. Jeffers 1969
Lois Gaynell Johnson 1969
Thelma Jones 1969
Dennis Jones 1969
Margaret Ann Karsner 1969
Jambut T. Khorzanoff 1969
Carolyn Marie Knighting 1969
Jacqueline Marie Kolbe 1969

Darlene Krahn 1969
Ann G. Lawson 1969
Mildred Lockhart 1969
V. Troy Lovett 1969
William Junior Lynch 1969
Calvin Coolige Lynch 1969
Warren Douglas Maggard 1969
Ruby Mardirossian 1969
Diana Ellen Meade 1969
Linda Meadows 1969
Phyllis Arlene Miracle 1969
Martin Ernest Miracle 1969
Carol Monhollen 1969
Larry Douglas Morrow 1969
Martha Elizabeth Murphy 1969
Gladys Napier 1969
Ruth A. Noe 1969
Rosie W. Owens 1969
Marilyn S. Owens 1969
Michael S. Parker 1969
Shirley Sue Partin 1969
Pat Phillips 1969
Sue K. Qualls 1969
Lolan J. Redden Jr. 1969
Ronald Wayne Redmon 1969
Raymond Roaden 1969
Millard D. Robbins 1969
William Joe Robinson 1969
James Monroe Samples 1969
Phyllis Darlene Sanders 1969
Jacqueline Navon Schwinn 1969
John Steven Schwinn 1969
Rinda C. Seither 1969
John J. Sergi 1969
Donald R. Shelton 1969
Steven E. Shoun 1969
Freda G. Simpson 1969
Lester R. Smith 1969
Anna Stephens 1969
Charles Tellie Sturgeon 1969
Christopher Wade Sullivan 1969
Maedean Sumner 1969
Paula Sue Sweeney 1969
Joyce M. Thomas 1969
Patricia Jean Treadway 1969
Rebecca Turner 1969
Bruce Vance Jr. 1969
Howard Voss 1969
Jo Ann Wade 1969
Carl Wayne Weaver 1969
Mary Etta White 1969
Harvey Sibert White 1969
Rose Nell Wilson 1969
Ray Winchester 1969
Nancy Carol Allen 1970
Willey David Alley 1970
Glinda Anderson 1970
James E. Artis 1970
Rita S. Ball 1970
Lynda Louise Barker 1970
Jennifer Barnes 1970
Alexander Begley 1970
Comman Blair 1970
Fay Eva Blevens 1970
Betty Ann Blunschi 1970
Janet Sue Bocock 1970
Linda Sue Bonaventure 1970
Joe B. Bowlin 1970
Billie Jean Bowling 1970
Thomas W. Branim 1970

Judy B. Brown 1970
Lorna Gail Bruce 1970
Jean Bryant 1970
James G. Buhel 1970
Phyllis Jean Burkhart 1970
Marcus A. Camacho 1970
William Big Red Campbell 1970
Elizabeth Carnahan 1970
Margaret Carson 1970
Florene L. Cathers 1970
Patricia Annise Centers 1970
Micci Jo Champion 1970
David Scott Childers 1970
Charles C. Chitwood 1970
Wanda Claypool 1970
Norma E. Clouse 1970
Judy Ann Cobb 1970
Wanda Fay Cobb 1970
Betty Sue Coffey 1970
Nellie Lou Cole 1970
Bill R. Collett 1970
Glenna M. Collins 1970
Charles Wayne Collins 1970
Gary Jerome Conley 1970
Rebecca A. Cordell 1970
Bonnie L. Couch 1970
Donna Katherine Cox 1970
Anna Cox 1970
Raymond Cox 1970
Jackie L. Creekmore 1970
Rebecca A. Davidson 1970
Nannie Sue Davis 1970
Sheryl Davis 1970
Jane Davis 1970
Teresa Deel 1970
Clara Faye Dennison 1970
Pam Doan 1970
Karen C. Ellis 1970
William M. Elsea 1970
Billy Roy Farmer 1970
Willard H. Farris 1970
Melvin Freeman 1970
Carl Edward Gant 1970
Quenton Wade Gayhart 1970
Phyllis Louise Glass-White 1970
Cheryl Jean Green 1970
Dorothy Janiece Gregory 1970
Susan Grimes 1970
Ron O. Hacker 1970
Judy Elaine Hamblin 1970
Harold Thomas Hammond 1970
Valena Harsh 1970
Patti A. Haun 1970
Daniel C. Hayes 1970
Glenna Faye Haynes 1970
Edna W. Helton 1970
William A. Hensley 1970
Jo Ann S. Herald 1970
Jimmy Ray Hicks 1970
Mossie Alberta Hodge 1970
Simeon P. Hodges 1970
David C. Hodson 1970
Glenna Hudson 1970
Eugene Hunley 1970
Kenneth D. Hurt 1970
Janrose L. Hurt 1970
Eugene Vernon Hyde Jr. 1970
Bobbie Pearl Jackson 1970
Faye R. Jeffers 1970
Elizabeth S. Jenkins 1970

Larry David Johnson 1970
Carolyn L. Jones 1970
John Paul Jones 1970
Kollen Karr 1970
David Joe Karsner 1970
Clifford E. Kohlmeyer 1970
Janet R. LaLance 1970
Kathy Langdon 1970
Delores Lynn Lawson 1970
Linda S. McClure 1970
Joyce A. McComb 1970
Sharon McNeeley 1970
Curtis L. Meadors 1970
Jan C. Melvin 1970
Harold Douglas Messer 1970
Lynette S. Mills 1970
Thomas Mills 1970
Cheryl Christine Moore 1970
Betty Jo Mullins 1970
Mary Alice Napier 1970
Jerry L. Neal 1970
Ruth E. Nickell-Cortes 1970
Dianna Parker 1970
Harold Eugene Peak 1970
Dan D. Pennington 1970
Larry E. Phelps 1970
Jimmy Charles Pierce 1970
Carolyn Sue Prewitt 1970
Linda Thompson Radford 1970
James L. Rains 1970
Linda J. Reisert 1970
Bernice Renfro 1970
Leslie Ann Reynolds 1970
Margie Rickard 1970
Janie Lou Ridenour 1970
Shelby J. Riggs 1970
Charlotte Riley 1970
Jerry L. Rismiller 1970
Daniel Risner 1970
Rebecca C. Rosenbaum 1970
Shirley Ruth 1970
William Sanders 1970
Brenda F. Seaver 1970
Rena Luella Sester 1970
James E. Shackleford 1970
Hugh Calloway Sharp 1970
Juanita Carolyn Sibert 1970
Linda G. Slusher 1970
Ellis Smith Jr. 1970
Rell B. Smith Jr. 1970
Janice Collett Smith 1970
Janet Smith 1970
Aaron L. Spaulding 1970
Pamela R. Stephens 1970
Alice C. Taylor 1970
Linda Teague 1970
Pamela S. Teague 1970
Harold Douglas Treadway 1970
Mary M. Tuttle 1970
Barbara J. Tyree 1970
Sharon Vanover 1970
Randall Ward 1970
Anita Sue Wells 1970
Jerry Wells 1970
Jane Ellie Ruth Whitaker 1970
Thelia White 1970
Rodney Wilson 1970
Lana R. Wilson 1970
Barbara Winstead 1970
Judy Carol Wolterman 1970

Vern Wooton 1970
Dorothy H. Yates 1970
George David Adams 1971
Joy Marie Allison 1971
Randall Delbert Baker 1971
Lindell Reed Ball 1971
Linda S. Barton 1971
Helen Barton 1971
Donald L. Beach 1971
Martha R. Begley 1971
Opal M. Bentley 1971
Charlotte A. Bialczak 1971
Marcus William Bibee 1971
Nelly Fay Blair 1971
Barbara F. Blair 1971
Janet E. Boyce 1971
Anna Pearl Brasel 1971
Jane Brock 1971
William Curtis Bruce 1971
Linda Kay Bryant 1971
Ocie Bunch 1971
Mary Volena Burchfield 1971
Shirley Faye Burgher 1971
Linda June Burkhart 1971
Paul D. Burns 1971
Judith Gayle Carmony 1971
Ronald W. Cawood 1971
Mary Evelyn Cobb 1971
Donna Jean Colegrove 1971
Jimmy Alan Collins 1971
Lana S. Combs 1971
Joan Combs 1971
Sharon Dale Cordell 1971
Charles McArthur Couch 1971
Jackie Ray Cupp 1971
Diana Sue Dalton 1971
Freddie Mae Daniels 1971
Sophia Davis 1971
Joe Mack Davis 1971
Larry Marshall Dean 1971
Carol Lynn Duncan 1971
Charles William Emory 1971
Larry Clark Farmer 1971
Ronnie Lester Faulkner 1971
Wanda Gray Frost 1971
Mary N. Gambrell 1971
Linda Gail Garrett 1971
Michael George Gerack Jr. 1971
Linda Carol Gibson 1971
Karen Elaine Graham 1971
Maxine Yvonne Gregg 1971
Beth Peele Harris 1971
Donald Eugene Harsh 1971
Patsy Henry 1971
Kay Silcox Hill 1971
Brenda Gay Hodges 1971
Betty Mae Hodges 1971
Patsy R. Howard 1971
Virginia C. Hubbard 1971
Barbara Lee Hubbard 1971
Scottie Gene Hubbard 1971
M. Oscar Hubbard 1971
Charles Hunley 1971
Ollie Kelly 1971
Wayne Kitts 1971
Joyce Ann Lane 1971
Minnie LeForce 1971
Garry Lynn Leger 1971
Elizabeth Constance Lipps 1971
Robert E. Long Jr. 1971

Martha Sue Lynch 1971
Anna Jayane Lynch 1971
Verlin C. Marsee 1971
Mack Webb Martin 1971
Sandra Kay Massey 1971
Alice Louverne McCrary 1971
Emogene McCutcheon 1971
Kathy Lou McDonald 1971
Charles N. McGinty 1971
Brenda Gail McKeehan 1971
Nancy Lynn McLain 1971
Linda C. McNabb 1971
Elaine A. Meadors 1971
Linda Lou Mills 1971
Helen Loretta Neal 1971
Christine Marie Neuner 1971
Roger C. Noe 1971
Barbara Noland 1971
Pamela John Owens 1971
Billy Gene Parsons 1971
Gwen Pavy 1971
Patsy Lee Phillips 1971
Steven Douglas Pope 1971
Jerian R. Powers 1971
Betty Sue Redden 1971
Betty Lou Richardson 1971
George Edward Robbins 1971
Veronica J. Roberts 1971
Louise Roberts 1971
Harold Wayne Robinson 1971
Wanda Lee Rowland 1971
Shirlene Rudder 1971
Janet Sagester 1971
Daniel L. Scott 1971
Daniel E. Sharkovitz 1971
Michael Dean Sherrow 1971
Janet Kay Shoemaker 1971
Curtis Eugene Slack 1971
Paula Kay Smiddy 1971
Brenda Kay Smith 1971
Hazelle A. Smith 1971
Larry Dean Smith 1971
Galia A. Stephens 1971
Sandra Stidham 1971
Robert Samuel Stringfield 1971
Linda W. Terry 1971
Sue H. Thomas 1971
Ann W. Titsworth 1971
Margaret Elaine Tucker 1971
Sondra Kay Turner 1971
Vicki L. Van De Griff 1971
Michael Lee Vowell 1971
Jackie D. Walden 1971
Janis Rose Walters 1971
Alma C. Walton 1971
Gregory Ward West 1971
Carl D. Westerfield 1971
Ford D. Whitaker 1971
Hazel White 1971
John T. White 1971
Carl Michael White 1971
Louis A. White 1971
Carla Watts Williams 1971
Phyllis Ann Williams 1971
Judith Wilson 1971
Terry Kermit Wilson 1971
Ronald Preston Wilson 1971
Jack D. Woods 1971
Betty A. Wright 1971
Ronnie Young 1971

Wanda Zins 1971
George Abner 1972
Sharon M. Afterkirk 1972
Norman Lee Alderman 1972
Bruce Rodney Arnett 1972
Julie Ashlock 1972
Sherry Gene Back 1972
Mary H. Bain 1972
William Forster Baird 1972
Anna Ruth Baird 1972
Lena N. Begley 1972
Loretta Begley 1972
Patricia Ann Bishop 1972
Virginia Cumy Blackwell 1972
Sharon Lee Blevins 1972
Louis M. Boyatt 1972
Mavis F. Broome 1972
Prudie Bundy 1972
Carcille Burchette 1972
Mary Elizabeth Byrd 1972
Gary Ray Calloway 1972
Mary Ann Calloway 1972
Emily Dianne Campbell 1972
Bobby R. Campbell 1972
Charlotte Jean Canter 1972
Lois Helen Carnes 1972
Lettie C. Chadwell 1972
Kenneth A. Clore 1972
Barbara Charlene Cobb 1972
Geraldine Collett 1972
Janice Susan Collins 1972
Sarah Conatser 1972
Gary Michael Cornelius 1972
Elbert Wayne Couch 1972
Max Allen Cox Sr. 1972
Sophie M. Crumpler 1972
Paula L. Davis 1972
Kenneth Warren Davis 1972
Deborah Lynn Davis 1972
Ruby Maxine Depew 1972
James Wallace Doane Jr. 1972
Pamela Jane Douglas 1972
Katherine Ann Dunn 1972
Pauline Estes 1972
Alvin Ray Evans 1972
Joan Leslie Flail 1972
Bettye L. Foister 1972
Sharon Gayle Gill 1972
Silas Thomas Golden 1972
China Mae Hackler 1972
James David Hale 1972
Janis Sue Hancock 1972
Patricia Ann Harris 1972
James E. Harris 1972
Elizabeth F. Harris 1972
Bobbie Jean Hatfield 1972
Linda Ann Henderson 1972
Bige Hensley Jr. 1972
Margaret Hensley 1972
Brenda Mae Hensley 1972
Donna Jean Hensley 1972
David W. Hensley 1972
Patricia Higginbotham 1972
Kathryn Y. Hoffman 1972
Barbara A. Hoskins 1972
Deania S. Hurst 1972
Jackie Hurst 1972
Johnny Hyde 1972
Ilene S. Irvin 1972
Eileen Johnson 1972

Dallas Edwin Johnson 1972
Patricia Ann Jones 1972
Lowell Jones 1972
Sharon Sue Kerr 1972
Diana Gwyn Kilpatrick 1972
Joe Marshall King 1972
Judith Ann Lakes 1972
Karen J. Lambdin 1972
Margaret Sue Landsaw 1972
John Thomas Larkey 1972
Doris R. Lawson 1972
Donna Kaye Ledden 1972
Harold E. Lester 1972
Brenda K. Maiden 1972
Joyce A. Martin 1972
James T. Martin 1972
Mary Jo McWilliams 1972
James M. Meadors 1972
Katherine Faye Miracle 1972
Cathy Sue Moretz 1972
Linda B. Mullen 1972
Madeline Murray 1972
Joyce L. Napier 1972
Maggie Evangeline Napier 1972
Vivian Jeanette Nickles 1972
Clarcie Yvonne Oerther 1972
Carole Darlene Owens 1972
Frances Estridge Parsons 1972
Joyce C. Partin 1972
Iona C. Patrick 1972
Mary Lou Payne 1972
Sharon Ann Perkins 1972
Martin E. Pierce MDiv 1972
Elizabeth Ann Pietrowski 1972
Jerry Wayne Pillow 1972
Ruth Ann Powell 1972
Magnolia Quillen 1972
Felecia Carol Reynolds 1972
Larry Eugene Richardson 1972
Ronita Lynn Rowe 1972
Troy Lee Rudder 1972
Sharon T. Scott 1972
Lawana Scoville 1972
Perry W. Sisson 1972
Mary Donna Skees 1972
Orville Smallwood Jr. 1972
Brenda Elaine Smith 1972
Dempsy Clive Smith 1972
Gary Gene Stanfill 1972
Monty Carl Stratton 1972
Billy Jack Tackett 1972
Jerry Wayne Taylor 1972
Mimi Vann Taylor 1972
Dorothy W. Thompson 1972
Joan B. Tompkins 1972
Patricia Ann Trundy 1972
Helen Turner 1972
Lois J. Wagers 1972
John Edward Watson 1972
Dennis Geoffrey Wells 1972
Eugenia L. West 1972
Shirley Anne West 1972
Sherry Sandra Wilder 1972
Martha A. Willard 1972
Linda Lou Williams 1972
Judy S. Williams 1972
Dennis Keith Wilson 1972
Linda Kay Wolfe 1972
Laura Christine Adams 1973
James David Arnett 1973

Sharon Pat Ayers 1973
Lawrence Bailey 1973
Donna Bandy 1973
Gary Wayne Bandy 1973
Deborah E. Boccio 1973
Norma Kaye Bowling 1973
Tommy Reed Brown 1973
Alfred Ronald Bunch 1973
William J. Burchwell Jr. 1973
Kathy S. Burke 1973
Linda Carey 1973
Mattie L. Childers 1973
Jerlyn Kay Clark 1973
Mary Ruth Coign 1973
Chris Combs 1973
Rodney E. Compton 1973
Mary Elizabeth Cook 1973
Karen Sue Cooper 1973
Linda W. Cooper 1973
Phyliss T. Coots 1973
Maudie P. Cornett 1973
Larry Wayne Cornett 1973
Alice Fay Cosimini 1973
Janice Kareen Costantine 1973
Myra Lu Davis 1973
D'Ila Mercer Deerman-Smith 1973
Bertha Lee Duncan 1973
Gregory Dyer 1973
Rickey Elliott 1973
Rex C. Estridge 1973
Andrea Jo Evans 1973
Charles W. Ferguson 1973
Patricia Ann Frueholz 1973
Marsha Lynn Gilbert 1973
Julie Ann Goodan 1973
Judy B. Gregory 1973
Gaylene Gross 1973
Jenny Lee Gullett 1973
Donald Ray Haynes 1973
Sharon F. Haynes 1973
Hamp C. Higginbotham 1973
Janice Hoh 1973
Robert Quentin Horn 1973
Thomas Sylvester Hornsby 1973
Donald Joe Irvin 1973
Ginny Lynne James 1973
Brenda Joyce Jody 1973
Janet Louise Johnson 1973
Janet E. Jones 1973
Brenda F. King 1973
Terry L. Landis 1973
Terry A. B. Ledford 1973
Mary Rowena Littrell 1973
Cheryl Anne Lowrey 1973
Linda Lois Moses 1973
Bobby Ray Nelson 1973
Constance L. Owens 1973
Terry V. Parks 1973
Maxine H. Partin 1973
Earlene Partin 1973
Glenna Pennington 1973
Cynthia Louise Perry 1973
Arlis Dean Polly 1973
Raymond Pryor 1973
Veronica Rains 1973
Debbie Ann Rains 1973
Pamela Marie Reynolds 1973
Ronald Wayne Reynolds 1973
Linda Ross 1973
Betty F. Saylor 1973

Judy Schmitt 1973
Janice C. Schneider 1973
Elizabeth E. Sergent 1973
Elizabeth Lee Smallwood 1973
Larry Charles Smith 1973
Kenneth Wilson Smith 1973
Linda Taylor 1973
Gary Lynn Taylor 1973
Wilma L. Teague 1973
Alice Tooley 1973
Janice Illene Vanzant 1973
Steven D. Weaver 1973
Brenda Lou West 1973
Nancy Lynn Widner 1973
Ted Williams 1973
Marilyn Sue Willis 1973
Kathryn L. Wilson 1973
Anna Belle Wright 1973
Murrel Thomas Albright 1974
Dennis J. Alldred 1974
Michael Lee Ashurst 1974
Mary Jane Ayers 1974
Portia Loretta Baker 1974
Janet Leigh Barnes 1974
John Wayne Barnes 1974
Billy Clay Barron 1974
Gail Begley 1974
Carl Morgan Biechler 1974
Irene Boggs 1974
Jerry Dean Borders 1974
Wanda Brown 1974
Pamela Joyce Brummett 1974
Diane L. Buckley 1974
Cathy Ann Bunch 1974
Linda Gail Camacho 1974
Sandra Campbell 1974
Diane Carnes 1974
Shirley Mae Chitwood 1974
Debra Billy Clouse 1974
Geraldine Joyce Coffey 1974
Leda Ann Coffman 1974
Farley Scott Coign 1974
James A. Combs 1974
Mary Compton 1974
Glenna Faye Cordell 1974
Karen Lee Creekmore 1974
Dennis Leo Crouch 1974
Diana H. Davis 1974
David Lytton Elliott 1974
Patricia Ann Elliott 1974
Jonna Lou Ellis 1974
Linda Jean Eversole 1974
Marsha Helen Foltz 1974
Lloyd Foster Jr. 1974
Betty Jean Golden 1974
Bobby Joe Golden 1974
Linda F. Green 1974
Brenda Kaye Greer 1974
Rebecca Rose Greer 1974
Lyle Edward Griffith 1974
Charlotte Sue Hackworth 1974
Kenneth R. Handley 1974
Linda Louise Hardwick 1974
Vickie Lynn Helvey 1974
Donald Lee Hendricks 1974
Judith V. Hensley 1974
Maureen Henson 1974
Ronald William Herold 1974
Patty Arlene Hibbs 1974
Richard Lee Hibbs 1974

Lena Marie Hill 1974
Glenda L. Hoffman 1974
Connie Howard 1974
Larry E. Hurt 1974
Jewel Dean Hutson 1974
Regina Irvin 1974
Charlotte Ivey 1974
Paula Asher Johnson 1974
Wayne Kelly Johnson 1974
Sue Ellen Johnson 1974
Donna Sue Kannady 1974
Vickie K. Kapitan 1974
Doyle Eugene King 1974
Linda C. King 1974
Sandra Lewis 1974
Bobbie Sue Lewis 1974
Neal R. Lickliter 1974
Crystal June Liming 1974
Phyllis R. Marlow 1974
Joseph Sherrill McDonald 1974
Ronald Wayne McIntosh 1974
Rebecca Ruth McLaughlin 1974
John Wesley Mercer 1974
Lou Ella Meredith 1974
Paul Mosley 1974
Sharon Mosley 1974
Barbara A. Myers 1974
Mary Frances Napier 1974
Kathryne Lynne Neal 1974
Inetta D. Nelson 1974
Edna S. Nichols 1974
Camille Partin 1974
Oscar Leroy Perry 1974
Kay Dianna Polly 1974
Ralph W. Pryor 1974
Donald Edmond Pyle 1974
David W. Reagan 1974
Carolyn W. Reaves 1974
Sadie Reynolds 1974
Danny Lee Rickett 1974
Patsy Gail Ridings 1974
Sandra L. Roberts 1974
Billy Robinson 1974
Richard A. Ross 1974
Barbara Faye Rouse 1974
Sally Ann Ruskaup 1974
Jolly Kay Sharp 1974
Flora Kay Sizemore 1974
Terry Lynn Smith 1974
John Smith 1974
Nancy L. Snider 1974
Kathy L. Stephens 1974
Kares Adrian Stonecipher 1974
Chris Lyndal Sutton 1974
Cindy Lou Taylor 1974
Alavene Templin 1974
Jennifer L. Townsend 1974
Judy Upchurch 1974
Nancy Catherine Vann 1974
Sally Carter Ward 1974
Carolyn Sue Wheeler 1974
Dalna Rena Whitaker 1974
Jacqueline Whitt 1974
Billy Joe Woods 1974
Sandra Lynn Wyatt 1974
Christine E. Bauchle 1975
David T. Bingham 1975
Frank Bizjack 1975
Donna D. Blanton 1975
Johnny Vestal Blevins 1975

Kathleen Bohman 1975
Jerry Bohman 1975
Victor Lee Boss 1975
Harold Dean Branam 1975
Dexter Lane Campbell 1975
Rosemary Carnes 1975
Marlene Kathy Cash 1975
Billy Joe Caudill 1975
Eva Chiari 1975
William Rodger Chiari 1975
Jeannie Carol Clem 1975
Marsha K. Cotsamire 1975
Michael Willard Croley 1975
Vicki Ann Foley 1975
Teri Ann Foltz 1975
Nancy Lou Fread 1975
Jackie Frost 1975
Sie Alvin Gilbert 1975
Mary Ellen Gladwell 1975
Marsha Joye Gordon 1975
Judith Ann Greis 1975
Cynthia L. Gross 1975
Ardana Rose Hacker 1975
Vaughn H. Hatcher 1975
Andrew Henry Helvey 1975
Karen G. Hendricks 1975
Michael R. Hensley 1975
Waynetta D. Howard 1975
Bobby Russell Howard 1975
Mary Susan Jaynes 1975
Ada M. Johnson 1975
Nola Mae Johnson 1975
Patricia Jones 1975
Sharon Fay Jones 1975
Emma Lee Keen 1975
Stephen J. Keener 1975
Deborah Elaine Kidd 1975
Nancy Lynn Kleemann 1975
Lynette Gail Latham 1975
Sandra Gail Lefevers 1975
Wilma Sue Lewis 1975
Robert Paul Liming 1975
William R. Lyttle 1975
C. Ray Martin 1975
Donna S. Masters 1975
Doris Ileene Mayes 1975
Georgeann McGaffee 1975
Pamela K. Meadors 1975
Jim Ed Miller 1975
Dennis David Miller 1975
Donald Eugene Miracle 1975
Joseph A. Moses 1975
Brenda K. Nelson 1975
Joyce Faye Ohler 1975
Audrey L. Pennington 1975
Lettie Myrtle Petree 1975
Preston Wolfe Potter 1975
Dixie L. Prewitt 1975
Neal Pucciarelli 1975
Nita Miniard Rezek 1975
Alice Ann Richter 1975
Linda Owens Ridenour 1975
Rick Rigel 1975
Keith A. Ritchey 1975
Darrell Edward Sawyers 1975
Robert Dwight Saylor 1975
John Benjamin Shipley 1975
Beverly Shipley 1975
Charlotte Sizemore 1975
Doris A. Slavey 1975

Judy Ann Smith 1975
Dewey R. Smith 1975
Dianne Rosemary Stanfill 1975
Burma Stephens 1975
Michael L. Stewart 1975
Norma Jean Stopher 1975
Geraldine Stroud 1975
Sandra Kay Sweet 1975
Connie Kay Thompson 1975
Stanley R. West 1975
Ruth Jean Whitaker 1975
Randall D. Williams 1975
John Steven Wilson 1975
David R. Wireman 1975
Ronald Wayne Young 1975
Michael Wayne Allen 1976
Beverly Ellen Anderson 1976
Vikki Lynne Ashurst 1976
Freda Joyce Bailey 1976
Belinda Jean Bass 1976
Robert S. Benge 1976
Judy F. Bingham 1976
Denise Lynn Bizjack 1976
Roger L. Blevins 1976
Regina Lynn Borden 1976
Mary Susan Bostick 1976
Patricia Lynn Boyes 1976
Jan C.B. Britton 1976
Stephen E. Brock 1976
Lenora Angel Bunch 1976
Julie Ann Buschor 1976
Damon Allen Carmical 1976
Joe R. Carson 1976
Samuel Reed Centers 1976
Alfred Hugh Cosimini 1976
Marilyn Criscillis 1976
Dixie Darlene Crouch 1976
Blanda Kay Crowe 1976
Mary Lou Disney 1976
Kenneth Lee Dryden 1976
Cynthia Thyine Duncan 1976
James Joseph Ehrhard 1976
Audrey E. Elliott 1976
Madeline Jo Ellis 1976
Linda Frances Elmore 1976
Eva Susan Estep 1976
William James Gray 1976
Millie Haar 1976
Karen Hall 1976
Roger Lynn Hall 1976
Donna Mae Housley 1976
Joe F. Hurst 1976
Shelley Bunyea King 1976
Victor B. King 1976
Mary Sharon Lewis 1976
Debra Ann Liford 1976
Bud Lockhart 1976
Theresa Louise Long 1976
Brenda Jackson Lyon 1976
Martha Ellis Mayer 1976
Evelyene Morgan 1976
Linda Napier 1976
Donna Meredith Norman 1976
Rick Osborn 1976
Sharon Lee Osborne 1976
Terry Layne Parks 1976
Lana Elaine Perkins 1976
Orville Dean Petrey 1976
Charlotte Q. Raney 1976
Catharine Blanton Renfro 1976

Janice Renfro 1976
Donold David Rhodes 1976
Sherry Elaine Richardson 1976
Bonita Richardson 1976
James Porta Rickett 1976
Mary Anne Roberts 1976
Thelma Frances Sasser 1976
Wendy J. Saylor 1976
Donna Shemwell 1976
Rosetta Sizemore 1976
Ray W. Snider 1976
Patricia Tate 1976
Karen Sue Taylor 1976
Henry R. Taylor Jr. 1976
Kimberly G. Tomberlin 1976
Deborah Van Hoose 1976
Pamela Elaine Weaver 1976
Dorothy E. West 1976
Pamela June White 1976
Lloyd Charles Wilson 1976
Patricia L. Wood 1976
Valrie A. Woodward 1976
Audrey S. Young 1976
Clyde Randolph Abney 1977
Doris Jean Adkins 1977
Brenda Darlene Albright 1977
Jackie Kenneth Baker 1977
Theresa Maria Barnes 1977
Anne Beckner 1977
Gerald Douglas Bingham 1977
Malissa A. Bowling 1977
Sheila Lynn Bowling 1977
Cheryl Ann Brock 1977
Alice Creech Brown 1977
Corinne L. Burns 1977
Larry Allen Carte 1977
Melissa Susan Chumley 1977
Linda W. Coleman 1977
Trenna C. Cornett 1977
Janice Couch 1977
Vanessa Cora Creekmore 1977
Mary J. Decker 1977
Timothy J. Erwin 1977
Regina Gail Flinchum 1977
Joyce Dale Fraley 1977
Linda T. Freeman 1977
Brenda Jo Fuson 1977
Judy L. Gabbard 1977
Darva D. Gibbs 1977
Rita C. Hamlin 1977
James Keith Hardy 1977
Thomas Calvin Hart 1977
James Earl Hays 1977
Judy Henard 1977
Linda P. Hollars 1977
Janet Lee Johnson 1977
Kenneth Dale Martin 1977
Judy Mobley 1977
Debbie Moore 1977
Sue Ellen Nidiffer 1977
Alice Perkins 1977
Flonnie Pearlene Perry 1977
David W. Powell 1977
Robert Queener 1977
Sandra Joyce Reeves-Watkins 1977
Kathy R. Renner 1977
Roger Samples 1977
Wuanita Kay Sawyers 1977
Phyllis Jean Scott 1977
Brenda Sue Shell 1977

Karen Lee Shonkwiler 1977
Constance Sue Somers 1977
Raymond Bradley Stearns 1977
David Stewart 1977
Edna Jane Taylor 1977
Valerie A. Taylor 1977
Daryl L. Varble DMin 1977
Barbara Vicars 1977
Donna Jean Walden 1977
Gail B. Young 1977
Cathy G. Armstrong 1978
Iris Hope Bailey 1978
Kenny B. Bates 1978
Rhodia Anne Berry 1978
Linda J. Blanton 1978
Mary Caroline Bowlin 1978
Peggy A. Brown 1978
Maxine Bunch 1978
Nita Karen Chadwell 1978
Dortha Hacker Cornett 1978
Melissa I. Correa-Connolly 1978
Beverly M. Covington 1978
Darrell C. Denney 1978
Debra Marie Dickerson 1978
Ray C. Duff 1978
Eugenia Lee Dunn 1978
Melissa Susan Edwards 1978
Clarence Eversole 1978
Joyce Pauline Feltner 1978
James Thomas Ford 1978
Donnie Lee Fox 1978
Minnie Pearl Goins 1978
Teresa Belle Harrell 1978
Curtiss Ray Hart 1978
Kathy Irene Henry 1978
Betty J. Hensley 1978
Connie Lou Hertzer 1978
Janet Kay Hibbard 1978
Vickie K. House 1978
Marilyn Jan Huddleston 1978
Judy Lynn Jones 1978
Brenda Kegley 1978
Wanda Faye Keith 1978
Donna Lee Kermos 1978
Shellia Elaine Kidd 1978
Deborah Kay Lamm 1978
Ella Kay Lewis 1978
Jann Ruth Lewis 1978
William Ralph Mays Jr. 1978
Donnie Ray McFarland 1978
Kay Mosley 1978
Marjorie Mullins 1978
E. Ann Naylor 1978
Ann Hurt Nebraski 1978
Mark Edwin Oxley Ph.D. 1978
Carolyn Sue Penix 1978
Bill Perkins 1978
David Michael Pinson 1978
Kathryn Elise Reed 1978
Kathryn Elise Reed 1978
Brenda Rae Rice 1978
Kathleen Ridner 1978
Patricia Brown Roaden 1978
Susan B. Roberts 1978
Reecia Samples 1978
Norma-Jean S. Scrivener 1978
Brenda Lou Shafer 1978
William David Simpson 1978
Cathy Sizemore 1978
Jennifer Ann Smith 1978

Richard Spencer 1978
Lois Spurlock 1978
Vicki Gilreath Strunk 1978
Evelyn Jean Tolliver 1978
LuAnn Tuttle 1978
Terri Jo Valentine 1978
Kenneth Allen Vann 1978
Patricia Suzan Venable 1978
Danny Alan Wasson 1978
Valerie Rose Williams 1978
Sharon Kaye Adkins 1979
Ivory Allen 1979
Mary Elizabeth Armstrong 1979
Billie Stone Baker 1979
Glynda F. Barner 1979
Jenise Bartholomew 1979
David James Bauer 1979
Janet Louise Belew 1979
Royce Gaylor Bell 1979
Nancy Black 1979
Lottie Kaye Bowers 1979
Brenda K. Brashear 1979
Wilma Mae Chitwood 1979
Helen Elizabeth Cornett 1979
Nancy C. Cox 1979
Joyce Ann Davidson 1979
Catherine Lynn Davis 1979
Kimberley Jo Dean 1979
Richard Clayton Dermon 1979
Richard T. Domm 1979
Kim Douglas 1979
Connie W. Drake 1979
Joseph Estill Dunn 1979
Rebecca Jayne Edwards 1979
Steven Anthony Finch 1979
Lois P. Ford 1979
Catherine Elaine Gaylor 1979
Emmalene D. Gibson 1979
Elizabeth Kathleen Harville 1979
Pauline D. Hickman 1979
Debra L. Hornyak 1979
Bridgett Gale Howell 1979
Beverly Kay Howison 1979
Dinia Emerine Howser 1979
Noah King 1979
Rita Jean Koon 1979
Edith Florine Lefevers 1979
Sandra Kay Lewis 1979
Pamela Marcum 1979
Patricia Ann Meadors 1979
Terry Keith Meadors 1979
Gwendolyn G. Meadows 1979
Donna Jean Morgan 1979
Deborah Sue Morris 1979
Glenna Rae Nicholson 1979
Gregory Alan Oxley 1979
Billie Denise Payne 1979
Rollie Burnett Pennington 1979
Bessie H. Perry 1979
Teresa Marie Phillips 1979
Glenda Kay Pucciarelli 1979
Myrtle Ledford Quinn 1979
Cynthia Elaine Reynolds 1979
Ryan Reese Riddle 1979
Cheryl Lynn Root 1979
La Vonne C. Ross 1979
Jerry Don Ross 1979
Randall Sawyers 1979
Jeanette Sears 1979
Lou Ann Steely 1979

Cynthia Stephens 1979
Dennis James Trickett 1979
Joyce K. Troxell 1979
Johnny Lewis Turnblazer II 1979
Susan Ann Vanover 1979
Paula Lynn White 1979
Julia C. Williams 1979
Alice F. Wooton 1979
Dennis Larry Anderson 1980
Sharon E. Apple 1980
Rebecca Jo Atchley 1980
Dwight D. Bailey 1980
Kelvin Bernard Blue 1980
Evie M. Brewer 1980
Donna Lee Bryant 1980
Meryl Ynona Burress 1980
Virginia Lee Carter 1980
Debbie J. Cash 1980
Marsha Sue Cheek 1980
Pamela Fay Cornett 1980
Chester Couch Jr. 1980
Don R. DeRose 1980
Clyde Ray Dixon 1980
Terri Lynn Dixon 1980
Mata Jo Douglas 1980
Rita Kay Dowden 1980
Kathie Drake 1980
Charles Ray Durham 1980
Franklin Dale Gay 1980
Claymon Gross 1980
Debbie Jo Halcomb 1980
Karen Elaine Hammons 1980
Vickie Kidwell Harbin 1980
Deborah A. Hart 1980
Verna Rae Hatcher 1980
Debra Lynn Hodge 1980
Wendell D. Howell 1980
Patricia Ann Jones 1980
Jo Ann Kinyon 1980
Linda Gail Lewis 1980
Cheryl Ann Marsh 1980
Rebecca Ellan Melton 1980
Lara B. Miller 1980
Yolanda D. Mitchell 1980
Billy Wayne Morgan 1980
Jessie Dianna Morgan 1980
Pamela Sue Muncy 1980
Kenneth Lloyd Nance 1980
Judy Starr Olliges 1980
Marisa G. Osborne 1980
William R. Parrott 1980
Jeanette Partin 1980
Nina L. Prewitt 1980
Deborah Sue Prewitt 1980
Kathy Lynn Pryor 1980
Glenn Willard Reeves Jr. 1980
Patricia M. Reeves 1980
Douglas Keith Roach 1980
Helen L. Robertson 1980
Cordelia Root 1980
Tracey Lynn Smith 1980
DinahGail Smith 1980
Margie L. Smith 1980
Phyllis D. Spivey 1980
Don Testerman 1980
Martha Howerton Thomas 1980
Nellie Jean Toppings 1980
Kimberly Gail Trammell 1980
Chad R. Velte 1980
Ben Watts 1980

Kathryn E. Wilkie 1980
Susan Zellner 1980
Stephen E. Ball 1981
Latin Renee Beets 1981
Anita Begley 1981
Rae Ann Bridge 1981
Cynthia Elizabeth Campbell 1981
Laura L. Caudle 1981
Tammie R. Chapman 1981
Linda Gail Collins 1981
Wanda Combs 1981
Dennis Allen Custard 1981
Peter M. DiMuro Jr. 1981
Debra Lee Dobson 1981
Pamela Denise Duncan 1981
T. O. Elliott 1981
Kimberly Ann Everhart 1981
Charles Douglas Felts 1981
Michael Francis Flynn 1981
Linda G. Freeman 1981
Lynne Marie Gritton 1981
Deborah Lavina Hale 1981
Rondal Wayne Harmon 1981
Tammy J. Hubbs 1981
Mary C. Isom 1981
Linda Lou Johnson 1981
David Alan Jones 1981
Lenora Eunice King 1981
Jacqueline Anita Kirby 1981
Rebecca A. Levi 1981
Jeanne Lose 1981
Alma Ruth Mays 1981
Mae W. McAtee 1981
Kimberly Elaine McCullah 1981
William Darrell McIntosh 1981
Sharyan L. McKinney 1981
Sandra K. Melton 1981
Anthony Melton 1981
Deita Renee Morgan 1981
Matt Allen Muncy 1981
Pete L. Murphy 1981
Kathleen Madonna Nixon 1981
Myra Lee Palmer 1981
Ronny Wayne Paul 1981
Lannie Jean Perkins 1981
Janet Elaine Preston 1981
Larry Wayne Rhodes 1981
Cindy Lou Richey 1981
William C. Riley Jr. 1981
Linda Gail Ruth 1981
Harold Dean Sexton Jr. 1981
Deborah Tywanna Smith 1981
Mary Ann Stanfill 1981
Patrick Steiner 1981
Timothy Scott Stephens 1981
Janis Lynn Traveny 1981
Gilbert L. Van Over Jr. 1981
Terry Curtis Watts 1981
Gloria D. Weigle 1981
Linda Ann Wells 1981
Tammie Renee White 1981
Cindy Lou Wilkerson 1981
Angela Renee Williams 1981
George Edward Wolfe Jr. 1981
Rebecca M. Wuerzer 1981
Connie Lou Anders 1982
Donna Dianne Anderson 1982
Doris Ann Baker 1982
Bonnie Lynn Balliet 1982
Betty C. Bishop 1982

Janice Sue Blankenship 1982
Donna Carole Branscum 1982
John Bosco Bunrasi 1982
Julia L. Cain 1982
Rebecca Carender 1982
Emily Faye Cornn 1982
Anita Lynn Daugherty 1982
Debbie Lynn Davidson 1982
David A. Fox 1982
Janet Lee Glover 1982
Roger James Greer 1982
Garnett Lynn Gritton 1982
Debbie Kay Hooks 1982
Victoria Hughes 1982
Vonna Valene Hutson 1982
Robert Howard Jones 1982
Sandra L. Jude 1982
Harold Lee Kendall 1982
Debbie J. Knuckles 1982
Barbara L. Longmire 1982
Richard Allen Lovitt 1982
Jerry L. Lunsford 1982
Marie Ann Mahan 1982
Phyllis D. Martin 1982
Zula Massengill 1982
Sandra Kay Massey 1982
Benita Caroll McBride 1982
Donna Lee McGeorge 1982
Patsy A. Miller 1982
Diana Lynn Mills 1982
Carrie Ann Newman 1982
Margaret Susan Oliver 1982
Anna Ruth Parrett 1982
Tommie L. Perkins 1982
Ira Stevie Powers 1982
Judith Diann Price 1982
Phyllis Robinson 1982
Debbie Sue Sexton 1982
Crystal Melanie Smothers 1982
Mark Alan Snider 1982
Susan Louise Stewart 1982
Douglas Carter Strunk 1982
Becky L. Swain 1982
Deborah Ann Tharpe 1982
Edward J. Traveny 1982
Donna F. Wagner 1982
Tracey E. Wessel 1982
Ann Louise White 1982
Regina C. White 1982
Petros Abraha 1983
Judy Ellen Alvarez 1983
Don Ricardo Barnett 1983
Susan Marie Barton 1983
Clara Hacker Bowling 1983
Carolyn B. Bowman 1983
Timothy L. Brown 1983
Judy B. Bruner 1983
Larry Glenn Bunch 1983
James Christopher Burt 1983
Donna Kaye Busic 1983
Patricia Lynn Centers 1983
Teresa L. Chitwood 1983
Melinda Kay Chitwood 1983
Linda Joyce Collins 1983
Joan R. Cottrell 1983
Rita Charlene Cox 1983
Sharon Odean Croley 1983
Lois M. Davis 1983
Jerry Dwayne Denney 1983
Susan Evans 1983

Teresa Gayle Feeback 1983
Martha Ruth Fleenor 1983
Theresa Karen Garrett 1983
Kathryn Lynn Hakes 1983
Melba Diane Hale 1983
Nannie L. Hays 1983
Kimberly Michelle Hembree 1983
Karen Elaine Hickey 1983
Linda Carol Hubbard 1983
Gilbert Earl Irvin 1983
Vickie Lynn Jackson 1983
Lily Augusta Jenkins 1983
Eugenia Jones 1983
Brenda Jones 1983
Patricia Ann Jones 1983
Lisa Faye Kassen 1983
David Kelly 1983
Gloria Sharon King 1983
Lisa Jo Kirby 1983
Ruby Jean Lee 1983
Vicki Lynne Meadors 1983
Carolyn Sue Mills 1983
Patricia H. Morgan 1983
Susan A. Morrow 1983
Reba Doris Morse 1983
Gary Granville Moses 1983
Susan Kay Mount 1983
Kathy B. Pavy 1983
Jodi Lynn Perry 1983
Sharon Inez Price 1983
Cheryl Lynn Puckett 1983
Sherry Anita Reed 1983
Lisa Gaye Richerson 1983
Woodie Joan Roberts 1983
Shena Ann Rose 1983
Karen Lynn Schoonover 1983
Dawn Marie Scroggins 1983
Marlene Selvidge 1983
Sandra Louise Sherwood 1983
Frances Carol Stout 1983
Sharon S. Strunk 1983
Bonita Swartz 1983
Mary Janice Sweat 1983
Linda Taylor 1983
Vicky Lynn Troxell 1983
Priscilla J. Vanhoose Nix 1983
Phyllis Ann Vaughn 1983
Terry Lynn Wagnon 1983
Tammy Jo Walters 1983
Albert Ray Watts 1983
Shanda Bunch Weddle 1983
Nila Nadine West 1983
Marta Lynn Whittington 1983
Doris June Williams 1983
Angela Joan Williamson 1983
Darrell L. Woods 1983
Teresa Darlene Wren 1983
Sandra Adkins 1984
Brenda Lee Alford 1984
Sharon Pat Ayers 1984
Tammie J. Baird 1984
James David Baker 1984
MaryAlice Elizabeth Bennett-Smith
1984
Rebecca C. Blevins 1984
Tammy L. Bowman 1984
Alesa Branham 1984
Kathy Ann Burgin 1984
Charlotte K. Cameron 1984
Rita K. Carroll 1984

Larry Allen Carte 1984
Kathryn Ann Clark 1984
Benita Kay Collins 1984
Cindy Lou Creech 1984
Sherri L. Davis 1984
Martha Emily Denny 1984
Dirk Richard DeVito 1984
Patricia Lynn Dugger 1984
Jackie Leland Duncan 1984
Anita Gay Edwards 1984
Joyce Sue Felts 1984
Paula Jean Felty 1984
Wanda Lee Fields' 1984
Joyce Dale Fraley 1984
Tracy Dean Gabbard 1984
Freda Kay Gay 1984
Lisa Kay Gilreath 1984
Brenda Sue Gipson 1984
Barbara Golden 1984
David Tilman Goodin 1984
Rosemary R. Grant 1984
Rosemary R. Grant 1984
Linda Kay Gray 1984
Debbie Ann Hamblin 1984
Kimberly Joy Hamlin 1984
John Fredrick Harris 1984
Roger Elvis Harrison 1984
Kenneth David Head 1984
Robin E. Head 1984
Patricia Ann Helton 1984
Scott Hensley 1984
Timothy D. Holland 1984
Connie M. Hunt 1984
Jackie William Jewell 1984
Virginia A. Jones 1984
Robert Howard Jones 1984
Evelyn King 1984
Lovada F. Kitts 1984
Marty Elaine Kuhl 1984
Joyce A. Landrum 1984
Jennifer F. Lanham 1984
Becky A. Lavender 1984
Rhonda D. Laxton 1984
Jamie Alesia Lay 1984
Sharon Lee Leach 1984
Penelope Leigh Lee 1984
Theresia D. Lewis 1984
Lori Donella Lewis 1984
Katherine G. Lisenbee 1984
Connie Loy 1984
Sandra L. Manning 1984
Stuart Douglas Manning 1984
Kimberly A. Marlow 1984
Stephanie J. Martin 1984
Betty Dale McIntosh 1984
Larry Wayne McKiddy 1984
Patricia Sue Meadors 1984
Elizabeth M. Nichols 1984
Patricia Ellen Nicholson 1984
Nancye Vanessa Noe-Scott 1984
William Brian Oberschlake 1984
Sharon Lynn Oberschlake 1984
Robert Wayne Parker 1984
Judith Ann Pennington-Price 1984
Terry Leon Petree 1984
Ronnie L. Rees 1984
Yvonne E. Rex 1984
Rhonda Maria Reynolds 1984
Roger Lee Richardson 1984
Betty F. Saylor 1984

Deborah Marie Shackleford 1984
Paula Louise Sinclair 1984
Lucretia Sizemore 1984
Rhonda Lynnell Smith 1984
Kimberly Ann Snodgrass 1984
Ginger L. Soden 1984
Bonnie H. Stokes 1984
Sherry Leigh Storm 1984
Deborah Kay Strunk 1984
Peggy Jean Taylor 1984
Martha Jane Taylor 1984
Cynthia Lynn Taylor 1984
Debra D. Tipton 1984
Janine L. Turner 1984
Ricky Allen Walton 1984
Gerald Weatherspoon 1984
Linda D. Woodson 1984
Wendell Worley 1984
Annita Gwenn Wylie 1984
Janet Louise Allen 1985
Vickie Jean Archer 1985
Carrie Ellen Banks 1985
Velva Jean Barker 1985
Michael D. Baumgarten 1985
June S. Begley 1985
Margaret E. Bowlin 1985
Rosemary Branham 1985
Alice Fae Bryant 1985
Donna Marie Bunch 1985
Kimberly L. Burress 1985
Donna Kaye Busic 1985
Alice S. Cantrell 1985
Terre Wanda Cobb 1985
Kathleen Chloe Cornett 1985
Velvet Cross 1985
Kenneth Davidson 1985
Deborah Ann Davidson 1985
Pamela Jean Emmert 1985
J. C. Engle 1985
Roger Dennis Fisher 1985
Deborah Ann Foley 1985
Mary Jean Gambrel 1985
Verda Fran Gay 1985
Tammy Gail Gibson 1985
Thalia Jo Gibson 1985
Marjorie M. Green 1985
Cecilia Diane Gregory 1985
Loretta M. Haddix 1985
Nicki Hammons 1985
Rosalee C. Hinkle 1985
Eugenia Jones 1985
Rebecca Jody King 1985
Deborah Kay Lamm 1985
Patricia Loriann Lay 1985
Jane Arlene Leach 1985
Jerry N. Leach 1985
Cathy Marie Lee 1985
Kimberly Kaye Lucas 1985
Donna R. Martin 1985
Bettye Lou McDaniel 1985
Rhonda Jean Metcalf 1985
Karen Denise Moore 1985
Randy E. Moses 1985
Billy Ray Mosley 1985
Phyllis A. Mullins 1985
Lisa K. Overbay 1985
Betsy Overbey 1985
Debra F. Payne 1985
Joan Darlene Phillips 1985
Darlene Lynn Prewitt 1985

Ricky Paul Rains 1985
Cynthia J. Rees 1985
Helen L. Robertson 1985
La Vonne C. Ross 1985
Lavonna J. Sams 1985
Cleston Anthony Saylor Jr. 1985
Cheryl Lynn Sergent 1985
Jennifer Ann Smith 1985
Jacqueline L. Spinelli 1985
Deborah Ann Tackett 1985
Bernice A. Taylor-Hyden 1985
Brenda Delaine Thomas 1985
Gerald Weatherspoon 1985
Eric Matthew Weibel 1985
Margaret Wells 1985
Laurel L. West 1985
Ruthie M. Willis 1985
Vicki Lynne Wilson 1985
Polly P. Wilson 1985
Cynthia Wells Woods 1985
Ben Worley 1985
Teresa Kay Yancey 1985
Ronald Dean Adkisson 1986
Shelia Jane Baker 1986
Doris Louise Beverly 1986
Cameron Eugene Black 1986
Novella Bowling 1986
Margaret Asher Bowman 1986
Cathy Jane Brown 1986
Gwendolyn R. Bryant 1986
Dorena Burns 1986
Janet Kay Carter 1986
Lawanna Chestnut 1986
Ruth Ellen Combs 1986
Vanessa Cora Creekmore 1986
Kimberly Sheryl Dorsey 1986
Angela Mary Douglas 1986
Elizabeth Ann Frazier 1986
Thalia Jo Gibson 1986
Tonya B. Gray 1986
Dawna Louise Grimes 1986
Laurel Elaine Grimm 1986
Denita Suzette Hall 1986
Pamela L. Hancock 1986
Kimberly R. Huff 1986
Brenda Gail Johnson 1986
Lana J. Karr 1986
Lara Lynn Koogler 1986
Karla Kim Lambdin 1986
Sharon Landers 1986
Melissa Langford 1986
James Randall Lawless 1986
Jane Arlene Leach 1986
Stuart Christopher Lockhart 1986
Kevin Dylan Lowrie 1986
Martina C. Lucas 1986
Darlene D. Lunsford 1986
Kelly McNiel 1986
Patricia Sue Meadors 1986
Lara B. Miller 1986
Gail Slusher Mixon 1986
Tracey Lynn Morgan 1986
Susan A. Morrow 1986
Judy Walker Parsons 1986
Tommie L. Perkins 1986
Debra G. Petrey 1986
Rhonda Beth Petrey-Collins 1986
Michael Dewayne Philpot 1986
Honora M. Pollard 1986
John F. Radecki 1986

Jeffrey L. Reed 1986
Lisa S. Reeder 1986
Perry D. Revlett 1986
Rick T. Richardson 1986
Ryan Reese Riddle 1986
Lesa Amburgy Roaden 1986
Georgia A. Rude 1986
Jeffrey Scott Schoonover 1986
Karen Lynn Schoonover 1986
Christine B. Shiflet 1986
Mike Sickafoose 1986
Darlene Hope Sparkman 1986
Joyce Sue Steely 1986
Mary Frances Steely 1986
Bonni Ellen Sutton 1986
Scott W. Thomas 1986
Robert Ray Turner 1986
Terry Lynn Wasson 1986
Teddy G. Weaver 1986
Jennifer Marie Whitt 1986
Roger Dale Wilson 1986
Jessie Ruby Wilson 1986
Sondra R. Worley 1986
Ben Worley 1986
Jennifer S. Adkisson 1987
Diane Ashley 1987
Thomas Allen Baker 1987
Nancy Kay Ball 1987
Royce Gaylor Bell 1987
Tonya Renee Bingham Casey 1987
Sandra J. Bradley 1987
R. Kevin Brashear 1987
Kelli Bryant 1987
James William Burke 1987
Samantha Ann Burton 1987
Jennifer Lynn Capo 1987
Ruby Jewell Carney 1987
Sally Rosina Christian 1987
Pamela Rose Clark 1987
Ruth Ellen Combs 1987
Shanee Lynn Cox Cummins 1987
Geff Davis 1987
Katrina E. Davis 1987
Mary Ann Day 1987
James B. Donahue 1987
Robert Manning Dubberly 1987
Diana Lynn Duckworth 1987
Janet Lynn Duncum 1987
Karen Lenore Gilreath 1987
Lisa Kay Gilreath 1987
Wilma Faye Grubbs 1987
Frederick Valdazze Hamn 1987
Sherry Ann Harper 1987
Maria Lynn Harrison 1987
Oliver Clay Hawkins Jr. 1987
Kimberly Marie Hooten 1987
Linda Carol Hubbard 1987
Sherry A. Huckaby 1987
Vickie Lynn Jackson 1987
Darlene Frances Jones 1987
Lisa F. Kelly 1987
Deborah Sue King 1987
Julia Florence King 1987
Karen H. Lawless 1987
Ruby Jean Lee 1987
Jean-Claude D. Liddie 1987
Joy Elizabeth Luke 1987
Steven M. Lyons 1987
Violet Irene Maiden 1987
John J. Maiden 1987

Kimberly Ann Maiden 1987
Bettye Lou McDaniel 1987
Karen Faye Moore 1987
Deita Renee Morgan 1987
Susan B. Morris 1987
Stephanie L. Nickel 1987
Cheryl A. Phero 1987
Jonathan Edward Ramey 1987
Linda S. Richardson 1987
Beverly Jones Roberts 1987
Judith Craft Shepherd 1987
Julie D. Shoemaker 1987
Lisa L. Smith 1987
Darlene W. Smith 1987
Mary Ann Stanfill 1987
Opal Hortense Strunk 1987
Edna Jane Taylor 1987
Deborah Lawson Thomas 1987
Marsha L. Tincher-Threlkeld 1987
Marlene S. Wells 1987
Barbara K. Wells 1987
Jack Ernest White 1987
Marjorie C. Wilson 1987
Ann Cherith Wohlfarth 1987
Joel Scott Woltz 1987
Annette Abner 1988
Azmy Sima'an Ackleh 1988
Michele Renee Anderson 1988
Rebecca Lynn Baird 1988
Lindell Reed Ball 1988
TaNesha Jo Belcher 1988
Rebecca C. Blevins 1988
Patti Ellen Byers 1988
Jana Dean Byrge 1988
Teresa L. Chitwood 1988
Janet Renee' Clifton 1988
Nancy Carolyn Cooper 1988
Candace C. Copes 1988
Charlene Creekmore 1988
Leta Rai Davenport 1988
Jana Riena Farmer 1988
Deborah Ann Foley 1988
Nancy Sue Forcht 1988
Jessica Ann Forrest 1988
Teddy Doyle Gabbard 1988
Patricia J. Gay 1988
Rosemary R. Grant 1988
Rosemary R. Grant 1988
Annette L. Gray 1988
L. Scott Gregory 1988
Cathy Lynn Gregory 1988
Jimmy Wayne Gross 1988
Betty Eileen Halcomb 1988
Deborah Lynne Hall 1988
Frederick Valdazze Hamn 1988
Dwayne Alvin Hatcher 1988
Julie Anne Hay 1988
Debra Lynn Hill 1988
Debra Lynn Hodge 1988
Tonya Rollanda Howard 1988
Donna Carol Hudson 1988
Benjamin Bray Johnson 1988
Kendra L. Klinglesmith 1988
Donna June Lair 1988
Karen H. Lawless 1988
Damita Gale Lee 1988
Pamela K. Lowe 1988
Kimberly A. Marlow 1988
Donna R. Martin 1988
Jaimie Lynn McNiel 1988

Terry Keith Meadors 1988
Anita F. Miller 1988
Medeana B. Miniard 1988
Patricia H. Morgan 1988
Susan R. Morris 1988
Joyce Ann Morris 1988
Marsha L. Morton 1988
Myron J. Moss 1988
Madonna Sue Mullins 1988
Ben T. Munsey 1988
Melissa N. Murphy 1988
Anna Ruth Parrett 1988
Janna Michelle Patrick 1988
Lisa Beth Payne 1988
Sharree Gail Payne 1988
Roy Lee Peace Jr. 1988
Kimberly Kay Perkins-Rabell 1988
Kendra Ann Perry 1988
Theodore Perry 1988
Eva Cheryl Potter 1988
Sherry Lynn Richards 1988
Teresa Sue Riley 1988
Michael David Roark 1988
Jennifer L. Halcomb Roll 1988
Sharon Denise Rosenberger 1988
Regina A. Sears 1988
Richard Dale Smiley 1988
Charlotte Sue Smith 1988
Barbara Gambrell Storms 1988
Robin Joyce Sweet 1988
Gina L. Thornton 1988
Rickey L. Vernon 1988
Penny Wagers 1988
Elizabeth Sue Walden 1988
Deborah Kay Whitehead 1988
Patricia Lynn Wilson 1988
William Keith Adams 1989
Vickie Jean Archer 1989
Linda Ray Baker 1989
Tammy Jo Ball-Neal 1989
Randall Lee Begley 1989
Etta Jean Burchfield 1989
Rodney Thomas Byrd 1989
Kimberly Lynn Cain 1989
Lee Ann Claypool 1989
Pamela Fay Cornett 1989
Jennifer Lee Couch 1989
Ella Fay Covington 1989
Cymbre A. Crisologo 1989
Donna Elizabeth Cummins 1989
Julie Marie Dick 1989
Greg Lee Duncum 1989
Mark Anthony Felts 1989
Patricia L. Floyd 1989
Donna Kaye Freeman 1989
David W. Gibbins 1989
Catherine L.C. Gibbs 1989
Tammy Gail Gibson 1989
Ann Hanson 1989
Arthur Lewis Hanson 1989
Tammy M. Harris 1989
Roger Elvis Harrison 1989
Robin E. Head 1989
Bobbie Lynn Huff 1989
Zohair D. Issac 1989
Lee Ann Jenkins-Freels 1989
Karen Sue Knuckles 1989
Donna M. Lauerman 1989
D. Kathy Lovitt 1989
Tammy Michelle Lowrie 1989

Jesse E. Males 1989
Pamela Brock Martin 1989
Anthony Joseph Mattia 1989
Edna A. McDaniel 1989
Angela McQueen 1989
Joy Harp Miller 1989
Vickie L. Nicholson 1989
Karin Erlandsson Pelfrey 1989
Jill A. Roaden 1989
Jeffrey Robbins 1989
Sondra Kay Robinson Frazier 1989
Cynthia Sharon Shook 1989
Viesta K. Skipper 1989
Cathy Sue Smith 1989
Charlotte Sue Smith 1989
Troy Douglas Stone 1989
Donald Keith Story 1989
Deborah Kay Strunk 1989
Sharon S. Strunk 1989
Jennifer M. Suttle 1989
Gayle Lenore Taylor 1989
Barbara Kay Thomas 1989
Robin Annette Widener 1989
Sharon P. Wilson 1989
Patrick James Wollam 1989
Sandra J. Allen 1990
Janet W. Anderson 1990
Mary Wynn Arnold 1990
Christopher Blake Baker 1990
Sherri Elaine Barnes 1990
Robin R. Baumgarten 1990
Lana J. Bay 1990
Penny Lynn Begley 1990
Melanie Jean Bloomer 1990
Justin Ervin Bozeman 1990
Justin Ervin Bozeman 1990
Michelle Bridges 1990
Vanessa Keri Burchfield 1990
Peggy Sue Burkey 1990
Lisa Renee Chitwood 1990
Janet Renee' Clifton 1990
Sharon C. Collett 1990
Mary Lou Corder 1990
Wesley Madison Cornett 1990
Vickie L. Corpuz 1990
Karla Rochelle Daniels 1990
Sherri L. Davis 1990
Mary Ann Day 1990
Angela Gail Dean 1990
Alvin Russell Draper 1990
Shane W. Early 1990
Sharon Lee Engle 1990
Melody Kay Estep 1990
Dawna Louise Grimes 1990
Todd Matthew Hamilton Ph.D. 1990
Nicki Hammons 1990
Debra Etta Helton 1990
Elizabeth Suzanne Hoskins 1990
Sheldon C. House 1990
Joan H. Hughes 1990
Harry C. Hunter Jr. 1990
Sheila K. Hurd 1990
Kathy Martin Jones 1990
Deborah LeAnn Justice 1990
Gloria Sharon King 1990
Brock Allen Lambdin 1990
Deanna Amelia Lemons 1990
Donna Logan 1990
Brian Keith Logan 1990
Kevin Dylan Lowrie 1990

Darlene D. Lunsford 1990
Rhonda Leigh Marlow 1990
Laura Faye Oakes McGill 1990
Kimberly Lee Miller 1990
Billy Wayne Morgan 1990
Lewis Dwayne Morris 1990
Lisa K. Overbay 1990
Janna Michelle Patrick 1990
Deana Suzanne Perkins 1990
Eleanor Ann Phillips 1990
David W. Powell 1990
Ira Stevie Powers 1990
Teresa J. Reasor 1990
Shari Lynn Rhodenbaugh 1990
Lisa M. Richardson 1990
Cynthia Abbott Rose 1990
Georgia A. Rude 1990
Kathy Smith 1990
Konnie Snyder 1990
Nora Swain 1990
Will Russell Waterson 1990
Rebecca C. Webb 1990
Mark Douglas Wells 1990
James David Wesley 1990
Laurel L. West 1990
Jennifer Diane White 1990
Marjorie C. Wilson 1990
Rita F. Wood 1990
Jacquelyn Gail Wood 1990
Linda Holmes Anderson 1991
Deborah Sue Barnes 1991
James Vincent Black 1991
Kelly Bryant 1991
Dennis Joe Bunch 1991
James William Burke 1991
Gussie Ann Burns 1991
Patti Ellen Byers 1991
Nerissa Lynn Calhoun 1991
Rita K. Carroll 1991
Sally Rosina Christian 1991
Lee Martin Cigliano 1991
Pamela Rose Clark 1991
Joy Marguerite Couch 1991
Donna Elizabeth Cummins 1991
Marion Aaron Fannin 1991
Becky Joan Fannin 1991
Lee Ann Fowler 1991
Emma Katherine Freeman 1991
Maria Lynn Harrison 1991
Lisa Marie Hartford 1991
Nannie L. Hays 1991
Pamela McGhee Hill 1991
Linda C. Hood 1991
Donna Gail House 1991
Patricia Lynn Howell 1991
Bobbie Lynn Huff 1991
Marcellous Johnson 1991
Carolyn Sue Johnston 1991
Verena Dean Jones 1991
Brenda Jones 1991
Sherry Lynn Jones-Durham 1991
Lana J. Karr 1991
Jerry Michael King 1991
Deborah Sue King 1991
Julia Florence King 1991
Jennifer Lynn Landry 1991
Rachel F. Layman 1991
Richard Allen Lovitt 1991
Clara W. McIntosh 1991
Betty Dale McIntosh 1991

Angela McQueen 1991
Melissa Lynn Mee 1991
Patricia Ruth Miller 1991
Phyllis A. Mullins 1991
Bennett R. Murphy 1991
Melissa Nadine Phillips 1991
Keith Edward Pray 1991
Melissa Marie Rains 1991
Donna J. Reid 1991
Sherry L. Rhodes 1991
Wendell Glenn Roberts 1991
Sherrie Lynn Robinson 1991
Martha K. Setters 1991
Christopher Paul Setters 1991
Bonnie Smith 1991
Darlene Hope Sparkman 1991
Matthew Alexander Stone 1991
Nora Swain 1991
Robin Joyce Sweet 1991
Anna Lou Taylor 1991
Bernice A. Taylor-Hyden 1991
Melissa Jean Weaver 1991
Tammy Diane Webb 1991
Rebecca Elaine Wollam 1991
Rhonda L. Woodlee 1991
Sondra R. Worley 1991
Tony Allen 1992
Carolyn S. Allen 1992
Gwendolyn A. Amburgy 1992
Veronica Lynn Arthur 1992
Jamie Carol Back 1992
Anita Miller Biles 1992
Karen Bowman 1992
Janie Sue Brooks 1992
Alice Fae Bryant 1992
Michael Wayne Cassidy 1992
Donna Collins-Martin 1992
Loren Lee Connell 1992
Harold Dean Cornett 1992
Rolandus D. Cox 1992
Stephanie Sue Credit 1992
Kimberly Denise Creekmore 1992
Paula K. Daniel 1992
Pamela Dixon 1992
Tonya Lynn Farmer 1992
Brenda Carolyn Fox 1992
Ronna Lea Garcia 1992
Jeffrey Neal Garmon 1992
Regina Gayle Griffin 1992
Garnett Lynn Gritton 1992
Cora Frances Hacker 1992
Betty Eileen Halcomb 1992
Pamela Fay Halstead 1992
Georgia Anne Herron 1992
Tina Lynne Holt 1992
Terry L. Huddleston 1992
Donna Carol Hudson 1992
April Gail Johnson 1992
Carolyn L. Jones 1992
Stephanie L. Jordan 1992
Claudia Nell Kelsey 1992
Dawn Michelle Lavey 1992
Serena Michell Lett 1992
Ronnie Steve Malicoat 1992
Rhonda Leigh Marlow 1992
Diana Kay Maxey 1992
Clara W. McIntosh 1992
Timothy Gene Messer 1992
Paul H. Mills 1992
Melissa Dean Moore 1992

Judith Elaine Patrick 1992
Amy Denise Robbins 1992
Charissa Lynn Sampson 1992
Tamra Rene Sams 1992
Jacalynn Jean Scott 1992
Mark L. Sizemore 1992
Susan Annette Soule 1992
Terry Jean Spradlin 1992
Reta Juanita Vann 1992
Penny Wagers 1992
Kimberly Jill Webb 1992
Alan Robert Ysidro 1992
Sara Jane Ash 1993
Velva Jean Barker 1993
Darlena Gibson Barton 1993
Deborah Sue Beagle 1993
Penny Lynn Begley 1993
Lonna Lynn Bledsoe 1993
Lawrence Randall Brown 1993
Karen Sue Browning 1993
Joy Lynn Burdette 1993
Samantha Ann Burton 1993
Debra Lynn Carver 1993
Dana Shoun Chitwood 1993
Michelle Elaine Chitwood 1993
Adam Danny Coleman 1993
Wesley Madison Cornett 1993
Ella Fay Covington 1993
Stephanie Brett Dotson LaRose 1993
Sulia Carpenter Douglas 1993
Tonia Ackerman Edwards 1993
Tara Ann Fields 1993
Wanda Lee Fields 1993
Patricia L. Floyd 1993
Joseph E. Frencl Jr. 1993
Trina Dinese Fuson 1993
Charles Richard Gallemore 1993
L. Bryon Green 1993
L. Bryon Green 1993
Laurel Elaine Grimm 1993
Margie Ann Hall 1993
Larina Faye Hall 1993
Kristie Michelle Harris 1993
Teresa Lynn Head 1993
Debra Etta Helton 1993
Judith V. Hensley 1993
Pamela McGhee Hill 1993
Jeannette R. Jewell Howard 1993
Jodi Jerri Huddleston 1993
Regina Leigh Hudson 1993
Lisa Jon Landers 1993
Janet Lynn Lashbrook 1993
Angela Joyce Lawson 1993
Lansford Hobert Lay Jr. 1993
Jerry N. Leach 1993
Margaret Ann Marsee 1993
Susan Ann McCall 1993
Vicki Lynne Meadors 1993
Anthony Melton 1993
Holly Elizabeth Nasinec 1993
Elizabeth M. Nichols 1993
Karen Susan Marie Osborne 1993
Rhonda F. Owens 1993
Cynthia Caroline Richardson 1993
Rhonda Kaye Roach 1993
Wanda E. Rose 1993
Kevin Paul Sanders 1993
Mildred Ann Sanders 1993
Terri Lynn Shelton 1993
Darlene W. Smith 1993

Lizbeth Marlene Staffey 1993
Bethany Lynn Stone 1993
Carol J. Sumner 1993
Larry Wayne Taylor 1993
Vicki Lynn Tsang 1993
Amy Lynn Whitaker 1993
Michael Douglas Whitaker 1993
Angela Joan Williamson 1993
Helen Annette Wormsley 1993
Melissa Dawn Zehr 1993
Annette Abner 1994
Dawn Marie Allen 1994
Hunter Robert Barber 1994
Amy Leigh Barr 1994
Stephanie Rae Begley 1994
Amanda Ruth Blair 1994
Bobby Blakley 1994
David Harold Bryant 1994
Peggy Darlene Burke 1994
Melody L. Coppock 1994
Mary Lou Corder 1994
Crissy Lynn Crubaugh 1994
Lucinda J. Daniels 1994
Faith M. Dykes 1994
Judith Ann Greis 1994
Candace Hope Hansford Ph.D. 1994
Stephanie Lynn Harmon 1994
Angela Renee' Haynes 1994
Laurel Shelley Herron 1994
Sheryl Ann Hicks 1994
DeAnna Lynn Jeffers 1994
Nena Lynnette Johnson 1994
Sherry Lynn Jones-Durham 1994
Sharon Zola Justice 1994
Carol Sue Lambdin 1994
Donna M. Lauerman 1994
Carolyn Sue Lawson 1994
Judy Eileen Lewallen 1994
Gary Hillard Lewis 1994
Elizabeth Gayle Lin 1994
Yvonne Marie Lowrie 1994
Tammy Michelle Lowrie 1994
Jacqueline Faye Marlow 1994
Pamela Brock Martin 1994
Michael Roger Maxey 1994
Deborah Ellen Mayberry 1994
Gary K. Merida 1994
Glenda J. Mitchell 1994
Matt Allen Muncy 1994
Joan Evelyn Raleigh 1994
Teresa J. Reasor 1994
Wayne Scott Reid 1994
Michael David Roark 1994
Karla Sue Roberts 1994
Gretchen Parrish Roland 1994
Shena Ann Rose 1994
Patricia Ann Ross 1994
Jill Lynette Sanders 1994
Michelle Renee' Shelley 1994
William Francis Shelley 1994
Michele Ann Shotwell 1994
Vivian L. Smiddy 1994
Douglas Wayne Smith 1994
Joyce Ann Steele 1994
Sonja Renee Stidham 1994
Nancy Carol Stokes 1994
Marea Jones Strunk 1994
Lisa Michelle Sweet 1994
Clark B. Teague 1994
Lesley Andrea Thomas 1994

Jeannene Ann Thompson 1994
Linda Kaye Watson 1994
Charles Steve Watson 1994
Johnnie Melinda Watters 1994
Judy Wells 1994
Leslie Brent West 1994
Margaret Lynne Wheeler 1994
Dawn Rachelle Woodruff 1994
Connie Lynn Blaylock 1995
Charlene Marie Blevins 1995
Cateresa Ann Boston 1995
Amy S. Bowlin 1995
Tamara Gay Bradley 1995
Sandra J. Bradley 1995
Alesa Branham 1995
Lesley Danielle Buckner 1995
Regina Gail Bunch 1995
Peggy Sue Burkey 1995
Gussie Ann Burns 1995
Jennifer Leigh Canter 1995
Veronica Reagan Carmical 1995
Michael Wayne Cassidy 1995
Tammie R. Chapman 1995
Sherry Renee Clark 1995
Krysti Rae Conlin 1995
Shanee Lynn Cox Cummins 1995
Jimmy Roger Dishman 1995
Eugenia Lee Dunn 1995
Melody Kay Estep 1995
Brenda Carolyn Fox 1995
Barbara Anne Gregory 1995
Charlotte Kay Hall 1995
Katherine Hampton 1995
Wanda M. Harris 1995
Leigh Ann Hayward 1995
Angela Renee Hilsenbeck 1995
Candy Leeann Holbrook 1995
Elizabeth Suzanne Hoskins 1995
Jennifer A. Hurst 1995
Rachel Yvette Jones 1995
Kathy Martin Jones 1995
Patricia Loriann Lay 1995
Jerry Wentfred Mansfield 1995
Elizabeth K. Martin 1995
Dale Allen Mayberry 1995
Vickie Lynn Mays 1995
Earl McDaniel 1995
Cathy McGinnis 1995
Bridgett Lee McWhorter 1995
Jack Byron McWilliams 1995
Joy Harp Miller 1995
Dana Louise Oak 1995
John Martin Penwell 1995
Melissa Nadine Phillips 1995
Kristie Lee Rae 1995
Ramsey Thomas Ross 1995
Mildred Ann Sanders 1995
Kindra Ann Scalf 1995
Mary Martha Sharp 1995
Gina Michelle Sharp 1995
Stuart Trent Shepherd 1995
Kenneth Allen Siler 1995
Amelia B. Stephens 1995
Tammy Denese Stevens 1995
Barbara Gambrell Storms 1995
Angela Colleen Swain 1995
Tammy Diane Webb 1995
Mackie Kay Whitley 1995
Amy Renee Wilson 1995
Susan Wilson 1995

Elizabeth Wyllie 1995
Shannon Leigh Aguinaldo 1996
Anthony Gene Arnold 1996
Laura Leigh Asbury 1996
Mitchell Bailey 1996
Mitchell Bailey 1996
Sherri Elaine Barnes 1996
Rebecca J. Blakley 1996
R. Kevin Brashear 1996
Elizabeth Ann Callahan 1996
Claudia Estelle Chandler 1996
Michael Eugene Cox 1996
Kimberly Denise Creekmore 1996
Gayla B. Daniels 1996
Richard Alan Deaver 1996
Norma Dillon 1996
Pamela Dixon 1996
Sulia Carpenter Douglas 1996
Kerry Kay Dugan 1996
Gloria Jean Dunham 1996
Shana Renee Dunn 1996
Becky Joan Fannin 1996
Connie Sue Floyd 1996
David W. Gibbins 1996
Sean Dewayne Gray 1996
Marjorie Ann Hanlon 1996
Michael John Hatfield 1996
Jodie Lynn Hill 1996
Janet Kay Howard 1996
Kristina L. Hulgan 1996
Sandra L. Hutson 1996
Leticia Dawn Johnson 1996
Brian Scott Kelley 1996
Kimberley Ray King 1996
Tania Gail Lewis-Sharp 1996
Jeffrey Michael Liddle 1996
Lisa A. Logsdon 1996
John Douglas Lovin 1996
Amy Renee Meadors 1996
Elizabeth Dawn Meadors 1996
Jennifer Lynn Meadors 1996
Cynthia JoAnn Moore-St. Germain
1996
Christene Elizabeth Moses 1996
Charles Curtis Palmer 1996
Lisa Gail Rains 1996
Melissa Danielle Retherford 1996
Jeremy Wade Roaden 1996
Chrischell Becky Samolis 1996
Kathy Sams 1996
Tamra Rene Sams 1996
Tracey Anne Schneeman 1996
Melissa Ann Schuyler 1996
Scotty Eugene Sexton 1996
Terri Lynn Shelton 1996
Terrylynn Skinner 1996
Deborah Lynn Slaven 1996
Lorraine Sue Stivers 1996
Carol J. Sumner 1996
Tammy Lynn Taylor 1996
Deborah Lawson Thomas 1996
Mari Elizabeth Thornsbury 1996
Jennie Leah Watkins 1996
Mary E. West 1996
Virginia LaDonna West 1996
Chad Ray Wetherill 1996
Cassondra Lynn Wheeler 1996
Helen Annette Wormsley 1996
Stephen Dale Young 1996
Michael Preston Abbott 1997

Sheila Marie Adams 1997
Amy Dawn Alder 1997
Claudia Sueann Anderson 1997
Eddie Lee Ball 1997
Darlena Gibson Barton 1997
Amy S. Bowlin 1997
Daryl Keith Bowman 1997
Kelcy Joy Burkhart 1997
Kimberly Renee' Carroll 1997
Tina Michele Cockerill 1997
Clinton Edward Coleman 1997
Patrick Stuart Conlin 1997
Krysti Rae Conlin 1997
Carole Colleen Cope 1997
Teresa Eileen Cornelius 1997
Carrie Lynn Cox 1997
Karen Deaton 1997
Greg Lee Duncum 1997
Gerald Edward Emerson 1997
Tracey Mullins Evans 1997
Jennifer Leigh Fischer 1997
Clay Michael Gibson 1997
William Patrick Giles 1997
Leigh Ann Gross-Ashcraft 1997
Margie Ann Hall 1997
Karen Diane Hammock 1997
Shane Hansen 1997
Beth Ann Hetzel 1997
Edith J. Huffman 1997
Camelia Carol Jackson 1997
Nena Lynnette Johnson 1997
Lora Renner Jones 1997
Stephanie Renee Jones 1997
Nancy Suzanne Lane 1997
Sherry Denise Lawson 1997
Carolyn Sue Lawson 1997
Pedano Lynn Lay 1997
Christy Diane Llewellyn 1997
Jeoffrey Chad Lynch 1997
Jacqueline Faye Marlow 1997
David W. Martin 1997
Patricia Lynn McKamey 1997
Martha Darlene Miller 1997
Lewis Dwayne Morris 1997
Angela Cooper Moses 1997
Debra B. Phillips 1997
Nathan William Pittenger 1997
Leah Paige Pizana 1997
Lisa Carol Potter-Smith 1997
Willie Scott Powell 1997
John W. Reeder Jr. 1997
Kimberly Jo Rewis 1997
Tessie Hale Rivero 1997
Tessie Hale Rivero 1997
Patricia Ann Ross 1997
Angela Lyn Schonauer 1997
Randall Lowell Sentman 1997
Elissa O'Bryan Settles 1997
Molly Amelia Shockey 1997
Michele Ann Shotwell 1997
Mary Juanelle Smith 1997
Kathy Smith 1997
Marea Jones Strunk 1997
Jennifer Renee Sulfridge 1997
Larry Wayne Taylor 1997
Carol Ann Thompson 1997
Cynthia Francine Thymius 1997
Cassandra Ann Trammell 1997
Chad D. Turner 1997
Susan Crabtree Vaden 1997

Amy Michelle Warfield 1997
Hannie Marie Wolfe 1997
Jennifer Renea Yarnell 1997
William Royd Allen 1998
Kellie Marie Anderson 1998
Brandon Tate Anderson 1998
Amanda Lynn Ayers 1998
Rebecca Lynn Baird 1998
Justin Ervin Bozeman 1998
Justin Ervin Bozeman 1998
Joy Lynn Brantley 1998
Evie M. Brewer 1998
Rebecca Leah Brothers 1998
Joshua Bryant 1998
Tonya Burdine 1998
Van Michael Burton 1998
Rebecca Ruth Burton 1998
Lucille Bussell 1998
Jeana Lana Carr 1998
Michele Lynn Clark 1998
Melissa Sue Conlin 1998
Carlee Ballard Cornett 1998
Amanda Ann Croley 1998
David Kyle Cupp 1998
Monica Denise Floyd 1998
Carol Ann Ford 1998
Teresa Gambrel 1998
Rebecca Lynne Graham 1998
Ann Hanson 1998
Laurel Shelley Herron 1998
Rosalee C. Hinkle 1998
Denice M. Hoffeditz 1998
Sandra Lynn Hughes 1998
Julie Denise Hurst 1998
Robin Rochelle Ingle 1998
Melissa Ann Jones 1998
Deanna Renee Kidd 1998
Derrick Wayne Lowrie 1998
Jodi Andrea Mackiewicz 1998
Amy Lorraine Manning 1998
Julie Megan McCarty 1998
April Denise McFalls 1998
Patricia Lynn McKamey 1998
Cynthia K. Moore 1998
Joseph Francis Orazen 1998
Karen Susan Marie Osborne 1998
James Memory Payne 1998
Gary Lee Peters 1998
Samantha Mary Ray 1998
Kathleen Ann Richie 1998
Kenneth Allen Siler 1998
Jennifer Renee Smith 1998
Konnie Snyder 1998
Lizbeth Marlene Staffey 1998
Kimberly Jo Sutton 1998
Theresa Toler 1998
Kellie Jo Weihe 1998
Joshua David Wellman 1998
Kara Lyn Wheeler 1998
Alan Robert Ysidro 1998
Melissa Dawn Zehr 1998
Mary Ruth Adkins 1999
Veronica Lynn Arthur 1999
Mitchell Bailey 1999
Mitchell Bailey 1999
Marilyn Lois Baird 1999
Tammy Jo Ball-Neal 1999
Stephanie Rae Begley 1999
Rebecca J. Blakley 1999
Kristi Leah Botner 1999

Felecia Jenee Breeding 1999
Malinda Sue Brooks 1999
Paula Jeanette Bruce 1999
Cynthia Fontae Bryant 1999
Matthew Shane Bryant 1999
Julie Ann Buschor 1999
Christopher James Bush 1999
Angela Tee Chestnut 1999
Melissa Lynn Chitwood 1999
Christy Renee Clark 1999
Christopher Lawrence Cool 1999
Vivian Cotterell 1999
Max Allen Cox Sr. 1999
Michelle K. Creekmore 1999
Tracy Jill Croley 1999
Angela Mary Douglas 1999
Marion Aaron Fannin 1999
Melanie Michelle Gover 1999
Leslie Ann Grillon-Patrick 1999
Sonia Kay Guffey 1999
Mary Elizabeth Haddix 1999
Tanya Lee Halcomb 1999
Ralph David Halcomb 1999
Pamela Fay Halstead 1999
Laura Janan Hamm 1999
Mary Jo Hannah 1999
Jamie Renee Hansen 1999
Susanna Jean Harper 1999
Juanita Leanna Hensley 1999
Sheryl Ann Hicks 1999
Sheila Kay Jennings 1999
Ann Marie Jewell 1999
Candy Martin Jones 1999
Jennifer Elizabeth Jones 1999
Lansford Hobert Lay Jr. 1999
Judy Eileen Lewallen 1999
Tania Gail Lewis-Sharp 1999
Yvonne Marie Lowrie 1999
Judy G. Lueking 1999
Kenneth Floyd McKinney 1999
Jennifer Courtney McKinney 1999
Rebecca Lynn McTaggart 1999
Marsha Renee McWilliams 1999
DeAnna Lynn Meadors 1999
Amy Renee Meadors 1999
Shelia Mullins Meece 1999
Rodney Gene Morris 1999
Sandra Joan Nantz 1999
Stephanie L. Nickel 1999
Derrick Scott Owens 1999
Jennifer Lynn Parsons 1999
Angela Denise Partin 1999
Tonya Kaye Pemberton 1999
Debra G. Petrey 1999
Stephanie C. Phillips 1999
Robert Wayne Powers 1999
Amber Brienne Rains 1999
Glenn Willard Reeves Jr. 1999
Katherine Susann Reid 1999
Larry Wayne Rhodes 1999
Larry Andrew Richardson 1999
Rhonda Kaye Roach 1999
Billy Ray Roberts 1999
Georgenia Dawn Rose 1999
Mary L. Ross 1999
Gina Michelle Sharp 1999
Regina Mahan Sharpe 1999
Stuart Trent Shepherd 1999
Robin Elaine Siler 1999
Michelle Lea Simpson 1999

Billy Wayne Simpson 1999
Deborah Lynn Slaven 1999
Hilary Page Sloat 1999
Mandi Marie Staton 1999
Joyce Ann Steele 1999
David Christopher Stephens Ph.D. 1999
Nancy Carol Stokes 1999
Jeffery David Stout 1999
David Ralph Strunk 1999
Cindy Ellen Sumner 1999
Patricia A. Thomas 1999
Stacie Lynn Trammell 1999
Carilyn Ann West 1999
Leslie Brent West 1999
Mackie Kay Whitley 1999
Stephen Dale Young 1999
Tonya Evyette Akins 2000
Amy Dawn Alder 2000
Dawn Marie Allen 2000
Mary Katherine Armstrong 2000
Amber Dawn Baird 2000
Mary Carol Baker 2000
Suzanne E. Baker 2000
Angela Helen Barrandeguy 2000
Brent L. Benning 2000
DeVonna Kay Blevins-Marble 2000
Cristel Gail Boggs 2000
Jennifer Elaine Bowlin 2000
Jill Ann Bradley 2000
Susan Marie Brashear 2000
Maggie Elizabeth Broughton 2000
Lesley Danielle Buckner 2000
Emily Susann Cain 2000
Melinda Gail Claxton 2000
Loren Lee Connell 2000
Paron Shane Creekmore 2000
Deidra Lee Etta Croley 2000
Janel Denise Cupp 2000
Jacqueline L. Daniels 2000
Dale Byron Davis 2000
Alvin Russell Draper 2000
Marsha Lynn Eads 2000
Karen Gail Fields 2000
Brian Lee Foley 2000
Laura Susan Galyen 2000
Melissa Mae Gilbert 2000
Latreca Denise Greer 2000
Dana Jo Hale 2000
Heather Marie Hamilton 2000
Susanna Jean Harper 2000
Vaughn Hartley Hatcher II 2000
Charles Edward Hayes 2000
Melissa J. Helton 2000
Tammie Lynn Henry 2000
Jodie Lynn Hill 2000
Staci Marie Howard 2000
Teresa Lynn Kidd 2000
Darla L. King 2000
Jerry Michael King 2000
Nancy Alicia Lay 2000
Amy Leigh Lewis 2000
Lisa M. Lindsay 2000
Amy Marie Madon 2000
Rachel Suzanne Madron 2000
John Myon Mahal Jr. 2000
Anthony Leo Martin 2000
Sherry Lynn Masters 2000
Diana Kay Maxey 2000
Dale Allen Mayberry 2000
Jaimie Lynn McNiel 2000

Elizabeth Dawn Meadors 2000
Timothy Gene Messer 2000
Cathy Marie Mitchell 2000
Bridgette Lee Napier 2000
Bethany Joy Nelson 2000
Sarah Len Nichter 2000
Anthony Hal Pietrowski 2000
Hope Ann Pohl 2000
Willie Scott Powell 2000
Lisa Gail Rains 2000
Tammy Lee Ramalho 2000
Amy Michelle Redfern 2000
John W. Reeder Jr. 2000
Sarah Elizabeth Rucker 2000
Amie Lou Rumph 2000
Sarah Elizabeth Shoemaker 2000
Jennifer Anne Simpson 2000
Shayla Lynn Smith 2000
John E. Smith II 2000
Richard Ray Soule Jr. 2000
Nancy Lee Stringer 2000
Randi Lynn Tallent 2000
Lora L. Todd 2000
Stacie Lynn Trammell 2000
Melinda Ann Wargacki 2000
Leslie Sue Weihe 2000
Carilyn Ann West 2000
Kay Ann Whitson 2000
Amy Renee Wilson 2000
Elizabeth Ruth Winkler 2000
Lori Kristine Worley 2000
Gwynne Elaine Baker 2001
Sacha Carman Bargo 2001
Tiffany Leigh Barnes 2001
Dana Renae Beattie 2001
Mary Elizabeth Blair 2001
Amie Louise Bowlin 2001
Brandi Marie Bray 2001
Rachael Rene Bresch 2001
Rhonda Clark Brown 2001
Gladys Lucille Brown 2001
Peggy Darlene Burke 2001
Jeana Lana Carr 2001
Kimberly Renee' Carroll 2001
Kimberly Nichole Clark 2001
Melissa Sue Conlin 2001
Patrick Stuart Conlin 2001
Kimberly Elaine Cooler 2001
Tonya Dale Corder 2001
Eric Weylin Corder 2001
Deidra Lee Etta Croley 2001
Lucinda J. Daniels 2001
Therese Carol Dixon 2001
Susan Diane Elza 2001
Monica Denise Floyd 2001
Lea Cheryl Fultz 2001
Jamie Belinda Garrett 2001
Amanda Gail Giles 2001
Susan Marie Gilreath 2001
Amanda Pennock Godbey 2001
Tanya Lee Halcomb 2001
Jamie Renee Hansen 2001
Sylvia Vera Hedrick 2001
Charles W. Higdon II 2001
Jennifer Marie Hinkle 2001
Lisa Kay Hopkins 2001
Melissa K. Howard 2001
Jodi Jerri Huddleston 2001
Cynthia Hudson 2001
Jenny Rebecca Iley 2001

Camelia Carol Jackson 2001
Sandy Kay Johnson 2001
April Gail Johnson 2001
Kenneth Allen Johnston 2001
Verena Dean Jones 2001
Angela Teresa Keeton 2001
Donna Marie Kennedy 2001
Susan Marie Kincaid 2001
Kasey Kathleen Lominac 2001
Derrick Wayne Lowrie 2001
Judy G. Lueking 2001
Jodi Andrea Mackiewicz 2001
Marie Ann Mahan 2001
Stacy Elizabeth Manning 2001
Michael Anthony Marciano Ph.D. 2001
Bridgett Lee McWhorter 2001
Catherine B. Mills 2001
Matthew Carl Mitchell 2001
Michelle Lee Morrow 2001
Christene Elizabeth Moses 2001
Jennifer Lee Murphy 2001
Holly Elizabeth Nasinec 2001
Dianna Lynn Olthof 2001
Pamela Lou Peters 2001
Amy Michelle Redfern 2001
Kristy Renee Reid 2001
Timmy Kay Roark 2001
John William Roden III 2001
Georgenia Dawn Rose 2001
Paula Michelle Russell 2001
Melissa Kristy Scott 2001
Heather Marie Shannon 2001
Cynthia Sharon Shook 2001
Justin Sims 2001
Patricia Jenene Singleton 2001
John Royce Smith 2001
Ranson Harold Smith 2001
Terry Jean Spradlin 2001
Bonnie Faye Stephens 2001
Amelia B. Stephens 2001
Sharon K. Stidham 2001
Darlene Stidham 2001
Kara Elizabeth Stille 2001
Melissa Kay Street 2001
Crisman Todd Strunk 2001
Joy Faye Strunk 2001
Jessica Susan Sulfridge 2001
Jennifer Renee Sulfridge 2001
Marc D. Taylor 2001
Jeff T. Terry 2001
Vicky Lynn Troxell 2001
Jaime Lynette Walden 2001
Amy Nicole Walker 2001
Linda Kaye Watson 2001
Charles Steve Watson 2001
Kevin Jarrett Weihe 2001
Judy L. Williams 2001
David Franklin Zinn 2001
Michael Preston Abbott 2002
Mary Ruth Adkins 2002
Diane Rene' Allen 2002
Brandon Tate Anderson 2002
Marilyn Lois Baird 2002
Eddie Lee Ball 2002
Amy Margaret Beard 2002
Melissa Irene Bennett 2002
Lori Lynn Bergman 2002
Lori Lynn Bergman 2002
Christopher Matthew Bishop 2002
Rodney Thomas Borders 2002

Brandi Marie Bray 2002
Dustin Kyle Brown 2002
Douglas Wade Burkhart 2002
Virginia Ann Cares 2002
Scott Damien Cash 2002
Heather Marie Cheney 2002
Melissa Lynn Chitwood 2002
Jenny Ruth Clifton 2002
Jo Ann Collins 2002
Misty Denise Croley 2002
Diana Woosley Cupp 2002
Lucy Orlena Davis-Chinn 2002
Lynn Arvilla Dill 2002
Jennifer Lynn Dukes 2002
James Rollie Durham 2002
Christian Leigh Faught 2002
Millie Gail Floyd 2002
Rebecca Elizabeth Ford 2002
Melissa Fox 2002
Emma Katherine Freeman 2002
Charlotte Christine Giles 2002
Mary Elizabeth Haddix 2002
Ralph David Halcomb 2002
Debra Ellen Hambrick 2002
Patricia D. Hamlin 2002
Shane Hansen 2002
Bernard Joseph Harrington 2002
Libby Joy Hicks 2002
Lora Jean Higginbotham 2002
Michael D. Irving 2002
Sindi Lowe Jeffers 2002
Sheila Kay Jennings 2002
Lora Renner Jones 2002
Christopher Michael Lackner 2002
Nolan Ryan LaVoie 2002
Andrea Michelle Lawler 2002
Sherry Denise Lawson 2002
Pedano Lynn Lay 2002
Jennifer Lynn Lee 2002
Amanda Susan Long 2002
Bryson Iran Loudermilk 2002
Cassie Beth Maples 2002
Jason Lee Martin 2002
Sarah Linda McCall 2002
DeAnna Lynn Meadors 2002
Shelia Mullins Meece 2002
Jackie Rees Melton 2002
Mary Beth Messer 2002
Tessa J. Miracle 2002
Michelle Lee Morrow 2002
Michelle R. Owens 2002
Cheryl Michelle Partin 2002
Anthony Hal Pietrowski 2002
Lindsay Blair Prather 2002
Tyrone Rakish Ramcharansingh 2002
Rheagan Leigh Redmond 2002
Jennifer Leigh Reser 2002
Charity Hope Reynolds 2002
Anita Beth Richardson 2002
Melissa Kay Rickett 2002
Audrea Louise Roark 2002
William Brandon Rogers 2002
Amie Lou Rumph 2002
Susan Gail Rutherford 2002
Floyd Michael Rutherford 2002
Mary Beth Salvato 2002
Rebecca Lynn Scalf 2002
John Luster Siler 2002
Billy Wayne Simpson 2002
Mary Juanelle Smith 2002

David Michael Sweet 2002
Shannon Renee Taylor 2002
Lindy Ann Terry 2002
Amanda Sue Thomas 2002
Christie Diane Willis 2002
Bradley Keith Woods 2002
Larry Shane Anderson 2003
Eric Ivary Anderson 2003
Heather Michelle Baird 2003
Shelia Jane Baker 2003
Magen Renee Ballard 2003
Robyn Mayree Bingham 2003
Patrick Wesley Bowlin 2003
Jamie Maria Bowman 2003
Steven Andrew Bryson 2003
Jennifer Sue Castle 2003
Michelle Elaine Chitwood 2003
Michele Lynn Clark 2003
Krissy Lynn Cobb 2003
Leigh Ann Cobb 2003
Dana Elaine Coffey 2003
Lynn Louise Collins 2003
Ginger Denise Crawford 2003
Lynn Arvilla Dill 2003
Elvenia W. Duff 2003
Wanda Jean Duncan 2003
Tiffany Lou Duvall 2003
Cheryl Renee Elmore 2003
Michelle Lynn Gross 2003
Laura Katherin Gumm 2003
Bernice Elizabeth Harris 2003
Jessica Lynn Holt 2003
Kyle Bryan Jones 2003
Stefanie Dawn Keene 2003
Wendy Michell King 2003
Brandie Rena Kinzel 2003
Susan Marie Lange 2003
Wanda Faye Larrigan 2003
Angela Joyce Lawson 2003
Nancy Alicia Lay 2003
Ellen Barnes LeRoy 2003
Christy Diane Llewellyn 2003
Judy Fay Lundy 2003
Amy Michelle Lunsford 2003
Kimberly Allison Mahne 2003
Nichole Brooke Mathews 2003
Katherine Rena Matta 2003
Jessica Leigh McGhee 2003
Jennifer Lynn Meadors 2003
Chad Matthew Muhlenkamp 2003
Gerald Ray Mullins 2003
Janice Marie Musick 2003
Misty Michelle Newberry 2003
William Carl Nichols 2003
Alicia Jan Nichols 2003
Danny Ray Oakes 2003
David Dwayne Owens 2003
Trina Jane Partin 2003
Josephine Lea Peters 2003
Keri Marie Polevchak 2003
Victoria Ann Pope 2003
Lana Michelle Powers 2003
Jason Brent Pullins 2003
Heather Danielle Ramey 2003
Jerrell Craig Reynolds 2003
John Allen Ritchie 2003
Jeremy Wade Roaden 2003
Sherrie Lynn Robinson 2003
Stephanie Gayle Ross 2003
Stephanie Renea Seale 2003

217

Jamie Faye Smith 2003
April Joy Spears 2003
Ashley Alaina Spradlin 2003
Chad Lee Starrett 2003
Edward Bryan Stewart 2003
Rebecca Lynn Taylor 2003
Elizabeth Brook Tillett 2003
Jessica Lynn West 2003
Angela Lea Whitus 2003
Angela Lea Whitus 2003
Robin Morene Wilson 2003
Casey Lachele Woods 2003
Teresa Kay Yancey 2003
Gary Steven Baker 2004
Sacha Carman Bargo 2004
Leslie Ann Bellar 2004
Melissa Irene Bennett 2004
Amie Louise Bowlin 2004
Charlie Robert Brock 2004
Melissa Ann Bruner 2004
Jamie Lynn Bryant 2004
LeAnne Danielle Burns 2004
Sharon Sue Capre 2004
Mary Lyn Carson 2004
Jennifer Sue Castle 2004
Angela Tee Chestnut 2004
Veronica Lynn Chitwood 2004
Rodney Jermaine Clarke 2004
Tamara Victoria Marie Coffey 2004
James Brian Crabtree 2004
Jennifer B. Crockett 2004
Amanda Ann Croley 2004
Tabitha Rebecca Cuomo 2004
Charles Franklin Davis II 2004
Stephanie Michelle Dobbs 2004
Jennifer Lynn Dukes 2004
Kenneth Michael Elam 2004
Jennifer Allison Farley 2004
Karen Gail Fields 2004
Amanda Montee Fowler 2004
Richard Carl Frazier 2004
Amanda Gail Giles 2004
Michelle Lynn Gross 2004
Julie Kay Grubb 2004
Winston Silas Harris 2004
Vaughn Hartley Hatcher II 2004
Tammie Lynn Henry 2004
Kim Yvonne Hooker 2004
MeLeea Jill Humfleet 2004
Christopher Lee Johnson 2004
Kathy Ann Jones 2004
Aimee Elizabeth Jones 2004
Rachel Yvette Jones 2004
John Curtis LaFevers 2004
Stephanie Leann Lawson 2004
Susannah Luise Lindsay 2004
Tammy Annette Marcum 2004
Tammy O. McDaniel 2004
Martha Darlene Miller 2004
Cynthia K. Moore 2004
Amanda Renee Mullen 2004
Amy Lynn Myers 2004
Cheryl Michelle Partin 2004
Rhonda Lynn Payne 2004
James Scott Prewitt 2004
Patrick Christian Reedy 2004
Norma Michelle Rice 2004
Patrick Edward Robinson 2004
Summer Destine Rogers 2004
Boyd Patrick Rowe 2004

Kimberly Ann Satterfield 2004
Sheridan Duncan Satterly 2004
Jessica Susan Sulfridge 2004
Cindy Ellen Sumner 2004
Jennifer E. Wendt 2004
Jessica Elaine Wilder 2004
Wyatt Lee Wilkie 2004
Ronda Fay Angel 2005
Carol Faye Asbury 2005
Jo Ann Baird 2005
Barry Lynn Baird 2005
Suzanne E. Baker 2005
Michelle Lynn Barrett 2005
Emily Shawn Benton 2005
Joshua David Bingham 2005
Amanda Jo Bowling 2005
Heather Lenora Bowling 2005
Susan Marie Brashear 2005
Felecia Jenee Breeding 2005
Bonnie Eloise Butcher 2005
Heather Nicole Cash 2005
Derek Todd Christerson 2005
Krissy Lynn Cobb 2005
Susan Beth Collett 2005
LeAnn Macey Collier 2005
Rhonda Fay Collins 2005
Rebecca Jill Conn 2005
William Kenneth Conn 2005
Misty Denise Croley 2005
Dana Michelle Davis 2005
Michal Renee Deaver 2005
Gloria Jean Dunham 2005
Joseph Clinton Durham 2005
Lindsey Donielle Engle 2005
Lindsey Cathern Evans 2005
Jason Craig Faulkner 2005
William Franklin Hackler 2005
Rebecca Faith Hackler 2005
Alyssa Ann Harmon 2005
Stephanie Elizabeth Harris 2005
Shona Vaughntella Hatfield 2005
Jason Breon Heath 2005
Stephanie Kaye Henderson 2005
Ashley Erin Hensley 2005
Christel Renee Hoskins 2005
Dara Eileen Johnson 2005
Laura Catherine Kegan 2005
Sharon Kathleen King 2005
Terri Lee King 2005
Steven Thomas Kissinger 2005
Angela Ruth Kubat 2005
Amy Heather Lawson 2005
Amanda Susan Long 2005
Addie Renee Maiden 2005
Andrea Beth Medaugh 2005
Misty Taylor Miller 2005
Sally Ruth Mitchell 2005
Steven Jay Moses 2005
April Kristen Napier 2005
Ronnie Dewayne Partin 2005
James Wesley Penny II 2005
Kristen Irene Phillips 2005
Robert Wayne Powers 2005
Tonya Elaine Proffitt 2005
Kristy Renee Reid 2005
Benjamin Thomas Reser 2005
Larry Andrew Richardson 2005
Michelle Pauline Rickett 2005
Johnathan David Owen Roberts 2005
Amber Nicole Romines 2005

Stephanie Renee Sanders 2005
Thomas John Scheithauer 2005
Jackson Delayne Sharp 2005
Robin Elaine Siler 2005
Ranson Harold Smith 2005
Jennifer Renee Smith 2005
Phyllis Kathryn Strunk 2005
Jacqueline Daphene Thompson 2005
Cassandra Ann Trammell 2005
Jaime Lynette Walden 2005
Kristen Lee Webb 2005
Stephanie Denise White 2005
Sarah Whitney White 2005
Katherine TeNeal Wilcox 2005
Justin Alan Williams 2005
Tiffany B. Wilson 2005
Heather Suzanne Wilson 2005
Paul Zachary Woodard 2005
Robert E. Angel 2006
James Nolan Baker 2006
Mary Carol Baker 2006
Joshua Lee Boston 2006
Alisha Renae Bruce 2006
David Harold Bryant 2006
Linda Joyce Collins 2006
Scott Michael Combs 2006
Melody Lois Creech 2006
Lisa Estelle Elliott 2006
Chasity Lynn Faulkner 2006
Violet A. Finch Helton 2006
Jessica Christina Foster 2006
Sonia Kay Guffey 2006
Amanda Brooke Hammonds 2006
Zachary Thomas Harris 2006
Carolyn Joyce Harris 2006
Bernice Elizabeth Harris 2006
Kelly Samantha Hart 2006
Crystal Dawn Hatfield 2006
Angela Marie Hayes 2006
Angela Marie Hayes 2006
Wayne Hensley 2006
Charlotte Ivey 2006
Mark Adam Jones 2006
Carrie Elizabeth Jones 2006
Melissa Ann Jones 2006
Ricky Lynn Kenney 2006
Carol Sue Lambdin 2006
Amy Marie Madon 2006
Joey Carl Marcum 2006
Kimberly Diana McPhetridge 2006
Jackie Rees Melton 2006
Kyle Lee Mink 2006
Kelly Sue Mocahbee 2006
Dan Everett Moody 2006
Kristi Layne Morgan 2006
Jessica Madison Morris 2006
Jennifer Lee Murphy 2006
Lesley Michelle Neal 2006
Jennifer Lynn Parsons 2006
Melanie Ruth Petzold 2006
Amber Brienne Rains 2006
Barbara Sue Root 2006
Dorcia F. Rose 2006
Debra Lynn Schneider 2006
Stephanie Renea Seale 2006
Tarrah Leigh Sexton 2006
Sarah Jane Shelly 2006
Natasha Tamara Singleton 2006
Kyle Daniel Singleton 2006
Brenda Rae Spanjer 2006

218

Robin B. Swisher 2006
Cathy Lynn Thomas 2006
Patricia A. Thomas 2006
Joyce K. Troxell 2006
Jeremy Lawrence Vaught 2006
Michelle Marie Warnky 2006
Joshua Lee White 2006
Joy Beth Williams 2006
Kristin Kay Allen 2007
Gretchen Lea Arzillo 2007
David Allen Atwood 2007
Barry Lynn Baird 2007
Tammie J. Baird 2007
Rebecca Jo Begley 2007
Joshua James Boggs 2007
Jennifer Elaine Bowlin 2007
April Michelle Bowman 2007
Tara Ann Brashear 2007
Jeannie Lorene Broyles 2007
Paula Jeanette Bruce 2007
Cheri Nicole Bumgardner 2007
Joni Allison Byrd 2007
Elizabeth Ann Callahan 2007
Jessica Michelle Carroll 2007
Scott Damien Cash 2007
Rachel B. Cima 2007
Melinda Gail Claxton 2007
Leigh Ann Cobb 2007
Treva Fugate Combs 2007
William Kenneth Conn 2007
Kelly Mae Cozmanciuc 2007
Kalie Lee Crowder 2007
Janel Denise Cupp 2007
Dana Michelle Davis 2007
Norma Dillon 2007
Sheryle Melissia Douglas 2007
Tiffany Rechelle Early 2007
Andrea Nichole Ellis 2007
Floyd Evan Friedman Sr. 2007
Richard Vance Gambrel 2007
Earl Noah Gregory 2007
Sarah Ann Hacker 2007
Kimberly Joy Hamlin 2007
Lora Jean Higginbotham 2007
Dena Nicole Hodge 2007
Lisa Ann Holt 2007
Stephen Brent Jackson 2007
Ryan Stewart Keeton 2007
Karla Kim Lambdin 2007
Samantha Jo Layne 2007
Angela Lonelle Loudermilk 2007
James Daniel Madden 2007
Jaime Jo Maiden 2007
Devlin Warren Marcum 2007
Samuel Alton Marple 2007
Steven Scott McClendon 2007
Steven Scott McClendon 2007
Kenneth Floyd McKinney 2007
Ana Lea Medders 2007
Rene Moreen Mortensen 2007
Gerald Ray Mullins 2007
Lindsay Elizabeth Musgrove 2007
Angela C.J. Owens 2007
Stephanie Ann Payne 2007
Larimie Richardson 2007
Susan Elizabeth Roberts 2007
Carl Lee Roberts 2007
Amber Nicole Romines 2007
Kimberly Ann Satterfield 2007
Shelly Anne Scheithauer 2007

Thomas John Scheithauer 2007
Laura Katherine Smith 2007
Angela Michelle Smith 2007
Phyllis Kathryn Strunk 2007
David Ralph Strunk 2007
Kimberly Jo Sutton 2007
Ashley Ann Terry 2007
Deborah Ann Tharpe 2007
Jessica Lynn West 2007
Chastity A. White 2007
Angela Lea Whitus 2007
Angela Lea Whitus 2007
Georgia Pauline Wilder 2007
Angela Nicole Wilson 2007
Claudia Sueann Anderson 2008
Gretchen Lea Arzillo 2008
Heather Michelle Baird 2008
Gwynne Elaine Baker 2008
Dionne M. Bates 2008
Stephen Christopher Bender 2008
Molli Erin Benge 2008
Chelsea Dale Boggs 2008
Jamie Maria Bowman 2008
ShaDon Quinn Brown 2008
Dustin Kyle Brown 2008
Amanda Rae Broyle 2008
Emily Susann Cain 2008
Stacy V. Calhoun 2008
Heather Fugate Campbell 2008
Jesse Danielle Clifton 2008
Jennifer Ann Coldiron 2008
Kevin Wayne Courtney 2008
Angel Marie Curry 2008
Laura Frances Curry 2008
Jami Rice Dailey 2008
Shawn Ray Decker 2008
Betsy Brooke Duell 2008
Denese H. Duncan 2008
Patrick Brian Durham 2008
Sandra G. Evans 2008
Jennifer Allison Farley 2008
Gregory Lee Foley 2008
Leslie Ann Foley 2008
Teresa Gambrel 2008
Melissa Joy Gray 2008
Kelly Samantha Hart 2008
Charles T. Houchens 2008
Jeannette R. Jewell Howard 2008
Patricia Ann Hubbard 2008
Mark Cordell Huff 2008
Lee Ann Jenkins-Freels 2008
Karla Danielle Johnson 2008
Candy Martin Jones 2008
Timothy David Kelley 2008
Christina Jane King 2008
Angela Ruth Kubat 2008
Christopher Michael Lay 2008
Margie Bevins Lowe 2008
Mary Crystal Lyttle 2008
Kristin Brooke Mack 2008
April Diana Manning 2008
Randall D. Mayfield 2008
Jacob Benjamin McKinney 2008
Edward Joseph Miller 2008
Matthew Dale Miller 2008
John Paul Mountjoy 2008
Amber Lee Murray 2008
April Kristen Napier 2008
Lori L. Newman 2008
Berna Dean Onkst 2008

Gillis Anthony Osborne 2008
Michelle R. Owens 2008
Michael Anthony Patterson 2008
Lakshmi Deepa Kumari Peddyreddy 2008
Heather Renee Powers 2008
Tonya Elaine Proffitt 2008
Carrol Lee Rice 2008
Shantel Jane Richardson 2008
Melissa Kay Rickett 2008
Jackie D. Robinson 2008
Ronika Pearl Roosa 2008
Rachael Dee Schwingen 2008
Joshua Emden Seabolt 2008
Tarrah Leigh Sexton 2008
Leena Shine 2008
Kristen Leigh Shockley 2008
Shannon Layne Sizemore 2008
Jessica Ann Smallwood 2008
Jamie Faye Smith 2008
Richard Ray Soule Jr. 2008
Ashley Alaina Spradlin 2008
Emma Jonel St. Jacques 2008
Elizabeth Suzanne Stack 2008
Sarah Deanna Strunk 2008
Kimberly Ann Teague 2008
Samantha Jo Thomas 2008
Jeffrey Dale Tingle 2008
April Marette Turpin 2008
Vicky Lynn Walden 2008
Ronda Ann Warren 2008
Matthew Joseph Watts 2008
Jamie Leighann Webb 2008
Tonette Lynn Weddle 2008
Patricia Ann Weiner 2008
Robin Morene Wilson 2008
Janie G. Wood 2008
Lindsey Alexandra Woodyard 2008
Amber R. Adams 2009
Kayla Michelle Adkins 2009
Travis Dale Anderson 2009
Justin Michael Arms 2009
Malissa Von Atkinson 2009
David Allen Atwood 2009
Casey Dawn Barnett 2009
Bobbie Lynn Barrier 2009
Aaron Clint Bass 2009
Matthew David Bastin 2009
Denise Lynn Bell 2009
Rahman Kolomo Bell 2009
Tiffani Anne Bertram 2009
Robert Drew Bigelow 2009
Renee Michelle Boggess 2009
Colleen Rene Boone 2009
Michael Roger Bowling 2009
James Richard C. Bridges 2009
Ernest John Bringer 2009
Debra Lynn Brock 2009
Sandra Dean Brown 2009
Delores Kay Burchett 2009
Angela Marie Burns 2009
Kimberly Dawn Canterbury 2009
Joseph Reginald Carr 2009
Barbara Joan Catt 2009
Christina Nicole Cecil 2009
Gabriel Philip Chapman 2009
Jamie Rae Chenault 2009
Jennifer Elaine Choate 2009
Jacquelyn Ann Clark 2009
Thomas Lloyd Coffey 2009

219

Sarah Elizabeth Collins 2009
Donna Kay Combs 2009
Larinda Layne Combs 2009
Tara Nicole Copas 2009
Kelly Mae Cozmanciuc 2009
Carla Elaine Crawford 2009
Paron Shane Creekmore 2009
Michelle K. Creekmore 2009
Benjamin Scott Croley 2009
Julie Denise Dailey 2009
Jessica Danielle Davis 2009
Grant Michael Davis 2009
Cathy Elizabeth Day 2009
Tonya Renee Decker 2009
Erica Nicole Denney 2009
Warren James Dickinson 2009
Kellie Rene Dillman 2009
Kelly Marie Dunn 2009
Jill Marie Durham 2009
Tiffany Rechelle Early 2009
Leslie Caron Edmondson 2009
Jennifer Nicole Faulkner 2009
Tyler Lee Faulkner 2009
Britney Lizetta Faulkner 2009
Crystal Darice Field 2009
Stephen Robert Fite 2009
Amanda Montee Fowler 2009
Tammy Maria Garnett 2009
Brandon Shane Gibson 2009
Melissa Mae Gilbert 2009
Charlotte Christine Giles 2009
Stephen Kyle Goodlett 2009
Sean Dewayne Gray 2009
Mona Rena Green 2009
Seth Jacob Green 2009
Steven Lance Gregory 2009
Cathy Lynn Gregory 2009
Cara Daniel' Griffey 2009
Crystal Michelle Grimes 2009
Jaziel Ramon Guerra 2009
Robin Gail Hacker 2009
Sarah Ann Hacker 2009
William Franklin Hackler 2009
Patrick Hart Hagan 2009
Jennifer Marcum Hagan 2009
Matthew Christopher Hall 2009
Amanda Brooke Hammonds 2009
Melissa Ann Harris 2009
Stephanie Elizabeth Harris 2009
Shona Vaughntella Hatfield 2009
Christopher Alan Hayes 2009
Brenda Sue Hayes 2009
Ashley Erin Hensley 2009
Lisa Ellen Hibbs 2009
James Dale Hicks 2009
Deidre Shanai Higgins 2009
Sharen Hill 2009
Amber Nicole Hobdy 2009
Brittney Elizabeth House 2009
Heather Ruth Housley 2009
Sherry Ann Hughley 2009
MeLeea Jill Humfleet 2009
Essien Dwright Jackson 2009
Connie Marie Jamieson 2009
Jason O. Jeffers 2009
Brittany Lea Jeffers 2009
Amy Christa Jeffers 2009
Danny Wayne Jett Jr. 2009
Roger Brian Johnson 2009
Christopher Lee Johnson 2009

Emily Lorene Jones 2009
Jessica Rebecca Keeton 2009
Eric Brent Keeton 2009
Barbara Jean Kenton 2009
Dawn Marie Kidd 2009
Wendy Michell King 2009
Kimberley Ray King 2009
Amy Elizabeth Klein 2009
Katie Scarlett Lanham 2009
Natasha Darlene Lanham 2009
Carol Dawn Latham 2009
Edith Renee Lawson 2009
Regina Lynn Ledington 2009
Christopher Michael Long 2009
Anne Louise Lopez 2009
Sherry Lynn Lovely 2009
Jody Brandon Madden 2009
John Myon Mahal Jr. 2009
Stacy Renee Marlar 2009
Michelle Lea Marnhout 2009
Jennifer Masterson 2009
Nichole Brooke Mathews 2009
Allison Lynn Maxey 2009
Christina Lynn McRay 2009
Jamie Ruth McWilliams 2009
Hunter Matthew Meade 2009
Christa Angelina Mendes 2009
Lindsay Nicole Mike 2009
Lana Renee' Mitchell 2009
Laura Vickerstaff Moberley 2009
Schann Rae Mobley 2009
Ashley Nicole Mofield 2009
Dan Everett Moody 2009
Michael Timothy Morgan 2009
Elizabeth Ashley Morris 2009
John Paul Mountjoy 2009
Robyn D. Mullins 2009
Lucian Anthony Musgrove 2009
Connie Denise Napier 2009
Kendall Sue Niemeyer 2009
Lonnie Glenn Nixon 2009
Katherine Elizabeth Owens 2009
Angela Dawn Parnell 2009
Robert Christopher Pash 2009
Amy Catherine Peropat 2009
Wendy Len Philpot 2009
Rebecca Wells Polsgrove 2009
Lisa Carol Potter-Smith 2009
Kristin Chinn Prewitt 2009
Lisa Nalley Ramsey 2009
Kevin Douglas Ray 2009
Chasity Ann Redmon 2009
Katherine Susann Reid 2009
Anita Beth Richardson 2009
Joshua Mitchell Roberts 2009
Susan Elizabeth Roberts 2009
Johnathan David Owen Roberts 2009
Carl Lee Roberts 2009
Judy Robinson 2009
Patrick Edward Robinson 2009
Calvin Ernest Rollyson Jr. 2009
Catherine Joy Rolph 2009
Crystal Nichole Ruckel 2009
Shelly Anne Scheithauer 2009
Sherry Lynne Schloemer 2009
Kris Ann Schuhmann 2009
Scott Anthony Self 2009
Tamitha Joy Sellers 2009
Richard Bryan Sester 2009
Sarah Jane Shelly 2009

Paula Marie Sidebottom 2009
Richard Jason Simpson 2009
Kyle Daniel Singleton 2009
Stefanie Renee Sizemore 2009
Michele Lea Smith 2009
Ashley Dara Smith 2009
John E. Smith II 2009
Geoffrey Paul Sprinkle 2009
Christina Mae Stearns 2009
John Stanley Steely 2009
Karen Stephens 2009
Robyn Kaye Stephens 2009
Lorene Marie Steward 2009
Lorene Marie Steward 2009
Christina Snider Strait 2009
Nathan Andrew Sutton 2009
Kathy Ann Taylor 2009
Andrea Lynn Thomas 2009
Cathy Lynn Thomas 2009
Stephanie Louise Thompson 2009
Christopher Allen Tucker 2009
Jay J. VanRyzin 2009
Allyson Lynn Vitato 2009
John Willard Walker 2009
Rachel Renee Walsh 2009
Sarah Gayle Watkins 2009
Sarah Gayle Watkins 2009
Joshua Thomas Watkins 2009
Ronald Lee Watkins 2009
Shandi Lynn Webb 2009
Kevin Jarrett Weihe 2009
Tara Nicole Wesley 2009
Kimberly Michelle Wethington 2009
Lisa Dianne Wheeler 2009
Lisa Dianne Wheeler 2009
Johnny Wade White 2009
Joshua Lee White 2009
Alicia Nan Whitworth 2009
Joy Beth Williams 2009
Janice Delores Willis 2009
Melissa Ann Winterland 2009
Troy Dean Wood 2009
Warry Ann Woodard 2009
Kaity Elizabeth Woods 2009
Kimberly Ann Young 2009
Ashley Lynn Adams 2010
Brian Lee Adkins 2010
Katie Jo Alexander 2010
Brittany Paige Alvey 2010
Gerald Scott Anderson 2010
Carol Ann Anderson 2010
Hollie Anne Arledge 2010
Roger Tyler Ayers 2010
Tessa D. Back 2010
Joel David Ball 2010
Kyle Wesley Ballou 2010
Jennifer Ramey Barnes 2010
Jennifer Jo Barnett 2010
James Vaughn Paul Bean 2010
Rebecca Jo Begley 2010
Stephen Christopher Bender 2010
Molli Erin Benge 2010
Leslie Dawn Bennett 2010
Heather Michelle Berry 2010
James Matthew Beshear 2010
Lisa Ann Biddle 2010
Joshua Ray Blevins 2010
Chelsea Dale Boggs 2010
Sarabeth Kristen Bollinger 2010
Lance Morgan Boston 2010

April Michelle Bowman 2010
Shanna Rose Brammell 2010
George Tyler Branham 2010
Teresa Lynn Brock 2010
Brandon Kyle Brockman 2010
Zaccheus David Brown 2010
Lawrence Randall Brown 2010
Jennifer Nicole Browning 2010
Katina Nicole Bruce 2010
Alexander Thomas Bumpas 2010
Traci Morris Burke 2010
Marsha Melissa Bush 2010
Brenda Gayle Caddell 2010
LeAnn Carrico 2010
Michael Hoyal Carroll 2010
Loretta Michelle Carson 2010
Tiarra Rochelle Cecil 2010
Trenda Dione Chapman 2010
Veronica Lynn Chitwood 2010
Phillip H. Clay Jr. 2010
Jason Matthew Clayman 2010
Tamara Victoria Marie Coffey 2010
Michael Joe Cole 2010
Carrie Ann Collins 2010
Joseph Randall Cook 2010
Terese Nicole Cooper 2010
Vicki Sue Cooper 2010
Teresa Eileen Cornelius 2010
Amy Jane Crabtree 2010
Mindy Lea Creekmore 2010
John Philip Crisologo 2010
Anna Jennifer Davidson 2010
Natalie Lorelle Davis 2010
Shelby Lynn Decker 2010
Janell Elizabeth Delaney 2010
Christopher Allen DeLotell 2010
Jennifer Ann Derifield 2010
Linda Faye Dial 2010
Phyllis Lynn Dickerson 2010
Ashley Dawn Dillow 2010
Rebecca Jean Dingess 2010
Stacy Kay Dunavent 2010
Donna Kathleen Duncan 2010
Cindy Lee Durham 2010
Emily Susan Duryea 2010
Edwina Gail Eldridge 2010
Lindsay Ann Elliott 2010
Alicia Guffey Emmick 2010
Rhea Anthony Faris Jr. 2010
Gregory Lee Foley 2010
Crystal Nicole Geary 2010
Heather Ruth Ann Geralds 2010
Lori Beth Gish 2010
Jennifer Leigh Gordon 2010
Leslie Anne Goss 2010
Chrystal Anne Graham 2010
Kelly Renee Gray 2010
Melissa Lynn Gregory 2010
Kathryn Ellen Gregory 2010
Christopher Charles Griffith 2010
Breanna Rushele Gross 2010
Maisie Lynette Gross 2010
Ashley Nacole Hackler 2010
Mark Allen Haddox 2010
Aaron Layton Hall 2010
Ashlie Brooke Hall 2010
Kelly Lynn Hall 2010
Amy Marie Hammond 2010
Holly Elizabeth Hance 2010
Tracy Lynn Harness 2010

Christel Dawn Harr 2010
Stephanie Elizabeth Harris 2010
Winston Silas Harris 2010
Kristen Renee Hart 2010
Michele Barnett Hawkins 2010
Christopher Alan Hayes 2010
Tonya Kay Heckman 2010
Tamara Nicole Herp 2010
Sandra Annette Herron 2010
April Marie Hertneck 2010
Megan Lyn Hibbs 2010
Jessica Lane Hill 2010
Teresa Ann Holland 2010
Carissa Ann Horn 2010
Mary Elizabeth Huckaby 2010
Donna Carol Hudson 2010
Larry Shane Humphrey 2010
Brandie Nicole Hutchins 2010
Bryan Thomas Hyatt 2010
Cortney Lynn Inklebarger 2010
Wesley Matthew Irvin 2010
Belinda Anita Jackson 2010
Holly Amanda Jacobs 2010
Michelle Leigh Jarvis 2010
Jordan Michael Jeffers 2010
Kendrick Devon Johnson 2010
Andrea Danielle Johnson 2010
Stephanie Ann Johnson 2010
Karla Danielle Johnson 2010
Mandy Meshea Jones 2010
Mark Adam Jones 2010
Bridget Hobing Karem 2010
Courtney Dawn Keene 2010
Natasha Shawnta Kelley 2010
Judy Lynn Kemper 2010
Jennifer Anne Kemper 2010
Joanna Case Kerr 2010
David Allen Kessler 2010
Rebecca Lea King 2010
Deatrik Germiles Kinney 2010
Gerald Luther Krebs Jr. 2010
Erika Maria Krebs 2010
Kelly Case Lane 2010
Cindi Rae Laney 2010
Lauren Elisabeth Larmon 2010
Michelle Ann Lawrence 2010
Alysonn Paige Lawson 2010
Michael Steven Lawson 2010
Amy Heather Lawson 2010
Stephen Wang Lin Jr. 2010
Mary Amanda Lipscomb 2010
George Bradley Lovely 2010
Miranda Leigh Lowe 2010
Terra Lynn Lyerla 2010
Naji Lakota Lyon 2010
Jody Brandon Madden 2010
James Daniel Madden 2010
Michael Anthony Marciano Ph.D. 2010
Rebecca Joann May 2010
Natosha Nicole McCarley 2010
Brandon Tyler McClain 2010
Shawn Dennis McDermott 2010
Jessica Leigh McGhee 2010
Jennifer Elizabeth McMillan 2010
Peggy Ann Meadows 2010
Satonya Dawn Melton 2010
Bradley Thomas Meredith 2010
Tammy Jo Merritt 2010
Timothy Gene Messer 2010
Kelly Marie Miller 2010

Janella Rae Miller 2010
Edward Joseph Miller 2010
Tamoreio Rashad Mincey 2010
Melissa Lynn Moore 2010
Melinda Renee Morgan 2010
Kristina Marie Morgan-Weber 2010
Christina Anne Morris 2010
Steven Jay Moses 2010
Julie C. Muntz 2010
Meranda Nicole Neace 2010
Lori Beth Neal 2010
Jamie Pearl Neal 2010
Kathy Elaine Waters Neal 2010
Melissa Ann Neeley 2010
Kara Lee Nixon 2010
Mitzi Robyn Norvell 2010
Alysha Ann O'Brien 2010
Kimberly Frances O'Bryan 2010
Michelle Marie Payne 2010
Lisa Nicole Payne 2010
Van Jason Peden 2010
Charles Jackson Perkins II 2010
David Lee Phillips 2010
Jacqueline Denise Phipps 2010
Debbie LeeAnn Pierce 2010
Tracy Poff 2010
Keri Marie Polevchak 2010
Jaime Leigh Posey 2010
Christy Michelle Prasch 2010
Megan Ashley Preis 2010
Heather Nicole Purdom 2010
Jason Richard Rahmel 2010
Bert Laurence Richey 2010
Heather Risch 2010
Robert Dean Ritter Jr. 2010
Anthony Patrick Rizzo 2010
Dennis Kyle Roberts 2010
Thomas Anthony Robertson 2010
Brandy Pauletta Rogers 2010
Heather Rooks 2010
Ronika Pearl Roosa 2010
Floyd Michael Rutherford 2010
Sandra Renee Sampson 2010
Samantha Ruth Schrage 2010
Sophia Renee Shepherd 2010
Brent Martin Shoemaker 2010
Leah Genan Shultz 2010
Erin Michelle Simpson 2010
Lincoln Tyler Spence 2010
Mark David St. Peter 2010
Rebecca Gayle Streeval 2010
Sarah Deanna Strunk 2010
Amy Michelle Sturgill 2010
Clint Earl Taylor 2010
Katherine Cole Thomas 2010
Adam Daniel Thomas 2010
Jacqueline Daphene Thompson 2010
Jeffrey Barrett Tingle 2010
Jessica Renee Tipton 2010
Suzanne Nicole Todd 2010
Amanda Carol Travers 2010
Paul Allan Treadway 2010
Carolyn Ann Trumble 2010
Chad D. Turner 2010
Vickie Ann Vance 2010
Melissa Lee Wall 2010
Daniel Ray Ward 2010
Mary Beth Warwick 2010
Ronald Lee Watkins 2010
Kimberly Ann Weaver 2010

Ashley Dawn Webb 2010
Suzanne Wehrman 2010
Ronda Ann Wendling 2010
Virginia LaDonna West 2010
Chad Ray Wetherill 2010
Benjamin Lee White 2010
Johnny Wade White 2010
Michael Lee Whitfill 2010
Britani Ann Whitis 2010
Amanda Joy Williams 2010
Jessica Faith Willis 2010
Matthew C. Willoughby 2010
Buddie Rae Wilmot 2010
Rachel Beth Wilson 2010
Colby Daniel Wilson 2010
Rachel Dawn Wingo 2010
Elizabeth Wolsey 2010
Kyla Layne Wombles 2010
Holly Deanna Wood 2010
Joanna Christina Yates 2010
Miranda Lynn Yonts 2010
Lauren Elizabeth York 2010
Lisa Michelle York 2010
Maria Danielle Zackery 2010
Arianne Marina Austin 2011
Mitchell Bailey 2011
Mitchell Bailey 2011
Joshua James Boggs 2011
Joshua Lee Boston 2011
Allison Perlina Carney 2011
Gabriel Philip Chapman 2011
Rachel B. Cima 2011
Kalie Lee Crowder 2011
Andrea Nichole Ellis 2011
Britney Lizetta Faulkner 2011
Jessica Christina Foster 2011
Catherine L.C. Gibbs 2011
Delanna Lynn Hardin 2011
Lora Jean Higginbotham 2011
Jennifer Marie Hinkle 2011
Dena Nicole Hodge 2011
Brittney Elizabeth House 2011
Sherry Ann Hughley 2011
Karra Elizabeth Jackson 2011
Jordan Michael Jeffers 2011
Amy Christa Jeffers 2011
Aimee Elizabeth Jones 2011
Angela Teresa Keeton 2011
Steven Thomas Kissinger 2011
Terry Lee Lanham 2011
Katie Scarlett Lanham 2011
Christopher Michael Lay 2011
Samantha Jo Layne 2011
LeRoy Bernard Madison Jr. 2011
Samuel Alton Marple 2011
Ana Lea Medders 2011
Kyle Lee Mink 2011
Berna Dean Onkst 2011
Karen Anita Patrick 2011
Michael Anthony Patterson 2011
Carolyn W. Reaves 2011
Megan Marie Reynolds 2011
Summer Destine Rogers 2011
Ashley Ann Terry 2011
Elizabeth Brook Tillett 2011
Suzanne Nicole Todd 2011
Christopher Allen Tucker 2011
Jeremy Lawrence Vaught 2011
Rosemary Macie Weddington 2011
Kimberly Michelle Wethington 2011

Alicia Nan Whitworth 2011
Katherine TeNeal Wilcox 2011
Justin Alan Williams 2011
Warry Ann Woodard 2011
Rebecca Anne Alicea 2012
Lacy DeNell Anderson 2012
Laurie Joan Angel 2012
Justin Michael Arms 2012
Roger Tyler Ayers 2012
Casey Dawn Barnett 2012
Robert Lewis Bauer 2012
Brandy Lee Beichler 2012
Joshua Adam Belcher 2012
Ashley Nicole Bender 2012
Heather Michelle Benson 2012
Sarah Le'Von Bertram 2012
Lisa Carol Bicknell 2012
Lisa Ann Biddle 2012
Sara Lynn Bijayananda 2012
Serena Monica Blevins 2012
Jennifer Annette Boggs 2012
Nellie Nicole Book 2012
Tanisha Dee Ann Bowen 2012
Sabrina Lynn Bowmer 2012
John Michael Bowmer 2012
Tara Ann Brashear 2012
James Richard C. Bridges 2012
Matthew Neil Brigance 2012
Alison Gwen Brown 2012
Crystal Lynette Caudill 2012
Ronald Scott Cheeks 2012
Benjamin Charles Citron 2012
Holly Lynn Clark 2012
Adam Todd Clary 2012
Kayla Marie Coburn 2012
Elizabeth Annette Coomer 2012
D'Artagnan Coots 2012
Meredith Leigh Cornwell 2012
Whitney Ellen Cox 2012
Samantha Michelle Creech 2012
Melody Lois Creech 2012
Jacqueline Anne Crigler 2012
Harvey J. Davis 2012
Dale Byron Davis 2012
Lucas Scott DeBord 2012
Mary Louis Dennison 2012
Lynn Arvilla Dill 2012
Kellie Rene Dillman 2012
Denise Ann Dodge 2012
Roger Lee Doss 2012
Carol Ann Dossett 2012
Stacy Suzanne Downs 2012
Elizabeth Ashley Dunnington 2012
Adam Lawrence Etienne 2012
Andrew Ryan Felker 2012
Susan Rene' Fields 2012
Victoria Lynn Finch 2012
Jacqueline Kay Flener 2012
Abby Sue Francis 2012
Christina Maria Frazier 2012
Richard Carl Frazier 2012
Adam Todd French 2012
Linda Cheryl Funke 2012
Brooke Michelle Gadberry 2012
Jennifer Margaret Gibson 2012
Jennifer Michelle Gilbert 2012
Lauren Elizabeth Good 2012
LeeWood Goodlett 2012
Andrea Jean Grant 2012
Cathy Lynn Gregory 2012

Kelley Kaye Griffith 2012
Donna Beth Hall 2012
Tritney Beth Hallmark 2012
Lauren Ingram Hamel 2012
Robin Rae Hancock 2012
Leah Roberts Harrison 2012
Jana Sue Harrison 2012
Andrea Elizabeth Hart 2012
Christopher Alan Hayes 2012
Anne Heltsley 2012
Katharine Scibal Hendrix 2012
Leigh Ann Henry 2012
Stephen Boyd Hibbard 2012
Bradley Dean Hill 2012
Richard West Hiller 2012
Taryn Nicole Hirsch 2012
Anthony Wayne Hite 2012
Brittney Elizabeth House 2012
Todd Aaron Houston 2012
Sheila Benita Huff 2012
Mark Cordell Huff 2012
Eric Wayne Hughes 2012
Daneika Nichole Hunt 2012
Rachel Lauren Jackson 2012
Karra Elizabeth Jackson 2012
Laura Catherine James 2012
Connie Marie Jamieson 2012
Brittany Lea Jeffers 2012
Bradley Howard Johnson 2012
Jenna Kay Jones 2012
LaTressa Dawn Jones 2012
Laura Catherine Kegan 2012
Betsy Renee Kennett 2012
Christina Jane King 2012
Kathryn Linn Kirkwood 2012
Emily Rebecca Kreyling 2012
Erin Elizabeth Larkin 2012
Lansford Hobert Lay Jr. 2012
Angela Lonelle Loudermilk 2012
Ramona Joy Luna 2012
Ashley Suzanne Lynn 2012
Kristin Brooke Mack 2012
LeRoy Bernard Madison Jr. 2012
Joanna Michelle Mahan 2012
Elizabeth Diane Marshall 2012
Jennifer Lynn Marshall 2012
Laura Martin 2012
Lora Anne Massey 2012
William Vernon Matthews Jr. 2012
Ashley LeAnn May 2012
Steven Scott McClendon 2012
Steven Scott McClendon 2012
Devin Ashley McFarland 2012
Ashley Marie McGaughey 2012
Chelsi Lynne McPherson 2012
Cecilia Ann Millay 2012
Sarah Marcole Miller 2012
Doris Annette Minor 2012
Heather Nicole Mulholland 2012
Amanda Leigh Mullins 2012
Melissa Ann Neeley 2012
Raven Lynn Norris 2012
Beth Gallagher Pack 2012
Kristen Brooke Potter 2012
Tiffany Suzanne Pugh 2012
Megan Marie Reynolds 2012
Karen Michelle Rice 2012
Jennifer Yvonne Romine 2012
Samantha Faye Rowe 2012
Sean Richard Russell 2012

Stephanie Renee Sanders 2012
Brittney Ann Sanderson 2012
Heather Michelle Sanderson 2012
Danielle Nicole Sarson 2012
Lindsay Brooke Seelow 2012
Carrie Ann Selby 2012
Amanda Marie Sigmon 2012
Jesse Daniel Simpson 2012
Jennifer Anne Simpson 2012
Billy Wayne Simpson 2012
Jody Kay Sizemore 2012
Shannon Layne Sizemore 2012
Steven Craig Slaughter 2012
Derek Justin Smith 2012
Ernest Lee Smith Jr. 2012
Margaret Alice Sporing 2012
Roger Scott Stainforth 2012
Rebecca Marlowe Steger 2012
Lindsay Brooke Stephens 2012

Amanda Dawn Stice 2012
Lisa Sue Stinson 2012
Micah Leigh Stokes 2012
Matthew Paul Stokes 2012
Dana Joyce Storey 2012
Jeffery David Stout 2012
Lynda Anne Sweeney 2012
Chelly Danielle Taylor-Stamps 2012
Kimberly Ann Teague 2012
Chelsey Brooke Tingle 2012
Jeffrey Barrett Tingle 2012
Cassandra Ann Trammell 2012
Dustin O'Neal Tuggle 2012
Darlene F. Turner 2012
Ashley Jane Von Schlutter 2012
Rachel Renee Walsh 2012
Ashley Dawn Webb 2012
Amy Dawne Webber 2012
Adam Michael Webster 2012

Michael David Weedman 2012
Anna F. Weiss 2012
Courtney Elizabeth Welte 2012
Sarah Elizabeth Wester 2012
Hannah R. Wheeler 2012
Dustin Edward Whitis 2012
Mallory Rae Wilkins 2012
Jonathan Wesley Williams 2012
Jason Lee Wilson 2012
Kayla Lizzie Marie Wilson 2012
Colby Daniel Wilson 2012
Amber Renee Wimsatt 2012
Bradley Keith Woods 2012
Anne Woodward 2012
Ashley Dawn Woosley 2012
Glenna Joyce Wright 2012
Stephen Allen Young 2012

TECHNICAL

Carolyn W. Stephens 1952
David Elbert Farris 1956
Melvin Clinton Gilreath 1956
Lowell Hubert Mayne 1957
Patsy Inez Moon 1957
Barbara S. Heimsness 1958
Louie Dills Jr. 1959
Jimmy Ray Partin 1964
James G. Owens 1967
Harold Moses 1968
Edward Lee Younce 1968
Jerry M. Brown 1969
Charles E. Centers 1969
George A. Harrison Jr. 1969
Stephen C. Keith 1969
Kenneth Ray Large 1969
James Burton Sexton 1970

Barbara W. Thompson 1970
Dennis R. Woods 1970
Douglas John Angel 1971
Eva Kay Stamper 1972
James H. Griffith 1973
Gary Everett Riner 1973
Kenneth Ray Robbins 1973
Gary Hackworth 1974
Roy Alan Samples 1974
William Craig Melton 1975
Paula Bradfield 1976
Sandra Kaye Cooley 1977
Larry Wayne Kapitan 1978
Linda Kay Maggard 1980
John M. Sharpe 1980
Daniel James Falvey 1981
Jackie E. Holloway 1982

Henry Wilson Middleton 1982
Catherine A. Jones 1984
Michael Owen Burson 1985
Helena Kay Bowden 1986
Alan C. Britton 1986
Gregory Lee Culver 1986
James Wade Beasley 1987
David Allen Brown 1987
Brian K. Raines 1989
Wayne Thomas Mattox 1991
Bryan Wayne Copeland 1994
Charles Richard Arndt II 1996
Kevin W. Brooks 1998
Eric Nicholas Cecil 2002
Courtney N. Boulds 2003
Jasmyne Laurel Isaacs 2006
Jarrod Lynn Johnson 2009

TELEVISION, RADIO, MEDIA, COMMUNICATIONS

Martha C. Ash 1944
William Alexander Fox 1948
Robert Lewis Donohew Ph.D. 1949
Donald Eugene Wheeler 1950
Naaman Nickell 1952
Charles E. Lovett 1953
Robert Whitecomb Alfred 1964
Bill D. Cody 1969
Sue B. Minton 1969
Randall Lynn Bennett 1970
Boyd Wayne Burkhart 1972
William Lewis Carroll 1972
Alpha Jane Bramel 1977
Byron Douglas Lutz Jr. 1978
Harry Joseph Browne 1981

Karen Joy Jones 1982
David K. Banks 1986
Scott K. Presley 1986
Ernest Kirk Belcher 1987
Timothy D. Chapman 1987
Karla Rochelle Daniels 1990
David Paul Estes 1990
Edith (Edie) Schmidt 1990
Charles Clayton Chitwood 1991
Daniel Lloyd Ashby 1993
Benjamin Michael Ozment 1996
William Henry Hill III 1997
Leshun Jabbar Letlow 1997
Lisa Carol Potter-Smith 1997
Brittney Nuskey 1998

Alyson Glaze 1999
Travis Wayne Wills 2001
Kristopher Chase Gilliam 2002
Joshua Jackson McKinney 2002
William Trevor Grigsby 2003
Amber Lynn Owens 2003
Leslie Nicole Fields 2004
Jared Michael Harmon 2004
Brenda McDaniel 2005
Pamela Martha Woody 2005
Jonathan Owen West 2006
LeNita Michelle Fugate 2009
Emily Pagee McKinney 2009
Lisa Carol Potter-Smith 2009

THERAPIST, THERAPIST MENTAL PHYSICAL, PHYSICAL THERAPY AID

Joyce Wilson 1965
Cheryl Bowdon 1966

Kennard David Jones 1966
Curtis Eugene Slack 1971

Theodore H. Hubble 1972
Raymond D. Sanders Sr. 1974

Herbert Carithers 1976
Brenda Kay Smith 1976
Thomas Hamilton Jr. 1977
Archie C. Pertiller 1977
Sharon Ruth Cates 1978
Peggy Scales Vance 1979
John Edwin Cates 1980
Lana Sue Haggard 1980
Michael Anthony Privette 1980
Patricia A. Baldwin 1981
Brenda Sue Ledbetter 1982
Mark A. Saxon 1982
James Paul Nelson 1983
Marcia Bird 1986
Willie Houston Murray 1986
Lawrence Clay Underwood 1987
Mike Worley 1988
Molly Ann Crockett 1989
Cindy Allison Moses 1989

Sandra G. Williams 1989
Jana N. del Rosario 1991
Julie H. Parker 1991
Stacey Lea Sutton 1991
Donna Lynn Pennington-Carroll 1992
Carrie Elizabeth Grierson 1993
Hunter Robert Barber 1994
Beverly Alice Carter 1994
Londa E. Holliday 1994
William Matthew Keene 1995
Shellie Nicole Hall 1996
Jason Gray Liddle 1996
Lisa Marie Gray 1997
Brenda Lea Linger 1997
Hazel Elizabeth McCray 1997
Samuel Anthony Miller 1997
Amber Denise Cary 1999
Jamie Lynn Morton 1999
Laura Anne Lawson 2000

Olivia Jo Hays 2001
Melissa Ann Jones 2001
Melissa Ann Jones 2001
Katrina LaRae Mounce 2001
April L. Coldiron 2002
Nancy Rae Epperson 2002
Stephanie Marie Mahal 2002
Jamie Lynn Ellis 2003
Jessica L. Wolfe 2004
Portia Leann Mozingo 2005
Jennifer Michelle Parham 2005
Ashley Lee Vanhook 2005
Erica Nicole Bright 2006
Walter Brent Stephens 2007
Morgan Len Lay 2008
Emily Sturgill Morrell 2008
Brittany Danielle Turner 2009
Buffie Denise Croft 2012

TRADE CRAFT, JEWELER, MECHANIC

Clarence Edward Bunch 1952
Jim B. Brown 1954
Noel Edwin Beatty 1955
Bonnie R. Holliday 1955
Jeanette Yvonne Bush 1972
Janie Lynn Kagy 1972

Thomas Edward Wade 1972
Herschel M. Love 1977
Phillip Gene Moore 1980
Mark Lee Struble 1980
Gary Ray Bryant 1981
Gregory Don Saylor 1985

Dwight Whitey Cope 1990
William Alan Endicott 1990
Randall Branden Heatherly 2002
Wendell L. Patterson 2009

TRANSPORTATION, TRUCK DRIVER

Betty Creech Collins 1949
Thomas Lemuel Coker 1952
Herbert H. Scalf 1952
H. Thomas Collins 1954
Charles E. Moore 1955
Paul Edwin Teague 1955
Duell Lester 1956
Robert Howard Wyatt 1956
Mark Daniels Jr. 1959
Jim Ray King 1959
Ronnie Jerrel Riggs 1959
Glennis Croley 1962
Patricia Cox 1963
Carl R. Roberts 1963
Leon I. Alder 1964
E. C. Barnes Jr. 1964
Russell Howard Stephens 1967

Ira Lee Barton 1970
David K. Engle 1970
Ronnie Dale Vaughn 1970
Raymond C. Henderson 1971
William Joseph Hensley 1971
Ronald Lloyd Rice 1971
Janet S. Ruggero 1971
Eddie M. Jones 1972
Emory L. McNew 1972
Ernest Eugene Sharp 1972
Eugene F. Sonnenberg 1972
Gary K. Vanover 1972
Robert W. Thurmond 1973
Marbeth Sue Carmack 1977
Rose Marie Bowen 1979
David L. Jones 1979
Stephen Craig Balderson 1981

Marvin Cress Sr. 1981
Gary James Miller 1982
Karl E. Perry 1985
Aleatha Oaks Muldrow 1989
Nicholas Lombardo 1990
Darrell Ball Jr. 1993
Derrick Kyle Messer 1995
Ansel Henry Smith 1995
Dennis Randle Fields Jr. 2000
Jeffrey Scott Stager 2000
Max Allen Cox Jr. 2002
Erin Margaret Schaffner 2004
James Robert Blanton 2005
Glenn Paul Napier II 2007
Scott James Nobles 2008
Anita Lou Hammons 2009

TRAVEL INDUSTRY, TRAVEL AGENT

Delores Davis 1963
Kenneth Thurston McNear 1968

Merle F. Bustle 1978
Kathy Urrely 1985

Timothy Scott Hoskins 1990
Renee Lynn Bock 1995

US POSTAL SERVICE

Golden Polly Angus 1927
Clarence C. Cox 1936
Cledith Mae Clark 1937
Lloyd Cornelius 1950
Pauline Fuson 1950
William Louis Sosh 1954
Roger H. Graves 1959

Johnny Everett Brown 1963
Ernest Lawson Whitt 1963
Donna Rae Beckett 1967
John M. Stone 1968
Gary L. Masters 1971
Millard Wayne Brown 1973
Tina Parsons 1973

Larry Lester Jones 1975
Gene Alan Richter 1975
Simon Ray Fincher 1976
Kerry Lee Greer 1978
Samuel R. Cordell 1979
Glen O. Martin 1980
Bruce Delynn Winchester 1980

William L. Taylor 1981

UTILITIES, WATER PLANT OPERATOR

Morris Mahone Trammel 1950
Roy L. Siler 1958
Ralph Hershel Robbins 1961
Theodore Madison Hampton 1962
Alice Jane Sharp 1965

Terry Bradley 1972
Albert Joseph Grillon 1974
Braden C. Condley 1977
Michael Howard Stevens 1977
Rick L. Brown 1981

Craig Creech 1987
Allen E. Robbins 1990
Kim A. Bush 1991
Jonathan Wood Thomas 1997
Joseph Barton Southerland 1999

VETERINARIAN, VETERINARIAN TECHNICIAN, ANIMAL SCIENCE VETERINARIAN

Carl L. Culver 1953
Bruce N. Catlett 1954
James Patrick Parks 1975
James R. White 1978

Alissa M. Smitley DVM 1990
David Scott Allen 1993
Laura Ann Berry 1993
Markus Daniel Brackett 1993

Danielle Rena Petker DVM 2000
Brandie DeShea Viars 2003
Cynthia Denise Swindall 2004

VOLUNTEER

Nicki Coyle 1954
Elizabeth S. Hummel 1959
Bonnie Lou Marx 1969
Jean Terry Hughes 1975

Ronald W. Parker 1979
Tina Jacobs 1982
Kelly Lynn Duncan 1983
Bruce Edward McCall 1989

Barbara Mae Grace 1999
Elizabeth Ann Hohman 2003

WRITING, FREE LANCE ABSTRACTOR, JOURNALISM

Smith G. Ross 1929
Lelia C. Wyatt 1938
Jacquelyn D. Owen 1948
Carolyn W. Stephens 1952
Wanda Carole Siler 1958

Anne Burton 1963
Eleanor Anne Nighbert 1963
John Thomas Cochran 1976
Richard Allen Evans 1988
Jeffrey Dewayne Harris 1990

Andrew Nichter 1997
Jacinda A. Andrews 2001
Tommie Lee Kendall 2004
Shane Hamilton Anglin 2010
Shane Hamilton Anglin 2011

YOUTH DIRECTOR

Denita M. Wright 1980
Michael David Cox 1995

Michael Douglas Williams 1995
LaTisha Michelle Cecil 2003

Andrew Deane Dukes 2004

Appendix A

ALUMNI HALL OF HONOR

1988 Hall of Honor Inductees

Mr. Harrison Allison '37
Miss Sylvia Marcia Angel '36
Mr. Fred Anness '70
Mr. Phillip Armstrong '70
Major General Benjamin R. Baker '44
Dr. Glen R. Baker, Jr.'64
Dr. Roger D. Baker '69
Dr. Charles D. Barnes '55
Dr. Nelda Ann Lambert Barton-Collings '78
Mrs. Eleanor Mitts Behrmann '36
Admiral Charles Adams Blakely '03
Dr. Vivian Bowling Blevins '58
Dr. Howard R. Boozer '42
Mr. James W. Bowling '58
Mr. Wallace Boyd '32
The Honorable Jerry D. Bryant '69
Mr. Tommy Warren Butler '51
Reverend Daniel W. Carroll '36
Mr. James B. Cheely '32
Lieutenant Theodore W. Clarke '41
Dr. Carl Thomas Cloer, Jr. '67
Dr. Michael Bruce Colegrove '71
Governor Bert T. Combs '30
Mrs. Jo Florence Cordell '68
Dr. James Lloyd Creech '07
Mr. Edgar Croley '39
Dr. James E. Croley, Jr. '43 ('47 DDS)
Mr. Arthur A. Dale '48
Mrs. Gertrude Angel Dale '32
Dr. Ralph Myers Denham '36
Mr. Edwin R. Denney '23
Miss Lela Dodson '56
Dr. Robert Michael Duncan '71
Brigadier General Roy W. Easley '10
Mr. Paul Estes '56
Mr. Joseph David Faulkner '58
Mr. Albert Robinson Evans '05
Dr. Charles E. Freeman '42
Mrs. Lillian Galloway '55
Mr. Ronald Leon Glass '70
Mr. Nick Greiwe '74
Miss Ethel Rebecca Harmon '32
Mr. Willard Marion Hamblin '56
Mr. Meriel D. Harris '33
Dr. Jerry Hayner '57
Dr. Jack Heneisen '68
Mr. John Heneisen '65
Mr. Jerry Hodges '71
Reverence R. B. Hooks, Jr. '51

Mr. David Nickell Huff '53
Dr. Billy Grey Hurt '51
Mrs. Mary Doyle Johnson '48
Mrs. Vivian McClure Johnston '33
The Honorable Pleas Jones '34
Mrs. Liz Young Krause '45
Mr. Eugene Adkins Lovett '31
Mr. V. Troy Lovett '69
Dr. Jerry D. Lowrie '58
Mr. E.T. Mackey '23
Mr. Conley Lee Manning '54
Ms. Rose Marlowe '12
Mr. Arloe W. Mayne '48
Dr. William A. McCall '11
Mr. A.. J. Meadors '1893
Reverend Bill Messer '68
Mrs. Frances Jones Mills '40
Mr. Dwight L. Moody – attended in 1930
Mr. Edwin P. Morrow
Dr. Harold L. Moses '56
Mayor Marcella Faulkner Mountjoy '43
Mr. Chester Allen Nevels '57
Mrs. Edna Jones Nicholson '18
Dr. Roger Noe '71
Mr. Floyd L. Parks
Dr. Howard Partin '61
Mr. Asbel Shakespeare Petrey '1893
Reverend Marshall Phillips '54
Mrs. Jean Ritchie Pickow '44
Dr. Darrel Estle Rains '59
Mr. Charles E. Reed '75
Mr. Benjamin Pleasant Roach 1899
Dr. Arliss L. Roaden '49
Dr. Mack Roberts '26
Dr. Martha Charlene Hill Robinson '59
Miss Besse Mahan Rose '09
Mrs. Judy Sizemore Rose '58
Mrs. Anna Frances Parker Rutherford '46
Mrs. Mary Farler Rutledge '56
Mr. James Boyd Scearce, Jr. '34
Mr. E.E. Sheils '30
Dr. Betty L. Siegel '50
The Honorable Eugene E. Siler Sr. '20
Mr. Mahan Siler '18
Ms. Doris J. Spafford '50
The Honorable Ronald Blaine Stewart '53
Dr. Donald A. Swanson '43
Mr. Walter E. Watson '22
Mr. Vernon West '68
Dr. Wayne F. Whitmer '69

Mr. Cratis Williams '30

1989 Hall of Honor Inductees
    Dr. David Denton '58
    Mrs. Ann Renfro Shelley '39
    Dr. Doris V. Spegal, '37

1990 Hall of Honor Inductees
    Mrs. Lucille Cottrell '50
    Mr. Ray Lipps '70

1991 Hall of Honor Inductees
    Dr. Jeroline Baker '52
    Mr. Gorman Jones Roberts '42

1992 Hall of Honor Inductees
    Mr. Kenneth Howard '61
    Mrs. Martha Victor '26

1993 Hall of Honor Inductees
    Mr. Barney Baker '12
    Mrs. Carolyn Siler Browning '51
    Mr. Howard Stephens '54

1994 Hall of Honor Inductees
    Rev. Robert Day, '84
    Rev. David Emmert, '85

1995 Hall of Honor Inductees
    Ms. Ethel Burrier, '28
    Ms. Lois Goldsmith, '25
    Ms. Rosella Shaw Smith, '46
    Dr. William Baylor Wilder, '39

1996 Hall of Honor Inductees
    Mr. Paul P. Steely, '49
    Dr. Merita L. Thompson, '65

No Hall of Honor Inductees: 1997-2006

2007 Hall of Honor Inductees
    Dr. Robert & Mrs. Sharon Finch, '77 Religious Service
    Mr. Ray Lipps, '70 Alumni Appreciation & Distinguished Service
    Dr. James H. Taylor, '68 Alumnus of the Year

2008 Hall of Honor Inductees
    Mr. Vaughn Hatcher, '75 Alumni Appreciation

2010 Hall of Honor Inductees
    Mr. H. Ray Hammons, '90, Alumnus of the Year
    Mr. Harry "Gippy" Graham, '50, Distinguished Alumnus
    Rev. Howard & Cora Elizabeth 'Libby' Atkinson, '71 & '70, Religious Service
    Mr. Teddy Byrd, '70, Alumni Appreciation
    Mr. David Atwood, '07, Young Alumnus

2011 Hall of Honor Inductees
    The Honorable Hubert Frank White, '23, Distinguished Alumnus Award (posthumous) January 17, 2011

2011 Hall of Honor Inductees during Homecoming
    Mr. David Jones, 1975-79, Alumnus of the Year
    Mr. William Anthony Wilburn, '80, Distinguished Alumnus
    Rev. Harold Dean Haun, '77, Religious Service
    Mr. Jerry Wayne Barker, '96, Young Alumnus

2012 Hall of Honor Inductees during Homecoming
    Joseph Craig King, '40, Alumnus of the Year
    Major General Kenneth W. Dowd, '79, Distinguished Alumnus
    Paul Falin, '65, Alumni Appreciation Award
    Carolyn Falin, '68, Alumni Appreciation Award
    Mike Wilson, '94, Service Award

2013 Hall of Honor Inductees during Homecoming
  Lloyd Abdoo, '80, Alumnus of the Year
  Frances Begley Morris, '53, Alumnae of the Year
  Sue Begley Stooksbury, '50, Alumnae of the Year
  Jeemes Akers, '70, Alumni Inspirational
  Jerry W. Croley, '78, Service Award
  Richard "Dick" Koeniger, '67, Alumni Appreciation Award
  Donnie Bruce Patrick, '92, Religious Service
  Brandon Hensley, '10, Young Alumni Award

Appendix B

ATHLETIC HALL OF FAME MEMBERS

**Deceased
* Inducted as individual and for other contributions to UC Athletics
highlighted rows indicated possible address of member (previously in lost)

Year Inducted	Sport	Class Year	Name
1997	Basketball	1991	Mrs. Hope Peace Akins
1997	Baseball	1984	Mr. Geff Davis
1997	Football *	1991	Mr. Orrin Scott Hamilton
1997	Basketball	1964	**Mr. Wilfort Jackson, Jr.
1997	Basketball	1971	Mr. Robert E. Long, Jr.
1997	Baseball Coach	1961-1982	**Mr. Walter Mathes
1997	Track	1968	Mr. Pete Melzoni
1997	Basketball	1984	Mr. Roger Richardson
1997	Ind. Cont.	1948	**Mr. James L. Smiddy
1997	Judo	1980	Mr. Leo White, Jr
1998	Golf	1981-1986	Mr. David Banks
1998	Basketball	1979-1981	Mr. James Crawford
1998	Judo Coach	1963-1986	**Mr. O. J. Helvey
1998	Basketball	1946-1947	Mr. Wade Scott Perkins
1998	Basketball	1980-1984	Ms. Soni Smith
1999	Basketball	1974	Mr. Maurice S. Byrd
1999	Basketball	1988	Mr. Garrett Gregory
1999	Judo	1983	Mr. Edward J. Liddie
1999	Basketball	1949	**Mr. John Renfro
1999	**Football**	**1988**	**1988 Football Team**
1999	Football	1990	Mr. V. C. Alcorn
1999	Football	1992	Mr. Tony Allen
1999	Football	1991	Mr. Russell Barker
1999	Football	1991	Mr. Mark Barrett
1999	Football	1991	Mr. Richard Bates
1999	Football	1989	Mr. Jeff Beach
1999	Football	1993	Mr. Kelvin Blackshear
1999	Football	1991	Mr. Romiach Blythe
1999	Football	1990	Mr. Terry Brady
1999	Football	1991	Mr. Anttarch Brandy
1999	Football	94, '06	Mr. David Bryant
1999	Football	1989	Mr. Rodney Byrd
1999	Football	1993	Mr. Craig Cain
1999	Football	1989	Mr. Jim Cain
1999	Football *	1990	Mr. David Carmichael
1999	Football	1987	Mr. Steve Campbell
1999	Football	1991	Mr. Mark Caldwell
1999	Football	1992	Mr. Mike Cassidy
1999	Football	1989	Mr. Donnie Cauchi
1999	Football	1989	Mr. Joel Clark
1999	Football	1994	Mr. Kelley Collier
1999	Football	1992	Mr. Alphonso Cox
1999	Football	1991	Mr. Tyronne Copeland

1999	Football		1992	Mr. Carl Croon
1999	Football		1993	Mr. Scott Detraz
1999	Football		1988	Mr. Todd Donohoe
1999	Football		1989	Mr. Mike Ellis
1999	Football		1988	Mr. Che English
1999	Football		1993	Mr. Brad Evans
1999	Football		1992	Mr. Tony Farmer
1999	Football		1989	Mr. Steve Feltner
1999	Football		1990	Mr. Greg Francis
1999	Football		1989	Mr. Shaun Francisco
1999	Football		1990	Mr. Brandon Gifford
1999	Football		1992	Mr. Wesley Griebel
1999	Football		1988	Mr. David Hamblin
1999	Football		1989	Mr. Linc Hamblin
1999	Football	*	1991	Mr. Orrin Scott Hamilton
1999	Football		1989	Mr. Scott Hicks
1999	Football		1991	Mr. John Hoff
1999	Football			Mr. Neil Hollingsworth
1999	Football		1990	Mr. Danny Howard
1999	Football		1989	Mr. Gregory Kirk Huff
1999	Football		1989	Mr. Walter Lamar Jackson
1999	Football	*	1991	Mr. Marcellous Johnson
1999	Football		1988	Mr. Rodney Johnson
1999	Football		1993	Mr. Brian Kearns
1999	Football			Mr. Dwight Kenon
1999	Football		1990	Mr. Mark Kirk
1999	Football		1992	Mr. John Lavey
1999	Football		1994	Mr. Anthony LeMaster
1999	Football		1992	Mr. Bryan Looney
1999	Football		1988	Mr. William Mahone
1999	Football		1989	Mr. Anthony Mattia
1999	Football		1989	Mr. Kenneth McAtee
1999	Football		1989	Mr. Mike McClellan
1999	Football		1988	Mr. Leon McQuay, Jr.
1999	Football	*	1990	Mr. Ralph McWilliams
1999	Football		1992	Mr. Dennis Bryan Miller, Jr.
1999	Football			Mr. David Miller
1999	Football		1992	Mr. Rusty Mitchell
1999	Football		1993	Mr. Dwayne Scott Mitchell
1999	Football		1991	Mr. Wayne Mattox
1999	Football		1988	Mr. Ben Munsey
1999	Football		1991	Mr. Ben Murphy
1999	Football		1988	Mr. Ronald Joseph Myers (Joey)
1999	Football		1989	Mr. Kevin Nicol
1999	Football		1989	Mr. Yardley Payne
1999	Football		1992	Mr. Anthony Pray
1999	Football		1991	Mr. Keith Pray
1999	Football		1990	Mr. Jeffery Renshaw
1999	Football		1990	Mr. Allen Robbins
1999	Football		1999	Mr. Paul Joseph Robinson
1999	Football		1988	Mr. Silas Robinson
1999	Football		1989	Mr. Leroy Ryals

1999	Football	1990	Mr. Leslie Sears
1999	Football	1993	Mr. David Shirah
1999	Football	2006	Mr. Kenny Smith
1999	Football	1998	Mr. James Matthew Smith
1999	Football	1989	Mr. Robert Smith
1999	Football	1991	Mr. Andrew Stallworth
1999	Football	1991	Mr. Danny Steely
1999	Football	1989	Mr. Darin Steely
1999	Football	1993	Mr. Dwayne Steven Steely
1999	Football		Mr. Troy Stone
1999	Football		Mr. Jamie Thomas
1999	Football	1988	Mr. Kevin Tilford
1999	Football	1990	Mr. Lance Treadway
1999	Football	1992	Mr. Ron Treadway
1999	Football	1989	Mr. Lawrence Oliver Twitty
1999	Football	1989	Mr. Phil Tyree
1999	Football	1990	Mr. Tim Walker
1999	Football	1992	Mr. Sherrod Ware
1999	Football	1990	Mr. Will Waterson
1999	Football	1992	Mr. Chris Watson
1999	Football	1991	Mr. Kevin Widener
1999	Football	1992	Mr. Thomas Jeffery Williams
1999	Football	1992	Mr. Corey Wilson
1999	Football	1991	Mr. Willie Lee Woods
1999	Football	1990	Mr. Jack LaRue Wright
1999	Football	1990	Mr. Michael Yeazel
1999	Football	1992	Mr. Mike Young
1999	Football	1992	Mr. Alan Ysidro
1999	Football Coach		Mr. Tom Dowling
1999	Football Coach		Mr. Scott McClanahan
1999	Football Coach		Mr. Paul H. Mills
1999	Football Coach		Mr. Dwayne Wells
1999	Football Coach		Mr. Dwayne Hatcher
1999	Football Coach		Mr. James Black
1999	Football Coach		Mr. Charles L. Graves
1999	Football Coach		Mr. James S. Ignoffo
1999	Football Coach		Mr. Michael Beagel
1999	Football Coach		Mr. Isaiah Hill
2000	Service		Mr. John D. Broome
2000	Basketball	1960	Mr. Bill Carlyle
2000	Track	1963	Mr. John Faulkner
2000	Basketball	1986	Mr. John McCoy
2001	Basketball	1957	**Mr. Henry J. Garrison
2001	Basketball/Golf	1968	Mr. Jim Rollins
2001	Basketball	1990	Ms. Barbara Spratling
2001	Coach Basketball *	1979-2000	Mr. Randy Vernon
2002	Basketball	1962	Mr. Don Bingham
2002	Football *	1985-1989	Mr. David Carmichael
2002	Golf	1988-1989	Mr. Scott Gardner
2002	Baseball	1964	Mr. Victor Morris
2002	Track/CC	1978	Mr. Tom Smith
2002	**Basketball**	**1985-1986**	**Men's Basketball Team**

231

2002 Basketball *	1998	Mr. Garrett Gregory
2002 Basketball	1987	Mr. Fred Hamn
2002 Basketball	1989	Mr. Art Hanson
2002 Basketball	1989	Mr. Marvin Junie Hemphill
2002 Basketball *	1986	Mr. John McCoy
2002 Basketball	1988	Mr. Myron Moss
2002 Basketball	1986	Mr. Randolph Scott Roark
2002 Basketball	1986	Mr. Ronnie Robinson
2002 Basketball	1988	Mr. Jeff Shoe
2002 Basketball	1986	Mr. Scott Thomas
2002 Basketball	1985	Mr. Quentin Worrell
2002 Basketball Coach	1985	Mr. Mike Baumgarten
2002 Basketball Coach	1986	Mr. Mike Sickafoose
2002 Basketball Coach*		Mr. Randy Vernon
2003 Basketball	1998	Mr. Mark Dillon
2003 Track	1977-1980	Mr. Carl Hanns
2003 Baseball Coach	1975	Mr. Terry Stigall
2003 Basketball	**1946-1947**	**1946-1947 Men's Basketball Team**
2003		**Mr. Harold Browning
2003 Basketball	1948	**Mr. Bill Caudill
2003		**Mr. Stanley Helton
2003		**Mr. Nixon Duncan
2003 Basketball	1950	Mr. J. B. Mountjoy
2003 Basketball	1948	Mr. Wade Scott Perkins
2003 Basketball		**Mr. Herbert Reeves
2003 Basketball		**Mr. James Smiddy
2003 Basketball		**Mr. John Taylor
2003 Basketball		Mr. Jess White
2003 Basketball	1948	Mr. Raymond White
2003 Basketball	1947	Mr. Jack Murphy
2003 Basketball Coach		**Mr. J. B. Scarce
2004 Ind. Cont.	1959-1995	Mr. John Duke
2004 Football *	1990	Mr. Ralph McWilliams
2004 Basketball	1987	Ms. Betsy Rains
2004 Ind. Cont.	1965	Mr. Zafer Roback
2005 Golf	1965	Mr. Frank Cameron
2005 Basketball	1979	Mr. Joseph Dallas
2005 Basketball	1967	Mr. William E. Fannin
2005 Track	1983	Mr. David Schaufuss
2006 Track/CC	1967	Mr. Gordon Bocock
2006 Basketball	1980-1982	Mr. Adrian Hayes
2006 Track	1980	Mr. Alvin Wadley
2007 Basketball	1970	Mr. Raymond Cox
2007 Basketball	1994	Ms. Melissa Irvin
2007 Football *	1991	Mr. Marcellous Johnson
2007 Golf	1978	Mr. Bill Sergent
2008 Basketball	1957	Mr. Alan LeForce
2008 Basketball	1956	Mr. Glenn Clarkston
2008 Track/Field	1965	Mr. Jack Agee Faulkner
2008 Basketball	1995	Mr. Brian Key
2008 Basketball	1999-2001	Ms. Nicole LaVan
2008 Golf	1968-1970	Mr. Jim Siler

2009 Softball	2000	Ms. Shannon Harrington
2009 Wrestling	2002	Mr. Michael Irving
2009 Track & Field Coach	1965	Mr. Alvin Sharpe
2009 Track & Field	1972	Mr. Dale Walker
2009 Basketball Coach	1958 &1963	Mr. John Dee Wilson
2010 Football *	1988-1991	Mr. Mark Barrett
2010 Track	2004	Mr. Anthony Kabara
2010 Baseball	1979	Mr. J. Wayne Seivers
2010 Track/X Country	2000	Mr. Gareth Wilford
2011 Baseball	2003	Mr. Jason S. Ellis
2011 Outstanding Service	Honorary 2008	Mr. Harold Hubbard
2011 Swimming	2001	Mr. Libor Janek
2011 Track & Field	1969	Dr. Fred B. Sagester
2011 Soccer	2002	Ms. Kelley Tragesser Wood
2012 Track & Field	1973	Mr. Ken Smith
2012 Track & Field	1975	Mr. Charles Reed
2012 Athletics Broadcasting	1990	Mr. David P. Estes
2012 Football Coach	1983-1995	Mr. Tom Dowling
2012 Swimming	2006	Mrs. Christen Heideman VonHertsenberg
2013 Track & Field	1975-1977	Mr. Mike Cooper
2013 Track/X Country	1971	Mr. Tim Henderlight
2013 Basketball	2003	Mr. Ivan Johnson
2013 Baseball	1966	Mr. Roger Morris
2013 Basketball	2001	Mr. Jerry Williams

Appendix C

HONORARY ALUMNI AWARD RECIPIENTS

<u>1971</u>
William M. Slusher

<u>1972</u>
Eugene Siler, Sr.

<u>1973</u>
Nell Moore
Wallace Boyd

<u>1977</u>
James Still
Carl Williams

<u>1978</u>
Ed Balloff
Robert A. Behrmann

<u>1979</u>
Billy C. Clark
C. R. Daley
Willie Dawahare
Andy Frost

<u>1981</u>
Mrs. T. E. Mahan

<u>1984</u>
Sam McGill

<u>1985</u>
Emma McPherson
Judge William R. Lamkin
Jim Roland
Dinah Taylor

<u>1986</u>
Roy Boatwright
Tal Bonham
Jim Hart
Harold Mauney
Sue Wylie

<u>1987</u>
Jim Byrge
Kenneth Shaw
Randy Vernon

<u>1988</u>
Doyle Gilbert
Jolene Gilbert
E. C. Masden
Patricia Neal
Eugene Siler, Jr.

<u>1989</u>
Lucy Paisley Moss
Ora Oliver

<u>1990</u>
Schyler Meyer
Martha Innes
J. Bazzel Mull
Ward Correll
Jerry Ikerd

<u>1991</u>
Ida Janie Hall
Virginia Lovett
Jeanette Palmer

<u>1993</u>
Elizabeth A. Hull
Will Junior Thacker
Dr. O. J. Helvey

<u>1994</u>
Marie Clark Croley
Marjorie Helvey
Maurine Kihlman
Albert and Bertha Tayman

<u>1995</u>
Jim Barna
John Peterson
Rev. Robert Williams

1996
Jeanette Oehring
Richardson McKinney
James and Mary Teer

1997
F. G. "Woody" and Carmen Ramsey
RADM Allan Roby

1998
Sam and Gracie Pettyjohn

2005
Whitey Richardson

2008
Harold Hubbard

2009
Cecil Moses

2011
Jerry and Carla Neeley

2013
Patricia Skeen Artman Lipps
Andy Croley

Appendix D

PAST ALUMNI DIRECTORS

Dr. John R. Heneisen, '65
1965-1968

Russel E. Bridges '51
Cumberland College – 1968

Dr. James H. Taylor '68
1968-1973

John E. Lancaster
1973-1975

Dr. Oline Carmical, Jr. '66
1975-1978

John E. Clinton '78
1978-1980

William H. Lynch '81
1980-1984

Dr. Brian L. Shoemaker '79
1984-1989

Patty Evans Bryant '81
1989-1990

R. Alan Coppock '87
1990-1994

Dr. Rick A. Fleenor '85
1994-2005

David S. Bergman '89
2006-present

Appendix E

PAST ALUMNI BOARD MEMBERS

1964-1967
Stanley Lovett '65
Johnny Reeves '57
Gwendolyn Renfro Goode '67
*E.E. Sheils '30
*Doris Spafford '50

1965-1968
*Tom Warren Butler '51
David Huff '53
Marcella Faulkner Mountjoy '43
*Harold Lee Patterson '58

1966-1969
Dr. Charles D. Barnes '55
William Reed Bryant '62
Nadine Maiden Siler '39
*Earl Woods '48

1967-1970
*John Wesley Faulkner, Jr. '63
Tom A. Gardner '67
Robert Leon "R.L." Miracle '62
Mary Kathryn Kirby Moss '64
*Ann Renfro Shelley '39

1968-1971
*The Honorable Bert T. Combs '30
*Dr. Darrel E. Rains '59
Donald B. Shelton '53
Ann Hollin Smith '56
*Marcus C. Yancey '27

1969-1972
Don J. Apking '58
*Sterling S. Brown '42
*Ken Howard '61
Mary Doyle Johnson '48**
*James E. McCreary '37

1970-1973
*Dr. Jerry D. Hayner '57
Dr. John R. Heneisen '65
Conley L. Manning '54
*Chester A. Nevels '57

1971-1974
Richard Brashear '63
Dr. Oline Carmical, Jr. '66
Dr. Howard Chitwood '51
*Dr. Cratis D. Williams '30

1972-1975

1973-1976
Earl C. Brady '69
Frances Hooks Catlett '55
Shelia Dinsmore Hollin '63
*The Honorable Eugene Siler, Sr. '20
*Dr. Cratis D. Williams '30

1974-1977
Lee A. Bishop '70
David L. Davies '55
Dr. Robert Michael Duncan '71
*Dr. M. Charlene Hill Robinson '61
*Dr. Clifton Raymond Smith '43 & '61

1975-1978
Ray C. Braden '74
*Meriel D. Harris '33
Dr. Judy S. Rose '58
Dr. Betty L. Siegel '50
*Doris Spafford '50

1976-1979
Gordon D. Bocock '67
*Ronald Glass '70
Ray Lipps '70
Martha Begley Lovett '46

1977-1980
Jerry Baker '67
*Lillian C. Galloway '55
Judson S. Harmon, Jr. '68
Linda Cox Miller '61
*R.C. Miller '26

1978-1981
Fred R. Conatser '77
Ray Cummins '55
Bill F. Freeman '49
*Meriel D. Harris '33

1979-1982
*Wallace Boyd '32
*Tom Warren Butler '51
Bob C. Jones '50
Mary Carolyn Farler Rutledge '56

1980-1983

*Jerry D. Bryant '69
Dr. Bernard C. Moses '72
George D. Roberts '50
Dr. Betty L. Siegel '50
Ike M. Slusher, Jr. '52

1981-1984
Lloyd Abdoo '80
Jo Florence Buhl Cordell '54
Dr. John R. Heneisen '65
Jerry L. Hodges '71

1982-1985
*Tom Warren Butler '51
Harold Glenn Clarkston '56
*Edger Croley '39
*Helen Campbell Hamblin '45
*Doris Jean Spafford '50

1983-1986
Martha Begley Lovett '46
Dr. Arliss L. Roaden '49
Dr. Judy S. Rose '58
Dr. Betty L. Siegel '50
Ann Hollin Smith '56

1984-1987
Dr. Frank H. Catron '53
Mary Doyle Johnson '48
Waunita Sowders Kearney '49
V. Troy Lovett '69
Larry W. Stewart '69

1985-1988
Fred Anness '70
Dr. Ralph M. Denham '36
*Dr. Jerry D. Hayner '57
Charles E. Reed '75

1986-1989
Nick F. Greiwe '74
Dr. Ralph W. Hodge '68
Zafer Roback '65
Anna P. Rutherford '46
*Doris Spafford '50

1987-1990
*The Honorable Jerry D. Bryant '69
Dr. Michael B. Colegrove '71
Ray Lipps '70
Dr. Carolyn Barnwell Petrey '71

1988-1991
*Dr. Verna Young Barefoot '34
Dr. Ronnie Day '63
Richard "Dick" Koeniger '76

Jim C. Wilder '61

1989-1992
David Davies '55
Rep. Tom Jensen '71
Donna Doan Ledden '72
Paul P. Steely '49

1990-1993
Glenna Mattingly Bryant '69
Jerry L. Connell '63
James M. Davis '72
Dr. David E. Ison '72

1991-1994
Anthony L. "Tony" Bell '89
Dr. Sue Ball Phelps '54
Dr. John R. Heneisen '65
*Doris Spafford '50

1992-1995
Dr. D. Terrell Bradley '81
Cathlene Lee '85
Dean Hawkins '81
*John L Turnblazer '49

1993-1996
*David L. Chitwood '68
Ray Lipps '70
Jenny Ruth Bryant Clifton '67 & '02
Jimmi Susan McIntosh '81

1994-1997
Jeff C. Clark '88
Bob C. Jones '50
Jo Florence Buhl Cordell '54
Ralph Souleyret '63

1995-1998
*Frank B. Abdoo '67
Martha Crume Ash '44
David Paul Estes '90
Bob Proud '81

1996-1999
Pamela Jean "P.J." Davis '77
Nick F. Greiwe '74
Sharon K. Parrott '68
Barry D. Pencek '68

1997-2000
Dr. Max Allen Cox '72 & '99
William Brian Oberschlake '84
Dr. Carolyn Barnwell Petrey '71
Laura J. Keown '82

1998-2001
Scott J. Burleigh '91
H. Ray Hammons '90
L.C. Madron '64
Dr. Leo R. Taylor '44
Donna Little Abner '76

1999-2002
Lee A. Bishop '70
Vince D. Henley '92
Ralph Lipps '70
Terry L. Wagnon '83

2000-2003
Teri Winkler Foltz '75
Andy O. Abbott '94
Mary Doyle Johnson '48**
Robert A. Kellough '75

2001-2004
Dr. Susan C. Hawkins '87
John W. McCauley '81
William Mike Sewell '72
V.L. Stonecipher '66
Brenda Phillips West '73

2002-2005
Ben F. Atchley, Jr. '82
David D. Close '93
Jimmy Huddleston '87
Kelly Partin Miller '97

2003-2006
Leigh Sexton Burke '90
William C. Gullett '71
Tracey Kidd Wessel '82
William R. Lyttle '75

2004-2007
Dr. Terry P. Dixon '68
John W. McCauley '81
Ralph Neal '80
Kime' Epsich Murphy '82
Dr. E. Wheeler Conover '87***

2005-2008
Colan Harrell '81
Ralph Lipps '70
Laura J. Keown '82
Sharon K. Parrott '68

*Deceased

**Appointed to fill vacancy

***Elected to special limited term

2006-2009
Andy O. Abbott '94
Jeffrey A. Barker '94
Mary Doyle Johnson '48**
David B. Rhodes '80

2007-2010
Susan Rice Bradley '98
Patti Mullins '91
Richard Prewitt '80
V. L. Stonecipher '66
Jimmy Huddleston '87***

2008-2011
Maureen "Cookie" Henson '74
Dr. John P. Hollingsworth '63
Mike Parsley '89
Allen E. Robbins '90
Jeffrey W. Davis '80

2009-2012
Jonathan Childers '00
Wesley Cornett '90
Dr. Terry P. Dixon '68
Melanie Mackey Evans '90
Shannon Evans Harrington '00
Dr. Duane Floro, '79 (filled two year vacancy 2010-12 by S. Harrington)

2010-2013
Tom Broyles, '80
Kathy Byrd, '83-'87
Brittney House, '09
Terry Stigall, '75
Amy Stroud, '04

2011-2014
Bill Hardin, '81
John Hollingsworth, '63
Lee Kendall, '82
Keith Pray, '90
Chuck Sheriff, '63

2012-2015
Willie Adkins, '03
Michael Bryant, II, '1987-'91
Amanda Farris, '08
Duane Floro, '79
Tony LeMaster, '94

Appendix F

PAST ALUMNI BOARD PRESIDENTS

1966-1967
Conley L. Manning '54

1967-1968
Wanda Bowling Freeman '61

1968-1969
*Dr. Jerry D. Hayner '57

1969-1970
*Robert K. Jones, '51

1970-1971
*Meriel D. Harris '33

1971-1972
*Dr. Howard R. Boozer '42

1972-1973
The Honorable Harry "Gippy" Graham '50

1973-1974
Ann Hollin Smith '56

1974-1975
**Mary Doyle Johnson '48

1975-1976
*Tom Warren Butler '51

1976-1977
Dr. John R. Heneisen '65

1977-1978
Dr. Chole Chitwood '49

1978-1979
David L. Davies '55

1979-1980
The Honorable Pleas Jones '34

1980-1981
Fred R. Conatser '77

1981-1982 (also 1970-1971)
*Meriel D. Harris '33

1982-1983
Lillian C. Galloway '55

1983-1984
Mary Farler Rutledge '56

1984-1985
Dr. James E. Croley, III '72

1985-1986
Jerry L. Hodges '71

1986-1987
Dr. Eleanor M. Behrmann '36

1987-1988
Phillip M. Armstrong, JD '70

1988-1989
Dr. Arliss L. Roaden '49

1989-1990
Kate Smith Hill, '63

1990-1991
Dr. Jerry Lowrie, '58

1991-1992
Ray Lipps, '70

1992-1993
*The Honorable Jerry Bryant, '69

1993-1994
**Richard "Dick" Koeniger '67

1994-1995
Paul P. Steely, Sr., '49

1995-1996
*Doris Jean Spafford '50

1996-1997
Dr. D. Terrell Bradley '81

1997-1998
Jimmi S. McIntosh '81

1998-1999
Jerry L. Connell '63

1999-2000
Bob Proud '81

2000-2001
Nick F. Greiwe '74

2001-2002
David Paul Estes '90

2002-2003
L.C. Madron '64

2003-2004
Ralph Lipps '70

2004-2005 (also 1974-1975)
**Mary Doyle Johnson '48

2005-2006
V. L. Stonecipher '66

2006-2007 (also 1993-1994)
**Richard "Dick" Koeniger '67

2007-2008
Dr. Terry Dixon '68

2008-2009
William R. Lyttle '75

2009-2010
David B. Rhodes, '80

2010-2011
Richard Prewitt, '80

2011-2012
Susan Rice Bradley, '98

2012-2013
Allen E. Robbins, '90

2013-2014
Jimmy Huddleston, '87

*Deceased

**Served twice as president

Appendix G

FACULTY AS OF JANUARY 1, 2013

Listed below are all faculty of the University as of January 1, 2013. Persons with a date following their name are full-time faculty and the date represents the year they started teaching at the University. Those with no date are part-time faculty employed as of January 1, 2013.

ACADEMIC AFFAIRS
Ronald Ray McKnight – 2012
Pearlie L. Wingeier
Debbie M. Harp
Carolyn West Reaves – 2007

ART
Geraldine Allen – 1995
Michael Kevin Joyce – 2011
Russell Scott Weedman – 1991

BIOLOGY
Dr. Sara Jane Ash – 2001
Dr. Leif D. Deyrup – 2008
Dr. Heather Leigh Eisler – 2011
Dr. Joan R. Hembree – 2001
Dr. John Andrew Hockert – 2007
Dr. Bret Kuss – 1989
Dr. Lisa K. Lyford – 2005
Dr. Renee B. Yetter – 2008
Dr. Todd C. Yetter – 1990

BUSINESS
Leetta Jackson Angel
Micaiah Bailey – 1973
Nicholas J Bergan
Edna Jane Carter – 1985
Dr. Margaret D. Combs – 2005
Gary Lee Gibson – 2008
Donald Kevin Grimes – 1994
Harold F. Hubbard – 1960
Dr. R. Michael LaGrone – 1998
Dr. Vernon L. McGlone – 2000
Dr. Douglas James Miller
Dr. Vonda K. Moore – 2008
Kenneth Stephen Sims – 1989
Dr. Chin Teck Tan – 1988

CHEMISTRY
Dr. Sharlene J. Dzugan – 1998
Dr. Thomas P. Dzugan – 1989
Jeffrey L. Schwarz
Dr. Julie Lay-Choo Tan
Jarrett Glenn Bourne – 2004

COMMUNICATIONS

Dr. Michael R. Dickman – 1993
Jeremiah Phillip Massengale – 2007
Dr. Kimberly Ann Miller – 2008
Ryan Scott Reed
Dr. Keith D. Semmel – 1990
John Martin Varley – 2011
Carl H Walling – 2010
Marianne Worthington – 1998

CRIMINAL JUSTICE
Melissa Charlene Bundy
Justin W DeCecca – 2010
David Dale Gray
Dr. Melvin Mahone – 2011
John Knox Mills – 2012
Richard Burton Mills
Robert Ernest Stephens

EDUCATION
Dr. Robbie Adell
Dr. Kenneth Ray Alford
Dr. Nathan Robert Ambrose
Aaron Dwight Anderson
Dr. Rhonda Ann Baldwin
Robert Seth Banks
Houston M Barber
Dr. Delia Beth Ben Chaabane
Dr. William Michael Bilyeu
Dr. Stanley L Bippus
Kimberly Jo Brown – 2009
Bonnie Eloise Mullins Butcher – 2012
Dr. Tyrone Bynoe – 2004
Dr. Melanie Jessee Cardell – 2010
Linda L. Carter – 1977
Jennifer Renee Chambers – 2012
Ms. Garnet Kindel Chrisman – 1994
Dr. Lawrence Lee Cockrum – 2005
Dr. Michael B. Colegrove – 1973
Dr. Melissa J. Comer
Amon Wesley Couch
Dr. Queenie Dalcoe
Deborah J Daniels
Dr. Vivian R Dugle
Dr. Donald Dunnigan
Deborah Ann Felts – 2012
Dr. Melissa R. Gibson

Dr. Robert Dodds Glass – 2008
Dr. Donald Gary Goff
Dr. Cristine Gail Goldberg
Dr. Karen Lenore Goldman – 2010
Dr. Robert Heffern
Dr. Mayford Dale Henry – 2012
Kevin F Hub
Mark Cordell Huff
Dr. Jean W. Hunt
Dr. Mary Ruth Isaacs – 2011
Jessica Ann Jones
Dr. Sarah Ann Keller
Dr. Nancy J Kolodziej
Dr. Hou Chun Kuong
Dr. Sandra M. Mancuso
Dr. Steven Tracy McAbee
Sylvia Darlene McBurney
Dr. Claud E McCary
Dr. Samuel William Misher
David A. Montgomery
Willette Andreen Nash
Dr. Carolyn H. Pate
Dr. Gary D. Pate - 2000
Iona Elizabeth Patrick
Dr. Deborah G. Richard 2012
Michael A Roadhouse
Dr. Susan Rardon Rose – 2009
Dr. Fred Sagester – 2010
Erica Scott-Lawrence
Dr. Jennifer Anne Simpson – 2012
Dr. Rebecca Starnes Smith
Linda Cox Story – 2012
Jamie Lee Stringer
Dr. Crystal Proctor Vail
Dr. Barry Aron Vann - 2008
Dr. Kathleen Ann Vettorello
Virginia LaDonna West
Dr. Jennifer Jo Woodruff - 2010
Dr. Mary Lynn Woolsey – 2008
Dr. Terry W. Worrell
Dr. Barbara Hawks Zwadyk

ENGLISH and Modern Foreign Language
Dr. Laura Dennis – 2001
Theresa Marie Dickman – 1998
Dr. Thomas Edward Fish – 1984
Kathy Griffith Fish – 1984
Dr. Thomas Brooks Frazier – 1976
Cristy Lynn Hall – 2011
Nicholas B. Harris – 2012
Dr. Gina Herring – 1990
Jennifer Susan Marsh – 2001
Cory McClellan – 2007
Dr. Ela Molina Morelock – 2008
Dr. Jolly Kay Sharp – 1991
Jamey Leann Temple – 2008

HEALTH,EXERCISE,SPORT SCIENCE
Sara Lindsay Baker
Ryan Wayne Bennett
Margaret A. Blackmore-Haus – 1990
Dr. Anita L. Bowman – 2004
Benjamin David Clayton
Connie Lou Howard – 1976
Jenine M Leskiw – 2012
Alvin D. Sharpe – 1971
Terry Stigall – 1982
Kristopher Thomas Strebeck
William J. Temple
Dr. Glenda A. Warren – 1984
Dr. Michael Joseph Welikonich – 2009

HISTORY AND POLITICAL SCIENCE
Dr. Oline Carmical – 1974
Dr. David Bruce Hicks – 1986
Dr. Christopher S. Leskiw – 2004
Dr. Charles A. Pilant – 1987
Dr. Melvin Charles Smith – 2005
Dr. Eric L. Wake – 1967

HUMAN SERVICES
Gina Lori Bowlin – 2008
Lindsey Ann Cockrum – 2012
Steven Lloyd Halstead – 2010
Jennifer Elaine Knuckles – 2010
Elissa Marie Price – 2012

MATH AND PHYSICS
Lenora Angel Bunch – 2006
Dr. Reid M. Davis – 2004
Dr. John A. Hymo – 1990
Diane Redman Jamison – 1989
Stuart Christopher Lockhart
Dr. James Ora Manning – 1987
Dr. Lawrence Allen Newquist – 1991
Gary R. Owens
Dr. Jonathan Edward Ramey – 1991

MILITARY SCIENCE
Eddie Dewayne Simpson

MISSIONS AND MINISTRY
Dr. Kirby L. Clark – 2001
Dr. Frederick B. Cummings – 2009
Dr. Robert C. Dunston – 1983
Stephen Edward Earle – 2012
Dr. Richard A. Fleenor
Travis A Freeman
Dr. Keith Dewayne Goforth – 2010
Albert Wayne Jones
Dean Whitaker

MUSIC
James R. Corcoran - 1997
Dr. David D. Etter - 1990
Kay Dawn McFarland
Dr. Jeff C. Smoak - 1994
Shawn Lynn Sudduth
Dr. Steven Sudduth - 2008
David M. Threlkeld – 1990
Dr. Patrick Tuck – 2007

PHYSICIAN ASSISTANT STUDIES
Will S. Massey
Dr. Edward Steely Perkins – 2008
Joseph Richard Reed – 2009
Kenneth Joe Reed – 2012

Lesley Anne Tipton – 2012
Dr. David B. Williams – 2009
Sonia Nicole Young – 2009

PSYCHOLOGY
Dr. Sam Aganov – 2012
Kara Lindsay Clemenz
Dr. Melanie Dyan Hetzel-Riggin
Bradford W. Humphrey
Dr. Kristy Marie Keefe – 2010
Dr. Eric Charles Stephens – 2001
Dr. Darren Vincent Testani – 2012
Dr. Dennis J. Trickett – 1997
Dr. Haley Crisp Turner – 2007
Jane Moir Whitaker - 2007

Appendix H

Support Staff as of January 1, 2013

Date Hired	Name	Position
8/21/2006	Carrie Mae Anderson	Housekeeper
6/1/1991	Stephen James Allen	Vice President - Financial Planning
1/1/1987	Bess O. Anderson	Resident Hall Director
4/1/2011	Shane Hamilton Anglin	Journalism & Special Events Coordinator
8/1/2008	Magan Elizabeth Atwood	Director of Appalachian Ministry
6/3/1975	Jana Kay Bailey	Vice President - Finance
8/18/1969	Pearl J Baker	Director - Human Resources
8/6/2012	Steven Charles Ball	Administrative Assistant -Financial Planning
7/21/1998	Lisa Irene Bartram	Director of Student Activities
8/9/2012	Timothy Larry Beauregard	Coach - Assistant W Basketball
2/1/2011	Brenton David Benware	Coach - Men Soccer
9/1/1990	David Bergman	Director of Alumni Services
4/14/2010	Alaina Berube	Coach - Women Wrestling
8/1/1990	Margaret A. Blackmore-Haus	Athletic Trainer
4/6/2006	John Malcolm Bland	Coach - Football
8/20/1998	Stephanie Renea Bowlin	Accounts Payable Manager
5/17/1999	Alice Jean Bowling	Administrative Assistant- President Office
12/10/2012	Megan Elizabeth Breeding	Office Assistant - Admissions
1/2/2013	Jared N Bright	Coach - Football Assistant
11/20/2002	Barbara Jane Broadwell	Manager- Business Services
9/15/1966	John David Broome	Advisor-Admissions
8/19/1998	Agnes Beatrice Brown-Oliphant	Secretary Business Administration
4/4/1994	Crystal Gail Broyles	Secretary Psychology/Human Services
7/25/1994	Mary K. Bryant	Administrative Assistant- Mountain Outreach
8/8/1976	Lenora Angel Bunch	Coordinator Pegasus Program
8/25/1989	Don Russel Butcher	Coach - Men Basketball
10/29/2012	Allison Brooke Byrd	Graduate Studies Admission Counselor
8/1/2007	Carrie Byrd*	Assistant Librarian
7/9/2003	Cleda Brown Caddell	Housekeeper
1/9/1998	Russell Edward Carr	Admissions Counselor
8/15/1977	Linda L. Carter*	Dean of Student Services
8/10/2011	Douglas J Carter	Coach - Women Basketball Assistant
3/1/2007	Kara Lindsay Clemenz	Coach - Women Volleyball
1/7/2011	Michael Todd Cline	Office Assistant -Information Technology
8/1/2012	Nathaniel Joshua Clouse	Admissions Counselor
6/1/2005	Lawrence Lee Cockrum	Vice President - Academics
9/1/2009	Nicholas L Cockrum	Associate Dean - Academics
7/1/1973	Michael B. Colegrove*	Vice President, Student Services
5/1/2006	Michael A. Collins	Coach - Football Assistant
7/3/2001	Kathy Claxton Cox	Secretary - Education
10/24/2012	Rachael Victoria Cox	Housekeeper
10/4/1993	Susan Elaine Croley	Office Assistant - Development
9/1/1983	Patsy L. Cross	Office Assistant - Development
4/12/2011	Gary Lynn Crusenberry	Maintenance Worker - Cumberland Inn
8/6/2012	Mirissa Kay Nicole Cumpston	Assistant - Student Health Clinic
4/1/2008	Robert R. Daniel	Assistant to President-Field Development
8/13/1996	Angela Gail Dean	Coach - Women Softball
10/30/2012	Rebecca Jean Dean	Telemarketer - Admissions
10/1/2003	Terry Chris Dillon	Security Guard

7/18/2011	Kristin Chlea Disney	Administrative Assistant- Music
8/13/2007	Shanna Renee Doan	Administrative Assistant- Business Services
8/30/1985	Sharon Lynne Douglas	Office Assistant - Development
5/14/1981	Georgia Jo Dupier	Bursar
4/27/1994	Charles Mayer Dupier, III	Registrar
6/22/1998	Susan Elizabeth Felts	Office Assistant - Bursar
7/3/1984	Thomas Edward Fish*	Associate Dean - Academics
5/1/1992	Richard A. Fleenor	Director - International Studies
8/14/2000	Gloria June Fritts	Secretary - Student Services
6/1/1985	Kyle Gilbert	Vice President - Operations
7/5/2010	Leah Faye Gray	Office Assistant - Registrar
1/14/2013	Duane Scott Grimes	Education Assessment Coordinator
5/22/1989	Donald Kevin Grimes*	Director of Information Technology
1/3/2012	Jordyne Lee Gunthert	Coordinator Admissions Social Media
8/29/2011	Gary Bradley Hall	Administrative Assistant - President Office
7/20/2005	George Hamlin Jr.	Security Guard
8/20/2012	Rebecca Jamirae Hammons	Manager Graduate Enrollment
5/1/1979	Debbie M. Harp	Director of Career Services
7/1/1985	Erica Ann Harris	Director of Undergraduate Admissions
6/1/2001	Nicholas B. Harris	Assistant - Library Staff
1/2/2013	Amy Michelle Hatcher	Office Assistant - Bursar
8/15/2011	Bobbi Anna Dean Hayes	Administrative Assistant -QEP
6/1/1988	Wanda L. Meyers Hensley	Secretary - International Studies
5/16/2005	John Marc Hensley	Director of Mountain Outreach
8/1/1994	Mark E. Hensley	Resident Hall Director/Security
9/29/2008	Justin Owen Hensley	IT Technician
12/20/2010	Brandon Lee Hensley	Multi Media - Sports Video/Radio Coordinator
1/3/2013	Bridgette Marie Herring	Office Assistant - Graduate Advising Associate
9/15/2011	James Arthur Hinkle	Maintenance Worker - Cumberland Inn
1/13/2009	Megan Hinkle	Office Assistant- Accounts Payable
2/14/2011	Kathy Hockert	Secretary-Biology
10/25/2009	Trina Curtis Holbrook	Assistant Manager-Cumberland Inn
5/17/2010	Meghann Helen Holmes	University Media & Publications Coordinator
3/30/2012	Robert Vernon Holmes	Night Auditor- Cumberland Inn
4/27/2007	Jessie David Hopkins	Manager Maintence Dept - Cumberland Inn
7/26/2010	Paul Jeffery Hughes	Coach - Football Assistant
5/12/1997	Melissa Elayne Irvin	Coach- Women Basketball
9/12/1983	Irma V. Ivey	Office Assistant - Development
6/4/1984	Lisa Whaley Jackson	Office Assistant - Development
3/7/2010	Lexie A Jackson	Housekeeper
8/2/2012	Nicklaus Ryan Jones	Night Auditor- Cumberland Inn
5/22/2007	Sherryll Renee Smith Jones	Secretary - Education Teacher Certification
12/2/1991	Sandra Lou Jones	Office Assistant - Registrar
6/2/2008	Jessica Ann Jones	Administrative Assistant-Graduate Advising
6/1/2004	Timothy Allen Kane	Office Assistant - Mail Room
5/29/2007	Terri Lynn Kane	Administrative Assistant- Criminal Justice
11/12/2012	Katherine J Kendall	Athletic Trainer
6/1/2010	Boyd Anthony Kidd	Sports Statistics & Photography Coordinator
10/10/2011	Cari Lynn Kidd	Office Assistant - Graduate Education
12/1/2007	Christopher Emory Kraftick	Coach-Men/Women Golf
7/19/2004	Sara Eliza Kroetsch	Office Assistant - Admissions
6/13/2011	Curtis Michael Ray Lawson	IT Technician
9/19/2012	Amber Lynn Lay	Housekeeper
8/1/2010	Matthew L Lowers	Coach - Men Wrestling
12/6/2010	Gregory Scott Manning	Administrative Assistant-Physicians Assistant
1/1/1984	Claudia Kay Manning	Development Office Manager

6/25/2010	Janet K Martin	Secretary - Student Services
12/3/2012	Carrie Leann Mattingly	Secretary - English and Religion
12/27/1999	Tonya Gail Maynard	Office Assistant - Accounts Payable
8/1/2005	Kay Dawn McFarland	Faculty Assistant - Music Department
10/23/2000	Linda B. McGarvey	Assistant Library Staff
8/2/2004	Melinda Joy McGlone	Telemarketer - Admissions
3/20/2003	Shelli Lynn McGrath	Office Assistant - Admissions Supervisor
6/2/2008	James Edward McGrath	Assistant to President-Field Development
8/20/1978	Karen Crawford McKinney	Assistant Director- Financial Planning
7/5/2011	Tabitha Kay McNealy	Secretary - Registrar
6/4/2012	Sonya R Meadors	Graduate Studies Admission Counselor
8/31/2012	Jason Eugene Meadors	Maintenance Worker - Cumberland Inn
2/5/2001	Jeffrey Scott Meadors	University Video & Streaming Coordinator
8/22/2002	Joshua Lee Meadors	Library Technologist
4/4/2010	Brittany Nicole Middleton	Sales Coordinator- Cumberland Inn
5/23/2011	Ashley Lynn Mills	Office Assistant-Graduate Advising Associate
7/11/1998	Steven J. Morris	Vice President, Business Services
8/1/1986	Shelleigh Lynn Broome Moses	Receptionist-Coordinator of Visits, Admissions
6/7/1996	Scottie Lee Mullins	Assistant to President-Field Development
8/1/2011	Sheila Kay Nantz	Secretary - Registrar
8/1/2011	Rebecca Gail Nantz	Resident Hall Director
8/16/2010	Angie Sunshine Nichols	Administrative Assistant-Information Technology
8/1/2012	Tonya Janelle Osborne	Social Media & Web Site Coordinator
4/13/2010	Lisa J Parks	Switchboard Operator
1/2/1987	Avis Fay Partin	Secretary - History and Political Science
3/15/2010	Priscilla Ann Partin	Manager - Cumberland Inn
10/15/1981	Pamelia Perkins	Office Assistant - Bursar
5/27/1974	Shanda M. Perkins	Coordinator-Campus Post Office
5/24/1982	Charles Wesley Perkins	IT Technician
12/15/2011	Willie Phillips	Athletic Trainer
12/7/2009	Shonda Renee Powers	Graduate Studies Admission Counselor
1/3/2012	Kendall Proffitt	Administrative Assistant- Student Services
9/21/2006	Carolyn West Reaves	Director- ARC
10/31/2011	Jennifer Nicole Reeder	IT Technician
1/14/2013	Kevin Joseph Reigle	Coach-Men/Women Bowling
5/10/2010	Hayley L Rice	Admissions Counselor
3/4/2012	Korrie Ann Richardson	Clerk- Front Desk Cumberland Inn
2/27/2012	Russell Eric Ridenour	Graduate Studies Admission Counselor
6/2/2008	Sherry Elaine Roaden	Administrative Assistant
8/15/2011	Ariel Dianne Robinson	Admissions Counselor
1/21/2011	Chelsea Robl	Athletic Trainer
5/15/2005	Jessica Renee Shearer	IT Technician
5/30/2001	Bradley Dwight Shelton	Coach - Baseball
5/3/1995	Nancy Kathryn Silcox	Housekeeper
12/3/2012	Melinda Silvers	Office Assistant - Admissions
7/1/2011	Eric Matthew Skelly	Coach - Swimming
1/7/2010	Tammy S Smith	Administrative Assistant - Academics
5/7/2012	Tiffney M. Sprague	Office Assistant - Mail Room
9/1/2009	Sharon Lynn Wilson Standifer	Administrative Assistant - Financial Planning
12/20/2005	Donna Sue Stanfill	Director of Graduate Admissions
2/1/2010	Paul E Stepp	Office Assistant - Academics
6/1/2004	Brina Kylene Strebeck	Athletic Trainer
7/1/2004	Kristopher Thomas Strebeck	Director of Intramurals
2/1/1974	Floyd C. Stroud	Coach - Cross Country/Track
6/1/1974	Linda C. Sutton	Administrative Assistant - Financial Planning
5/17/2011	Stephanie Leigh Taylor	Administrative Assistant - Alumni

9/1/1984	Dinah L. Taylor	Assistant to President-Field Development
1/1/1968	James H. Taylor*	President
3/28/2005	Randle Lee Teague	Controller - Finance
1/1/2001	William J. Temple	Coach - Cross Country/Track Assistant
7/1/2012	Stephen Elliott Thompson	Administrative Assistant - Church Relations
10/19/2009	Stephen Bradley Tipton	IT Technician
8/15/2012	Joseph Adam Townsend	Coach - Women Soccer
6/1/2012	Chandler Huntington Camp Tygard	Coach - Football Assistant
8/1/2008	Amy Elizabeth Vann	Secretary - Chemistry
4/21/1979	Randall L. Vernon	Vice President - Athletics
8/17/2005	Mark Alexander Vernon	Coach - Men Basketball Assistant
9/4/2012	Nicole Bryant Wake	Admissions Counselor
10/15/1973	Sue Wake	VP - Institutional Advancement/Development
6/1/1999	Jennifer Wake-Floyd*	Director - Multi Media and Athletics Services
6/3/2005	Amanda Gail Walton	Admissions Counselor
7/1/2012	Rebecca Ann Watkins	Graduate Studies Admission Counselor
8/1/2005	Susan Jean Weaver	Director -QEP
6/1/2006	Edgar A. Weiser	Coach - Football Assistant
9/1/2011	Jonathan Leigh Welch	Clerk- Front Desk Cumberland Inn
6/29/1992	Lana Kay West	Administrative Assistant - Athletics
8/16/2010	Kimberly White	Office Manager - Education
8/23/1999	Phyllis Marie Wilson	Payroll Clerk - Personnel Records
5/9/2011	Lacy Brooklyn Wilson	Publications Sports & Graphic Services Coordinator
11/14/2003	Travis Lee Wilson	Manager Telecommunications
4/29/1985	Pearlie L. Wingeier	Resident Hall Director
2/9/2009	Andrew Philip Wolfe	Supervisor Tele Marketers - Admissions
3/21/2011	Debbie Carol Wood	Administrative Assistant - EDD
1/19/2012	Lois Ann Woods	Office Assistant-Graduate Advising Associate
3/22/2010	Peggy Daphne Woods	Dean of Student Labor
8/21/2006	Beth Ann Wooley	Secretary - Health Education and Sports/Art
8/9/2012	Steven Bruce Wright	Coach - M Basketball Assistant
1/13/2009	Bethel T. Wyatt	Assistant to President-Field Development

* Also has faculty rank

Appendix I

Members of The Board of Trustees
OF
WILLIAMSBURG INSTITUTE, CUMBERLAND COLLEGE AND
UNIVERSITY OF THE CUMBERLANDS

The first date following each name indicates the first year of service on the Board while the second date indicates the last year of service. The first members of the Board, appointed at meetings of the Mt. Zion Association in 1887 and 1888, oversaw the founding of the Institute. In 1889 after the school opened its doors, additional members were added. Members of the first Board, then called the Board of Directors, are indicated with an * while current members of the Board of Trustees are indicated with **. In 1960 the College's Charter was changed regarding length of service of Trustees. Since that time Trustees have been elected to serve a four-year term. They are then eligible for reelection for another four-year term. After eight years, however, a Trustee must remain off the Board for a period of one year before being eligible for another four-year, renewable appointment. This process can continue indefinitely. In some of the earlier records the title for the chairman of the Board is listed as president of the Board and the vice-chairman's title is listed as vice-president of the Board.

William Adcock, 1998-1999; Partial 2000; Partial 2001; 2002-2009

N. A. Archer, 1911-1946

Phillip M. Armstrong, 1997-2004; 2006-2013**

Robert Asher, 1908-1914

Frank Atkins, 1992-1999; 2002-2009

A. Doyle Baker, 1999-2002; Partial 2003-2004; 2005-2008; 2010-2013**

Samuel D. Ballou, 1975-1982; Chairman 1981-1982; 1984-1991; 2001-2008; 2010-2011

Charles Barnes, 1970-1986; Chairman 1980

Jesse Bell, 1964-1971

C. V. Bennett, III, 1999-2001

John A. Black, 1889*

Charles Boggs, II, 2008-2011

Haskell Bolding, 1965-1969; Secretary 1969

Linda D. Booth, 2013**

Ben Brewer, 1990-1997; 2004-2005

William Brown, 1967-1968

Robert Browning, 1986-1993; 1995-1998

Charles Buhl, Sr., 1966-1986

Maurice Byrd, 2008 – 2011

249

Arnold Caddell, 1992-1999

W. J.Caudill, 1898-1902

Mrs. W. T. Chappell, 1971-1978; Secretary 1973-1978

B. E. Cheely, 1930-1966

W. J. Chestnut, 1961-1968

Velma Childers, 1997-2004

Paul Chitwood, 2007-2010

Josephine Cochran, 1996-2003

Jo Florence Cordell, 1995-2002; Secretary 1997-2002

Edgar Croley, 1991-1998

James Croley, Jr., 1964-1981; Vice Chairman 1969

Arthur Dale, 1969-1978

Robert Daniel, 1957-1974; Chairman 1966-1974

Hywell Davies, 1904-1908

J. H. Davis, 1893-1903; Secretary 1897-1899

Roy Dobyns, 1998-2005

E. O. Edwards, 1955; (Elected to serve unexpired term of A. T. Siler)

C. G. Ellison, 1898-1939; Secretary 1900-1939

Donald R. Ellison, 2006-2010

J. M. Ellison, 1895-1942; Vice Chairman 1906-1907; Vice Chairman and Assistant Treasurer
    1907-1910; Vice Chairman and Treasurer 1911-1942

W. A. Ellison, 1940-1942

William Ellison, 1889*

Don Estep, 1989-1996; 2000-2007; 2009

Paul Estes, 1976-1983; Vice Chairman 1979-1982; Chairman 1983; 1985-1992; 1996-2003;
    Secretary 2003; 2005-2012; Chairman, 2011

J. Donald Faulkner, 1977-1984

W. H. Felix, 1902-1912

Charles E. Freeman, 1969-1980; Vice Chairman 1975; Chairman 1976

H. H. Fuson, 1923-1964

L. S. Gaines, 1927-1928

Georgetta Gannon, Partial 2007; 2008-2011; Vice Chairman 2011; 2013**

Oliver Keith Gannon, Partial 2007; 2008-2011; 2013**

David Gardner, 1996-2003

Gilbert Garrard, 1889*

Charles Garringer, 1964-1965

Ancil Gatliff, 1888*-1918; Chairman 1888-1918

E. M. Gatliff, 1949

J. B. Gatliff, 1918-1964; Chairman 1931-1964

J. B. Gatliff, Jr., 1946-1965; Vice Chairman 1958-1965

J. G. Gatliff, 1894-1897

H. C. Gentry, 1889*

George Griffin, 1966-1985; Chairman 1975; 1988-1995

Orville Griffin, 1996-2003

William Gullett, 2006-2013**

Bill Hacker, 1982-1985; 1987-1994; 2001-2008; 2010-2013**

Mrs. William Hagan, 1957

E. D. Hall, 1949-1953

H. Ray Hammons, Jr., 2008-2013**

Tony Hancock, 2002-2009; 2012-2013**

Jim Hannah, 1990-1997; 2004-2005

French Harmon, Partial 2011-2013**

William "Bill" Henard, 2009-2013**

Maureen "Cookie" Henson, 2011-2013**

Oscar Hornsby, 1996-2003; 2009-2012

David Huff, 1969; 1980-1987; Secretary 1987; 1989-1996; Secretary 1993-1996; 1998-2005; Secretary 2004-2005; 2007-2013**

Billy G. Hurt, 1980-1987; 1989-1996; 1999-2006

J. D. Johnson, 1969-1970

C. H. Keeton, 1893-1899

Ray Kelly, 1987-1990

Richard Knock, 1997-2004; Chairman 2003-2004; 2010-2013**

William Lamkin, 1987-1994; Vice Chairman 1989-1994

Raymond Lawrence, 1971

Joseph J. Leary, 1972-1979

Herman E. Leick, 1972; Vice Chairman 1977; 1981-1988; Vice Chairman 1984-1988;
   1990-1997; 2001-2002

J. W. Logsdon, 1900-1902

E. C. Mahan, 1915-1948

J. M. Mahan, 1896-1936

J. P. Mahan, 1888*-1906; Vice Chairman 1888-1906

T. B. Mahan, 1896-1930; Chairman 1918-1930

T. E. Mahan, 1950-1970; Secretary 1960-1961; Chairman 1965-1966

Howard Mann, 2010-2013**

John Meadors, 1889-1896

Bill Messer, 1998-2001

W. H. Moody, 1916-1918

E. S. Moss, 1888*-1904; Chairman (temporary)1888; Secretary 1888

Roland Mullins, 1993-2000; 2002-2009; 2011-2013**

George Munro, 1966; Vice Chairman 1972; 1980-1987

S. W. McComb, 1919-1945

O. G. Nicholson, 1957-1967

Kenneth Nighbert, 1991-1994

James Oaks, 1985-1992; Chairman 1989-1992; 1994-2001; Chairman 1995-2001; 2003-2010;
   Vice Chairman 2003-2004; Chairman 2005-2010; 2012-2013; Chairman 2012-2013**

Charles Osborne, 1979-1986; Secretary 1984-1986; 1988-1995; Chairman 1993; 1997-2000

Robert Palmer, 1961-1968

Donnie Patrick,1993-2000; 2003-2010; Secretary 2008-2010; 2012-2013**

J. Q. Pearce, 1889*

George Pedigo, 1961-1963

J. Hunt Perkins, 2011; Partial 2012; 2013**

N. B. Perkins, 1917-1955

Mrs. N. B. Perkins, 1957-1964

Carolyn Petrey, 2011-2013**

Dallas Petrey, 2005-2012

Calvin Perry, 1987-1994; 2004-2007

John N. Prestridge, 1893-1896; Secretary 1895-1896

Elmer G. Prewitt, 1968-1975

Floyd Price, 1982-1989

Donnie Rains, Partial 1987; 1988-1995; 2000-2007; Secretary 2006-2007; 2009; 2013**

William Ramsay, 1961-1969

Tom Raper, 1995-2002; 2005-2012

S. M. Reams, 1946-1948

M. A. Reese, 1972; Secretary 1979-1980; 1982-1989

A.A. Richardson, 1935-1956

Gorman J. Roberts, 1956-1979

T. J. Roberts, 1936-1959; Secretary and Treasurer 1939-1959

Charles Roesel, 2011-2013**

James Roland, 1974; 1978-1981; Secretary 1981; 1983-1990

B. F. Rose, 1911-1921

Judy Rose, 1986-1993; 1995-2002; Vice Chair 1995-2001; Chair 2002; 2005-2008

J. R. Sampson, 1888*-1915; Secretary 1888

R. D. Sanders, 1960-1978

Carl D. Sears, 1974-1981

N. M. Scales, 1889*

Lynwood Schrader, 1995-1998

P. Norris Shockley, Jr., 1994-2001

A.T. Siler, 1901-1953; Vice Chairman 1946-1953

E. E. Siler, Sr., 1946-1965

E. E. Siler, Jr., 1966; Vice Chairman 1966-1967; 1970-1971; Vice Chairman1983; Chairman 1984-1988

J. W. Siler, 1887*-1912; Treasurer (temporary) 1887; Treasurer 1889-1912

Mahan M. Siler, 1948-1956

M. V. Siler, 1916-1934

J. Charles Smiddy, 1995-2002; 2004-2009

Joseph Smiddy, 1998-2001

C. L. Smith, 1956-1963

Keith P. Smith, 1965-1972

S. Stanfill, 1889-1897

Joe M. Stanford, 1977-1984

E. N. Steely, 1889-1893

Paul Steely, Partial 2005; Partial 2006; 2007-2010; 2011-2013**

Ezra Stephens, 1905-1916

Scott Thompson, 2003-2010; Vice Chair 2005-2010; 2013**

John Mark Toby, Partial 2011-2013**

Lonnie Walden, 2003-2006; 2008-2013; Secretary 2011-2013**

Eugene M. West, Partial 2005

Jon Westbrook, 2003-2010; 2012-2013; Vice Chair 2012-2013**

Jerry Winchester, 2010-2011; Partial 2012; Partial 2013**

INDEX

ENDNOTES

[1] Chester R. Young, *"To Win The Prize": The Story of the First Baptist Church at Williamsburg, Kentucky, 1883-1983* (Williamsburg: Centennial Committee, First Baptist Church, 1983) 182.

[2] *Baptist Evangelist*, "Smith's Obituary," A copy of this original article is contained in the official records of the College's Board of Trustees, 1895.

[3] Young, 13.

[4] Mount Zion Association, Record Book No. 1: 52-53.

[5] Young, 5.

[6] Ida Janie Hall, "The Hostory of Cumberland College" (unpublished Master's thesis, University of Tennessee, 1962) 14.

[7] Williamsburg Institute, *Catalogue 1892-1893*: 24.

[8] H. H. Hibbs, "Tender Memories," in *Doctor Ancil Gatliff*, 20.

[9] Eugene Siler, "Heads or Tales," *The Whitley Republican*, 19 March 1981.

[10] "Henry Clay Frick," The McGraw-Hill Encyclopedia of World Biography, 1973 ed., vol. 4, cited by permission of Heraty Associates, Encyclopedia Division, Palatine, Illinois in James H. Taylor and Elizabeth Sue Wake, eds., *A Bright Shining City set on a Hill: a Centennial History* (Williamsburg, KY: Cumberland College, 1988) 3.

[11] Taylor, 65.

[12] Robert Cummin[g]s Medaris, *Blazing the Gospel Trail*, 2nd ed. (Williamsburg, KY, 1920) 20.

[13] *Western Recorder*, 17January 1889: 5.

[14] Wallace Buttrick, "Memorandum Regarding Cumberland College," 23 June 1921, New York, New York: Rockefeller Archive Center cited in Taylor, 2

[15] Claire Collier, personal correspondence, 6 June 1985, New York: Rockefeller Archive Center cited in Taylor, 2.

[16] Siler, 19 March 1981.

[17] Williamsburg Institute Board of Trustees, *Minutes*, 28 January 1905.

[18] Cumberland College, *Catalogue 1928-29*: 9.

[19] Cumberland College, *Catalogue 1928-29*: 9.

[20] Letter from Clara Wright Hines, 18 November 1982 cited in Taylor, 35.

[21] *Whitley News Journal*, 11 September 1996.

[22] Quoted by permission, courtesy of Lincoln Perseverance Motivational Poster by Successories.com LLC.

[23] Young, 186-189.

[24] Williamsburg Institute, *Catalogue*.

[25] *Corbin Times Tribune*, 27 February 2002.

[26] Information provided by Mrs. Homer Davis, Sister of General Easley, as cited in Taylor, 17.

[27] "Major General Floyd Parks," *The Whitley Republican*, 31 May 1951 as cited in Taylor, 16.

[28] Siler, 10 February 1977 as cited in Taylor, 15.

[29] Simon L. Renfro, *Renfro Revelations*, Vol. III, No. 4, April 1946: 87 as cited in Taylor, 15.

[30] Bert T. Combs, Address and interview at Homecoming, 22 November 1980 as cited in Taylor, 128-130.

[31] www.historykygovernors.com/edwinporchmorrow.htm

[32] Siler, 12 January 1984 cited in Taylor, 19.

[33] Siler, 17 July 1980 cited in Taylor, 150.

[34] Williamsburg Institute, Board of Trustees, *Minutes*, 20 December 1904, 17 June 1906 and 23 March 1912 cited in Taylor, 83.